The New Century Hymnal

The New Century Hymnal

Jesus Christ is the same yesterday and today and forever.
Hebrews 13:8

The Pilgrim Press
Cleveland, Ohio

The New Century Hymnal

ISBN 0-8298-1051-X Pew Edition
ISBN 0-8298-1053-6 Gift/Pulpit Edition
ISBN 0-8298-1055-2 Accompanist Edition
ISBN 0-8298-1057-9 Large Print Edition

Printed in the U.S.A. on acid-free paper.

CONTENTS

Foreword	vii
Preface and Introduction	viii
Acknowledgments	xi
Editor's Notes	xii
ORDERS OF WORSHIP	Pages 1–14
Service of the Word I	1
Service of the Word II	5
Morning Prayer	8
Evening Prayer	11
HYMNS	Numbers 1–617
HYMNS OF PRAISE	
The Holy Trinity	
God	1–39
Jesus Christ	40–55
Holy Spirit	56–64
Opening of Worship	65–74
Close of Worship	75–82
Morning	83–91
Evening	92–100
HYMNS FOR THE CHRISTIAN YEAR	
Advent	101–123
Christmas	124–153
Epiphany	154–181
Baptism of Jesus	167–169
Transfiguration	182–184
Lent	185–212
Ash Wednesday	185–188
Palm/Passion Sunday	213–217
Holy Week	218–229
Easter	230–245
Easter Season	246–256
Ascension	257–260
Pentecost	261–272
Trinity Sunday	273–280
Hymns of the Spirit	281–294
All Saints Day	295–299
Reign of Christ	300–305
HYMNS FOR THE FAITH AND ORDER OF THE CHURCH	
The Church	306–314
The Bible	315–321
Ministry, Sacraments, and Rites	
Holy Baptism	322–328
Holy Communion	329–349
Confirmation	350–354
Commissioning, Ordination, and Installation	355–360
Marriage	361–364
Burial and Memorial	365–368
Anniversaries and Dedications	369–373
Communion of Saints	374–385
Christian Unity	386–402
Faith	403–418
Seasons	
Thanksgiving	419–425
Festival of the Christian Home	426–429
Changing Seasons	430–435

HYMNS FOR THE LIFE AND WORK OF THE CHURCH
Pilgrimage
Struggle and Conflict 436–447
Consecration 448–457
Nurture 458–471
Comfort and Assurance 472–490
Discipleship 491–504
Prayer 505–521
Mission
Witness 522–531
Service 532–543
Healing and Forgiveness 544–555
Stewardship and Creation 556–569
Justice and Peace 570–590
Citizenship 591–594
HYMNS OF CHRISTIAN HOPE
Eternal Life 595–606
Realm of God 607–617

PSALMS AND CANTICLES Pages 618–740
Introduction and Psalm Tones 618–620
Psalms 621–731
Canticles and Ancient Songs 732–740

SERVICE MUSIC Numbers 741–815
Call to Worship 741–744
Prayer for Mercy (Trisagion and Kyrie) 745–753
Song of Praise (Gloria) 754–760
Scripture Response 761–764
Alleluia 765–768
Prayer Response, Meditation 769–775
Doxology 776–782
Offertory 783–785
Invitation to Communion 786–788
Holy, Holy, Holy, (Sanctus, Seraphic Hymn) 789–795
Memorial Acclamation 796–799
Lamb of God (Agnus Dei) 800–804
Blessing, Song of Simeon (Nunc Dimittis) 805–809
Amens 810–815

WORSHIP RESOURCES Numbers 816–887
Prayers Before Worship 816–818
Opening Words 819–825
Invocations 826–831
Confessions, Words of Assurance 832–841
Offertory Sentences and Prayers 842–845
Prayers 846–866
Prayers for Home Use 867–871
Prayers of Benediction 872–877
Litanies 878–880
Creeds, Affirmations of Faith 881–887

INDEXES AND COPYRIGHT ACKNOWLEDGMENTS Pages 888–934
Copyright Acknowledgments 888
Author, Composer, and Source Index 896
Metrical Index 902
Tune Index 907
Scriptural Index 910
Lectionary Index 912
Topical Index 918
First Line Index 928
Descant Index 934

FOREWORD

The praise of God proclaimed through music begins in scripture with the song of Miriam and Moses at the Exodus and culminates in a reprise of their anthem by an apocalyptic choir of the saints at the close of history. For Jews and Christians the faithful people of God at worship are preeminently a community of song.

The psalmist calls us to celebrate our living faith not only in hymns from the past but in every "new song" inspired by the marvelous deeds of God across all time. The Christian story itself was sung by Mary, by the angelic choir at Bethlehem, at the gathering in the Upper Room, and throughout the churches of the New Testament. Hymns that touched the hearts of the faithful in enduring ways became part of the memory of the church. Today we sing the poetry of Ambrose of Milan and Hildegard of Bingen with fresh language made possible by new understandings of their words. We also sing the testimony of contemporary hymnwriters who remind us that God is not without witnesses in any age.

In the metaphor of centuries of hymnody, ancient and modern, we discern that God is always more than our human words are able to express. Our reverence for the mystery of God's being invites humility as we seek language that opens human hearts to the good news of God's love for all creation. We acknowledge the limitations of our words while we confess that in Jesus Christ the Word of God became flesh and lived within history.

Where language fails us, we live with confidence that the Holy Spirit intercedes for us with sighs too deep for words. Our hymns are a testimony to this ministry of the Holy Spirit. Hymns are more than the sum of their parts. They become for us a language that transcends human speech. They are the poetry of eternity within time. They are signs of grace that comes from beyond ourselves.

The New Century Hymnal does not claim to reach the heights of this vision of hymnody. It is, at best, the contribution of the United Church of Christ to the larger quest of the universal church to praise God faithfully in each generation. It is, however, a hymnal boldly committed to a spirit of inclusiveness. It welcomes and celebrates the diversity of all the people of God as surely as it confesses the mystery of diversity within God the Holy Trinity.

Thousands of people have participated in the preparation of this hymnal. One among them, however, with indefatigable courage and conviction, inspired the vision that has resulted in the pages that follow. We are indebted to Ansley Coe Throckmorton for her deep faith, scholarly gifts, and pastoral heart, without which this hymnal would not have been possible.

Thomas E. Dipko
Executive Vice President
United Church Board for Homeland Ministries

PREFACE

"Jesus Christ is the same yesterday and today and forever." *The New Century Hymnal* is rooted in that conviction, in the conviction that the unchanging Jesus Christ, whose story is told through the centuries, in many images and languages, is the same Jesus Christ of the gospels and epistles. Seers and saints, poets and prophets of many ages have told of the unchanging Jesus Christ in their own ways. This hymnbook, following the common lectionary, also tells that same story in many ways.

Believers know that images of Christ have always preceded Christology, and that those images of Christ lie behind the confessions and creeds of the church. This book retains not only the images of other periods of history—images of shepherd, sovereign, healer, teacher, liberator, and so on—but it also contains the images of poets, prophets, and saints of our time who sing of the changeless Jesus Christ in images of our own age and for the new century now upon us.

Bernard of Clairvaux once observed that we must drink from our own wells. And the South American pastor and theologian Gustavo Gutiérrez brought that observation to bear on the lives of his people. So likewise Hildegard of Bingen, Martin Luther, Charles Wesley, Isaac Watts, Sarah Flower Adams, Madeleine Marshall, and Brian Wren—and each of us does the same. To drink from one's own well in this matter is to live, sing, and pray in the spirit of the unchanging Jesus Christ, as each of us has encountered Christ, to discern the mysterious connection between that life and our lives.

One of the great gifts to our time is the spirit now moving among us calling us to affirm the fullness of God, the goodness of creation, and the value of every person. The search for language and metaphor to express that breadth and richness marks this book.

In doing these things this hymnbook preserves much of the best hymnody of the past, and of the present, and it leads to a future we begin dimly to see. We have shaped a book that expresses the faith of the church in the unchanging Jesus Christ in words and images of our time. In whatsoever way it is faithful to these high standards, it is offered *Deo Gloria*.

Ansley Coe Throckmorton
General Secretary for Education and Publication
United Church Board for Homeland Ministries

INTRODUCTION

In 1977, General Synod XI of the United Church of Christ directed the Executive Council to create a new official hymnal using language that is inclusive. In October 1989 the United Church Board for Homeland Ministries set aside resources to develop the hymnal. The project was completed in three phases. First, the Board of Directors of the United Church Board for Homeland Ministries appointed an advisory Hymnal Committee of thirteen members to function within its Division of Education and Publication, which provided appropriate staffing, research tools, and logistical support. The committee consisted of men and women from various geographical regions and traditions within the United Church of Christ. Each member brought liturgical sensibility, professional skill, cultural perspective, theological acumen, and particular musical erudition. As a result, the committee proved far greater than the sum of its parts.

The committee met between February 1990 and January 1993 in churches all across the continental United States, in Hawaii, and at the national offices in Cleveland. At its meetings and at thirty-five public forums the committee, in conversation with United Church of Christ local church members, considered hymns celebrating a diversity of liturgical, mission-oriented, and topical emphases. They invited and tested hymns from communities of Asian Americans, Native Americans, African Americans, and Latinos/Latinas. A significant portion of this hymnal can be credited to the probing questions and insightful observations of United Church of Christ members and others.

As a corollary to the hymnal forums, a churchwide research project that ran from the summer of 1990 through the summer of 1991 sought information from every local church in the denomination: "What do you sing? What do you want to sing? In a new hymnal, what might be a help or a hindrance?" From thousands of responses, two major findings surfaced: the majority of congregations that would buy hymnals in the next decade seek, first, new music, and second, inclusive metaphors for God and the human community. These findings confirmed the vision of General Synod in 1977 for an inclusive-language hymnal, and they were the foundation for the work of the advisory Hymnal Committee as it sought to design a hymnal for current and future worshipers in the United Church of Christ. In April 1993 the committee completed the first phase of the development process. It had reviewed more than ten thousand hymns, designed the contents, selected the repertory, and wrestled with every imaginable nuance, subtlety, and challenge of the language of love, justice, and worship of God.

For the second phase, the Hymnal Committee was succeeded by an Editorial Panel appointed by the Board of Directors of the United Church Board for Homeland Ministries. The board charged the panel with refining and completing the vast work submitted by the Hymnal Committee. The panel set about the delicate work of balancing hymnal components, texts and tunes included, and reviewing the language of all texts. The panel's work concluded in the fall of 1994.

In the final phase, the editors and the hymnal office staff prepared the hymnal layout, edited the manuscript, garnered the copyrights, monitored the typesetting, and pursued everything necessary to produce a hymn collection suited for the ecumenical church.

Within the historic Protestant traditions that shape the United Church of Christ, the hymnbook serves as a primary vehicle to nurture the faith of church members. All who worked on this project were guided by the affirmation that *The New Century Hymnal* should provide rich, varied metaphors for singing about God, and language to sing about people that excludes no one—words that all people can sing.

This work was done amid what can only be called a new reformation. It recognized that its task was to do more than select six hundred historic and familiar hymns. It was also asked to consider hundreds of submitted manuscripts and new hymns that emerged from a wide variety of global traditions. The committee also reviewed newly published hymnals within the ecumenical community that presented even more possibilities. Each religious and cultural tradition presented its own treasured core hymnody. The Board for Homeland Ministries, the Hymnal Committee, and the Editorial Panel, in concert with the stated convictions of General Synod, believe the fullness of God is greater than exclusively masculine words and images. Thus the Hymnal Committee sought to broaden the traditional divine references so that they included the feminine. It searched for hymns containing similes, parables, analogies, and metaphors that point to the fullness of God.

In addition to this broad process of selection, every text underwent careful scrutiny of its metaphors and pronouns that refer to God, Christ, and the Spirit. Why the scrutiny? Because for nearly two millennia these words have tended toward exclusively masculine characterization, bearing painful consequences, especially for women. Every effort was made to ensure that all hymns spoke to and for all God's people, equally. This resulted in the examination of language from racial, ethnic, and sociocultural perspectives, and the review of language that could be diminishing to people with physical disabilities. Consideration was also given to imagery to assure that it relate to the scientific understandings of a coming generation.

For the required text revisions, contemporary poets and hymn lyricists explored the scriptures, the prophets, mystics, and seers to forge fresh forms to address the living God and describe our world. Just as translators have rendered scriptures in present-day language, the poets were asked to revise language, yet maintain the nuance and intent of the original. In fact, numerous Latin and German hymns were newly translated for this hymnal. As a result, in the next century, as in preceding centuries, the church will be able to worship in the common language of the day.

It is the hope of all who labored on *The New Century Hymnal* that the church will discover a language that stretches the dimensions of justice and helps reveal the unfathomable depths of the God of biblical faith. It represents an attempt to embody a faith and joyous hope to sustain the church in a new millennium. May it serve as a transforming witness to the church of Jesus Christ as it celebrates public worship and sings gratefully—buoyantly—with the psalmist, "Praise God! Praise God from the heavens; Praise God in the heights; Praise God all the angels; Praise God, all you Host! Let everything that breathes, praise the living God! Praise God."

James W. Crawford
Chair, Hymnal Committee

ACKNOWLEDGMENTS

Hymnal Committee

Janet Satre Ahrend, James W. Crawford (Chair), Daniel L. Johnson, Joyce Finch Johnson, Dorothy Lester *(ex officio, Office of Church Life and Leadership)*, Luis Olivieri, Jeffrey Radford, Linda Jambor Robinson, A. Knighton Stanley, Catherine Thiedt, and Stephen Wayles

Editorial Panel

Stephen W. Camp, Cesar A. Coloma, James W. Crawford, Martha S. Due *(Chair)*, and Miriam Therese Winter

United Church Board for Homeland Ministries Staff

Charles Shelby Rooks, *Executive Vice President, 1984–1992**
Thomas E. Dipko, *Executive Vice President from 1992*+*
Ansley Coe Throckmorton, *General Secretary, Division of Education and Publication*+*
Arthur G. Clyde, *Hymnal Editor+*
Kristen Lundstrom Forman, *Assistant Editor*
Jonathan B. McNair, *Assistant Editor, Music*
Sylvia Penny, *Copyright Specialist*
Lynne M. Deming, *Publisher*
(*members ex officio of the Hymnal Committee)
(+members ex officio of the Editorial Panel)

Grateful Appreciation to

Gene Paul Strayer, *who was succeeded on the committee by* Stephen Wayles.

Lavon Bayler, Dosia Carlson, Carl P. Daw Jr., Ruth Duck, Sylvia G. Dunstan, Marty Haugen, Carolyn Jennings, Madeleine Forell Marshall, Elizabeth C. Ragan, Thomas H. Troeger, and Miriam Therese Winter, *who assisted in the revision of hymn texts.*

Bede Kotlinski, O.S.B., *who consulted on the Latin texts.*

Jon Michael Spencer, Marilyn K. Stulken, and Mary Louise VanDyke, *who assisted in the preparation of historical notes.*

Burton H. Throckmorton Jr., *who was consulted on the versification and language of the psalms.*

June Christine Goudey and Robert D. Witham, *who helped compile the worship resources.*

Jo Shelnutt Melendy and Howard H. Tobak, *who assisted in the preparation of scriptural references.*

Joan Menocal, *who designed the divider pages.*

EDITOR'S NOTES

As worshipers begin to use the hymn section of this book, they will find a pattern throughout the pages. Preceding each hymn are the first line, scriptural references, and source(s) of the text. As is customary, *alt.* indicates that the original text has been altered; *adapt.* indicates more extensive revision. There are three noteworthy elements of style. First, in many instances, a non-English text precedes the English translation in recognition of the culture of origin. Second, poetic capitalization has been dealt with uniformly by using capitals at musical cadence points to achieve consistency in appearance. Third, in verses outside the music score, hyphens have been added for singing ease.

The historical notes following the hymns provide background, however brief, on the circumstances of origin. The composer, tune name, meter, and other information pertaining to the music also follow the hymn, making a clear distinction between music and text information. Dates appearing in the citations indicate, for the most part, the year of creation or first publication. Birth and death dates are located in the index. Users will find extensive indexes to aid in selecting hymns for the lectionary year. In addition, traditional topical and scriptural indexing have been provided.

Much care has been taken to present music that most congregations will find within their abilities. At the same time, the hymnal provides an occasional challenge that may require some practice and effort. The majority of settings are harmonized to allow for part singing. When unison settings appear, it is often because they were conceived that way, and usually it indicates a strong, vigorous melody. Performance directives are few, since worship tradition, occasion, architecture, instrumentation, and other factors can greatly alter the choice of tempo or dynamic. The collection allows for experimentation, and enthusiastic participation will sometimes be preferred to absolute "correctness" of style. All are encouraged to try the many languages and styles that have been included in the book to gain a sense of the church's diversity. This can provide opportunities to invite those who know this music to introduce it.

The New Century Hymnal was compiled with anticipation of the joy it will bring. It was also prepared with the hope that its musical and poetic offerings will be true both to past traditions and to the desire of the church to renew its worship. As in every age, texts have been changed to provide for worship in the vernacular. The wisdom of using skilled hymnwriters to perform this task should be evident as the hymns are sung. Many classic texts are reclaimed through new translations, which in some instances restore verses that had fallen into disuse. Throughout, the goal has been not to achieve the perfect or ultimate version, but to make the hymns live in our own time to be passed into the hands of coming generations, for their use and adaptations.

Arthur G. Clyde
Editor, The New Century Hymnal

ORDERS FOR WORSHIP

In the Orders for Worship that follow, the word "Sovereign" may be said instead of the word "Lord."

Service of the Word I

Prelude

The service may begin with music as the congregation gathers. The hymn or introit may follow, according to local custom.

Call to Worship

A leader may use one of the following or may offer other words appropriate to the season.

A LEADER

Morning has broken. Let us give thanks for the gift of life and for the presence of the Holy One among us. Let us worship God together.

B LEADER

Our help is in the name of God, who made heaven and earth. Let us worship God.

PEOPLE

Thanks be to God!

Hymn of Adoration

All may be invited to stand. This may be a processional.

Introit

An introit related to the season may be said or sung.

Prayer of Confession

All may be seated. A leader may offer a prayer based on scripture, may use his or her own words, or may use one of the following prayers.

LEADER

Let us confess our sins before God and one another.

A ALL

Almighty and merciful God, you created and are creating still. In your presence our limits lie stark before us. We confess our unclean lips, our cold hearts, our turning away from neighbors, our broken promises, and our unrepentant hours. Forgive us, O Holy One. We confess that we have squandered the gifts you have given. We have neglected the land. We have grasped for goods. We have used each other. We have loved power more than people. Forgive us, O Holy One. Cleanse from us the illusion of innocence. Come into our hearts, and make us new again. We pray in the name of Jesus. Amen.

B ALL

Most merciful God, we confess that we are in bondage to sin and cannot free ourselves. We have sinned against you in thought, word, and deed, by what we have done and by what we have left undone. We have not loved you with our whole heart. We have not loved our neighbors as ourselves. For the sake of Jesus Christ, have mercy on us. Forgive us, renew us, and lead us, so that we may delight in your will and follow in your ways, to the glory of your holy name. Amen.[1]

SILENCE

Silence may be observed for reflection and prayer.

ASSURANCE OF PARDON

A leader may speak of God's pardon or mercy in her or his own words or may use one of the following.

A LEADER

In Jesus Christ, God knows and
receives us as we are. Listen, give
thanks, and live.

B LEADER

Almighty God, who is great in mercy
and promises forgiveness of sin to all
who truly repent and are sincere in
faith, have mercy on you, pardon and
deliver you from all sin, confirm and
strengthen you in all goodness, and
bring you to everlasting life.

PEOPLE

Amen.

Thanks be to God.

PASSING THE PEACE

As a sign of their reconciliation with God and each other, all may greet those around them with an embrace or a handshake, accompanied by such words as: "The peace of God be with you," and the response: "And also with you."

All may be invited to stand for the passing of the peace. Leaders of the service may move among the congregation to share the signs of peace.

PSALM OR RESPONSIVE READING

A psalm may be sung or read responsively or in unison.

GLORIA

All may be invited to stand for a gloria or another hymn of praise. Musical settings, 754–760.

READING OF SCRIPTURE

The people may be seated as the scripture lessons are introduced. It is recommended that the schedule of readings found in the ecumenical lectionary be used. If it is not, care should be taken to maintain a balance in readings from the Old Testament, the Epistles, and the Gospels.

A collect for illumination, a seasonal collect, or an extemporaneous prayer asking for attentive hearts may precede the first reading. A brief introduction to the theme of each lesson may be offered. In order to distinguish the lesson from the commentary, the leader may announce the lesson.

OLD TESTAMENT LESSON

READER *before the lesson*

Listen for the word of God in _____.

After the lesson, a psalm may be said or sung, followed by a gloria, unless one has been said or sung earlier, or the following or a similar announcement may be made.

READER

Here ends the Old Testament lesson.

Epistle Lesson

READER *before the lesson*
Listen for the word of God in _____.

READER *following the lesson*
Here ends the Epistle lesson.

Gospel Lesson

In some local churches, standing, for those who are able, for the reading of the Gospel is customary as it is a sign of respect for Jesus Christ, who addresses the congregation in words remembered by the early church. The responses before and after this lesson may be said or sung. (See 761–764.)

READER *before the lesson*
Listen to the Gospel of Jesus Christ according to _____.

PEOPLE
Glory to you, O Christ.

READER *following the lesson*
This is the good news.

PEOPLE
Praise to you, O Christ.

Sermon

Affirmation of Faith

All may be invited to stand for a form of the Statement of Faith of the United Church of Christ, a creed, or a church covenant. (See 881–887.)

Hymn, Anthem, or Other Music

Prayers of the People

The people may be seated. Leaders may announce special concerns for prayers and invite the people to indicate needs or to name causes for thanksgiving. Intercessions may include prayers for:

- *The church universal, including ecumenical councils, specific churches in other places, the United Church of Christ and its leaders, and this local church.*
- *The nations and all in authority.*
- *Justice and peace in all the world.*
- *The health of those who suffer in body, mind, or spirit.*
- *The needs of families, single people, and the lonely.*
- *Reconciliation with adversaries.*
- *The local community and all other communities.*
- *All who are oppressed or in prison.*

A litany of prayers and responses, with silences, may be used; a pastoral prayer may be offered; petitions may be offered by anyone present, ending with a phrase to which all may respond, such as those below. A longer period of silence may precede or follow the prayers.

A LEADER
Christ, in your mercy,

PEOPLE
Hear our prayer.

B LEADER
Holy Spirit, our Comforter,

PEOPLE
Receive our prayer.

LORD'S PRAYER

Standing, sitting, or kneeling, all may sing or say the prayer received from Jesus Christ.

CONCERNS OF THE CHURCH

The people may be seated. A leader and the people may announce information concerning the program, ministry, and people of the church.

OFFERTORY

A leader may use his or her own words or one of the following to introduce the offertory.

A LEADER

Let everyone give, not grudgingly or of necessity, but from the fullness of our gratitude to God.

B LEADER

Let us give, as each is able, according to the blessings God has given each of us.

Music may be offered to God's glory while the tithes and offerings are being received. Silence is also appropriate. The people may express their dedication and thanksgiving to God through music, prayers, dance, and other acts. The people may be invited to stand as representatives bring the gifts to the table. A doxology may be sung, and a prayer of dedication may be said. Musical settings, 776–782, 784, 785.

HYMN

COMMISSIONING AND BENEDICTION

A LEADER

The blessing of the God of Sarah and of Abraham; the blessing of Jesus Christ, born of Mary; the blessing of the Holy Spirit, who broods over us as a mother over her children; be with you all. Amen.[2]

B LEADER

Go forth into the world to serve God with gladness; be of good courage; hold fast to that which is good; render to no one evil for evil; strengthen the fainthearted; support the weak; help the afflicted; honor all people; love and serve God, rejoicing in the power of the Holy Spirit.[3]

The grace of Jesus Christ, the love of God, and the communion of the Holy Spirit, be with you all.[4] Amen.

POSTLUDE

The congregation may be seated and remain until the postlude is concluded.

Service of the Word II

Concerns of the Church

Leaders and the people may announce information concerning the program, ministry, and people of the church now or at the offertory.

Prelude

The service may begin with music as the congregation gathers. The call to worship or hymn may follow, according to local custom.

Call to Worship

All may be invited to stand. A leader may offer one of the following or other words appropriate to the season.

A LEADER

Rejoice, for God is among us. Give thanks, for in Christ we are a new people. Sing praise, for we come to worship God.

B LEADER

Come from the east and the west, the north and the south, and worship the God of our fathers and mothers, the God of Jesus Christ. Amen. The grace of Jesus Christ and the love of God and the communion of the Holy Spirit be with us all.[5]

PEOPLE

Amen.

Hymn of Adoration

All may be invited to stand. This may be a processional hymn.

Invocation

All may be invited to stand. A leader may offer a prayer in her or his own words or may use one of these, asking for the worshipers to be made responsive to the presence of God.

A LEADER

Christ is with us.

PEOPLE

Christ is in our midst.

LEADER

Let us pray.

B LEADER

God be with you.

PEOPLE

And also with you.

LEADER

Let us pray.

AND

A ALL

O God, distant yet near, we gather as witnesses to your promise that if we seek you with all our hearts, we will find you. Be among us this day. Hear the confessions of our mouths and the yearnings of our hearts. Help us

B ALL

Gracious God, gentle in your power and strong in your tenderness, you have brought us forth from the womb of your being and breathed into us the breath of life. We know that we do not live by bread alone

5

change the narrowness of our vision and the pettiness of our living. Make us new again with your holy grace. Grant us the maturity to accept your many gifts in humility and to use them with faithfulness. Grant to us your spirit that our worship may have integrity and energy, ever witnessing to your holy presence in our lives. We praise and give thanks to you, Eternal Presence; through Jesus Christ we pray. Amen.

but by every word that comes from you. Feed our deep hungers with the living bread that you give us in Jesus Christ. May Jesus' promise, "Where two or three are gathered in my name, there am I in the midst of them,"[6] be fulfilled in us. Make us a joyful company of your people so that with the faithful in every place and time we may praise and honor you, God Most High. Amen.

Prayer of Our Savior

LEADER
Let us pray as Christ our Savior has taught us.
Standing, sitting, or kneeling, all may sing or say the prayer received from Jesus Christ.

Psalm or Responsive Reading

A psalm may be sung or read responsively or in unison.

Gloria

All may be invited to stand for a gloria or another hymn of praise. Musical settings, 754–760.

Prayer for Illumination or Collect for the Day

The people may be seated. A leader may offer a prayer for illumination in her or his own words asking for open hearts and attentive minds, may use a seasonal collect, or may use one of these.

A LEADER
Eternal God, in the reading of the scripture, may your word be heard; in the meditations of our hearts, may your word be known; and in the faithfulness of our lives, may your word be shown. Amen.

B LEADER
Almighty God, you have revealed yourself to us as one God; give us grace to continue steadfast in the living of our faith and constant in our worship of you, for you live and reign, one God, now and for ever. Amen.

Reading of Scripture

It is recommended that the schedule of readings found in the ecumenical lectionary be used. If it is not, care should be taken to maintain a balance in readings from the Old Testament, the Epistles, and the Gospels.

A brief introduction to the theme of each lesson may be offered. In order to distinguish the lesson from the commentary, the reader may announce: "A reading from _____" and may conclude: "Here ends the lesson."

Sermon

Hymn, Anthem, or Other Music

Prayers of the People

The people may be seated. Leaders may announce special concerns for prayers and invite the people to indicate needs or to name causes for thanksgiving. See page 3 for topics for intercessions. A litany of prayers and responses, with silences, may be used; a pastoral prayer may be offered; petitions may be offered by anyone present, ending with a phrase to which all may respond, such as those below. A longer period of silence may precede or follow the prayers.

A LEADER

Merciful God,

PEOPLE

Hear our prayer.

B LEADER

Healing Spirit,

PEOPLE

Receive our prayer.

Passing the Peace

As a sign of their reconciliation with God and each other, all may greet those around them with an embrace or a handshake, accompanied by such words as: "The peace of God be with you," and the response: "And also with you." All who are able may rise for the passing of the peace. Leaders of the service may move among the congregation to share the signs of peace.

Offertory

As part of the offering of life and labor, significant announcements concerning the mission of the church may be made. Music may be offered to God's glory while the tithes and offerings are being received. Silence is also appropriate. The people may express their dedication and thanksgiving to God through music, prayers, dance, and other acts. Upon presentation of the offerings, a leader may offer a prayer of dedication, and a doxology may be sung. Musical settings, 776–782, 784, 785.

Hymn

Commissioning and Benediction

A LEADER

Let us go forth into the new seasons of our lives.

PEOPLE

We go forth into growing and changing and living.

LEADER

Let us go with caring awareness for the world and all that is in it.

PEOPLE

We go to discover the needs and opportunities around us.

LEADER

Let us go forth in peace and be led out in joy.

ALL

We go in God's continuing presence, with the power to love and the strength to serve. Amen.[7]

B LEADER

God's peace go with you into the worlds in which you live; be nurtured by the time of gathering, be faithful in the time apart. Love and serve each other in the name of the faithful God, who calls us to be God's people; and the blessing of God, Creator, Redeemer, and Sanctifier, be with us always. Amen.

Postlude

The congregation may be seated and remain until the postlude is concluded.

Morning Prayer

The practice of Christian morning prayer came from our Jewish heritage. This suggested service of prayer is based on traditions of early Christian daily public worship. Appropriate for any gathering for morning worship, morning prayer can be adapted for use in the home by family or for individual devotions. A daily lectionary may be used to provide scripture and psalm selections.

Opening Sentence

All may stand or, if desired, remain seated throughout.
O God, open my lips.
And my mouth shall proclaim your praise.

Doxology

The following or other praise of the Trinity may be said or sung. (See also 776–782.) Alleluia is omitted in the season of Lent.

Praise to the holy and undivided Trinity, one God:
as it was in the beginning, is now, and will be forever. Amen.

Throughout Lent

Alleluia!
Alleluia!

Praise to you, O Christ,
Sovereign of eternal Glory.

Morning Hymn or Canticle (Optional)

A morning hymn or canticle may be sung. See Morning hymns; "Canticle of the Three," 738.

Morning Psalm

One of the following psalms, or others, may be used: Psalm 51, 63, 67, or 95. (See Psalter section, pp. 621–731.) Following the morning psalm, the people may be seated.

Psalms

An additional psalm for the day or other psalms may be sung or said. Following each psalm is a period of silence for reflection.

Reading from Scripture

One or more readings from scripture are announced and read, followed by

A
The word of truth.
Thanks be to God.

B *following a Gospel reading*
This is the good news.
Praise to you, O Christ.

After a silence for reflection following the reading of scripture, an appropriate meditation or a reading other than scripture may be offered. Silence may follow.

Canticle of Zechariah

May be sung or spoken. A hymn version, 110, may be used, or the pointed version in the Psalter, p. 733.

Blessed be the Sovereign God of Israel,
who has looked favorably on the people and redeemed them.
God has raised up a mighty savior for us
in the house of God's servant David;
as God spoke through the mouth of the holy prophets from of old,
that we would be saved from our enemies and from the hand of all who hate us.
Thus God has shown the mercy
promised to our ancestors,

and has remembered God's holy covenant,

the oath that God swore to our ancestor Abraham,

to grant us that we, being rescued from the hands of our enemies,

might serve God without fear, in holiness and righteousness
before God all our days.

And you, child, will be called the prophet of the Most High,

for you will go before God to prepare God's ways;
to give knowledge of salvation to the people
by the forgiveness of their sins.

By the tender mercy of our God,

the dawn from on high will break upon us,

to give light to those who sit in night and in the shadow of death,

to guide our feet into the way of peace.

PRAYERS

One of the following prayers for mercy may be said. (Musical settings, 745–753.)

A

God be with you.

And also with you.

(Let us pray, saying "Christ have mercy.")

That there may be purpose and fulfillment, O God, in all that we do,

Christ have mercy.

That we may show others this day the love that you have taught us,

Christ have mercy.

That the church throughout the world may respond to your call for peace and justice,

Christ have mercy.

That those who are in need be helped and comforted,

Christ have mercy.

(Other intercessions may be added.)

That we may be strengthened by your grace for the tasks of this day,

Christ have mercy.

B	**C**	**D**
Holy God,	Lord, have mercy.	Sovereign, have mercy.
Holy and Mighty One,	**Christ, have mercy.**	**Christ, have mercy.**
Holy Immortal One,	Lord, have mercy.	Sovereign, have mercy.
Have mercy upon us.		

PRAYER OF OUR SAVIOR

One of the following versions or another version may be said.

A	**B**
Our Father in heaven,	**Our Father-Mother, who is in the heavens,**
hallowed be your name,	**may your name be made holy,**
your kingdom come,	**may your dominion come,**
your will be done,	**may your will be done,**
on earth as in heaven.	**on the earth as it is in heaven.**

Give us today our daily bread.	Give us today the bread we need;
Forgive us our sins	and forgive us our debts,
as we forgive those who sin against us.	as we have forgiven our debtors;
Save us from the time of trial	and do not put us to the test,
and deliver us from evil.	but rescue us from evil.
For the kingdom, the power,	For yours is the dominion, and the power,
and the glory are yours,	and the glory forever. Amen.
now and for ever. Amen.	

COLLECT

God be with you.
And also with you.

One of the following prayers or another may be used.

General

Almighty God, give us faith to live this day not knowing where it will lead, but with the assurance that your love and guidance are with us always; through Jesus Christ. **Amen.**

Advent

Stir up our hearts, O God, to prepare the way for the coming of the Promised One. Help us to spend our days open to the presence of Christ in our lives. **Amen.**

Christmastide

Almighty God, you have given us the Word in flesh. Let the Word be the wisdom for all that we do in our lives; through Jesus Christ, this Word, who reigns with you and the Holy Spirit, one God, now and forever. **Amen.**

Epiphany

Almighty God, as you have led us to your Child by a star, lead us to seek faithfully your presence in our lives this day; through Jesus Christ, the light of the world. **Amen.**

Lent

Most merciful God, all have sinned and fall short of your glory; but you have given us your only begotten Child that we may have eternal life. Keep us ever mindful of this gift that we may gratefully serve you all of our days. **Amen.**

Eastertide

Almighty God, in Christ you have embraced all of life through the one who is the way, the truth, and the life. Pour out your grace upon us that we may love all of life as you have loved us. **Amen.**

A concluding hymn may be sung (optional).

May the God of hope fill you with all joy and peace in believing, so that you may abound in hope by the power of the Holy Spirit.

Let us bless God.
Thanks be to God.

Evening Prayer

The practice of Christian evening prayer came from our Jewish heritage. This suggested service of prayer is based on traditions of early Christian daily public worship. Appropriate for any gathering for evening worship, this order for prayer can be adapted for use in the home by family or for individual devotions. In the earliest tradition, lamps are lighted as the hymn of praise is sung to Christ, the radiant light. If evening prayer is the final prayer of the night, a penitential prayer may be said following the opening sentence. A daily lectionary may be used to provide scripture and psalm selections.

Service of Light

For the lighting of candles or lamps (optional).

Jesus Christ is the light of the world.
The light shines in the deepest night,
and the night cannot overcome it.
Stay with us now, for it is evening,
and the day is almost over.
Let your light disperse the shadows
and shine within us here.

Evening Hymn

A hymn is sung when the candles or lamps have been lit. "O Holy Radiance," 736, "O Wisdom," 737, "Christ, Mighty Savior," 93, or another evening hymn may be used. If the preceding Service of Light is not used, Evening Prayer may begin with the Opening Sentence and Doxology, and an evening hymn may be inserted before the Evening Psalm.

Opening Sentence

All may stand or, if desired, remain seated throughout.

O God, come to my aid.
Hear my voice when I cry to you.

Doxology

The following or other praise of the Trinity may be said or sung. (See also 776–782.) Alleluia is omitted in the season of Lent.

Praise to the holy and undivided Trinity, one God:
as it was in the beginning, is now, and will be forever. Amen.

	Throughout Lent
Alleluia!	Praise to you, O Christ,
Alleluia!	**Sovereign of eternal Glory.**

Evening Psalm

Psalm 141 is said or sung. (See Psalter, pp. 716, 730, 731.) In keeping with the intention of Psalm 141, incense may be used. Following the psalm, the people may be seated.

Psalm

Following the evening psalm, one or more psalms may be said or sung, especially Psalms 110–117; 120–133; 135–147. Following each psalm is a period of silence for reflection.

Reading from Scripture

One or more readings from scripture are announced and read, followed by

A	**B**	**C** *following a Gospel reading*
God have mercy on us.	The word of truth.	This is the good news.
Thanks be to God.	**Thanks be to God.**	**Praise to you, O Christ.**

After a silence for reflection following the reading of scripture, an appropriate meditation or a reading other than scripture may be offered. Silence may follow.

THE SONG OF MARY

May be sung or spoken. Hymn versions, 106, 119 may be used, or the pointed version in the Psalter, p. 732.

My soul magnifies the Sovereign,
> **and my spirit rejoices in God my Savior;**
for God has looked with favor on the lowliness of God's servant.
> **Surely, from now on all generations will call me blessed;**
for the Mighty One has done great things for me,
> **the Mighty One whose name is holy.**
God's mercy is for those who fear God
> **from generation to generation.**
God has shown great strength;
> **and has scattered the proud in the thoughts of their hearts.**
God has brought down the powerful from their thrones,
> **and lifted up the lowly;**
God has filled the hungry with good things,
> **and sent the rich away empty.**
God has helped God's servant Israel,
> **in remembrance of God's mercy,**
according to the promise made to our ancestors,
> **to Abraham and Sarah and to their descendants forever.**

PRAYERS

One of the following prayers for mercy may be said (Musical settings, 745–753.)

A

God be with you.
And also with you.

(Let us pray, saying "O God, hear our prayer.")
For the peace from on high and for our salvation, let us pray,
O God, hear our prayer.

For the welfare of all churches, and for those who lead us in the faith,
O God, hear our prayer.

For our nation and our community, and for those who preside in public offices,
O God, hear our prayer.

For all who hunger, are sick, and in pain,
O God, hear our prayer.

(Other intercessions may be added.)
For a peaceful evening and safety this night,
O God, hear our prayer.

B	**C**	**D**
Holy God,	Lord, have mercy.	Sovereign, have mercy.
Holy and Mighty One,	**Christ, have mercy.**	**Christ, have mercy.**
Holy Immortal One,	Lord, have mercy.	Sovereign, have mercy.
Have mercy upon us.		

PRAYER OF OUR SAVIOR

One of the following versions or another version may be said.

A

Our Father in heaven,
    hallowed be your name,
    your kingdom come,
    your will be done,
    on earth as in heaven.
Give us today our daily bread.
Forgive us our sins
    as we forgive those who sin against us.
Save us from the time of trial
    and deliver us from evil.
For the kingdom, the power,
    and the glory are yours,
    now and for ever. Amen.

B

Our Father-Mother, who is in the heavens,
    may your name be made holy.
    may your dominion come,
    may your will be done,
    on the earth as it is in heaven.
Give us today the bread we need;
    and forgive us our debts,
    as we have forgiven our debtors;
    and do not put us to the test,
    but rescue us from evil.
For yours is the dominion, and the power,
    and the glory forever. Amen.

COLLECT

God be with you.
And also with you.

The following or others may be used.

General

Almighty God, you have brought us to the ending of this day; release us from all chains of strife and draw us close with your gentle bands of peace. **Amen.**

Advent

Almighty God, as you have sent the Word to be the light of the world, let that light shine in our hearts that we may be filled with the joy and peace that you alone can provide. **Amen.**

Christmastide

Almighty God, may the light that shines from the cradle in Bethlehem be the light in our hearts that guides us and protects us; we pray in the name of the Christ, who is the way, the truth, and the light. **Amen.**

Epiphany

Eternal Light, you have shone your glory upon us in Christ, the Word made flesh. May our lives ever be a reflection of your gift of salvation to us. **Amen.**

Lent

O Jesus, Sun of Salvation, shine in our inmost beings this night; be the lamp to our way, and our beacon of hope. We pray in the name of Christ, the light of the world. **Amen.**

Eastertide

Almighty God, you have given us the gift of eternal life in the risen Christ. May the glory light of the resurrection shine within us forevermore, through Jesus Christ we pray. **Amen.**

A concluding hymn may be sung (optional).

A

Let us bless God.
Thanks be to God.

B

May God bless us and protect us.
**May God bring us to everlasting light.
Amen.**

HYMNS

Immortal, Invisible, God Only Wise

1

Walter C. Smith, 1867; alt.

1 Tim. 1:17; Ps. 36:6

1 Im - mor - tal, in - vis - i - ble, God on - ly wise,
2 Un - rest - ing, un - hast - ing, and si - lent as light,
3 Your life is life - giv - ing— to both great and small;
4 So per - fect your glo - ry, so bril - liant your light,

in light in - ac - ces - si - ble hid from our eyes,
not want - ing, not wast - ing, but rul - ing in might;
in all life you're liv - ing, the true life of all;
your an - gels a - dore you, all veil - ing their sight;

Most bless - ed, most glo - rious, the An - cient of Days,
Your jus - tice like moun - tains high soar - ing a - bove,
We blos - som and flour - ish as leaves and as flowers,
All praise we now ren - der as your an - gels do:

al - might - y, vic - to - rious, your great name we praise.
your clouds which are foun - tains of good - ness and love.
then with - er and per - ish— but naught dims your powers.
in awe at the splen - dor of light hid - ing you.

Walter C. Smith, minister of the Free Church of Scotland and
later moderator of the Assembly, wrote poetry as a retreat from
work and to say what could not be fully expressed in the pulpit.

Tune: ST. DENIO 11.11.11.11.
Adapt. from a Welsh ballad in John Roberts'
Caniadaeth y Cysegr, *1839*

Glory, Glory Hallelujah

Exod. 15:20; Gen. 28:12; Ps. 81:6

African-American spiritual

1 Glo - ry, glo - ry hal - le - lu - jah, since I laid my bur - dens down. Glo - ry, glo - ry hal - le - lu - jah, since I laid my bur - dens down.
2 I feel bet - ter, so much bet - ter, since I laid my bur - dens down. I feel bet - ter, so much bet - ter, since I laid my bur - dens down.
3 Feel like shout - ing "Hal - le - lu - jah!" since I laid my bur - dens down. Feel like shout - ing "Hal - le - lu - jah!" since I laid my bur - dens down.
4 I am danc - ing Mir - iam's dance now, since I laid my bur - dens down. I am danc - ing Mir - iam's dance now, since I laid my bur - dens down.
5 I am climb - ing Ja - cob's lad - der, since I laid my bur - dens down. I am climb - ing Ja - cob's lad - der, since I laid my bur - dens down.
6 Ev - ery round goes higher and high - er, since I laid my bur - dens down. Ev - ery round goes higher and high - er, since I laid my bur - dens down.

Despite their physical captivity, the enslaved of antebellum America often found an inward freedom through their faith in Jesus the liberator. This liberation, which permitted them to sing rejoicingly, anticipated their eventual physical emancipation.

Tune: GLORY, GLORY 8.7.8.7.
African-American spiritual
Arr. Joyce Finch Johnson, 1992

Wakantanka Taku Nitawa

3

(Many and Great, O God, Are Your Works)

Dakota hymn, Joseph R. Renville, 1842
Paraphr. by R. Philip Frazier, 1929; alt.
For another translation, see 341

Ps. 104:24–25; Jer. 10:12–13; 2 Esd. 16:56–60

Optional hand-drum rhythm: ♩ ♩ ♩

1 Wa - kan - tan - ka   ta - ku   ni - ta - wa   tan - ka - ya
2 Wo - eh - da - ku   ni - ta - wa kin   he   mi - na - gi

1 Man - y and   great,   O   God,   are your   works,   Mak - er of
2 Grant un - to   us   com - mu - nion with   you,   O   star a -

qa   o - ta;   Ma - hpi - ya   kin   e - ya - hna - ke   ca,
kin   qu   wo;   Ma - hpi - ya   kin   i - wan - kam ya - ti,

earth and   sky;   Your hands have   set   the   heav - ens with   stars,
bid - ing   One;   Come un - to   us   and   dwell with   us:

ma - ka kin   he   du - o - wan - ca,   Mni - o - wan -
wi - co - wa - śte   yu - ha   nan - ka,   Wi - co - ni

your   fin - gers spread   the   moun - tains and   plains.   Lo,   at your
with   you   are   found   the   gifts   of   life.   Bless   us with

ca   śbe - ya   wan - ke   cin,   he - na o - ya - ki - hi.
kin   he   ma - ya - qu   nun,   o - wi - han - ke   wa - nin.

word   the   wa - ters were formed;   deep seas o - bey your   voice.
life   that   has   no   end,   e - ter - nal   life with   you.

Probably the best-known Native American hymn, "Many and Great" is sung with great reverence by the Dakota people in worship, at communion, and for births, funerals, and burials. Renville helped establish the Lac qui Parle mission in Minnesota. Frazier, a Native American, was a Congregational minister.

Tune: LACQUIPARLE 9.6.9.9.9.6.
Native American melody (Dakota)
Adapt. Joseph R. Renville, 1842
Harm. James R. Murray, 1877

4
Joyful, Joyful, We Adore You

Ps. 145:10; Isa. 49:13

Henry van Dyke, 1907; alt.

1 Joy - ful, joy - ful, we a - dore you, God of glo - ry, God of love;
2 All your works with joy sur-round you, earth and heaven re - flect your rays,
3 You are giv - ing and for - giv - ing, ev - er bless-ing, ev - er blessed,
4 Mor-tals, join the might-y cho - rus which the morn-ing stars be - gan;

Hearts un - fold like flowers be - fore you, open-ing to the sun a - bove.
Stars and an - gels sing a - round you, cen - ter of un - bro - ken praise.
Well-spring of the joy of liv - ing, o - cean depth of hap - py rest!
Bound-less love is reign-ing o'er us, re - con - cil - ing race and clan.

Melt the clouds of sin and sad - ness, drive the storms of doubt a - way;
Field and for - est, vale and moun-tain, flower-y mead-ow, flash-ing sea,
Lov - ing Spir - it, Fa - ther, Moth-er, all who love be - long to you;
Ev - er sing-ing, move we for - ward, faith - ful in the midst of strife,

Giv - er of im - mor - tal glad-ness, fill us with the light of day.
Chant-ing bird and flow-ing foun-tain, teach us what our praise should be.
Teach us how to love each oth - er, by that love our joy re - new.
Joy - ful mu - sic leads us on - ward in the tri - umph song of life.

Henry van Dyke was a noted church leader, U.S. ambassador,
Navy chaplain, and prolific writer. Many people associate this
hymn with Beethoven's ninth symphony, but few are aware
of the original poem by the German classicist F. Schiller
(1759–1805) that inspired Beethoven.

Tune: HYMN TO JOY 8.7.8.7.D.
Ludwig van Beethoven, 1824
Adapt. and harm. Edward Hodges, 1846

Praise to God

Nobuaki Hanaoka, 1980; alt.

Rom. 14:11; John 3:16; Eph. 5:16–20; Ps. 68:4, 32

Unison

1 Praise to God, praise to God, for the green - ness
2 Thanks to God, thanks to God, for the gift of
3 Sing to God, sing to God, for the grace of

of the trees, for the beau - ty of the flowers, for the bless - ing
friends in Christ, for the church, our house of faith, for the gift of
Je - sus Christ, for the love of par - ent God, for the com - fort

of the sky, for the great - ness of the sea.
won - drous love, for the gift of end - less grace.
and the strength of the Spir - it, ho - ly God.

Praise to God, praise to God, now and for - ev - er - more.
Thanks to God, thanks to God, now and for - ev - er - more.
Sing to God, sing to God, now and for - ev - er - more.

Nobuaki Hanaoka was born in Japan and has earned degrees in theology from Japanese and American schools. Hanaoka has served as a pastor in Sacramento, California, and has published articles in both Japanese and English. He is the author of Nihilism and Nothingness, 1968.

Tune: SAKURA 6.7.7.7.7.6.6.
Traditional Japanese melody
Harm. Jonathan McNair, 1993

6   Sing Praise to God, Our Highest Good

Ps. 105; 1 Chron. 16:9; 1 Pet. 1:3–7

Johann J. Schütz, 1675
Transl. Madeleine Forell Marshall, 1993

1 Sing praise to God, our high-est good, pro - found re - spect ex -
2 Cre - a - tion thanks you, Ho - ly One: you made us and re -
3 What God has made, God will pre-serve, with righ-teous-ness un -
4 I cry to God, in pain and grief, "Please, God of mer - cy,

press - ing. God gives us health, life, live - li - hood, with ev - ery
new us. De - light-ed at what you have done, you show your
fail - ing. Re - gard-less what we may de - serve, we see this
hear me!" My cer - tain help pro - vides re - lief, faith, hope, and

need - ed bless - ing. To God, who won-drous works per-forms, cre -
great - ness through us. So may all liv - ing things pro-claim the
good pre - vail - ing. To God who gov - erns ev - er-more with
love to cheer me. So let me sing, joy - ful and free: ah,

a - ting life and calm-ing storms, to God give praise and glo - ry!
won-ders of their Mak-er's name: to God give praise and glo - ry!
jus - tice serv - ing rich and poor, to God give praise and glo - ry!
thank-ful Chris-tians, sing with me: to God give praise and glo - ry!

5 For-ev-er with us, God is here,
　　Nor ev-er will de-sert us.
　So dear-ly loved, we shall not fear:
　　there's noth-ing that can hurt us.
　We place our trust in God's com-mand,
　who leads us with a moth-er's hand:
　to God give praise and glo-ry!

6 Dear Chris-tian friends, we bear the name
　　of Christ, our sure sal-va-tion.
　Let us re-call Christ Je-sus came,
　　most ho-ly in-car-na-tion,
　Came from the one God we a-dore,
　came with new life for-ev-er-more:
　to God give praise and glo-ry!

*Johann Jakob Schütz practiced both civil and canon law in
Frankfurt, Germany, throughout his life. He had an interest in the
company that purchased land in Germantown, Pennsylvania, from
William Penn in 1683. Schütz published two collections of hymns.*

Tune:　MIT FREUDEN ZART　8.7.8.7.8.8.7.
Bohemian Brethren's Kirchengesäng, *1566*
Harm. Maurice F. Bell, 1906

All People That on Earth Do Dwell　　　　7

William Kethe, 1561　　　　　　　　　　　　　　　　　　　　*Ps. 100*
Adapt. Thomas H. Troeger, 1992

1 All peo-ple that on earth do dwell, sing
2 Know that there is one God, in-deed, who
3 En-ter the sa-cred gates with praise, with
4 Pro-claim a-gain that God is good, whose

out your faith with cheer-ful voice; De-light in God whose
fash-ions us with-out our aid, Who claims us, gives us
joy ap-proach the tem-ple walls. Ex-tol and bless our
mer-cy is for-ev-er sure, Whose truth at all times

praise you tell, whose pres-ence calls you to re-joice.
all we need, whose ten-der care will nev-er fade.
God al-ways as peo-ple whom the Spir-it calls.
firm-ly stood, and shall from age to age en-dure.

*Old Hundredth is perhaps the best known and most widely used
of all psalm tunes. It came into English use in 1561 with Kethe's
paraphrase of Psalm 100 and has been associated with it ever since.*

Tune:　OLD HUNDREDTH　L.M.
Attrib. to Louis Bourgeois (c. 1510–c. 1561)
Trente quatre Pseaumes, *Geneva, 1551*

8

Praise to the Living God

Ps. 84:1–2

Curtis Beach, 1966; alt.

1 Praise to the liv - ing God, the God of love and light, Whose
2 Praise to the liv - ing God, from whom all things de - rive, Whose
3 Praise to the liv - ing God, who knows our joy and pain, Who
4 Praise to the liv - ing God, a - round, with - in, a - bove, Be -

word brought forth the myr - iad suns and set the worlds in flight;
Spir - it formed up - on this sphere the first faint seeds of life;
shares with us our com - mon life, the sa - cred and pro - fane.
yond the grasp of hu - man mind, but whom we know as love.

Whose in - fi - nite de - sign, which we but dim - ly see, Per -
Who caused them to e - volve, un - wit - ting, toward God's goal, Till
God toils wher-e'er we toil, in home and mart and mill; And
In these tu - mul-tuous days, so full of hope and strife, May

vades all na - ture, mak-ing all a cos - mic u - ni - ty.
hu - man-kind stood on the earth, as liv - ing, think-ing souls.
deep with - in the hu - man heart God leads us for - ward still.
we bear wit - ness to the Way, O Source and Goal of life.

Curtis Beach, born into a family of several generations of
ministers, was educated at Harvard University, the Boston
University School of Theology, and the University of Southern
California. A minister in the United Church of Christ, Beach
authored The Gospel of Mark: Its Making and Meaning.

Tune: DIADEMATA S.M.D.
George J. Elvey, 1868

We Sing to You, O God

9

Gracia Grindal, 1985, 1989

1 We sing to you, O God, the Rock who gave us birth, let
2 We wan-dered far from home out in a des-ert land, you
3 You bear us through the world, an ea-gle to her young, who
4 O God, e-ter-nal God, we hide with-in your wings, the

our re-joic-ing sing your name in all the earth. To you, O
shield-ed with your love our fear-ful pil-grim band. You kept us
ris-es on her wings and bears us toward the sun. We ride the
ev-er-last-ing arms to whom our prais-es ring. Your word is

God, let songs be raised, in joy-ful hymns, our feast of praise.
safe with-in your arms and shel-tered us a-gainst the storm.
vaults of light and air and trust in your un-fail-ing care.
true, your way is just, you are the God in whom we trust.

Poet, author, and teacher of poetry and writing, Gracia Grindal
has held editorial and consultant positions for several hymnic
publications. She has served as professor of pastoral theology
and ministry communication at Luther Northwestern
Theological Seminary, Minneapolis.

Tune: CAMANO 6.6.6.6.4.4.4.4.
Richard Proulx, 1979
Alternate tune: DARWALL'S 148TH

10

Maoz Tsur Y'shuati
(Rock of Ages)

Jewish traditional
Transl. Marcus Jastrow and Gustave Gottheil, 20th century

1 Ma - oz tsur y' - shu - a - ti l'-cha na - eh l'-sha - bei - ach,
1 Rock of a - ges, let our song praise your sav - ing pow - er;
2 Chil-dren of the Ho - ly God, wheth - er free or fet - tered,

ti - kon beit t' - fi - la - ti v'-sham to - dah n' - za - bei - ach.
you, a - mid the rag - ing foe, were our shel - tering tow - er.
wake the ech-oes of that song where you may be scat - tered.

L'-eit ta-chin mat - bei - ach mi - tzar ham'-na - bei - ach,
Fu - rious it as - sailed us, but your arm a - vailed us,
Yours the mes - sage cheer - ing that the time is near - ing

az eg - mor b'shir miz-mor cha - na - kat ha miz bei - ach.
and your word broke its sword when our own strength failed us.
which will see all set free, ty - rants no more fear - ing.

This traditional Jewish hymn and its tune are sung during Hanukkah. Instituted by Judas Maccabeus and the congregation of Israel in 165 B.C.E., Hanukkah commemorates the rededication of the Jerusalem temple after the victory that year over Antiochus Epiphanes.

Tune: MAOZ TSUR 7.6.7.6.6.6.3.3.6.
(ROCK OF AGES)
Traditional Hebrew melody

Bring Many Names

11

Brian Wren, 1989

Gen. 1:27

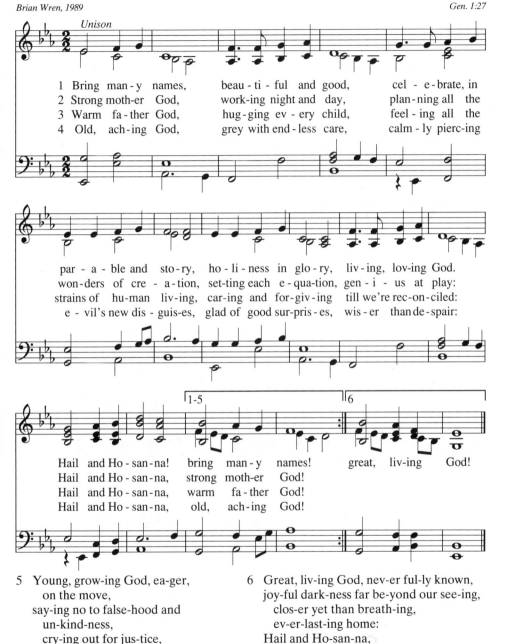

1 Bring man-y names, beau-ti-ful and good, cel-e-brate, in
2 Strong moth-er God, work-ing night and day, plan-ning all the
3 Warm fa-ther God, hug-ging ev-er-y child, feel-ing all the
4 Old, ach-ing God, grey with end-less care, calm-ly pierc-ing

par-a-ble and sto-ry, ho-li-ness in glo-ry, liv-ing, lov-ing God.
won-ders of cre-a-tion, set-ting each e-qua-tion, gen-i-us at play:
strains of hu-man liv-ing, car-ing and for-giv-ing till we're rec-on-ciled:
e-vil's new dis-guis-es, glad of good sur-pris-es, wis-er than de-spair:

Hail and Ho-san-na! bring man-y names! great, liv-ing God!
Hail and Ho-san-na, strong moth-er God!
Hail and Ho-san-na, warm fa-ther God!
Hail and Ho-san-na, old, ach-ing God!

5 Young, grow-ing God, ea-ger,
   on the move,
   say-ing no to false-hood and
   un-kind-ness,
   cry-ing out for jus-tice,
   giv-ing all you have:
   Hail and Ho-san-na,
   young, grow-ing God!

6 Great, liv-ing God, nev-er ful-ly known,
   joy-ful dark-ness far be-yond our see-ing,
   clos-er yet than breath-ing,
   ev-er-last-ing home:
   Hail and Ho-san-na,
   great, liv-ing God!

The author states that aspects of the divine are revealed in our maleness, femaleness, youth, and age in a moving, growing matrix of life in God. The tune Westchase was composed especially for this text.

Tune: WESTCHASE 9.10.11.9.
Carlton Young, 1989

12   I Sing the Mighty Power of God

Ps. 136:5–9; James 1:17

Isaac Watts, 1715; alt.

Descant

3 On earth there's not a plant or flower but makes your glo - ry known.

1 I sing the might - y power of God that made the moun - tains rise,
2 I sing the good-ness of our God that filled the earth with food;
3 On earth there's not a plant or flower but makes your glo - ry known.

The clouds a - rise and spread their showers by or - der from your throne.

That spread the flow-ing seas a - broad, and built the loft - y skies.
God formed the crea-tures with a word, and then pro - nounced them good.
The clouds a - rise and spread their showers by or - der from your throne.

All life is but a gift from you and ev - er in your care;

I sing the wis-dom that or - dained the sun to rule the day;
Oh, how your won-ders are dis - played, wher - e'er I turn my eye:
All life is but a gift from you and ev - er in your care;

The tune Ellacombe *was named for a place in Devonshire, England. It was first published in a collection of tunes used in the private chapel of the Duke of Wirtemberg, and was possibly sung with the text "Ave Maria, klärer."*

Tune: ELLACOMBE C.M.D.
Gesangbuch der herzoglichen
Wirtembergischen katholischen Hofkapelle, *1784*
Descant, The New Century Hymnal, *1993*

Wher - ev - er peo-ple gath - er, you, O God, are pres - ent there.

The moon shines full at God's com-mand, and all the stars o - bey.
If I sur - vey the ground I tread, or gaze up - on the sky!
Wher - ev - er peo-ple gath - er, you, O God, are pres-ent there.

O My Soul, Bless Your Creator 13

Anon.
United Presbyterian Book of Psalms, *1871; alt.*

Ps. 103

1 O my soul, bless your Cre - a - tor; all with-in me bless God's name;
2 God for-gives all your trans-gres-sions, all who suf - fer, gen - tly heals;
3 Far as east from west is dis-tant, God has put a - way our sin;
4 As it was with - out be - gin-ning, so it lasts with - out an end;
5 Un - to all who keep God's cov-enant and are stead-fast in God's way;

Bless your Mak - er, and for-get not all God's mer - cies to pro-claim.
God re - deems you from de-struc-tion, and with you so kind-ly deals.
Like a moth - er and a fa - ther, God com - pas - sion - ate has been.
To their chil - dren's chil-dren ev - er shall God's righ - teous - ness ex - tend:
Un - to all who still re-mem-ber God's com-mand-ments and o - bey.

Psalm 103, a beautiful psalm of thanksgiving for God's forgiveness and steadfast love, is summed up in the lines of this hymn. The author of the paraphrase is unknown.

Tune: STUTTGART 8.7.8.7.
Attrib. to Christian F. Witt
Psalmodia Sacra, *Gotha, 1715*

14

How Can I Say Thanks

Ps. 115:1

Andraé Crouch, 1971; alt.

How can I say thanks for the things you have done for me?

Things so un-de-served, yet you gave to prove your love for me; the

voic-es of a mil-lion an-gels could not ex-press my grat-i-tude. All that I

am, and ev-er hope to be; I owe it all to you.

To God be the glo-ry, to God be the glo-ry, to

God be the glo - ry for the things you have done.

Refrain

With your blood you have saved me; with your power you have raised me;

Second time, end

to God be the glo - ry for the things you have done.

Just let me live my life— let it be pleas-ing un-to you;

to Refrain ℅

And if I gain an - y praise, let it go to glo - ri - fy you.

Andraé Crouch, the son of a bishop in the Church of God in Christ, belongs to the contemporary gospel era. Beginning in 1969 this new gospel music was made to "rock" with the help of electronic instrumentation.

Tune: MY TRIBUTE Irr. with refrain
Andraé Crouch, 1971

My Heart Is Overflowing
(The Song of Hannah)

1 Sam. 2:1–10

Miriam Therese Winter, 1993

Unison

1 My heart is ov - er - flow-ing   with glad-ness and with praise.
2 The liv - ing God has spo - ken.   Earth an - swers with a song.
3 All who are poor and low - ly   will have a heaven-ly home.
4 The pow - er of com-pas - sion   can turn the world a - round.
5 The One who once cre - a - ted   and now sus - tains the earth,

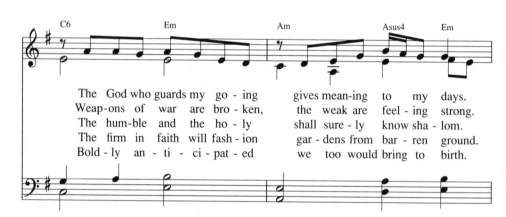

The God who guards my go - ing   gives mean-ing to my days.
Weap-ons of war are bro - ken,   the weak are feel - ing strong.
The hum-ble and the ho - ly   shall sure - ly know sha - lom.
The firm in faith will fash - ion   gar - dens from bar - ren ground.
Bold - ly an - ti - ci - pat - ed   we too would bring to birth.

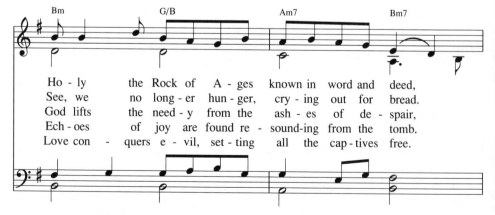

Ho - ly   the Rock of A - ges   known in word and deed,
See, we   no long - er hun - ger,   cry - ing out for bread.
God lifts   the need - y from the   ash - es of de - spair,
Ech - oes   of joy are found re - sound-ing from the tomb.
Love con - quers e - vil, set - ting   all the cap - tives free.

*In this song, Hannah, after many childless years, celebrates the
birth of Samuel with gratitude for God's faithfulness and
concern for the oppressed. This canticle is echoed later in the
New Testament "Song of Mary" or "Magnificat."*

Tune: TOLLEFSON 7.6.7.6.6.6.7.6.
Paulette Tollefson, 1971

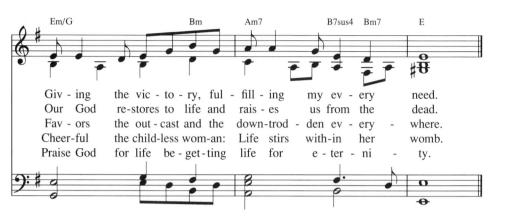

Giv - ing the vic - to - ry, ful - fill - ing my ev - ery need.
Our God re-stores to life and rais - es us from the dead.
Fav - ors the out - cast and the down-trod - den ev - ery - where.
Cheer-ful the child-less wom-an: Life stirs with-in her womb.
Praise God for life be - get-ting life for e - ter - ni - ty.

Let Us with a Joyful Mind

16

John Milton, 1624
Adapt. Thomas H. Troeger, 1993

Ps. 136

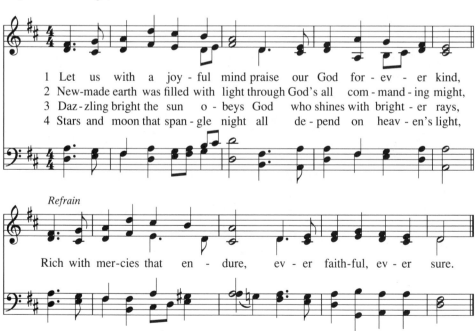

1 Let us with a joy - ful mind praise our God for - ev - er kind,
2 New-made earth was filled with light through God's all com - mand - ing might,
3 Daz - zling bright the sun o - beys God who shines with bright - er rays,
4 Stars and moon that span - gle night all de - pend on heav - en's light,

Refrain

Rich with mer-cies that en - dure, ev - er faith-ful, ev - er sure.

5 Crea-tures of the sea and land
  all are fed by God's own hand,
Rich with mer-cies that en-dure,
ev-er faith-ful, ev-er sure.

6 There-fore with a joy-ful mind,
  praise our God for-ev-er kind,
Rich with mer-cies that en-dure
ev-er faith-ful, ev-er sure.

As a youth of fifteen, John Milton composed a lengthy, elaborate paraphrase of Psalm 136 from which these lines have been selected. Milton, an English Puritan and Congregationalist, is best known for Paradise Lost.

Tune: INNOCENTS 7.7.7.7.
The Parish Choir, 1850

17

To You, O God, All Creatures Sing

Ps. 148

St. Francis of Assisi, 1225
Adapt. Miriam Therese Winter, 1993

Descant
4 To you, God, day af-ter day, earth in

Unison
1 To you, O God, all crea-tures sing, and all cre - a - tion, ev - ery-
2 Your wind that blows the tem-pest by, your clouds that sail a-cross the
3 Your flow-ing wa - ters, crys - tal clear, make mel - o - dies for you to
4 To you, O God, day af - ter day, your plan - et earth in ev - ery

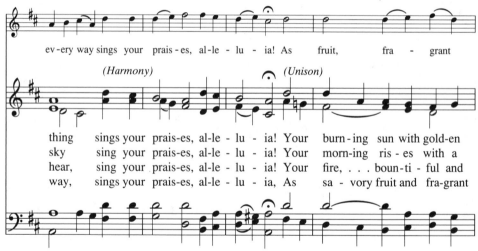

ev-ery way sings your prais - es, al-le - lu - ia! As fruit, fra - grant

(Harmony)   (Unison)

thing sings your prais-es, al-le - lu - ia! Your burn-ing sun with gold-en
sky sing your prais-es, al-le - lu - ia! Your morn-ing ris - es with a
hear, sing your prais-es, al-le - lu - ia! Your fire, . . . boun-ti - ful and
way, sings your prais-es, al-le - lu - ia, As sa - vory fruit and fra-grant

Miriam Therese Winter described her thoughts about adapting
this text: "As I entered into communion with the word and spirit
of the hymn, I felt called to enable that unknown-to-me poet's
wisdom to live on into the future, a moving commission, and
also felt a bond with the one who had gone before."

Tune: LASST UNS ERFREUEN
8.8.4.4.8.8. with alleluias
Geistliche Kirchengesäng, Cologne, 1623
Harm. Ralph Vaughan Williams, 1906
Descant, The New Century Hymnal, 1993

flower show forth glo - ry and power, sing - ing prais - es, al - le -

(Harmony)

beam, your sil - ver moon with soft - er gleam sing your prais - es,
song, and lights of eve - ning sing a - long, sing your prais - es, al - le -
bright, re - mem - bering your warmth and light, sings your prais - es,
flower show forth your glo - ry and your power, sing - ing prais - es,

lu - ia, al - le - lu - ia, al - le - lu - ia, al - le - lu - ia!

(Unison)

lu - ia, al - le - lu - ia, al - le - lu - ia, al - le - lu - ia.

5 Now we who are of ten-der heart,
   for-giv-ing oth-ers, take our part,
     sing your prais-es, al-le-lu-ia!
   To you we lift our pain and care,
   re-ceive the bur-dens that we bear,
     sing-ing prais-es, al-le-lu-ia,
     al-le-lu-ia, al-le-lu-ia, al-le-lu-ia.

6 In you, a kind and gen-tle death
   pre-pares to hush our fi-nal breath,
     sing-ing prais-es, al-le-lu-ia!
   Christ goes be-fore us to re-new
   the way that leads us home to you.
     Hear our prais-es, al-le-lu-ia,
     al-le-lu-ia, al-le-lu-ia, al-le-lu-ia.

18 Guide Me, O My Great Redeemer

Exod. 13:21; 16:4; 17:6; Ps. 105:39–44; Rev. 22:1–2

William Williams, 1745
St. 1, transl. Peter Williams, 1771; alt.
St. 2–3, transl. William Williams, 1772; alt.

1 Guide me, O my great Re - deem - er, pil - grim through this
2 O - pen now the crys - tal foun - tain, where the heal - ing
3 When I reach the Riv - er Jor - dan, bid my anx - ious

bar - ren land; I am weak, but you are might - y;
wa - ters flow. Let the fire and cloud - y pil - lar
fears sub - side. Death of death, and hell's de - struc - tion,

hold me with your power-ful hand. Bread of heav - en, bread of heav - en,
lead me all my jour - ney through. Strong de-liv - er - er, strong de-liv - er - er,
land me safe on heav-en's side. Songs of prais - es, songs of prais - es

feed me till I want no more, feed me till I want no more.
ev - er be my strength and shield, ev - er be my strength and shield.
I will ev - er sing to you, I will ev - er sing to you.

*John Hughes, a railroad official by trade, composed this tune
for the 1907 anniversary of Capel Rhondda, Pontypridd, Wales.
Cwm Rhondda refers to the "low valley" area surrounding the
urban district of Rhondda in southern Wales.*

Tune: CWM RHONDDA 8.7.8.7.8.7.7.
John Hughes, 1907
Alternate setting: ZION

Guide Me, O My Great Redeemer

William Williams, 1745
St. 1, transl. Peter Williams, 1771; alt.
St. 2-3, transl. William Williams, 1772; alt.

Exod. 13:21; 16:4; 17:6; Ps. 105:39–44; Rev. 22:1–2

1 Guide me, O my great Re-deem-er, pil-grim through this bar-ren
2 O-pen now the crys-tal foun-tain, where the heal-ing wa-ters
3 When I reach the Riv-er Jor-dan, bid my anx-ious fears sub-

land; I am weak, but you are might-y; hold me with your power-ful
flow. Let the fire and cloud-y pil-lar lead me all my jour-ney
side. Death of death, and hell's de-struc-tion, land me safe on heav-en's

hand. Bread of heav-en, feed me till I want no more,
through. Strong de-liv-er-er, ev-er be my strength and shield,
side. Songs of prais-es I will ev-er sing to you,

bread of heav-en, feed me till I want no more.
strong de-liv-er-er, ev-er be my strength and shield.
songs of prais-es I will ev-er sing to you.

The Thomas Hastings tune for this text is popular in the United States. A self-taught musician, Hastings was a colleague of Lowell Mason in New York City, where they worked together to raise the standard of worship music.

Tune: ZION 8.7.8.7.4.7.4.7.
Thomas Hastings, 1830
Alternate setting: CWM RHONDDA

20

God of Abraham and Sarah

James Gertmenian, 1986; alt.

1 God of A - bra - ham and Sar-ah, God of Mo - ses, Mir - iam's Guide;
2 God who danc - es in cre - a - tion, spin - ning stars a - bove our heads;
3 God who loves the poor in spir - it, God who com-forts those who mourn;
4 In our lives from birth to dy - ing, depth of sor - row, height of joy:

God of Da - vid and the proph-ets, God in Je - sus glo - ri - fied:
God whose face is scribed in mu - sic, by whose hand the earth is fed:
Balm for wounds, the friend of sin - ners, tak-ing the side of earth's for - lorn:
Prais-ing God in ev - ery sea - son, let ev - ery key our hearts em - ploy.

Up from the dust you raise a peo - ple, breathe in the breath of life, of soul;
Up from the ground you raise the moun-tains, raise our spir - its, lift our eyes;
Up from the depths you raise your peo - ple, giv - ing them cour-age for the day;
Praise is the heal - ing, praise, the glo - ry, praise is the fin - al mys-ter - y;

Down through the years the peo - ple praise you till al - le-lu-ias make them whole!
Down through the years your peo - ple praise you till al - le-lu-ias flood the skies!
Down through the years the peo - ple praise you till al - le-lu-ias light their way!
Down through the years let peo - ple praise you till al - le-lu-ias set them free!

*The healing power of praise and the history of God's dealings
with humankind are the themes of this hymn, written by a United
Church of Christ minister who is the grandson of Armenian
immigrants. The tune is named for his father.*

Tune: CONSTANTINE 8.7.8.7.D.
*Melody by James Gertmenian, 1986
Harm. Ronald Huntington, 1986; alt.*

God Reigns o'er All the Earth

Jane Parker Huber, 1981   *Isa. 52:7–10*

1 God reigns o'er all the earth! Green hills and val-leys low, the
2 God reigns o'er hu-man life! Through youth and ag-ing years, in
3 God reigns o'er time and space! In his-tory's by-gone days, Christ's
4 God reigns! Em-man-u-el! God with us ev-ery day, in

farms and towns in golds and browns God's grace and beau-ty show.
death, in birth, in grief, in mirth, in all our hopes and fears.
faith-ful folk in rev-erence spoke to bring God earn-est praise.
all our past and to the last, our com-fort and our stay.

God reigns o'er all the earth! Stone banks and spread-ing plains, in
God reigns o'er hu-man life! Our in-spi-ra-tion still. Through
God reigns o'er time and space! O'er gal-ax-y and sun, through
God reigns! Em-man-u-el! Let praise to Christ be sung! God's

rain-bow hues— reds, yel-lows, blues— of streams and coun-try lanes.
all our schemes, in all our dreams, we see God's reign-ing will.
time-less years the cos-mos hears the heaven-ly mu-sic run.
pres-ence here makes all things dear. Let joy-ful bells be rung!

The author's notes on this text describe it as a progression of awareness of God's reign among us—in physical surroundings, in the various stages of life, in time and space, and supremely in Christ, God with us.

Tune: TERRA BEATA S.M.D.
Traditional English melody
Adapt. Franklin L. Sheppard, 1915

22 Sing Praise to God, Who Has Shaped

Ps. 68:4, 32; Ps. 105

Joachim Neander, 1680
Transl. Madeleine Forell Marshall, 1993

1 Sing praise to God, who has shaped and sus - tains all cre -
2 Praise God, our guard - ian, who lov - ing - ly of - fers cor -
3 Sing praise to God, with sin - cere thanks for all your suc -
4 Sing praise, my soul, the great name of your high God com -

a - tion! Sing praise, my soul, in pro - found and com -
rec - tion, Who, as on ea - gle's wings, saves us from
cess - es. Mer - ci - ful God ev - er loves to en -
mend - ing. All that have life and breath join you, their

plete ad - o - ra - tion! Glad-some re - joice— or - gan and
sin - ful de - jec - tion. Have you ob - served, how we are
cour - age and bless us. On - ly con - ceive, what god - ly
notes sweet-ly blend - ing. God is your light! Soul, ev - er

trum - pet and voice— join - ing God's great con-gre - ga - tion.
al - ways pre - served by God's pa - ren - tal af - fec - tion?
strength can a - chieve: strength that would touch and car - ess us.
keep this in sight: a - men, a - men nev - er end - ing.

Joachim Neander was a dedicated, caring pastor of the Reformed Church in Düsseldorf, Germany. This was the most familiar of his fifty-six hymn texts, which were published along with many of his original tunes in 1680, the year of his death.

Tune: LOBE DEN HERREN 14.14.4.7.8.
Erneuerten Gesangbuch, *Stralsund, 1665*
Adapt. and harm. William S. Bennett, 1863

There's a Wideness in God's Mercy

Frederick William Faber, 1854; alt.

1 There's a wide-ness in God's mer-cy, like the wide-ness of the sea;
2 For the love of God is broad-er than the mea-sures of our minds;

there's a kind-ness in God's jus-tice, which is more than lib-er-ty.
and the heart of the E-ter-nal is most won-der-ful-ly kind.

There's no place where earth-ly sor-rows are more felt than in God's heaven;
If our love were but more faith-ful, we would glad-ly trust God's word;

there's no place where earth-ly fail-ings have such kind-ly judg-ment given.
and our lives would show thanks-giv-ing for the good-ness of our God.

Of Huguenot Protestant ancestry, Frederick William Faber was influenced by the Oxford Movement and eventually became a Catholic priest. He wrote 150 hymns to correspond to the number of psalms.

Tune: IN BABILONE 8.7.8.7.D.
Dutch melody
Arr. Julius Röntgen, 1906
Alternate tune: HOLY MANNA

24

Yigdal Elohim Chai
(The God of Abraham Praise)

Gen. 12:1; 17:15–16; Exod. 3:14; Isa. 44:6; Rev. 4:8

Moses Maimonides, 12th century
Versification attrib. to Daniel ben Judah, c. 1400
Transl. Max Landsberg and Newton Mann, 1884; alt.

1 Yig - dal e - lo - him chai v' - yish - ta - bach,
1 The God of A - braham praise, all prais - es to God's name,
2 God's spir - it free - ly flows, high surg - ing where it will;
3 God has e - ter - nal life im - plant - ed in the soul;
4 The God of Sar - ah praise, all prais - es to God's name,

nim - tza v' - ein eit el m' - tzi - u - to
who was and is and is to be, for - e'er the same!
God spoke of old in proph - et's word; that word speaks still.
God's love shall be our strength and stay, while a - ges roll.
who was and is and is to be, for - e'er the same!

E - chad v' - ein ya - chid k' - yi - chu - do,
The one e - ter - nal God, be - fore what now ap - pears;
Es - tab - lished is God's law, and change-less it shall stand,
All praise the liv - ing God! Ex - tol that hal - lowed name,
The one e - ter - nal God, be - fore what now ap - pears;

The twelfth-century scholar Moses Maimonides drew up the thirteen articles of the Hebrew creed, which were subsequently cast in metrical form (the Yigdal). This translation represents an ecumenical collaboration between Rabbi Landsberg and Unitarian minister Mann.

Tune: LEONI 6.6.8.4.D.
Traditional Yigdal melody
Adapt. Meyer Lyon, 1770

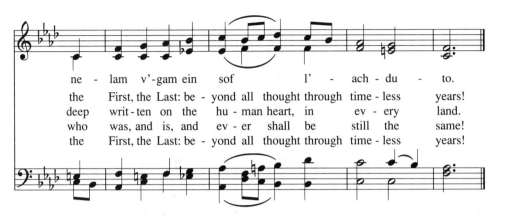

ne - lam v'-gam ein sof l' - ach - du - to.
the First, the Last: be - yond all thought through time - less years!
deep writ - ten on the hu - man heart, in ev - ery land.
who was, and is, and ev - er shall be still the same!
the First, the Last: be - yond all thought through time - less years!

O God, Our Help in Ages Past 25

Isaac Watts, 1719; alt.   *Ps. 90:1–2, 4–5*

1 O God, our help in a - ges past, our hope for years to come,
2 Un - der the shad - ow of your throne your saints have dwelt se - cure;
3 Be - fore the hills in or - der stood or earth re - ceived its frame,
4 A thou - sand a - ges in your sight are like an eve - ning gone,

Our shel - ter from the storm - y blast, and our e - ter - nal home:
Suf - fi - cient is your arm a - lone, and our de - fense is sure.
From ev - er - last - ing you are God, to end - less years the same.
Short as the watch that ends the night be - fore the ris - ing sun.

5 Time, like an ev-er-roll-ing stream,
    soon bears us all away;
We fly for-got-ten, as a dream
    fades at the o-pening day.

6 O God, our help in a-ges past,
    our hope for years to come,
Still be our God while trou-bles last,
    and our e-ter-nal home!

Watts, minister of a Congregational church in London, wrote
theological and philosophical works and hundreds of "hymns
of human composure" (everyday language). He augmented the
congregational singing of psalms with a new style of hymnody.

Tune: ST. ANNE C.M.
William Croft, 1708

26 We Worship You, God

Ps. 104:2–6, 10–13

Robert Grant, 1833; alt.

1 We worship you, God; your power and your love
2 We tell of your might, we sing of your grace,
3 The earth, with its store of won-ders un-told,
4 Your boun-ti-ful care, what tongue can re-cite?
5 Frail chil-dren of dust, and fee-ble as frail,

are bla-zoned a-broad, a-round, and a-bove:
whose robe is the light, whose can-o-py space;
Al-might-y, your power has found-ed of old,
It breathes in the air, it shines in the light;
in you do we trust, nor find you to fail;

Our Shield and De-fend-er, the An-cient of Days,
Your char-iots of wrath the deep thun-der-clouds form,
Es-tab-lished it fast by a change-less de-cree,
It streams from the hills, it de-scends to the plain,
Your mer-cies how ten-der, how firm to the end,

pa-vil-ioned in splen-dor, and gird-ed with praise.
and broad is your path on the wings of the storm.
and round it you cast, like a man-tle, the sea.
and sweet-ly dis-tills in the dew and the rain.
our Mak-er, De-fend-er, Re-deem-er, and Friend!

Born in Bengal, India, Robert Grant became a lawyer in England, a member of Parliament, and for the last four years of his life was governor of Bombay. This text was inspired by William Kethe's paraphrase of Psalm 104.

Tune: LYONS 10.10.11.11.
Attrib. to J. Michael Haydn (1737–1806)
Alternate tune: HANOVER

From All That Dwell below the Skies

Isaac Watts, 1719; alt.

Ps. 117

1 From all that dwell be-low the skies let the Cre - a-tor's praise a -
2 E - ter-nal are your mer-cies, God; your truth stands ev - er high and

rise; Al-le - lu - ia! Al-le - lu - ia! Let the Re - deem-er's name be
broad: Al-le - lu - ia! Al-le - lu - ia! Your praise shall sound from shore to

sung through ev - ery land, by ev-ery tongue. Al-le - lu - ia, al-le -
shore till suns shall rise and set no more.

lu - ia, al-le - lu - ia, al-le - lu - ia, al - le - lu - ia!

Isaac Watts, author of more than 600 hymns, paraphrased the two verses of Psalm 117 into this two-stanza hymn, which was included in his Psalms of David, 1719. The tune originated in a German Catholic hymnal.

Tune: LASST UNS ERFREUEN
8.8.4.4.8.8. with alleluias
Geistliche Kirchengesäng, *Cologne, 1623*
Harm. Ralph Vaughan Williams, 1906

28

For the Beauty of the Earth

St. 1–3, Folliott S. Pierpoint, 1864; alt.
St. 4, Miriam Therese Winter, 1993

1 For the beau-ty of the earth, for the splen-dor of the skies,
2 For the won-der of each hour of the day and of the night,
3 For the joy of hu-man love, broth-er, sis-ter, par-ent, child,
4 For the good that love in-spires, for a world where none ex-clude,

For the love which from our birth o-ver and a-round us lies,
Hill and vale, and tree and flower, sun and moon, and stars of light,
Friends on earth, and friends a-bove, for all gen-tle thoughts and mild,
For a faith that nev-er tires, and for ev-ery heart re-newed,

Refrain

God of all, to you we raise this our hymn of grate-ful praise.

*Folliott S. Pierpoint, author of numerous hymns, penned these
verses near his native city of Bath, England, on a late spring day
when flowers were in full bloom and all the earth seemed to rejoice.*

Tune: DIX 7.7.7.7. with refrain
Conrad Kocher, 1838
Adapt. William H. Monk, 1861

29

Let Heaven Your Wonders Proclaim

Ps. 89:1–2, 8–17

The Iona Community, 1991

Refrain, in unison

Let heav-en your won-ders pro-claim, let an-gels your faith-ful-ness praise,

Last time, end

for who in the heights or the depths can e-qual your maj-es-ty, O God?

In harmony (Melody in tenor)

1 Your strength rules the rage of the sea, your
2 The heav - ens are yours and the earth: you
3 All tough - ness and val - or are yours, and
4 So glad are the peo - ple who praise you, who

(Melody in tenor)

(Basses, hum)

faith - ful-ness calms its wild waves, you quell ev-ery fear of the
found-ed the world and its wealth; The north and the south show your
strong is your hand lift-ed high; Yet jus - tice is found at your
live in the light of your love; In you, God a-lone, is their

(all sing)

to Refrain

deep, and scat - ter your en - e - mies a - far.
skill, the east and the west at - test your fame.
throne, and love is for - ev - er by your side.
strength, their hon - or, their jus - tice, and their joy.

This beautiful and simple melody, composed by Salvador Martinez, is in the style of a Philippine folk tune. It may be sung with a simple guitar accompaniment.

Tune: MARTINEZ 8.8.8.9. with refrain
Salvador T. Martinez, 1989
Arr. The Iona Community, 1991

30

Colorful Creator

Ruth Duck, 1992

Unison

1 Col - or - ful Cre - a - tor, God of mys - ter - y,
2 Har - mo - ny of a - ges, God of lis - ten - ing ear,
3 Au - thor of our jour - ney, God of near and far,
4 God of truth and beau - ty, Po - et of the Word,

thank you for the art - ist teach - ing us to see glimps - es of the
thank you for com - pos - ers tun - ing us to hear ech - oes of the
praise for tale and dra - ma tell - ing who we are, strip - ping to the
may we be cre - a - tors by the Spir - it stirred, o - pen to your

mean - ing of the com - mon - place, vi - sions of the
Gos - pel in the songs we sing, sounds of love and
es - sence strug - gles of our day, times of change and
pres - ence in our joy and strife, ves - sels of the

1–3
ho - ly in each hu - man face.
long - ing from the deep - est spring.
con - flict when we choose our way.
4
ho - ly cours - ing through our life.

This hymn was written for the 1992 installation of Linda Clark
as Houghton Scholar of Sacred Music at Boston University,
where Ruth Duck earned her Th.D. degree. It praises the Artist
who inspires our creativity.

Tune: HOUGHTON 11.11.11.11.
Carlton R. Young, 1992

All Things Bright and Beautiful

Cecil F. Alexander, 1848; alt.

Unison
Refrain

All things bright and beau-ti-ful, all crea-tures great and small,

Last time, end

All things wise and won-der-ful, our dear God made them all.

1 Each lit-tle flower that o-pens, each lit-tle bird that sings,
2 The pur-ple-head-ed moun-tain, the riv-er run-ning by,
3 The cold wind in the win-ter, the pleas-ant sum-mer sun,

to Refrain

God made their glow-ing col-ors, and made their ti-ny wings.
The sun-set, and the morn-ing that bright-ens up the sky.
The ripe fruits in the gar-den, God made them ev-ery one.

This hymn for children is based on the first article of the Apostles' Creed: "Maker of heaven and earth." The English hymnwriter Cecil Frances Alexander was married to William Alexander, who became bishop of Ireland.

Tune: ROYAL OAK 7.6.7.6. with refrain
English melody
Adapt. Martin Shaw, 1915

32 God of the Sparrow God of the Whale

1 Thess. 5: 18; Ps. 136

Jaroslav J. Vajda, 1983

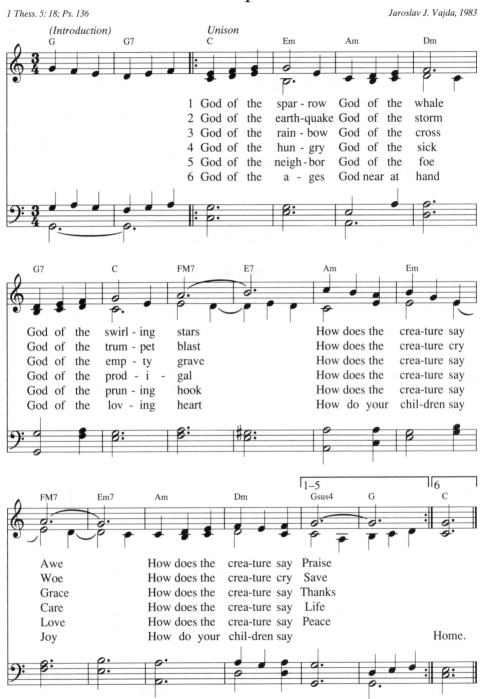

1 God of the spar-row God of the whale
2 God of the earth-quake God of the storm
3 God of the rain-bow God of the cross
4 God of the hun-gry God of the sick
5 God of the neigh-bor God of the foe
6 God of the a-ges God near at hand

God of the swirl-ing stars How does the crea-ture say
God of the trum-pet blast How does the crea-ture cry
God of the emp-ty grave How does the crea-ture say
God of the prod-i-gal How does the crea-ture say
God of the prun-ing hook How does the crea-ture say
God of the lov-ing heart How do your chil-dren say

Awe How does the crea-ture say Praise
Woe How does the crea-ture cry Save
Grace How does the crea-ture say Thanks
Care How does the crea-ture say Life
Love How does the crea-ture say Peace
Joy How do your chil-dren say Home.

After forty years in the ministry, Jaroslav Vajda wrote this text to provoke answers to how and why we serve God. By creating new poetic forms and adapting ageless ideas and expressions, Vajda speaks in the language of his time.

Tune: ROEDER 5.4.6.7.7.
Carl F. Schalk, 1983

God Created Heaven and Earth

Taiwanese hymn
Transl. Boris and Clare Anderson, 1981

Ps. 148; Gen. 1:1–5

1 God cre - a - ted heaven and earth, all things per - fect
2 Let us praise God's mer - cy great, all our needs that
3 God is one, will ev - er be: i - dols are mere
4 But God's grace be - yond com - pare saves us all from

brought to birth; God's great power made
love a - wait; God, who fash - ions
van - i - ty; Hand-made gods of
death's de - spair; So earth's crea - tures

dark and light, earth re - volv-ing day and night.
all that lives, to each one a bless - ing gives.
wood and clay can - not help us when we pray.
small and great give thanks for that bless - ed state.

This popular Taiwanese hymn speaks in symbols that
are universal. I-to Loh is a professor of church music
and ethnomusicology and is a leader in the development
of indigenous Christian hymnody in Asia.

Tune: TŌA-SĪA 7.7.7.7.
Pi-po melody
Harm. I-to Loh, 1963; rev. 1982

Alabanza
(As the Rain Is Falling)

Ps. 96

Pablo Fernández Badillo, 1977
Transl. Roberto Escamilla and Elise S. Eslinger, 1983

Estribillo (Refrain)

To - da flor sil - ves - tre, la ma - ya, el cun-dea - mor.
¡Có - mo se te_a - la - ba en to - da la cre - a - ción!
All God's great cre - a - tion is sing - ing songs of love,
How all of cre - a - tion has joined in prais - ing God.

1.
¡To - do ma - ni - fies - ta la glo - ria de mi Dios!
in beau-ty is shown the glo - ry of our God!

2.
Yo qui - sie - ra_ha - cer - lo en for - ma_i - gual, mi Dios.
I al - so shall of - fer my songs of praise to you.

Coquí: a small frog-like creature, found only in Puerto Rico, that "sings." Duende: a small, purple flower.

Tune: ALABANZA 6.6.6.6.D. with refrain
Pablo Fernández Badillo, 1977

Pablo Fernández Badillo, a Presbyterian musician from Puerto Rico, writes in both traditional and contemporary hymnic styles, often incorporating elements of folk or popular music. This was one of 104 of his hymns published in "Himnario Criollo" (1977).

35   O Mighty God, When I Survey in Wonder

Carl Boberg, 1885
Transl. The New Century Hymnal, *1994*

1 O might-y God, when I sur-vey in won-der the world that
2 When your voice speaks in rolls of thun-der peal-ing, your light-ning
3 The Bi-ble tells the sto-ry of your bless-ing so free-ly
4 And when, at last, the clouds of doubt dis-pers-ing, you will re-

formed when once the word you said, The strands of life all wo-ven close to-
pow-er bursts in bright sur-prise; When cool-ing rain, your gen-tle love re-
shed up-on all hu-man life; Your con-stant mer-cy, ev-ery care ad-
veal what we but dim-ly see; With trum-pet call, our great re-birth an-

Refrain

geth-er, the whole cre-a-tion at your ta-ble fed,
veal-ing, re-flects your prom-ise, arc-ing through the skies, (1–3) My soul cries
dress-ing, re-liev-ing bur-dened souls from sin and strife.
nounc-ing, we shall re-join you for e-ter-ni-ty, (4) Then we will

out in songs of praise to you, O might-y God! O might-y God! My soul cries
sing your praise for-ev-er more, O might-y God! O might-y God! Then we will

out in songs of praise to you, O might-y God! O might-y God!
sing your praise for-ev-er-more, O might-y God! O might-y God!

Carl Boberg, a popular evangelical minister and teacher in Sweden, wrote his poem "O Store Gud" in the summer of 1885. Several years later, he was surprised to hear it sung with this old Swedish melody, with which it has been associated ever since. The first literal English translation by E. Gustav Johnson was published in the United States in 1925. The hymn also became known in Germany and Russia, where the British missionary Stuart K. Hine was inspired to create his English paraphrase known as "How great thou art." This translation and arrangement were created for The New Century Hymnal *to restore the meaning and flavor of Boberg's original hymn.*

Tune: O STORE GUD
11.10.11.10. with refrain
Swedish folk melody
Harm. The New Century Hymnal, *1994*

To God Compose a Song of Joy   36

Ruth Duck, 1986   *Ps. 98*

1 To God com-pose a song of joy; to God make mel-o-dy,
2 Be-fore the na-tions God re-veals a just and righ-teous will,
3 In ev-ery cor-ner of the earth, God comes to save and free;
4 With trum-pet, with the sound of horns, with strings, yes, with the lyre,

Whose arm of strength does won-drous things, whose hand brings vic-to-ry!
Re-mem-ber-ing in faith-ful love the house of Is-ra-el.
Break forth with shouts of ho-ly joy; all lands, make mel-o-dy.
With voic-es praise the sov-ereign God, a lust-y, joy-ous choir.

5 Let seas in all their full-ness roar;
    sing, peo-ple of all lands;
    Let moun-tains join and sing for joy;
    let riv-ers clap their hands.

6 The God of jus-tice comes to save;
    let earth make mel-o-dy;
    For God will judge with righ-teous-ness
    and rule with eq-ui-ty.

Ruth Duck is associate professor of worship and dean of the chapel at Garrett Evangelical Theological Seminary in Evanston, Illinois. A minister in the United Church of Christ, she has edited several books of worship resources and hymns.

Tune: RICHMOND C.M.
Thomas Haweis, 1792

Our God, to Whom We Turn

Edward Grubb, 1925; alt.

1 Our God, to whom we turn when wea-ry with il - lu-sion,
2 You are in - deed the truth; though we, who deign to find you,
3 All beau-ty your de - cree: the moun-tains and the riv - ers,
4 O hid-den fount of truth, of love, and peace, and beau-ty,

whose stars se - rene-ly burn a - bove this earth's con - fu-sion,
have tried, with thought un - couth, in fee - ble words to bind you.
the line of lift - ed sea, where spread-ing moon-light quiv-ers.
in - spire us from our youth with joy and strength for du - ty.

Yours is the might - y plan, the stead-fast or - der sure,
It is be - cause you are we're driv - en to the quest;
The deep-toned or - gan blast that rolls through arch - es dim,
May your fresh light a - rise with - in each heart ob - scure,

in which the world be - gan, en - dures, and shall en - dure.
till truth from false-hood part, our souls can find no rest.
hints of the mu - sic vast of heaven's e - ter - nal hymn.
till, bar - ing all dis - guise, we know you true and sure!

The English Quaker Edward Grubb was owner and editor of a
monthly periodical, The British Friend. *He also wrote and*
lectured on biblical and religious history and related subjects.

Tune: STEADFAST 6.7.6.7.6.6.6.6.
(O GOTT, DU FROMMER GOTT, *Hanover, 1646*)
Neu Ordentlich Gesangbuch, *1646*
Harm. from J. S. Bach (1685–1750)
Alternate tune: DARMSTADT

"Lift Up Your Hearts!"

Henry M. Butler, 1881; alt.

1 "Lift up your hearts!" We lift them up to you,
2 A-bove the lev - el of the for-mer years,
3 Lift ev-ery gift that God to us has given;
4 Then as the trum - pet call, in af-ter years,

for in your pres - ence it is right to do;
the mire of sin, the weight of guilt - y fears,
low lies the best till blessed by God in heaven;
"Lift up your hearts!" rings peal - ing in our ears,

"Lift up your hearts!" In joy to - geth - er laud,
The mist of doubt, the blight of love's de - cay,
Low lie the bound - ing heart, the teem - ing brain,
With spir - its one, with hearts in - spired and awed,

"We lift them up, we lift them up to God."
O God of life, lift all our hearts to - day!
till, once more, they re - turn to God a - gain.
"We lift them up, we lift them up to God!"

This text is a meditation written for students at Harrow School, England. It is based on a liturgical dialogue, Sursum Corda, used since the third century in the Eastern and Western church to introduce the eucharisteō *or prayer of consecration.*

Tune: WOODLANDS 10.10.10.10.
Walter Greatorex, 1916

39

Cantemos al Creador
(Creator God We Sing)

Ps. 68:4, 32

Carlos Rosas, 1976; alt.
Transl. Dimas Planas-Belfort; alt.

1 Can - te - mos al Crea - dor   un him - no de a - le - grí - a,
2 Can - te - mos al Crea - dor   un him - no de a - la - ban - za
1 Cre - a - tor God we sing,   a hymn of joy we're mak - ing;
2 Cre - a - tor God we sing,   your power and wis - dom bless - ing;

de a - gra - de - ci - do a - mor   al na - cer el nue - vo dí - a.   Pues
que ex - pre - se ad - mi - ra - ción,   ma - ra - vi - lla y es - pe - ran - za,   Pues
our grate - ful love we bring,   as the new day's light is break - ing.   God
our hope and won - der bring,   ad - mir - a - tion now ex - press - ing.   The

hi - zo el cie - lo, el mar,   el sol y las es - tre - llas,   y en e - llos vio bon-
to - da la crea - ción   pre - go - na su gran - de - za: a - sí nues - tro can-
made the sea and land;   the sun and stars came roll - ing   from God's own lov - ing
u - ni - verse main - tains   that God in might is dwell - ing;   and we, in hum - ble

Estribillo (Refrain)

dad,   pues sus o - bras e - ran be - llas.
tar   va a - nun - cian - do su be - lle - za.   ¡A - le - lu - ya;
hand,   their Cre - a - tor's love ex - tol - ling.
strains,   of God's beau - ty here are tell - ing.   Al - le - lu - ia,

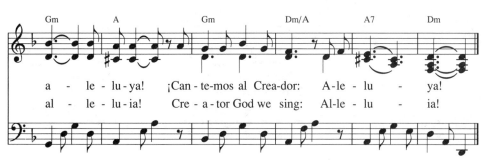

Gm   A   Gm   Dm/A   A7   Dm

a - le - lu - ya! ¡Can - te-mos al Crea-dor: A-le - lu - ya!
al - le - lu - ia! Cre - a - tor God we sing: Al-le - lu - ia!

This processional hymn by Mexican composer and hymnwriter
Carlos Rosas was originally the second movement in his mass
setting "Rosas Del Tepeyac." Rosas has served as director of the
Mexican-American Cultural Center in San Antonio, Texas.

Tune: ROSAS 6.7.6.8.D. with refrain
Carlos Rosas, 1976
Harm. *The New Century Hymnal, 1993*

You Are the Way   40

George W. Doane, 1824; alt.   *John 14:6*

1 You are the way; through you a - lone   can we   the true God   find;
2 You are the truth; your word a - lone   true wis - dom can im - part;
3 You are the life; the   o - pen tomb   pro-claims God's love a - new;
4 You are the way, the   truth, the life;   grant us   that way to   know,

In you, O Christ, is   now re-vealed   God's heart and will and   mind.
You on - ly can in - form the mind   and pur - i - fy   the   heart.
And God will ne'er for - sake the one   who trusts, O Christ, in   you.
That truth to keep, that life to win,   whose joys e - ter - nal   flow.

Jesus' words to Thomas, "I am the way, and the truth, and the
life," inspired this hymn. George W. Doane, a powerful leader in
the Episcopal church in the United States, served as parish priest,
professor, and bishop of New Jersey.

Tune: NUN DANKET ALL' C.M.
(GRÄFENBERG)
Johann Crüger, 1647, in
Praxis Pietatis Melica

41

I Thank You, Jesus

Kenneth Morris, 1948

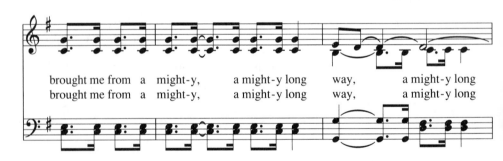

This is one of countless hymns of African-American worship that are known as "testimony hymns." Such congregational songs emphasize personal experiences with God, especially the way God has delivered people from the tribulations of life.

Tune: THANK YOU, JESUS Irr.
Kenneth Morris, 1948
Adapt. and arr. Joyce Finch Johnson, 1992

thank you, Je-sus,   my Sav-ior God,   for you brought me, yes, you
been my sis-ter,   my broth-er, too,   for you brought me, yes, you

way.

brought me from a might-y, a might-y long way, a might-y long way.
brought me from a might-y, a might-y long way, a might-y long way.

O for a Thousand Tongues to Sing   42

Charles Wesley, 1740; alt.

1 O   for a thou-sand tongues to sing my   great Re-deem-er's   praise,
2 My   gra-cious Sav-ior and my God, as - sist me to pro-claim,
3 Je - sus! the name that calms our fears, that bids our sor-rows cease
4 Glo - ry to God, and love and praise be ev - er, ev - er given

The glo - ries ev - er ech - o - ing the tri - umphs of God's grace!
To spread through all the earth a - broad the hon - ors of your name.
Is mu - sic in the sin-ner's ears, is life, and health, and peace!
By all the saints in ev - ery age, the church in earth and heaven.

The hymn is a cento from a longer poem of eighteen stanzas written by Charles Wesley on the first anniversary of his conversion. The present form of the hymn is one edited by John Wesley for The Wesleyan Hymn Book, 1780.

Tune: AZMON C.M.
Carl G. Gläser, 1828
Adapt. in L. Mason's Modern Psalmody, *1839*
Alternate tune: RICHMOND

43 Love Divine, All Loves Excelling

Mal. 3:1; 2 Cor. 3:18; 5:17; Eph. 5:27   *Charles Wesley, 1747; alt.*

1 Love di-vine, all loves ex-cel-ling, joy of heaven, on earth be found,
2 Breathe, O breathe your lov-ing Spir-it in-to ev-ery trou-bled breast;
3 Come, al-might-y to de-liv-er, let us all your life re-ceive;
4 Fin-ish, then, your new cre-a-tion; pure and spot-less may we prove;

Fix in us a hum-ble dwell-ing, all your faith-ful mer-cies crown;
Let us all in you in-her-it, let us find your prom-ised rest;
Sud-den-ly re-turn, and ne-ver, ne-ver-more your tem-ples leave.
Let us see your great sal-va-tion per-fect-ly re-stored in you;

Je-sus, you are all com-pas-sion; pure, un-bound-ed love im-part.
Take a-way our love of sin-ning; Al-pha and O-me-ga be;
You we would be al-ways bless-ing, love you as your an-gels love,
Changed from glo-ry in-to glo-ry, till in heaven we take our place,

Vis-it us with your sal-va-tion, en-ter ev-ery trem-bling heart.
End of faith, as its be-gin-ning, set our hearts at lib-er-ty.
Pray and praise for your un-fail-ing, wound-ed arms out-stretched a-bove.
Crowned as saints, we ev-er shall be lost in won-der, love, and praise.

This hymn is said to have been suggested by a "Song of Venus"
from Dryden's King Arthur. *It is one of 6,500 written by Charles*
Wesley, the "sweet singer of Methodism," who was skilled at
interweaving literary and scriptural images.

Tune: BEECHER 8.7.8.7.D.
John Zundel, 1855
Alternate tune: HYFRYDOL
For another harmonization, see 368, 495

Beautiful Jesus

Münster Gesangbuch, *1677*
Transl. Madeleine Forell Marshall, 1993

1 Beau - ti - ful Je - sus, Head of all cre - a - tion,
2 Beau - ti - ful spring - time, love - ly, green, and hope - ful,
3 Beau - ti - ful sun - shine, clear, so love - ly, moon - light,
4 All earth - ly beau - ty, all ce - les - tial ra - diance

God and the bless - ed Mar - y's child: I want to love you,
all earth ex - hales its sweet per - fume: Je - sus is sweet - er,
stars shine like an - gels, ranked through space: Je - sus shines bright - er,
fade when com - pared to Je - sus' face. Let me not cher - ish

praise and a - dore you, joy of my soul, so long de - sired.
Je - sus is pur - er, sad hearts at this, re - joice and bloom.
Je - sus shines clear - er, in per - fect beau - ty, love, and grace.
beau - ties that per - ish; let me this love - ly good em - brace.

This text, which has also been translated as "Fairest Lord Jesus"
and "Beautiful Savior," was included in a German Catholic
hymnal published in Münster. The melody, known by various
names, is thought to be a Silesian folk tune.

Tune: SCHÖNSTER HERR JESU 5.6.8.5.5.8.
Silesian folk melody
Harm. Richard S. Willis, 1850

45

Cristo es la peña de Horeb
(Christ Is the Mountain of Horeb)

Exod. 17:6; Song of Sol. 2:1–2; John 4:7–14

Anonymous; alt.
Transl. The New Century Hymnal, 1993

1 Cris-to es la pe - ña de Ho - reb, que es-tá bro - tan - do,
2 Cris-to es el li - rio del va - lle de las flo - res,
1 Christ is the Moun - tain of Ho - reb which is flow - ing:
2 Flow-er of flow - ers, the Lil - y of the Val - ley,

a - gua de vi - da sa - lu - da - ble pa - ra ti.
Cris - to es la ro - sa her-mo - sa y pu - ra de Sa - rón.
wa - ter of life pour forth to heal, to make us whole.
the Rose of Shar - on, bloom-ing pure and free for you.

Cris - to es la pe - ña de Ho - reb, que es-tá bro - tan - do,
Cris - to es la vi - da y a - mor de los a - mo - res,
Christ is the Moun - tain of Ho - reb which is flow - ing:
O Christ, the path - way of love a - bove all loves,

a - gua de vi - da sa - lu - da - ble pa - ra ti.
Cris - to es la e - ter - na fuen-te de la sal - va - ción.
wa - ter of life pour forth to heal, to make us whole.
E - ter - nal Foun-tain of sal - va - tion flow-ing free.

This anonymous hymn has been sung since the 1930s and is especially popular among the pentecostal churches of Puerto Rico. The arrangement, in the "pasodoble" rhythm, captures the style in which it is most often performed in its country of origin.

Tune: CRISTO ES LA PEÑA 12.12.12.12.D.
Puerto Rican melody
Arr. Luis Olivieri, 1993

Ven, a to - mar - la que_es más dul - ce que la miel,
Ven, a bus - car - la cuan - do en tris - te - za_es - tés,
Sweet-er than hon-ey is the stream, come taste and see—
Come seek the One who un - der - stands your grief and pain,

Re - fres-ca_el al - ma, re - fres - ca to - do tu ser.
Re - fres-ca_el al - ma, re - fres - ca to - do tu ser.
Re - fresh your be - ing, re - fresh your heart and mind.
Re - fresh your be - ing, re - fresh your heart and mind.

Cris - to_es la pe - ña de Ho - reb, que_es-tá bro - tan - do,
Cris - to_es el li - rio del va - lle de las flo - res,
Christ is the Moun - tain of Ho - reb which is flow - ing:
Flow - er of flow - ers, the Lil - y of the Val - ley,

a - gua de vi - da sa - lu - da-ble pa - ra ti.
Cris - to_es la ro-sa_her-mo - sa_y pu - ra de Sa - rón.
wa - ter of life pour forth to heal, to make us whole.
the Rose of Shar-on, bloom-ing pure and free for you.

46

Hope of the World

Georgia Harkness, 1954; alt.

1 Hope of the world, O Christ of great com-pas - sion,
speak to our fear - ful hearts by con - flict torn.
Save us your peo - ple from con - sum - ing pas - sion,
from false pur - suits through which our lives are worn.

2 Hope of the world, God's gift of our re-demp - tion,
bring - ing to hun - gry souls the bread of life,
Still let your Spir - it un - to us be giv - en
to heal earth's wounds and end its bit - ter strife.

3 Hope of the world, who by the cross did save us
from death and sad de - spair, from sin and guilt,
We ren - der back the love your mer - cy gave us;
take back our lives and use them as you will.

4 Hope of the world, O Christ, o'er death vic - to - rious,
who by this sign did con - quer grief and pain,
We would be faith - ful to your gos - pel glo - rious;
our Sov - ereign who for - ev - er - more shall reign!

*Author of many books in her field and an internationally
recognized teacher, Georgia Harkness was one of the leading
women theologians of her generation. This text was written for the
Second General Assembly of the World Council of Churches.*

Tune: ANCIENT OF DAYS 11.10.11.10
J. Albert Jeffrey, 1886
Adapt. The New Century Hymnal, 1992

O Christ Jesus, Sent from Heaven

47

James W. Crawford, 1994

John 17:17–23

1 O Christ Je - sus, sent from heav-en, Love E - ter - nal,
2 O Christ Je - sus, our sal - va - tion, Shep-herd kind, life's
3 O Christ Je - sus, Fa - ther - Moth-er, Spir - it, Tri - une
4 O Christ Je - sus, preached down a - ges, in the womb of

cru - ci - fied, wel - come Sav - ior, mis - sion bear - ing,
Bread and Wine, Word Made Flesh, God's Bless - ed Ser - vant,
Source of all, claim our wound - ed, halt - ing wit - ness;
God be - gun, pray re - store your bro - ken Bod - y,

dwell a - mong us, now re - side. Al - le - lu - ia!
wash - ing feet shows your de - sign. Al - le - lu - ia!
we sur - ren - der to your thrall. Al - le - lu - ia!
born when Cal - vary's work was done. Al - le - lu - ia!

Way of An - guish, sow your peace, with us a - bide.
Liv - ing Wa - ter, slake our hearts with grace di - vine.
Truth In - car - nate, stir us with your ser - vant call.
Life for Oth - ers, hear our plea: "May all be one!"

James W. Crawford served as minister of the Old South Church in Boston for more than twenty years. His text uses imagery from the Gospel of John to indicate that the church's unity lies in the risk and hope of loving service.

Tune: WESTMINSTER ABBEY 8.7.8.7.8.7.
Henry Purcell, c. 1680
Arr. Ernest Hawkins, 1842
Alternate tune: REGENT SQUARE

48

Jesus the Christ Says

John 6:48; 14:6; 11:25; 8:12; 9:5

Urdu, anon.; alt.

1 Je - sus the Christ says, I am the bread, the bread of life for the world am I. The bread of life for the world am I, the bread of life for the world am I. Je - sus the Christ says, I am the bread, the bread of life for the world am I.

2 Je - sus the Christ says, I am the way, the way and the truth and the life am I. The way and the truth and the life am I, the way and the truth and the life am I. Je - sus the Christ says, I am the way, the way and the truth and the life am I.

3 Je - sus the Christ says, I am the light, the one true light of the world am I. The one true light of the world am I, the one true light of the world am I. Je - sus the Christ says, I am the light, the one true light of the world am I.

4 Je - sus the Christ says, I am the life, the res - ur - rec-tion and the life am I. The res - ur - rec-tion and the life am I, the res - ur - rec-tion and the life am I. Je - sus the Christ says, I am the life, the res - ur - rec-tion and the life am I.

This anonymous hymn, both text and tune, originated in Pakistan or northern India and has been sung around the world since its publication by the East Asia Christian Council and the World Council of Churches.

Tune: YISU NE KAHA 9.9.9.9.9.9.
Urdu melody
Arr. Francis B. Westbrook, 1950

Ask Me What Great Thing I Know

49

Johann C. Schwedler, 1741
Transl. Benjamin H. Kennedy, 1863; alt.

1 Cor. 2:2; Gal. 6:14

1 Ask me what great thing I know that de - lights and stirs me so,
2 Who de - feats my fierc-est foes? Who con - soles my sad - dest woes?
3 Who is life in life to me? Who the death of death will be?
4 This is that great thing I know; this de - lights and stirs me so:

What the high re - ward I win, whose the name I
Who re - vives my faint - ing heart, heal - ing all that
Who holds all my days se - cure, in God's heart where
Faith in Christ who died to save, Christ who tri - umphed

glo - ry in: Je - sus Christ, the cru - ci - fied.
grief im - parts? Je - sus Christ, the cru - ci - fied.
love is sure? Je - sus Christ, the cru - ci - fied.
o'er the grave, Je - sus Christ, the cru - ci - fied.

Johann Christoph Schwedler, one of the most powerful preachers of Germany, was author of more than 450 hymns. This hymn was frequently used at funerals in Schwedler's native Silesia.

Tune: HENDON 7.7.7.7.7.
H. A. César Malan, 1827

50

I Sing the Praise of Love Almighty

Gerhard Tersteegen, 1757
Transl. Madeleine Forell Marshall, 1993

1 I sing the praise of Love al-might-y, which shines re-vealed in
2 How lov-ing-kind you are, how gen-tle, how your heart reach-es
3 Se-cure my heart and all my be-ing, in you, my Sav-ior,
4 May my heart bear the deep im-pres-sion of love that Je-sus

Je-sus' face. I of-fer up all that de-lights me,
af-ter mine! My heart re-sponds in el-e-men-tal
cru-ci-fied. You gave your life to work my heal-ing,
shares with me, My life be-come a pure ex-pres-sion

all mean de-sires, each fond em-brace, Turn from my-self, in
sym-pa-thy, beat-ing per-fect time. This mu-tual love, this
bleed-ing for me, you groaned and died. Be-lov-ed Je-sus,
of all that Chris-tian love can be: Each word, each act, a

pure de-vo-tion, and ea-ger plunge in love's vast o-cean.
strong at-trac-tion, I know no oth-er sat-is-fac-tion.
my sal-va-tion, you have, through love, re-stored cre-a-tion.
bright re-flec-tion of joy in Love's own res-ur-rec-tion.

Gerhard Tersteegen was an eighteenth-century hymnwriter and
mystic, nurtured in the German Reformed Church. The four
stanzas that comprise "Ich bete an die Macht der Liebe" were
drawn from a longer poem and became popular in this form
when published by Pastor Johannes Evangelist Gossner in his
Choralbuch *of 1825.*

Tune: ST. PETERSBURG 9.8.9.8.9.9.
Dimitri Bortniansky, 1825

O Sing a Song of Bethlehem

51

Louis F. Benson, 1899; alt.

Luke 2:8–20, 25–32; Matt. 14:22–33; Mark 4:39; 6:47–52; John 6:16–21; Acts 5:30–31; 10:39–43

1 O sing a song of Beth-le-hem, of shep-herds watch-ing there,
2 O sing a song of Naz-a-reth, of days of joy and sun,
3 O sing a song of Gal-i-lee, of lake and woods and hill,
4 O sing a song of Cal-va-ry, its glo-ry and dis-may,

and of the news that came to them from an-gels in the air:
O sing of fra-grant flo-wers' breath, and of the sin-less One:
of One who walked up-on the sea and bade its waves be still:
of One who hung up-on the tree, and took our sins a-way:

The light that shone on Beth-le-hem fills all the world to-day;
For now the flowers of Naz-a-reth in ev-ery heart may grow;
For though, like waves on Gal-i-lee, rough seas of trou-ble roll,
For Christ who died on Cal-va-ry is ris-en from the grave;

of Je-sus' birth and peace on earth the an-gels sing al-way.
now spreads the fame of Je-sus' name on all the winds that blow.
when faith has heard the Sav-ior's word, falls peace up-on the soul.
God's sov-ereign Child, who rec-on-ciled, is might-y now to save.

Using four biblical locations important to the story, the American hymnwriter Louis F. Benson has summarized the life of Jesus and related it to the present. Benson edited several Presbyterian hymnals and wrote a number of books on hymnody.

Tune: KINGSFOLD C.M.D.
Traditional English melody
Arr. Ralph Vaughan Williams, 1906

52

There Is a Name I Love to Hear
(O How I Love Jesus)

Frederick Whitfield, 1855; alt.

1 There is a name I love to hear, I love to sing its worth;
2 It tells my Sav - ior's love for all; Christ died to set us free;
3 It bids me serve a - mid the wrath God's peo - ple face each day,

It sounds like mu - sic to my ear, the sweet - est name on earth.
What - ev - er prob - lems may be - fall, we'll live in dig - ni - ty.
And sheds a - long life's trou - bled path bright sun - shine on my way.

Refrain

O how I love Je - sus, O how I love Je - sus,

O how I love Je - sus, whose love has first found me.

Frederick Whitfield was ordained in the Church of England and served several English parishes. This hymn is a combination of Whitfield's stanzas and a refrain by an unknown author, both set to an existing nineteenth-century tune. The text was published in a leaflet in 1855.

Tune: O HOW I LOVE JESUS C.M. with refrain
United States, 19th century

Glorious Is Your Name, O Jesus

53

Robert J. Fryson, 1982; alt.

Glo-rious is your name, O Je-sus, prais-es to your name. Oh, glo-ri-ous and right-teous and ho-ly is your name. Oh, glo-ri-ous is your name.

I feel your pres-ence in this place, your Spir-it makes me whole; I can feel your warm em-brace and all the joy with-in my soul, Oh, glo-ri-ous is your name, Oh, glo-ri-ous is your name.

Composer Robert J. Fryson served as minister of music for the Amistad United Church of Christ, as well as choral director for several other Washington, D.C., churches. Fryson also was active as a soloist and recording artist with his sacred music group, "The Voices-Supreme."

Tune: GLORIOUS IS YOUR NAME Irr.
Robert J. Fryson, 1982

54

O Praise the Gracious Power

Eph. 2:11–22

Thomas H. Troeger, 1984

1 O praise the gra-cious power that tum - bles walls of fear And
2 O praise per - sis - tent truth that o - pens fist - ed minds And
3 O praise in - clu - sive love, en - cir - cling ev - ery race, Ob -
4 O praise the word of faith that claims us as God's own, A
5 O praise the tide of grace that laps at ev - ery shore With

gath - ers in one house of faith all stran - gers far and near:
eas - es from their anx - ious clutch the prej - u - dice that binds:
liv - i - ous to gen - der, wealth, to so - cial rank or place:
liv - ing tem - ple built on Christ, our rock and cor - ner - stone:
vi - sions of a world at peace, no long - er bled by war:

Refrain

We praise you, Christ! Your cross has made us one!

Thomas H. Troeger and Carol Doran have collaborated on several collections of new hymnody that utilize selected lectionary readings as their inspiration. This text focuses on the unifying power of Christ, to which Paul attests in the letter to the Ephesians.

Tune: CHRISTPRAISE RAY S.M. with refrain
Carol Doran, 1984
Alternate tune: MARION

6 O praise the power, the truth,
   the love, the word, the tide,
   Yet more than these, O praise their source,
   praise Christ the cru-ci-fied:
   We praise you, Christ!
   Your cross has made us one!

7 O praise the liv-ing Christ
   with faith's bright song-ful voice!
   An-nounce the gos-pel to the world
   and with these words re-joice:
   We praise you, Christ!
   Your cross has made us one!

Rejoice, You Pure in Heart 55

Edward H. Plumptre, 1865; alt.   *Ps. 20:5; Phil. 4:4*

1 Re - joice, you   pure in   heart;   lift   prais - es   to the   sky;
2 Bright youth and   sea - soned   age,   strong souls and   spir - its   meek,
3 With   voice as   full and   strong   as   o - cean's surg-ing   praise,
4 Yes,   on   through life's long   path,   still   chant-ing   as you   go,
5 Praise God who   rules all   worlds,   the   ris - en   Christ a - dore,

Your fes - tal ban - ner   wave with joy,   the   cross of Christ raise   high!
Raise high your free, ex - ult - ing   song, God's won-drous prais - es   speak.
Send forth the hymns the   saints have loved, the   psalms of   an - cient   days.
From youth to   age, by   night and day,   in   glad-ness and   in   woe:
Praise God the Spir - it,   Ho - ly   Fire,   one God for   ev - er - more!

Refrain

Re - joice,   re - joice,   re - joice, give thanks and   sing.
Re - joice   Re - joice

*This hymn, inspired by Philippians 4:4, was written for the
Choral Festival held at Peterborough Cathedral in England. The
author was an Anglican priest and a professor of theology
at Oxford University.*

Tune: MARION S.M. with refrain
*Arthur H. Messiter, 1883
For an alternate setting, see 71
Alternate tune: CHRISTPRAISE RAY*

56

Soplo de Dios viviente
(Breath of the Living God)

Osvaldo Catena; alt.
Transl. The New Century Hymnal, *1993*

Unison

1 So - plo de Dios vi - vien - te que̯en el prin - ci - pio cu - bris - te̯el a - gua;
2 So - plo de Dios vi - vien - te por quien el ver - bo se hi - zo car - ne,
1 Breath of the liv - ing God, who in the be - gin - ning moved o'er the wa - ters,
2 Breath of the liv - ing God, whose e - ter - nal Word came to dwell a - mong us,

So - plo de Dios vi - vien - te que fe - cun - das - te la cre - a - ción.
So - plo de Dios vi - vien - te que re - no - vas - te la cre - a - ción.
Breath of the liv - ing God, by whom all cre - a - tion was first con - ceived:
Breath of the liv - ing God, by whom all cre - a - tion has been re - newed:

Estribillo (Refrain)

¡Ven hoy a nues - tras vi - das, in - fún - de - nos tus do - nes,
Come now and live with - in us, come, let your gifts en - rich us,

So - plo de Dios vi - vien - te, oh San - to̯Es - pí - ri - tu Cre - a - dor!
Breath of the liv - ing God, our Cre - a - tor Spir - it, e - ter - nal Source.

This text by the contemporary Argentinian hymnwriter and composer Osvaldo Catena utilizes a traditional melody from Norway. The hymn was published in Cancionero Abierto IV *in 1979.*

Tune: FLORINDEZ Irr. with refrain
Norwegian traditional melody
Arr. Lorraine Floríndez, 1991

3 So-plo de Dios vi-vien-te
     por quien na-ce-mos en el bau-tis-mo;
  So-plo de Dios vi-vien-te
     que con-sa-gras-te la cre-a-ción.
        (Estribillo)

3 Breath of the liv-ing God,
     source of life a-new
     through our ho-ly Bap-tism,
  Breath of the liv-ing God,
     by whom all cre-a-tion is sanc-ti-fied:
        (Refrain)

O Holy Spirit, Root of Life 57

Jean Janzen, 1991; based on writings by
Hildegard, Abbess of Bingen, 12th century

1 O Ho - ly Spir - it, Root of life, Cre - a - tor,
2 E - ter - nal Vig - or, Sav - ing One, you free us
3 O Ho - ly Wis - dom, Soar - ing Power, en - com - pass

cleans - er of all things, a - noint our wounds, a -
by your liv - ing Word, be - com - ing flesh to
us with wings un - furled, and car - ry us, en -

wak - en us with lus - trous move - ment of your wings.
wear our pain, and all cre - a - tion is re - stored.
cir - cling all, a - bove, be - low, and through the world.

Hildegard of Bingen (1098–1179) was a "woman for all
seasons." A German abbess, she was a prolific liturgical
composer and poet, artist and mystic, and scientist and
theologian whose works exhibit deep spirituality. This new text
combines rich images from Hildegard's songs "De Spiritu
Sancto," "O Virtus Sapientiae," and "O Vis Aeternitatis."

Tune: PUER NOBIS NASCITUR L.M.
Melody from "Piae Cantiones," 1582
Adapt. Michael Praetorius, 1609

58

Spirit of Love

Shirley Erena Murray, 1992

1 Spir - it of love, you move with - in cre - a - tion,
2 Though we have frayed the fab - ric of your mak - ing,
3 Great loom of God, where his - to - ry is wo - ven,

draw - ing the threads to col - or and de - sign:
tear - ing a - way from all that you in - tend,
you are the frame that holds us to the truth,

Life in - to life, you knit our true sal - va - tion,
Yet, to be whole, hu - man - i - ty is ach - ing—
Christ is the theme, the pat - tern you have giv - en—

come, work with us, and weave us in - to one.
come, work with us, and weave us in - to one.
come, work with us, and weave us in - to one.

Originally titled "Weaver Spirit," this text was written for the World Council of Churches Assembly at Canberra. It addressed one of the themes of that meeting—"Come, Holy Spirit, Reconcile Your People."

Tune: PERFECT LOVE 11.10.11.10.
Joseph Barnby, 1889

Holy Spirit, Ever Dwelling

59

Timothy Rees, 1922; alt.

1 Ho-ly Spir-it, ev-er dwell-ing in the ho-liest realms of light;
2 Ho-ly Spir-it, ev-er breath-ing on the church the breath of life;
3 Ho-ly Spir-it, ev-er work-ing through the church's min-is-try—

Ho-ly Spir-it, ev-er brood-ing o'er a world of gloom and
Ho-ly Spir-it, ev-er striv-ing through your peo-ple's cease-less
Quick-ening, strength-ening, and ab-solv-ing, set-ting cap-tive sin-ners

blight; Ho-ly Spir-it, ev-er rais-ing earth-bound souls to glo-ry
strife; Ho-ly Spir-it, ev-er form-ing in the church the mind of
free; Ho-ly Spir-it, ev-er bind-ing age to age and soul to

high; Liv-ing, life-im-part-ing Spir-it; you we praise and mag-ni-fy.
Christ: In our wor-ship we will praise you for your fruit and gifts un-priced.
soul, In com-mu-ni-ty un-end-ing you we wor-ship and ex-tol.

*Timothy Rees, Welsh curate, lecturer, chaplain, and winner of
the Military Cross in World War I, was appointed Bishop of
Llandaff in 1931. These words were written for the Anglican
Community of Mirfield, Yorkshire, of which he was a member.*

Tune: NETTLETON 8.7.8.7.D.
John Wyeth's Repository of Sacred Music, *1813*

60

O Spirit of God

Rom. 8:1–2, 9–17

Johann Niedling, c. 1650
Transl. Madeleine Forell Marshall, 1993

1 O Spir-it of God, O life-giv-ing breath! You com-fort us in life and death. When hu-mans gasp in pain and grief, you breathe as-sur-ance and re-lief:

2 O Spir-it of God, O ho-li-est flame! Ig-nite our love, our hearts re-claim, That we, a blessed com-mu-ni-ty, may lov-ing Chris-tian ser-vants be:

3 O Spir-it of God, O life-giv-ing power! In-crease our faith, bring it to flower. With-out that strength which you sup-ply, our life in Christ will fade and die:

4 O Spir-it of God, O ho-li-est light! Il-lu-mine, by your Word, our night. Our Mak-er's power and glo-ry show, and Je-sus, whom we joy to know:

5 O Spir-it of God, our com-fort and guide, In life, in death, close by our side: For this, we hon-or you with song, ex-press-ing thanks our whole life long:

The German hymnwriter Johann Niedling taught school in
Altenburg, Saxony. Among the six collections he compiled
was the popular Lutherische Handbüchlein.

Tune: O HEILIGER GEIST 10.8.8.8.10.
(O JESULEIN SÜSS)
Geistliche Kirchengesäng, 1623
Harm. adapt. from J. S. Bach, 1993

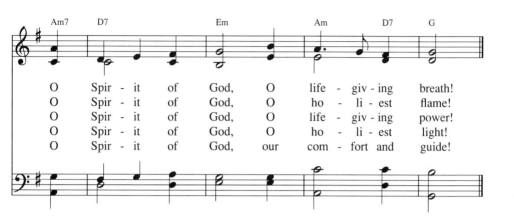

O Spir - it of God, O life - giv - ing breath!
O Spir - it of God, O ho - li - est flame!
O Spir - it of God, O life - giv - ing power!
O Spir - it of God, O ho - li - est light!
O Spir - it of God, our com - fort and guide!

Gracious Spirit, Holy Ghost 61

Christopher Wordsworth, 1862; alt. *1 Cor. 13:1–14*

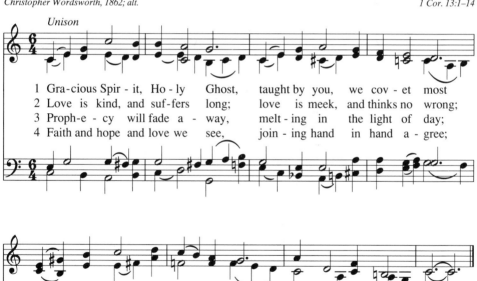

Unison

1 Gra-cious Spir - it, Ho - ly Ghost, taught by you, we cov - et most
2 Love is kind, and suf-fers long; love is meek, and thinks no wrong;
3 Proph-e - cy will fade a - way, melt - ing in the light of day;
4 Faith and hope and love we see, join - ing hand in hand a - gree;

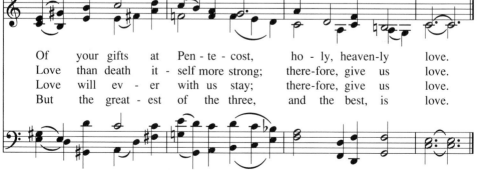

Of your gifts at Pen - te - cost, ho - ly, heaven-ly love.
Love than death it - self more strong; there-fore, give us love.
Love will ev - er with us stay; there-fore, give us love.
But the great - est of the three, and the best, is love.

The author, a nephew of poet William Wordsworth and a celebrated Greek scholar, served as Bishop of London. Jane Marshall is known as a church music composer, educator, and editor.

Tune: ANDERSON 7.7.7.5.
Jane Marshall, 1985

62

Come, Share the Spirit

Luke 4:18–19; Isa. 61   *Vicki Vogel Schmidt, 1987; alt.*

With a happy, driving beat
Unison

1 Come, share the Spir - it, mov-ing a - mong us, weav-ing
2 Come, Rush-ing Wa - ters, let jus - tice roll like an
3 Come, Gen - tle Breez-es, breath of all lov - ing, giv - en

in and through this place; break-ing down the walls that
ev - er - flow - ing stream; till the poor find strength as they
to God's cho - sen band; let us dance and feast with the

split and di - vide, bring-ing whole-ness to em - brace.
hear the good news, and the rich a - dopt new dreams.
bro - ken ones, bring com - pas - sion to our land.

Come, Liv - ing Spir - it, bloom in our hearts as when the
Come, Blaz-ing Fire, a - noint our tongues with the
Come! Lift our hands in joy - ful ap - plause to the

Vicki Vogel Schmidt wrote this hymn for a meeting of the
Northwest Minnesota Synod of the Evangelical Lutheran
Church in America. It utilizes the theme for the merger of
Lutheran denominations in 1987—"Come, share the Spirit."

Tune: SHARE THE SPIRIT Irr.
Vicki Vogel Schmidt, 1987
Arr. The New Century Hymnal, 1993

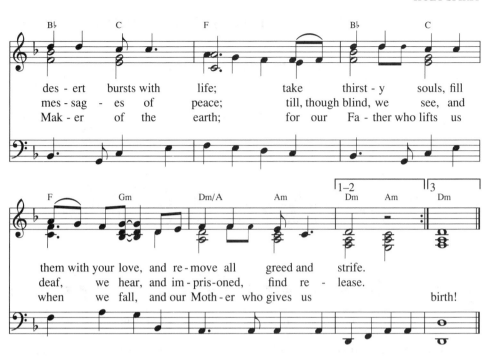

des - ert   bursts with   life;   take   thirst - y   souls, fill
mes - sag - es   of   peace;   till, though blind, we   see, and
Mak - er   of   the   earth;   for   our   Fa - ther who lifts   us

them with your love, and re - move all   greed and   strife.
deaf,   we   hear, and im - pris - oned,   find   re - lease.
when   we   fall,   and our Moth - er who gives us   birth!

Holy Spirit, Truth Divine   63

Samuel Longfellow, 1864; alt.

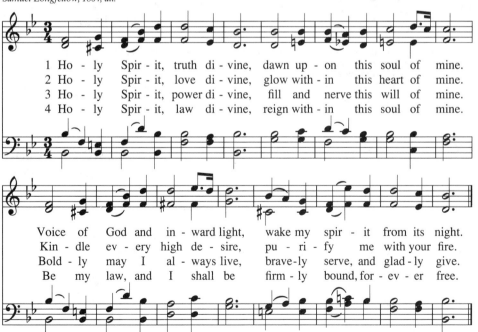

1 Ho - ly   Spir - it, truth di - vine, dawn up - on   this soul of   mine.
2 Ho - ly   Spir - it, love di - vine, glow with - in   this heart of   mine.
3 Ho - ly   Spir - it, power di - vine, fill and   nerve this will of   mine.
4 Ho - ly   Spir - it, law di - vine, reign with - in   this soul of   mine.

Voice   of   God   and   in - ward light,   wake my   spir - it   from its   night.
Kin - dle   ev - ery   high de - sire,   pu - ri - fy   me with your   fire.
Bold - ly   may   I   al - ways live,   brave-ly   serve, and   glad - ly   give.
Be   my   law, and   I   shall be   firm - ly   bound, for - ev - er   free.

*Louis Moreau Gottschalk was the first American musician to be
acclaimed at home and abroad as a virtuoso pianist and gifted
composer, often incorporating folk and popular tunes into his
own concert music. Mercy was arranged from his piano
composition, "The Last Hope."*

Tune: MERCY 7.7.7.7.
*Louis Moreau Gottschalk, 1867
Arr. Edwin Parker, 1888*

64 Fire of God, Undying Flame

Acts 2:1–21   *Albert F. Bayly (1901–1984); alt.*

1 Fire   of God, un - dy - ing Flame,   Spir - it who in splen-dor came,
2 Breath of God, that   swept in power   in   the Pen - te - cos - tal hour,
3 Strength of God, your   might with - in   con - quers sor - row, pain, and sin.
4 Truth of God, your   pierc - ing rays   pen - e - trate my   se - cret ways.
5 Love of God, your   grace pro-found   knows not ei - ther age   or bound.

Let   your heat   my   soul   re - fine,   till   it glows with   love di - vine.
Ho - ly Breath, be   now   in   me   source of vi - tal   en - er - gy.
For - ti - fy   from   e - vil's art   all   the gate - ways   of   my heart.
May the light that shames my   sin   guide me ho - lier   paths to win.
Come, my heart's own guest   to   be;   dwell for - ev - er - more in me.

*Albert F. Bayly, an English Congregational minister, wrote his
first hymn after age forty and subsequently published several
collections of hymnody. Most hymnals published since 1950
have included at least one of his hymns.*

Words Copyright © 1988 Oxford University Press.

Tune: NUN KOMM DER HEIDEN HEILAND
7.7.7.7.
*Plainsong melody; adapt. Johann Walther in
Geistliche Gesangbuchlein, Wittenberg, 1524
Harm. Melchior Vulpius (c. 1560–1616)*

65 Este es el día
(This Is the Day)

Ps. 118:19–29   *Pablo D. Sosa, 1983; alt.*
Transl. Roberto Escamilla and Elise S. Eslinger, 1983

Estribillo (Refrain)
Unison   FM7/C   Bb   Bb9/A   Gm7   Am7   Gm7   C11

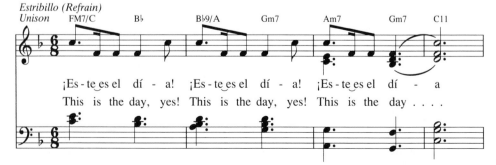

¡Es - te es el   dí - a!   ¡Es - te es el   dí - a!   ¡Es - te es el   dí - a
This   is the day, yes!   This   is the day, yes!   This   is the   day . . . .

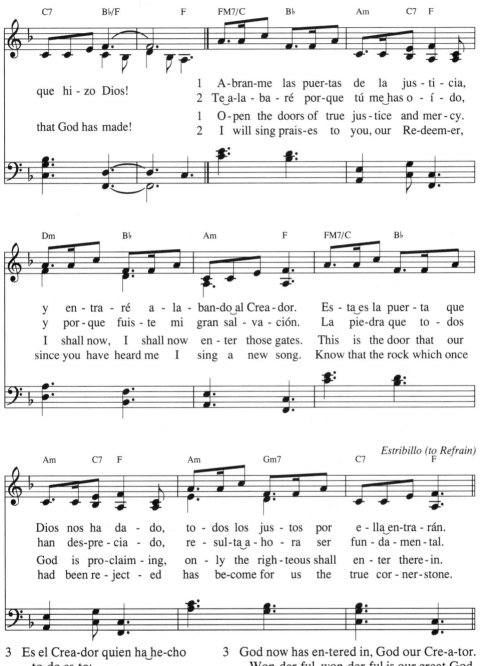

que hi - zo Dios!

that God has made!

1 A-bran-me las puer-tas de la jus - ti - cia,
2 Te a-la - ba - ré por-que tú me has o - í - do,

1 O-pen the doors of true jus-tice and mer - cy.
2 I will sing prais-es to you, our Re-deem-er,

y en - tra - ré a - la - ban-do al Crea - dor. Es - ta es la puer - ta que
y por - que fuis - te mi gran sal - va - ción. La pie-dra que to - dos

I shall now, I shall now en - ter those gates. This is the door that our
since you have heard me I sing a new song. Know that the rock which once

Dios nos ha da - do, to - dos los jus - tos por e - lla en-tra - rán.
han des-pre - cia - do, re - sul-ta a - ho - ra ser fun - da - men - tal.

God is pro-claim - ing, on - ly the righ-teous shall en - ter there-in.
had been re - ject - ed has be-come for us the true cor - ner-stone.

Estribillo (to Refrain)

3 Es el Crea-dor quien ha he-cho
to-do es-to;
¡qué ma-ra-vi-lla po-der ver-lo hoy!
Es-te es el dí-a que Dios ha he-cho,
con a-le-grí-a go-ce-mos en él.
(*Estribillo*)

3 God now has en-tered in, God our Cre-a-tor.
Won-der-ful, won-der-ful is our great God.
This is the day that our Mak-er has of-fered.
Let us re-joice and be glad and sing praise.
(*Refrain*)

*The refrain of this psalm setting from Argentina was inspired by
the echoing voices of gauchos (cowboys) calling to greet each
other as they rode through the fields.*

Tune: ESTE ES EL DIA 11.10.11.10. with refrain
Pablo D. Sosa, 1983
Arr. Roberto Milano, 1984

66 O Day of Radiant Gladness

St. 1–2, Christopher Wordsworth, 1862; alt.
St. 3, Charles P. Price, 1980; alt.
St. 4, The Hymnal 1982; alt.

1 O day of ra-diant glad - ness, O day of joy and light;
2 This day at the cre - a - tion the light first had its birth;
3 This day God's peo-ple, meet - ing, the Ho - ly Scrip-ture hear;
4 That light our hope sus - tain - ing, up - on the pil-grim way,

O balm of care and sad - ness, most beau - ti - ful, most bright;
this day for our sal - va - tion Christ rose from depths of earth;
Christ's liv - ing pres-ence greet - ing, through bread and cup made near.
at length our rest at - tain - ing, our end - less Sab - bath day.

This day the high and low - ly, through a - ges joined in tune,
This day our God vic - to - rious the Spir - it sent from heaven,
We jour-ney on, be - liev - ing, re - newed with heaven-ly might,
We sing to you our prais - es, our Hope, our Joy, our Sun:

sing "Ho - ly, ho - ly, ho - ly" to the great God tri - une.
and thus this day most glo - rious a tri - ple light was given.
from grace more grace re - ceiv - ing on this blessed day of light.
the church its voice up - rais - es to you, blessed Three in One.

Christopher Wordsworth, Anglican priest, wrote voluminously on the Bible and church history in addition to his hymn writing. This hymn is from his Holy Year, 1862.

Tune: ES FLOG EIN KLEINS WALDVÖGELEIN
7.6.7.6.D.
*Memmingen manuscript, 17th century
Harm. George R. Woodward, 1904*

Let Me Enter God's Own Dwelling

67

Benjamin Schmolck, 1732
Transl. Madeleine Forell Marshall, 1993

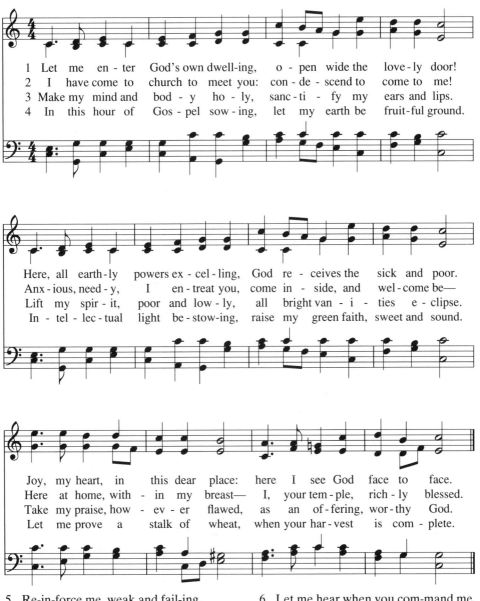

1 Let me en-ter God's own dwell-ing, o-pen wide the love-ly door!
2 I have come to church to meet you: con-de-scend to come to me!
3 Make my mind and bod-y ho-ly, sanc-ti-fy my ears and lips.
4 In this hour of Gos-pel sow-ing, let my earth be fruit-ful ground.

Here, all earth-ly powers ex-cel-ling, God re-ceives the sick and poor.
Anx-ious, need-y, I en-treat you, come in-side, and wel-come be—
Lift my spir-it, poor and low-ly, all bright van-i-ties e-clipse.
In-tel-lec-tual light be-stow-ing, raise my green faith, sweet and sound.

Joy, my heart, in this dear place: here I see God face to face.
Here at home, with-in my breast— I, your tem-ple, rich-ly blessed.
Take my praise, how-ev-er flawed, as an of-fering, wor-thy God.
Let me prove a stalk of wheat, when your har-vest is com-plete.

5 Re-in-force me, weak and fail-ing,
   mak-ing sure your pre-cious word—
   (Thieves and e-vil un-a-vail-ing)—
   lives with-in my heart se-cured.
   Shin-ing word, my star-ry guide,
   plant-ed for me, deep in-side.

6 Let me hear when you com-mand me,
   let me leap to do your will.
   When I wan-der, rep-ri-mand me,
   com-fort me when I lie ill.
   In the hour of si-lent dread,
   feed me with your heaven-ly bread.

A native of Silesia, Benjamin Schmolck was ordained a Lutheran pastor. Although he was one of only three clergy serving thirty-six villages, he wrote more than 1,000 hymns. Joachim Neander, an important Reformed musician, wrote the music.

Tune: UNSER HERRSCHER 8.7.8.7.7.7.
Joachim Neander, 1680

68   God Is Truly with Us

Matt. 1:23; 2 Cor. 9:8; Rev. 4:8–11   *Gerhard Tersteegen, 1729*
                                             Transl. Frederick W. Foster and others; alt.

1 God is tru-ly with us; sing we and a - dore   now: praise the One we
2 God is tru-ly with us; loud our praise re - sound - ing! Ech - oes of the
3 Source of ev-ery bless - ing, bless the ones who name   you, let our words and

come be - fore   now. Here with-in this tem - ple, here in sound and
saints sur - round - ing! "Ho - ly, ho - ly, ho - ly," hear the hymn as -
deeds pro - claim   you. Like the saints and an - gels prais-ing you in

si - lence, wor-ship God in deep - est rev - erence. You a - lone,
cend - ing, an - gels, saints, their voic - es blend - ing! Bow your ear
glo - ry, may your ser - vants sing your sto - ry. And in all,

God, we own, you, our God and Sav - ior; praise to you for - ev - er.
to us here; hear, O Christ, the prais - es that your Church now rais - es.
great and small, may we do most near - ly what you love most dear - ly.

Gerhard Tersteegen, an important German hymnwriter of the   Tune: WUNDERBARER KÖNIG 6.6.8.6.6.8.3.3.6.6.
Reformed Church, began preaching at prayer meetings and   *Joachim Neander, in A und Ω,*
gained a considerable following. He devoted his life to praying,   Glaubund Liebesübung, Bremen, 1680
preaching, visiting the poor, and writing and translating
devotional material.

Come, God, Creator, Be Our Shield

69

Marion M. Meyer, 1990

Ps. 84:8–12

1 Come, God, Cre - a - tor, be our shield, the
2 Come, gra - cious Je - sus, be our guest, our
3 Come, Ho - ly Spir - it, be our guide, our

One to whom our cares we yield;
morn - ing joy, our eve - ning rest;
strength to risk a - gainst the tide,

And in our wor - ship, faith im - part, your
And in our dai - ly lives im - part, your
That in God's world we shall im - part, your

grace and calm to ev - ery heart.
love and peace to ev - ery heart.
light and hope to ev - ery heart.

After serving as a teacher in Baghdad, Iraq, Marion Meyer joined the staff of The Pilgrim Press and United Church Press in 1958. She retired thirty years later as senior editor. Her tune, named for Old First Reformed Church, U.C.C., in Philadelphia, was composed as a setting for the traditional table grace she adapted in stanza two.

Tune: OLD FIRST L.M.
Marion M. Meyer, 1990
Harm. The New Century Hymnal, 1994

70 God Is Here! As We Your People Meet

Fred Pratt Green, 1978; alt.

1 God is here! As we your peo-ple meet to of - fer praise and prayer,
2 Here are sym-bols to re - mind us of our life - long need of grace;
3 Here our chil-dren find a wel-come in the Shep - herd's flock and fold;
4 Sov - ereign God, of earth and heav-en, in an age of change and doubt

May we find in full - er mea-sure what it is in Christ we share.
Here are ta - ble, font, and pul - pit, here the cross has cen - tral place.
Here as bread and wine are tak - en, Christ sus - tains us as of old.
Keep us faith - ful to the gos - pel, help us work your pur - pose out.

Here, as in the world a - round us, all our var - ied skills and arts
Here in hon - es - ty of preach-ing, here in si - lence, as in speech,
Here the ser - vants of the Ser - vant seek in wor-ship to ex - plore
Here, in this day's ded - i - ca - tion, all we have to give, re - ceive;

wait the com - ing of the Spir - it in - to o - pen minds and hearts.
here, in new-ness and re - new-al, God the Spir - it comes to each.
what it means in dai - ly liv-ing to be - lieve and to a - dore.
we, who can - not live with-out you, we a - dore you! We be - lieve!

Though he retired in 1969, this distinguished British poet has continued to write hymns. In addition to administering several circuits and local congregations, Fred Pratt Green published plays, translations, and poems. Emory University in Atlanta awarded him an honorary doctorate.

Tune: ABBOT'S LEIGH 8.7.8.7.D.
Cyril V. Taylor, 1941

Rejoice, You Pure in Heart

Edward H. Plumptre, 1865; alt.   *Ps. 20:5; Phil. 4:4*

1 Re - joice, you pure in heart; lift prais - es to the
2 Bright youth and sea - soned age, strong souls and spir - its
3 With voice as full and strong as o - cean's surg - ing
4 Yes, on through life's long path, still chant - ing as you
5 Praise God who rules all worlds, the ris - en Christ a -

sky; Your fes - tal ban - ner wave with joy, the
meek, Raise high your free, ex - ult - ing song, God's
praise, Send forth the hymns the saints have loved, the
go, From youth to age, by night and day, in
dore, Praise God the Spir - it, Ho - ly Fire, one

cross of Christ raise high!
won-drous prais - es speak.
psalms of an - cient days.   Ho - san - na! Ho -
glad - ness and in woe:
God for ev - er - more!

Refrain

san - na! Re - joice, give thanks and sing.

Richard Wayne Dirksen served on the musical staff of the Washington Cathedral for more than forty years, and was the first layperson in an American cathedral to be appointed precentor. Dirksen composed this tune for the installation of John M. Allin as presiding bishop of the Episcopal church.

Tune: VINEYARD HAVEN S.M. with refrain
Richard Wayne Dirksen, 1974
For an alternate setting, see 55

72

Sekai no Tomo
(Here, O God, Your Servants Gather)

John 14:6; Rom. 10:12–13; Eph. 1:7–14

Tokuo Yamaguchi, 1958; alt.
Phonetic transcription, I-to Loh, 1958
Transl. Everett M. Stowe, 1958; alt.

1 Se - ka - i no to - mo to te o tsu - na - gi,
1 Here, O God, your ser - vants gath - er, hand we link in hand;
2 Man - y are the tongues we speak, scat-tered are the lands,
3 Na - ture's se - crets o - pen wide, chan-ges nev - er cease;
4 Grant, O God, an age re - newed, show us how love thrives,

Jyu - ji - ka no mo - to ni ta - tsu wa - re - ra,
look - ing toward our Sav - ior's cross, joined in love we stand.
yet our hearts are one in God, one in love's de - mands.
where, O where, can wea - ry souls find the source of peace?
help us as we work and pray, send us for our lives

Ka - mi no mi - ku - ni o me - a - te to - shi,
As we seek the realm of God, we u - nite to pray:
In de - spair our hope ap - pears, call - ing age and youth:
Un - to all those sore dis - tressed, torn by end - less strife:
Truth and cour - age, faith and power need - ed in our strife:

Shu Ye-su no mi-chi o su-su-mi-yu kan.
Je-sus, Sav-ior, guide our steps, for you are the Way.
Je-sus, Teach-er, dwell with us, for you are the Truth.
Je-sus, Heal-er, bring your balm, for you are the Life.
Je-sus, Lead-er, be our Way, be our Truth, our Life.

This hymn was composed for the fourteenth World Council of Christian Education, 1958. Tokuo Yamaguchi has served many Japanese parishes and since 1979 has been pastor emeritus of Toyohashi Church, Aichi Prefecture. His translation of The Journal of John Wesley *won official commendation.*

Tune: TOKYO 7.5.7.5.D.
Japanese gagaku mode
Arr. Isao Koizumi, 1958

Enter, Rejoice, and Come In 73

Louise Ruspini; alt. *Ps. 100*

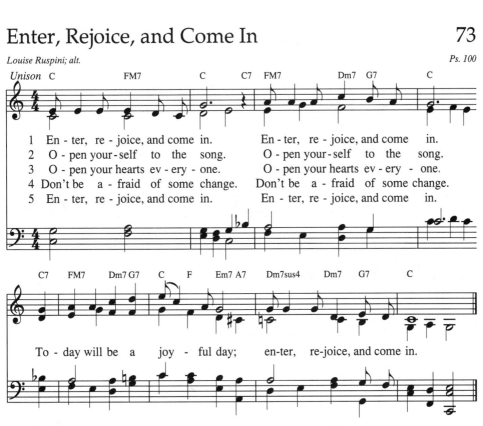

1 En-ter, re-joice, and come in. En-ter, re-joice, and come in.
2 O-pen your-self to the song. O-pen your-self to the song.
3 O-pen your hearts ev-ery-one. O-pen your hearts ev-ery-one.
4 Don't be a-fraid of some change. Don't be a-fraid of some change.
5 En-ter, re-joice, and come in. En-ter, re-joice, and come in.

To-day will be a joy-ful day; en-ter, re-joice, and come in.

This song, based on Psalm 100, became popular in the 1970s in the United States. It works equally well with organ, piano, or guitar accompaniment.

Tune: ENTER, REJOICE 7.7.8.7.
Louise Ruspini
Harm. The New Century Hymnal, *1993*

74   We Have Gathered, Jesus Dear

Tobias Clausnitzer, 1663
Transl. Madeleine Forell Marshall, 1993

1 We have gath-ered, Je-sus dear, we have come to
2 All our in-tel-lec-tual dreams come to noth-ing,
3 Born of God, true light of light, Ho-ly Spir-it,

watch and lis - ten. Fix our minds, our sens-es clear,
fade at day - break. All our hope-ful plots and schemes,
pure, un-fail - ing: All our fac-ul-ties ex - cite,

to re-ceive your heaven-ly les - son. Please im-prove our
start in pre-tense, end in heart - ache. Thought-ful speech, and
ears and heart and mouth un-seal - ing: Then, through Je - sus'

con-cen-tra-tion: draw us in-to con-tem-pla - tion.
ac-tive jus-tice, you ac-com-plish these with-in us.
me-di-a-tion, God will hear our sup-pli-ca - tion.

Written to precede the sermon, this hymn briefly reflects the
Nicene Creed in the third stanza. Tobias Clausnitzer, a German
Lutheran pastor, served for a time as a chaplain to a Swedish
regiment and later as a parish pastor.

Tune: LIEBSTER JESU 7.8.7.8.8.8.
Johann R. Ahle, 1664
Harm. Das grosse Cantional, Darmstadt, 1687

Lord, Make Me More Holy

African-American spiritual

1 Lord, make me more ho - ly. Lord, make me more ho - ly.

Lord, make me more ho - ly, un - til we meet a - gain.

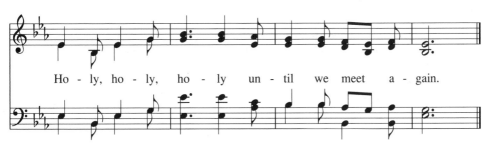

Ho - ly, ho - ly, ho - ly un - til we meet a - gain.

2 Lord, make me more faith-ful, . . . Faith-ful, . . . un-til we meet a-gain.
3 Lord, make me more hum-ble, . . . Hum-ble, . . . un-til we meet a-gain.
4 Lord, make me more righ-teous, . . . Righ-teous, . . . un-til we meet a-gain.

The origins of this African-American spiritual have been traced to the area of Charleston, South Carolina, where it may have been sung as a closing hymn for worship. It is one of a number of devotional songs expressing the desire to attain the spiritual character of Jesus.

Tune: LORD, MAKE ME MORE HOLY
6.6.6.6.6.6.
African-American spiritual

76 Sent Forth by God's Blessing

Omer Westendorf, 1964

Omer Westendorf, author of numerous hymns, compiler of several hymnals, and founder of World Library Publications, included this hymn in People's Mass Book, *1964, the first vernacular Roman Catholic hymn and service book to implement the decrees of Vatican II.*

Tune: THE ASH GROVE 6.6.11.6.6.11.D.
Welsh folk melody
Harm. Leland Sateren, 1972
Descant, The New Century Hymnal, *1993*

77   Lord, Dismiss Us with Your Blessing

Luke 2:29; Rom. 1:16   *Attrib. to John Fawcett, 1773; alt.*

Influenced by George Whitefield's preaching, John Fawcett joined the Baptist church, and served as minister in Wainsgate, England, for fifty-four years. Yielding to the persuasion of his parishioners, he declined invitations to move elsewhere. He wrote more than 160 hymns.

Tune: SICILIAN MARINERS 8.7.8.7.8.7.
Sicilian melody, 18th century
The European Magazine and Review, *1792*

Part in Peace 78

Sarah Flower Adams (1805–1848); alt.

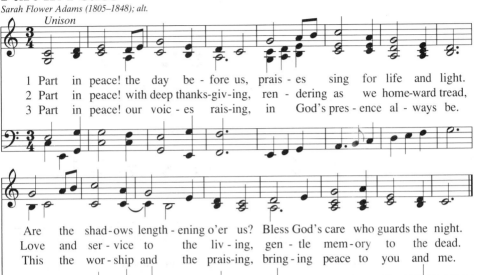

Unison

1 Part in peace! the day be - fore us, prais - es sing for life and light.
2 Part in peace! with deep thanks-giv-ing, ren - dering as we home-ward tread,
3 Part in peace! our voic - es rais-ing, in God's pres - ence al - ways be.

Are the shad-ows length - ening o'er us? Bless God's care who guards the night.
Love and ser - vice to the liv - ing, gen - tle mem-ory to the dead.
This the wor - ship and the prais-ing, bring - ing peace to you and me.

Daughter of an editor, Sarah Flower Adams gave up a successful acting career in London to continue writing poems and hymns. One of her best-known texts is "Nearer, my God, to thee."

Tune: CHARLESTOWN 8.7.8.7.
Southern Harmony, 1835
Harm. Carlton R. Young, 1964

May the Sending One Defend You 79

Brian Wren, 1989; rev. 1993

Unison

1 May the Send - ing One de - fend you, may the Seek - ing One a - mend you,
2 May the Giv - en One re - trieve you, may the Gift - ed One re - lieve you,
3 May the Bind - ing One u - nite you— may the One Be-loved in - vite you—

May the Keep - ing One be - friend you, in your glad - ness and in your griev - ing.
May the Giv - ing One re - ceive you, in your fall - ing and your re - stor - ing.
May the Lov - ing One de - light you— Three-in - One, joy in life un - end - ing.

Brian Wren wrote this text during a visit with composer Mikkel Thompson on Bainbridge Island, Washington. When he first heard the tune, Wren said, "It cried out for a text, and suggested the style of ancient Celtic blessings."

Tune: ROLLINGBAY 8.8.8.9.
Mikkel Thompson, 1989

80 Savior, Again to Your Dear Name

Ps. 141:3–4a; 139:11–12; John 14:27 *John Ellerton, 1866; alt.*

1 Savior, again to your dear name we raise
2 Grant us your peace upon our home-ward way;
3 Grant us your peace, as day turns into night;
4 Grant us your peace throughout our earth-ly life,

with one ac-cord our part-ing hymn of praise;
with you be-gan, with you shall end the day;
stay with us till the com-ing of the light;
our balm in sor-row, and our stay in strife;

We join to bless you ere our wor-ship cease,
Guard all the lips from sin, the hearts from shame,
Keep safe all those who call up-on your name,
Then, when your voice shall bid our con-flict cease,

then, in the si-lence, wait your word of peace.
that in this house have called up-on your name.
for dark and light to you are both the same.
call us, O God, to your e-ter-nal peace.

John Ellerton, a priest of the Church of England, wrote this hymn for a choral association festival. The final stanza was sung at his funeral. Ellerton edited and contributed to numerous hymnals.

Tune: ELLERS 10.10.10.10.
Edward J. Hopkins, 1869

God Be with You 81

Jeremiah E. Rankin, 1880; alt.

1 God be with you till we meet a-gain; By good coun-sel guide, up-hold you,
2 God be with you till we meet a-gain; Wings of shel-ter safe-ly hide you,
3 God be with you till we meet a-gain; When life's per-ils thick con-found you,
4 God be with you till we meet a-gain; Keep love's ban-ner float-ing o'er you,

With a shep-herd's care en-fold you: God be with you till we meet a-gain.
Dai-ly man-na still pro-vide you: God be with you till we meet a-gain.
Put un-fail-ing arms a-round you: God be with you till we meet a-gain.
Smite death's threat-ening wave be-fore you: God be with you till we meet a-gain.

Refrain

Till we meet, till we meet, till we meet at Je-sus' feet;
till we meet, till we meet a-gain, till we meet,

till we meet, till we meet, God be with you till we meet a-gain.
till we meet, till we meet a-gain,

Written during his last pastorate, at First Congregational Church in Washington, D.C., Jeremiah Rankin's hymn spread quickly throughout America and England by way of Moody and Sankey's revival meetings. Rankin later served as the seventh president of Howard University.

Tune: GOD BE WITH YOU 9.8.8.9. with refrain
William G. Tomer, 1880

82 Go, My Children, with My Blessing

Jaroslav J. Vajda, 1983, 1990; alt.

1 Go, my chil-dren, with my bless-ing, nev - er a - lone;
2 Go, my chil-dren, fed and nour-ished, clos - er to me;

Wak - ing, sleep-ing, I am with you, you are my own;
Grow in love and love by serv-ing, joy - ful and free.

In my love's bap - tis-mal riv - er I have made you mine for-ev - er,
Here my Spir - it's pow-er filled you, here with ten - der com-fort stilled you;

Go, my chil-dren, with my bless-ing, you are my own.
Go, my chil-dren, fed and nour-ished, joy - ful and free.

For marriage services, this stanza may be sung between stanzas 1 and 2 above.

In this un-ion I have joined you hus-band and wife,
Now, my chil-dren, live to-geth-er as heirs of life:
Each the oth-er's glad-ness shar-ing,
each the oth-er's bur-dens bear-ing,
Now, my chil-dren, live to-geth-er as heirs of life.

American hymnwriter and translator Jaroslav Vajda crafted this benediction text as though God were "dismissing the congregation after worship, while drawing together a review of the events that transpired during the service." The wedding stanza was a later addition.

Tune: AR HYD Y NOS 8.4.8.4.8.8.8.4.
Traditional Welsh melody
For another harmonization, see 425

I Sing as I Arise Today 83

Attrib. to St. Patrick (372–466)
Transl. anon.

1 I sing as I a - rise to - day! I
2 The word of God to be my speech, The
3 Al - le - lu - ia, al - le - lu - ia, Al -

call on my Cre - a - tor's might: The will of God to
hand of God to be my stay, The shield of God to
le - lu - ia, al - le - lu - ia, Al - le - lu - ia, al -

be my guide, The eye of God to be my sight,
be my strength, The path of God to be my way.
le - lu - ia, Al - le - lu - ia, al - le - lu - ia.

The prayer known as "Breastplate" has been traditionally
ascribed to St. Patrick, who is said to have brought Christianity
to Ireland. It appears in many versions, including this
anonymous morning hymn.

Tune: SEED OF LIFE L.M.
William P. Rowan, 1986

84

This Is the Day

Ps. 118:24; Luke 24:1–7; Acts 2:1–4

St. 1 paraphr. by Les Garrett, 1967; alt.
St. 2–3, traditional; alt.

1 This is the day, this is the day that our God has made, that our
2 This is the day, this is the day Je-sus rose a-gain, Je-sus
3 This is the day, this is the day when the Spir-it came, when the

God has made; we will re-joice, we will re-joice and be glad in it, and be
rose a-gain; we will re-joice, we will re-joice and be glad in it, and be
Spir-it came; we will re-joice, we will re-joice and be glad in it, and be

glad in it. This is the day that our God has made, we will re-joice and be
glad in it. This is the day Je-sus rose a-gain, we will re-joice and be
glad in it. This is the day when the Spir-it came, we will re-joice and be

glad in it; This is the day, this is the day that our God has made.
glad in it; This is the day, this is the day Je-sus rose a-gain.
glad in it; This is the day, this is the day when the Spir-it came.

The first stanza of this hymn was written by Leslie Garrett, who was born in New Zealand and served as pastor of a church in western Australia. The other two stanzas are anonymous.

Tune: THIS IS THE DAY Irr.
Les Garrett, 1967

I Woke Up This Morning

African-American traditional

The spirituals that were passed down through the African-American oral tradition were not only enduring but also adaptable. During the civil rights movement of the 1960s this spiritual was sung as "Woke up this morning with my mind on freedom."

Tune: WOKE UP THIS MORNING Irr.
African-American spiritual
Arr. Jeffrey Radford, 1993

86

When Morning Gilds the Skies

Ps. 5:3; 59:16–17

Katholisches Gesangbuch, *1828*
Transl. Edward Caswall, *1854; alt.*

1 When morn - ing gilds the skies, my heart a - wak-ing cries,
2 New strength comes night or day when from the heart we say,
3 Dis - cor - dant hu - man - kind, in this your con-cord find,
4 Be this, while life is mine, my can - ti - cle di - vine,

may Je - sus Christ be praised! A - like at work and prayer,
may Je - sus Christ be praised! Let sin and e - vil fear,
may Je - sus Christ be praised! Let all the earth a - round
may Je - sus Christ be praised! Be this the e - ter - nal song,

one pur-pose I de - clare: may Je - sus Christ be praised!
when this sweet chant they hear: may Je - sus Christ be praised!
ring joy - ous with the sound: may Je - sus Christ be praised!
through all the a - ges long: may Je - sus Christ be praised!

*This anonymous German Catholic hymn was translated to
English by Edward Caswall, an Anglican—and later, Roman
Catholic—priest. Among the scripture references is Psalm 5:3,
"O God, in the morning you hear my voice. . . ."*

Tune: LAUDES DOMINI 6.6.6.6.6.6.
Joseph Barnby, 1868

O Splendor of God's Glory Bright

Ambrose of Milan (c. 340–c. 397)
Transl. composite The New Century Hymnal, 1993

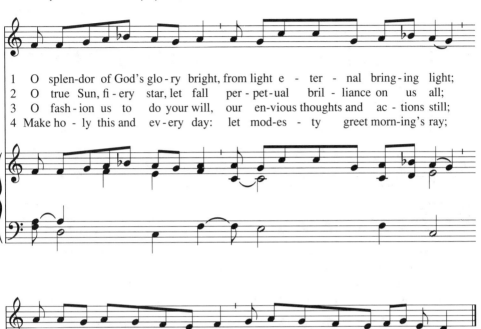

1 O splen-dor of God's glo-ry bright, from light e - ter - nal bring-ing light;
2 O true Sun, fi - ery star, let fall per - pet-ual bril - liance on us all;
3 O fash - ion us to do your will, our en-vious thoughts and ac - tions still;
4 Make ho - ly this and ev-ery day: let mod-es - ty greet morn-ing's ray;

O light of light, light's liv - ing spring, O day of days, il - lu - min-ing.
The Ho - ly Spir - it's ra - diant beam up - on our earth - ly sens - es stream.
In ev - ery chal - lenge may we find the grace which guides both heart and mind.
And faith-ful love, the noon-day light; and hope, the sun - set calm and bright.

St. Ambrose is noted for introducing congregational and antiphonal singing to the Western church. This hymn is an example of an early "protest song" written to preserve orthodox views of the divinity of Christ, which were threatened by the rise of Arianism in the fourth century.

Tune: SPLENDOR PATERNAE L.M.
Sarum plainsong, mode 1
Alternate tune: PUER NOBIS NASCITUR

88

Pero Queda Cristo
(My Soul Overflows with Praise)

Alfredo Colom M., 1954; alt.
English version by Carolyn Jennings, 1993

1 Por la ma-ña-na di-ri-gi-mos la a-la-ban-za a Dios que ha
2 Cuan-do la no-che se a-pro-xi-ma, te-ne-bro-sa, en e-le-
1 At ear-ly dawn we sing a song of ad-o-ra-tion to God who
2 When night ap-proach-es and would cause us to be fear-ful, we lift our

si-do nues-tra ú-ni-ca es-pe-ran-za. Por la ma-ña-na le in-vo-
var-le u-na o-ra-ción el ser se go-za; Sien-te su paz i-na-go-
is our on-ly hope and our sal-va-tion. At ear-ly dawn we raise our
souls to God in prayer with spir-it cheer-ful. God's sooth-ing peace and com-fort

ca-mos con el al-ma, le su-pli-ca-mos que nos dé su dul-ce
ta-ble, dul-ce y gra-ta por-que te-mo-res y an-sie-dad, Je-sús nos
long-ing in-vo-ca-tion; for God's sweet calm we beg in fer-vent sup-pli-
fill our hearts with glad-ness, and Christ con-tin-ues to dis-pel our fear and

cal-ma. Dios nos es-cu-cha, pues nos a-ma tan-to, y nos a-
qui-ta. Y nues-tro cán-ti-co se e-le-va al cie-lo cuan-do a la
ca-tion. God's heart is full of love and mer-cy for us, from all our
sad-ness. Though shad-ows thick-en ev-ery-where a-round us, the sav-ing

Born in Guatemala in 1904, Alfredo Colom M. was an
evangelist and prolific writer and composer of hymns, although
he did not have any formal musical training.

Tune: POR LA MAÑANA 13.13.D.11.11.D.
Alfredo Colom M., 1954

li - via de cual-quier que - bran - to. Nos da su ma - no po - de - ro - sa y
tie - rra ba - ja os - cu - ro ve - lo. El sol se o - cul - ta, pe - ro que - da
bro-ken-ness God will re - store us. Our God is strong and will for-sake us
love of God will still sur - round us. The sun has gone but Christ is ev - er

fuer - te, pa - ra li - brar - nos de la mis - ma muer - te.
Cris - to, que nues-tros o - jos en el sue - ño han vis - to.
nev - er, from death it - self God sets us free for - ev - er.
near us, with - in our dreams a con - stant hope to cheer us.

3 Bri-lla su lum-bre bien-he-
      cho-ra so-bre to-dos;
   su ma-no po-ne so-bre los
      que es-tán en-fer-mos.
   Nos for-ta-le-ce, nos a-lien-ta
      con el sue-ño;
   es nues-tro Dios, el Re-den-tor
      y nues-tro due-ño.
   En la ma-ña-na al
      des-per-tar sen-ti-mos
   que Dios in-va-de el
      ser y el pen-sa-mien-to;
   Ve-mos a Cris-to el
      Re-den-tor a-ma-do,
   pa-ra sal-var-nos, en la
      cruz cla-va-do.

3 The light of God shines over us
      while we are sleep-ing;
   our health and life and ver-y breath
      are in God's keep-ing.
   Through-out the night we trust in God
      to stay be-side us,
   the ver-y God who owns our be-ing
      and re-deems us.
   And when we wak-en
      in the light of morn-ing,
   the face of Je-sus,
      still our thoughts a-dorn-ing,
   Re-minds us that God came
      and died to save us,
   and through the cross
      the joy of heav-en gave us.

89   Awake, Awake to Love and Work

Geoffrey A. Studdert-Kennedy, 1921; alt.

1 A - wake, a - wake to love and work! The lark is in the sky;
2 Come, let your voice be one with theirs, shout with their shout of praise;
3 To give and give, and give a - gain, as God's own grace is free;

the fields are wet with dia - mond dew; The worlds a - wake to cry
See how the gi - ant sun soars up, God's gift for all your days!
To spend your-self nor count the cost; To serve most glo - rious - ly

their prais - es to the Fount of Life; Christ Je - sus pass - es by.
So let the love of Je - sus come and set your soul a - blaze,
the God who gave all worlds that are, and all that are to be.

Geoffrey Studdert-Kennedy was known in the United States as an
eloquent preacher. He was a famed chaplain (Woodbine Willie)
in World War I and later chaplain to the King of England. This
hymn is part of a longer poem, "At a Harvest Festival."

Tune: MORNING SONG 8.6.8.6.8.6.
Kentucky Harmony, 1816
Harm. C. Winfred Douglas, 1940

Rising in Darkness

Attrib. to Gregory the Great (540–604)
Transl. The New Century Hymnal, *1993*

1 Ris - ing in dark - ness, let us all keep watch - ing, let psalms pro -
2 As we might prais - es bring a ho - ly rul - er, so may we
3 Grant, O blessed God - head, this our prayer at dawn - ing, that we re -

vide our source of med - i - ta - tion; And sing with all our strength;
sing, your heaven-ly courts to en - ter, There with the saints to join,
flect the good-ness of your pres - ence; Your beau-ty shines, O Light,

hymns of ad - o - ra - tion to our Cre - a - tor bring.
now and ev - er af - ter, bless-ings on us con - fer.
O Sun, O Ra - diance, glo - ry re - ech - o - ing.

"Nocte surgentes" has been attributed to Gregory the Great, who
was the fourth of the traditional Latin "Doctors of the Church"
(including Ambrose, Augustine, and Jerome). It was written for
use at Matins—a service held in the hours before dawn.

Tune: CHRISTE SANCTORUM 11.11.12.6.
La Feillée's Méthode de plain-chant, *1782*

91

Wake, My Soul

Heb. 12:28; Ps. 30:4–5, 11–12

Friedrich R. L. von Canitz (1654–1699)
Transl. Madeleine Forell Marshall, 1993

1 Wake, my soul, with all things liv - ing, thanks be giv - ing to the
2 All your hope - ful plans con - fess - ing, ask for bless - ing on that
3 Cry for help, when griefs as - sail you, good friends fail you, life is
4 Af - ter one last night of weep - ing, one last sleep-ing, you shall

Source of life and day. Sun - light comes and gone con -
good which you would do; But if you should need cor -
hope - less, death ap - pears. One whose child knew deep af -
wake to pure de - light. You at last shall know per -

fu - sion, night's il - lu - sion, like the star - light, fades a - way.
rec - tion, ask di - rec - tion, pray for pur - pose, clear and new.
flic - tion, cru - ci - fix - ion, ev - er waits to dry your tears.
fec - tion, pure af - fec - tion, bathed in God's own morn - ing light.

Baron Friedrich R. L. von Canitz was famous in his lifetime as a successful diplomat—educated, refined, and gracious to all people. He allowed none of his hymns or poetry to be published during his lifetime.

Tune: HAYDN 8.4.7.8.4.7.
Franz Joseph Haydn, 1791

Day Is Done

92

James Quinn, S. J., 1969; alt.

1 Day is done, but love un-fail-ing dwells ev - er here;
2 Dusk de-scends, but light un-end-ing shines through our night;
3 Eyes will close, but you un-sleep-ing watch by our side;

Shad - ows fall, but hope, pre-vail-ing, calms ev - ery fear.
You are with us, ev - er lend-ing new strength to sight:
Death may come, in love's safe-keep-ing still we a - bide.

God, our Mak - er, none for-sak - ing, take our hearts, of Love's own mak-ing,
One in love, your truth con-fess - ing, one in hope of heav - en's bless-ing,
God of love, all e - vil quell - ing, sin for-giv - ing, fear dis - pel-ling,

Watch our sleep-ing, guard our wak - ing, be al - ways near.
May we see, in love's pos-sess - ing, love's end - less light!
Stay with us, our hearts in-dwell-ing, this e - ven - tide.

*Father James Quinn, S. J., has taught at several colleges in
Scotland and is the author of articles and books, as well as
hymns. He is active in ecumenical affairs and is one of the most
distinguished hymnwriters of the Roman Catholic Church.*

Tune: AR HYD Y NOS 8.4.8.4.8.8.8.4.
Traditional Welsh melody
For another harmonization, see 425

93   Christ, Mighty Savior

Mozarabic hymn, 10th century
Transl. Alan McDougall, 1916; rev. by Anne LeCroy, 1982

Unison

1 Christ, might - y Sav - ior, Light of all cre - a - tion, you make the
2 Now comes the day's end as the sun is set - ting: mir - ror of
3 There - fore we come now eve - ning rites to of - fer, joy - ful - ly
4 Give heed, we pray you, to our sup - pli - ca - tion: that you may
5 Though bod - ies slum - ber, hearts shall keep their vig - il, for - ev - er

day - time ra - diant with the sun - light And to the night give
day - break, pledge of res - ur - rec - tion; While in the heav - ens
chant - ing ho - ly hymns to praise you, With all cre - a - tion
grant us par - don for of - fens - es, Strength for our weak hearts,
rest - ing in the peace of Je - sus, In light or dark - ness

glit - ter - ing a - dorn - ment, stars . . . . in the heav - - ens.
choirs of stars ap - pear - ing hal - - low the night - - fall.
join - ing hearts and voic - es sing - - ing your glo - - ry.
rest for ach - ing bod - ies, sooth - - ing the wea - - ry.
wor - ship - ing our Sav - ior now . . . . and for - ev - - - er.

"Christe lux mundi," a nine-stanza evening hymn of the
Mozarabic rite, is the basis for the present hymn. "Mozarabic"
refers to a body of rites and hymnody of the Spanish church
before 1085.

Tune: MIGHTY SAVIOR 11.11.11.5.
David Hurd, 1984

Now All the Woods Are Sleeping

Paul Gerhardt, 1647
Transl. The Lutheran Book of Worship, *1978; alt.*

1 Now all the woods are sleep - ing, through fields the shad-ows
2 The ra - diant sun has van - ished, its gold - en rays are
3 Now all the heaven-ly splen - dor breaks forth in star - light

creep - ing, and cit - ies pause to rest; Let
ban - ished from deep - ening skies of night; But
ten - der from myr - iad worlds un - known; And

us, as night is fall - ing, on God our Mak - er
Christ, the sun of glad - ness, dis - pel - ling all our
we, this mar - vel see - ing, for - get our self - ish

call - ing, sing praise to God who loves us best.
sad - ness, shines in our hearts with warm - est light.
be - ing and know a beau - ty not our own.

Though beset with many professional difficulties and
personal losses, the German hymnwriter Paul Gerhardt
wrote more than one hundred hymns, including some of the
finest and most beloved of Christian hymnody. This hymn
was a favorite of the poet himself.

Tune: NUN RUHEN ALLE WÄLDER 7.7.6.7.7.8.
(INNSBRUCK)
Heinrich Isaac (1455–1517)

95 The Day You Gave Us, God, Is Ended

John Ellerton, 1870; alt.

1 The day you gave us, God, is end-ed, the light now
2 We thank you that your Church, un-sleep-ing while earth rolls
3 As o'er each con-ti-nent and is-land the dawn leads
4 The sun that bids us rest is wak-ing our fam-ily
5 So be it, God. Your reign shall nev-er, like earth's proud

fades at your re-quest; To you our morn-ing hymns as-
on-ward in-to light, Through all the world its watch is
on an-oth-er day, The voice of prayer is nev-er
mem-bers far a-way, Who, while we sleep, are glad-ly
em-pires, fade and fall. Your reign en-dures, and grows for-

cend-ed, your praise shall sanc-ti-fy our rest.
keep-ing, and rests not now by day or night.
si-lent, nor dies the strain of praise a-way.
tak-ing their turn to wor-ship you and pray.
ev-er till all your crea-tures heed your call.

John Ellerton, a priest of the Church of England, wrote many hymns and edited numerous hymnals. This text and music have been together since they appeared in an important book edited by Arthur Sullivan.

Tune: ST. CLEMENT 9.8.9.8.
Clement E. Scholefield, 1874

Sun of My Soul, O Savior Dear

96

John Keble, 1820; alt.

Luke 24:29; John 15:4–5

1 Sun of my soul, O Sav - ior dear, it is not
2 A - bide with me from morn till eve, for with - out
3 Watch by the sick; en - rich the poor with bless - ings
4 Come near and bless us when we wake, as through the

night if you are near; O may no earth - born
you I can - not live; A - bide with me when
from your bound - less store; Be ev - ery mourn - er's
world our way we take, Till through your love which

cloud a - rise to hide you from your ser - vant's eyes.
night is nigh, for with - out you I dare not die.
sleep to - night, like in - fants' slum - bers, pure and light.
knows no end we gain at last the peace of heaven.

John Keble, known for his volume of poems The Christian
Year, *helped to initiate the Oxford Movement in 1833 with his
sermon on "National Apostasy." This movement sought to
reinstate the liturgical practices of the medieval church.*

Tune: HURSLEY L.M.
Adapt. from GROSSER GOTT, WIR LOBEN DICH
Katholisches Gesangbuch, Vienna, c. 1774

97

Salup na ang Adlaw
(Now the Sun Is Setting)

Elena G. Maquiso, 1970; alt.
Transl. Fé Nebres, 1993

Filipino hymnwriter *Elena G. Maquiso* has composed nearly
400 hymns and other sacred choral pieces, many of which have
appeared in international publications. Her tune Moning *bears*
the nickname of a classmate at the Divinity School, Silliman
University.

Tune: MONING 6.6.6.6.6.6.5.6.5.
Elena G. Maquiso, 1970

3 Kon du-nay na-sa-kit,
  gu-mi-kan ka-na-mo,
  bi-san wa hi-baw-i
  un-sa ang hi-nung-dan,
  I-tu-got-ka-na-mo,
  pag-pa-sig-u-li,
  I-mong ka-bu-but-on
  ma-tu-man ga-yud.

4 Pa-sa-la-ma-tan, Ka,
  sa ad-law'ng na-ta-pos,
  ma-nga ka-say-pa-nan,
  I-mong hi-ka-lim-tan,
  Ka-li-naw ha-ta-gi
  sa pag-pa-hu-lay,
  mag-ma-ta sa bun-tag
  sa ka-bag-o-han.

3 If to some a-round us
  pain we may have giv-en,
  Caused un-know-ing-ly some
  soul a wound-ed heart,
  Grant to us your mer-cy,
  bring us back a-gain.
  May your love em-brace us,
  may your will be done.

4 Thank you, lov-ing God, for
  this day that has end-ed;
  For our man-y fail-ures
  grant your grace and par-don.
  On our sleep be-stow-ing
  peace and calm-ness, too.
  Strength-ened for to-mor-row,
  Prais-ing each new day.

Now the Day Is Over 98

Sabine Baring-Gould, 1865; alt. *Matt. 11:28*

1 Now the day is o - ver, night is draw-ing nigh,
2 Je - sus, give the wear - y calm and sweet re - pose;
3 Grant to lit - tle chil - dren vi - sions of your care;
4 Com-fort ev - ery suf - ferer watch-ing late in pain;
5 When the morn-ing wak - ens, then may we a - rise

Shad - ows of the eve - ning steal a - cross the sky.
With your ten - der bless - ing may our eye - lids close.
Keep our trav - els safe by sea and land and air.
Those who plan some e - vil from their sin re - strain.
Pure and fresh and sin - less in your ho - ly eyes.

Sabine Baring-Gould, author of a prodigious amount of literature in a wide variety of fields, was a priest of the Church of England. He wrote this hymn for the children of Horbury Bridge, Yorkshire, during his ministry there.

Tune: MERRIAL 6.5.6.5.
Joseph Barnby, 1868

99

Abide with Me

Luke 24:29; 1 Cor. 15:55

Henry F. Lyte, 1847; alt.

1 A - bide with me; fast falls the e - ven - tide;
2 Swift to its close ebbs out life's lit - tle day;
3 I need your pres - ence ev - ery pass - ing hour;
4 I fear no foe, with you at hand to bless;
5 Hold now your cross be - fore my clos - ing eyes;

The shad - ows deep - en, Lord, with me a - bide;
Earth's joys grow dim, its glo - ries pass a - way;
I need your grace to foil the tempt-er's power.
Ills have no weight and tears no bit - ter - ness;
Shine through the gloom and point me to the skies;

When oth - er help - ers fail, and com - forts flee,
Change and de - cay in all a - round I see;
Give me your love my guide and stay to be.
Where is death's sting? where, grave, your vic - to - ry?
Heaven's morn-ing breaks, and earth's vain shad-ows flee;

Help of the help - less, O a - bide with me.
O Christ who chang - es not, a - bide with me.
Through cloud and sun - shine, O a - bide with me.
I tri - umph still if you a - bide with me.
In life, in death, O Christ, a - bide with me.

Following the final sermon of his career, Henry F. Lyte handed a copy of this recently written hymn to a relative. He died two months later. The tune by W. H. Monk has contributed greatly to the popularity of the hymn.

Tune: EVENTIDE 10.10.10.10.
William H. Monk, 1861

All Praise Be Yours, My God, This Night   100

St. 1–3, Thomas Ken, 1692; alt.
St. 4, Carl P. Daw, Jr., 1992

1 All praise be yours, my God, this night, for all the bless-ings of the light; Keep me, kind Mak - er of all things, be - neath the shel - ter of your wings.

2 For - give me, by Christ's vic - tory won, the ill that I this day have done, That from the fear of sin set free, I, ere I sleep, at peace may be.

3 O let me on your love re - pose, let wel - come sleep my eye - lids close, Sleep from whose balm new strength I take to serve my God when I a - wake.

4 Praise God who gives all bless-ings birth; praise God all crea - tures on the earth; Praise God, who makes, sus - tains, sets free: one ho - ly God in per - sons three.

Thomas Ken was a priest at Winchester Cathedral and College and later ministered to the English royal family. Tallis' "Canon" was one of the nine tunes composed for a book of metrical psalms by Matthew Parker. The new fourth stanza was written for The New Century Hymnal.

Tune: TALLIS' CANON L.M.
Thomas Tallis, c. 1567

101

Comfort, Comfort O My People

Isa. 40:1–8

Johannes Olearius, 1671
Transl. Catherine Winkworth, 1863; alt.

1 "Com - fort, com - fort O my peo - ple, tell of peace," thus says our God;
2 For the her - ald's voice is call - ing in the des - ert far and near,
3 Straight shall be what long was crook-ed, and the rough - er pla - ces plain!

Com-fort those whose hearts are shroud-ed, mourn-ing un - der sor-row's load.
Bid-ding us to make re - pen - tance since the realm of God is here.
Let your hearts be true and hum - ble, for Mes-si - ah's ho - ly reign.

Speak un - to Je - ru - sa - lem of the peace that waits for them;
Oh, that warn - ing cry o - bey! Now pre-pare for God a way;
For God's glo - ry ev - er-more shall be known o'er all the world;

Tell them that their sins I cov - er, and their war-fare now is o - ver.
Let the val - leys rise in meet-ing and the hills bow down in greet-ing.
And all flesh shall see the to - ken that God's word is nev - er bro - ken.

Written for John the Baptist's Day, June 24, this hymn clearly
reflects the Isaiah text. Johannes Olearius, a Lutheran pastor,
held a faculty appointment at Wittenberg University as well as
church administration positions in his region.

Tune: PSALM 42 8.7.8.7.7.7.8.8.
(FREU DICH SEHR)
Trente quatre Pseaumes, Geneva, 1551

O How Shall I Receive You

Paul Gerhardt, 1653
Transl. Catherine Winkworth, 1863, and others; alt.

1 O how shall I re - ceive you, how meet you on your way,
2 Love caused your in - car - na - tion; love brought you un - to me;
3 You come, O Christ, with glad - ness, in mer - cy and good - will,

blessed hope of ev - ery peo - ple, my soul's de - light and stay?
your thirst for my sal - va - tion pro - cured my lib - er - ty.
to bring an end to sad - ness and bid our fears be still.

O Je - sus, Je - sus, give me now by your own pure light,
O love be - yond all tell - ing, that led you to em - brace
In pa - tient ex - pec - ta - tion we live for that great day

to know what-e'er is pleas - ing and wel - come in your sight.
in love, all love ex - cel - ling, our lost and fall - en race.
when a re - newed cre - a - tion your glo - ry shall dis - play.

As a German Lutheran pastor serving during the Thirty Years'
War, Paul Gerhardt's trials were legion. In the midst of it all, he
composed more than a hundred hymns, among them some of the
finest and most beloved in Christian hymnody.

Tune: ST. THEODULPH 7.6.7.6.D.
(VALET WILL ICH DIR GEBEN)
Melchior Teschner, 1615

103   Watcher, Tell Us of the Night

Isa. 21:11–12   *John Bowring, 1825; alt.*

1 Watch-er, tell us of the night, what its signs of prom-ise are.
2 Watch-er, tell us of the night, high-er yet that star as-cends.
3 Watch-er, tell us of the night, for the morn-ing seems to dawn.

Trav - eler, O a won-drous sight! See that glo-ry - beam - ing star!
Trav - eler, bless-ed - ness and light, peace and truth its course por - tends.
Trav - eler, shad-ows take their flight, doubt and ter - ror are with-drawn.

Watch-er, does its beau - teous ray news of joy or hope fore - tell?
Watch-er, will its beams a - lone gild the spot that gave them birth?
Watch-er, you may go your way; has - ten to your qui - et home.

Trav-eler, yes; it brings the day, prom - ised day of Is - ra - el!
Trav-eler, a - ges are its own; see, it bursts o'er all the earth!
Trav-eler, I re - joice to - day, for Em - man - u - el has come!

This hymn, a dialogue between watcher and traveler, was
suggested by the dialogue in Isaiah 21:11–12. John Bowring was
a gifted linguist, worker for political and social reform, member
of Parliament, and governor of Hong Kong.

Tune: ABERYSTWYTH 7.7.7.7.D.
Joseph Parry, 1879
Alternate tune: *ST. GEORGE'S WINDSOR*

We Hail You God's Anointed

James Montgomery, 1821; alt.

104

Ps. 72

1 We hail you God's a - noint - ed, the long - a - wait - ed One!
2 You shall come down like show - ers up - on the fruit - ful earth;
3 The wise shall bow be - fore you and gold and in - cense bring;
4 O'er ev - ery foe vic - to - rious, you on your throne shall rest;

Hail in the time ap - point - ed, your reign on earth be - gun!
and joy and hope, like flow - ers, spring in your path to birth.
all na - tions shall a - dore you, and praise all peo - ples sing;
from age to age more glo - rious, all - bless-ing and all - blessed:

You come to break op - pres - sion, to set the cap-tive free;
Be - fore you on the moun - tains shall peace, the her - ald, go,
To you shall prayer un - ceas - ing and dai - ly vows be said,
The tide of time shall nev - er your cov - e - nant re - move;

to take a - way trans - gres - sion, and rule in eq - ui - ty.
and righ - teous-ness, in foun - tains, from hill to val - ley flow.
your realm is still in - creas - ing, with you, O Christ, as head.
your name shall stand for - ev - er, your change-less name of Love.

Written as a Christmas hymn for the Moravian settlement in Yorkshire, England, this hymn has enjoyed widespread popularity from the beginning. It is characteristic of Montgomery's deep faith and passion for social justice.

Tune: ELLACOMBE C.M.D.
Gesangbuch der herzoglichen Wirtembergischen katholischen Hofkapelle, *1784*

105   Gentle Joseph, Joseph Dear

Matt. 1:18–25

German carol, 15th century
Paraphr. by Carol Birkland, 1993

1 "Gen - tle Jo - seph, Jo - seph dear,   stay with me, for the ba - by's near;   God will sure - ly your good - ness hear, as you will love this new - born child," says Mar - y.

2 "Glad - ly Mar - y, Mar - y mine,   I will cra - dle the child di - vine;   Here will heav - en and earth com - bine, for you will bear God's child, O dear - est Mar - y."

3 "Peace to all and God's good-will,"   heaven and earth with this song will fill;   Soon will God, in the eve - ning still, be born in Beth - le - hem, the child of Mar - y.

The German carol on which this is based appears in a mystery play, c. 1500. It is one of a group of related carols that also includes "In dulci jubilo"—"Good Christian friends, rejoice."

Tune: JOSEPH LIEBER, JOSEPH MEIN   7.8.8.11.
German carol, 15th century
Harm. The New Century Hymnal, 1993

My Heart Sings Out with Joyful Praise

106

Ruth Duck, 1985

Luke 1:46–55

1 My heart sings out with joy - ful praise to God who rais - es me,
2 The arm of God is strong and just to scat - ter all the proud.
3 The prom-ise made in a - ges past at last has come to be,

Who came to me when I was low and changed my des - ti - ny.
The ty - rants tum - ble from their thrones and van - ish like a cloud.
for God has come in power to save, to set all peo - ple free.

The Ho - ly One, the Liv - ing God, is al - ways full of grace
The hun - gry all are sat - is - fied; the rich are sent a - way.
Re - mem-bering those who wait to see sal - va - tion's dawn-ing day,

To those who seek their Mak-er's will in ev - ery time and place.
The poor of earth who suf - fer long will wel-come God's new day.
Our Sav - ior comes to all who weep to wipe their tears a - way.

The "Magnificat," a traditional text for evening prayer as well as Advent, is paraphrased here by Ruth Duck. She developed it to make the ancient rite of evening prayer available to her own worshipping communities.

Tune: MARIAS LOVSÅNG C.M.D.
Swedish folk melody
Alternate tunes: *ELLACOMBE, TALLIS' THIRD*

107   Awake! Awake, and Greet the New Morn

Isa. 12:6; 26:9; 35:6; Matt. 11:5   *Marty Haugen, 1983; rev. 1993*

1 A - wake! a - wake, and greet the new morn, for
2 To us, to all in sor - row and fear, Em -
3 In deep - est night Christ's com - ing shall be, when
4 Re - joice, re - joice, take heart in the night, though

an - gels her - ald its dawn-ing,   sing out your joy, for
man - u - el comes a - sing-ing,   whose hum - ble song is
all the world is de - spair-ing,   as morn - ing light so
cold the win - ter and cheer-less,   the ris - ing sun shall

Je - sus is born, be - hold! the Child of our long - ing.
qui - et and near, yet fills the earth with its ring - ing.
qui - et and free, so warm and gen - tle and car - ing.
crown you with light, be strong and lov - ing and fear - less;

Liturgical composer Marty Haugen wrote both words and music for this Advent hymn with the twofold aim of providing an easy congregational chorale and utilizing the images of the Isaiah passages.

Tune: REJOICE, REJOICE   9.8.9.8.8.7.8.9.
Marty Haugen, 1983

108   Isaiah the Prophet Has Written of Old

Isa. 11:6–9; 55:10–13   *Joy F. Patterson, 1982; rev. 1993*

1 I - sa - iah the proph-et has writ-ten of old how God's new cre - a - tion shall come. In - stead of the thorn tree, the fir tree shall grow; the wolf shall lie down with the

2 The moun-tains and hills shall break forth in - to song, the peo - ples be led forth in peace; The earth shall be filled with the knowl-edge of God as the wa - ters cov - er the

3 Yet na - tions still prey on the meek of the world, and con - flict turns par-ent from child. Your peo - ple de - spoil all the sweet-ness of earth; the brier and the thorn tree grow

4 God, bring to fru - i - tion your will for the earth, that no one shall hurt or de - stroy, That wis - dom and jus - tice shall reign in the land and your peo - ple shall go forth in

Joy Patterson, of Wausau, Wisconsin, served on the editorial
committee for The Presbyterian Hymnal, *1990. This text was one*
of seven winning hymns published in New Hymns for Children
by Choristers Guild and The Hymn Society of America.

Tune: JUDAS AND MARY   Irr.
Sydney Carter, 1964

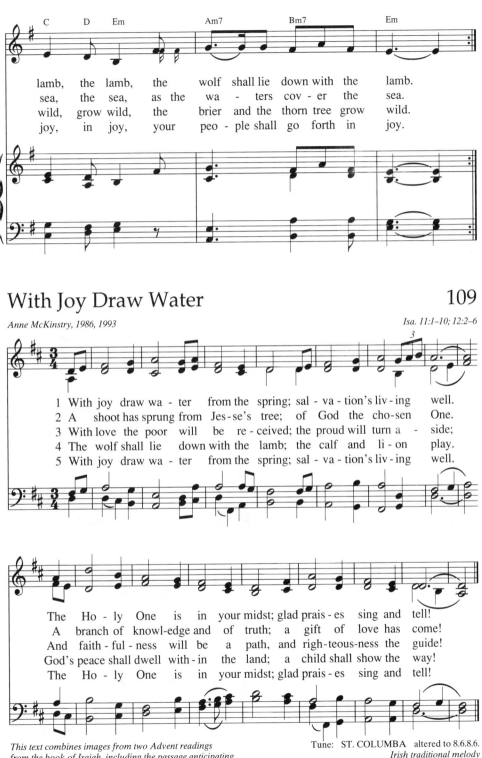

lamb, the lamb, the wolf shall lie down with the lamb.
sea, the sea, as the wa - ters cov - er the sea.
wild, grow wild, the brier and the thorn tree grow wild.
joy, in joy, your peo - ple shall go forth in joy.

With Joy Draw Water

109

Anne McKinstry, 1986, 1993

Isa. 11:1–10; 12:2–6

1 With joy draw wa - ter from the spring; sal - va - tion's liv - ing well.
2 A shoot has sprung from Jes - se's tree; of God the cho - sen One.
3 With love the poor will be re - ceived; the proud will turn a - side;
4 The wolf shall lie down with the lamb; the calf and li - on play.
5 With joy draw wa - ter from the spring; sal - va - tion's liv - ing well.

The Ho - ly One is in your midst; glad prais - es sing and tell!
A branch of knowl - edge and of truth; a gift of love has come!
And faith - ful - ness will be a path, and right - eous - ness the guide!
God's peace shall dwell with - in the land; a child shall show the way!
The Ho - ly One is in your midst; glad prais - es sing and tell!

*This text combines images from two Advent readings
from the book of Isaiah, including the passage anticipating
the reign of peace. The author, Anne McKinstry, has served
as a writer-in-residence at Otis United Church of Christ in
Massachusetts.*

Tune: ST. COLUMBA altered to 8.6.8.6.
Irish traditional melody
Harm. Charles V. Stanford, 1906

110

Now Bless the God of Israel

Luke 1:68–79; Ps. 18:1–3; Isa. 9:2–7

Ruth Duck, 1985

1 Now bless the God of Is - ra - el, who comes in love and power,
who rais - es from the roy - al house de - liv - erance in this hour.
Through ho - ly proph-ets God has sworn to free us from a - larm,
to save us from the heav - y hand of all who wish us harm.

2 Re - mem-ber-ing the cov - e - nant, God res - cues us from fear,
that we might serve in hol - i - ness and peace from year to year;
And you, my child, shall go be - fore to preach, to proph-e - sy,
that all may know the ten - der love, the grace of God most high.

3 In ten - der mer-cy, God will send the day - spring from on high,
our ris - ing sun, the light of life for those who sit and sigh.
God comes to guide our way to peace, that death shall reign no more.
Sing prais-es to the Ho - ly One! O wor - ship and a - dore!

This text by United Church of Christ clergywoman Ruth Duck
is a paraphrase of the "Benedictus," which is often sung at
morning prayer. She came to appreciate daily prayer while
studying at the University of Notre Dame.

Tune: FOREST GREEN C.M.D.
Traditional English melody
Harm. Ralph Vaughan Williams, 1906

O Loving Founder of the Stars

Latin, anon., 9th century; transl. The New Century Hymnal, *1993*

Luke 2:1–7; John 1:1–5; Phil. 2:5–11

1 O lov - ing found - er of the stars, to all of faith light
2 Who griev - ing at the cry of pain— the an - guish of our
3 As Sav - ior from the heav - ens forth, when earth draws near its
4 O Christ, who braved earth's deep - est pain, all kneel - ing low your
5 Your judg - ment of this world draws near, O Ho - ly One, un -

with - out end, O Christ, re - deem - er of us all,
dy - ing race— Did death it - self for us de - stroy,
fi - nal hour, You from the vir - gin moth - er's womb
name a - dore; All heaven and earth your name con - fess
til that day pro - tect us all your faith - ful ones

to earn - est prayers your mer - cy lend.
and guilt as - sume through lov - ing grace:
ap - peared in love's re - deem - ing power.
and praise you, Sov - ereign, ev - er - more.
a - gainst the Faith - less One, we pray.

The original Latin hymn, dating from the early Middle Ages, was sung at Vespers (sunset) during Advent. The tune referred to in old service books as the "Ambrosian Advent Hymn" is thought to be one of the earliest church tunes.

Tune: CONDITOR ALME L.M.
ancient Sarum plainsong, mode IV

112   Keep Awake, Be Always Ready

Isa. 2:1–5; 60:1–3; 64:1–9; Matt. 24:36–44;
Rom. 13:11–14; 1 Cor. 1:3–9; 1 Thess. 3:9–13

Arthur G. Clyde, 1993

1 Keep a-wake, be al - ways rea - dy, God's time ap - proach-es
2 Rise and shine for One is com - ing whose love will quench all

sure and stea - dy, God's strength will keep your heart from blame.
na - ture's thirst - ing to be made whole for - ev - er more.

Clouds, the Spir - it's light con - ceal - ing, dis - perse, God's pur - est
On that day to end all weep - ing, death's swords trans - formed to

light re - veal - ing; cre - a - tion will its Sov-ereign name. Dry
tools of reap - ing, the God of might will mer - cy pour. In -

This new text, written to reflect the readings for the first
Sunday in Advent, is set to a traditional tune of the season
by sixteenth-century Lutheran pastor Philipp Nicolai.

Tune: WACHET AUF 8.9.8.8.9.8.6.6.4.8.8.
Philipp Nicolai, 1599
Harm. J. S. Bach, 1731

branch - es burst forth green, God's ad - vent signs are seen: Hal - le - lu - jah!
car - nate, God ap - pears em - brac - ing all our tears: Hal - le - lu - jah!

Christ's judg - ment won, God's will be done; God's new do - min - ion thus be - gun.
God's maj - es - ty e - ter - nal - ly re - vealed to set the cos-mos free.

Little Bethlehem of Judah

113

Calvin Seerveld, 1986; alt.

Mic. 5:2–4

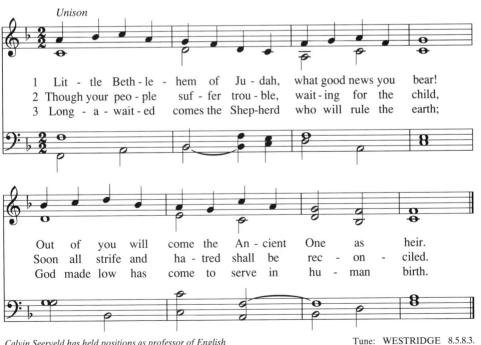

Unison

1 Lit - tle Beth - le - hem of Ju - dah, what good news you bear!
2 Though your peo - ple suf - fer trou - ble, wait - ing for the child,
3 Long - a - wait - ed comes the Shep-herd who will rule the earth;

Out of you will come the An - cient One as heir.
Soon all strife and ha - tred shall be rec - on - ciled.
God made low has come to serve in hu - man birth.

Calvin Seerveld has held positions as professor of English literature and philosophy and, since 1972, has been senior member in the Institute for Christian Studies in Toronto. He was on the committee appointed to revise the Psalter Hymnal.

Tune: WESTRIDGE 8.5.8.3.
Martin F. Shaw, 1929

114 Return, My People

Joel 2:12–23; Isa. 11:1–12   *James F. D. Martin, 1981; alt.*

1 Re - turn, my peo - ple, Is - ra - el, with pen - i - ten - tial tear;
2 Fear not, be - lov - ed, hear - ken now: our God has done great things!
3 Then to the faith - ful of the earth the call of God rings clear:

just as the proph - et did fore - tell the ad - vent of Em - man - u - el,
Your vin - di - ca - tion shall pour down like rain up - on the bar - ren ground,
"Re - turn, my peo - ple, claim your worth, pre - par - ing for your Sav - ior's birth;

God's reign on earth is near! God's reign on earth is near!
glad tid - ings to you bring, glad tid - ings to you bring.
my reign on earth is near. My reign on earth is near."

This new Advent text by United Church of Christ minister James Martin is set to a tune by British composer Charles Hubert Hastings Parry, who is also known for his symphonies, organ works, and cantatas.

Tune: REPTON 8.6.8.8.6.6.
C. Hubert H. Parry, 1888
Alternate tune: REST

The Baptist Shouts on Jordan's Shore 115

Charles Coffin, 1736
Transl. The New Century Hymnal, *1993*

John 1:6–8, 19–28; Mark 1:1–8;
Luke 3:2–6, 15–18; Matt. 3:1–6, 11–12

1 The Bap - tist shouts on Jor - dan's shore, the
2 The earth and sky and sea now feel that
3 Clean up your hearts, lay down the way, for
4 Through you, O Je - sus, you a - lone sal -

earth shakes with the might - y roar, A - wake, let laz - y
which their Au - thor will re - veal: The Child now leap - ing
God ap - proach-es day by day; Pre - pare for such a
va - tion, so - lace, strength are known; With - out your love we

sleep now flee: be - hold, the voice of proph - e - cy!
in the womb as God does hu - man form as - sume.
wor - thy heir, for such a guest your house pre - pare.
fade like grass, like wilt - ed flowers our lives will pass.

5 Your hands ex-tend, our pain em-brace,
   lift up the pros-trate, show your face;
   Though we in part your beau-ty know,
   O blos-som forth, your splen-dor show.

6 O One who comes to set us free,
   O Child, to you our song will be,
   With Fa-ther, Spir-it moth-er-ing,
   to you shall praise for-ev-er ring!

Charles Coffin, distinguished scholar and Latin author,
was rector of the University of Paris for a time. The hymn,
appearing here in a new translation, is from a breviary ordered
by the archbishop of Paris to replace ancient Latin hymns with
newer ones.

Tune: WINCHESTER NEW L.M.
Musikalisches Handbuch, *Hamburg, 1690*

116 O Come, O Come, Emmanuel

Isa. 11:1–12; Exod. 19–20:17

Psalteriolum Cantionum Catholicarum, *1710*
Based on ancient antiphons from Advent Vespers
Transl. John Mason Neale, 1851, and others; alt.
St. 2, 7, transl. Henry Sloane Coffin, 1916; alt.

Unison

1 O come, O come, Em - man - u - el, and
2 O come, O Wis - dom from on high, and
3 O come, O come, O A - do - nai, who
4 O come, O shoot of Jes - se, free your
5 O come, O Key of Da - vid, come, and

ran - som cap - tive Is - ra - el That mourns in lone - ly
or - der all things far and nigh; To us the path of
came to all on Si - nai high, And from its peak a
own from Sa - tan's tyr - an - ny, From depths of hell your
o - pen wide your heaven - ly home; Make safe the path to

ex - ile here, un - til the Child of God ap - pear.
knowl - edge show, and help us in that way to go.
sin - gle law pro - claimed in maj - es - ty and awe.
peo - ple save, and give them vic - tory o'er the grave.
end - less day, to hell's de - struc - tion close the way.

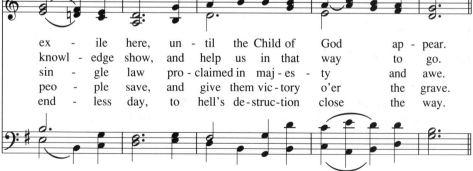

In the medieval Western church, seven "Great O" antiphons,
the basis for this hymn, were sung consecutively on the
seven days before Christmas, ending with what appears
above as the first stanza.

Tune: VENI EMMANUEL L.M. with refrain
Melody from a 15th-century French "Processional"
Arr. Thomas Helmore, 1854

Refrain

Re - joice! Re - joice! Em - man - u - el shall come to you, O Is - ra - el!

6 O come, O Day-spring, come and cheer
  our spir-its by your ad-vent here;
  Love stir with-in the womb of night,
  and death's own shad-ows put to flight.
  (Refrain)

7 O come, De-sire of Na-tions, bind
  all peo-ples in one heart and mind;
  Make en-vy, strife, and quar-rels cease;
  fill the whole world with heav-en's peace.
  (Refrain)

Lift Up Your Heads, O Mighty Gates 117

Georg Weissel, 1641   *Ps. 24:7–10*
Transl. Catherine Winkworth, 1865; alt.

1 Lift up your heads, O might-y gates; be-hold the glo - rious Rul - er waits!
2 Fling wide the por - tals of your heart; make it a tem - ple, set a - part
3 Re - deem - er, come! I o - pen wide my heart to you; here, Christ, a - bide!
4 So come, my Sov-ereign; en - ter in! Let new and no - bler life be - gin;

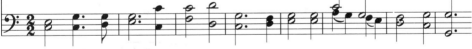

The Sov-ereign One is draw - ing near; the Sav - ior of the world is here.
From earth - ly use for heaven's em - ploy, a - dorned with prayer and love and joy.
Let me your in-ner pres - ence feel; your grace and love in me re - veal.
Your Ho - ly Spir-it guide us on, un - til the glo - rious crown be won.

Georg Weissel, a Lutheran pastor, served a church in
Königsberg, East Prussia. He wrote some twenty hymns,
most of them for the great festivals of the church year.
This hymn was written for Advent.

Tune: TRURO L.M.
Thomas Williams' Psalmodia Evangelica, *1789*

118   Of the Parent's Heart Begotten

Marcus Aurelius Clemens Prudentius (348–413)
Col. 1:15–17; John 1:1–5, 14   *Transl.* The New Century Hymnal, *1993*

1 Of the Par - ent's heart be - got - ten when the worlds were yet to be,
2 By this Word was all cre - a - ted, by this Word were all things done:
3 Bless - ed dawn - ing of sal - va - tion as the Word is breathed in grace
4 Now be - hold the One whom proph - ets have fore - told for a - ges long
5 Depths and heights break forth in sing - ing, an - gels, saints make mel - o - dy,

One there was with no be - gin - ning, One who is e - ter - nal - ly—
Land and air and deep - est o - cean, har - mo - ny of three in one,
In - to earth - ly flesh re - ceiv - ing— God in - car - nate tak - ing place;
On the faith - ful page of scrip - ture, seers and sag - es in their song;
All do - min - ions, ev - ery power sing, make new psalms of ec - sta - sy,

Source and End - ing of all things that have been,
And all grow - ing in the lu - mi - nance
Now the light of God re - vealed . . . .
Now the Prom - ised One shines forth! . . . .
Let no heart re - frain from prais - ing God,

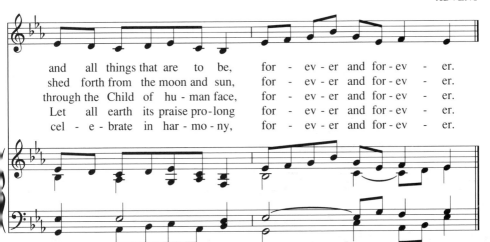

and all things that are to be, for - ev - er and for - ev - er.
shed forth from the moon and sun, for - ev - er and for - ev - er.
through the Child of hu - man face, for - ev - er and for - ev - er.
Let all earth its praise pro-long for - ev - er and for - ev - er.
cel - e - brate in har - mo - ny, for - ev - er and for - ev - er.

"Corde natus ex parentis" is taken from twelve poems for the daily hours by Clemens Prudentius, who gave up a court office to enter a monastery, where he wrote a number of important and influential works.

Tune: DIVINUM MYSTERIUM 8.7.8.7.8.7.7.
Adapt. from a medieval plainsong in Petri's Piae Cantiones, *1582*
Harm. C. Winfred Douglas, 1940

My Soul Gives Glory to My God 119

Miriam Therese Winter, 1987   Luke 1:46b–55; 1 Sam. 2:1–10

1 My soul gives glo - ry to my God. My heart pours out its praise.
2 My God has done great things for me: yes, ho - ly is God's name.
3 From age to age, to all who fear, such mer - cy love im - parts,
4 Love casts the might-y from their thrones, pro-motes the in - se - cure,
5 Praise God, whose lov - ing cov - e - nant sup-ports those in dis - tress,

God lift - ed up my low - li - ness in man - y mar-vel-ous ways.
All peo - ple will de - clare me blessed, and bless - ings they shall claim.
dis - pens-ing jus-tice far and near, dis - miss - ing self - ish hearts.
leaves hun - gry spir-its sat - is - fied, the rich seem sud-den-ly poor.
re - mem-ber-ing past prom-is - es with pres - ent faith - ful - ness.

This New Testament canticle, with its mosaic of liberation motifs that proclaim the justice of God, is known as the "Magnificat," the opening word of its Latin translation.

Tune: MORNING SONG C.M.
Melody from Kentucky Harmony, *1816*
Harm. C. Winfred Douglas, 1940

120   There's a Voice in the Wilderness

Isa. 40:3–11; Ps. 103:15–17   *J. Lewis Milligan, 1925; alt.*

1 There's a voice in the wil - der - ness cry - ing, a
2 O Zi - on, who of - fers good tid - ings, to the
3 But the word of our God is for - ev - er, our De -

call from the ways un - trod: Pre - pare in the des - ert a
height of the moun-tains dare! Lift your voice to the cit - ies of
fend - er's will is strong; God stands in the midst of

high - way, a high - way for our God! The
Ju - dah: "Be - hold your God!" de - clare. Like the
na - tions, to ren - der right the wrong. Then

Before moving to Canada, J. Lewis Milligan was a successful
British journalist and poet. This text was written in 1925 to
celebrate the union of three churches into The United Church
of Canada, a body he served as public relations director.

Tune: ASCENSION Irr.
H. Hugh Bancroft, 1938

val - leys shall be ex - alt - ed, the loft - y hills brought
flowers of the field we per - ish, our hu - man works de -
God shall be as a shep-herd, the lambs gath-ered to God's

low: make straight all the crook - ed pla - ces
cay, the power and pomp of na - tions
breast; and pas - tures of peace shall greet them,

where Em - man - u - el may go!
shall pass like a dream a - way.
to give to the wea - ry rest.

121

Toda la Tierra
(All Earth Is Waiting)

Isa. 40:3–5; Luke 3:4–6; Matt. 1:23

Alberto Taulé, 1972; alt.
Transl. Gertrude C. Suppe, 1987; alt.

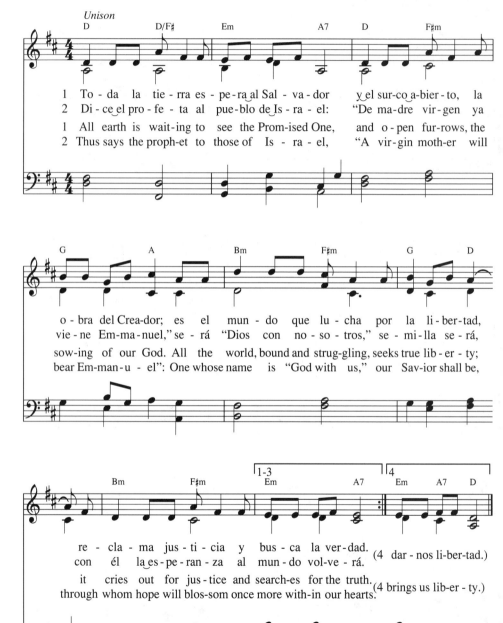

1 To - da la tie - rra es - pe - ra al Sal - va - dor y el sur-co a-bier - to, la
2 Di - ce el pro - fe - ta al pue-blo de Is - ra - el: "De ma-dre vir - gen ya
1 All earth is wait-ing to see the Prom-ised One, and o - pen fur-rows, the
2 Thus says the proph-et to those of Is - ra - el, "A vir-gin moth-er will

o - bra del Crea-dor; es el mun - do que lu - cha por la li - ber-tad,
vie - ne Em-ma-nuel," se - rá "Dios con no - so - tros," se - mi - lla se - rá,
sow-ing of our God. All the world, bound and strug-gling, seeks true lib - er - ty;
bear Em-man-u - el": One whose name is "God with us," our Sav-ior shall be,

re - cla - ma jus - ti - cia y bus - ca la ver-dad. (4 dar - nos li-ber-tad.)
con él la es - pe - ran - za al mun - do vol-ve - rá.
it cries out for jus - tice and search-es for the truth. (4 brings us lib-er - ty.)
through whom hope will blos-som once more with-in our hearts.

Alberto Taulé, composer and author of this new Advent hymn, has served as a parish priest and music editor for the Roman Catholic Church in Spain. This hymn was his first to be published in the United States.

Tune: TAULE 11.11.12.12.
Alberto Taulé, 1972
Harm. Skinner Chávez-Melo, 1988

3 Mon-tes y va-lles
  ha-brá que pre-pa-rar;
  nue-vos ca-mi-nos
  te-ne-mos que tra-zar.
  Dios es-tá ya muy cer-ca,
  ve-nid-lo a en-con-trar,
  y to-das las puer-tas
  a-brid de par en par.

3 Moun-tains and val-leys will
  have to be made plain;
  o-pen new high-ways,
  new high-ways for our God,
  Who is now com-ing closer,
  so come all and see,
  and o-pen the door-ways
  as wide as wide can be.

4 En un pe-se-bre
  Je-sús a-pa-re-ció,
  pe-ro en el mun-do
  es-tá pre-sen-te hoy.
  Vi-ve en-tre la gen-te,
  con e-llas es-tá;
  y vuel-ve de nue-vo
  a dar-nos li-ber-tad.

4 In low-ly sta-ble
  the Prom-ised One ap-peared,
  yet feel that pres-ence
  through-out the earth to-day,
  For Christ lives in all Chris-tians
  and is with us now;
  a-gain, on ar-riv-ing
  Christ brings us lib-er-ty.

Come, O Long-Expected Jesus 122

Charles Wesley, 1744; alt.

1 Come, O long - ex - pect-ed Je - sus, born to set all peo-ple free;
2 Is - rael's strength and con - so - la - tion, hope to all the earth im - part;
3 Born all peo - ple to de - liv - er, born a child, you came to reign!
4 By your own e - ter - nal Spir - it, come to claim us as your own;

From our fears and sins re - lease us; grant us your true lib - er - ty.
Dear de - sire of ev - ery na - tion, en - ter ev - ery long - ing heart.
Born to rule on earth for - ev - er, come, be known to us a - gain.
By your all - suf - fi - cient mer - it, let us share your cross and crown.

Charles Wesley, the brother of John, was one of the students known as "Methodists" at Oxford University. He wrote hymns for every occasion. This is from his small collection Hymns for the Nativity.

Tune: STUTTGART 8.7.8.7.
Melody attrib. to Christian F. Witt (1660–1716)
from Psalmodia Sacra, Gotha, 1715
Alternate tune: IN BABILONE

123 Mary, Woman of the Promise

Luke 1:39–55 *Mary Frances Fleischaker, 1988*

1 Mar - y, wom - an of the prom - ise; ves - sel
2 Mar - y, song of ho - ly wis - dom sung be -
3 Mar - y, morn - ing star of jus - tice; mir - ror
4 Mar - y, mod - el of com - pas - sion; wound - ed
5 Mar - y, wom - an of the gos - pel; hum - ble

of your peo - ple's dreams: Through your o - pen,
fore the world be - gan: Faith - ful to the
of the Ra - diant Light: In the shad - ows
by your off - spring's pain: When our hearts are
home for trea - sured seed: Help us to be

will - ing spir - it wa - ters of God's good - ness streamed.
Word with - in you, as you bore God's won - drous plan.
of life's jour - ney, be a bea - con for our sight.
torn by sor - row, teach us how to love a - gain.
true dis - ci - ples, bear - ing fruit in word and deed.

This text, selected as the winner in a regional Hymn Society competition seeking contemporary Marian hymns, portrays Mary's many roles in fulfilling God's promise. The author is an Adrian Dominican sister whose ministry has focused on worship and the arts.

Tune: QUEM PASTORES 8.7.8.7.
German carol, 14th century
Harm. Ralph Vaughan Williams, 1906

Away in a Manger

Anon., United States, 1885; st. 3, 1892; alt.

Luke 2:7

1 A - way in a man - ger, no crib for a bed, the
2 The cat - tle are low - ing, the poor ba - by wakes, but
3 Be near me, Lord Je - sus; I ask you to stay close

lit - tle Lord Je - sus laid down his sweet head. The
lit - tle Lord Je - sus, no cry - ing he makes. I
by me for - ev - er and love me, I pray. Bless

stars in the sky looked down where he lay, the
love you, Lord Je - sus; pro - tect me, I pray, and
all the dear chil - dren in your ten - der care, and

lit - tle Lord Je - sus, a - sleep on the hay.
stay by my side un - til night turns to day.
fit us for heav - en to live with you there.

This anonymous United States carol is often misattributed to Luther. The poem first appeared in a Lutheran hymnal for schools and families. Though he never credited himself with it, the tune most likely was composed by Murray.

Tune: AWAY IN A MANGER 11.11.11.11.
(MÜLLER)
Attrib. to James R. Murray, 1887

125 Angels We Have Heard on High

Luke 2:15

Traditional French carol
Transl. st. 1–3, "Crown of Jesus Music II," 1862; alt.
St. 4, "Carols Old and Carols New," Boston, 1916; alt.

1 An - gels we have heard on high, sweet - ly sing - ing o'er the plains,
2 Shep-herds, why this ju - bi - lee? Why your joy - ous strains pro - long?
3 Come to Beth-le - hem and see Christ whose birth the an - gels sing;
4 See the babe in man - ger laid whom the choirs of an - gels praise;

And the moun-tains in re - ply, ech - o back their joy - ous strains.
Say what may the tid - ings be, which in - spire your heaven-ly song.
Come a - dore on bend - ed knee, God, our world now en - ter - ing.
Mar - y, Jo - seph, lend your aid, while our hearts in love we raise.

Refrain

Glo - - - - - - ri - a

in ex - cel - sis De - o, Glo - - - -

The earliest version of this anonymous French carol was first published in 1855. There have been numerous English translations since the 1860s, but the carol did not gain widespread ecumenical usage until the first half of the twentieth century.

Tune: GLORIA 7.7.7.7. with refrain
(LES ANGES DANS NOS CAMPAGNES)
French carol melody

- - - ri - a   in ex-cel-sis De - o.

Angels, from the Realms of Glory   126

James Montgomery, 1816; alt.   *Luke 2:8–20; Matt. 2:1–2, 9–11*

1 An - gels, from the realms of glo - ry, wing your flight o'er all the earth;
2 Shep-herds, in the fields a - bid - ing, watch-ing o'er your flocks by night,
3 Sag - es, leave your con - tem-pla-tions, bright-er vi - sions beam a - far;
4 Saints, be - fore the al - tar bend-ing, watch-ing long in hope and fear,

As you sang cre - a - tion's sto - ry, now pro-claim Mes - si - ah's birth:
God with us is now re - sid - ing, yon - der shines the in - fant light:
Seek the great De - sire of Na - tions, guid - ed by Christ's na - tal star:
Sud-den - ly, your prayers at - tend-ing, Christ be - side you shall ap - pear.

Refrain

Come and wor-ship, come and wor-ship, wor-ship Christ, give thanks and sing.

James Montgomery, English journalist, raised a strong voice against injustice in his newspaper Sheffield Iris, *in which this hymn was first printed on December 24, 1816. The tune is named for Regent Square Church in London, today a congregation of the United Reformed Church in England and Wales.*

Tune: REGENT SQUARE 8.7.8.7.8.7.
Henry T. Smart, 1867

127

Es ist ein' Ros entsprungen
(Lo, How a Rose E'er Blooming)

Isa. 11:1

German, 15th century; transl. Theodore Baker, 1894; alt.

ein - er Wur- zel

1 Es ist ein' Ros ent - sprun-gen aus ein - er Wur - zel zart,
1 Lo, how a Rose e'er bloom-ing from ten - der stem has sprung!
2 I - sa-iah had fore - told it, the Rose I have in mind,

Jes - se kam die

wie uns die Al - ten sun - gen: von Jes - se kam die Art
Of Jes-se's lin-eage com - ing as saints of old have sung.
With Mar-y we be - hold it, the Vir - gin Moth - er kind.

und hat ein Blüm-lein bracht mit - ten im kal - ten
It came a flower-et bright, a - mid the cold of
To show God's love a - right, she bore to us a

der. . . . hal- ben

Win - ter wohl zu der hal - ben Nacht.
win - ter, when half spent was the night.
Sav - ior, when half spent was the night.

Possibly dating from the fifteenth century, this anonymous hymn
was first published in a Catholic hymnal in Germany, where the
rose was held in special regard and was employed as a symbol
for Mary or for Christ.

Tune: ES IST EIN' ROS 7.6.7.6.6.7.6.
Catholische Geistliche Kirchengesäng, *Cologne, 1599*
Harm. Michael Praetorius, 1609

In the Bleak Midwinter

128

Christina G. Rossetti, 1872; alt.

1. In the bleak mid - win - ter, frost - y wind made moan,
2. Our God tran-scends all heav - en, earth, and its do - main;
3. An - gels and arch - an - gels may have gath - ered there,
4. What can I of - fer, poor as I am?

earth stood hard as i - ron, wa - ter like a stone;
heaven and earth shall flee a-way when Christ comes to reign;
cher - u - bim and ser - a-phim thronged the mid - night air;
If I were a shep - herd, I would bring a lamb.

Snow had fall - en, snow on snow, snow on snow,
In the bleak mid - win - ter a sta - ble place suf - ficed the
But his moth - er on - ly, in her maid - en bliss,
If I were a wise one, I would do my part; but

in the bleak mid - win - ter, long a - go.
sov - ereign God al - might - y, Je - sus Christ.
wor - shiped the be - lov - ed with a kiss.
what can I of - fer: all my heart.

Christina Rossetti has portrayed the Christmas story, not in warm Bethlehem, but in the winter of her native England. Rossetti was an accomplished writer of poetry and prose, noted for her deep spirituality.

Tune: CRANHAM Irr.
Gustav Holst, 1906

129 Good Christian Friends, Rejoice

German and Latin, 14th century
Transl. John Mason Neale, 1855; alt.

Descant

3 Good Chris - tian friends, re-joice with heart and soul and voice;

1 Good Chris-tian friends, re - joice with heart and soul and voice;
2 Good Chris-tian friends, re - joice with heart and soul and voice;
3 Good Chris-tian friends, re - joice with heart and soul and voice;

now you need not fear the grave: Je - sus Christ was born to save!

now give heed to what we say: Je - sus Christ is born to - day;
now you know of end - less bliss: Je - sus Christ was born for this!
now you need not fear the grave: Je - sus Christ was born to save!

Calls you one and calls you all to gain the ev - er -

Ox and ass be - fore him bow, a - sleep with - in the
God has o - pened heav - en's door, and you are blessed for -
Calls you one and calls you all to gain the ev - er -

This carol is very old. Heinrich Suso, a German mystic who died
in 1366, related a vision in which angels, singing this carol, drew
him into a dance. The words were originally macaronic,
combining Latin phrases with the vernacular.

Tune: IN DULCI JUBILO 6.6.7.7.7.8.5.5.
German melody, 14th century
Harm. adapt. from John Stainer, 1871
Descant, H. A. Chambers, 1931

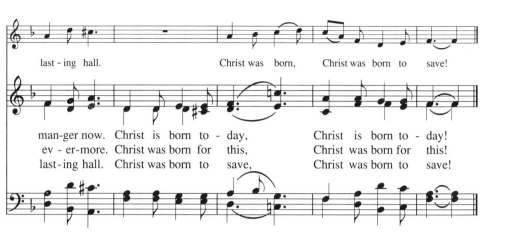

last - ing hall.   Christ was born,   Christ was born to   save!

man-ger now. Christ is born to - day,   Christ is born to - day!
ev - er-more. Christ was born for this,   Christ was born for this!
last-ing hall. Christ was born to save,   Christ was born to save!

From Heaven unto Earth I Come   130

Martin Luther, c. 1535
St. 1–2, transl. Catherine Winkworth, 1855; alt.
St. 3–5, transl. Lutheran Book of Worship, 1978; alt.

Luke 2:1–14

1 "From heav-en un - to earth I come to bear good news to ev - ery - one!
2 "To you, this night, is born a child of Mar - y, cho - sen moth-er mild;
3 O dear-est Je - sus, ho - ly child, pre-pare a bed, soft, un - de - filed,
4 My heart for ver - y joy now leaps; my voice no long - er si - lence keeps;
5 "Glo - ry to God," the an-gels sing, "and peace on earth," let heav-en ring.

Glad tid-ings of great joy I bring where-of I now will glad-ly sing:
This lit - tle child, in Jo-seph's arms, with joy shall con-quer all earth's harms."
A ho - ly shrine, with-in my heart, that you and I need nev - er part.
I too must join the an - gel throng to sing this joy-ous cra - dle song.
With voic-es raised we greet the birth: a glad new year to all the earth.

Martin Luther used a singing-game song as the model for the
first stanza of this hymn, then added fourteen more stanzas. The
hymn was written for his family's Christmas Eve celebration in
1534, and published the following year.

Tune: VOM HIMMEL HOCH L.M.
Valentin Schumann's Geistliche Lieder, *1539*
Harm. Hans Leo Hassler in Kirchengesäng,
Psalmen und Geistliche Lieder, *Nürnberg, 1608*

131   It Came upon the Midnight Clear

Luke 2:8–14   *Edmund H. Sears, 1849; alt.*

1 It came up-on the mid-night clear, that glo-rious song of old,
2 Still through the clo-ven skies they come, with peace-ful wings un-furled,
3 And you, be-neath life's crush-ing load, whose forms are bend-ing low,
4 For lo, the days are hasten-ing on, by proph-et bards fore-told,

from an-gels bend-ing near the earth to touch their harps of gold;
and still their heaven-ly mu-sic floats o'er all the wea-ry world;
who toil a-long the climb-ing way, with pain-ful steps and slow,
when with the ev-er-cir-cling years comes round the age of gold;

"Peace on the earth, good will to all, great news of joy we bring."
A-bove its sad and low-ly plains they bend on hover-ing wing,
Look now, for glad and gold-en hours come swift-ly on the wing;
When peace shall o-ver all the earth its an-cient splen-dors fling,

The world in sol-emn still-ness lay to hear the an-gels sing.
and ev-er o'er its Ba-bel sounds the bless-ed an-gels sing.
O rest be-side the wea-ry road, and hear the an-gels sing!
and all the world send back the song which now the an-gels sing.

Edmund Sears, a Unitarian minister who served a number of
congregations in the Boston area, wrote this Christmas hymn
emphasizing the social implications of the Gospel for his
congregation at Wayland, Massachusetts.

Tune: CAROL C.M.D.
Richard S. Willis, 1850

Joy to the World! 132

Isaac Watts, 1719; alt. Ps. 98:4–9; Luke 2:11–15

1 Joy to the world! the Lord is come: let earth its
2 Joy to the earth! the Sav - ior reigns! Let all their
3 Christ rules the world with truth and grace, and makes the

prais - es bring; Let ev - ery heart pre - pare Christ room,
songs em - ploy; While fields and floods, rocks, hills, and plains
na - tions prove The glo - ries of God's righ - teous - ness

and heaven and na - ture sing, and heaven and na - ture
re - peat the sound-ing joy, re - peat the sound-ing
and won - ders of God's love, and won - ders of God's

and heaven and na - ture sing, and
re - peat the sound-ing joy, re -
and won - ders of God's love, and

sing, and heaven, and heaven and na - ture sing.
joy, re - peat, re - peat the sound-ing joy.
love, and won - ders, won - ders of God's love.

heaven and na - ture sing,
peat the sound-ing joy,
won - ders of God's love,

Stanza 1 may be sung, "Joy to the world! the Sovereign comes: . . ."

Isaac Watts, an English Congregationalist, freely paraphrased
Old Testament psalms to glorify Christ and here develops a
hymn of advent and nativity from a psalm.

Tune: ANTIOCH C.M.
Lowell Mason, 1836

133   O Little Town of Bethlehem

Mic. 5:2; Luke 2:4–7   *Phillips Brooks, 1868; alt.*

1 O lit - tle town of Beth - le - hem, how still we see you lie!
2 For Christ is born of Mar - y, and gath - ered all a - bove,
3 How si - lent - ly, how si - lent - ly, the won - drous gift is given!
4 O ho - ly Child of Beth - le - hem, de - scend to us, we pray;

A - bove your deep and dream-less sleep the si - lent stars go by;
While mor - tals sleep, the an - gels keep their watch of won-dering love.
So God im - parts to hu - man hearts the glo - rious love of heaven.
Cast out our sin and en - ter in; be born in us to - day.

Yet in your dark streets shines forth the ev - er - last - ing light,
O morn-ing stars, to - geth - er pro - claim the ho - ly birth!
No one dis - cerns God's com - ing, but in this world of sin,
We hear the Christ-mas an - gels the great glad tid - ings tell;

The hopes and fears of all the years are met in you to - night.
And prais - es sing, and voic - es ring with peace to all on earth.
Where yearn-ing souls long to be whole, the dear Christ en - ters in.
O come to us, a - bide with us, our Lord Em - man - u - el!

Inspired by a visit to Bethlehem, Phillips Brooks, minister of   Tune: ST. LOUIS 8.6.8.6.7.6.8.6.
Holy Trinity Church, Philadelphia, wrote this hymn for the   *Lewis H. Redner, 1868*
Sunday School's Christmas service. The tune was hastily   *Alternate tune: FOREST GREEN*
sketched by the church organist in time for the service.

Silent Night, Holy Night

Joseph Mohr, 1818
Transl. John F. Young, c. 1863; alt.

Luke 2:1–20

1 Si - lent night, ho - ly night, all is calm, all is bright
2 Si - lent night, ho - ly night, shep-herds quake at the sight,
3 Si - lent night, ho - ly night, Child of God, love's pure light,

Round yon vir - gin moth-er and child. Ho - ly in - fant so ten - der and mild,
Glo - ries stream from heav-en a - far, heaven-ly hosts sing Al - le - lu - ia;
Ra - diant beams from your ho-ly face bring the dawn of re - deem - ing grace;

Sleep in heav - en - ly peace, sleep in heav - en - ly peace.
Christ the Sav - ior is born, Christ the Sav - ior is born.
Je - sus Christ at your birth, Je - sus Christ at your birth.

Stil-le Nacht, hei-li-ge Nacht!
Al-les schläft, ein-sam wacht
Nur das trau-te, hoch-hei-li-ge Paar
Hol-der Kna-be im lock-i-gen Haar,
Schlaf in himm-li-scher Ruh,
Schlaf in himm-li-scher Ruh!
(Original German text by Joseph Mohr)

¡No-che de paz; no-che de a-mor!
To-do duer-me en de-rre-dor.
En-tre los as-tros que es-par-cen su luz,
be-lla, a-nun-cian-do al ni-ñi-to Je-sús,
bri-lla la es-tre-lla de paz;
bri-lla la es-tre-lla de paz.
(Spanish transl. Federico Fliedner; alt.)

Po-la'i e, po kama-ha'o,
Ma-lu-hia, Ma-lama-lama,
Ka ma-kua-hi-ne a-lo-ha, e,
Me ke kei-ki He-mo-lele e,
Moe me ka ma-lu-hia la-ni,
Moe me ka ma-lu-hia la-ni.
(Hawaiian transl. Stephen Desha)

Csen-des éj, szent-sé-ges éj!
Min-de-nek nyug-ta mély;
Nincs fenn más, csak a szent szü-le pár,
Drá-ga kis-de-dük ál-ma-i-nál.
Szent fi-ú a-lud-jál,
Szent fi-ú a-lud-jál!
(Hungarian transl. anon.)

This beloved carol was created when, the day before Christmas,
the organ broke down in an Alpine village church. The priest,
Joseph Mohr, gave a new poem to the organist, Franz Gruber,
to be set to music. Gruber composed the music on the guitar,
and it was sung with guitar on Christmas.

Tune: STILLE NACHT Irr.
Franz Gruber, 1818

135

Adeste Fideles
(O Come, All You Faithful)

Luke 2:11–15; John 1:14

Latin, 18th century; attrib. to John Francis Wade
Transl. Frederick Oakeley, 1841, and others; alt.

1 A - des - te, fi - de - les, lae - ti tri - um - phan - tes; ve -
1 O come, all you faith - ful, joy - ful and tri - um - phant, O
2 God of true God . . . Light of true Light . . .
3 Sing, choirs of an - gels, sing in ex - ul - ta - tion,
4 A - men, Lord, we greet you, born this hap - py morn - ing;

ni - te, ve - ni - te in Beth - le - hem.
come now, O come now to Beth - le - hem.
born of the Vir - gin's womb in hu - man form;
sing, all you mes - sen - gers of heaven - ly love:
Je - sus to you shall all glo - ry be given;

Na - tum vi - de - te Re - gem an - ge - lo - rum.
Come and be - hold the rul - er of all an - gels:
Tru - ly our God, be - got - ten, not cre - at - ed:
"Glo - ry to God, all glo - ry in the high - est":
Word of our God . . . . now in flesh ap - pear - ing:

Refrain

Ve - ni - te a - do - re - mus, ve - ni - te a - do - re - mus,
O come in ad - o - ra - tion, O come in ad - o - ra - tion,

The Latin text and tune of this familiar hymn are found
together in several eighteenth-century manuscripts signed
by John F. Wade. Wade lived among a group of English
Catholic refugees in northern France.

Tune: ADESTE FIDELES Irr. with refrain
English melody, 18th century
John F. Wade's *Cantus Diversi, c. 1743*
Harm. Collections of Motets or Antiphons, *1792*

ve - ni - te   a - do - re - mus,   Do - mi - num.
O   come in   ad - o - ra - tion: Christ   is   Lord!

Jesus, Jesus, Oh, What a Wonderful Child   136

African-American traditional; alt.   *Luke 1:30–35; 2:8–14*

Je - sus,   Je - sus,   oh,   what a won-der-ful child.

Je - sus,   Je - sus,   so ho - ly,   meek, and mild;   new

life,   new hope   the   Child will bring.   Lis - ten   to the

an-gels sing,   "Glo-ry,   glo-ry,   glo - ry," let the heav-ens   ring!

This gospel song praising the newborn Child might be effectively used by repeating it several times. It could be sung softly as a background for dance, story, or drama. Finger-snaps on the off-beats might be used to fill the rests.

Tune: WONDERFUL CHILD 11.10.8.7.11.
African-American traditional
Arr. Jeffrey Radford, 1992

137

Hitsuji wa nemureri
(Sheep Fast Asleep)

Luke 2:8–14; Matt. 1:23; 2:1–2, 9–11

Genzō Miwa, 1907
Transl. John Moss, 1957; alt.

1 Hi - tsu-ji wa / ne - mu-re - ri, / Ku - sa - no, / to - ko ni,
2 Ma - hi-ru ni / o - to-ra-nu / Ku - shi - ki / hi - ka - ri,

1 Sheep fast a-sleep, / there on a hill, / grass for a bed; / all is still.
2 Star in the sky / shin-ing; so bright! / Si - lent and pure, / won-drous light!

Sa - e - yu - ku / fu - yu no yo, / Shi - mo mo mi - e - tsu.
Mi - so - ra no / ka - na - ta ni / Te - ri - ka - ka - ya ku.

Cold win-ter night, the / frost ap-pears; / shep-herds keep watch by their fire.
What tid-ings brings it / Is - ra - el? / Can we new hope in it find?

Ha - ru - ka ni, / hi - bi-ku wa / Ka - ze - ka, / mi - zu ka,
Su - ku - i wo / mo - ta-ra-su / Ka - mi no / mi - ko no

Soft there a sound, / far, far a-way; / is it the stream? winds at play?
Good news it brings! / "Fear not, I pray! / Born is God's Child, born to-day!

I - na - to yo / mi - tsu - ka - i / U - ta - u / mi - u - ta.
U - ma - re-shi / yo - ro - ko - bi / Tsu - gu - ru / ho - shi ka.

Nay, friend, it is the / heaven-ly choir, / sing-ing through-out the spheres.
God's gift of love to / all the earth, / Je - sus, Em - man - u - el."

*Written by Genzō Miwa in 1907, the text of this popular
Japanese Christmas hymn was later revised and published in
Kyodan Sambika (1954) with the current tune. Translator John
Moss has served as a United Church of Christ missionary in
Niigata, Japan.*

Tune: KŌRIN 8.7.8.7.8.7.8.6.
Chūgorō Torii, 1941

Jesus, Our Brother, Strong and Good 138

French carol, 12th century   Luke 2:1–7; Matt. 1:23
Transl. anon.

1 Je - sus, our broth - er, strong and good, was hum - bly
2 "I," said the don - key, shag - gy and brown, "I car - ried your
3 "I," said the cow, all white and red, "I gave you my
4 "I," said the sheep with curl - y horn, "I gave you my

born in a sta - ble rude, and the friend - ly beasts a -
moth - er up - hill and down, I car - ried your moth - er to
man - ger for your bed, I gave my hay to
wool for a blan - ket warm, you wore my coat on

round him stood, Je - sus our broth - er, strong and good.
Beth - le - hem town; I," said the don - key, shag - gy and brown.
pil - low your head; I," said the cow, all white and red.
Christ - mas morn; I," said the sheep with curl - y horn.

5 "I," said the dove, from the raf-ters high,
   "I cooed you to sleep that you should not cry,
   we cooed you to sleep, my love and I;
   I," said the dove, from the raf-ters high.

6 Thus all the beasts, by some good spell,
   in the sta-ble dark were glad to tell
   of the gifts they gave Em-man-u-el,
   the gifts they gave Em-man-u-el.

Little is known of either the origins of this French text or its
translation. The melody comes from a medieval French
cathedral festival recognizing the role of the donkey in the flight
into Egypt.

Tune: ORIENTIS PARTIBUS 7.7.7.7.
French melody, early 13th century
Harm. Ralph Vaughan Williams, 1906

139

The First Nowell

Luke 2:8–20; Matt. 2:1–12

Traditional English carol; alt.

1 The first Now - ell, the an - gel did say,
2 They looked a - bove and saw a star
3 And by the light of that same star
4 This star shone bright in the north - west,
5 Then en - tered in those ma - gi three,

was to cer - tain poor shep - herds in fields as they lay;
shin-ing in the east, be - yond them far,
three sag - es came from coun - try far;
o'er Beth - le - hem it seemed to rest,
and bend - ing low up - on their knee,

In fields where they lay keep - ing their sheep,
And to the earth it gave great light,
To seek for a king was their in - tent,
And there it did both stop and stay,
They of - fered there, in great rev - erence,

on a   cold win - ter's   night   that   was   so   deep.
and   so it   con - tin - ued   both   day   and   night.
and to fol - low   the   star   wher - ev - er   it   went.
right   o - ver   the   place   where   Je - sus   lay.
their   gold   and   myrrh   and   frank - in - cense.

Refrain

Refrain

Now - ell,   now - ell,   now - ell,   now -

ell,   born in a   man - ger, Em - man - u - el.

Though perhaps of earlier origins, this anonymous English carol first appeared in print in the nineteenth century. "Nowell" stems from the Latin novellae *(news) and is used as a joyous greeting to celebrate Jesus' birth.*

Tune: THE FIRST NOWELL   Irr. with refrain
Traditional English melody
Harm. Christmas Carols New and Old, *1871*
Descant, Edward Shippen Barnes, 1937

140 Break Forth, O Beauteous Heavenly Light

Luke 2:8–14

St. 1, Johann Rist, 1641
Transl. John Troutbeck, c. 1885; alt.
St. 2, Fred Pratt Green, 1989

1 Break forth, O beau-teous heaven - ly light, and ush - er in the
2 Come, dear - est child, in - to our hearts, and leave your crib be -

morn - ing; O shep - herds, shud - der not in fright, but
hind you! Let this be where the new life starts for

hear the an - gel's warn - ing. "This child, now weak in
all who seek and find you. To you the hon - or,

in - fan - cy, our con - fi - dence and joy shall be, the
thanks, and praise, for all your gifts this time of grace; come,

This hymn combines the great talents of German artistry: seventeenth-century Rist, the prolific poet; Schop, brilliant instrumentalist of the same time; and Bach, who in the eighteenth century arranged both in a memorable setting for the "Christmas Oratorio."

Tune: ERMUNTRE DICH 8.7.8.7.8.8.7.7.
Johann Schop, 1641
Harm. J. S. Bach, 1734

Carol Our Christmas 141

Shirley Erena Murray, 1986

1 Car - ol our Christ-mas, an up - side - down Christ-mas: snow is not
2 Sing of the gold and the green and the spar - kle, wa - ter and
3 Shep - herds and mus - ter - ers move o - ver hill - side, find - ing, not
4 Right - side - up Christ-mas be - longs to the u - ni - verse, made in the

fall - ing and trees are not bare. Car - ol the sum - mer, and
riv - er and lure of the beach. Sing in the hap - pi - ness
an - gels, but sheep to be shorn; Wise ones make jour - neys, what -
mo - ment a wom - an gives birth; Hope is the Je - sus gift,

wel-come the Christ Child, warm in our sun-shine and sweet-ness of air.
of o - pen spac - es, sing a na - tiv - i - ty sum - mer can reach!
ev - er the sea - son, search-ing for signs of the truth to be born.
love is the of - fering, ev - ery-where, an - y - where, here on the earth.

*Shirley Erena Murray, who lives in New Zealand, paints a
picture of Christmas as it is experienced in the midst of summer
in the southern hemisphere. Composer Colin Gibson has
collaborated frequently with Murray. A "musterer" is a rancher.*

Tune: REVERSI 11.10.11.10.
Colin Gibson, 1986

142

Manglakat na Kita sa Belen
(Let Us Even Now Go to Bethlehem)

Luke 2:15; John 1:14–18

St. 1, Angel Sotto; st. 2–3, Lois Bello, 1981; rev. 1993

1 Mang - la - kat na ki - ta sa Be -
1 Let us e - ven now go to Beth - le - hem, go to
2 Let us e - ven now of - fer love and praise to our
3 Let us e - ven now sing with heart and soul: "Christ was

len sa Hu - di - ya. Kay ang Ha - ri
Beth - le-hem of Ju - de - a. Je - sus Christ,
God a-bove, to our God a-bove; who from heav - en's throne
born to save! Christ was born to save!" Let us sing our praise

sa ma - nga ha - ri sa Be - len na - ta - wo
who is our Sov - ereign, now in Beth - le - hem is
has sent a gift of love, Je - sus Christ, God's on - ly
that all the world may know, all the world may know God's

na, sa Be - len na - ta - wo na.
born! now in Beth - le - hem is born!
Child, Je - sus Christ, God's on - ly Child.
love, all the world may know God's love.

This carol is part of a longer Christmas narrative originating in the Philippines, in which singers and dancers parade from house to house, often joined by neighbors and family members as they go.

Tune: MANGLAKAT 10.10.11.7.7.
Angel Sotto, 1981
Arr. Vérne de la Peña, 1994

On Christmas Night All Christians Sing 143

Traditional English carol Luke 2:8–14; John 1:1–5, 14; Acts 13:38–39

1 On Christ-mas night all Chris - tians sing, to hear the news the
2 Then why should we on earth be sad, since our Re - deem - er
3 From out of mys - tery came the Light, which made the an - gels

an - gels bring; On Christ-mas night all Chris - tians sing, to
made us glad; Then why should we on earth be sad, since
sing this night; From out of mys - tery came the Light, which

hear the news the an - gels bring— News of great
our Re - deem - er made us glad, When from our
made the an - gels sing this night: "Glo - ry to

joy, news of great mirth, news of our gra - cious Rul - er's birth.
sin Christ set us free, all for to gain our lib - er - ty.
God and peace to all, for - ev - er - more, Al - le - lu - ia!"

The Puritan era in England sent the medieval carols underground. Many were not rediscovered until the early twentieth century when Ralph Vaughan Williams, Cecil Sharp, and others began collecting them. This tune is one found by Vaughan Williams in Sussex.

Tune: SUSSEX CAROL 8.8.8.8.8.8.
English traditional melody
Harm. Jonathan McNair, 1993

144

Hark! The Herald Angels Sing

Luke 2:10–11, 25–32; 24:46–51;
1 Thess. 4:13–18; Isa. 60:19–20

Charles Wesley, 1739; alt.

1 Hark! the her - ald an - gels sing, "Glo - ry to the Christ-child bring;
2 Christ, by high - est heaven a - dored, Christ the ev - er - last - ing Lord!
3 Hail the Bear - er of God's peace! Hail the Sun of righ - teous-ness,

Peace on earth and mer - cy mild, God and sin - ner rec - on - ciled!"
Late in time the Sav - ior comes, off - spring of the Vir-gin's womb.
Light and life our Sav - ior brings, risen with ra - diant, heal-ing wings.

Joy - ful, all you saints a - rise, join the tri - umph of the skies;
Veiled in flesh, the God-head see; hail the in-car - nate De - i - ty,
Mild - ly lay - ing glo - ry by, born that we no more may die,

With the an - gel host pro - claim, "Christ is born in Beth - le - hem!"
Pleased on earth with us to dwell, Je - sus, our Em - man - u - el.
Born to raise us all from earth, born to give us sec - ond birth.

This hymn by Charles Wesley, one of the founders of Methodism,
is firmly wedded to Felix Mendelssohn's music. Composed for the
four hundredth anniversary of the invention of printing, the music
was adapted to this hymn fifteen years later.

Tune: MENDELSSOHN 7.7.7.7.D. with refrain
From Felix Mendelssohn's "Festgesang," 1840
Arr. William H. Cummings, 1855

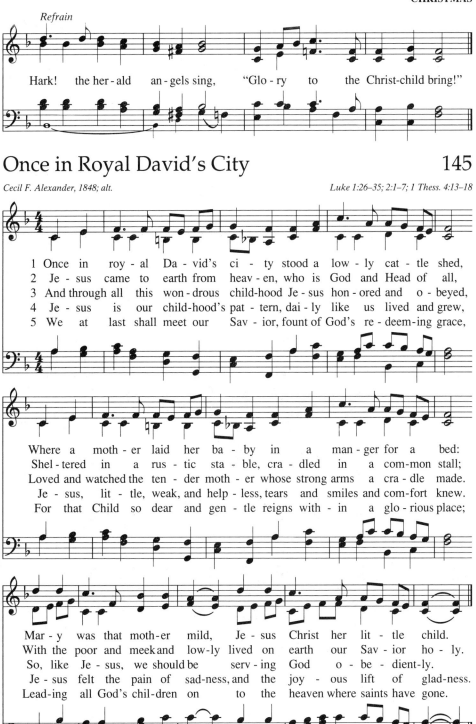

Refrain

Hark! the her-ald an-gels sing, "Glo - ry to the Christ-child bring!"

Once in Royal David's City 145

Cecil F. Alexander, 1848; alt. *Luke 1:26–35; 2:1–7; 1 Thess. 4:13–18*

1 Once in roy - al Da - vid's ci - ty stood a low - ly cat - tle shed,
2 Je - sus came to earth from heav - en, who is God and Head of all,
3 And through all this won - drous child-hood Je - sus hon - ored and o - beyed,
4 Je - sus is our child-hood's pat - tern, dai - ly like us lived and grew,
5 We at last shall meet our Sav - ior, fount of God's re - deem-ing grace,

Where a moth - er laid her ba - by in a man - ger for a bed:
Shel - tered in a rus - tic sta - ble, cra - dled in a com - mon stall;
Loved and watched the ten - der moth - er whose strong arms a cra - dle made.
Je - sus, lit - tle, weak, and help - less, tears and smiles and com-fort knew.
For that Child so dear and gen - tle reigns with - in a glo - rious place;

Mar - y was that moth-er mild, Je - sus Christ her lit - tle child.
With the poor and meek and low-ly lived on earth our Sav - ior ho - ly.
So, like Je - sus, we should be serv - ing God o - be - dient-ly.
Je - sus felt the pain of sad-ness, and the joy - ous lift of glad-ness.
Lead-ing all God's chil-dren on to the heaven where saints have gone.

Cecil Frances Alexander, wife of the bishop of Ireland, wrote a series of children's hymns commenting on the Apostles' Creed. This hymn, elaborating on the words ". . . born of the Virgin Mary," tells the whole life of Christ.

Tune: IRBY 8.7.8.7.7.7.
Henry J. Gauntlett, 1849
Harm. A. H. Mann, 1919

146

Nu Oli
(Glad Tidings)

Luke 2:10–11

Fanny Crosby, 1873; alt.
Transl. Laiana (Lorenzo Lyons, 1807–1886)

1 Nu - o - li! nu - o - li! he nu ka - ma - ha'o!
1 Glad tid - ings! glad tid - ings! O won - der - ful love!
2 Nu - o - li! nu - o - li! ua pi - li ia nu
3 Nu - o - li! nu - o - li! hau - o - li ou - kou,

He nu no ke o - la mai lu - na mai no,
A mes - sage has come from the an - gels a - bove:
Ika po'e i - li - hu - ne, ka po - e lu'u - lu'u,
Ka po'e a - ka - hai, a ha'a - ha'a ka na - au;

No ka - na - ka nu - i, no ka - ma - li'i nei,
Good news of great joy comes to young and to old,
Ne'e mai a pau - le - le, ha - hai ia Ie - su,
Na Ie - su e ka - la a ho'o - ha - nau hou,

A oi ka na - ni i ke gu - la a'i - a'i.
For Je - sus brings mer - cy more pre - cious than gold.
A pau no ka hu - ne, a ma - ha ou - kou.
A ka'i mai nei a'e i ka na - ni ma - o.

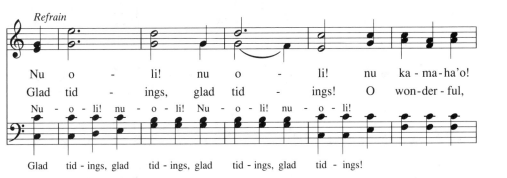

Refrain

Nu o - li! nu o - li! nu ka - ma - ha'o!
Glad tid - ings, glad tid - ings! O won - der - ful,

Nu - o - li! nu - o - li! Nu - o - li! nu - o - li!

Glad tid - ings, glad tid - ings, glad tid - ings, glad tid - ings!

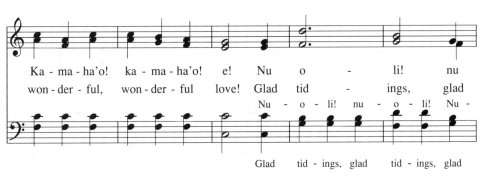

Ka - ma - ha'o! ka - ma - ha'o! e! Nu o - li! nu
won - der - ful, won - der - ful love! Glad tid - ings, glad

Nu - o - li! nu - o - li! Nu -

Glad tid - ings, glad tid - ings, glad

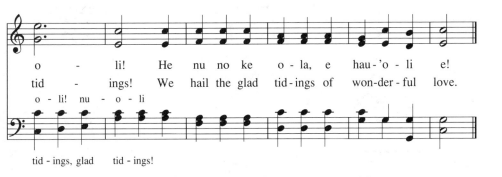

o - li! He nu no ke o - la, e hau - 'o - li e!
tid - ings! We hail the glad tid - ings of won - der - ful love.
o - li! nu - o - li

tid - ings, glad tid - ings!

In 1831 newly ordained Lorenzo Lyons and Betsy, his wife,
sailed to Hawaii with the Sandwich Islands Mission. He served
there over fifty years. Father Lyons (or "Laiana") translated a
great number of hymns into Hawaiian. This one is very popular
and is sung at Christmas.

Tune: NU OLI 11.11.11.11. with refrain
(GLAD TIDINGS)
Robert Lowry, 1873

147
See the Little Baby

Luke 2:7–14; Matt. 2:1–2, 9–11 — Donald Swift, 1983; alt.

Refrain

See the lit-tle ba-by born in a man-ger, on this Christ-mas morn-ing,

bright as the an-gels; See the lit-tle ba-by born in a man-ger,

Last time, end

sing No-el! Sing No-el!

Sing No-el!

1 There were shep-herds keep-ing their watch
2 "Come and see," said Mar-y and Jo-seph;

o - ver sheep as the an - gels sang. There were sa - ges
"Come and see what a won-der-ful child." Sheep and ox all

to Refrain

fol-low-ing the star. Sing No - el! Sing No - el!
gath-er-ing a - round. Sing No - el! Sing No - el!

*This song was first performed in a choral arrangement by the
Spelman-Morehouse College Glee Clubs in 1985. Composer
Donald Swift is a graduate of Morehouse College, whose work
includes chamber pieces and choral collections such as "Three
Easter Spirituals."*

Tune: LITTLE BABY Irr. with refrain
Donald Swift, 1983

What Child Is This

148

William C. Dix, 1865; alt.

Luke 2:7–14, 25–32; Matt. 2:11; John 1:14;
John 19:16b–18, 34

1 What child is this, who, laid to rest, on Mar-y's lap is sleep-ing?
2 Why lies the Child in man-ger bare where ox and ass are feed-ing?
3 Bring gifts of in-cense, gold, and myrrh; come, join in ju-bi-la-tion;

Whom an-gels greet with an-thems sweet while shep-herds watch are keep-ing?
Give heed, draw near; for sin-ners here the si-lent Word is plead-ing.
The Ho-ly Child, though meek and mild, has come with God's sal-va-tion.

This, this, the an-gels sing, is Christ, God's ho-ly of-fer-ing;
Nails, spear shall pierce him through, the cross be borne for me, for you;
Raise, raise the song on high, the moth-er sings her lul-la-by;

Haste, haste your praise to bring the babe, the child of Mar-y!
Hail, hail the Word made flesh, the babe, the child of Mar-y!
Joy, joy, for Christ is born, the babe, the child of Mar-y!

William Chatterton Dix, manager of an English marine insurance company, wrote a number of fine hymns. This one is always sung to the tune Greensleeves, *which first appeared in England in 1580 and is mentioned in one of Shakespeare's plays.*

Tune: GREENSLEEVES 8.7.8.7.6.8.6.7. with refrain
English traditional melody, 16th century

149

Pastores a Belén
(As Shepherds Filled with Joy)

Traditional Puerto Rican carol
Transl. The New Century Hymnal, *1993*

1 Pas - to - res a Be - lén va - mos con a - le - grí - a,
2 Oh ni - ño ce - les - tial, ben - di - ce a los pas - to - res,
1 As shep-herds filled with joy, to Beth - le - hem we're go - ing,
2 O ho - ly, heaven-ly Child, the shep-herds seek your bless - ing,

que ha na - ci - do ya el hi - jo de Ma - rí - a.
que co - rren al por - tal can - tan - do tus lo - o - res.
for Mar - y's child is born this bless - ed Christ-mas morn - ing.
while sing - ing hap - py songs, our hope and joy con - fess - ing.

A - llí, a - llí, nos es - pe - ra Je - sús.
Co - rred, vo - lad, sus glo - rias a al - can - zar.
See there, see there, the ba - by Je - sus waits.
We run, we fly, to greet the glo - rious Child.

A - llí A - llí nos es - pe - ra Je - sús.
Co - rred, vo - lad, sus glo - rias a al - can - zar.
See there, see there, the ba - by Je - sus waits.
We run, we fly, to greet the glo - rious Child.

Lle - ve - mos pues tu - rro-nes y miel pa - ra o-fre - cer-le al ni - ño Ma-nuel.
O - fre - ce a mil a - mor y vir-tud, tra - ed, za - gal, al ni - ño Je - sús.
O let us bring our hon-ey so sweet, an of-fering for the Child to eat.
With thank-ful hearts we of-fer our best to Je - sus, at the man-ger we'll rest.

Lle - ve - mos pues tu - rro - nes y miel pa - ra o - fre - cer - le al
O - fre - ce a mil a - mor y vir - tud, tra - ed, za - gal, al
O let us bring our hon - ey so sweet, an of - fering for the
With thank - ful hearts we of - fer our best to Je - sus, at the

ni - ño Ma - nuel. Va - mos, va - mos, va-mos a ver, va-mos a ver al
ni - ño Je - sús. Va - mos, va - mos, va-mos a ver, va-mos a ver al
Child to eat. Hur - ry, hur - ry, hur-ry and see, hur-ry and see the
man - ger we'll rest. Hur - ry, hur - ry, hur-ry and see, hur-ry and see the

re - cién na - ci - do, va - mos a ver al ni - ño Ma - nuel.
re - cién na - ci - do, va - mos a ver al ni - ño Ma - nuel.
child born of Mar - y. Let's go and see Em - man - u - el.
child born of Mar - y. Let's go and see Em - man - u - el.

This traditional carol from Puerto Rico invites the singer to
experience the wonder and joy of the shepherds as they came
to greet the Holy Child in the Bethlehem stable.

Tune: PASTORES A BELEN Irr.
Traditional Puerto Rican melody
Harm. Allena Luce, 1949

150 Sing a Different Song

Isa. 9:2, 6–7; 42:10–11; Matt. 1:23

The Iona Community, 1987; alt.

Vigorously

1 Sing a dif-ferent song now
2 Shout a dif-ferent shout now
3 Love a dif-ferent love now
4 Dance a dif-ferent dance now

(Introduction)

Christ-mas is here, sing a song of peo-ple know-ing God's
Christ-mas is here, shout a shout of joy and gen - u - ine
Christ-mas is here, love with-out con-di - tion, love with - out
Christ-mas is here, dance a dance of war on suf - fering and

near: The Mes - si - ah is born in the
cheer: Fill the earth and the sky with the
fear: With the hum - ble and poor, with the
fear: Peace and jus - tice are one, in the

face of our scorn, sing a dif-ferent song to
news from on high, shout a dif-ferent shout that
shy and un - sure, love a dif-ferent love. Let
light of the sun. Dance a dif-ferent dance. God's

wel-come and warn.
all may come by.
Christ be the cure!
reign has be - gun!

This lively new carol from The Iona Community of Scotland
can be accompanied by drums and tambourines to enhance its
dance-like quality. The text invites enthusiastic participation in
celebrating the Christmas event.

Tune: DIFFERENT SONG 10.10.6.6.10.
John L. Bell, 1987

151 'Twas in the Moon of Wintertime

Matt. 1:23; Luke 2:11

Jean de Brébeuf, c. 1643
Transl. Jesse Edgar Middleton, 1926; alt.

1 'Twas in the moon of win-ter-time, when all the birds had fled, that might-y Git-chi Man-i-tou sent an-gel choirs in-stead; Be-fore their light the stars grew dim, and won-dering hunt-ers heard the hymn:

2 With-in a lodge of bro-ken bark the ten-der babe was found; a rag-ged robe of rab-bit skin en-wrapped his beau-ty round; But as the hunt-er braves drew nigh, the an-gel song rang loud and high:

3 The ear-liest moon of win-ter-time is not so round and fair as was the ring of glo-ry on the help-less in-fant there. The chiefs from far be-fore him knelt with gifts of fox and bea-ver pelt.

4 O chil-dren of the for-est free, O seed of Man-i-tou, the ho-ly Child of earth and heaven is born to-day for you. Come kneel be-fore the ra-diant Child, who brings you beau-ty, peace, so mild.

Jean de Brébeuf, a Jesuit priest, started a mission among native Huron people in Canada in the early seventeenth century. Jesse Middleton's translation moves beyond the original French poem to include Huron folk symbols such as "rabbit skin" for "swaddling clothes."

Tune: UNE JEUNE PUCELLE
8.6.8.6.8.8. with refrain
French folk melody, 16th century
Harm. Jonathan McNair, 1993

Refrain

Je-sus Em-man-u - el, Je - sus is born, in ex-cel-sis glo - ri - a.

Born in the Night, Mary's Child 152

Geoffrey Ainger, 1964; alt.

Luke 2:1–7; Mark 10:18; John 1:1–5, 14;
John 19:16b–18

Unison

1 Born in the night, Mar-y's Child, a long way from your home;
2 Clear shin-ing light, Mar-y's Child, your face lights up our way;
3 Truth of our life, Mar-y's Child, you tell us God is good;
4 Hope of the world, Mar-y's Child, you're com-ing soon to reign;

Com - ing in need, Mar-y's Child, born in a bor-rowed room.
Light of the world, Mar-y's Child, dawn on our shad-owed day.
Prove it is true, Mar-y's Child, go to your cross of wood.
Sov - ereign of earth, Mar-y's Child, walk in our streets a - gain.

Methodist minister Geoffrey Ainger's song was part of a drama he
wrote for youth at his church in Loughton. Set in this section of
London, the play depicted Mary and Joe arriving on the subway,
with baby Jesus being born in a room above a filling station. The
carol made its way around the world, and on Christmas 1969,
Ainger recalls, it was being sung in India, Australia, in South
Pacific islands, and at Festival Hall in London.

Tune: MARY'S CHILD 7.6.7.6.
Geoffrey Ainger, 1964
Harm. Richard D. Wetzel, 1972

153 Who Would Think That What Was Needed

Isa. 11:1–6; Matt. 2:1–11; Luke 2:8–14   *John Bell and Graham Maule, 1990; alt.*

1 Who would think that what was need-ed   to trans-form and save the earth
2 Shep-herds watch and sag - es won-der,   mon-archs scorn and an - gels sing;
3 Cen - tu - ries of skill and sci-ence span the past from which we move,

might not be   a   plan or   ar - my   proud in pur - pose, proved in worth?
such a place as none would reck - on hosts a ho - ly, help - less thing;
yet ex - per-ience ques-tions wheth-er with such prog-ress we im - prove.

Who would think, de - spite de - ri - sion, that a child should lead the way?
Sta - bled beasts and pass-ing strang-ers watch a ba - by laid in hay:
In our search for sense and mean-ing, lest our hopes and hu-mor fray,

God sur - pris - es earth with heav-en, com-ing here on Christ-mas Day.
God sur - pris - es earth with heav-en, com-ing here on Christ-mas Day.
God sur - pris - es earth with heav-en, com-ing here on Christ-mas Day.

This song was written by The Iona Community in Scotland, which frequently develops hymn texts through a collaborative process, often employing traditional tunes from the British Isles such as "Scarlet Ribbons."

Tune: SCARLET RIBBONS 8.7.8.7.D.
English traditional melody
Arr. John Bell and others, 1990

Go Tell It on the Mountain

African-American spiritual
Arr. John W. Work II, 1907

Luke 2:8–20; Isa. 18:3; 52:7

Refrain

Go tell it on the moun - tain, o - ver the hill and ev - ery - where.

Go tell it on the moun - tain, that Je - sus Christ is born!

1 While shep-herds kept their watch-ing o'er si - lent flocks by night,
2 The shep-herds feared and trem-bled when lo! a - bove the earth
3 Down in a low - ly man - ger the hum - ble Christ was born,

Be - hold through-out the heav-ens there shone a ho - ly light.
Rang out the an - gel cho - rus that hailed our Sav - ior's birth.
And God sent us sal - va - tion that bless - ed Christ-mas morn.

This is one of the few spirituals heard inside as well as outside African-American churches. It was adapted by John Wesley Work II, who is remembered as the director of the Jubilee Singers of Fisk University.

Tune: African-American spiritual
Adapt. Joyce Finch Johnson, 1992

155 Los magos que llegaron a Belén
(The Magi Who to Bethlehem Did Go)

Matt. 2:1–12

Manuel Fernández Juncas
English version, Carolyn Jennings, 1993

Introduction (one time only)

Los ma-gos que lle-ga-ron a Be-lén a - nun-cia-ron la lle - ga - da del Me -
The ma - gi who to Beth-le-hem did go were the her-alds of the com-ing of Mes -

sí-as y no - so-tros, con a - le - grí - a, la a-nun - cia - mos hoy tam-bién.
si-ah; And with joy we al-so would has-ten to an-nounce the news to - day.

Stanzas

1 De tie - rra le - ja - na ve - ni - mos a ver - te,
2 Al re-cién na - ci - do que es Rey de los re - yes,
1 From a dis - tant land we come with hum-ble greet - ing,
2 To the new-born Child who has no earth-ly trea - sure

nos sir - ve de guí - a la es-tre - lla de O - rien - te.
o - ro le re - ga - lo pa-ra or-nar sus sie - nes.
where the east - ern star our car - a - van is lead - ing.
I have come with gold to bring de - light and plea - sure.

This traditional Puerto Rican carol is frequently sung during one of the most cherished celebrations of the church year—the epiphany. The music is in the popular style of a "danza," a traditional dance form.

Tune: LOS MAGOS 12.12. with refrain
Traditional Puerto Rican carol

Estribillo (Refrain)

(1–3) Oh bri - llan-te es-tre - lla que a-nun - cias la au - ro - ra   no nos
(4) Glo-ria en las al - tu - ras   al   Hi - jo   de   Dios,   Glo-ria en
(1–3) Ev - er - shin-ing star,   God's bril - liant dawn re - veal - ing,   ev - er
(4) Glo - ry   be   to   God,   who sent the Child of Heav-en,   Glo - ry

fal - te   nun - ca   tu   luz bien-he - cho-ra.
las   al - tu - ras   (4) y en la tie-rra a-mor.
guide our   way,   God's pres-ence still as - sur - ing.
be   to   God,   and   (4) peace to all on earth.

3. Co-mo es Dios el ni-ño
   le re-ga-lo in-cien-so,
   con a-ro-ma dul-ce
   que su-be has-ta el cie-lo.
   Estribillo

4. Al ni-ño del cie-lo
   que ba-jó a la tie-rra,
   le re-ga-lo mi-rra
   que ins-pi-ra tris-te-za.
   Estribillo

3. To the Child of God
   rich in-cense I am bring-ing,
   With a-ro-ma sweet
   that heav-en-ward is wing-ing.
   Refrain

4. To the Child who came
   to bring us heav-en's glad-ness,
   I have come with myrrh,
   a sign of com-ing sad-ness.
   Refrain

156

Brightest and Best

Matt. 2:9–11; Luke 2:10–14

Reginald Heber, 1811; alt.

1 Bright - est and best of the stars of the morn - ing,
2 Cold on the cra - dle the dew - drops are shin - ing,
3 Shall we not of - fer our cost - ly de - vo - tion,
4 Vain - ly we of - fer each am - ple ob - la - tion,

dawn on our mid - night and lend us your aid.
God's ho - ly Child with the beasts of the stall;
fra - grance of E - dom and of - ferings di - vine,
vain - ly with gifts would we fa - vor se - cure;

Star of the East the ho - ri - zon a - dorn - ing,
An - gels a - dore while this ba - by lies sleep - ing,
Gems of the moun - tain and pearls of the o - cean,
Rich - er by far is the heart's ad - o - ra - tion;

guide where our in - fant Re - deem - er is laid.
Mak - er and Mon - arch and Sav - ior of all.
myrrh from the for - est or gold from the mine?
dear - er to God are the prayers of the poor.

This is thought to be one of the earliest tunes to which "Brightest and Best" was sung in the United States. It appears to be named for William Walker, the compiler of Southern Harmony, *a nineteenth-century collection of American tunes.*

Tune: WALKER 11.10.11.10
Southern Harmony, *1835*
Harm. Jonathan McNair, *1994*
Alternate setting: MORNING STAR

Brightest and Best

157

Reginald Heber, 1811; alt.

Matt. 2:9–11; Luke 2:10–14

1 Bright - est and best of the stars of the morn - ing,
2 Cold on the cra - dle the dew - drops are shin - ing,
3 Shall we not of - fer our cost - ly de - vo - tion,
4 Vain - ly we of - fer each am - ple ob - la - tion,

dawn on our mid - night and lend us your aid.
God's ho - ly Child with the beasts of the stall;
fra - grance of E - dom and of - ferings di - vine,
vain - ly with gifts would we fa - vor se - cure;

Star of the East the ho - ri - zon a - dorn - ing,
An - gels a - dore while this ba - by lies sleep - ing,
Gems of the moun - tain and pearls of the o - cean,
Rich - er by far is the heart's ad - o - ra - tion,

guide where our in - fant Re - deem - er is laid.
Mak - er and Mon - arch and Sav - ior of all.
myrrh from the for - est or gold from the mine?
dear - er to God are the prayers of the poor.

An Anglican priest, Reginald Heber became bishop of Calcutta (including all of India), where he died of exhaustion at age forty-three. His Hymns (1827) was the first modern English hymnal arranged according to the church year.

Tune: MORNING STAR 11.10.11.10.
James P. Harding, 1892
The New Psalms and Hymns, Richmond, Va., 1901
Alternate setting: WALKER

158   O Morning Star, How Clear and Bright

Isa. 60:19–20; Rom. 15:7–13

Philipp Nicolai, 1598
Transl. Catherine Winkworth, 1863; alt.

1 O Morn-ing Star, how clear and bright, your beam shines forth in
2 Come heaven-ly Bright-ness, Light di - vine, and deep with - in my

truth and light! My Sov-ereign meek and low - ly! O Root of Jes - se,
heart now shine, there make your - self an al - tar! Fill me with joy and

Prom - ised One, my God and Rul - er, you have won my heart to serve you
strength to be your mem-ber, joined e - ter - nal - ly in love that can - not

sole - ly! You are ho - ly, great and glo-rious, all - vic - to - rious,
fal - ter; Long-ing for you does pos - sess me; turn and bless me;

This German chorale by Lutheran pastor Philipp Nicolai became so popular that its tune was chimed by church bells and its words engraved on pottery. It has been called "the queen of chorales."

Tune: WIE SCHÖN LEUCHTET 8.8.7.8.8.7.4.8.4.8.
Philipp Nicolai, 1598
Harm. J. S. Bach, c. 1731

Rich in bless - ing, rule and might o'er all pos - sess - ing.
Here in sad - ness eye and heart long for your glad - ness.

As with Gladness Those of Old 159

William C. Dix, 1861; alt.   Matt. 2:1–12

1 As with glad-ness those of old did the guid-ing star be-hold;
2 As with joy-ful steps they sped to that low-ly man-ger bed,
3 As they of-fered gifts most rare at that man-ger plain and bare,
4 Ho-ly Je-sus, ev-ery day keep us in the nar-row way;

As with joy they hailed its light, lead-ing on-ward, beam-ing bright;
There to bend the knee be-fore One whom heaven and earth a-dore;
So may we with ho-ly joy, pure and free from sin's al-loy,
And when mor-tal things are past, bring our ran-somed souls at last

So, true Morn-ing Star, may we ev-er-more your splen-dor see.
So may we with will-ing feet ev-er seek your mer-cy seat.
All our cost-liest trea-sures bring, Christ, to you from whom they spring.
Where they need no star to guide, where no clouds your glo-ry hide.

After reading the Epiphany gospel, William C. Dix penned this hymn. Dix, the manager of a marine insurance company, was also a gifted hymnwriter. Among his many fine contributions is "What Child Is This."

Tune: DIX 7.7.7.7.7.7.
Conrad Kocher, 1838
Adapt. William H. Monk, 1861

160

Hark! the Herald Angels Sing
(Jesus, the Light of the World)

John 8:12; 9:5   *Charles Wesley, 1739; alt.; adapt. George D. Elderkin; alt*

1 Hark! the her-ald an-gels sing, Je-sus, the light of the world;
2 Joy-ful, all you saints a-rise, Je-sus, the light of the world;
3 Christ, by high-est heaven a-dored, Je-sus, the light of the world;
4 Hail the Bear-er of God's peace! Je-sus, the light of the world;

Glo-ry to the Christ-child bring, Je-sus, the light of the world.
Join the tri-umph of the skies, Je-sus, the light of the world.
Christ, the ev-er-last-ing Word, Je-sus, the light of the world.
Hail the Sun of righ-teous-ness! Je-sus, the light of the world.

Refrain

We will fol-low the light, beau-ti-ful light, come where the dew-drops of mer-cy are bright, Shine all a-round us by day and by night, Je-sus, the light of the world.

The original version of Charles Wesley's hymn has received various alterations throughout the years. This adaptation by George Elderkin utilizes a repeated ascription, "Jesus, the light of the world," and a refrain to create a rousing carol of praise.

Tune: ELDERKIN 7.7.7.7. with refrain
*George D. Elderkin
Arr. Jeffrey Radford, 1993*

Amen, Amen

African-American spiritual

Mark 3:7–10; Luke 2:7, 46–47; Rom. 6:6–10

Congregation/choir

A - men, a - men, a - men, a - men,

Solo

1 O   see the lit-tle ba-by   ly-ing in a man-ger
2 See   Je-sus in the tem-ple   talk-ing to the el-ders;
3 See   Je-sus at the sea-shore   preach-ing to the peo-ple,
4 See   Je-sus on the cross ....   bear-ing all my sins ....
5 Yes, Je-sus died to save us,   rose on Eas-ter morn-ing,
6 We're sing-ing Al-le-lu-ia!   Je-sus is my Sav-ior,

(Congregation/choir)

a - men!   A - men,

on Christ-mas   morn-ing.   (2 See)
how they   all   mar-veled!   (3 See)
       heal-ing all the sick ones!   (4 See)
in bit-ter   ag-o-ny!   (5 Yes,)
and lives   for-ev-er!   (6 We're)
who lives   for-ev-er!

a - men,   a - men, a - men, a - men!

This is one of the many spirituals that found fame during
the civil rights movement of the 1960s. Its pattern of
call-and-response allowed the lead singer to create new
verses while those gathered sang the response of "Amen."

Tune: AMEN Irr.
African-American spiritual
Arr. Nelsie T. Johnson, 1988

162

In a Lowly Manger Born

Matt. 8:20; John 19:5; Phil. 2:5–11; Heb. 5:1–11

Kō Yūki, 1923
Transl. Vern Rossman; alt.

1 In a low-ly man-ger born, hum-ble life be-gun in scorn.
2 Vis-it-ing each out-cast soul, bring-ing peace to make them whole,
3 Came to earth for you and me, gave up life up-on the tree;

In a work-shop Je-sus grew, work-er's strug-gles knew.
Giv-ing self-less-ly in love, God's own love to prove.
There we saw God's love re-vealed, through that pain were healed.

Knew the suf-fering of the weak, knew the long-ing of the meek,
Sin-ners glad-ly heard Christ call, righ-teous ones did hum-ble fall.
Lives a-gain in glo-ry bright, lives a-gain in power and might,

Knew the poor and suf-fering ones; this is God, the Hu-man One!
And in Christ new life be-gun, wor-shipped God, the Hu-man One!
Our sal-va-tion now has come, gift of God, the Hu-man One!

In 1971 Kō Yūki was named pastor emeritus of a Tokyo church he had served for fifty years. He is known as a Christian educator, Pascal scholar, and prolific hymnwriter. Translator Vern Rossman was an American missionary to Japan.

Tune: MABUNE 7.7.7.7.D.
Seigi Abe, 1930

Many Are the Lightbeams

Cyprian of Carthage, "De unitate ecclesiae," 252 C.E.
Swedish paraphr. by Anders Frostenson (b. 1906)
Transl. David Lewis, 1983

John 8:12; 9:5; 15:1–5; 1 Cor. 12:4–27; Gal. 3:28

1 Man - y are the light-beams from the one light. Our one
2 Man - y are the branch-es of the one tree. Our one
3 Man - y are the gifts given, love is all one. Love's the
4 Man - y ways to serve God, the Spir - it is one; ser - vant
5 Man - y are the mem - bers, the bod - y is one; mem - bers

light is Je - sus. Man - y are the light-beams
tree is Je - sus. Man - y are the branch-es
gift of Je - sus. Man - y are the gifts given,
spir - it of Je - sus. Man - y ways to serve God, the
all of Je - sus. Man - y are the mem - bers, the

from the one light; we are one in Christ.
of the one tree; we are one in Christ.
love is all one; we are one in Christ.
Spir - it is one; we are one in Christ.
bod - y is one; we are one in Christ.

The text upon which this hymn is based is by a bishop of the
early church, Cyprian of Carthage. It was paraphrased from his
252 C.E. work, "De unitate ecclesiae" (Of church unity). He was
martyred in Carthage c. 258.

Tune: LIGHTBEAMS Irr.
Olle Widestrand (b. 1906)
Arr. Darryl Nixon, 1987

164   Arise, Your Light Is Come

Isa. 60:1; 61:1–2; Luke 4:14–21   *Ruth Duck, 1973*

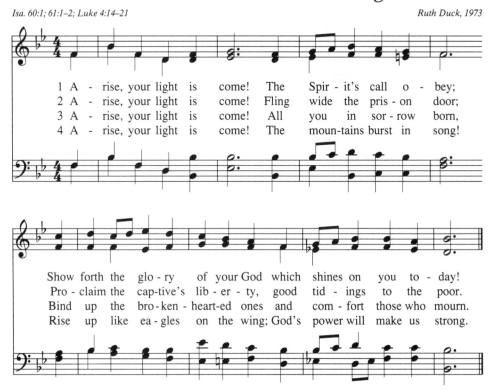

1 A - rise, your light is come! The Spir - it's call o - bey;
2 A - rise, your light is come! Fling wide the pris - on door;
3 A - rise, your light is come! All you in sor - row born,
4 A - rise, your light is come! The moun-tains burst in song!

Show forth the glo - ry of your God which shines on you to - day!
Pro - claim the cap-tive's lib - er - ty, good tid - ings to the poor.
Bind up the bro-ken - heart-ed ones and com - fort those who mourn.
Rise up like ea - gles on the wing; God's power will make us strong.

This hymn was first published by the Ecumenical Women's Center of Chicago in the 1974 collection of hymn adaptations, Because We Are One People. Ruth Duck later included it in her own collection, Dancing in the Universe.

Tune: FESTAL SONG S.M.
William Walter, 1872

165   Love Came Down at Christmas

Matt. 2:1–11; Luke 2:8–18   *Christina G. Rossetti, 1885; alt.*

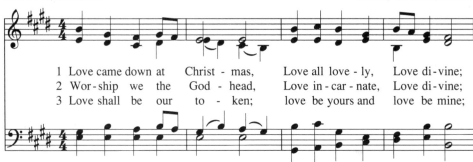

1 Love came down at Christ - mas, Love all love - ly, Love di - vine:
2 Wor - ship we the God - head, Love in - car - nate, Love di - vine:
3 Love shall be our to - ken; love be yours and love be mine;

Christina Rossetti, author of the more familiar carol "In the Bleak Midwinter," lived a very quiet life in England. This text has been described by the noted editor Percy Dearmer as a "gem, where so much is said in so little space."

Tune: WHITNEY 6.7.6.7.
Maurice C. Whitney, 1962

Love was born at Christ-mas; star and an-gels gave the sign.
Wor-ship we our Je - sus, but where is God's sa - cred sign?
Love to God and neigh - bor, love for plea and gift and sign.

Immortal Love, Forever Full 166

John Greenleaf Whittier, 1867; alt. *Phil. 2:9–11; Rom. 10:6–7; Mark 5:25–29*

1 Im - mor - tal Love, for - ev - er full, for - ev - er flow - ing free,
2 Our out - ward lips con - fess the Name all oth - er names a - bove;
3 We may not climb the heaven-ly steeps to bring the Sov-ereign down;
4 But warm, sweet, ten - der, ev - en yet this One our help will be;

For - ev - er shared, for - ev - er whole, a nev - er - ebb - ing sea!
Love on - ly knows from where it came and com - pre-hends God's love.
In vain we search the low - est deeps for One no depths can drown.
For faith has still its Ol - i - vet, and love its Gal - i - lee.

5 The heal-ing of Christ's seam-less dress
   still soothes our beds of pain;
  We touch it in life's throng and press,
  and we are whole a-gain.

6 Through Christ our ear-liest prayers are said
  with words we scarce can frame;
  The last low whis-pers of our dead
  still ech-o with Christ's name.

Though the American poet John Greenleaf Whittier did not write hymnody as such, a number of hymns have been drawn from his devotional poetry. This hymn was selected from The Tent on the Beach and Other Poems.

Tune: SERENITY C.M.
Arr. from William V. Wallace, 1856
Alternate tune: BEATITUDO

167   Mark How the Lamb of God's Self-Offering

Matt. 3:13–17; 4:1–2; Mark 1:9–13; Luke 3:21–22;
Acts 10:34–38; 2:38–42

Carl P. Daw, Jr., 1990

1 Mark how the Lamb of God's self - of - fering our hu - man
2 From this as - sur - ance of God's fa - vor Je - sus goes
3 Grant us, O God, the strength and cour - age to live the

sin - ful-ness takes on In the birth - wa-ters of the Jor - dan
to the wil - der - ness, There to en - dure a time of test - ing
faith our lips de - clare; Bless us in our bap-tis-mal call - ing;

as Je - sus is bap-tized by John. Hear how the voice from heav-en
that read-ied him to teach and bless. So we, by wa - ter and the
Christ's roy - al priest-hood help us share. Turn us from ev - ery false al -

thun - ders, "Lo, this is my be - lov - ed Son." See how in
Spir - it bap - tized in - to Christ's min - is - try, Are of - ten
le - giance, that we may trust in Christ a - lone: Raise up in

Regarding this hymn for the first Sunday after the Epiphany,
hymnwriter Carl P. Daw, Jr., writes that "the Baptism of Christ
is one of the regular occasions for baptisms and for the making
and renewing of baptismal vows."

Tune: RENDEZ À DIEU 9.8.9.8.D.
Louis Bourgeois (c. 1510–c. 1561)
Trente quatre Pseaumes, Geneva, 1551

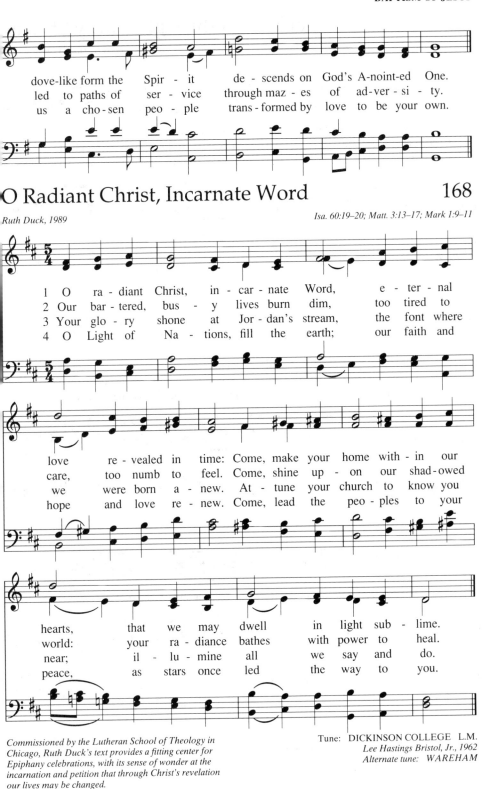

dove-like form the Spir - it de - scends on God's A-noint-ed One.
led to paths of ser - vice through maz - es of ad-ver - si - ty.
us a cho-sen peo - ple trans-formed by love to be your own.

O Radiant Christ, Incarnate Word   168

Ruth Duck, 1989   *Isa. 60:19–20; Matt. 3:13–17; Mark 1:9–11*

1 O ra - diant Christ, in - car - nate Word, e - ter - nal
2 Our bar - tered, bus - y lives burn dim, too tired to
3 Your glo - ry shone at Jor - dan's stream, the font where
4 O Light of Na - tions, fill the earth; our faith and

love re - vealed in time: Come, make your home with - in our
care, too numb to feel. Come, shine up - on our shad - owed
we were born a - new. At - tune your church to know you
hope and love re - new. Come, lead the peo - ples to your

hearts, that we may dwell in light sub - lime.
world: your ra - diance bathes with power to heal.
near; il - lu - mine all we say and do.
peace, as stars once led the way to you.

Commissioned by the Lutheran School of Theology in
Chicago, Ruth Duck's text provides a fitting center for
Epiphany celebrations, with its sense of wonder at the
incarnation and petition that through Christ's revelation
our lives may be changed.

Tune: DICKINSON COLLEGE L.M.
Lee Hastings Bristol, Jr., 1962
Alternate tune: WAREHAM

169   What Ruler Wades through Murky Streams

Matt. 3:13–17; Mark 1:9–11; Luke 3:21–22;
Col. 2:9–12

Thomas H. Troeger, 1984; rev. 1993

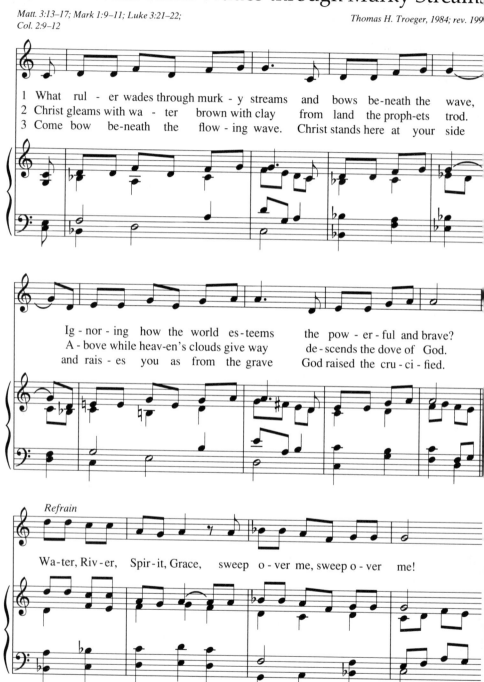

1 What rul - er wades through murk - y streams and bows be-neath the wave,
2 Christ gleams with wa - ter brown with clay from land the proph-ets trod.
3 Come bow be-neath the flow - ing wave. Christ stands here at your side

Ig - nor - ing how the world es - teems the pow - er - ful and brave?
A - bove while heav-en's clouds give way de - scends the dove of God.
and rais - es you as from the grave God raised the cru - ci - fied.

Refrain

Wa-ter, Riv-er, Spir-it, Grace, sweep o - ver me, sweep o - ver me!

*Thomas H. Troeger commented that this text "was inspired by
seeing a picture of a muddy Jordan River and realizing the
materiality of Christ's experience at baptism." The new musical
setting was provided by David Hurd at the invitation of The
New Century Hymnal.*

Tune: WATER OF BAPTISM C.M. with refrain
David Hurd, 1994

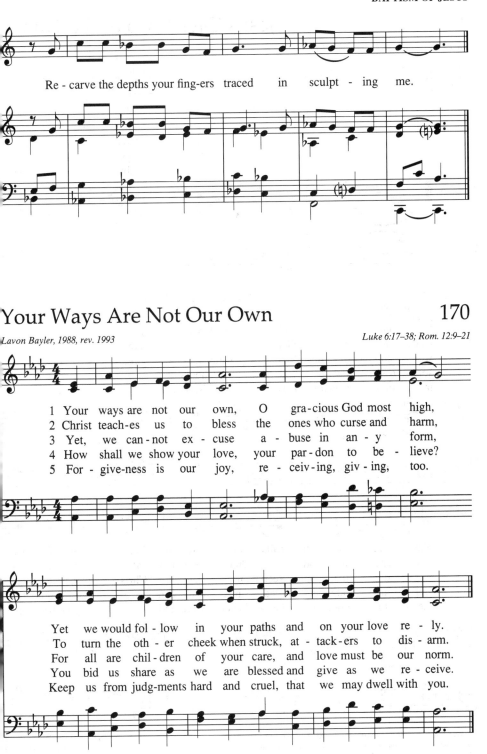

Re - carve the depths your fing-ers traced in sculpt - ing me.

Your Ways Are Not Our Own

170

Lavon Bayler, 1988, rev. 1993

Luke 6:17–38; Rom. 12:9–21

1 Your ways are not our own, O gra-cious God most high,
2 Christ teach-es us to bless the ones who curse and harm,
3 Yet, we can-not ex - cuse a - buse in an - y form,
4 How shall we show your love, your par-don to be - lieve?
5 For - give-ness is our joy, re - ceiv-ing, giv - ing, too.

Yet we would fol - low in your paths and on your love re - ly.
To turn the oth - er cheek when struck, at - tack-ers to dis - arm.
For all are chil - dren of your care, and love must be our norm.
You bid us share as we are blessed and give as we re - ceive.
Keep us from judg-ments hard and cruel, that we may dwell with you.

Lavon Bayler has served on the Illinois Conference staff of the United Church of Christ beginning in 1979. She maintains a faithful practice of writing worship materials as part of her daily spiritual discipline and has published several books of resources.

Tune: SCHUMANN S.M.
Cantica Laudis,
Lowell Mason and G. J. Webb, 1850

171 Jesus Calls Us, o'er the Tumul

Matt. 4:18–22; Mark 1:16–20; John 21:15

Cecil F. Alexander, 1852; a

1 Je - sus calls us, o'er the
2 As of old, Saint An - drew
3 Je - sus calls us from the
4 In our joys and in our
5 Je - sus calls us! By your

tu - mult of our life's wild, rest-less sea; Day by
heard it by the Gal - i - le - an lake, Turned from
wor - ship of the trea - sures we a - dore, From each
sor - rows, days of toil and hours of ease, Je - sus
mer - cies, Sav-ior, may we hear your call, Give our

day that voice still calls us, say - ing, "Chris - tian, fol - low
home and toil and kin - dred, leav - ing all for Je - sus'
i - dol that would keep us, say - ing, "Chris - tian, love me
calls, in cares and plea - sures, "Chris-tian, love me more than
hearts to your o - be - dience, serve and love you best of

*David Hurd is an internationally recognized organist
and composer who has served on the faculty of General
Theological Seminary and Manhattan School of Music.
This tune was composed especially for this text and
should be performed simply, like a folk song.*

Tune: ST. ANDREW 8.7.8.7.7
*David Hurd, 198(
Alternate setting: GALILEE*

Last time only

me," say - ing, "Chris - tian, fol - low me."
sake, leav - ing all for Je - sus' sake.
more," say - ing, "Chris - tian, love me more."
these, Chris-tian, love me more than these."
all, serve and love you best of all.

Last time only

Jesus Calls Us, o'er the Tumult   172

Cecil F. Alexander, 1852; alt.   *Matt. 4:18–22; Mark 1:16–20; John 21:15*

1 Je-sus calls us, o'er the tu - mult of our life's wild, rest-less sea;
2 As of old, Saint An-drew heard it by the Gal - i - le - an lake,
3 Je-sus calls us from the wor-ship of the trea - sures we a - dore,
4 In our joys and in our sor-rows, days of toil and hours of ease,
5 Je-sus calls us! By your mer-cies, Sav-ior, may we hear your call,

Day by day that voice still calls us, say - ing, "Chris-tian, fol - low me."
Turned from home and toil and kin-dred, leav - ing all for Je - sus' sake.
From each i - dol that would keep us, say - ing, "Chris-tian, love me more."
Je - sus calls, in cares and plea-sures, "Chris-tian, love me more than these."
Give our hearts to your o - be-dience, serve and love you best of all.

*Cecil Alexander, who in Ireland wrote sacred verse to teach
children the meaning of the catechism and liturgy, designated
this poem for St. Andrew's Day. Many years later Galilee was
composed for this text by an English organist, William Jude.*

Tune: GALILEE 8.7.8.7.
William H. Jude, 1887
Alternate setting: ST. ANDREW

173

Tú has venido a la orilla
(You Have Come down to the Lakeshore)

Matt. 4:18–22; Mark 1:16–20; Luke 5:1–11

Cesáreo Gabaraín, 1979; alt.
Transl. Madeleine Forell Marshall, 1989; alt.

1 Tú has ve - ni - do a la o - ri - lla, no has bus -
2 Tú sa - bes bien lo que ten - go: en mi
1 You have come down to the lake - shore seek - ing
2 You know full well my pos - ses - sions. Nei - ther

ca - do ni a sa - bios, ni a ri - cos, tan só - lo
bar - ca no hay o - ro ni es-pa - das; tan só - lo
nei - ther the wise nor the wealth - y, But on - ly
trea - sure nor weap-ons for con - quest, Just these my

Estribillo (Refrain)

quie - res que yo te si - ga. Je -
re - des y mi tra - ba - jo.
ask - ing for me to fol - low. O
fish - nets and will for work - ing.

sús, me has mi - ra - do a los o - jos;
Je - sus, you have looked in - to my eyes;

One of the most popular hymns to emerge from the 1970s revival of religious songs in Spain, this text has been translated into nearly eighty languages. The Spanish composer-author was a parish priest known for his work among youth.

Tune: PESCADOR DE HOMBRES
8.10.10. with refrain
Cesáreo Gabaraín, 1979
Harm. Skinner Chávez-Melo, 1987

son - ri - en - do, has di - cho mi nom - bre;
kind - ly smil - ing, you've called out my name.

en la a - re - na he de - ja - do mi bar - ca;
On the sand I have a - ban - doned my small boat;

jun - to a ti bus - ca - ré o - tro mar.
now with you I will seek oth - er seas.

3. Tú ne-ce-si-tas mis ma-nos,
   mi can-san-cio que a o-tros des-can-se,
   a-mor que quie-ra se-guir a-man-do.
   Estribillo

3. You need my hands, my ex-haus-tion,
   work-ing love for the rest of the
   wea-ry—
   A love that's will-ing to go on lov-ing.
   Refrain

4. Tú, Pes-ca-dor de o-tros ma-res,
   an-sia e-ter-na de al-mas que es-pe-ran.
   A-mi-go bue-no, que a-sí me lla-mas.
   Estribillo

4. You who have fished oth-er wa-ters;
   you, the long-ing of souls that are
   yearn-ing:
   As lov-ing Friend, you have come
   to call me.
   Refrain

174   Hear the Voice of God, So Tender

Mark 2:21–22; Ps. 103   *Lavon Bayler, 1987; rev. 1993*

1 Hear the voice of God, so ten-der, gath-ering
2 God is heal-ing and for-giv-ing crea-tures
3 Lis-tening to the Spir-it's guid-ing, breath be-
4 Shed the old wine-skins of war-fare for the

us in righ-teous-ness, Giv-ing, as our sure de-fend-er,
who are sore dis-tressed, O-pening doors to hope-ful liv-ing,
yond the writ-ten code, We, in cov-e-nant a-bid-ing,
fresh new wines of peace, Know-ing God sus-tains our wel-fare

stead-fast love and faith-ful-ness. Bless God's ho-ly name to-geth-er,
as, by love, we're dai-ly blessed. Bless God's ho-ly name to-geth-er,
seek to write our let-ters bold. Bless God's ho-ly name to-geth-er,
with a love that will not cease. Bless God's ho-ly name to-geth-er,

as the Spir-it brings new life. Giv-ing, as our sure de-
as the Spir-it brings new life. O-pening doors to hope-ful
as the Spir-it brings new life. We, in cov-e-nant a-
as the Spir-it brings new life. Know-ing God sus-tains our

This is one of the hundreds of hymn texts Lavon Bayler has provided in her books of liturgical resources related to the common lectionary. It appears in the volume for year B, aptly titled Whispers of God.

Tune: RAQUEL 8.7.8.7.D.
Skinner Chávez-Melo, 1985
Alternate tune: *BEACH SPRING*

fend	-	er,	stead-fast	love and faith - ful	-	ness.
liv	-	ing,	as, by	love, we're dai	-	ly	blessed.
bid	-	ing,	seek to	write our let	-	ters	bold.
wel	-	fare	with a	love that will	not	cease.

O Christ, the Healer, We Have Come   175

Fred Pratt Green, 1967   *Matt. 8:5–13; 15:21–28; Mark 5:25–34; Luke 7:1–10; 9:37–43a*

Unison

1 O Christ, the heal - er, we have come to
2 From ev - ery ail - ment flesh en - dures our
3 In con - flicts that de - stroy our health we
4 Grant that we all, made one in faith, in

pray for health, to plead for friends. How can we fail to be re -
bod - ies clam - or to be freed. Yet in our hearts we would con -
rec - og - nize the world's dis - ease; Our com - mon life de - clares our
your com-mu - ni - ty may find. The whole-ness that, en - rich - ing

stored when reached by love that nev - er ends?
fess that whole-ness is our deep - est need.
ills. Is there no cure, O Christ, for these?
us, shall reach and pros - per hu - man - kind.

*Fred Pratt Green wrote this hymn in 1967 at the suggestion of
the committee compiling* Hymns and Songs, *when they noted the
need for a new healing text. Green immediately produced this
prayer for wholeness of body, mind, and spirit.*

Tune: KENTRIDGE L.M.
Richard Gieseke, 1988
Alternate tune: *TALLIS' CANON*

176   "Silence! Frenzied, Unclean Spirit"

Mark 1:21–28; Luke 4:33–37   *Thomas H. Troeger, 1984; rev. 1993*

1 "Si - lence! Fren - zied, un-clean spir - it," cried God's heal - ing, Ho - ly One.
2 Christ, the de - mons still are thriv-ing in the grey cells of the mind:
3 Si - lence, Christ, the un-clean spir - it, in our mind and in our heart.

"Cease your rant - ing! Flesh can't bear it. Flee as night be - fore the sun."
Ty - rant voic - es, shrill and driv-ing, twist-ed thoughts that grip and bind,
Speak your word that when we hear it all our de - mons shall de - part.

At Christ's voice the de - mon trem - bled, from its vic - tim
Doubts that stir the heart to pan - ic, fears dis - tort - ing
Clear our thought and calm our feel - ing, still the frac - tured,

mad - ly rushed,   While the crowd that   was   as - sem - bled
rea - son's sight,   Guilt that makes our   lov - ing   fran - tic,
war - ring soul.   By   the   pow - er   of   your   heal - ing

1–2

3

stood   in   won - der,   stunned and   hushed.
dreams that   cloud   the   soul   with   fright.
make   us   faith - ful,   true,   and   whole.

Thomas H. Troeger has stated: "'Silence! Frenzied Unclean Spirit' represented my personal desperation to come to terms with the meaning of demons and the profound emotional turmoil I encountered in many people when I was a pastor. I wanted to draw on the strength of Christ's exorcism for facing these painful situations."

Tune: AUTHORITY 8.7.8.7.D.
Carol Doran, 1984
Alternate tune: JEFFERSON

177 God of Change and Glory

1 Cor. 12:4–27

Al Carmines, 1973

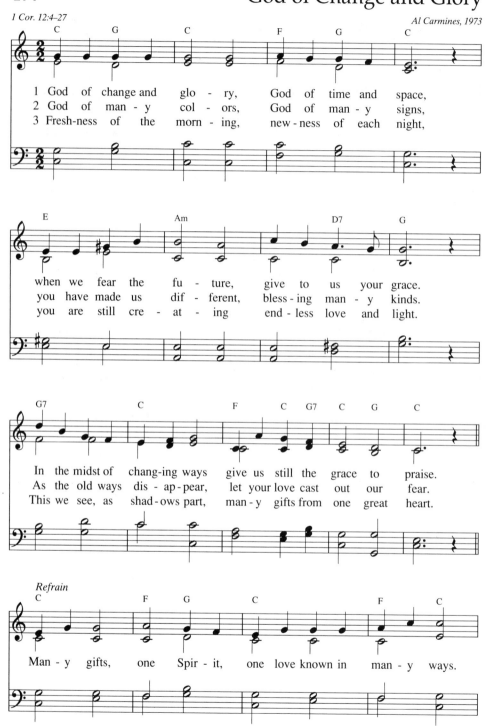

1 God of change and glo - ry, God of time and space,
2 God of man - y col - ors, God of man - y signs,
3 Fresh-ness of the morn - ing, new - ness of each night,

when we fear the fu - ture, give to us your grace.
you have made us dif - ferent, bless - ing man - y kinds.
you are still cre - at - ing end - less love and light.

In the midst of chang-ing ways give us still the grace to praise.
As the old ways dis - ap-pear, let your love cast out our fear.
This we see, as shad-ows part, man - y gifts from one great heart.

Refrain

Man - y gifts, one Spir - it, one love known in man - y ways.

Al Carmines, composer, playwright, performer, and teacher, has
served as minister for two United Church of Christ congregations
in New York City. This hymn, commissioned in 1973, was one
of the first modern texts to claim diversity as a gift from God.

Tune: KATHERINE 6.5.6.5.7.7.
Al Carmines, 1973

In our dif - fer - ence is bless-ing, from di - ver - si - ty we praise
one Giv-er, one Word, one Spir-it, one God known in man-y ways,
hal-low-ing our days. For the Giv-er, for the gifts, praise, praise, praise!

178 We Have the Strength to Lift and Bear

Mark 2:1–12   *Thomas H. Troeger, 1985; rev. 1993*

1 We have the strength to lift   and bear   a   friend's im - mo - bile weight,
2 It   was this hope   and trust that filled the   four who walked the road
3 The awk-ward-ness   of match-ing strides and one   an - oth - er's pace
4 Christ, give your church that sin - gle hope by   which those faith - ful four

The strength to watch and   nurse and care through hours   long and late,
And bore their friend whose limbs were stilled be - neath some hid - den load.
While hold - ing up   the   bed's two sides to keep their friend in place,
Could low - er down their friend by rope while oth - ers blocked the door.

Be - cause we trust in ways un-known the springs of health are stirred,
Each foot   a stone, each leg a rod, for years he lay in bed,
The   crowd - ed street, the roof of clay, the scribes who took of-fense—
Though we may lack your gift to heal, this task   is sure - ly ours:

And thus the mind, the flesh and bone re - ceive Christ's heal - ing word.
in   ter - ror of   a judg - ing god and par - a - lyzed by dread.
Not all of these could turn a - way those stub - born lov - ing friends.
To   bring to you the lost who feel their need of   gra - cious powers.

In writing this text based on the Mark narrative, Thomas H.   Tune: TALLIS' THIRD TUNE C.M.D.
Troeger recalled his own observations of various people,   *Thomas Tallis, c. 1557*
particularly nurses and spouses, who care for stroke victims.

We Yearn, O Christ, for Wholeness

179

Dosia Carlson, 1986; rev. 1993

1 We yearn, O Christ, for whole - ness and for your heal-ing touch;
2 We long to have com - pan - ions who trav - el by our side,
3 We need your liv - ing pres - ence, O Christ of Gal - i - lee,

too long have we felt help - less; our bur - dens seemed too much.
strong friends to call and an - swer with whom we are al - lied;
a pres-ence that re - vives us and sets our spir - its free.

For - get - ting all pre - tens - es we make our plead-ings heard,
As we lift up each oth - er when strug-gles lay us low,
No long - er are we fear - ful, your love per - vades each place.

in hope and ex - pec - ta - tion a - wait your gra-cious Word.
com - mu - ni - ty de - vel - ops; our faith and car - ing grow.
Em - pow - er us with cour - age to claim your heal-ing grace.

Dosia Carlson is noted for her ministry at Beatitudes United
Church of Christ in Phoenix, Arizona, and for her hymnwriting.
This text was inspired by a sermon given by Harold Wilke
during the International Year of Persons with Disabilities (1983).

Tune: PASSION CHORALE 7.6.7.6.D.
Hans Leo Hassler, 1601
Harm. J. S. Bach, 1719
For another harmonization, see 202

180   Blessed Are the Poor in Spirit

Matt. 5:3–12; Luke 6:20–23; John 20:29; 2 Cor. 5:17–18   *Rusty Edwards, 1993*

Unison

1 Blessed are the poor in spir-it: heav-en will some-day   be theirs.
2 Blessed all who thirst or hun-ger: right-eous-ly they will   be fed.
3 Each seek-ing peace and jus-tice   shall be known as God's own heir.

Blessed are the mourn-ing chil-dren: com-fort comes from One who cares.
Those who re-spond with mer-cy   will see mer-cy up a-head.
Blessed, too, are those ill-treat-ed   for what's good and right and fair.

Blessed the meek and pa-tient,   hav-ing cour-age to hang on.
Blessed the clean in spir-it—   beau-ti-ful, the pure in heart;
Blessed the New Cre-a-tion,   joy be-yond what we con-ceive;

Soon all earth they will in-her-it;   times of tri-als will be gone.
One day they will see their Mak-er,   nev-er-more to live a-part.
Blessed all those who trust the prom-ise: with-out see-ing, they be-lieve!

Howard M. Edwards III, who writes as Rusty Edwards, is an   Tune: ANNIKA'S DANCE   7.7.7.7.6.7.8.7.
ordained Lutheran pastor from Illinois. The tune for this new   *Jane Marshall, 1993*
Beatitudes paraphrase was composed especially to be interpreted
by liturgical dancer Annika Gustafson.

You Are Salt for the Earth, O People

181

Paraphr. by Marty Haugen, 1986; alt.

Matt. 5:13–15

1 You are salt for the earth, O peo-ple: salt for the reign of God!
2 You are a light on the hill, O peo-ple: light for the Cit-y of God!
3 You are a seed of the Word, O peo-ple: bring forth the reign of God!
4 We are a blessed and a pil-grim peo-ple: bound for the reign of God!

Share the fla-vor of life, O peo-ple: life in the Cit-y of God!
Shine so ho-ly and bright, O peo-ple: shine for the Cit-y of God!
Seeds of mer-cy and seeds of jus-tice, grow in the Cit-y of God!
Love our jour-ney and love our home-land: love is the Cit-y of God!

Refrain

Bring forth the reign of mer-cy, bring forth the reign of peace;

Bring forth the reign of jus-tice, bring forth the Cit-y of God!

During a residency at Holden Village, a retreat center in the state of Washington, Marty Haugen wrote this hymn to be used as a "processing song" for outdoor worship. The lectionary readings focusing on Jesus' teaching about the "reign of God" provided the basis for the text.

Tune: BRING FORTH Irr. with refrain
Marty Haugen, 1986

182   We Have Come at Christ's Own Bidding

Matt. 17:1–8; Mark 9:2–8; Luke 9:28–36   *Carl P. Daw, Jr., 1988*

1 We have come at Christ's own bid - ding to this high and
2 Light breaks through our clouds and shad - ows, splen - dor bathes the
3 Strength-ened by this glimpse of glo - ry, fear - ful lest our

ho - ly place, Where we wait with hope and long - ing for some
flesh-joined Word, Mo - ses and E - li - jah mar - vel as the
faith de - cline, We, like Pe - ter, find it tempt-ing to re -

to - ken of God's grace. Here we pray for new as -
heav - enly voice is heard. Eyes and hearts be - hold with
main and build a shrine. But true wor - ship gives us

sur - ance that our faith is not in vain, Search - ing
won - der how the Law and Proph - ets meet: Christ with
cour - age to pro - claim what we pro - fess, That our

like those first dis - ci - ples for a sign both clear and plain.
gar - ments drenched in bright - ness, stands trans - fig - ured and com-plete.
dai - ly lives may prove us peo - ple of the God we bless.

In his commentary on the text, hymnwriter Carl P. Daw, Jr.,
describes the "implicit comparison between the attitudes and
assumptions of the disciples on the Mount of the Transfiguration
and the expectations of present-day Christians as they gather
for worship."

Tune: HYFRYDOL 8.7.8.7.D.
Rowland H. Prichard, 1844
Arr. Ralph Vaughan Williams, 1906

Words Copyright © 1988 by Hope Publishing Company
Arrangement Copyright ©, Oxford University Press. From *The English Hymnal 1906.*

Jesus, Take Us to the Mountain   183

Jaroslav J. Vajda, 1991; alt.

Matt. 17:1–8; Mark 9:2–8; Luke 9:28–36;
John 19:30; Matt. 27:50–54; Mark 15:37–39

Unison

1 Je - sus, take us to the moun-tain, where, with Pe - ter, James, and John,
2 What do you want us to see there, that your close com-pan - ions saw?
3 What do you want us to hear there, that your dear dis - ci - ples heard?
4 Take us to that oth - er moun-tain where we see you glo - ri - fied,
5 We who have be - held your glo - ry, ris - en and as - cend - ed Christ,

We are daz-zled by your glo - ry, light as blind-ing as the sun.
Your di - vin - i - ty re - vealed there fills us with the self - same awe.
Once a - gain the voice from heav - en says of the In - car - nate Word:
Where you shout-ed, "It is fin - ished!" where for all the world you died.
Can - not help but tell the sto - ry, all that you have sac - ri - ficed;

There pre - pare us for the night by the vi - sion of that sight.
Clothed in flesh like ours you go matched to meet our dead - liest foe.
"Lis - ten, lis - ten, ev - ery - one, this is my be - lov - ed One!"
Hear the stunned cen - tu - ri - on: "This was God's be - lov - ed One!"
Say with Pe - ter, James, and John: "You are God's be - lov - ed One!"

Both text and tune were commissioned by St. Luke Lutheran
Church, Silver Spring, Maryland, to commemorate its fiftieth
anniversary. The hymnwriter, Jaroslav Vajda, tells of being
"as much at a loss for words contemplating the glory of the
transfigured Christ as were the disciples."

Tune: SILVER SPRING 8.7.8.7.7.7.
Carl F. Schalk, 1991
Alternate tune: IRBY

Music Copyright © 1991 by G.I.A. Publications, Inc.

184   O Wondrous Sight, O Vision Fair

Luke 9:28–36; Matt. 17:1–5; Mark 9:2–7   *Latin, "Sarum Breviary," 1495*
Transl. John Mason Neale, 1851; alt.

1. O won - drous sight, O vi - sion fair of glo - ry
2. From age to age the tale de - clare, how with the
3. The law and proph - ets there have place, two cho - sen
4. With shin - ing face and bright ar - ray, Christ deigns to
5. And faith - ful hearts are raised on high by this great

that the church shall share, Which Christ up - on the
three dis - ci - ples there, Where Mo - ses and E -
wit - ness - es of grace; The voice of God out
man - i - fest to - day What glo - ry shall be
vi - sion's mys - ter - y, For which in joy - ful

moun-tain shows, where bright - er than the sun, Christ glows!
li - jah meet, they with the Christ God's fu - ture greet.
from the cloud pro - claims the Hu - man One a - loud.
theirs be - yond, who live with - in God's lov - ing bond.
strains we raise the voice of prayer, the hymn of praise.

This tune was composed in honor of the defeat of France at Agincourt by England under Henry V. The words, "Deo gracias . . . ," were added in honor of the English king's wish that the glory for the victory be given to God.

Tune: DEO GRACIAS L.M.
"The Agincourt Song," England, c. 1415
For other harmonizations, see 209, 259

Savior, When in Tears and Dust

185

Robert Grant, 1815; alt.

1 Sav - ior, when in tears and dust, low we bow to you in trust,
2 By your help-less in - fant years, by your life of want and tears,
3 By your hour of dire de - spair, by your ag - o - ny of prayer,
4 By your deep ex - pir - ing groan, by the sad se - pul-chral stone,

When re - pen - tant, to the skies scarce we lift our weep-ing eyes,
By your days of sore dis-tress in the sav - age wil - der - ness,
By the cross, the nail, the thorn, pierc-ing spear, and tor - turing scorn,
By the vault whose cold a - bode held in vain the ris - ing God:

Mind-ful how you suf - fered pain that God's love in us might reign—
By the dread mys - te - rious hour of the in-sult - ing tempt-er's power:
By the gloom that veiled the skies o'er the dread-ful sac - ri - fice:
O from earth to realms of light, Christ re - stored in power and might,

Help us claim what we would be, hear our sol - emn lit - a - ny.
Turn, O turn a fa - voring eye, hear our sol - emn lit - a - ny.
Lis - ten to our hum-ble cry, hear our sol - emn lit - a - ny.
Lis - ten, lis - ten to the cry of our sol - emn lit - a - ny.

Robert Grant—English lawyer, member of Parliament, advocate general, humanitarian, and author of a number of significant hymns—was born in India. He returned near the end of his life to become governor of Bombay.

Tune: SPANISH HYMN 7.7.7.7.D.
Traditional melody
Arr. Benjamin Carr, 1824

186 Dust and Ashes Touch Our Face

Gen. 3:17–19; Ps. 51:1–12 *Brian Wren, 1989*

This hymn, exploring the different dimensions of repentance, was written for the choir of the United Church, Hyde Park, Chicago, with Ash Wednesday in mind. Brian Wren reminds us that the Holy Spirit is always with us, not only at Pentecost.

Tune: DUST AND ASHES Irr. with refrain
Hal H. Hopson, 1989

bring us liv-ing wa-ter, Ho - ly Spir - it, come.

Again We Keep This Solemn Fast

187

"Ex more docti mystico"
Attrib. to Gregory the Great (c. 540–604)
Transl. Peter J. Scagnelli (b. 1949); alt.

Matt. 6:1–6, 16–21

To be sung freely

1 A - gain we keep this sol-emn fast, a   gift   of   faith from a - ges past, This
2 The   law and proph-ets from of   old   in   fig - ured ways this Lent fore-told, Which
3 More spar-ing, there-fore, let   us make the words we speak, the food we take, Our
4 Let   us   a - void each harm-ful way that lures the   care - less mind a - stray; By
5 We   pray, O   bless-ed Three-in - One, our God while end - less   a - ges run, That

Lent which binds us   lov - ing - ly   to   faith   and   hope   and char - i - ty.
Christ, all   a - ges' Sov-ereign Guide, in   these   last   days   has sanc - ti - fied.
sleep, our   laugh-ter, ev - ery   sense, learn peace through ho - ly pen - i - tence.
watch-ful   prayer our spir - its   free   from schem - ing   of   the En - e - my.
this, our   Lent of   for - ty   days, may   bring   us   growth and give you praise.

Ascribed by some to Gregory the Great, this Latin hymn, "Ex more docti mystico," has been found in several manuscripts, the earliest dating from the tenth century.

Tune: ERHALT UNS, HERR L.M.
Adapt. from "Jesu, dulce cordium" in
Klug's Geistliche Lieder, *1543*
Harm. The New Century Hymnal, *1993*

188 Give Me a Clean Heart

Ps. 51:1–12 Margaret J. Douroux, 1970; alt.

Give me a clean heart so I may serve you.
God, fix my heart so that I may be used by you.
For I'm not wor - thy of all these bless - ings.
Give me a clean heart and I'll fol-low you.

Margaret J. Douroux, the daughter of a Baptist minister, is
known especially for this gospel song, which was recorded by
singer James Cleveland. Among her other popular songs found
in church hymnals is "God Is Not Dead."

Tune: DOUROUX 10.12.10.10.
Margaret J. Douroux, 1970
Arr. Albert Denis Tessier, 1987

Down at the Cross

189

Elisha A. Hoffman (1839–1929); alt.

Gal. 2:20

1 Down at the cross where my Sav - ior died, down where for cleans-ing from
2 I am so won-drous-ly saved from sin, Je - sus so sweet-ly a -
3 O pre-cious foun-tain that saves from sin, I am so glad I have
4 Come to this foun-tain so rich and sweet, cast your poor soul at the

sin I cried, there to my heart was the blood ap - plied—
bides with - in; there at the cross where Christ took me in—
en - tered in; there Je - sus saves me and keeps me clean—
Sav - ior's feet; plunge in to - day and be made com - plete—

Refrain

(1–4) Glo - ry to Christ's name. Glo - ry to Christ's name, glo - ry to Christ's

name; There to my heart was the blood ap-plied; glo-ry to Christ's name.

While Elisha Hoffman pastored several congregations, he was associated with evangelical publishing houses as editor or compiler of fifty songbooks. Although never formally trained in music, he wrote texts and tunes for more than 200 hymns.

Tune: DOWN AT THE CROSS
9.9.9.5. with refrain
John H. Stockton (1813–1877)

190 Beneath the Cross of Jesus

Isa. 32:2; Gal. 6:14   *Elizabeth C. Clephane, 1872; alt.*

1 Be - neath the cross of Je - sus I glad - ly take my stand,
2 Up - on the cross of Je - sus with - in my mind I see
3 I take, O cross, your shad - ow for my a - bid - ing place;

the shad - ow of a might - y rock with - in a wea - ry land;
the ver - y dy - ing form of One who suf - fered there for me;
I ask no oth - er sun - shine than the sun - shine of Christ's face;

A home with - in the wil - der - ness, a rest up - on the way,
And from my griev - ing heart with tears two won - ders I con - fess—
Con - tent to let the world go by, to know no gain or loss,

from the burn - ing of the noon - tide heat, and the bur - den of the day.
the won - ders of Christ's glo - rious love and my un - wor - thi - ness.
my sin - ful self my on - ly shame, my glo - ry all the cross.

Elizabeth Clephane was known during her short lifetime for her charitable work in her hometown of Melrose, Scotland. After her death, this hymn was compiled from several stanzas of a longer poem that had appeared in a popular Scottish religious magazine.

Tune: ST. CHRISTOPHER 7.6.8.6.8.6.8.6.
Frederick C. Maker, 1881

Before Your Cross, O Jesus

191

Ferdinand Q. Blanchard, 1929; alt.

Mark 8:34; Gal. 6:14; Phil. 1:27; 3:7–10

1 Be-fore your cross, O Je-sus,
   our lives are judged to-day;
   the mean-ing of our ea-ger strife
   is test-ed by your way.
   A-cross our rest-less liv--ing
   the light streams from your cross,
   and by its clear, re-veal-ing beams
   we mea-sure gain and loss.

2 The hopes that lead us on-ward,
   the fears that hold us back,
   our will to dare great things for God,
   the cour-age that we lack,
   The faith we keep in good--ness,
   our love, as low or pure,
   on all, the judg-ment of the cross
   falls stead-y, clear, and sure.

3 Yet hum-bly, in our striv-ing,
   we rise to face its test.
   We crave the power to do your will
   as once you did it best.
   On us let now the heal--ing
   of your great Spir-it fall,
   and make us brave and full of joy
   to an-swer to your call.

Ferdinand Q. Blanchard, moderator of the General Council of Congregational Churches (1942–1944), was active in missions and was a leading advocate of educational opportunity for African-Americans. This hymn was written for Euclid Avenue Congregational Church in Cleveland, Ohio, which he served for forty years.

Tune: ST. CHRISTOPHER 7.6.8.6.8.6.8.6.
Frederick C. Maker, 1881

When Jesus Wept

192

William Billings, 1770

John 11:35

1 When Je - sus wept, the fall - ing tear in mer - cy

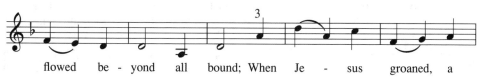

flowed be - yond all bound; When Je - sus groaned, a

trem - bling fear seized all the guilt - y world a - round.

William Billings served as choir leader at Old South Church (Congregational) in Boston. A self-taught singing-school teacher and composer, he also worked as a tanner. "When Jesus Wept" is especially beautiful when sung as a canon, with groups entering as indicated by the numbers above.

Tune: WHEN JESUS WEPT L.M.
William Billings, 1770
New England Psalm Singer

193

In the Cross of Christ I Glory

Gal. 6:14

John Bowring, 1825

1 In the cross of Christ I glo - ry, tower - ing
2 When the woes of life o'er - take me, hopes de -
3 When the sun of bliss is beam - ing light and
4 Bane and bless - ing, pain and plea - sure, by the
5 In the cross of Christ I glo - ry, tower - ing

o'er the wrecks of time; All the light of
ceive, and fears an - noy, Nev - er shall the
love up - on my way, From the cross the
cross are sanc - ti - fied; Peace is there that
o'er the wrecks of time; All the light of

sa - cred sto - ry gath - ers 'round its head sub - lime.
cross for - sake me: Lo! it glows with peace and joy.
ra - diance stream-ing adds more lus - ter to the day.
knows no mea - sure, joys that through all time a - bide.
sa - cred sto - ry gath - ers 'round its head sub - lime.

John Bowring's goal "to do something which may connect my work with the literature of the age" was attained with this enduring hymn. The gifted Bowring studied 200 languages and wrote extensively in many fields.

Tune: RATHBUN 8.7.8.7.
Ithamar Conkey, 1849
Alternate setting: TOMTER

In the Cross of Christ I Glory

John Bowring, 1825

Gal. 6:14

1 & 5 In the cross of Christ I glo - ry, tower - ing o'er the
2 When the woes of life o'er - take me, hopes de - ceive, and
3 When the sun of bliss is beam-ing light and love up -
4 Bane and bless - ing, pain and plea-sure, by the cross are

wrecks of time; All the light of sa - cred
fears an - noy, Nev - er shall the cross for -
on my way, From the cross the ra - diance
sanc - ti - fied; Peace is there that knows no

sto - ry gath - ers 'round its head sub - lime.
sake me: Lo! it glows with peace and joy.
stream-ing adds more lus - ter to the day.
mea - sure, joys that through all time a - bide. *(repeat first stanza)*

Composer Bruce Neswick wrote this tune to provide an alternative to the traditional one. It is named for Episcopal priest Patrick Tomter, in whose parish Neswick served as organist during his undergraduate studies at Pacific Lutheran University.

Tune: TOMTER 8.7.8.7.
Bruce Neswick (b. 1956)
Alternate setting: RATHBUN

195

On a Hill Far Away
(The Old Rugged Cross)

Heb. 12:2; James 1:12   *George Bennard, 1913; alt.*

1 On a hill far a-way stood an old rug-ged cross, the
2 Oh, that old rug-ged cross, so de-spised by the world, has a
3 In that old rug-ged cross, which bore Love so di-vine, a
4 To the old rug-ged cross I will ev-er be true, its

em-blem of suf-fering and shame; And I love that old cross where the
won-drous at-trac-tion for me; For the dear Lamb of God left the
won-drous beau-ty I see, For up-on that old cross Je-sus
shame and re-proach glad-ly bear; When God calls me some-day to my

dear-est and best for a world of lost sin-ners was slain.
glo-ry of heaven to bear it to cold Cal-va-ry.
suf-fered and died to par-don and sanc-ti-fy me.
home far a-way, there God's glo-ry for-ev-er I'll share.

Refrain

So I'll cher-ish the old rug-ged cross, till my
cross, the old rug-ged cross,

After serving as an officer in the Salvation Army, George Bennard was ordained by the Methodist Episcopal Church. In the midst of his travels through the Midwest conducting revival services, he was inspired to write this hymn.

Tune: THE OLD RUGGED CROSS Irr.
George Bennard, 1913

tro - phies at last I lay down; I will cling to the old rug - ged cross, the

cross, and ex - change it some-day for a crown.
old rug - ged cross,

When, like the Woman at the Well 196

Edith Sinclair Downing, 1992   *John 4:5–42*

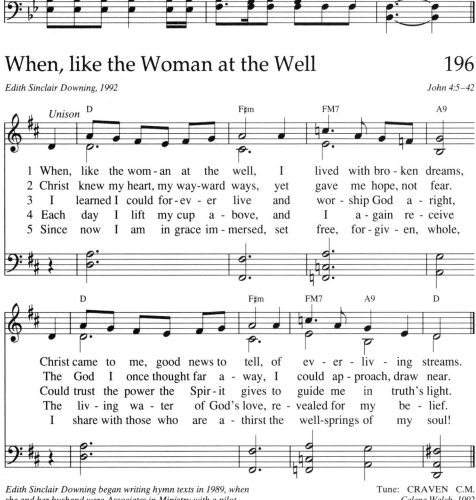

Unison   D   F♯m   FM7   A9

1 When, like the wom - an at the well, I lived with bro - ken dreams,
2 Christ knew my heart, my way-ward ways, yet gave me hope, not fear.
3 I learned I could for - ev - er live and wor - ship God a - right,
4 Each day I lift my cup a - bove, and I a - gain re - ceive
5 Since now I am in grace im - mersed, set free, for - giv - en, whole,

D   F♯m   FM7   A9   D

Christ came to me, good news to tell, of ev - er - liv - ing streams.
The God I once thought far a - way, I could ap - proach, draw near.
Could trust the power the Spir - it gives to guide me in truth's light.
The liv - ing wa - ter of God's love, re - vealed for my be - lief.
I share with those who are a - thirst the well-springs of my soul!

Edith Sinclair Downing began writing hymn texts in 1989, when
she and her husband were Associates in Ministry with a pilot
project of The Presbyterian Church (USA). Composer Celene
Welch named her tune in honor of professor Toni Craven of
Texas Christian University.

Tune: CRAVEN C.M.
Celene Welch, 1992

197 Jesus, Keep Me near the Cross

Gal. 6:14; Rev. 22:1–5   *Fanny Crosby, 1869; alt.*

1 Je - sus, keep me near the cross; there a pre - cious foun - tain,
2 Near the cross, a trem - bling soul, love and mer - cy found me;
3 Near the cross! O Lamb of God, bring its scenes be - fore me;
4 Near the cross I'll watch and wait, hop - ing, trust - ing ev - er,

free to all, a heal - ing stream, flows from Cal - vary's moun - tain.
there the bright and morn - ing star sheds its beams a - round me.
help me live from day to day with its shad - ow o'er me.
till I reach the gold - en strand just be - yond the riv - er.

Refrain

In the cross, in the cross, be my glo - ry ev - er,

till my ran - somed soul shall find rest be - yond the riv - er.

"Aunt Fanny" Crosby was an inspiration to people around the world. Blind from infancy, she wrote about 8,000 gospel hymns using more than 200 pseudonyms. William H. Doane, an active layperson and philanthropist in Cincinnati and close personal friend, often collaborated with her.

Tune: NEAR THE CROSS 7.6.7.6. with refrain
William H. Doane, 1869

Lift High the Cross

George William Kitchin (1827–1912)
Rev. by Michael Robert Newbolt, 1916; alt.

John 1:29–34; Rom. 5:6–11; 6:3–8; Rev. 7:9–17; 22:1–5

Refrain, in unison

Lift high the cross, the love of Christ pro-claim; Let

Last time, end

all a-dore and praise that sa-cred name.

Stanzas, in harmony

1	Come,	Chris-tians, fol-low	where our Sav-ior	trod, the
2	Each	new-born ser-vant	of the Cru-ci-	fied bears
3	O	Christ, once lift-ed	on the glo-rious	tree, your
4	Set	up your throne, that	earth's de-spair may	cease, be-
5	So	shall our song of	tri-umph ev-er	be: praise

to Refrain

Lamb	vic-to-rious,	Christ the Child of	God.
on	the brow the	seal of Christ who	died.
death	has brought us	life e-ter-nal-	ly.
neath	the shad-ow	of its heal-ing	peace.
to	the Cru-ci-	fied for vic-to-	ry.

Since its first inclusion in a U.S. hymnal in the 1970s, this hymn has become enormously popular. G. W. Kitchin and M. R. Newbolt were Church of England ministers. Sydney Nicholson was organist of Westminster Abbey.

Tune: CRUCIFER 10.10. with refrain
Sydney Hugo Nicholson, 1916

199

Alas! and Did My Savior Bleed
(At the Cross)

Gal. 2:20; 6:14; Phil. 2:2–12; Heb. 12:1–3

Isaac Watts, 1707; alt.
Refrain by Ralph E. Hudson, 1885; alt.

1 A - las! and did my Sav-ior bleed, and did my Sov-ereign die?
2 Was it for crimes that I have done, Christ groaned up-on the tree?
3 Well might the sun in shad-ows hide, and shut its glo-ries in,
4 But tears of grief can-not re-pay the debt of love I owe;

Would God de-vote that sa-cred head for sin-ners such as I?
A - maz-ing pit-y! Grace un-known! And love be-yond de-gree!
When Je-sus Christ my Sav-ior died for hu-man crea-tures' sin.
Here, Christ, I give my-self a-way as all that I can do!

Refrain

At the cross, at the cross where I first found the light, and the

bur-den of my heart rolled a-way,
rolled a-way, It was there by faith all my

After discharge from the Union army, Ralph Hudson taught music at Mt. Union College in Alliance, Ohio, where he founded a publishing company. He wrote the music for this Isaac Watts text and added a familiar camp-meeting chorus as a refrain.

Tune: HUDSON C.M. with refrain
Ralph E. Hudson, 1885
Alternate setting: MARTYRDOM

fears took flight, and now I am hap-py all the day.

Alas! and Did My Savior Bleed

200

Isaac Watts, 1707; alt.

Gal. 2:20; 6:14; Phil. 2:2–12; Heb. 12:1–3

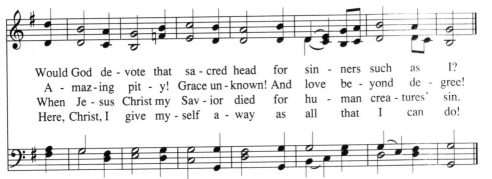

1 A - las! and did my Sav - ior bleed, and did my Sov-ereign die?
2 Was it for crimes that I have done, Christ groaned up - on the tree?
3 Well might the sun in shad-ows hide, and shut its glo - ries in,
4 But tears of grief can - not re - pay the debt of love I owe;

Would God de - vote that sa - cred head for sin - ners such as I?
A - maz-ing pit - y! Grace un - known! And love be - yond de - gree!
When Je - sus Christ my Sav - ior died for hu - man crea - tures' sin.
Here, Christ, I give my - self a - way as all that I can do!

This tune has also been called Avon, Fenwick, Drumclog, Inverness, and All Saints. Although published by Hugh Wilson (1827) and Robert Smith (1825), some claim it to be a Scottish folk tune. In early America, the hymn appeared in shape note books to at least five other tunes.

Tune: MARTYRDOM C.M.
(AVON)
Scottish folk tune
Alternate setting: HUDSON

201

An Outcast among Outcasts

Luke 17:11–19; Mark 15:32

Richard D. Leach, 199.

1 An out-cast a-mong out-casts, dis - missed with dou - ble scorn,
2 An out-cast a-mong out-casts, where three were cru - ci - fied,
3 For out-casts a-mong out-casts the bound-aries are re - drawn,

be - lit - tled by the la - bels: "un - clean" and "for-eign born"—
de - rid - ed by the oth - ers as they hung side by side—
by words, "Your faith has saved you," by cross and Eas-ter dawn.

came back with thanks for Je - sus, and then went on his way:
came back from death with pow - er, God had the fi - nal say:
The dis - tant longed-for cen - ters of pow - er, peace, and care,

An out - cast a-mong out - casts showed grate - ful faith that day.
An out - cast a-mong out - casts shows God to us to - day.
where life is free to flour - ish, are found now ev - ery-where.

United Church of Christ minister Richard D. Leach has served churches in Connecticut since 1978, when he graduated from Princeton Theological Seminary. He began writing hymns in 1987 and had his first texts published in 1989.

Tune: POST STREET 7.6.7.6.D.
Dan Damon, 1994

O God, How We Have Wandered 202

Kevin Nichols, 1980; alt.

Luke 15:11–32; 2 Cor. 5:16–20

1 O God, how we have wan - dered and hid - den from your face;
2 And now at length dis - cern - ing the e - vil that we do,
3 O God of all the liv - ing, both ban - ished and re - stored,

In fool - ish - ness have squan - dered your leg - a - cy of grace.
By faith we are re - turn - ing with hope and trust in you.
Com - pas - sion-ate, for - giv - ing, our peace and hope as - sured.

But how, in ex - ile dwell - ing, we turn with fear and shame,
In haste you come to meet us, and home re - joic-ing bring,
Grant now that our trans - gress - ing, our faith-less-ness may cease.

As dis - tant but com - pell - ing, you call us each by name.
In glad - ness there to greet us with calf and robe and ring.
Stretch out your hand in bless - ing, in par - don, and in peace.

The tune for this contemporary text appears five times in J. S. Bach's St. Matthew Passion, *and first appeared as a hymn setting in the early 1800s. It has an ecumenical history reaching back many centuries. Originally it was a German love song.*

Tune: PASSION CHORALE 7.6.7.6.D.
(HERZLICH TUT MICH VERLANGEN)
Melody by Hans Leo Hassler, 1601
Harm. J. S. Bach, 1729
For another harmonization, see 179

203 Ah, What Shame I Have to Bear

Luke 15:11–19

Sogo Matsumoto, 189
Transl. Esther Hibbard, 196

1 Ah, what shame I have to bear,
2 In this hut I sleep and wake,
3 Tat - tered sleeves are wet with dew

for I left my home To pur - sue an
tak - ing care of swine; No one has pit -
when I think of home. Wak - ing from my

emp - ty dream, spent my life in vain!
y on me: loud blows chil - ly wind.
fool - ish dreams, to my home I'll go.

This Japanese text provides an opportunity to imagine and enter into the experience of the prodigal child who longs for the forgiveness of a parent. Translator Esther Hibbard was a United Church of Christ missionary in Japan for many years.

Tune: IMAYO 7.5.7.5.
Japanese melody, 12th century

204 "Take Up Your Cross," the Savior Said

Mark 8:34

Charles W. Everest, 1883; alt.

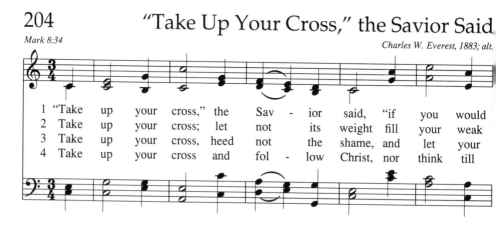

1 "Take up your cross," the Sav - ior said, "if you would
2 Take up your cross; let not its weight fill your weak
3 Take up your cross, heed not the shame, and let your
4 Take up your cross and fol - low Christ, nor think till

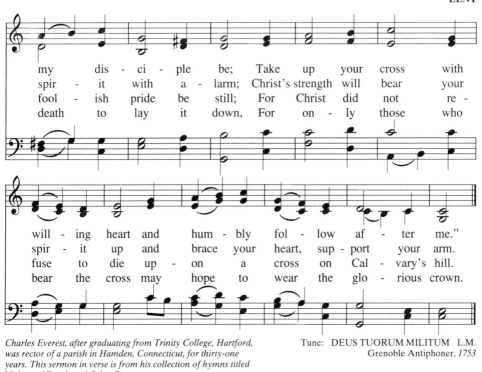

my	dis - ci - ple	be;	Take	up	your	cross	with
spir - it	with	a - larm;	Christ's	strength	will	bear	your
fool - ish	pride	be	still;	For	Christ	did	not	re -
death	to	lay	it	down,	For	on - ly	those	who

will - ing	heart and	hum - bly	fol - low	af - ter	me."
spir - it	up and	brace	your	heart,	sup - port	your	arm.
fuse	to die	up - on	a	cross	on	Cal - vary's	hill.
bear	the cross may	hope	to	wear	the	glo - rious	crown.

Charles Everest, after graduating from Trinity College, Hartford, was rector of a parish in Hamden, Connecticut, for thirty-one years. This sermon in verse is from his collection of hymns titled Visions of Death and Other Poems.

Tune: DEUS TUORUM MILITUM L.M.
Grenoble Antiphoner, 1753

Forty Days and Forty Nights   205

George Hunt Smyttan, 1856; alt.   Matt. 4:1–11; Heb. 2:18

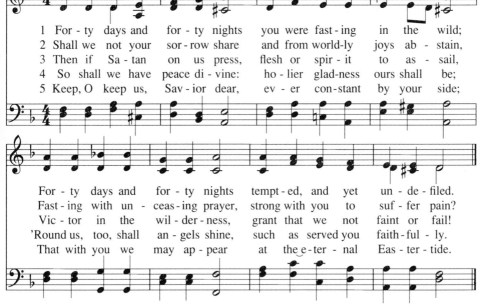

1 For - ty days and	for - ty nights	you were fast - ing	in the	wild;
2 Shall we not your	sor - row share	and from world - ly	joys ab - stain,
3 Then if Sa - tan	on us press,	flesh or spir - it	to as - sail,
4 So shall we have	peace di - vine:	ho - lier glad - ness	ours shall	be;
5 Keep, O keep us,	Sav - ior dear,	ev - er con-stant	by your	side;

For - ty days and	for - ty nights	tempt - ed, and	yet	un - de - filed.
Fast - ing with un - ceas-ing prayer,	strong with you	to	suf - fer pain?
Vic - tor in the	wil - der - ness,	grant that we	not	faint or fail!
'Round us, too, shall	an - gels shine,	such as served you	faith - ful - ly.
That with you we	may ap - pear	at the e - ter - nal	Eas - ter - tide.

The son of a doctor in Bombay, George Hunt Smyttan became a priest in the Church of England. He published several collections of verse. This hymn was one of three Lenten hymns that appeared in The Penny Post (1856).

Tune: HEINLEIN 7.7.7.7.
Attrib. to Martin Herbst, 1676

A Woman Came Who Did Not Count the Cost

Mark 14:3–9   Richard D. Leach, 1990

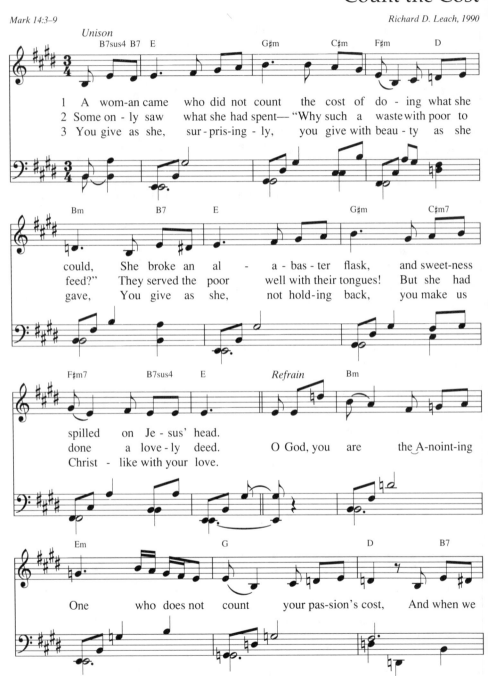

1 A wom-an came who did not count the cost of do - ing what she
2 Some on - ly saw what she had spent— "Why such a waste with poor to
3 You give as she, sur - pris-ing - ly, you give with beau - ty as she

could, She broke an al - a - bas - ter flask, and sweet-ness
feed?" They served the poor well with their tongues! But she had
gave, You give as she, not hold-ing back, you make us

spilled on Je - sus' head.
done a love - ly deed. *Refrain* O God, you are the A-noint-ing
Christ - like with your love.

One who does not count your pas-sion's cost, And when we

United Church of Christ minister Richard D. Leach has stated
that much of his inspiration as a hymnwriter comes during his
sermon preparations. The theme of this text—God anointing us,
as the woman anointed Jesus with perfume—was first developed
in a sermon, and then given poetic form.

Tune: WEXFORD CAROL L.M.D.
Irish folk melody
Arr. Arthur G. Clyde, 1994

gath - er you will spill the sweet-ness of your grace on us.

Just as I Am   207

Charlotte Elliott, 1836; alt.   *John 6:37; Eph. 2:14*

1 Just as I am, with - out one plea but that your
2 Just as I am, though tossed a - bout with man - y a
3 Just as I am, you will re - ceive, will wel - come,
4 Just as I am, your love un - known has bro - ken

blood was shed for me, And that you called in -
con - flict, many a doubt, Fight - ings and fears with -
par - don, cleanse, re - lieve; Be - cause your prom - ise
ev - ery bar - rier down; Now to be yours, and

vit - ing me, O Lamb of God, I come, I come!
in, with - out, O Lamb of God, I come, I come!
I be - lieve, O Lamb of God, I come, I come!
yours a - lone, O Lamb of God, I come, I come!

This text appeared in Charlotte Elliott's Invalid's Hymn Book,
published in England in 1836. Disabled at age thirty, she
continued a career of writing and editing. This hymn has been
translated into many languages.

Tune: WOODWORTH L.M.
William B. Bradbury, 1849

208

God Loved the World

John 3:16–17

Heiliges Lippen und Herzens Opfer, *Stettin, 1778*
Transl. August Crull, 1845; alt

1 God loved the world, and lov - ing gave
2 Christ Je - sus is the ground of faith,
3 If you are sick, if death is near,
4 Be of good cheer, for God in Christ

a won - drous gift, the lost to save,
who was made flesh and suf - fered death;
this truth your trou - bled heart can cheer;
for - gives the flock, by sin en - ticed,

That all who would in Christ be - lieve
All who con - fide in Christ a - lone
Christ Je - sus saves us all from death;
And jus - ti - fied by Je - sus' blood,

should ev - er - last - ing life re - ceive.
are built on this chief cor - ner - stone.
that is the firm - est ground of faith.
your bap - tism grants the high - est good.

Edward Miller, a skilled flutist in G. F. Handel's orchestra,
adapted Rockingham *from the tune* Tunbridge. *Miller named it*
for the Marquis of Rockingham, a patron and friend, and prime
minister of Great Britain.

Tune: ROCKINGHAM L.M.
Anon.
Adapt. Edward Miller, 1790

O Love, How Vast, How Flowing Free 209

Latin, 15th century
Transl. The New Century Hymnal, *1994*

*Matt. 4:1–11; Luke 4:1–13; Phil. 2:5–11;
John 17:1–26; 19:1–3, 16–18*

1 O Love, how vast, how flow - ing free, O Love how
2 Not as an an - gel vis - it - ing, nor form ce -
3 For us bap - tized, and fast - ing long, for us was
4 For us was beat - en, whipped, and tried, and tak - en

filled with ec - sta - sy, That God a hu - man
les - tial or - bit - ing, But born in flesh God
tempt - ed by the wrong, For us the pangs of
to be cru - ci - fied, So Love all this for

form should take, and mor - tal be for mor-tals' sake.
chose to be, robed in our own hu - man - i - ty.
hun - ger knew; for us the Tempt - er o - ver - threw.
us en - dured, and dy - ing, life for us pro - cured.

5 A-ris-ing from the dead a-gain,
    our Sov-ereign goes on high to reign;
    And sends the Spir-it to a-bide
    for strength and sol-ace at our side.

6 Then for God's bound-less love
        sing praise
    through end-less a-ges, count-less days;
    By Love we have been rec-on-ciled:
    sal-va-tion gained through
        God's own Child.

*Recounting the life of Christ, this hymn comes from an
anonymous fifteenth-century Latin hymn of twenty-three
stanzas. It has been described as a precursor of Christmas
and Epiphany carols.*

Tune: DEO GRACIAS L.M.
"The Agincourt Song," England, c. 1415
For another harmonization, see 184, 259

210

Said Judas to Mary

John 12:1–8

Sydney Carter, 1964; alt

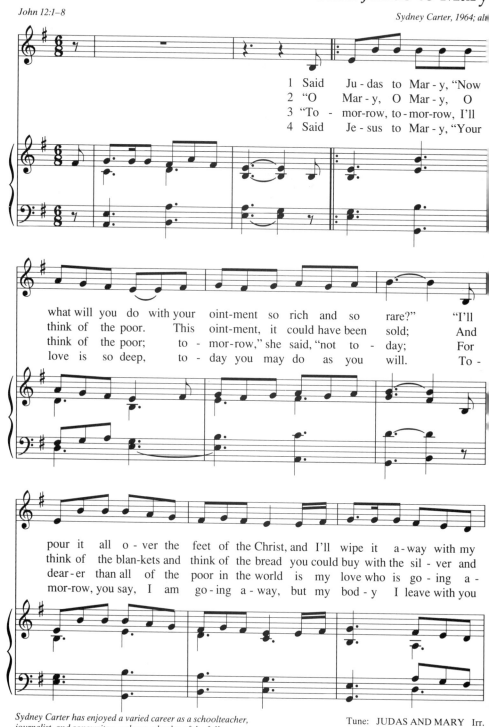

1 Said Ju - das to Mar - y, "Now
2 "O Mar - y, O Mar - y, O
3 "To - mor-row, to - mor-row, I'll
4 Said Je - sus to Mar - y, "Your

what will you do with your oint-ment so rich and so rare?" "I'll
think of the poor. This oint-ment, it could have been sold; And
think of the poor; to - mor-row," she said, "not to - day; For
love is so deep, to - day you may do as you will. To -

pour it all o - ver the feet of the Christ, and I'll wipe it a - way with my
think of the blan-kets and think of the bread you could buy with the sil - ver and
dear - er than all of the poor in the world is my love who is go - ing a -
mor-row, you say, I am go - ing a - way, but my bod - y I leave with you

Sydney Carter has enjoyed a varied career as a schoolteacher, journalist, and songwriter, and was a leader of the folk-song renaissance in English church music in the early 1960s. This hymn imagines the dialogue between Mary of Bethany, Judas Iscariot, and Jesus.

Tune: JUDAS AND MARY Irr.
Sydney Carter, 1964

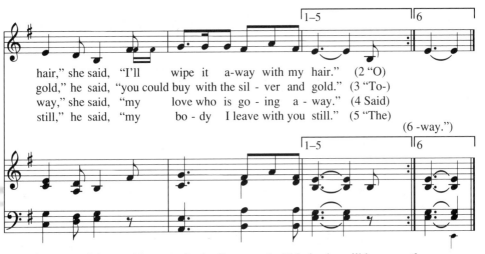

hair," she said, "I'll wipe it a-way with my hair." (2 "O)
gold," he said, "you could buy with the sil - ver and gold." (3 "To-)
way," she said, "my love who is go - ing a - way." (4 Said)
still," he said, "my bo - dy I leave with you still." (5 "The)

(6 -way.")

5 "The poor of the world are my bod-y,"
he said,
"to the end of the world they shall be.
The bread and the blan-kets you give
to the poor
you will know you have giv-en to me,"
he said,
"you'll know you have giv-en to me."

6 "My bod-y will hang on the cross
of the world
to-mor-row," he said, "not to-day.
And Mar-tha and Mar-y will find me
a-gain
and wash all my sor-row a-way,"
he said,
"and wash all my sor-row a-way."

Lord Jesus, Who through Forty Days 211

Claudia F. I. Hernaman, 1873; alt.   *Mark 1:12–13; Luke 4:1–13*

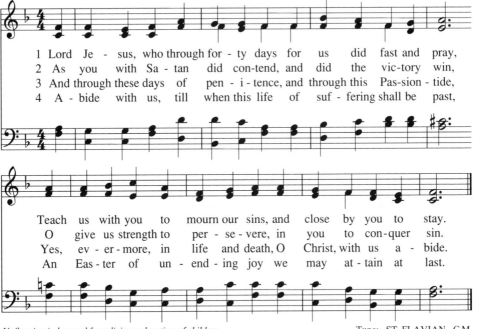

1 Lord Je - sus, who through for - ty days for us did fast and pray,
2 As you with Sa - tan did con-tend, and did the vic-tory win,
3 And through these days of pen - i - tence, and through this Pas-sion - tide,
4 A - bide with us, till when this life of suf - fering shall be past,

Teach us with you to mourn our sins, and close by you to stay.
O give us strength to per - se - vere, in you to con-quer sin.
Yes, ev - er - more, in life and death, O Christ, with us a - bide.
An Eas-ter of un - end - ing joy we may at - tain at last.

Unflagging in her zeal for religious education of children,
Claudia F. I. Hernaman wrote some 150 hymns. This one
appeared in her Child's Book of Praise *(1873).*

Tune: ST. FLAVIAN C.M.
Day's The Whole Booke of Psalms, *1562*

212   O Jesus Christ, May Grateful Hymns

Matt. 23:37–39; Luke 13:34–35   *Bradford Gray Webster, 1954; alt.*

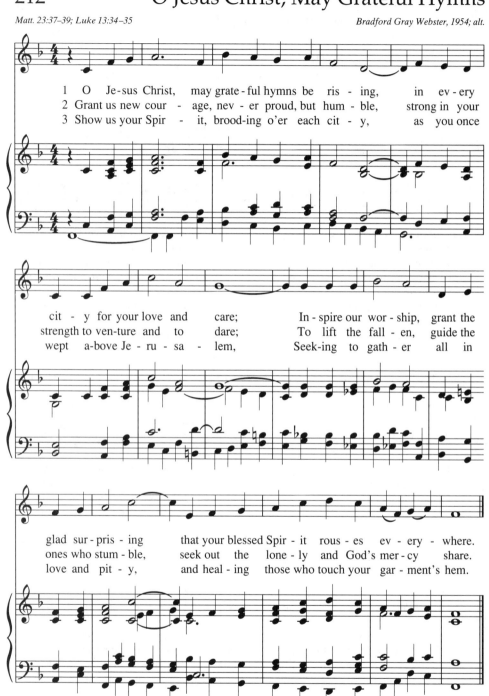

1 O Je-sus Christ, may grate-ful hymns be ris - ing, in ev-ery
2 Grant us new cour - age, nev - er proud, but hum - ble, strong in your
3 Show us your Spir - it, brood-ing o'er each cit - y, as you once

cit - y for your love and care; In - spire our wor - ship, grant the
strength to ven-ture and to dare; To lift the fall - en, guide the
wept a-bove Je - ru - sa - lem, Seek-ing to gath - er all in

glad sur - pris - ing that your blessed Spir - it rous - es ev - ery - where.
ones who stum - ble, seek out the lone - ly and God's mer - cy share.
love and pit - y, and heal - ing those who touch your gar - ment's hem.

This text, written for a Convocation of Urban Life in America,
was chosen by The Hymn Society for publication in Five New
Hymns on the City. *Bradford Webster, a Methodist minister,*
served churches in his native New York state for forty years.

Tune: CHARTERHOUSE 11.10.11.10.
David Evans, 1927

"Hosanna, Loud Hosanna"

213

Jennette Threlfall, 1873; alt.   *Mark 11:8–10; Matt. 21:15*

1 "Ho - san - na, loud ho - san - na," the lit - tle chil - dren sang;
2 From Ol - i - vet they fol - lowed a - mid a cheer-ing crowd,
3 "Ho - san - na in the high - est!" That an - cient song is ours.

through pil - lared court and tem - ple the love - ly an - them rang;
the vic - tor palm branch wav - ing, and chant-ing clear and loud.
We hail our great Re - deem - er and sing with all our powers:

To Je - sus, who had blessed them close fold - ed to his breast,
The one whom an - gels wor - ship rode on in low - ly state,
"Ho - san - na, Christ, we praise you with heart and life and voice.

the chil - dren sang their prais - es, the sim - plest and the best.
and glad to see the chil - dren, slowed down the don-key's gait.
Ho - san - na! In your pres - ence for - ev - er we'll re - joice!"

Jennette Threlfall of England, who was disabled by two accidents,
wrote hymns that inspired hope and courage in others. This text was
published in her collection Sunshine and Shadow.

Tune: ELLACOMBE C.M.D.
Gesangbuch der herzoglichen Wirtembergischen
katholischen Hofkapelle, *1784*

214

Mantos y Ramos
(Filled with Excitement)

Matt. 21:6–9; Luke 19:35–38; Mark 11:7; John 12:12–15

Rubén Ruíz Avila, 1972; alt.
Transl. Gertrude C. Suppe, 1979, 1987; alt.

1 Man - tos y ra - mos es - par - cien - do va
2 Co - mo en la en - tra - da a Je - ru - sa - lén,
1 Filled with ex - cite - ment, all the hap - py throng
2 As in that en - trance to Je - ru - sa - lem,

el pue - blo a - le - gre de Je - ru - sa - lén.
to - dos can - ta - mos a Je - sús el rey,
spread cloaks and branch-es on the cit - y streets.
ho - san - nas we will sing to Je - sus Christ,

A - llá a lo
al Cris - to
There in the
To our Re -

le - jos se vis - lum - bra ya
vi - vo que nos lla - ma hoy
dis-tance they be - gin to see,
deem-er who still calls to - day,

en un po - lli - no al Sal - va -
pa - ra se - guir - le con a -
there on a don-key, comes the
asks us to fol - low with our

Estribillo (Refrain)

dor Je - sús.
mor y fe.
Sav - ior, Christ.
love and faith.

Mien - tras mil vo - ces re - sue - nan por do - quier; ho -
From ev - ery cor - ner a thou-sand voic - es sing

Mexican church musician Rubén Ruíz Avila composed
this hymn for the choir of the United Methodist Church in
Covington, Virginia. It was first published in Canciones de Fe y
Compromiso *(1978) in the arrangement by Alvin Schutmaat.*

Tune: HOSANNA 10.10.10.10. with refrain
Rubén Ruíz Avila, 1972
Arr. Alvin Schutmaat, 1979

215   Ride On! Ride On in Majesty

Luke 19:36–38; Zech. 9:9   *Henry H. Milman, 1827; adapt. Lavon Bayler, 1993*

1 Ride on! Ride on in maj - es - ty!
2 Ride on! Ride on in maj - es - ty!
3 Ride on! Ride on in maj - es - ty!
4 Ride on! Ride on in maj - es - ty!

O Christ, with brave hu - mil - i - ty,
As crowds of peo - ple come to see
Ride on in hum - ble dig - ni - ty;
For you have set your peo - ple free

On low - ly colt, your road pur - sue,
And shout ho - san - nas, lift - ing high
Be - hold the ones you came to save
And we, re - mem - bering all your pain,

as palms and cloaks are spread for you.
their praise for one a - bout to die.
from sense - less life and end - less grave.
now meet a - gain to hail your reign.

Henry H. Milman, a priest of the Church of England,
served successively as professor of poetry at Oxford,
canon of Westminster, and dean of St. Paul's Cathedral,
London. He was also a successful playwright and historian.

Tune: ST. DROSTANE L.M.
John B. Dykes, 1862
Alternate tune: WINCHESTER NEW

All Glory, Laud, and Honor

216

Theodulph of Orléans, 9th century
Transl. John Mason Neale, 1854; alt.

Matt. 21:8–9

1 All glo - ry, laud, and hon - or to you, O Christ, we sing,
2 O Prom-ised One of Is - rael, of Da - vid's roy - al line,
3 As you re-ceived their prais - es, re - ceive our prayers to - day,

to whom the lips of chil - dren made sweet ho - san-nas ring!
the one called "God's be - lov - ed," of flesh and yet di - vine,
whose jus - tice and whose mer - cy and sov-ereign-ty hold sway.

The peo-ple of the He - brews with palms a - dorned your way;
To you, be - fore your pas - sion, they sang their hymns of praise;
All glo-ry, laud, and hon - or to you, O Christ, we sing,

our praise and prayer and an - thems we of - fer you this day.
to you, now high ex - alt - ed, our mel - o - dy we raise.
to whom the lips of chil - dren made sweet ho - san-nas ring!

Brought to France by Charlemagne, Theodulph became
bishop of Orléans but was later imprisoned by Charlemagne's
successor. According to legend, he was released when the
king, Louis the Pious, heard him sing this hymn from prison.

Tune: ST. THEODULPH 7.6.7.6.D.
(VALET WILL ICH DIR GEBEN)
Melchior Teschner, 1615
For another setting, see 217

217

All Glory, Laud, and Honor

Matt. 21:8–9

Theodulph of Orléans, 9th century
Transl. John Mason Neale, 1854; alt.

1 All glo - ry, laud, and hon - or to you, O Christ, we
2 O Prom - ised One of Is - rael, of Da - vid's roy - al
3 As you re - ceived their prais - es, re - ceive our prayers to -

sing, to whom the lips of chil - dren made sweet ho -
line, the one called "God's be - lov - ed," of flesh, and
day, whose jus - tice and whose mer - cy, and sov - ereign -

san - nas ring! The peo - ple of the He - brews with
yet, di - vine, To you, be - fore your pas - sion, they
ty hold sway. All glo - ry, laud, and hon - or to

palms a - dorned your way; our praise and prayer and
sang their hymns of praise; to you, now high ex -
you, O Christ, we sing, to whom the lips of

*Vérne de la Peña is a Philippine composer and ethno-
musicologist whose studies have focused on the music of
indigenous peoples of Southeast Asia and the Pacific. His
tune, Eulogia, is reminiscent of that music through the use
of the "tritone" and ostinato accompaniment.*

Tune: EULOGIA 7.6.7.6.D.
Vérne de la Peña, 1994
For another setting, see 216

an - thems   we   of - fer you this   day.
alt - ed,   our   mel - o - dy we   raise.
chil-dren   made sweet ho - san-nas   ring!

Ah, Holy Jesus   218

Johann Heermann, 1630
Paraphr. by Robert Bridges, 1899; alt.

Isa. 53:3–5; John 1:11; 18:15–17

1 Ah, ho - ly Je - sus, how have you of - fend - ed, that mor-tal
2 Who was the guilt - y? Who brought this up - on you? It is my
3 For me, kind Je - sus, was your in - car - na - tion, your mor-tal
4 There-fore, kind Je - sus, since I can-not pay you, I do a -

judg - ment has on you de - scend - ed? By foes de - rid - ed,
trea - son, Je - sus, that has slain you. And I, dear Je - sus,
sor - row, and your life's ob - la - tion, Your death of an - guish
dore you, and will ev - er pray you, Think on your pit - y

by your own re - ject - ed, O most af - flict - ed!
I it was de - nied you; I cru - ci - fied you.
and your bit - ter pas - sion, for my sal - va - tion.
and your love un - swerv - ing, not my de - serv - ing.

Based on an eleventh-century Latin meditation by Jean de
Fécamp, this is one of many fine hymns by Johann Heermann.
Though poor, Heermann's parents prepared him for the
Lutheran pastorate. Much of his ministry took place during
the Thirty Years' War.

Tune: HERZLIEBSTER JESU 11.11.11.5.
Johann Crüger, 1640

219 Journey to Gethsemane

John 18:1–20:18 *James Montgomery, 1820; alt.*

1 Jour - ney to Geth - se - ma - ne, go and feel the
2 Fol - low then to Pi - late's hall, view the Lord of
3 Cal - vary's mourn - ful moun - tain climb, see the Sav - ior
4 Ear - ly has - ten to the tomb, hear the cry of

tempt - er's power; Your Re - deem - er's con - flict see,
life ar - raigned; Crowned with thorns and mocked by all,
lift - ed high, Mark the mir - a - cle of time,
great sur - prise; Then the si - lence in the room,

watch the an - guish of this hour; Do not hide or
faith - ful - ly this pain sus - tained; Great - er still than
God's own Child is sac - ri - ficed; "It is fin - ished!"
Je - sus there no long - er lies: Christ is ris - en!

turn a - way: learn from Je - sus how to pray.
shame or loss, Je - sus now must face the cross.
Je - sus cries: learn from Je - sus how to die.
Re - al - ize that with Christ we, too, may rise.

James Montgomery, born of Moravian missionary parents,
edited a newspaper in England. Risking imprisonment, he
published articles advocating human rights, including the
abolition of slavery. He wrote more than 400 hymns.

Tune: REDHEAD NO. 76 7.7.7.7.7.7.
Richard Redhead, 1853

Sing, My Tongue

220

Venantius Honorius Fortunatus (530–609)
Transl. The New Century Hymnal, 1995

Unison

1 Sing, my tongue, the glo - rious bat - tle, right has tri - umphed
2 Since the first tree brought earth sor - row, griev - ing, God then
3 Thir - ty years of life com - plet - ed, now the hu - man
4 Of all trees is none so faith - ful, none of such no -

o - ver wrong; Now the cross stands as the to - ken
chose the way: Chose the tree to bear the Sav - ior,
form is spent; Born to fill this sa - cred mo - ment,
bil - i - ty As the cross, whose leaves, and blo - ssoms,

of the strug - gle, fierce and long; Christ the vic - tim
chose in man - ger poor to lay; Thus the plan of
fac - ing death with full in - tent, For the sac - ri -
and whose fruit shall match - less be— Sweet - est wood and

now is vic - tor, sing the no - ble tri - umph song.
our sal - va - tion: God for all our sin would pay.
fice of a - ges, to the cross the Lamb is sent.
nails of i - ron, sweet weight bear - ing grace - ful - ly.

Taken from a long poem by Fortunatus, bishop of Poitiers,
France, this hymn tells a story beginning with the tree in the
Garden of Eden and ending with the cross. It was found in
most medieval breviaries and missals.

Tune: FORTUNATUS NEW   8.7.8.7.8.7.
Carl Schalk (b. 1929)

221   The Royal Banners Forward Fly

Venantius Honorius Fortunatus (530–609)

Isa. 52:13; 53:4–5; John 19:17–18, 31–34   *Transl.* The New Century Hymnal, *1994*

1 The roy - al ban - ners for - ward fly, the cross, their
2 O sa - cred bod - y, wound-ed side by cru - el
3 The mys - tic proph - e - cy of old, which Da - vid
4 O won-drous tree by God or - dained, though now with

stan - dard, lights the sky; The mys - ter - y: as
spear is o - pened wide, That wa - ter stream - ing
faith - ful - ly fore - told: That God on earth should
roy - al pur - ple stained, Your bur - den once to

Life was slain, through death, e - ter - nal life to gain.
mixed with blood might cleanse us in the pre - cious flood.
sov - ereign be, ful - filled as God reigns from a tree.
all dis - played, the limbs on which our sin was weighed.

*This early hymn by Fortunatus was first sung as a processional
on November 19, 569, and has been in general use at Passiontide
at least since the tenth century. In more recent tradition it is sung
on Good Friday.*

Tune: GONFALON ROYAL L.M.
Percy C. Buck, 1918
Alternate tune: ERHALT UNS, HERR

My Song Is Love Unknown

222

Samuel Crossman, 1664; alt.

2 Cor. 5:15–19; Heb. 5:7–10

1 My song is love un - known, my Sav - ior's love to me,
2 God left the rich - est throne sal - va - tion to be - stow;
3 Some - times they threw down palms and sweet - est prais - es sang.
4 What has my Sov - ereign done? What makes this rage and spite?
5 I sing my plain be - lief, one song my heart out - pours:

Love to the love - less shown, that they might love - ly be.
But Christ as flesh and bone the world re - fused to know.
Ho - san - nas and glad psalms through streets and mar - kets rang.
Christ gave new strength to run, re - stored the gift of sight.
Nev - er was pain nor grief, nev - er was love like yours.

O who am I, that for my sake my God should take frail
But, O my Friend, my Friend in - deed, who at my need did
Then "Cru - ci - fy!" is all their breath, for blood and death they
Sweet in - ju - ries! Yet they at these them - selves dis - please, and
This is my Friend, in whose sweet praise I all my days could

flesh and die? My God should take frail flesh and die?
life ex - pend; who at my need did life ex - pend.
thirst and cry; for blood and death they thirst and cry.
'gainst Christ rise; them - selves dis - please, and 'gainst Christ rise.
glad - ly spend; I all my days could glad - ly spend.

First published in 1664 by Samuel Crossman, one of the first writers of English hymns, this hymn of praise for Christ's love was not appreciated until 200 years later. The tune was named for the parish in northeastern Wales where the composer served as vicar.

Tune: RHOSYMEDRE 6.6.6.6.8.8.8.
John D. Edwards, c. 1840

223   What Wondrous Love Is This

John 19:17; Rev. 5:13

19th century, United States; alt.
First published in Mercer's Cluster, 1836

1 What won-drous love is this, O my soul! O my soul! What
2 To God and to the Lamb I will sing, I will sing, to
3 And when from death I'm free, I'll sing on, I'll sing on, and

won-drous love is this, O my soul!   What won-drous love is
God and to the Lamb, I will sing;   To God and to the
when from death I'm free, I'll sing on!   And when from death I'm

this! that Christ should come in bliss to bear the heav-y cross for my
Lamb who is the great I Am, while mil - lions join the theme, I will
free, I'll sing and joy - ful be, and through e - ter - ni - ty I'll sing

soul, for my soul, to bear the heav-y cross for my soul!
sing, I will sing; while mil - lions join the theme, I will sing.
on, I'll sing on, and through e - ter - ni - ty I'll sing on!

This anonymous folk hymn, with its modal (dorian) tune, has appeared in many versions. William Walker, compiler of Southern Harmony, one of the most important nineteenth-century tune books in the United States, lived and died in Spartanburg, South Carolina.

Tune: WONDROUS LOVE 12.9.12.12.9.
(CHRISTOPHER)
Appendix to Wm. Walker's Southern Harmony, c. 1843
Harm. The New Century Hymnal, 1993

When I Survey the Wondrous Cross 224

Isaac Watts, 1707; alt. Gal. 6:14; Phil. 3:7–8

1 When I sur - vey the won - drous cross,
2 For - bid it, then, that I should boast,
3 From sa - cred head, from hands, and feet,
4 Were the whole realm of na - ture mine,

on which the Christ of glo - ry died,
save in the death of Christ, my God;
sor - row and love flow min - gled down!
that were a pres - ent far too small;

My rich - est gain I count but loss,
All the vain things that charm me most
Did e'er such love and sor - row meet,
Love so a - maz - ing, so di - vine,

and pour con - tempt on all my pride.
I sac - ri - fice them to Christ's blood.
or thorns com - pose so rich a crown?
de - mands my soul, my life, my all.

Originally titled "Crucifixion to the World by the Cross of Christ," this hymn has been acclaimed as one of the finest in the English language. Isaac Watts' hymnody grew out of his dissatisfaction with the restraints of the metrical psalters.

Tune: HAMBURG L.M.
Lowell Mason, 1825

225   It Was a Sad and Solemn Night

Mark 14:22–25; 1 Cor. 11:23–26   *Isaac Watts, 1709; alt.*

1 It was a sad and sol - emn night, when powers of earth
2 Be - fore the mourn-ful scene be - gan, our Je - sus blessed
3 "This is my bod - y, broke for sin, re - ceive and eat
4 "Share this, my feast, till time shall end, in mem - ory of
5 O Christ your feast we cel - e - brate; we show your death,

and hell a - rose A - gainst the Child of
and broke the bread; What love through all these
the liv - ing food"; Then took the cup and
your dy - ing friend: Meet at my ta - ble
we sing your name, Till you re - turn, and

God's de - light, whom friends be - trayed to wick - ed foes.
ac - tions ran, what won-drous words of love were said!
blessed the wine, "This the new cov - enant in my blood."
and re - call the love which God has shown to all."
we shall eat the mar - riage sup - per of the Lamb.

Isaac Watts, often considered the founder of English hymnody, recalls very powerfully in this hymn the Maundy Thursday events. The meal in the upper room is recounted, and the great marriage feast of the Lamb is anticipated.

Tune: BOURBON L.M.
Melody attrib. to Freeman Lewis, 1825
Harm. Louise McAllister (1913–1960)
Alternate tune: ERHALT UNS, HERR

O Sacred Head, Now Wounded   226

Medieval Latin, attrib. to Bernard of Clairvaux (1091–1153)   Isa. 53; John 19:1–3
German paraphr. by Paul Gerhardt, 1656
Transl. James W. Alexander, 1830; alt.

1 O sa - cred Head, now wound - ed, with grief and shame weighed down,
2 What you, dear Sav - ior, suf - fered was all for sin - ners' gain;
3 What lan - guage shall I bor - row to thank you, dear - est friend;

Now scorn - ful - ly sur - round - ed with thorns, your on - ly crown,
Mine, mine was the trans - gres - sion, but yours the dead - ly pain.
For this your dy - ing sor - row, your pit - y with - out end?

How pale you are with an - guish, with sore a - buse and scorn!
Lo, here I fall, my Sav - ior, for I de - serve your place;
May I be yours for - ev - er; and though my days be few,

How does your vis - age lan - guish which once was bright as morn!
Look on me with your fa - vor, O grant to me your grace.
O Sav - ior, let me nev - er out - live my love for you!

This hymn is drawn from an extended Latin poem in seven sections, each addressed to a member of Christ's body on the cross. It comes to us by way of a German translation by Lutheran pastor and hymnwriter Paul Gerhardt.

Tune: PASSION CHORALE 7.6.7.6.D.
(HERZLICH TUT MICH VERLANGEN)
Melody by Hans Leo Hassler, 1601
Harm. J. S. Bach, 1729
For another harmonization, see 179

227   Christ at Table There with Friends

Matt. 26:39; Mark 14:36; Luke 22:42;
John 6:47–51; 1 Cor. 11:23–25

Anabel S. Miller, 1982; rev. 1994

1 Christ at ta - ble there with friends shar - ing bread and wine, and then
2 In the gar - den Je - sus bows. Harsh the cry that ris - es now:
3 "Yet, your will, not mine, be done. For this pur - pose I am come.
4 At our ta - ble Je - sus stands, Word of God with nail - scarred hands.

Speak - ing words of mys - ter - y:
"Fa - ther, some way let it be!
Thus to make all peo - ple new I
"Come, re - ceive the mys - ter - y.

"Thus re - mem - ber me, thus re - mem - ber me."
Take this cup from me, take this cup from me!"
take this cup from you, I take this cup from you."
Take this cup from me, take this cup from me."

Anabel Miller, born in China of American missionary parents,
wrote this poem during Lent in 1982. Ten years later, she shared
it with composer Emma Lou Diemer, who served as organist at
her Presbyterian church in California. Diemer recognized its
potential as a hymn text, and supplied the musical setting.

Tune: MAUNDY THURSDAY 7.7.7.5.5.
Emma Lou Diemer, 1992

Ruler of Life, We Crown You Now   228

Jennie Evelyn Hussey, 1921; alt.   *Matt. 26:36–39; Mark 14:32–36; 16:1–2; Luke 24:1–10; John 19:2; 20:11–13*

1 Rul - er of life, we crown you now as we your glo - ry see;
2 Show us the tomb where you were laid, ten - der - ly mourned and wept;
3 Let us, like Mar - y, through the gloom, come with a gift for you;
4 May we be will - ing, Christ, to bear dai - ly our cross for you,

Lest we for - get your thorn-crowned brow, lead us to Cal - va - ry.
An - gels in robes of light ar - rayed guard-ed you while you slept.
Show to us now the emp - ty tomb lead - ing to life a - new.
E - ven your cup of grief to share; your love will see us through.

Refrain

Lest we for-get Geth - sem - a - ne, lest we for-get your ag - o - ny,

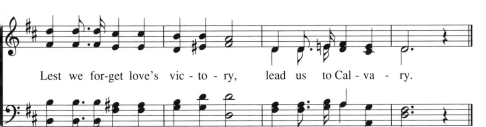

Lest we for-get love's vic - to - ry, lead us to Cal - va - ry.

A lifelong resident of New Hampshire, Jennie Evelyn Hussey began to write poems when she was eight and published her first hymns when she was twenty-four. Although her family had Congregational ties, Hussey was active in the Society of Friends.

Tune: DUNCANNON C.M. with refrain
William J. Kirkpatrick, 1921

229

Were You There?

John 19:16–18; 20:11–17

African-American spiritual

1 Were you there when they cru - ci - fied my Lord?
2 Were you there when they nailed him to the tree? Were you there?
3 Were you there when God wept at Mar - y's cry?
4 Were you there when Christ rose up from the tomb?

Were you there when they cru - ci - fied my Lord?
Were you there when they nailed him to the tree? Were you there?
Were you there when God wept at Mar - y's cry?
Were you there when Christ rose up from the tomb?

O some-times it caus-es me to trem-ble, trem-ble, trem-ble.

Were you there when they cru - ci - fied my Lord?
Were you there when they nailed him to the tree? Were you there?
Were you there when God wept at Mar - y's cry?
Were you there when Christ rose up from the tomb?

While many spirituals begin solemnly but end on a high pitch of praise, this is one of the true "sorrow songs" that W. E. B. DuBois spoke about in his book The Souls of Black Folk.

Tune: WERE YOU THERE Ir▪
African-American spiritua
Arr. Joyce Finch Johnson, 199▪

Come, You Faithful, Raise the Strain

230

Attrib. to John of Damascus (c. 696–c. 754 C.E.)
Transl. John Mason Neale, 1872; alt.

Exod. 15; Luke 24

1 Come, you faith - ful, raise the strain of tri - um - phant glad - ness;
2 Spring has dawned on earth to - day; Christ has burst from pris - on,
3 Now the joy - ous sea - son, bright with the day of splen - dor,
4 Nei - ther might the gates of death, nor the tomb's dim por - tal,

God has brought all Is - ra - el in - to joy from sad - ness;
And from three days' sleep in death as the sun has ris - en;
With the roy - al feast of feasts, comes its joys to ren - der;
Nor the watch - ers, nor the seal hold you as a mor - tal;

Loosed from Pha - raoh's bit - ter yoke Ja - cob's sons and daugh - ters;
All the win - ter of our sins, long and gray, is fly - ing
Comes to glad Je - ru - sa - lem who with true af - fec - tion
But to - day a - mid the twelve you still stand, be - stow - ing

Led them with un - moist-ened foot through the Red Sea wa - ters.
From the Light, to whom we give laud and praise un - dy - ing.
Wel-comes in un - wear - ied strains Je - sus' res - ur - rec - tion.
Peace and joy which ev - er - more pass - es hu - man know - ing.

Little is known of St. John of Damascus, an early Greek theologian, but his writings have survived. Among these are poems that have been made into hymns and some that have been integrated into Greek Orthodox liturgy.

Tune: ST. KEVIN 7.6.7.6.D.
Arthur S. Sullivan, 1872

231   Because You Live, O Christ

Luke 24:1–10   Shirley Erena Murray, 198?

1 Be - cause you live, O Christ, the gar - den of the
2 Be - cause you live, O Christ, the spir - it bird of
3 Be - cause you live, O Christ, the rain - bow of your

world has come to flow - er, the shad-ows of the tomb
hope is freed for fly - ing, our ca - ges of de - spair
peace will span cre - a - tion, the col - ors of your love

are flood - ed with your res - ur - rec - tion pow - er.
no long - er keep us closed and life - de - ny - ing.
will draw all hu - man - kind to ad - o - ra - tion.

The stone has rolled a - way and death can - not im - pris - on! O

*New Zealand hymnwriter Shirley Erena Murray expressed
her aims in writing this new text for the beloved Easter tune
Vruechten: "I wanted a fresh expression of community
joyfulness, with light, color, and the vision of the covenant
rainbow through the Resurrection."*

Tune: VRUECHTEN 6.7.6.7.D.
*Melody in David's Psalmen, 1685
J. Oudaen, Amsterdam*

sing this   Eas - ter   Day,   for   Je - sus Christ has   ris - en,   has

ris - en, has   ris - en, has   ris   -   en!

This Joyful Eastertide

232

George R. Woodward, 1894; alt.

This text may be used with the above tune as a canticle for Easter.

This joy-ful Eas-ter-tide, a-way with sin and sor---row!
My love, the Cru-ci-fied, has sprung to life this mor---row.
Had Christ, who once was slain,
    not burst from three days' pris-on,
    Our faith had been in vain.
But now has Christ a-ris-en, a-ris-en, a-ris-en;
    But now has Christ a-ris---en!

George R. Woodward was a Cambridge Scholar and served various parishes in England. He collaborated on the editing and publishing of several collections of carols and hymns.

Tune: VRUECHTEN 6.7.6.7.D.
Melody in David's Psalmen, 1685
J. Oudaen, Amsterdam

233 Christ the Lord Is Risen Today

Matt. 28:5–8; 1 Cor. 15:20–22; 54–57

Charles Wesley, 1739; alt.

1 Christ the Lord is risen to-day, Al - le - lu - ia!
2 Let the Vic-tor's peo-ple sing, Al - le - lu - ia!
3 Love's re-deem-ing work is done, Al - le - lu - ia!
4 Soar we now where Christ has led, Al - le - lu - ia!

Mor - tal tongues and an - gels say: Al - le - lu - ia!
Where, O death, is now your sting? Al - le - lu - ia!
Fought the fight, the bat - tle won, Al - le - lu - ia!
Fol - lowing our ex - alt - ed Head, Al - le - lu - ia!

Raise your joys and tri - umphs high, Al - le - lu - ia!
Dy - ing once, Christ lives to save, Al - le - lu - ia!
Death in vain for - bids Christ rise, Al - le - lu - ia!
Made like Christ, like Christ we rise, Al - le - lu - ia!

Sing, glad heavens, and earth re - ply: Al - le - lu - ia!
Where your vic - to - ry, O grave? Al - le - lu - ia!
God has o - pened par - a - dise, Al - le - lu - ia!
Ours the cross, the grave, the skies, Al - le - lu - ia!

The unknown editor of Lyra Davidica *wanted music with more movement and spirit than found in the grave, slow-paced psalm tunes, with one note to a syllable. Easter Hymn was among the first of a new popular style.*

Tune: EASTER HYMN 7.7.7.7. with alleluias
Arr. from Lyra Davidica, *London, 1708*

I'll Shout the Name of Christ Who Lives

234

Vivincio L. Vinluan, 1980; alt.

Rom. 6:5–11

1 I'll shout the name of Christ who lives,
2 Dear broth - ers sing a - mong all here,
3 Once more we shout our joy and praise

who lives, who lives, that all might live;
and leap with joy, my sis - ters dear;
to One we love, whose throne is grace,

Christ broke death's power at Cal - va - ry,
A - lone at home we seek our peace,
Whose way is Life, whose Word ful - fills

and now I know from sin I'm free.
there Je - sus comes to bring re - lease.
as we in glad - ness do God's will.

This contemporary Filipino hymn incorporates a musical motive from a traditional folk song, "Bahay Kubo." It was published in the 1983 collection of Asian-American hymns, Hymns from the Four Winds, edited by I-to Loh.

Tune: BAHAY KUBO L.M.
Wesley Tactay Tabayoyong, 1981
Based on a Philippine folk song

¡Cristo Vive
(Christ Is Living)

1 Cor. 15:54–57; Luke 24:1–10; Col. 1:15–20; Rom. 5:12–21

Nicolás Martínez, 1960; alt.
English version, Carolyn Jennings, 199

At a lively tempo
Unison

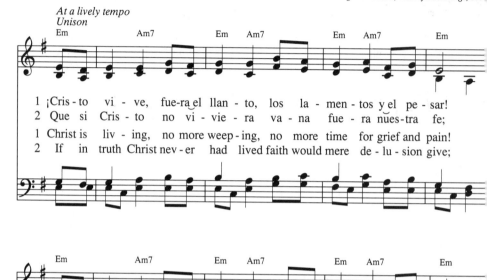

1 ¡Cris - to vi - ve, fue-ra el llan - to, los la - men - tos y el pe - sar!
2 Que si Cris - to no vi - vie - ra va - na fue - ra nues-tra fe;
1 Christ is liv - ing, no more weep-ing, no more time for grief and pain!
2 If in truth Christ nev - er had lived faith would mere de - lu - sion give;

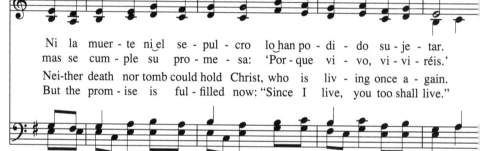

Ni la muer - te ni el se - pul - cro lo han po - di - do su - je - tar.
mas se cum - ple su pro - me - sa: 'Por - que vi - vo, vi - vi - réis.'
Nei-ther death nor tomb could hold Christ, who is liv - ing once a - gain.
But the prom - ise is ful - filled now: "Since I live, you too shall live."

No bus - quéis en - tre los muer-tos al que siem-pre ha de vi - vir,
Si en A - dán en - tró la muer-te, por Je - sús la vi - da en - tró:
Do not look a - mong the dead for one who lives most cer - tain - ly;
If through Ad - am death came in, through Je - sus Christ came life in - stead;

This resurrection hymn is the product of two Argentinean talents. Author Nicolás Martínez was a Disciples of Christ pastor, poet, and editor. Composer Pablo D. Sosa is known as an international leader in liturgical music.

Tune: CENTRAL 8.7.8.7.D.
Pablo D. Sosa, 1960

| Em | | | F♯7 | Bm | CM7 | Em | | Bm | Em |

¡Cris-to vi - ve! es - tas nue - vas por do - quier de - jad o - ír.
No te - máis, el triun-fo es nues - tro: ¡Cris - to ya re - su - ci - tó!
Christ is liv - ing! Hear the good news that re - sounds so joy - ful - ly.
Have no fear! Ours is the tri - umph; Christ is ris - en from the dead.

3 Si es ver-dad que de la muer-te
   el pe-ca-do es a-gui-jón,
   no te-máis pues Je-su-cris-to
   nos da vi-da y sal-va-ción.
   Gra-cias de-mos a Dios siem-pre
   que nos da se-gu-ri-dad,
   que quien si-gue a Je-su-cris-to
   vi-ve por la e-ter-ni-dad.

3 E-ven if the sting of death is
   tru-ly found in hu-man sin,
   Be not fear-ful, for Christ Je-sus
   came our lib-er-ty to win.
   We give end-less thanks to God,
   who is our sure se-cu-ri-ty;
   Those who fol-low Christ the Sav-ior
   will have life e-ter-nal-ly.

Halleluja   236

Traditional

| A | | | E | A | D | | | Bm | E |

Hal-le, hal-le, hal - le - lu - ja. Hal-le, hal-le, hal - le - lu - ja.

| A | | | C♯7 | F♯m | | Bm | | E7sus4 E7 | A |

Hal-le, hal-le, hal - le - lu - ja. Hal-le - lu-ja, hal - le - lu - ja.

This joyous response may be used following readings of scripture,
or as a processional or recessional, especially during Easter.

Tune: HALLELUJA
Caribbean melody

237

I Come to the Garden Alone
(In the Garden)

John 20:14–18

C. Austin Miles, 1912

1 I come to the gar-den a-lone, while the dew is still on the
2 He speaks, and the sound of his voice is so sweet the birds hush their
3 I'd stay in the gar-den with him, though the night a-round me be

ros - es; And the voice I hear, fall-ing on my ear, the
sing - ing; And the mel - o - dy that he gave to me with-
fall - ing; But he bids me go; through the voice of woe his

Refrain

Son of God dis - clos - es.
in my heart is ring - ing. And he walks with me, and he
voice to me is call - ing.

talks with me, and he tells me I am his own, And the

joy we share as we tar - ry there, none oth-er has ev - er known.

C. Austin Miles wrote this hymn and its music to tell the story of
Mary Magdalene's encounter with Jesus at the tomb, when she
recognizes him and calls him "Rabboni" ("Teacher").

Tune: GARDEN 8.9.5.5.7. with refrain
C. Austin Miles, 1912

Now the Green Blade Rises

238

John M. C. Crum, 1928; alt.

Matt. 27:57–28:7; Luke 23:50–24:12

1 Now the green blade ris - es from the bur - ied grain;
2 In the grave they laid their Love whom hate had slain,
3 Christ came forth at Eas - ter, like the ris - en grain,
4 When our hearts are win - try, griev - ing, or in pain,

Wheat that in dark earth for man - y days has lain;
Think - ing that their Love would nev - er wake a - gain,
Je - sus, who for three days in the grave had lain,
Christ's warm touch can call us back to life a - gain,

Love lives a - gain, that with the dead has been:
Laid in the earth like grain that sleeps un - seen:
Quick from the dead the ris - en One is seen:
Fields of our hearts that dead and bare have been:

Refrain

Love is come a - gain like wheat that ris - es green.

John M. C. Crum, an English priest who was canon of Canterbury for fifteen years, wrote these words for this ancient French Christmas carol tune when it was included in the Oxford Book of Carols *(1928).*

Tune: NOËL NOUVELET 11.10.10.11.
French noel, 15th century
Harm. Martin F. Shaw, 1928

239 Christ Rose Up from the Dead

Matt. 28:2–6; John 19:16–18; 19:38–20:18

African-American traditional; alt.

Refrain

Christ rose, Christ rose, Christ rose up from the dead, Christ rose,
a-rose a-rose, a-rose,

Christ rose, Christ rose from the dead, Christ rose Christ rose,
a-rose a-rose, a-rose,

Last time, end

Christ rose up from the dead, and God's grace will bear my spir-it home.

1 They cru-ci-fied my Sav-ior up-on a com-mon cross, they
2 And Jo-seph begged his bod-y, and laid it in the tomb, and
3 An an-gel came from heav-en and rolled a-way the stone, an
4 Oh, Mar-y, she came run-ning and found an emp-ty tomb, oh,

This jubilee song, collected by K. D. Reddick and arranged by Phil V. S. Lindsley, appeared around 1918 in shape note style in a collection titled The National Jubilee Melodies, published by the National Baptist Publishing Board.

Tune: ASCENSIUS 7.6.7.6.7.6.9. with refrain
African-American traditional
Arr. Phil V. S. Lindsley, 20th century

cru - ci - fied my Sav - ior up - on a com - mon cross, They
Jo - seph begged his bod - y, and laid it in the tomb, And
an - gel came from heav - en and rolled a - way the stone, An
Mar - y, she came run - ning and found an emp - ty tomb, Oh,

cru - ci - fied my Sav - ior up - on a com - mon cross,
Jo - seph begged his bod - y, and laid it in the tomb,
an - gel came from heav - en and rolled a - way the stone,
Mar - y, she came run - ning and found an emp - ty tomb,

to Refrain

(1–4) and God's grace will bear my spir - it home.

240   Jesus Christ Is Risen Today

Matt. 28:1–10; Mark 16:1–8; Luke 24:1–10   *St. 1 transl.*, Lyra Davidica, *London, 1708*
                                                      St. 2–5 transl., The New Century Hymnal, *1994*

1. Je - sus Christ is risen to - day,   Al - le - lu - ia!
2. To the tomb the wom - en bring,   Al - le - lu - ia!
3. There the an - gel clothed in white,   Al - le - lu - ia!
4. "Has - ten now to Gal - i - lee,"   Al - le - lu - ia!
5. Christ ap - pears in full ar - ray,   Al - le - lu - ia!

Our tri - um - phant ho - ly day,   Al - le - lu - ia!
Spic - es rich, an of - fer - ing,   Al - le - lu - ia!
Tells the news with great de - light,   Al - le - lu - ia!
"Tell the oth - ers what you see!"   Al - le - lu - ia!
Sing with joy this Pas - chal day,   Al - le - lu - ia!

Who did once up - on the cross,   Al - le - lu - ia!
Ask - ing where might Je - sus be,   Al - le - lu - ia!
This the news the an - gel gives,   Al - le - lu - ia!
With ex - cite - ment trem - bling,   Al - le - lu - ia!
Christ now from the dead is raised,   Al - le - lu - ia!

In 1749, an English translation of this fourteenth-century Latin hymn dropped all but the first stanza of the original. Most hymnbooks have used that (1749) version. In this new translation the original Latin verses of the medieval text are restored, thus bringing to life the original Easter narrative.

Tune: LLANFAIR 7.7.7.7. with alleluias
Robert Williams, 1817
Harm. John Roberts (1822–1877)

Unison

Suf - fer	to	re - deem our	loss,	Al	-	le	-	lu	-	ia!
Sav - ior	come to	set us	free,	Al	-	le	-	lu	-	ia!
That the	Sov-ereign glo - rious	lives,		Al	-	le	-	lu	-	ia!
Off they	run, good news to	bring,		Al	-	le	-	lu	-	ia!
Ho - ly	Trin - i - ty be	praised,		Al	-	le	-	lu	-	ia!

Joy Dawned Again on Easter Day   241

Latin, c. 5th century
Transl. John Mason Neale, 1851; alt.

Luke 24:36–37

1 Joy dawned a - gain on Eas - ter Day, the sun shone
2 O Je - sus, Sav - ior, Gen - tle One, come take our
3 O Sov - ereign One, with us a - bide in this our

out with bright ar - ray; For when the A - pos - tles
hearts to be your own, That we may give you
joy - ful Eas - ter - tide; From ev - ery weap - on

hid in fear, the Ris - en Christ to them ap - peared.
all our days the will - ing trib - ute of our praise.
death can wield, your own re - deemed for - ev - er shield.

This anonymous Latin hymn of uncertain date is one of the two
earliest hymns assigned to a special season. From that beginning
grew a full list of medieval Latin hymns assigned to specific times
and seasons.

Tune: PUER NOBIS NASCITUR L.M.
German carol, 15th century
Adapt. Michael Praetorius, 1609
Harm. George R. Woodward, 1910

242

The Strife Is O'er

1 Cor. 15:53–57

Latin, c. 1695
Transl. Francis Pott, 1861; alt.

Refrain (before st. 1 and after st. 4)

Al - le - lu - ia, al - le - lu - ia, al - le - lu - ia!

1 The strife is o'er, the bat - tle done, the vic - to -
2 The powers of death have done their worst, but Christ their
3 The three sad days are quick - ly sped, Christ ris - es
4 Christ, by your wounds on Cal - va - ry from death's dread

ry of life is won; The song of tri - umph
le - gions has dis - persed: Let shouts of ho - ly
glo - rious from the dead: All glo - ry to our
sting your ser - vants free, That we may live e -

has be - gun. Al - le - lu - ia!
joy out - burst. Al - le - lu - ia!
ris - en Head! Al - le - lu - ia!
ter - nal - ly. Al - le - lu - ia! *to Refrain*

A seventeenth-century Jesuit collection published in Cologne,
Germany, is the earliest known source of this Latin hymn. The
hymn is firmly associated with this musical setting from a
Magnificat by the Italian composer Palestrina.

Tune: VICTORY 8.8.8. with alleluias
Giovanni Perluigi da Palestrina, 1591
Arr. William H. Monk, 1861

Alleluia! Alleluia! Hearts to Heaven 243

Christopher Wordsworth, 1872; alt.   Matt. 28:5–8; Rom. 5:21; 6:4–11; 1 Cor. 15:20–22

1 Al - le - lu - ia! Al - le - lu - ia! Hearts to heaven and voic - es raise;
2 Now the i - ron bars are bro - ken, Christ from death to life is born;
3 Christ is ris - en, we are ris - en; shed up - on us heaven-ly grace,
4 Al - le - lu - ia! Al - le - lu - ia! Glo - ry to the God of joy;

Sing to God a hymn of glad-ness, sing to God a hymn of praise.
Glo-rious life, and life im - mor - tal on this ho - ly Eas - ter morn;
Rain and dew, and gleams of glo - ry from the bright - ness of your face;
Al - le - lu - ia to the Sav - ior who came death's bonds to de - stroy;

Je - sus on the cross as Sav - ior for the world's sal - va - tion bled;
Christ has tri - umphed, and we con-quer by God's lib - er - at - ing deed;
That we, with our hearts in heav-en, here on earth may fruit-ful be,
Al - le - lu - ia to the Spir - it, Fount of love and sanc-ti - ty;

But the cru - ci - fied Re - deem-er now is ris - en from the dead!
Now the Christ with us a - bid - ing to e - ter - nal life shall lead.
And by an - gel hands be gath-ered, and be yours e - ter - nal - ly.
Al - le - lu - ia! Al - le - lu - ia! To the Tri - une Maj - es - ty.

Christopher Wordsworth, gifted nephew of poet William   Tune: WEISSE FLAGGEN 8.7.8.7.D.
Wordsworth, served the Church of England successively as canon   Tochter Sion, Cologne, 1741
at Westminster, parish priest in Berkshire, and, finally, bishop of   Alternate tune: HYFRYDOL
Lincoln. This Easter hymn is one of his most enduring.

244   O Sons and Daughters, Let Us Sing

Mark 16:1–7; John 20:19–29

Attrib. to Jean Tisserand (d. 1494)
Transl. John Mason Neale, 1851; alt.

Antiphon (may be sung at beginning and end)

Al - le - lu - ia!   Al - le - lu - ia!   Al - le-lu - ia!   Al - le-lu - ia!

1. O sons and daugh-ters, let us sing the flower of heaven, a -
2. That Eas - ter morn at break of day, the faith - ful wom - en
3. An an - gel clad in white they see, who sat and spoke un -
4. When Thom - as first the tid - ings heard, he count - ed what they

live as spring, o'er death to - day rose
went their way to seek the tomb where
to the three, "Christ waits for you in
said ab - surd, but see - ing Christ his

tri - umph-ing, Al - le - lu - ia! Al - le - lu - ia!
Je - sus lay, Al - le - lu - ia! Al - le - lu - ia!
Gal - i - lee." Al - le - lu - ia! Al - le - lu - ia!
faith was stirred: Al - le - lu - ia! Al - le - lu - ia!

Jean Tisserand, a Franciscan preaching friar, was well known in Paris. He founded an order for women and wrote a history commemorating some Franciscans martyred in Morocco in 1220.

Tune: O FILII ET FILIAE 8.8.8. with alleluias
Airs sur les hymnes sacrez, *Paris, 1623*

5 How blessed are they who have not seen
and yet whose faith has con-stant been;
for they e-ter--nal life shall win,
Al-le-lu-ia! Al-le-lu-ia!

6 On this most ho-ly day of days,
our hearts and voic-es, Christ, we raise
to you in ju--bi-lee and praise.
Al-le-lu-ia! Al-le-lu-ia! *(Antiphon)*

The Day of Resurrection 245

John of Damascus, 8th century
Transl. John Mason Neale, 1862; alt.

Mark 16:1–6

1 The day of res-ur-rec-tion! Earth, tell it out a-broad;
2 Our hearts be pure from e-vil, that we may see a-right
3 Now let the heavens be joy-ful, let earth its song be-gin,

the Pass-o-ver of glad-ness, the Pass-o-ver of God.
the Christ who reigns e-ter-nal in res-ur-rec-tion light;
the whole world keep high tri-umph, and all that is there-in;

From death to life e-ter-nal, from earth un-to the sky,
We lis-ten for the teach-ings once heard so calm and plain,
Let all things seen and un-seen their notes of glad-ness blend,

our Christ has brought us o-ver with hymns of vic-to-ry.
for we, too, want to fol-low and raise the vic-tor strain.
for Christ a-gain has ris-en, our joy that has no end.

A Greek canon—an extended poem of eight or nine odes, each based on a scriptural canticle—was the source of this hymn. John of Damascus gave up a high government position to enter a monastery.

Tune: LANCASHIRE 7.6.7.6.D.
Henry T. Smart, 1836

246

Hoy celebramos con gozo al Dios
(Come, Celebrate with Thanksgiving)

Mortimer Arias; alt.
Transl. Roberto Escamilla and Elise S. Eslinger, 1981; alt.

1 Hoy ce-le-bra-mos con go-zo al Dios to-do-po-de-
2 Hoy ce-le-bra-mos fes-ti-vos al Dios de li-be-ra-
1 Come, cel-e-brate with thanks-giv - ing, come and wor-ship God al-
2 Come, cel-e-brate in your feast - ing that the God of lib-er-

ro - so, al cre-a-dor de la tie - rra y da-
ción, que da vi-da y es-pe-ran - za y se
might - y, Who is cre-a-tor of all things, and the
a - tion Brings us to new life, new whole - ness, and for-

dor de to - do bien; al que vi-no has-ta no-
go - za en el per - dón. Con vo-ces y con pan-
giv - er of good gifts; Who came to be one a-
gives in joy and love. With voic-es and hap-py

so - tros y mu - rió en u - na cruz,
de - ros en-to - na-mos la can - ción,
mong us, e - ven dy - ing on a cross.
drum - ming let us sing the tri - umph song.

This hymn by Bolivian Methodists Mortimer Arias and Antonio Auza employs the Latin American "cueca" rhythm which juxtaposes contrasting meters. In Buenos Aires, Argentina, women whose husbands have 'disappeared' sometimes dance the "cueca" around a central square.

Tune: CHUQUISACA 8.8.8.7.D. with refrain
Antonio Auza
Arr. Homero Perera

que ha ven-ci - do a las ti - nie - blas y a la muer-te des - tru - yó.
ce - le-bran-do al Dios vi - vien - te dan - za nues-tro co - ra - zón.
E - vil has been o - ver-come, and now death has been de - stroyed.
God is a - live and a - mong us, now our danc-ing hearts re - joice!

Estribillo (Refrain)

¡Cris-to vi - ve! Ce - le - bre - mos y es-pe - re - mos su gran
Cel - e - brate that Christ is liv - ing and then wait for God's great

don; San-to Es-pí - ri - tu di - vi - no, ven a nues-tro co - ra -
gift: The di - vine and ho - ly Spir - it now may come in-to our

zón. nues - tro co - ra - zón.
hearts. come in - to our hearts.

3 Hoy a-cu-di-mos a-le-gres
   a es-ta fies-ta del a-mor;
   res-pon-dien-do fer-vo-ro-sos
   a la san-ta in-vi-ta-ción.
   En a-mor hoy ce-le-bra-mos
   es-ta san-ta co-mu-nión;
   es-tre-chán-do-nos las ma-nos
   so-mos pue-blo del Crea-dor.
   (Estribillo)

3 Come, cel-e-brate all to-geth-er
   in this feast of heaven-ly love.
   We come at God's in-vi-ta-tion
   on this hap-py, ho-ly day.
   Joy-ful-ly, let us now gath-er,
   cel-e-brat-ing u-ni-ty,
   Join-ing our hands in thanks-giv-ing
   as the fam-i-ly of God.
   (Refrain)

247 My Shepherd Is the Living God

Ps. 23; John 10:11, 27–30　　　　　*Composite from Thomas Sternhold, 1549, and Isaac Watts, 1719; alt.*

1 My shep-herd is the liv-ing God, I there-fore noth-ing need;
2 When I walk through the shades of death, your pres-ence is my stay;
3 The sure pro-vi-sions of my God at-tend me all my days;

In pas-tures fair, near pleas-ant streams you set-tle me to feed.
A word of your sup-port-ing breath drives all my fears a-way.
O may your house be my a-bode, and all my work be praise.

You bring my wan-dering spir-it back when I for-sake your ways,
Your hand, in sight of all my foes, does still my ta-ble spread;
There would I find a set-tled rest, while oth-ers come and go—

And lead me for your mer-cy's sake in paths of truth and grace.
My cup with bless-ings o-ver-flows, your oil a-noints my head.
No more a strang-er or a guest, but like a child at home.

Isaac Watts, London's leading Congregational minister, wrote
more than 600 hymns. His paraphrase of Psalm 23 has been
altered here by combining a few phrases from Thomas
Sternhold, a sixteenth-century English hymnwriter who also
wrote metrical psalm texts.

Tune: CONSOLATION C.M.D.
Southern Harmony, 1835
Harm. Erik Routley, 1976
Alternate tune: *CRIMOND (Each stanza*
above becomes two stanzas.)

Such Perfect Love My Shepherd Shows 248

Henry W. Baker, 1868; alt. *Ps. 23*

1 Such per - fect love my Shep - herd shows, whose
2 Where streams of liv - ing wa - ter flow, my
3 When vain and fool - ish oft I strayed, you,
4 I do not fear death's shad - owed vale when

good - ness fails me nev - er, Whose hand all things I
lov - ing Shep - herd leads me, And where the ver - dant
faith - ful Shep - herd, sought me, And on your shoul - der
you are here be - side me; Your rod and staff and

need be - stows and watch - es me for - ev - er.
pas - tures grow with food from heav - en feeds me.
gent - ly laid, then home re - joic - ing brought me.
strength pre - vail to com - fort and to guide me.

5 You spread a ta-ble in my sight,
your gifts of grace be-stow-ing;
And from your chal-ice I de-light
to taste your mer-cy flow-ing.

6 And so through all the length of days
your good-ness fails me nev-er;
Good Shep-herd, may I sing your praise
with-in your house for-ev-er.

*English clergyman Henry Baker greatly influenced hymnody in
England and the United States through his leadership in
preparing* Hymns Ancient and Modern *(1861). Baker's hymn is
a recast of a George Herbert poem.*

Tune: DOMINUS REGIT ME 8.7.8.7.
John B. Dykes, 1868
Alternate tune: ST. COLUMBA

249   Peace I Leave with You, My Friends

John 14:18–29   *Ray Repp, 1967*

Refrain

Peace I leave with you, my friends, sha-lom, my peace, in
all you do. Peace I leave with you, my friends. I give to
you so you can give to oth - ers, too.

1 To share God's love   is   why   I   came,
2 Take my hand   and   be   at   peace;
3 With this love   now   all   will   know

to show God's kind - ness with - out end.
the spir - it of our love I send.
that lone - li - ness is at an end.

Songwriter Ray Repp has composed and recorded numerous
albums of liturgical songs since 1965, when he introduced guitar
into worship with his "Mass for Young Americans."

Tune: PEACE, MY FRIENDS   Irr. with refrain
Ray Repp, 1967
Arr. The New Century Hymnal, *1994*

Go now, my friends, and do the same,
And with this love you will be free,
Re - joice, my friends, al - though I go,

un - til I come a - gain.
un - til I come a - gain.
for I will come a - gain.

Listen to Your Savior Call   250

William Cowper, 1768; alt.   John 21:15–16

1 Lis - ten to your Sav - ior call, "Do you love me most of all?"
2 "I de - liv - ered you when bound, and, when bleed - ing, healed your wound.
3 "Mine is an un - chang - ing love, high - er than the heights a - bove,
4 O my Sav - ior, hear my need: though my love is faint in - deed,

Je - sus speaks, and speaks to you: "Love me as I first loved you."
Sought you wan - dering, set you right, for your path - way gave you light."
Deep - er than the depths be - neath, free and faith - ful, strong as death."
Still I love you and a - dore— oh, for grace to love you more!

William Cowper was trained as a barrister. He suffered from
severe depression, but during a time of wellness he wrote this
hymn based on John 21:15—a dialogue between Jesus and
the individual.

Tune: ORIENTIS PARTIBUS 7.7.7.7.
French melody, early 13th century
Arr. Richard Redhead, 1853

251 I Greet You, Sure Redeemer

John 11:25–27

Anon., from Strasbourg Psalter, *1545*
Transl. Elizabeth L. Smith, 1868; alt.

1 I greet you, sure Re - deem - er, with my heart,
glad for the sav - ing love that you im - part,
Who pain did un - der - go for my poor sake;
I pray you from our hearts all cares to take.

2 You are the source of mer - cy and of grace,
reign - ing om - ni - po - tent in ev - ery place;
So rule in us and our whole be - ing sway.
Shine on us with the light of your pure day.

3 You are the life, by which a - lone we live,
and all our sub - stance and our strength re - ceive.
Sus - tain us by your faith and by your power,
and give us strength in ev - ery try - ing hour.

4 You have the true and per - fect gen - tle - ness,
no harsh - ness have you and no bit - ter - ness;
Grant us the grace that flows in you so free
that we may dwell in per - fect u - ni - ty.

5 Our hope is all in you and you a - lone;
we trust the prom - ise that your word makes known.
O dear Re - deem - er, make us calm and sure,
that in your strength we ev - er - more en - dure.

This hymn first appeared in a sixteenth-century Strasbourg Psalter edited by John Calvin. The original tune Old 124th and text were both shortened to the present meter—the tune for an early English psalter and the text for the 1920 Hymnal of the Reformed Church in the United States.

Tune: TOULON 10.10.10.10.
Adapt. from OLD 124th
Trente quatre Pseaumes, *Geneva, 1551*

Savior, like a Shepherd Lead Us 252

Attrib. to Dorothy A. Thrupp (1779–1847) John 10:1–29
From Hymns for the Young, *1836; alt.*
St. 1 transl. to Hawaiian by Laiana (1807–1886)

1 Sav-ior, like a shep-herd lead us, much we need your ten-der care;
1 Ie-su no ke Ka-hu-hi-pa, Ka-hu-hi-pa ma'i-ka'i e,
2 We are yours, in love be-friend us, be the guard-ian of our way;
3 Let us al-ways seek your fa-vor; let us al-ways do your will;

in your pleas-ant pas-tures feed us, for our use your folds pre-pare.
Ei-a ma-kou ka 'o-ha-na ke ho'o-lo-he a ha-hai:
keep your flock, from sin de-fend us, seek us when we go a-stray.
Je-sus Christ our on-ly Sav-ior, with your love our spir-its fill.

Bless-ed Je-sus, bless-ed Je-sus, you have bought us, yours we are;
E a-lo-ha, e a-lo-ha, a-la-ka'i a ha-nai mai,
Bless-ed Je-sus, bless-ed Je-sus, hear your chil-dren when we pray;
Bless-ed Je-sus, bless-ed Je-sus, you have loved us, love us still;

Bless-ed Je-sus, bless-ed Je-sus, you have bought us, yours we are.
E a-lo-ha, e a-lo-ha, a-la-ka'i a ha-nai mai.
Bless-ed Je-sus, bless-ed Je-sus, hear your chil-dren when we pray.
Bless-ed Je-sus, bless-ed Je-sus, you have loved us, love us still.

The theme of Christ as shepherd is familiar and beloved to Christians. Emma Lyons Doyle, granddaughter of Laiana (translator Lorenzo Lyons), once said, "If you want to know the full beauty of this hymn, hear it sung in Hawaiian."

Tune: BRADBURY 8.7.8.7.D.
William B. Bradbury, 1859

253

A toi la gloire, ô Ressuscité!
(Yours Is the Glory, Resurrected One!)

Matt. 28:1–10; John 20:19–29; 1 Cor. 15:54–55

Edmond L. Budry, 1904
Transl. The New Century Hymnal, *1993*

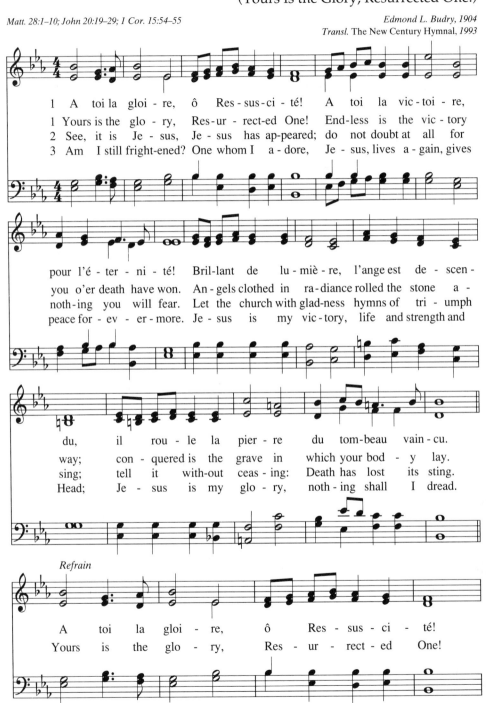

1 A toi la gloi - re, ô Res - sus - ci - té! A toi la vic - toi - re,
1 Yours is the glo - ry, Res - ur - rect-ed One! End-less is the vic - tory
2 See, it is Je - sus, Je - sus has ap-peared; do not doubt at all for
3 Am I still fright-ened? One whom I a - dore, Je - sus, lives a - gain, gives

pour l'é - ter - ni - té! Bril-lant de lu - miè - re, l'ange est de - scen -
you o'er death have won. An - gels clothed in ra - diance rolled the stone a -
noth-ing you will fear. Let the church with glad-ness hymns of tri - umph
peace for - ev - er - more. Je - sus is my vic - tory, life and strength and

du, il rou - le la pier - re du tom-beau vain - cu.
way; con - quered is the grave in which your bod - y lay.
sing; tell it with-out ceas - ing: Death has lost its sting.
Head; Je - sus is my glo - ry, noth - ing shall I dread.

Refrain

A toi la gloi - re, ô Res - sus - ci - té!
Yours is the glo - ry, Res - ur - rect - ed One!

Swiss pastor Edmond L. Budry may have drawn his inspiration
for this hymn from a German Advent poem set to Handel's
triumphant music. The tune Judas Maccabeus *is adapted from a*
chorus in Handel's oratorio of the same name.

Tune: JUDAS MACCABEUS
5.5.6.5.6.5.6.5. with refrain
G. F. Handel, 1751

A toi la vic - toi - re, pour l'é - ter - ni - té!
End - less is the vic - tory you o'er death have won.

These Things Did Thomas Count

254

Thomas H. Troeger, 1984

John 20:19–31

1 These things did Thom - as count as real: the warmth of
2 The vi - sion of his skep - tic mind was keen e -
3 His rea - soned cer - tain - ties de - nied that one could
4 May we, O God, by grace be - lieve and thus the

blood, the chill of steel, The grain of wood, the heft of
nough to make him blind To an - y un - ex - pect - ed
live when one had died, Un - til his fin - gers read like
ris - en Christ re - ceive, Whose raw, im - print - ed palms reached

stone, the last frail twitch of flesh and bone.
act too large for his small world of fact.
Braille the mark - ings of the spear and nail.
out and beck - oned Thom - as from his doubt.

The author cites his "reading of twentieth-century theology and
its coming to terms with the limits of the enlightenment and
rational cognition" as the foundational thought for this text.

Tune: DISTRESS L.M.
The Sacred Harp, *1844*
Arr. Jonathan McNair, 1993

255

Jesus, Sovereign, Savior

Luke 24:13–48; John 20:19–23

Patrick M. Kirkland (1857–1943); alt.

1 Je - sus, Sov - ereign, Sav - ior, once for sin - ners slain,
2 Faith-ful ones com - mun - ing towards the close of day,
3 In the up - per cham - ber, fol - low-ers, in fear,

cru - ci - fied in weak - ness, raised in power to reign,
des - o - late and wea - ry, met you on the way.
gath-ered sad and trou - bled, there you did ap - pear.

Dwell-ing now im - mor - tal, end-less in your days,
So, when sun is set - ting, come to us and show
Christ, be pres - ent with us, bid our sor - rows cease;

un - to you be glo - ry, hon - or, bless - ing, praise.
your truth, and with - in us make our hearts to glow.
breath - ing on us, Sav - ior, say, "I give you peace."

*Patrick M. Kirkland ministered to a Presbyterian church in
Cheshire, England, for forty years. Named for a village near
Bristol, King's Weston is one of several fine hymn tunes written
by the English composer Ralph Vaughan Williams.*

Tune: KING'S WESTON 6.5.6.5.D.
Ralph Vaughan Williams, 1925

We Live by Faith and Not by Sight 256

Henry Alford, 1844; alt.   *John 20:24–29*

Unison

1 We live by faith and not by sight;
2 We may not touch Christ's hands and side,
3 Help then, O Christ, our un - be - lief;
4 That, when our life of faith is done,

no gra - cious words we hear From Christ who spoke as
nor fol - low where Christ trod; But in con - fess - ing
and may our faith a - bound To call on you when
in realms of clear - er light We may be - hold you

none e'er spoke, who still we know is near.
we re - joice: our Sav - ior and our God!
you are near and seek where you are found:
as you are, with full and end - less sight.

As dean of Canterbury, Henry Alford exemplified ecumenism by working closely with non-Anglican groups. He promoted New Testament scholarship with his famous commentary on the Greek New Testament, one of fifty books he published during his lifetime.

Tune: DUNLAP'S CREEK C.M.
Samuel McFarland, c. 1816
Harm. Richard Proulx, 1986

257

Alleluia! Gracious Jesus!

Eph. 1:15–23; Heb. 9:11–14   *William C. Dix, 1867; alt.*

1 Al - le - lu - ia! Gra - cious Je - sus! Yours the
2 Al - le - lu - ia! Not as or - phans are we
3 Al - le - lu - ia! Bread of an - gels, you on
4 Al - le - lu - ia! Christ e - ter - nal, noth - ing

scep - ter, yours the throne! Al - le - lu - ia! Yours the
left in sor - row now. Al - le - lu - ia! You are
earth our food, our stay. Al - le - lu - ia! Here the
can dis - rupt your reign; Al - le - lu - ia! Born of

tri - umph, yours the vic - to - ry a - lone!
near us; faith be - lieves, nor ques - tions how.
sin - ful flee to you from day to day.
Mar - y, heaven and earth are your do - main.

Hark! the songs of peace - ful Zi - on
Though the cloud from sight re - ceived you
In - ter - ces - sor, friend of sin - ners,
Hu - man life you ful - ly en - tered,

thun - der	like	a	might - y	flood;	Je	- sus,	out	of
when the	for -	ty	days	were o'er,	shall	our	hearts	for -
earth's Re -	deem -	er,	plead	for me,	and	the	songs	that
tend - ing	those	we	count	the least,	serv -	ing	both	as

ev - ery	na	- tion you've	re -	deemed us	by	your	blood.
get	your	prom -	ise, "I	am	with	you	ev - er - more."
sound	in	heav -	en will	re -	peat	your	gra - cious plea.
Priest	and	Vic -	tim in	the	eu -	cha - ris - tic	feast.

William C. Dix, manager of a marine insurance company, was
also a gifted writer who made a significant contribution to
hymnody. This hymn was written to fill a need for communion
hymns in Church of England hymnals.

Tune: HYFRYDOL 8.7.8.7.D.
Rowland H. Prichard, 1844
Arr. Ralph Vaughan Williams, 1906

258   Christ, Enthroned in Heavenly Splendor

John 6:51; Heb. 9:26; 1 Cor. 10:4   *George Hugh Bourne, 1874; alt.*

1 Christ, en-throned in heaven-ly splen-dor, first be-got-ten from the dead,
2 Here our hum - ble hom - age pay we, here in lov - ing rev - erence bow;
3 Pas - chal Lamb, your of - fering fin - ished once for all when you were slain,
4 Life - im - part - ing heaven-ly man - na, strick-en rock with stream-ing side,

You a - lone, our strong de - fend - er, now lift up your peo - ple's head.
Here for faith's dis - cern-ment pray we, lest we fail to know you now.
In its full - ness un - di - min-ished shall for - ev - er - more re - main,
Heaven and earth with loud ho - san - na wor-ship you, the Lamb who died,

Al - le - lu - ia! Al - le - lu - ia! Al - le - lu - ia!
Al - le - lu - ia! Al - le - lu - ia! Al - le - lu - ia!
Al - le - lu - ia! Al - le - lu - ia! Al - le - lu - ia!
Al - le - lu - ia! Al - le - lu - ia! Al - le - lu - ia!

Christ, our true and liv - ing Bread. Christ, our true and liv - ing Bread.
You are here, we ask not how. You are here, we ask not how.
Cleans-ing hearts from ev - ery stain. Cleans-ing hearts from ev - ery stain.
Risen, as-cend - ed, glo - ri - fied! Risen, as - cend - ed, glo - ri - fied!

This post-communion hymn was one of seven by Anglican clergyman Bourne, who was headmaster at Chardstock College in England. It was first published in the United States in The Hymnal *of the Evangelical and Reformed Church (1941).*

Tune: BRYN CALFARIA 8.7.8.7.4.7.
William Owen, Y Perl Cerddoral, 1852

A Hymn of Glory Let Us Sing

259

The Venerable Bede (673–735)
1–2, transl. Elizabeth R. Charles, 1858; alt.
3, transl. Benjamin Webb, 1854; alt.

Phil. 2:1–11; Eph. 1:15–23

Fanfare (introduction and coda, and interlude if desired)

1 A hymn of glo - ry let us sing, new
2 You are a pres - ent joy, O Christ, tri -
3 O ris - en Christ, as - cend-ed now, to

hymns through-out the world shall ring; By a new way none
um - phant love once sac - ri - ficed, And great the light in
your blessed name all knees shall bow; You are, while end - less

ev - er trod Christ shares once more the throne of God.
you we see to guide us to e - ter - ni - ty.
a - ges run, in Tri - une God - head ev - er One.

This Latin hymn by the Venerable Bede is possibly among the first Christian hymns written in England. Bede's Historia Ecclesiastica is an important source of early English history.

Tune: DEO GRACIAS L.M.
"The Agincourt Song," England, c. 1415
Arr. E. Power Biggs, 1947; adapt. Richard Proulx, 1985
For another harmonization, see 184, 209

260 Hail the Day That Sees Christ Ris

Acts 1:6–11; John 14:16

Charles Wesley, 1739; a

1 Hail the day that sees Christ rise, Al - le - lu - ia!
2 Christ, for you high tri - umph waits, Al - le - lu - ia!
3 See! The nail - marked hands a - bove; Al - le - lu - ia!
4 Christ for us still in - ter - cede, Al - le - lu - ia!

To a throne in par - a - dise; Al - le - lu - ia!
Lift your heads, e - ter - nal gates! Al - le - lu - ia!
Sing of God's re - deem - ing love; Al - le - lu - ia!
By your suf - fering for us plead; Al - le - lu - ia!

Christ, the Lamb for sin - ners given, Al - le - lu - ia!
You have con - quered death and sin; Al - le - lu - ia!
Hark! Christ's words our hearts as - sure: Al - le - lu - ia!
Make us wor - thy of the place, Al - le - lu - ia!

En - ters now the high - est heaven. Al - le - lu - ia!
You, our Sov - ereign, en - ter in! Al - le - lu - ia!
"I will send a Com - fort - er!" Al - le - lu - ia!
Which you of - fer us by grace. Al - le - lu - ia!

Charles Wesley's original text was written for Ascension Day 1739 and had no alleluias; these were added in 1852 by G. E. White. Joseph Jones' tune bears the name of a twelfth-century bard and a town in Wales.

Tune: GWALCHMAI 7.7.7.7. with alleluia
Joseph David Jones, 186
Alternate tune: LLANFAII

5 Now, though part-ed from our sight,
   Al-le-lu-ia!
   In the depths of star-ry night,
   Al-le-lu-ia!
   May our souls with you a-rise,
   Al-le-lu-ia!
   Seek-ing whole-ness at your side.
   Al-le-lu-ia!

6 There we will with you re-main,
   Al-le-lu-ia!
   Heirs in your e-ter-nal reign;
   Al-le-lu-ia!
   In the pres-ence of your face,
   Al-le-lu-ia!
   We will dwell in heav-en's grace.
   Al-le-lu-ia!

Let Every Christian Pray   261

Fred Pratt Green, 1970; rev. 1994   *Acts 2*

1 Let ev-ery Chris-tian pray, this day and ev-ery day,
2 The Spir-it brought to birth the church of Christ on earth
3 On-ly the Spir-it's power can fit us for this hour:

come, Ho-ly Spir-it, come! Was not the church we love
to seek and save the lost: God nev-er has with-drawn,
come, Ho-ly Spir-it, come! U-nite, in-struct, in-spire

com-mis-sioned from a-bove? Come, Ho-ly Spir-it, come!
since that tre-men-dous dawn, the gifts of Pen-te-cost.
and fill us with your fire: come, Ho-ly Spir-it, come!

Noted contemporary British hymnwriter Fred Pratt Green retired from the parish ministry in 1969 and only then commenced his prolific output of hymn texts, which can be found in every major hymnal publication of the late twentieth century.

Tune: LAUDES DOMINI 6.6.6.6.6.6.
Joseph Barnby, 1868

Words Copyright © 1971 by Hope Publishing Company

262

Hail, O Festal Day

Luke 24:1–12; Acts 1:6–11; 2:1–4; 3:12–21

Venantius Honorius Fortunatus (c. 530–609
Stanzas 3, 5, 6 and Pentecost from York Processionals, 153
Transl. The New Century Hymnal, 199

Refrain (sing once to begin and after each stanza)
Unison

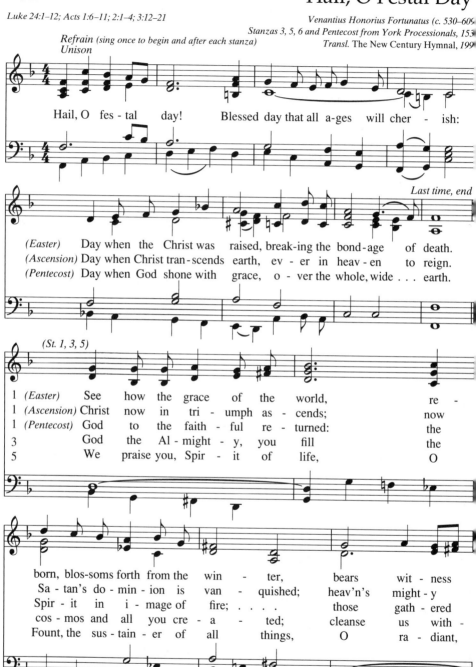

Hail, O fes - tal day! Blessed day that all a-ges will cher - ish:

Last time, end

(Easter) Day when the Christ was raised, break-ing the bond-age of death.
(Ascension) Day when Christ tran-scends earth, ev - er in heav - en to reign.
(Pentecost) Day when God shone with grace, o - ver the whole, wide . . . earth.

(St. 1, 3, 5)

1 *(Easter)* See how the grace of the world, re -
1 *(Ascension)* Christ now in tri - umph as - cends; now
1 *(Pentecost)* God to the faith - ful re - turned: the
3 God the Al - might - y, you fill the
5 We praise you, Spir - it of life, O

born, blos-soms forth from the win - ter, bears wit - ness
Sa - tan's do - min - ion is van - quished; heav'n's might - y
Spir - it in i - mage of fire; . . . . those gath - ered
cos - mos and all you cre - a - ted; cleanse us with -
Fount, the sus - tain - er of all things, O ra - diant,

A poem of 110 lines by Fortunatus comparing the Resurrection to springtime and the renewal of nature is the basis for this ages-old hymn. It was adapted for major festivals, and new, anonymous verses and responses were added. This version takes centos found in the processionals used at York in 1530.

Tune: SALVE FESTA DIES Irr. with refrain
Ralph Vaughan Williams, 1906

to Christ's re - turn: life's ver - y gift is re - newed.
gates o - pen wide, spil - ling forth in - crease of light.
tell of Christ's deeds, in ev - ery lan - guage on earth.
in, make us pure, that we your ves - sel may be.
life - giv - ing Light, re - new - ing life with your grace.

(St. 2, 4, 6)

2 *(Easter)* Now on the third day re - turned, a - rise now, O
2 *(Ascension)* The laws of hell now op - pressed, cre - a - tion re -
2 *(Pentecost)* Now to our lips the bright coal touch gen - tly, so
4 O Christ, Re - deem - er of all, our Sav - ior, the
6 Sov - ereign of all that is good, your sweet balm of

Christ, who was bur - ied; fill - ing your prom-ise of
sounds in thanks-giv - ing; field and sea, light and sky
we, too, are kin - dled— your love a - flame in our
Au - thor of good - ness, On - ly Be - got - ten of
peace pour up - on us; give us the wis - dom that

to Refrain

faith; nour - ish - ing Pow - er a - rise.
sing at the re - turn of their God.
hearts, lit from your own end - less love.
God, touch us with your heal - ing grace.
guides the u - ni - verse on its way.

263

O Spirit of the Living God

Acts 2:1–4, 17–21

Henry Hallam Tweedy, 1933; a

1 O Spir - it of the liv - ing God, pure Light and Fire Di -
2 Blow, Wind of God! With wis - dom blow, dis - perse and put to
3 Teach us to ut - ter liv - ing words of truth which all may
4 So shall we know the power of Christ, the strength of love to

vine: burn bright - ly in your church once more, its life and
flight the mists of er - ror, clouds of doubt which hide you
hear, the lan - guage all can un - der - stand when love speaks
save, so shall we rise with Christ to life which soars be -

faith re - fine, Fill it with love and joy and power, with
from our sight. Burn, Wing - ed Fire! In - spire our lips, re -
loud and clear; Till ev - ery na - tion, age, and race shall
yond the grave; And earth shall win true ho - li - ness, which

righ - teous - ness and peace, till Christ shall dwell in
new in us your call to preach with zeal your
blend their creeds in one, and all to - geth - er
makes your chil - dren whole, and draws us on by

hu - man hearts, and sin and sor - row cease.
great good news: God's love ex - tends to all.
use their gifts to see your will is done.
grace to reach cre - a - tion's glo - rious goal!

Henry Hallam Tweedy served Congregational churches in New York and Connecticut from 1898 to 1909 before joining the faculty of Yale University Divinity School.

Tune: ST. MATTHEW C.M.D.
William Croft, 1708

Holy Spirit, Come, Confirm Us 264

Brian Foley, 1971; alt.   John 14:25–27; 15:26–16:15

1 Ho - ly Spir - it, come, con - firm us in the
2 Ho - ly Spir - it, come, con - sole us, come as
3 Ho - ly Spir - it, come, re - new us, come your -
4 Ho - ly Spir - it, come, ful - fill us, you the

truth that Christ makes known; We have faith and un - der -
ad - vo - cate to plead; Lov - ing Spir - it stand be -
self to make us live; Make us ho - ly through your
love of Three in One; Bring our lives to full com -

stand - ing through your help - ing gifts a - lone.
side us, grant in Christ the help we need.
pres - ence, ho - ly through the gifts you give.
ple - tion through your work in us be - gun.

Author Brian Foley has served as a Roman Catholic priest in his native England since 1945. This text is a distillation of several scriptural passages, an example of his conviction that hymns should be based on theology, not mere sentiment.

Tune: FOR THE BREAD 8.7.8.7.
V. Earle Copes, 1960

265 Come, O Spirit, with Your Sound

Acts 2:1–24, 32–47; Joel 2:28

John A. Dalles, 1983; rev. 1993

1 Come, O Spir-it, with your sound like a wind, quick rush-ing;
2 Come, O Spir-it, with your flame, leap-ing tongues of fire; . . .
3 Come, O Spir-it, fill your church, mak-ing strong our mis-sion;

come from heav-en, stir our hearts, each dis-ci-ple touch-ing!
come, and with your glo-rious light all our thoughts in-spire! . . .
fill your daugh-ters and your sons with a might-y vi-sion,

Mold our ac-tions to your will, you our ser-vice giv-ing;
Rest up-on each ser-vant's head till each one is speak-ing
Till the great and glo-rious day when the whole cre-a-tion

move in our com-mu-ni-ty, trans-form now our liv-ing!
of our Christ, the Ho-ly One all the earth is seek-ing!
sings your praise as Sov-ereign One, giv-er of sal-va-tion!

This hymn text was written for the Pentecost Worship Celebration of Wabash Valley (Indiana) Presbytery in 1983 and was first published in The Presbyterian Hymnal *(1990). John A. Dalles, a Presbyterian minister, is a graduate of Lancaster Theological Seminary.*

Tune: BOUNDLESS MERCY 7.6.7.6.D.
Union Harmony, *1836*
Harm. Hilton Rufty, *1934*
Alternate tune: ST. KEVIN

Filled with the Spirit's Power

266

John R. Peacey, 1969; alt.

Acts 2:1–24, 32–47

1 Filled with the Spir - it's power, all hearts as one,
2 Now with the mind of Christ set us on fire,
3 Wid - en our love, good Spir - it, to em - brace

the in - fant church con-fessed Christ's vic - tory won.
that u - ni - ty may be our great de - sire.
in your strong care all those of ev - ery race.

O Ho - ly Spir - it, in the church to - day
Give joy and peace; give faith to know your call,
Like wind and fire with life a - mong us move,

no less your un - i - fy - ing power dis - play.
and read - i - ness in each to work for all.
till we are known as Christ's, and Chris - tians prove.

Following service during World War I with the British army in France, canon John Peacey was administrator and chaplain for colleges in England and India. He returned to England in 1945 and began writing hymns only after retiring in 1967.

Tune: SHELDONIAN 10.10.10.10.
Cyril V. Taylor, 1951

267   Come, O Spirit, Dwell among Us

Acts 2:1–36; Exod. 13:18–22; Ps. 118:19–29   *Janie Alford, 1979; alt.*

1 Come, O Spir - it, dwell a - mong us, come with Pen - te -
2 We would raise our al - le - lu - ias for the grace of
3 Come, O Spir - it, dwell a - mong us; give us words of

cos - tal power; give the church a strong - er vi - sion,
for - mer years; for to - mor - row's un - known path - way,
fire and flame. Help our strug-gling voic - es praise you,

help us face each cru - cial hour. Built up - on a firm foun - da - tion,
hear, O God, our hum - ble prayers. In the church's pil - grim jour-ney
glo - ri - fy your ho - ly name. Good Cre - a - tor, Sav-ior, Spir - it,

Je - sus Christ, the Cor - ner - stone, still the church is
you have led us all the way, still in pres - ence
Three in One: what mys - ter - y! We would sing our

Janie Alford is often described as "the Grandma Moses of hymnody." In her nineties, this retired medical secretary and Nashville, Tennessee, shop owner remained an active church worker and wrote many hymns. Nine of her texts were published in 1979.

Tune: EBENEZER (TON-Y-BOTEL) 8.7.8.7.D.
Thomas J. Williams, 1890

called to mis - sion that God's love shall be made known.
move be - fore us, fire by night and cloud by day.
loud ho - san - nas now and through e - ter - ni - ty.

Creator Spirit, Come, We Pray 268

Latin, 9th century; attrib. to Rhabanus Maurus (d. 856)
Transl. The New Century Hymnal, 1995

1 Cre - a - tor Spir - it, come we pray, and vis - it
2 From God on high you are the gift: O Fount of
3 En - kin - dle us, set us a - glow, pour out your
4 De - fend us al - ways from the foe; on those who

ev - ery mind to - day; May hearts you made to be your
Life, your name we lift, O Par - a - clete, our Char - i -
love till hearts o'er - flow; To be made whole we sore - ly
fear, your peace be - stow; Pro - tect our jour - ney, be our

own be filled with heav - enly grace a - lone.
ty, O Fire, blessed Unc - tion flow - ing free.
long; O heal us, Spir - it ev - er strong.
guide, that we in safe - ty may a - bide.

Although the author of this hymn is unknown, it is often attributed to Rhabanus Maurus, archbishop of Mainz. Manuscripts date from as early as the tenth century when it was used in the daily office during Pentecost.

Tune: DICKINSON COLLEGE L.M.
Lee Hastings Bristol, Jr., 1962
Alternate tune: PUER NOBIS NASCITUR

269 Sweet Delight, Most Lovely

Paul Gerhardt, 1648
Transl. Madeleine Forell Marshall, 1993

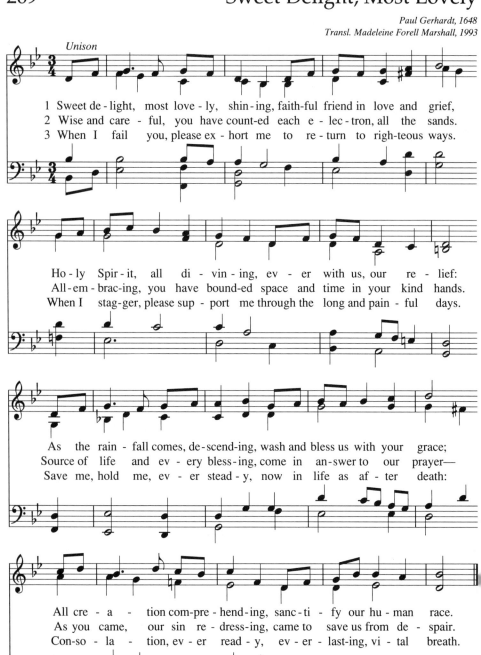

Unison

1 Sweet de-light, most love-ly, shin-ing, faith-ful friend in love and grief,
2 Wise and care-ful, you have count-ed each e-lec-tron, all the sands.
3 When I fail you, please ex-hort me to re-turn to righ-teous ways.

Ho-ly Spir-it, all di-vin-ing, ev-er with us, our re-lief:
All-em-brac-ing, you have bound-ed space and time in your kind hands.
When I stag-ger, please sup-port me through the long and pain-ful days.

As the rain-fall comes, de-scend-ing, wash and bless us with your grace;
Source of life and ev-ery bless-ing, come in an-swer to our prayer—
Save me, hold me, ev-er stead-y, now in life as af-ter death:

All cre-a-tion com-pre-hend-ing, sanc-ti-fy our hu-man race.
As you came, our sin re-dress-ing, came to save us from de-spair.
Con-so-la-tion, ev-er read-y, ev-er-last-ing, vi-tal breath.

This text is one of numerous new translations of German hymns written for The New Century Hymnal by Madeleine Forell Marshall. A comparative literary historian and professor, Marshall specializes in devotional poetry and hymnody. She has worked to support women who are victims of poverty and abuse, and to facilitate intercultural communication.

Tune: JOEL 8.7.8.7.D.
Sally Ann Morris, 1991
Alternate tune: NETTLETON

Like the Murmur of the Dove's Song 270

Carl P. Daw, Jr., 1982   *Isa. 38:14; Rom. 8:26; 12:4–5; John 15:1–5*

1 Like the mur - mur of the dove's song, like the chal - lenge of her
2 To the mem - bers of Christ's bod - y, to the branch - es of the
3 With the heal - ing of di - vi - sion, with the cease - less voice of

flight, like the vig - or of the wind's rush, like the
Vine, to the church in faith as - sem - bled, to our
prayer, with the power to love and wit - ness, with the

new flame's ea - ger might: Come, Ho - ly Spir - it, come.
midst as gift and sign: Come, Ho - ly Spir - it, come.
peace be - yond com - pare: Come, Ho - ly Spir - it, come.

Carl P. Daw, Jr., wrote this text for The Hymnal 1982
(Episcopal), and expressly for the tune Bridegroom. *Born and
educated in England, composer Peter Cutts has served as music
director for churches in Massachusetts and on the faculty of
Andover Newton Theological School.*

Tune: BRIDEGROOM 8.7.8.7.6.
Peter Cutts, 1969

271   Wind Who Makes All Winds That Blow

Acts 2:1–21   *Thomas H. Troeger, 1983*

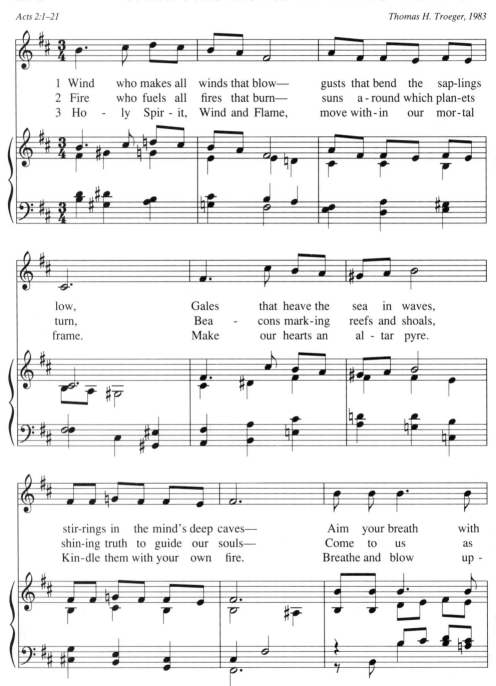

1 Wind who makes all winds that blow—
gusts that bend the sap-lings
2 Fire who fuels all fires that burn—
suns a-round which plan-ets
3 Ho - ly Spir - it, Wind and Flame,
move with-in our mor-tal

low, Gales that heave the sea in waves,
turn, Bea - cons mark-ing reefs and shoals,
frame. Make our hearts an al - tar pyre.

stir-rings in the mind's deep caves—
Aim your breath with
shin-ing truth to guide our souls—
Come to us as
Kin-dle them with your own fire.
Breathe and blow up -

Hymnwriter Thomas H. Troeger and composer Carol Doran
collaborated on this new hymn for a Pentecost celebration. The
tune is named for Father Sebastian Falcone, director of St.
Bernard's Institute of Rochester, New York, for whom the text
was written.

Tune: FALCONE 7.7.7.7.D.
Carol Doran, 1985
Alternate tune: ABERYSTWYTH

stead - y power on your church, this day, this hour.
once you came: burst in tongues of sa - cred flame!
on that blaze till our lives, our deeds and ways

Raise, re - new the life we've lost, Spir-it God of Pen - te - cost.
Light and Pow - er, Might and Strength, fill your church, its breadth and length.
Speak that tongue which ev - ery land by your grace shall un - der-stand.

272   On Pentecost They Gathered

Acts 2:1–24, 32–47   *Jane Parker Huber, 1981; rev. 1993*

1 On Pen - te - cost they gath - ered quite ear - ly in the day,
2 The peo - ple all a - round them were star - tled and a - mazed
3 God pours the Ho - ly Spir - it on all who would be - lieve,
4 O Spir - it, sent from heav - en on that day long a - go,

a band of Christ's dis - ci - ples to wor - ship, sing, and pray.
to un - der-stand their lan - guage, as God in Christ they praised.
on wom-en, men, and chil - dren who would God's grace re - ceive.
re - kin-dle faith a - mong us in all life's ebb and flow.

A might-y wind came blow - ing, filled all the swirl - ing air,
What un - i - ver - sal mes - sage, what great good news was here?
That Spir - it knows no lim - it, be - stow-ing life and power.
O give us hearts to lis - ten and tongues a - flame with praise,

and tongues of fire a - glow-ing in - spired each per - son there.
That Christ, once dead, is ris - en to van - quish all our fear.
The church, formed and re - form - ing, re - sponds in ev - ery hour.
so folk of ev - ery na - tion glad songs of joy shall raise.

Jane Parker Huber explained that she wrote this text in 1981
"to fill a gap in current hymnody," in that "many of the hymns
concerning the activity of the Holy Spirit do not mention
Pentecost."

Tune: MUNICH 7.6.7.6.D.
Neuvermehrtes Gesangbuch, *Meiningen, 1693*
Harm. Felix Mendelssohn, *1847*

Praise with Joy the World's Creator

273

The Iona Community, 1985; alt.

1 Praise with joy the world's Cre - a - tor, God of jus - tice,
2 Praise to Christ who feeds the hun - gry, frees the cap - tive,
3 Praise the Spir - it sent a - mong us, lib - er - a - ting
4 Praise the Mak - er, Christ, and Spir - it, one God in Com-

love, and peace, Source and end of hu - man knowl-edge,
finds the lost, Heals the sick, up - sets re - li - gion,
truth from pride, Forg - ing bonds where race or gen - der,
mu - ni - ty, Call - ing Christ-ians to em - bod - y

grace be - stow - ing with - out cease. Cel - e - brate the
fear - less both of fate and cost. Cel - e - brate Christ's
age or na - tion dare di - vide. Cel - e - brate the
one - ness and di - ver - si - ty. Thus the world shall

Ma - ker's glo - ry, power to res - cue and re - lease.
con - stant pres-ence— Friend and Strang-er, Guest and Host.
Spir - it's trea-sure— fool - ish - ness none dare de - ride.
yet be - lieve when shown Christ's vi - brant un - i - ty.

The Iona Community works and worships in a tenth-century abbey on the remote island of Iona, Scotland. Their output of hymns and songs includes this one written for the anniversary gathering of the World Student Christian Federation in Edinburgh in 1985.

Tune: LAUDA ANIMA (PRAISE MY SOUL)
8.7.8.7.8.7.
John Goss, 1869

274 Womb of Life, and Source of Being

John 1:14; 20:19–23   *Ruth Duck, 1986, 1990*

1 Womb of life, and source of be - ing, home of ev - ery rest - less heart, in your arms the worlds a - wak - ened; you have loved us from the start.

2 Word in flesh, our broth - er Je - sus, born to bring us sec - ond birth, you have come to stand be - side us, know - ing weak - ness, know - ing earth.

3 Brood - ing Spir - it, move a - mong us; be our part - ner, be our friend. When our mem - ory fails, re - mind us whose we are, what we in - tend.

4 Moth - er, Broth - er, ho - ly Part - ner; Fa - ther, Spir - it, On - ly Son: we would praise your name for - ev - er, one - in - three, and three - in - one.

This hymn, which mixes old and new metaphors to express faith and praise to God, known to us as Source, Word, and Spirit (and many other names!), borrows a phrase from Charles Wesley: "Born to give us second birth." According to Ruth Duck, Trinitarian theology provides a model for the life of community.

Tune: LADUE CHAPEL 8.7.8.7.D.
Ronald Arnatt, 1968
Alternate tunes: HYMN TO JOY; CENTRAL

275 Come Now, Almighty God

Anon., English, c. 1757; alt.

1 Come now, Al - might - y God, help us your
2 Come now, In - car - nate Word, by heaven and
3 Come, Ho - ly Com - fort - er, your sa - cred
4 To you, great One in Three, e - ter - nal

name to laud; our songs we raise:
earth a - dored; our prayer at - tend:
wit - ness bear in this glad hour.
prais - es be for ev - er - more.

Rul - er all glo - ri - ous, o'er all vic - to - ri - ous,
Come, and your peo - ple bless, and give your word suc - cess;
Your grace to us im - part, now rule in ev - ery heart,
Your sov - ereign maj - es - ty may we in glo - ry see,

come and reign o - ver us, An - cient of Days!
grant us your ho - li - ness, Sav - ior and Friend!
nev - er from us de - part, Spir - it of power!
and to e - ter - ni - ty love and a - dore.

This anonymous English hymn to the Trinity was first published in George Whitefield's Collection, *1757. This tune was composed especially for this text by Giardini, who was a brilliant violinist.*

Tune: ITALIAN HYMN 6.6.4.6.6.6.4.
Felice de Giardini, 1769

Holy God, We Praise Your Name

276

Anon., German, c. 1774
Transl. Clarence Alphonsus Walworth, 1853; alt.

Rev. 4:8–11

1 Ho - ly God, we praise your name; Sov - ereign God, we bow be - fore you; All on earth your scep - ter claim, all the heaven - ly hosts a - dore you. In - fi - nite your vast do - main, ev - er - last - ing is your reign.

2 Hark, the glad ce - les - tial hymn an - gel choirs a - round are rais - ing; Cher - u - bim and ser - a - phim, in un - ceas - ing cho - rus prais - ing, Fill the heavens with joys a - flame: ho - ly, ho - ly is your name.

3 All a - pos - tles join the strain as your sa - cred name they hal - low; Proph - ets swell the glad re - frain, and the bless - ed mar - tyrs fol - low; And from morn to set of sun, through the church the song goes on.

4 Ho - ly Fa - ther, Ho - ly Son, Ho - ly Spir - it, Three we name you, While in es - sence tru - ly one, un - di - vid - ed God we claim you; So we gath - er rev - erent - ly to a - dore the mys - ter - y.

This German Catholic hymn, based on the Te Deum Laudamus, *appeared with this tune in a hymnal published by command of Austrian empress Maria Theresa. In the nineteenth century it became popular in Protestant worship.*

Tune: GROSSER GOTT, WIR LOBEN DICH
7.8.7.8.7.7.
Katholisches Gesangbuch, Vienna, c. 1774
Alt. Johann Gottfried Schicht, 1819

277 Holy, Holy, Holy

Rev. 4:8–11; Isa. 6:1–8

Reginald Heber, 1826; alt.

Descant

4 Ho - ly, ho - ly, ho - ly!

1 Ho - ly, ho - ly, ho - ly,   God   the Al - might - y!
2 Ho - ly, ho - ly, ho - ly!   Saints a - dore you   tru - ly,
3 Ho - ly, ho - ly, ho - ly!   Though we know but   dim - ly,
4 Ho - ly, ho - ly, ho - ly,   God   the Al - might - y!

Ho - ly, ho - ly, ho - ly!

Ear - ly   in   the   morn - ing   we   praise your maj - es - ty.
Cast - ing down their gold - en crowns a - round the glass - y   sea;
Though the eyes   of   hum - an - kind your glo - ry may not   see,
All   your works shall praise your name in   earth and sky and sea.

Ho - ly, ho - ly, ho - ly!

Ho - ly, ho - ly   ho - ly!   Mer - ci - ful and   might - y!
Cher - u - bim and   ser - a - phim   bow   be - fore you   on - ly,
You a - lone are   ho - ly,   you   a - lone are   wor - thy,
Ho - ly, ho - ly, ho - ly!   Mer - ci - ful and   might - y!

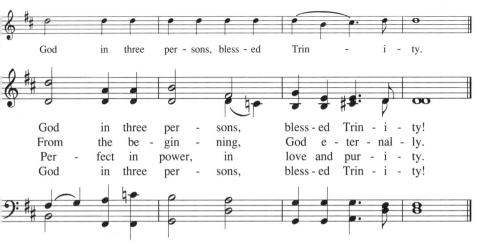

God in three per - sons, bless - ed Trin - i - ty.

God in three per - sons, bless - ed Trin - i - ty!
From the be - gin - ning, God e - ter - nal - ly.
Per - fect in power, in love and pur - i - ty.
God in three per - sons, bless - ed Trin - i - ty!

This hymn by Reginald Heber was published in a book of
hymns for Banbury Parish Church in England. Nicaea, one of
nearly 300 tunes by John B. Dykes, was named for the famous
council that defined the doctrine of the Trinity.

Tune: NICAEA 11.12.12.10.
John B. Dykes, 1861
Descant David McK.Williams, 1948

Creator God, Creating Still 278

Jane Parker Huber, 1977; rev. 1993

Rom. 5:1–5

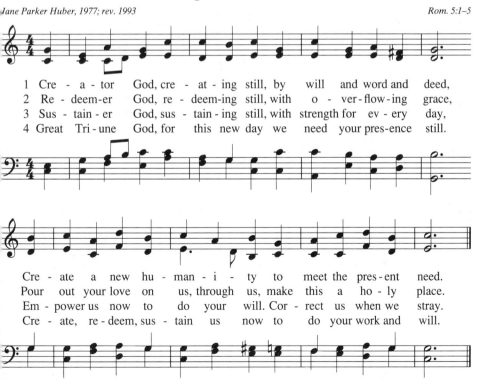

1 Cre - a - tor God, cre - at - ing still, by will and word and deed,
2 Re - deem-er God, re - deem-ing still, with o - ver-flow-ing grace,
3 Sus - tain - er God, sus - tain - ing still, with strength for ev - ery day,
4 Great Tri - une God, for this new day we need your pres-ence still.

Cre - ate a new hu - man - i - ty to meet the pres-ent need.
Pour out your love on us, through us, make this a ho - ly place.
Em - power us now to do your will. Cor - rect us when we stray.
Cre - ate, re - deem, sus - tain us now to do your work and will.

*Jane Parker Huber's second hymn was written during a time of
particular focus on language. By describing the Triune God in
terms of function rather than in terms of persons, she hoped to
avoid a tendency to think we know God by knowing formulas.*

Tune: ST. ANNE C.M.
William Croft, 1708

279 O God in Heaven

John 14:15–19, 25–27

Elena G. Maquiso, 1961
Transl. D. T. Niles, 1964; alt.

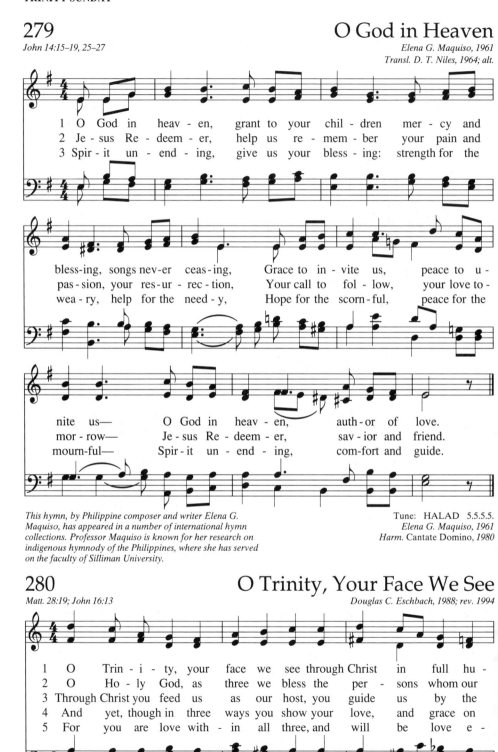

1 O God in heav - en, grant to your chil - dren mer - cy and
2 Je - sus Re - deem - er, help us re - mem - ber your pain and
3 Spir - it un - end - ing, give us your bless - ing: strength for the

bless - ing, songs nev - er ceas - ing, Grace to in - vite us, peace to u -
pas - sion, your res - ur - rec - tion, Your call to fol - low, your love to -
wea - ry, help for the need - y, Hope for the scorn - ful, peace for the

nite us— O God in heav - en, auth - or of love.
mor - row— Je - sus Re - deem - er, sav - ior and friend.
mourn-ful— Spir - it un - end - ing, com-fort and guide.

This hymn, by Philippine composer and writer Elena G. Maquiso, has appeared in a number of international hymn collections. Professor Maquiso is known for her research on indigenous hymnody of the Philippines, where she has served on the faculty of Silliman University.

Tune: HALAD 5.5.5.5.
Elena G. Maquiso, 1961
Harm. Cantate Domino, 1980

280 O Trinity, Your Face We See

Matt. 28:19; John 16:13

Douglas C. Eschbach, 1988; rev. 1994

1 O Trin - i - ty, your face we see through Christ in full hu -
2 O Ho - ly God, as three we bless the per - sons whom our
3 Through Christ you feed us as our host, you guide us by the
4 And yet, though in three ways you show your love, and grace on
5 For you are love with - in all three, and will be love e -

man - i - ty; For flesh has held di -
creeds con - fess; But each is nei - ther
Ho - ly Ghost. You fa - ther us in
us be - stow, our faith will e - ven
ter - nal - ly; May we in your love

vin - i - ty, that we might share your mys - ter - y.
more nor less, for all make up your ho - li - ness.
ways that boast of love for those who need you most.
strong - er grow when through each one all three we know.
ev - er be, most bless - ed Ho - ly Trin - i - ty.

Douglas Eschbach was serving as minister at St. Paul Lutheran Church in Telford, Pennsylvania, and Arthur Clyde was director of music at Zwingli United Church of Christ in Souderton, Pennsylvania when they collaborated on this hymn.

Tune: RELIANCE L.M.
Arthur G. Clyde, 1988
Alternate tune: WINCHESTER NEW

Come, Holy Spirit, Heavenly Dove   281
Isaac Watts, 1707; alt.   *John 1:32*

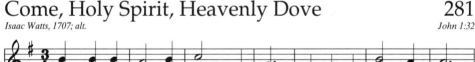

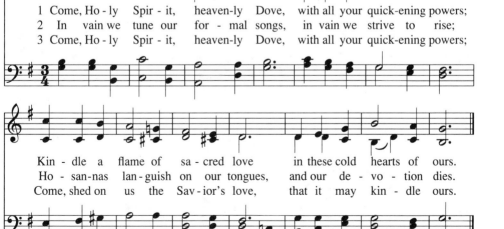

1 Come, Ho - ly Spir - it, heaven-ly Dove, with all your quick-ening powers;
2 In vain we tune our for - mal songs, in vain we strive to rise;
3 Come, Ho - ly Spir - it, heaven-ly Dove, with all your quick-ening powers;

Kin - dle a flame of sa - cred love in these cold hearts of ours.
Ho - san-nas lan - guish on our tongues, and our de - vo - tion dies.
Come, shed on us the Sav - ior's love, that it may kin - dle ours.

This text from an early collection of Watts' Hymns and Spiritual Songs (1707) has seen many modifications through the years, including some made by John Wesley on theological grounds.

Tune: ST. AGNES C.M.
John B. Dykes, 1866

282

Every Time I Feel the Spirit

2 Sam. 22:9; Ps. 18:8

African-American spiritual

Among the thousands of spirituals that exist today are songs of gladness and songs of sorrow. This well-known spiritual is a song of joy, captured not only in the words, but in the lively rhythms.

Tune: African-American spiritual
Arr. Joyce Finch Johnson, 1992

Spirit of the Living God

283

Daniel Iverson, 1926

Acts 11:15; 2 Cor. 3:1–6; Gal. 5:25

Presbyterian minister Daniel Iverson was inspired to write this chorus one evening while attending revival services led by the George T. Stephans Evangelistic Party in Orlando, Florida, in 1926. It became widely popular at similar meetings before it was published several years later.

Tune: IVERSON 7.5.7.5.8.7.5.
Daniel Iverson, 1926

284   Joys Are Flowing like a River
(Blessed Quietness)

Matt. 8:26; John 14:16; Ps. 46:4   *Manie Payne Ferguson (b. 1850); alt.*

1 Joys are flow-ing like a riv - er, since the Com - fort - er has
2 Bring-ing life and health and glad-ness all a - round, this heaven-ly
3 Like the rain that falls from heav - en, like the sun - light from the
4 See, a fruit-ful field is grow-ing, bless-ed fruit of righ - teous -
5 What a won - der - ful sal - va - tion, when we al - ways see Christ's

come;   Christ a - bides with us for - ev - er, makes the
Guest   Ban-ished un - be - lief and sad - ness, changed our
sky,   So the Spir - it too is giv - en, com - ing
ness;   And the streams of life are flow - ing in the
face,   What a per - fect hab - i - ta - tion, what a

Refrain

trust - ing heart a home.
wea - ri - ness to rest.
on us from on high.   Bless-ed qui - et - ness, ho - ly
lone - ly wil - der - ness.
qui - et rest - ing place.

qui - et - ness, what as - sur - ance in my soul. On the

storm-y sea, Je-sus speaks to me, and the bil-lows cease to roll.

Manie Payne Ferguson, born in Ireland, was married to a
Wesleyan evangelist who established several missions on
England's west coast. Ferguson's hymns were published
in Echoes from Beulah.

Tune: BLESSED QUIETNESS 8.7.8.7. with refrain
W. S. Marshall
Arr. J. Jefferson Cleveland
and Verolga Nix, 1981

O Holy Dove of God Descending

285

Bryan Jeffery Leech, 1976

Unison

1 O ho-ly Dove of God de-scend-ing, you are the love that knows no end-ing,
2 O ho-ly Wind of God now blow-ing, you are the seed that God is sow-ing,
3 O ho-ly Rain of God now fall-ing, you make the Word of God en-thrall-ing,
4 O ho-ly Flame of God now burn-ing, you are the power of Christ re-turn-ing,

All of our shat-tered dreams you're mend-ing: Spir-it, now live in me.
You are the life that starts us grow-ing: Spir-it, now live in me.
You are the in-ner voice now call-ing: Spir-it, now live in me.
You are the an-swer to our yearn-ing: Spir-it, now live in me.

Bryan Jeffery Leech, educated in Britain and the United States,
has served American churches since 1955. He has also written
musical plays, assisted in preparing and editing hymnals, and
co-edited The Hymnal Companion *(1979).*

Tune: O HOLY DOVE 9.9.9.6.
Bryan Jeffery Leech, 1976

286

Spirit, Spirit of Gentleness

James K. Manley, 1978; alt.

*Reduced-size notes may be played with organ pedals in lieu of or in combination with the other notes.

This popular hymn by songwriter James K. Manley grew out of a sabbatical leave at the School of Theology at Claremont, California. It was first sung at Waiokeola Congregational Church in Honolulu, after which Manley added the fourth stanza at the suggestion of a church member.

Tune: SPIRIT Irr.
James K. Manley, 1978
Arr. The New Century Hymnal, *1993*

287 Come, Teach Us, Spirit of Our God

Shirley Erena Murray, 1990

Unison

1 Come, teach us, Spir - it of our God, the
2 Ex - cite our minds to fol - low you, to
3 En - gage our wits to dance with you, to
4 In - spire our spark to light from you to
5 De - light our hearts to wor - ship you, to

lan - guage of your way, the les - sons
trace new truths in store, new flight paths
leap from log - ic's base, to cap - ture
catch cre - a - tion's flair, new ar - tis -
learn com - pas - sion's code, to live in

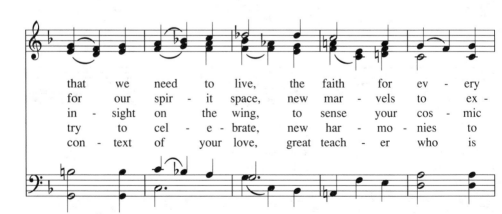

that we need to live, the faith for ev - ery
for our spir - it space, new mar - vels to ex -
in - sight on the wing, to sense your cos - mic
try to cel - e - brate, new har - mo - nies to
con - text of your love, great teach - er who is

For a hymn search sponsored by an educational institution,
Shirley Erena Murray sought to utilize various images of
creativity in learning. The tune was composed especially
for this text.

Tune: MURRAY C.M. extended
Arthur G. Clyde, 1993

day;		the	faith	for	ev -	ery	day.
plore:		new	mar -	vels	to	ex -	plore:
grace:		to	sense	your	cos -	mic	grace:
dare:		new	har -	mo -	nies	to	dare:
God!		Great	teach -	er	who	is	God!

Let It Breathe on Me

288

Magnolia Lewis-Butts, 1941; alt.

Job 33:4; Ezek. 37:1–14; John 20:19–23

1 Let it breathe on me, let it breathe on me, let the breath of the
2 While I'm work - ing, God, in your vine - yard here, I can - not
3 When the path - way, God, I can - not see, when the way is

Spir - it breathe on me. Let it breathe on me, let it
serve with - out you near; O come, blessed Spir - it, so
hard, O breathe on me; Give me grace to know when

breathe on me, let the breath of God now breathe on me.
close to me that I may feel you breathe on me.
you are near, then, I pray, O Spir - it, breathe on me.

Songwriter Magnolia Lewis-Butts helped form the National
Convention of Gospel Choirs and Choruses in 1932, which was
the model for all subsequent gospel music conventions.

Tune: BREATHE ON ME Irr.
Magnolia Lewis-Butts, 1941

289

Come Forth, O Love Divine

Acts 2:1–4

Bianco da Siena (d. 1434)
Transl. Richard F. Littledale, 1867; alt

1 Come forth, O Love di - vine, seek now this soul of
2 O let it free - ly burn, till earth - ly pas - sions
3 And so the yearn - ing strong with which the soul will

mine, and vis - it it with your own ar - dor glow - ing;
turn to dust and ash - es in its heat con - sum - ing;
long, shall far out - pass the power of hu - man tell - ing;

O Com-fort - er, draw near, with - in my heart ap - pear,
And let your glo - rious light shine ev - er on my sight,
For none can guess its grace, till love cre - ate a place

and kin - dle it, your ho - ly flame be - stow - ing.
and clothe me round, the while my path il - lum - ing.
where - in the Ho - ly Spir - it makes a dwell - ing.

Bianco da Siena lived in Venice, where he was a member
of a religious order following the rule of St. Augustine.
Ralph Vaughan Williams' tune composed for this hymn
was named for his birthplace in England.

Tune: DOWN AMPNEY 6.6.11.D.
Ralph Vaughan Williams, 1906

Spirit of God, Descend upon My Heart 290

George Croly, 1854; alt. *Gal. 5:25; Matt. 22:37; John 1:32*

1 Spir - it of God, de - scend up - on my heart;
2 I ask no dream, no proph - et ec - sta - sies,
3 Have you not bid us love you ev - ery way?
4 Teach me to feel that you are al - ways nigh;
5 Teach me to love you as your an - gels love,

wean it from earth, through all its puls - es move;
no sud - den rend - ing of the veil of clay,
All, all your own: soul, heart, and strength, and mind;
teach me the strug - gles of the soul to bear,
one ho - ly pas - sion fill - ing all my frame;

Stoop to my weak - ness, might - y as you are,
No an - gel vis - i - tant, no o - pening skies;
I see your cross— there teach my heart to stay:
To check the ris - ing doubt, the reb - el sigh;
The bap - tism of the heaven - de - scend - ed dove,

and make me love you as I ought to love.
but take the dim - ness of my soul a - way.
O let me seek you, and O let me find.
teach me the pa - tience of un - an - swered prayer.
my heart an al - tar, and your love the flame.

George Croly, ordained in the Church of Ireland, was well known in London literary circles and served a poor parish. This hymn is from a collection he compiled for that congregation. Hellespont was the original name for the tune Morecambe.

Tune: MORECAMBE 10.10.10.10.
Frederick C. Atkinson, 1870

291

O God the Creator

Ps. 104:24–30; Acts 4:32–35

Elizabeth Haile and Cecil Corbett, 1977; alt

1 O God, the Cre - a - tor, the Three - in -
2 For the earth is our moth - er where all things
3 We are one in the Spir - it, in the great mys-ter -
4 God, we ask you for lead - ers with your wis - dom

One, the Cre - a - tor of earth and moon and
grow, and her val - leys are green where the wa - ters
y, joined to - geth - er in beau-ty as we dwell in har-mo -
blessed, and we pray you will join us in our vi - sion

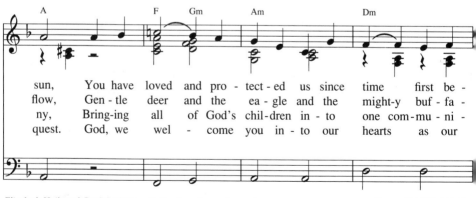

sun, You have loved and pro - tect - ed us since time first be -
flow, Gen - tle deer and the ea - gle and the might-y buf - fa -
ny, Bring-ing all of God's chil-dren in - to one com-mu - ni -
quest. God, we wel - come you in - to our hearts as our

Elizabeth Haile and Cecil Corbett are Native Americans who wrote this text as the theme song of the 1977 Indian Youth Conference in Tulsa, Oklahoma. It was published with Joy Patterson's tune in The Presbyterian Hymnal *(1990). A "vision quest," referred to in stanza four, is a Lakota Indian ritual of prayer and fasting carried out in the form of a circle and a cross. Through this spiritual exercise, an individual seeks wisdom and communion with "Wakan-Tanka" (the Great Spirit), and may receive healing or new direction in life.*

Tune: KASTAAK Irr.
Joy F. Patterson, 1989

Refrain

gun,
lo,
ty,
guest,

And we're broth - ers and sis - ters in God's love, in God's

love, and we're broth-ers and sis - ters in God's love.

Breathe on Me, Breath of God 292

Edwin Hatch, 1886; alt.

1 Breathe on me, Breath of God, fill me with life a - new
2 Breathe on me, Breath of God, un - til my heart is pure,
3 Breathe on me, Breath of God, stir in me one de - sire:
4 Breathe on me, Breath of God, so shall I nev - er die,

That I may love the way you love and do what you would do.
Un - til with you I will one will, to do and to en - dure.
That ev - ery earth - ly part of me may glow with ho - ly fire.
But live with you the per - fect life of your e - ter - ni - ty.

*Between parish assignments in London, Edwin Hatch taught
classics at Trinity College, Quebec, and lectured at Oxford. This
hymn appeared in a leaflet, "Between Doubt and Prayer"
(1878). Other hymns were published posthumously in* Towards
Fields of Light, *London (1890).*

Tune: TRENTHAM S.M.
Robert Jackson, 1894

293

Sweet, Sweet Spirit

2 Cor. 3:17–5:5

Doris Akers, 1962; alt

Slowly

1 There's a sweet, sweet Spir-it in this place, and I
2 There are bless-ings you can-not re-ceive till you

know that it's the Spir-it of the Lord; there are
know that Spir-it's full-ness and be-lieve; you're the

sweet ex-pres-sions on each face, and I
one to prof-it when you say, "I am

to Refrain

know they feel the pres-ence of the Lord.
going to stay with Je-sus all the way."

This is one of the most popular gospel songs from the corpus of African-American songwriters who emerged during the golden age of gospel (1930–1969). Although this era was dominated by the Baptists, Doris Akers had Methodist roots.

Tune: SWEET, SWEET SPIRIT
9.11.9.11. with refrain
Doris Akers, 1962

Refrain

Sweet Ho - ly Spir - it, sweet heav-en-ly Dove, stay right here with us, fill-ing us with your love; And for these bless-ings we lift our hearts in praise. With-out a doubt we'll know that we have been re - vived when we shall leave this place.

294   There's a Spirit in the Air

John 6:24–35, 51–58; 1 Cor. 2:9–16; 1 John 4   *Brian Wren, 1969; rev. 1987*

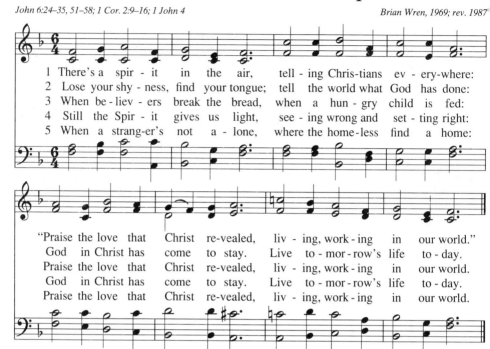

1 There's a spir - it in the air, tell - ing Chris-tians ev - ery-where:
2 Lose your shy - ness, find your tongue; tell the world what God has done:
3 When be - liev - ers break the bread, when a hun - gry child is fed:
4 Still the Spir - it gives us light, see - ing wrong and set - ting right:
5 When a strang-er's not a - lone, where the home-less find a home:

"Praise the love that Christ re-vealed, liv - ing, work - ing in our world."
God in Christ has come to stay. Live to - mor - row's life to - day.
Praise the love that Christ re-vealed, liv - ing, work - ing in our world.
God in Christ has come to stay. Live to - mor - row's life to - day.
Praise the love that Christ re-vealed, liv - ing, work - ing in our world.

6   May the Spir-it fill our praise,
     guide our thoughts and change our ways.
     God in Christ has come to stay.
     Live to-mor-row's life to-day.

7   There's a Spir-it in the air,
     call-ing peo-ple ev-ery-where:
     Praise the love that Christ re-vealed,
     liv-ing, work-ing in our world.

Brian Wren celebrates the Spirit's work in the world in this text written for Pentecost at Hockley, England. In it, Wren borrows a poetic device from the Isaac Watts hymn "Give to Our God Immortal Praise" with the alternating repetition of two choruses.

Tune: ORIENTIS PARTIBUS 7.7.7.7.
Medieval French melody
Harm. Richard Redhead, 1853

295   I Sing a Song of the Saints of God

Lesbia Scott, 1929; alt.

Unison

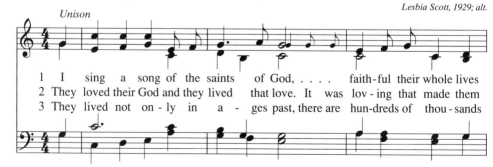

1 I sing a song of the saints of God, ... faith-ful their whole lives
2 They loved their God and they lived that love. It was lov - ing that made them
3 They lived not on - ly in a - ges past, there are hun-dreds of thou - sands

This text was included in Lesbia Scott's Everyday Hymns for Little Children with her original words, music, and illustrations. A native of Britain, Scott was also the author of six published plays and enjoyed painting until her death in 1986.

Tune: GRAND ISLE Irr.
John H. Hopkins, 1940

through, who brave-ly la-bored, lived, and died for the God they
strong. They did what was right, for Je-sus' sake, lived just-ly their
still. The world is filled with liv-ing saints who choose to

loved and knew. And one was a doc-tor, and one was a queen, and an-
whole lives long. And one was a proph-et, and one was a priest, and an-
do God's will. You can meet them in school, on the road, or at sea, in a

oth-er a shep-herd in pas-tures green: they were saints of God, if you
oth-er was slain by a fierce wild beast: there is no earth-ly rea-son,
church, in a train, in a shop, or at tea: for the saints are folk like

know what I mean. God, help me to be one, too.
none in the least, why I should-n't be one, too.
you and like me, and I mean to be one, too.

296   Behold the Host All Robed in Light

Rev. 7:9–17

Hans A. Brorson, c. 1764
Transl. Carl Doving, 1909; alt.

1 Be - hold the host all   robed in   light, ar -   rayed like   snow - clad
2 Their work was hard, their   jour - ney long, but   by   God's grace their

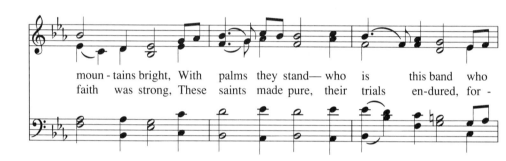

moun - tains bright, With   palms they stand— who   is   this band   who
faith   was strong, These   saints made pure, their   trials   en-dured, for -

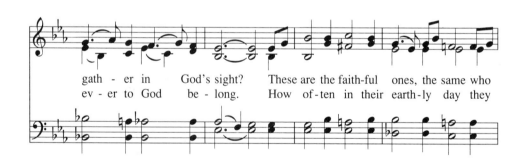

gath - er in   God's sight?   These are the faith-ful   ones, the same who
ev - er to God   be - long.   How of-ten in their earth-ly day they

through   the time   of   tri -   al came, Who   Christ has raised that
si -   lent - ly   did   weep   and pray, But   con - flicts past, brought

Danish Lutheran pastor and hymnwriter Hans A. Brorson
was bishop of Ribe for many years, a position in which he was
greatly loved and respected. The Norwegian folk melody from
Heddal was harmonized by Norwegian composer Edvard Grieg.

Tune: DEN STORE HVIDE FLOK   8.8.4.4.6. Triple
Norwegian folk tune
Arr. Edvard Grieg (1843–1907)

they might praise un - end - ing - ly God's name;
home at last, God wiped their tears a - way;

And now their jour - ney fin - ished they with
No hun - ger now, nor thirst they know; op -

joy - ful voic - es join to pray, glad songs they sing. Their
pres - sion can - not cause them woe. The Shep - herd feeds and

thanks they bring to God both night and day.
gent - ly leads where liv - ing wa - ters flow.

297
Give Thanks for Life

1 Thess. 5:18; Rom. 16:1–16; Eph. 1:15–16

Shirley Erena Murray, 1986

1 Give thanks for life, the mea-sure of our days,
2 Give thanks for those who made their life a light
3 And for our own, our liv-ing and our dead,
4 Give thanks for hope, that like the wheat, the grain

mor - tal, we pass through beau - ty that de - cays,
caught from the Christ-flame, burst-ing through the night,
thanks for the love by which our life is fed,
that lies in dark - ness does its life re - tain

Yet sing to God our hope, our love, our praise,
Who touched the truth, who burned for what was right,
A love not changed by time or death or dread,
In res - ur - rec - tion to grow green a - gain,

Shirley Erena Murray wrote this text "as a celebration for someone who has lived a full life." The tune by Nancy M. René was originally composed as a setting for her own version of "For All the Saints," and was dedicated to her mother and grandmother.

Tune: ROBINSON 10.10.10. with alleluias
Nancy M. René, 1994

Al - le-lu-ia, Al-le - lu - ia! ia!

O Savior, for the Saints 298

Richard Mant, 1837; alt. *Rom. 14:7–9*

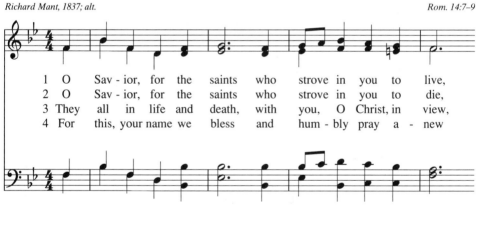

1 O Sav - ior, for the saints who strove in you to live,
2 O Sav - ior, for the saints who strove in you to die,
3 They all in life and death, with you, O Christ, in view,
4 For this, your name we bless and hum - bly pray a - new

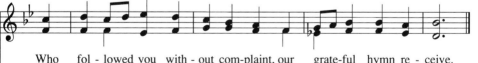

Who fol - lowed you with - out com-plaint, our grate-ful hymn re - ceive.
Who loved and served with - out re - straint, ac - cept our thank-ful cry.
Learned from the Ho - ly Spir-it's breath to suf - fer and to do.
That we, like them, in ho - li - ness may live and die in you.

This was one of several original hymns appended to Richard
Mant's book of translations of Latin hymns from the Roman
Breviary. A priest of the Church of England, Mant was for
many years a bishop in Ireland.

Tune: FESTAL SONG S.M.
William Walter, 1872

299
For All the Saints

Heb. 12:1   *William W. How, 1864; alt.*

1 For all the saints who from their la - bors rest,
2 You were their rock, their ref - uge, and their might:
3 Still may your peo - ple, faith - ful, true, and bold,
4 Ringed by this cloud of wit - ness - es di - vine,
5 And when the strife is fierce, the war - fare long,

who to the
you, Christ, the
live as the
we fee - bly
steals on the

world their stead-fast faith con - fessed, your name, O Je - sus,
hope that put their fears to flight; 'mid gloom and doubt, you
saints who no - bly fought of old, and share with them a
strug - gle, they in glo - ry shine; yet in your love our
ear the dis - tant tri - umph song, then hearts are brave a -

be for - ev - er blessed.
were their one true light.
glo - rious crown of gold. Al - le - lu - ia! Al - le - lu - ia!
faith - ful lives en - twine.
gain, and faith grows strong.

*This traditional All Saints Day hymn originally consisted
of eleven stanzas written for the* Sarum Hymnal *(1869) and
set to a tune by that name,* Sarum. *It has grown in popularity
since it was later paired with the enduring* Sine Nomine *in*
The English Hymnal *(1906).*

Tune: SINE NOMINE 10.10.10.4.
Ralph Vaughan Williams, 1906

Jesus Shall Reign

300

Isaac Watts, 1719; alt.

Ps. 72; Rev. 1:4b–8

1 Je - sus shall reign wher - e'er the sun
2 Through Christ shall end - less prayer be made,
3 Peo - ple and realms of ev - ery tongue
4 Bless - ings a - bound where - e'er Christ reigns:
5 Let ev - ery crea - ture rise and bring

does its suc - ces - sive jour - neys run;
borne by the Spir - it's cease - less aid;
dwell on God's love with sweet - est song,
the pris - oners leap to lose their chains,
trib - utes of praise for all to sing;

God's realm shall stretch from shore to shore
Like sweet per - fume new hymns shall rise
And in - fant voic - es shall pro - claim
The wea - ry find e - ter - nal rest,
An - gels de - scend with songs a - gain,

till moons shall wax and wane no more.
with ev - ery morn - ing sac - ri - fice.
their ear - liest prayers in Je - sus' name.
and all who suf - fer want are blessed.
and earth re - peat the loud a - men.

The second half of a longer paraphrase of Psalm 72, this hymn was included in Isaac Watts' Psalms of David, a collection of psalm-based poems with New Testament orientation. John Hatton once lived on Duke Street in St. Helen's, Lancaster, England.

Tune: DUKE STREET L.M.
Attrib. to John Hatton, c. 1793

301 Crown with Your Richest Crowns

John 19:16–18, 31–34; Rev. 7:9–10

Matthew Bridges, 1851, and Godfrey Thring, 1874
Adapt. Thomas H. Troeger, 1993

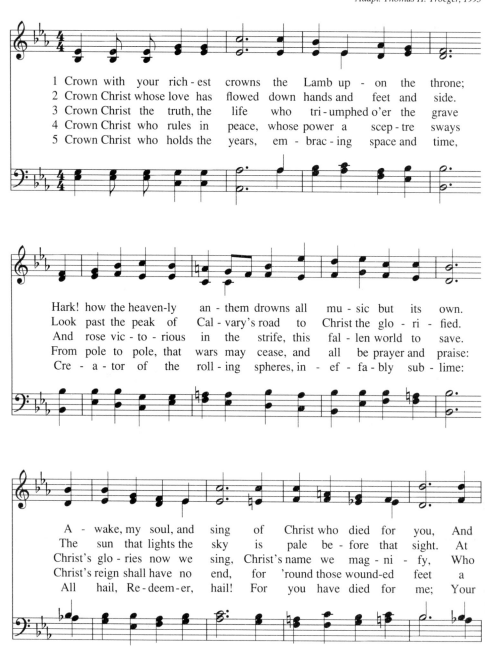

1 Crown with your rich-est crowns the Lamb up-on the throne;
2 Crown Christ whose love has flowed down hands and feet and side.
3 Crown Christ the truth, the life who tri-umphed o'er the grave
4 Crown Christ who rules in peace, whose power a scep-tre sways
5 Crown Christ who holds the years, em-brac-ing space and time,

Hark! how the heaven-ly an-them drowns all mu-sic but its own.
Look past the peak of Cal-vary's road to Christ the glo-ri-fied.
And rose vic-to-rious in the strife, this fal-len world to save.
From pole to pole, that wars may cease, and all be prayer and praise:
Cre-a-tor of the roll-ing spheres, in-ef-fa-bly sub-lime:

A-wake, my soul, and sing of Christ who died for you, And
The sun that lights the sky is pale be-fore that sight. At
Christ's glo-ries now we sing, Christ's name we mag-ni-fy, Who
Christ's reign shall have no end, for 'round those wound-ed feet a
All hail, Re-deem-er, hail! For you have died for me; Your

This hymn has evolved as a composite of the original text by Matthew Bridges and Godfrey Thring's version written twenty-three years later. Diademata was composed for Bridges' text and is titled for the Greek word meaning "crowns."

Tune: DIADEMATA S.M.D.
George J. Elvey, 1868

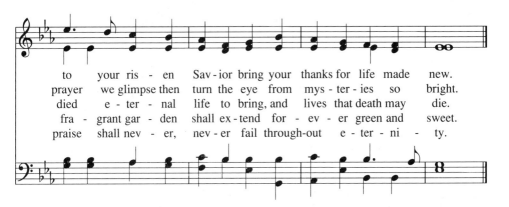

to   your ris - en   Sav-ior bring your   thanks for life made   new.
prayer   we glimpse then   turn the eye from   mys - ter - ies   so   bright.
died   e - ter - nal   life to bring, and   lives that death may   die.
fra - grant gar - den   shall ex - tend for - ev - er green and   sweet.
praise   shall nev - er,   nev - er fail through-out   e - ter - ni -   ty.

Eternal Christ, You Rule   302

Dan Damon, 1990   Eph. 1:15–23; 5:1–2

Unison

1 E - ter-nal Christ, you rule   keep-ing com - pa - ny   with pain;
2 E - ter-nal Christ, you rule   speak-ing par - don from the cross;
3 E - ter-nal Christ, you rule   tak - ing chil - dren by the hand;
4 E - ter-nal Christ, you rule   fast - ing for - ty days a - lone;
5 E - ter-nal Christ, you rule   keep-ing com - pa - ny   with pain;

en - dur-ing rid - i - cule,   re - ject - ed, still you reign.
for - giv-ing pound-ed nails;   death did its worst and lost.
the   proud re - turn to school; the meek re - ceive the land.
the   tempt-er played the fool, ex - pect - ing bread from stone.
with love and truth as tools, come build in us your reign.

*Hymnwriter Daniel Charles Damon credits a sermon given by
United Church of Christ minister Ansley Coe Throckmorton at
Pacific School of Religion in Berkeley, California, as his
inspiration for this text. To the question, "How does Christ
rule?" Throckmorton replied, "By keeping company with pain."*

Tune: THROCKMORTON 6.7.6.6.
Dan Damon, 1990

303   Rejoice, Give Thanks and Sing

Phil. 4:4; Rev. 3:7; 19:6–7   *Charles Wesley, 1746; alt.*

1 Re - joice, give thanks and   sing;   your   Sov-ereign God   a - dore!
2 Our   Sav - ior   Je - sus   reigns,   the   God   of   truth   and   love;
3 Christ   Je - sus   can - not   fail   to   rule both earth   and   heaven;
4 Re - joice in   glo - rious   hope,   for   Christ the   Judge shall   come,

For   Christ has robbed death's   sting and tri - umphs ev - er -   more. Lift
The   Lamb who purged our   stains is crowned with power a -   bove. Lift
The   keys   of   death   and   hell are to   the   Sav - ior   given. Lift
And   take   the   faith - ful   up   to their   e - ter - nal   home. We

up   your   heart, lift   up   your voice! Re - joice, a - gain   I   say,   re - joice.
up   your   heart, lift   up   your voice! Re - joice, a - gain   I   say,   re - joice.
up   your   heart, lift   up   your voice! Re - joice, a - gain   I   say,   re - joice.
soon shall   hear   a   heaven-ly   voice a - bove the trum-pet's sound, "Re - joice!"

This Ascension text, one of the festival hymns by Charles Wesley,
was published originally in John Wesley's Moral and Sacred Poems
(1744). Somewhat altered, it appeared in this familiar version in
Charles' *1746 collection,* Hymns for Our Lord's Resurrection.

Tune: DARWALL'S 148th 6.6.6.6.8.8.
John Darwall, 1770

All Hail the Power of Jesus' Name 304

St. 1–3, Edward Perronet, 1779, 1780; alt.
St. 4, John Rippon, 1787; alt.

Rev. 19; 5:9; Phil. 2:9–11

1 All hail the power of Je - sus' name! Let an - gels pros - trate fall;
2 A - dorn, O mar - tyred saints of old, the cor - o - na - tion hall;
3 All heirs of Is - rael's chos - en race, now ran-somed from the fall,
4 Be - fore the cross, with heav-en's throng, we on our knees shall fall;

Bring forth the roy - al di - a - dem, and crown Christ ser - vant of all.
Ex - tol the wound-ed One fore - told, and crown Christ bear - er of all.
Pro - claim the won - ders of God's grace, and crown Christ heal - er of all.
We'll join the ev - er - last - ing song, and crown Christ sav - ior of all.

At - tend the Sav - ior's sov - ereign claim, and crown Christ ser - vant of all.
Ex - tol the wound-ed One fore - told, and crown Christ bear - er of all.
Pro - claim the won - ders of God's grace, and crown Christ heal - er of all.
We'll join the ev - er - last - ing song, and crown Christ sav - ior of all.

Edward Perronet, long a worker for English Methodism, later became a Congregational minister near Canterbury. John Rippon, an English Baptist minister, wrote more than 1,000 hymns. The tune is by Oliver Holden, an early American carpenter, legislator, musician, and hymnal editor.

Tune: CORONATION C.M.
Oliver Holden, 1793

305 You Servants of God, Your Sovereign Proclaim

Rev. 4:9–11; 5:11–14   *Charles Wesley, 1744; alt.*

1 You ser - vants of God, your Sov - ereign pro - claim,
2 God rules from on high, al - might - y to save,
3 Sal - va - tion to God who sits on the throne!
4 Then let us a - dore and ren - der God's right,

and pub - lish a - broad that won - der - ful name:
and still God is nigh, whose pres - ence we have.
Let all cry a - loud for what God has done.
all glo - ry and power, all wis - dom and might,

The name, all vic - to - rious, of Je - sus ex - tol,
The great con - gre - ga - tion God's tri - umphs shall praise,
The prais - es of Je - sus the an - gels pro - claim,
All hon - or and bless - ing with an - gels a - bove,

who, sov - ereign and glo - rious, now rules o - ver all.
as - crib - ing sal - va - tion to Je - sus al - ways.
still veil - ing their fac - es, they wor - ship the Lamb.
and thanks nev - er ceas - ing and in - fin - ite love.

Written at a time of anti-Methodist sentiment, this hymn was included in Charles Wesley's Hymns for Times of Trouble and Persecution. *The tune is attributed to William Croft, composer at England's Chapel Royal and organist at Westminster Abbey.*

Tune: HANOVER 10.10.11.11.
Attrib. to William Croft, 1708

The Church of Christ, in Every Age 306

Fred Pratt Green, 1969

1 The church of Christ, in ev - ery age be -
2 A - cross the world, a - cross the street, the
3 Then let the ser - vant church a - rise, a

set by change, but Spir - it led, Must
vic - tims of in - jus - tice cry For
car - ing church that longs to be A

claim and test its her - i - tage and
shel - ter and for bread to eat, and
part - ner in Christ's sac - ri - fice, and

keep on ris - ing from the dead.
nev - er live be - fore they die.
clothed in Christ's hu - man - i - ty.

*Poet Fred Pratt Green has been a chaplain, parish minister,
administrator, and playwright. Since retiring from parish
responsibilities in 1969, he has been an active hymnwriter
and makes his home in Norwich, England.*

Tune: WAREHAM L.M.
William Knapp, 1738

307   Glorious Things of You Are Spoken

Ps. 87:3; Isa. 33:20–21; 60:18; 26:4; Exod. 13:22   *John Newton, 1779; alt.*

1 Glo - rious things of you are spo-ken, Zi - on, cit - y of our God;
2 See! the streams of liv-ing wa - ters, spring - ing from e - ter - nal Love,
3 'Round each hab - i - ta-tion hov-ering, see the cloud and fire ap - pear
4 Sav - ior, if of Zi-on's cit - y we through grace a part may claim,

One whose word can - not be bro - ken formed you for a blessed a - bode.
Well sup - ply your sons and daugh-ters, and all fear of want re - move.
For a glo - ry and a cov - ering, show - ing that their God is near!
Let the world de - ride or pit - y, we will glo - ry in your name.

On the Rock of A - ges found-ed, what can shake your sure re - pose?
Who can faint, while such a riv - er ev - er will their thirst as - suage:
Thus de - riv - ing from their ban - ner light by night and shade by day,
Fad - ing is all world-ly plea - sure, all earth's boast - ed pomp and show;

With sal - va-tion's walls sur-round-ed, you may smile at all your foes.
Grace which, like our God, the Giv - er, nev - er fails from age to age?
Safe they feed up - on the man - na which God gives them when they pray.
Sol - id joys and last - ing trea - sures, none but Zi - on's chil - dren know.

Filled with Old Testament scriptural allusions, this was one of few hymns of praise included among the many subjective, sometimes brooding, hymns in Newton and Cowper's Olney Hymns. *It has enjoyed great popularity in many English-speaking countries.*

Tune: AUSTRIAN HYMN 8.7.8.7.D.
Franz Joseph Haydn, 1797
Alternate tune: *ABBOT'S LEIGH*

At the Font We Start Our Journey

308

Jeffery Rowthorn, 1992

Col. 3:15; Acts 10:36–43

1 At the font we start our jour-ney, in the Eas - ter
2 At the pul - pit we are fash-ioned by the Eas - ter
3 At the al - tar we are nour-ished with the Eas - ter
4 At the door we are com - mis-sioned, now the Eas - ter

faith bap - tized; doubts and fears no long - er blind us,
tale re - told in - to wit - nes - ses and proph - ets,
gift of bread; in our break - ing it to piec - es
vic - tory's won, to re - store a world di - vid - ed

by the light of Christ sur - prised. Al - le - lu - ia,
by the power of Christ made bold. Al - le - lu - ia,
see the love of Christ out - spread. Al - le - lu - ia,
to the peace of Christ as one. Al - le - lu - ia,

al - le - lu - ia! Hope held out and re - al - ized.
al - le - lu - ia! Faith pro - claimed, yet still un - told.
al - le - lu - ia! Life em - braced, yet free - ly shed.
al - le - lu - ia! Eas - ter's work must still be done.

This text was written for a parish in the Episcopal Diocese of
Connecticut, where the author served as bishop suffragan. Born
and educated in Britain, Rowthorn has held positions at Union
Theological Seminary and Yale University Divinity School, and
more recently was appointed bishop in charge of the
Convocation of American Churches in Europe.

Tune: WESTMINSTER ABBEY 8.7.8.7.8.7.
Henry Purcell, c. 1680
Arr. Ernest Hawkins, 1842

309

We Are Your People

Brian Wren, 1973; rev. 1993

Unison

1 We are your peo - ple: Spir - it of grace,
2 Joined in com - mu - ni - ty, trea - sured and fed,
3 Rich in di - ver - si - ty, help us to live
4 Glad of tra - di - tion, help us to see

you dare to make us Christ to our neigh - bors
may we dis - cov - er gifts in each oth - er,
clos - er than neigh-bors, o - pen to strang - ers,
in all life's chang-ing, where Christ is lead - ing,

1 & 6   *Last time, end* | 2–5

of ev - ery cul - ture and place.
will - ing to lead and be led.
a - ble to clash and for - give.
where our best ef - forts should be.

5 Give, as we ven-ture
jus-tice and care
(peace-ful, in-sist-ing,
risk-ing, re-sist-ing),
wis-dom to know when and where.

6 Spir-it, u-nite us,
make us, by grace,
will-ing and read-y,
Christ's liv-ing bod-y,
lov-ing the whole hu-man race.

*Originally written in 1973 for the hymnal of the United
Reformed Church in England and Wales,* New Church Praise,
*this text was revised by Brian Wren in 1993. The tune is named
for the composer's father-in-law, who served as chair of the
Congregational Union of England and Wales.*

Tune: WHITFIELD Irr.
John Wilson, 1975

It's the Old Ship of Zion

310

African-American spiritual

Refrain

It's the old ship of Zi - on, it's the old ship of Zi - on,

It's the old ship of Zi - on, get on board, get on board.

Last time, end

Leader   **All**

1 It has land-ed man-y a thou-sand, it has land-ed man-y a thou-sand,
2 There's no dan-ger in the wa - ter, there's no dan-ger in the wa - ter,

to Refrain

It has land-ed man-y a thou-sand, get on board, get on board.
There's no dan - ger in the wa - ter, get on board, get on board.

3 It was good for my dear moth-er, . . . Get on board.
4 It was good for my dear fa-ther, . . . Get on board.
5 It will take us home to Glo-ry, . . . Get on board.

The image of the ship is like the image of the train in many other spirituals, where the same train that carried relatives of the enslaved to freedom would return tomorrow. In each instance, everyone is encouraged to "get on board."

Tune: OLD SHIP OF ZION 8.8.8.6. with refrain
African-American spiritual

311 Renew Your Church

Matt. 5:13–16; Luke 11:1–4; Mark 12:28–34　　　　　　　　*Kenneth L. Cober, 1960; alt.*

1 Re - new your church, its min - is - tries re - store: both to serve
2 Teach us your word, re - veal its truth di - vine; on our path
3 Teach us to pray, for you are ev - er near; your still voice
4 Teach us to love, with strength of heart and mind, each and all—

and a - dore. Make us a - gain as salt through-out the land,
let it shine. Tell of your works, your might - y acts of grace;
let us hear. Our souls are rest - less till they rest in you;
hu - man-kind! Break down old walls of prej - u - dice and hate;

and as light from a stand. 'Mid som - ber shad - ows
from each page show your face. As you have sent your
this is life, full and true. Be - fore your pres - ence
leave us not to our fate. As you have loved and

of the night, where greed and ha - tred spread their blight, O
Christ to save, in love to tri - umph o'er the grave, O
keep us still that we may find for us your will And
given your life to end hos - til - i - ty and strife, Your

Kenneth L. Cober grew up in Puerto Rico, the son of missionary
parents. Cober has served churches in many states and has
written several books about church education.

Tune: ALL IS WELL 10.6.10.6.8.8.8.6.
Traditional English melody

send us forth	with	power en-dued.	Help us, God,	be	re-newed.
let our hearts	with	love be stirred.	Help us, God,	know your word.
seek your guid-ance	ev-ery day.	Teach us, God,	how to pray.
grace we must	be	mind-ful of:	Teach us, God,	how to love.

We Love Your Realm, O God 312

Timothy Dwight, 1801
Adapt. Lavon Bayler, 1992

Ps. 26:8

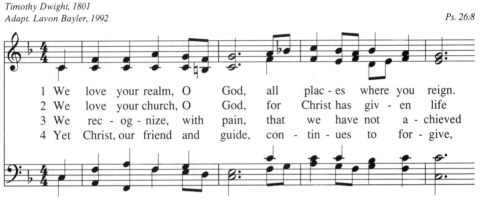

1 We love your realm, O God, all plac-es where you reign.
2 We love your church, O God, for Christ has giv-en life
3 We rec-og-nize, with pain, that we have not a-chieved
4 Yet Christ, our friend and guide, con-tin-ues to for-give,

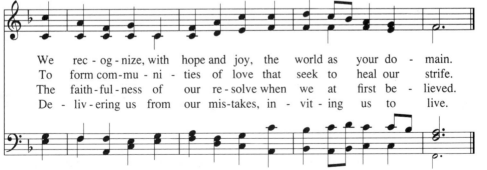

We rec-og-nize, with hope and joy, the world as your do-main.
To form com-mu-ni-ties of love that seek to heal our strife.
The faith-ful-ness of our re-solve when we at first be-lieved.
De-liv-ering us from our mis-takes, in-vit-ing us to live.

5 Be-yond our bro-ken-ness,
   we seek to know your ways
   Of deep com-mu-nion, sol-emn vows,
   and hymns of love and praise.

6 We know your truth will last.
   We trust your reign is sure.
   E-quip us for those dai-ly tasks
   that help your world en-dure.

This poem by Lavon Bayler, a United Church of Christ minister,
was inspired by and modeled after the oldest commonly used
American hymn, "I Love Thy Kingdom" by Timothy Dwight.

Tune: ST. THOMAS S.M.
Williams' New Universal Psalmodist, 1770

313

Like a Tree beside the Waters

Jer. 17:7–8

James F. D. Martin, 1992

Unison

1 Like a tree be-side the wa-ters, nur-tured by your lov - ing care,
2 Like a tree be-side the riv - er, draw-ing life from ho - ly streams,
3 We, be - side the liv-ing wa-ters, drink from your e - ter - nal life.

We, O God, your sons and daugh-ters, your en - dur-ing wit - ness bear.
Fill us with your love for - ev - er; re - cre - ate our hopes and dreams.
Give to all, your sons and daugh-ters, faith that ris - es o - ver strife.

In each pass - ing gen - er - a - tion may your voice of love be heard.
Through the storms of life sus - tain us by the wis-dom of your grace.
O Liv - ing God, most glo-rious, strength-en us for life to - day.

Bless, we pray, this con - gre - ga - tion with your ho - ly, liv - ing Word.
May the chang-ing of the sea-sons find us in your warm em - brace.
By the hope of time-less prom-ise guide your church up - on the Way.

*James Martin wrote this text at the invitation of Campbellsport
(Wisconsin) United Church of Christ for the celebration of its 125th
anniversary year in 1993. Ordained to the United Church of Christ in
1980, Martin has served as pastor to churches in Wisconsin.*

Tune: SILVER CREEK 8.7.8.7.D.
Roy Hopp, 1989
Alternate tune: HYFRYDOL

Community of Christ

314

Shirley Erena Murray, 1985

1 Com - mu - ni - ty of Christ, who make the Cross your own,
2 Com - mu - ni - ty of Christ, look past the church's door
3 Com - mu - ni - ty of Christ, through whom the word must sound—
4 When men-ace melts a - way, so shall God's will be done,

live out your creed and risk your life for God a - lone:
and see the ref - u - gee, the hun - gry, and the poor.
cry out for jus - tice and for peace the whole world 'round:
the cli - mate of the world be peace and Christ its Sun;

The God who wears your face, to whom all worlds be - long,
Take hands with the op - pressed, the job - less in your street,
Dis - arm the powers that war and all that can de - stroy,
Our cur - ren - cy be love and kind - li - ness our law,

whose chil - dren are of ev - ery race and ev - ery song.
take towel and wa - ter, that you wash your neigh-bor's feet.
turn bombs to bread, and tears of an - guish in - to joy.
our food and faith be shared as one for ev - er - more.

Shirley Erena Murray has grown up within the Ecumenical Movement and addresses related themes such as Christian unity and social justice in her hymnody. This text was first sung at the General Assembly of the Presbyterian Church of New Zealand.

Tune: LEONI 6.6.8.4.D.
Traditional Hebrew melody
Adapt. Meyer Lyon, 1770

315

O Word of God Incarnate

Ps. 119:105

William W. How, 1867; alt.

1 O Word of God in - car - nate, O Wis - dom from on high,
2 O God, we hold this trea - sure from you, its source di - vine,
3 O make your church, dear Sav - ior, a lamp of pur - est gold,

O Truth un-changed, un - chang-ing, O Light of cloud - ed sky:
a light that to all a - ges through-out the earth will shine;
to bear be - fore all peo - ple your true light as of old!

We praise you for the ra - diance that from the hal-lowed page,
It is the chart and com - pass that all life's voy-age through,
O teach your wan-dering pil - grims by this their path to trace,

a lan - tern to our foot - steps, shines on from age to age.
'mid mists and rocks and tem - pest, still guides, O God, to you.
till, doubt and striv - ing end - ed, they meet you face to face.

William W. How, author and hymnwriter, is remembered
especially for his work among the poor of London's East End.
Felix Mendelssohn harmonized this German hymn tune, which
appeared with a different text for his oratorio Elijah.

Tune: MUNICH 7.6.7.6.D.
Neuvermehrtes Gesangbuch, Meiningen, 1693
Harm. Felix Mendelssohn, 1847

We Limit Not the Truth of God

316

George Rawson, 1853; alt.

1 We lim-it not the truth of God to our poor reach of mind,
2 Who dares to bind to one's own sense the or-a-cles of heaven,
3 E-ter-nal God, In - car-nate Word, Spir-it of flame and dove:

to no-tions of our day and place, crude, par-tial, and con - fined;
for all the na-tions, tongues, and climes and all the a - ges given?
en-large, ex-pand all liv - ing souls to com-pre-hend your love;

No, let a new and bet - ter hope with-in our hearts be stirred:
That u - ni-verse, how much un - known! that o-cean un - ex-plored!
And help us all to seek your will with wis-er powers con-ferred:

O God, grant yet more light and truth to break forth from your Word.

George Rawson based this text on the parting words of Pastor
John Robinson to the Pilgrim founders in 1620.

Tune: OLD 22nd C.M.D.
Anglo-Genevan Psalter, *1556*
Alternate tunes: FOREST GREEN; ELLACOMBE

317

Mikotoba o kudasai
(Make a Gift of Your Holy Word)

Deut. 32:1–2; Amos 8:11; Matt. 8:8

Yasushige Imakoma, 1965; transl. Paul R. Gregory, 199-

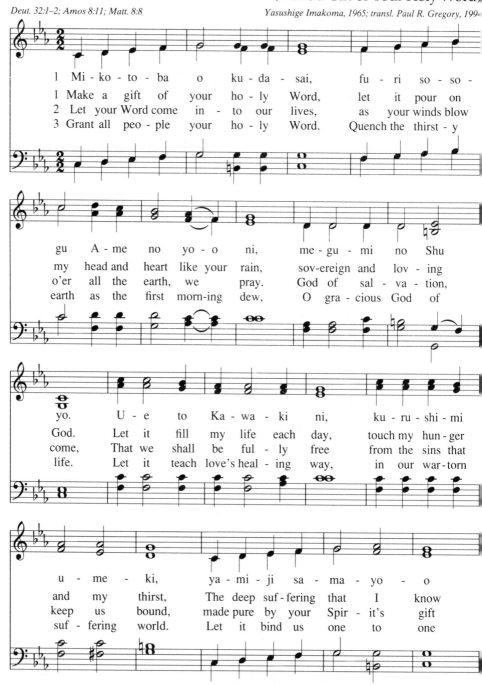

1 Mi - ko - to - ba o ku - da - sai, fu - ri so - so -
1 Make a gift of your ho - ly Word, let it pour on
2 Let your Word come in - to our lives, as your winds blow
3 Grant all peo - ple your ho - ly Word. Quench the thirst - y

gu A - me no yo - o ni, me - gu - mi no Shu
my head and heart like your rain, sov-ereign and lov - ing
o'er all the earth, we pray. God of sal - va - tion,
earth as the first morn-ing dew, O gra - cious God of

yo. U - e to Ka - wa - ki ni, ku - ru - shi - mi
God. Let it fill my life each day, touch my hun - ger
come, That we shall be ful - ly free from the sins that
life. Let it teach love's heal - ing way, in our war-torn

u - me - ki, ya - mi - ji sa - ma - yo - o
and my thirst, The deep suf - fering that I know
keep us bound, made pure by your Spir - it's gift
suf - fering world. Let it bind us one to one

Selected by the Hymnal Committee of the United Church of
Christ in Japan from many original submissions, this hymn
was first published in Sambike (Hymns of Praise), 1967. The
winning tune provided by Shōzō Koyama was the composer's
first encounter with a text in colloquial Japanese verse and
moved him deeply.

Tune: MIKOTOBA 8.11.6.7.7.7.7.
Shōzō Koyama, 1965

I - no - chi no ta - me ni.
on life's lone - ly, wan - dering way.
of re - sound - ing vic - to - ry.
toward a just and peace - ful day.

Almighty God, Your Word Is Cast 318

John Cawood, 1815; alt.

Matt. 13:1–9, 18–23

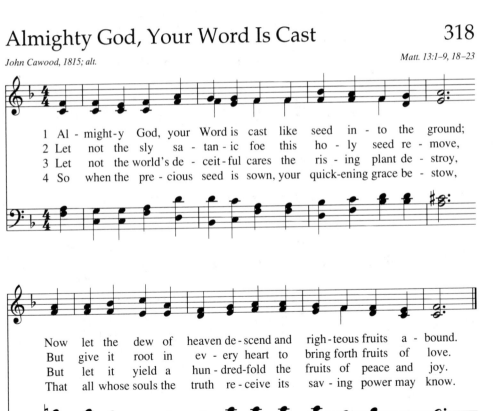

1 Al - might-y God, your Word is cast like seed in - to the ground;
2 Let not the sly sa - tan - ic foe this ho - ly seed re - move,
3 Let not the world's de - ceit - ful cares the ris - ing plant de - stroy,
4 So when the pre - cious seed is sown, your quick-ening grace be - stow,

Now let the dew of heaven de - scend and righ - teous fruits a - bound.
But give it root in ev - ery heart to bring forth fruits of love.
But let it yield a hun - dred-fold the fruits of peace and joy.
That all whose souls the truth re - ceive its sav - ing power may know.

The parable of the sower from Matthew's Gospel was the basis for this hymn. Growing up on a small farm, John Cawood, a priest of the Church of England, surely had a special understanding of this parable.

Tune: ST. FLAVIAN C.M.
Day, The Whole Booke of Psalms, 1562

319

Sing Them Over Again to Me
(Wonderful Words of Life)

Philip P. Bliss, 1874; alt

1 Sing them o - ver a - gain to me, won-der-ful words of life;
2 Christ, the bless-ed one, gives to all won-der-ful words of life;
3 Sweet - ly ech - o the gos - pel call, won-der-ful words of life;

let me more of their beau - ty see, won-der - ful words of life;
sin - ner, wake to the lov - ing call, won-der - ful words of life;
of - fer par-don and peace to all, won-der - ful words of life;

Words of life and beau - ty teach me faith and du - ty.
All so free - ly giv - en, our sure hope of heav - en.
Je - sus, on - ly Sav - ior, keep me with you for - ev - er.

Refrain

Beau-ti - ful words, won-der-ful words, won-der-ful words of life.

Beau-ti - ful words, won-der-ful words, won-der-ful words of life.

Philip Bliss wrote this text and tune for the first issue of Words
*of Life (1874). A few years later it was sung as a duet during an
evangelistic campaign and became popular immediately.*

Tune: WORDS OF LIFE C.M. with refrain
Philip P. Bliss, 1874

Deep in the Shadows of the Past

320

Brian Wren, 1973; rev. 1993

1 Deep in the shad-ows of the past, far out from set-tled lands,
2 While oth-ers bowed to change-less gods, they met a mys-ter-y:
3 From A-bra-ham to Naz-a-reth the prom-ise changed and grew,
4 For all the writ-ings that sur-vived, for lead-ers, long a-go,

some no-mads trav-eled with their God a-cross the des-ert sands.
a hid-den, un-com-plet-ed Name— "I AM WHAT I WILL BE";
while some, re-mem-ber-ing the past, re-cord-ed what they knew,
who sift-ed, cop-ied, and pre-served the Bi-ble that we know,

The dawn-ing hope of hu-man-kind by them was sensed and shown:
And by their tents, a-round their fires, in sto-ry, song, and law,
and some, in let-ters and la-ments, in proph-e-cy and praise,
Give thanks and find its sto-ry yet our prom-ise, strength, and call:

a prom-ise call-ing them a-head, a fu-ture yet un-known.
they praised, re-mem-bered, hand-ed on, a past that prom-ised more.
re-cov-ered, kin-dled, and ex-pressed new hope for chang-ing days.
the work-ing-mod-el of our faith, a-live with hope for all.

Brian Wren has commented: "The hymn tries to tell the story of the Bible in a manner acceptable to different beliefs about its inspiration." Wren credits James Barr's The Bible in the Modern World *for the idea of the Bible as a "working-model" of our faith.*

Tune: SHEPHERDS' PIPES C.M.D.
Annabeth McClelland Gay, 1952

321 Break Now the Bread of Life

Matt. 14:13–21; Mark 6:30–44

Mary A. Lathbury, 1877; alt.

1 Break now the bread of life, Sav - ior, to me, as you once
2 Bless now the truth, dear Christ, to me, to me, as you once

broke the loaves be - side the sea; Be - yond the sa - cred page
blessed the bread by Gal - i - lee; Then shall all bond-age cease,

I seek you, Lord; my spir-it yearns for you, O Liv - ing Word.
all shack-les fall, and I shall find my peace, my all in all.

*Mary Lathbury, "poet laureate of Chautauqua," wrote her
prayer hymn to enrich the lives of those gathered for summer
study at the lakeside conferences near Jamestown, New York.
The tune was written for it by the chorus director of Chautauqua
that same season.*

Tune: BREAD OF LIFE 6.4.6.4.D.
William F. Sherwin, 1877

322 Take Me to the Water

Acts 8:36–39; 10:47–48

African-American spiritual

1 Take me to the wa - ter, take me to the wa -
2 None but the righ - teous, none but the righ -
3 I love Je - sus, I love Je -
4 Je - sus is my Sav - ior, Je - sus is my Sav -

ter,   take me to the   wa - ter   to   be bap - tized.
teous,   none but the   righ - teous . . .   shall see God.
sus,   I   love   Je - sus, . . .   yes, I   do.
ior,   Je - sus is my Sav - ior   for - ev - er   more.

During the antebellum era the enslaved either worshipped secretly in the woods or in small one-room churches built on the plantations. This spiritual reminds us that in either case baptisms were done down at the riverside.

Tune: African-American spiritual
Arr. Jeffrey Radford, 1993

Little Children, Welcome   323

Fred Pratt Green, 1973

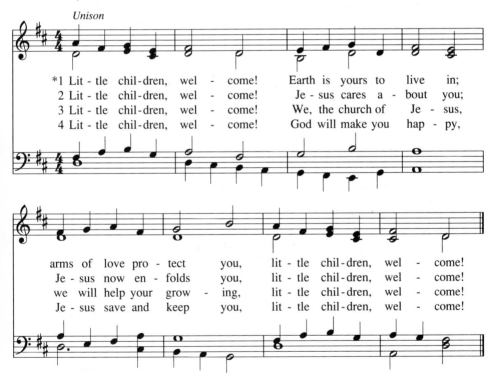

Unison

*1 Lit - tle chil-dren, wel - come!   Earth is yours to   live in;
 2 Lit - tle chil-dren, wel - come!   Je - sus cares a - bout you;
 3 Lit - tle chil-dren, wel - come!   We, the church of Je - sus,
 4 Lit - tle chil-dren, wel - come!   God will make you hap - py,

arms of love pro - tect   you,   lit - tle chil-dren, wel - come!
Je - sus now en - folds   you,   lit - tle chil-dren, wel - come!
we will help your grow - ing,   lit - tle chil-dren, wel - come!
Je - sus save and keep   you,   lit - tle chil-dren, wel - come!

Other words may be substituted as appropriate; for example, "Sisters, brothers, welcome!" "Little sister, welcome!" or "Little brother, welcome!"

Fred Pratt Green is a noted British hymnwriter who was awarded an honorary doctorate from Emory University in Atlanta, Georgia, where his papers will be held. The uncomplicated tune by contemporary composer Roy Hopp makes this an easy hymn for people of all ages.

Tune: SAIPAN 6.6.6.6.
Roy Hopp, 1988

324   Baptized into Your Name Most Holy

Matt. 28:19; Rom. 6:1–3, 10–11

Johann J. Rambach, 1734
Transl. Catherine Winkworth (1829–1878); alt.

1 Bap-tized in - to your name most ho - ly, O Fa - ther, Son,
2 My lov - ing Fa - ther, here you take me hence-forth to be
3 O faith-ful God, you nev - er fail me; your cov-enant sure -
4 All that I am and love most dear - ly, re - ceive it all,

and Ho - ly Ghost, I claim a place, though weak and low - ly,
your child and heir; My faith-ful Sav - ior, here you make me
ly will a - bide. Let not e - ter - nal death as - sail me
O God, from me. Oh, let me make my vows sin - cere - ly,

A - mong your seed, your cho - sen host. Bu - ried with
The fruit of all your sor - rows share; O Ho - ly
should I trans - gress it on my side! Have mer - cy
and help me your own child to be! Let noth - ing

Christ and dead to sin, I have your Spir - it now with - in.
Ghost, you com-fort me though threat-ening clouds a - round I see.
when I come de - filed; for - give, lift up, re - store your child.
that I am or own serve an - y will but yours a - lone.

Although this hymn originated in eighteenth-century Germany, it could be found two centuries later in the United States in hymnals of the Evangelical and German Congregational churches. Johann Jakob Rambach was a popular preacher and professor of theology.

Tune: O DASS ICH TAUSEND ZUNGEN HÄTTE
9.8.9.8.8.8.
Johann B. König, Harmonischer Liederschatz, 1738

Child of Blessing, Child of Promise 325

Ronald S. Cole-Turner, 1981

1 Child of bless-ing, child of prom-ise, bap - tized with the Spir-it's sign;
2 Child of love, our love's ex - pres-sion, love's cre - a - tion, loved in - deed!
3 Child of joy, our dear - est trea-sure, God's you are, from God you came.
4 Child of God your lov - ing Par - ent, learn to know whose child you are.

With this wa - ter God has sealed you un - to love and grace di - vine.
Fresh from God, re - fresh our spir - its, in - to joy and laugh - ter lead.
Back to God we hum-bly give you; live as one who bears Christ's name.
Grow to laugh and sing and wor - ship, trust and love God more than all.

Ronald Cole-Turner, a teacher of theology, is an ordained minister of the United Church of Christ. He is an award-winning author on the interface of science and religion.

Tune: STUTTGART 8.7.8.7.
Attrib. to Christian F. Witt (1660–1716), in
Psalmodia Sacra, Gotha, 1715

Crashing Waters at Creation 326

Sylvia G. Dunstan, 1991   Gen. 1:1–5; Exod. 14:21–22; Mark 1:9–11; John 4:13–14

1 Crash-ing wa-ters at cre-a-tion
   or-dered by the Spir-it's breath,
   First to wit-ness day's be-gin-ning
   from the bright-ness of night's death.

2 Part-ing wa-ter stood and trem-bled
   as the cap-tives passed on through,
   Wash-ing off the chains of bond-age—
   chan-nel to a life made new.

3 Cleans-ing wa-ter once at Jor-dan
   closed a-round the One fore-told,
   O-pened to re-veal the glo-ry
   ev-er new and ev-er old.

4 Liv-ing wa-ter, nev-er end-ing,
   quench the thirst and flood the soul.
   Well-spring, Source of life e-ter-nal,
   drench our dry-ness, make us whole.

Hymnwriter Sylvia Dunstan wrote this text to accompany a prayer for blessing the water in the United Church of Canada baptismal rites. She has credited the work of Miriam Therese Winter as her inspiration for some of the imagery in the last stanza.

Tune: STUTTGART 8.7.8.7.
Attrib. to Christian F. Witt (1660–1716), in
Psalmodia Sacra, Gotha, 1715

327

Jesus Loves Me

St. 1, Anna B. Warner, 1860
St. 2–3, David Rutherford McGuire, 1971

1 Je - sus loves me! This I know, for the Bi - ble tells me so.
2 Je - sus loves me! This I know, as he loved so long a - go,
3 Je - sus loves me! Still to - day, walk-ing with me on my way,

Lit - tle ones to him be - long; they are weak, but he is strong.
Tak - ing chil - dren on his knee, say - ing, "Let them come to me."
Want-ing as a friend to give light and love to all who live.

Refrain

Yes, Je - sus loves me! Yes, Je - sus loves me!

Yes, Je - sus loves me! The Bi - ble tells me so.

1 Deer He-soos zis guh see-reh,
   eem soorp keer-kus ice guh-seh,
Inch koo-tov ink un-toon-etz
   po-ker dug-hak, yev orh-netz.

   Vo, guh see-reh ziss!
   Vo, guh see-reh ziss!
   Vo, guh see-reh ziss!
   Soorp Kirk-uh ice guh-seh.
(Armenian transliteration Vartan Hartunian)

1 Lo'u A-lii ua faa-fe-tai
   I lou sa-ga a-lo-fa-mai
Ua i-lo-a-ti-no ai
   I lou tau-si pe-a mai.

   O lou a-lo-fa!
   O lou a-lo-fa!
   O lou a-lo-fa!
   E si-li la-va lea.
(Samoan transl. anon.)

Anna B. Warner collaborated with her sister, Susan, on several novels. In one, Say and Seal, *this hymn was sung to comfort a sick child. Two new stanzas have been provided by Canadian David R. McGuire, an Anglican priest.*

Tune: JESUS LOVES ME 7.7.7.7. with refrain
William B. Bradbury, 186

1 Cris-to me a-ma, bien lo sé,
   Su pa-la-bra me ha-ce ver
   Que los ni-ños son de A-quél,
   Quien es nues-tro A-mi-go fiel.

   Cris-to me a-ma,
   Cris-to me a-ma,
   Cris-to me a-ma,
   La Bib-lia di-ce a-sí.
(Spanish transl. Himnario Metodista, *1968)*

1 Saq wa-re o a-i-su,
   Saq wa tsu-yo ke-re ba,
   Wa-re yo-wa-ku-to-mo,
   O-so-re wa a-ra-ji.

   Wa-ga Shu ye-su,
   Wa-ga Shu ye-su,
   Wa-ga Shu ye-su,
   Wa-re o a-i-su.
*(Japanese phonetic transcription
Mas Kawashima, 1988)*

1 Je-sus liebt mich ganz ge-wiss,
   Denn die Bi-bel sagt mir dies,
   Al-le Kind-er schwach und klein,
   Lad't Er herz-lich zu sich ein.

   Ja, Je-sus liebt mich,
   Ja, Je-sus liebt mich,
   Ja, Je-sus liebt mich,
   Die Bi-bel sagt mir dies.
(German transl. Psalter und Harfe, *1876)*

1 Ye-su sa-rang Ha-si-man
   Geo-ruk-ha-sin ma-ril-sei
   Wo-o-ri-drn Ya-ka-na
   Ye-su gwon-sei man-to-da.

   Nal sa-rang ha-sim
   Nal sa-rang ha-sim
   Nal sa-rang ha-sim
   Seong gyon-gei sse-oit-ne.
*(Korean transl. anon. in
Hymnal: A Worship Book, 1992)*

1 Je-sus Christ wa-śte-ma-da,
   Wo-wa-pi Wa-kan he-ye:
   Mi-ye on te hi qon he,
   Wan-na he wa-na-ka-ja.

   Han Je-sus wa-śte;
   Han Je-sus wa-śte;
   Han Je-sus wa-śte;
   Wa-śte ma-da-ka ye.
(Lakota transl. Dakota Odowan, *1842)*

1 He a-lo-ha ko Ie-su
   I ke kei-ki li'i-li'i no,
   No-na no ka po'e li'i-li'i,
   No-na wau ka po-ki'i nei.

   Kei-ki a-lo-ha!
   Kei-ki a-lo-ha!
   Kei-ki a-lo-ha!
   Ke a-lo-ha! o Ie-su!
(Hawaiian transl. Laiana, 19th century)

1 En-gem sze-ret Jé-zu-som,
   Bib-li-ám-ból jól tu-dom.
   Mind ö-vé a kis gyer-mek,
   E-rőt ád a gyön-gék-nek!

   Úgy van ő sze-ret,
   Ő sze-ret na-gyon;
   Úgy van ő sze-ret,
   Í-gé-jé-ből tudom.
(Hungarian transl. János Victor)

1 Me-nya be Ye-su lɔa mí.
   E-fe nya gblɔ ne-ne-ma.
   E-lɔa ɖe-vi-wo ka-tã
   'La-be e-fe dɔ-me nyo.

   Ẽ, Ye-su lɔa mí,
   Ẽ, Ye-su lɔa mí,
   Ẽ, Ye-su lɔa mí,
   'La-be e-fe dɔ-me nyo.
(Ghanaian transl. anon.)

328 Wonder of Wonders, Here Revealed

Jane Parker Huber, 1980

1 Won - der of won - ders, here re - vealed;
God's cov - e - nant with us is sealed.
And long be - fore we know or pray,
God's love en - folds us ev - ery day.

2 Here in this sac - ra - ment we see
God's grace un - bound, for all, for me!
May we re - spond with joy - ful praise
in lov - ing ser - vice all our days.

3 This child of God, though young or old,
we wel - come now in - to Christ's fold,
To know with us God's lov - ing care;
here all our joys and sor - rows share.

4 Now we our vow of faith re - new,
stretch wide our sights to glob - al view,
And claim with Chris - tians far and near
a larg - er fam - i - ly held dear.

Jane Parker Huber has noted two important ideas she addressed in this text: "The fact that God loves each of us before we know how to love in return, and . . . in baptism we become part of a worldwide family."

Tune: PENTECOST L.M.
William Boyd, 1864

Jesus, the Joy of Loving Hearts

329

Attrib. to Bernard of Clairvaux, c. 1150
Transl. Ray Palmer, 1858; alt.

John 6:52–58; Heb. 13:8

1 Je - sus, the joy of lov - ing hearts, fount of our lives, and
2 Your truth un - changed has ev - er stood; you plead with all to
3 We taste of you, the liv - ing bread, and long to feast up -
4 For you our rest - less spir - its yearn, wher-e'er our chang - ing
5 O Je - sus, ev - er with us stay! Make all our mo - ments

light of all: From ev - ery bliss that earth im - parts
call on you; To those still seek - ing, you are good;
on you still; We drink of you, the foun - tain - head;
lot is cast; Glad, when your smile on us you turn,
calm and bright! Oh, chase the cloud of sin a - way!

we turn, un - filled, to hear your call.
to those who find you, life is new.
our thirst - y souls from you we fill.
blessed, when by faith we hold you fast.
Shed o'er the world your ho - ly light.

Bernard, founder of the monastery at Clairvaux, was respected
by popes and royalty alike. From the forty-two-verse Latin
poem, American Congregational minister Ray Palmer freely
translated selected verses to create this version.

Tune: HESPERUS L.M.
(QUEBEC)
Henry W. Baker, 1854

330

Let Us Break Bread Together

Acts 2:42

African-American spiritual

1 Let us break bread to-geth-er on our knees;
* 2 Let us drink wine to-geth-er on our knees;
3 Let us praise God to-geth-er on our knees;

let us break bread to-geth-er on our knees.
let us drink wine to-geth-er on our knees.
let us praise God to-geth-er on our knees.

Refrain

When I fall on my knees, with my face to the ris-ing sun,

* "Share the cup" *may be substituted for* "drink wine."

*The earliest version of this spiritual probably began with the
current stanza three, and was a song some of the enslaved in
Virginia used when gathering for secret meetings. The
communion stanzas were added some time after the Civil War.*

Tune: LET US BREAK BREAD
10.10. with refrain
Harm. David Hurd, 1983

Come, My Way, My Truth, My Life 331

George Herbert, 1633; alt.   *John 8:12; 14:1–7; 15:11*

1 Come, my Way, my Truth, my Life: such a way as gives us
2 Come, my Light, my Feast, my Strength: such a light as shows a
3 Come, my Joy, my Love, my Heart: such a joy as none can

breath; Such a truth as ends all strife;
feast; Such a feast as mends in length;
move; Such a love as none can part;

such a life as con - - - quers death.
such a strength as makes a guest.
such a heart as joys in love.

Shortly before his death, the poet George Herbert entrusted his manuscript of The Temple *(including this hymn) to a friend for publication. The musical setting by English composer Ralph Vaughan Williams is from* Five Mystical Songs from George Herbert.

Tune: THE CALL 7.7.7.7.
Ralph Vaughan Williams, 1911

332

As We Gather at Your Table

Matt. 22:1–10; Luke 14:16–24

Carl P. Daw, Jr., 1989

1 As we gath-er at your ta - ble, as we lis-ten to your word,
2 Turn our wor-ship in-to wit - ness in the sac-ra-ment of life;
3 Gra-cious Spir-it, help us sum-mon oth-er guests to share that feast

help us know, O God, your pres-ence; let our hearts and minds be stirred.
send us forth to love and serve you, bring-ing peace where there is strife.
where tri-um-phant Love will wel-come those who had been last and least.

Nour-ish us with sa-cred sto - ry till we claim it as our own;
Give us, Christ, your great com-pas - sion to for-give as you for-gave;
There no more will en-vy bind us nor will pride our peace de-stroy,

teach us through this ho - ly ban-quet how to make Love's vic-tory known.
may we still be-hold your im-age in the world you died to save.
as we join with saints and an-gels to re-peat the sound-ing joy.

In this hymn, commissioned by an Episcopal parish in Virginia
for the celebration of its tricentennial, Carl P. Daw, Jr., utilized a
familiar phrase from Isaac Watts' "Joy to the World," which was
the motto for the celebration: "Repeat the sounding joy."

Tune: BEACH SPRING 8.7.8.7.D.
The Sacred Harp, *1844*
Harm. The New Century Hymnal, *1992*

Words Copyright © 1989 by Hope Publishing Company

O Bread of Life

333

Timothy Tingfang Lew, 1934
Transl. Greer Anne Wenh-In Ng, 1986

John 6:35

1 O Bread of life, for all things break - ing,
2 We come this day in hum - ble wor - ship - ing;
3 Stand in our midst, eyes and hearts o - pen - ing;

the bit - ter cup on Cal - vary drain - ing;
our land is scarred, earth's peo - ple suf - fering;
your mys - tic self to us re - veal - ing;

Re - deemed by grace, we join in feast - ing,
O sa - cred face, blood and tears min - gling,
U - nite us in life ev - er - last - ing,

at your com - mand the past re - mem - bering.
all hu - man pain you are still bear - ing.
Im - man - u - el, bless - ing un - end - ing.

One of fifty indigenous hymns to be included in the Protestant
Chinese publication Hymns of Universal Praise, *this text*
employs some Buddhist terms and images with which many
Chinese people can identify. The tune can be translated as
"God's, or holy, grace."

Tune: SHENG EN 9.9.9.9.
Yin-Lan Su, 1936
Arr. Darryl Nixon, 1986

334   Graced with Garments of Great Gladness

Isa. 61:10; John 6:35–58

Johann Franck, c. 1649
Transl. Catherine Winkworth, 1863; alt.

1 Graced with gar-ments of great glad - ness, I shall leave the depths of
2 Bright - ness, that my life so bright - ens, Light, that all my soul en -
3 Je - sus, Bread of Life, I pray you, let me glad-ly here o -

sad - ness, En - ter in - to glo-ry's splen - dor, there with
light - ens, Joy, that joins my heart in know - ing, Fount, that
bey you, To your ta - ble here in - vit - ed be your

joy my prais-es ren - der To the One whose grace un-bound - ed
is all be-ing flow - ing, At your name I cry, "My Mak - er!"
love by love re-quit - ed. From this ban-quet let me mea - sure,

has this won-drous ban-quet found - ed. Sing my soul, your sto - ry
Let me be a fit par-tak - er Of this bless-ed food from
oh, how vast, how deep its trea - sure. Through the mer-cies that you

One of Germany's leading hymnwriters, Johann Franck was
also a secular poet of some renown. Born at the beginning of
the Thirty Years' War, Franck became a lawyer and served as
a councillor, a mayor, and finally a provincial representative.

Tune: SCHMÜCKE DICH L.M.D.
Johann Crüger, 1649
Harm. The English Hymnal, 1906

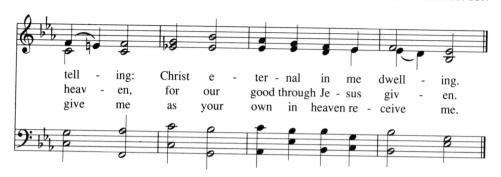

tell - ing: Christ e - ter - nal in me dwell - ing.
heav - en, for our good through Je - sus giv - en.
give me as your own in heaven re - ceive me.

Come, Gather in This Special Place 335

Phil Porter, 1991

1 & 4 Come, gath - er in this spe - cial place; the ta - ble here is
2 The grapes have yield - ed es - sence pure, a drink to quench the
3 The bread is fresh - ly baked to - day, a fra - grant feast of

long and wide; For all who heed com - mu - nion's call, there's
grav - est thirst; The cup is passed from hand to hand, and
grain sup - plied; And e - ven crumbs that dust our palms will

room for thou - sands side by side.
each will sense de - spair re - versed.
leave souls ful - ly sat - is - fied.

Elaine Kirkland and Phil Porter, both United Church of Christ artists, have been composing songs, hymns, and chants together since 1989. This is the first communion hymn they created, which appeared in their collection Fire Will Shine.

Tune: GATHER L.M.
Elaine Kirkland, 1991

336 Here, O My Lord, I See You Face to Face

Horatius Bonar, 1855; alt.

1 Here, O my Lord, I see you face to face;
here would I touch and han - dle things un - seen;
Here grasp with firm - er hand the e - ter - nal grace,
And all my wea - ri - ness up - on you lean.

2 Here would I feed up - on the bread of God,
here share the cup, the gra - cious gift of heaven;
Here would I lay a - side each earth - ly load,
here taste a - fresh the calm of sin for - given.

3 This is the hour of ban - quet and of song;
this is the heaven - ly ta - ble spread a - new;
Here let me feast, and, feast - ing, still pro - long
the brief, bright hour to - geth - er here with you.

4 Too soon we rise; the sym - bols dis - ap - pear;
the meal, but not your love, is past and gone.
This joy - ful feast con - firms that you are here,
now and for - ev - er, as our shield and sun.

5 We have no help but yours, nor do we need
an - oth - er strength than yours to lean up - on.
It is e - nough, O Lord, e - nough in - deed;
our faith is in your might, your might a - lone.

Horatius Bonar, a founder of the Free Church of Scotland and author of 600 hymns, wrote this hymn at his brother's request. It was first printed in a leaflet for the author's church, St. Andrew's Free Church in Greenock, Scotland.

Tune: MORECAMBE 10.10.10.10.
Frederick C. Atkinson, 1870
Alternate tune: LANGRAN

Draw Us in the Spirit's Tether

337

Percy Dearmer, 1925; alt.

Matt. 18:20

1 Draw us in the Spir-it's teth - er, for when hum - bly
2 As dis - ci - ples used to gath - er in the name of
3 All our meals and all our liv - ing make as sac - ra -

in your name, two or three are met to - geth - er,
Christ to sup, then with thanks to God the Giv - er,
ments of you, that by car - ing, help-ing, giv - ing,

you are in the midst of them; Al - le - lu - ia!
break the bread and bless the cup, Al - le - lu - ia!
we may be dis - ci - ples true. Al - le - lu - ia!

Al - le - lu - ia! Touch we now your gar - ment's hem.
Al - le - lu - ia! So now bind our friend - ship up.
Al - le - lu - ia! We may serve with faith a - new.

British hymnal editor Percy Dearmer originally wrote these stanzas under a pseudonym as part of a postcommunion hymn by George H. Bourne. The tune was adapted from an anthem by Harold Friedell and is named for Union Theological Seminary in New York.

Tune: UNION SEMINARY 8.7.8.7.4.4.7.
Harold Friedell, 1957
Adapt. Jet Turner, 1967

338

Una Espiga
(Sheaves of Summer)

Cesáreo Gabaraín, 1973; alt.
Transl. George Lockwood, 1989

1 U - na es - pi - ga do - ra - do por el sol, el ra -
2 Com - par - ti - mos la mis - ma co - mu - nión, so - mos

1 Sheaves of sum-mer turned gold-en by the sun, grapes in
2 We are shar-ing the same com-mu-nion meal; we are

ci - mo que cor - ta el vi - ña - dor, Com-par -
tri - go del mis - mo sem-bra - dor, Un mo -

bunch-es cut down when ripe and red, Are con -
wheat by the same great Sow-er sown; Like a

ti - mos a - hor - ra en pan y vi - no de a - mor: que son
li - no, la vi - da, nos tri - tu - ra con do - lor, Dios nos

vert - ed in - to the bread and wine of God's love in the
mill-stone life grinds us down with sor - row and pain, but God

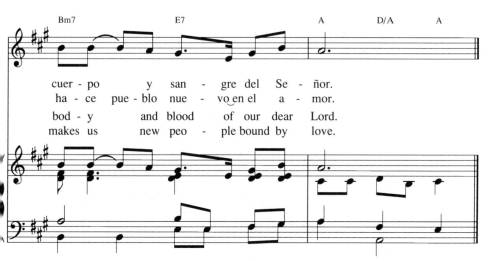

cuer - po   y   san - gre del Se - ñor.
ha - ce   pue - blo nue - vo en el   a - mor.
bod - y   and blood   of our dear Lord.
makes us   new peo - ple bound by   love.

3 Co-mo gra-nos que han
    he-cho el mis-mo pan,
    co-mo no-tas que te-jen un can-tar,
    Co-mo go-tas de a-gua que se
    fun-den en el mar,
    los cris-tia-nos un cuer-po
    for-ma-rán.

4 A la me-sa de Dios se
    sen-ta-rán,
    co-mo i-gle-sia su pan
    com-par-ti-rán,
    U-na mis-ma es-pe-ran-za
    ca-mi-nan-do can-ta-rán,
    en la vi-da her-ma-na-dos
    se a-ma-rán.

3 Like the grains which be-come
    one same whole loaf,
    like the notes that are wo-ven in-to song,
    Like the drop-lets of wa-ter
    that are blend-ed in the sea,
    we, as Chris-tians, one bod-y
    shall be-come.

4 At God's ta-ble to-geth-er
    we shall sit.
    As God's chil-dren, Christ's
    bod-y we will share.
    One same hope we will sing
    to-geth-er as we walk a-long.
    Broth-ers, sis-ters, in life,
    in love, we'll be.

Author and composer of a number of Spanish hymns that have gained
widespread popularity in the late twentieth century, Cesáreo Gabaraín
was a parish priest who received postgraduate degrees in theology,
journalism, and musicology from the University of Madrid.

Tune: UNA ESPIGA Irr.
Cesáreo Gabaraín, 1973
Harm. Skinner Chávez-Melo, 1987

339

Adoro te devote
(Truth Whom We Adore)

Thomas Aquinas c. 1260
Transl. The New Century Hymnal, 1995

Gently flowing
Unison

1 A - do - ro te de - vo - te, la - tens De - i - tas,
1 Truth whom we a - dore though hid - den you may be,
2 Of your death, O Sav - ior, this me - mo - ri - al:
3 Je - sus, now but dim - ly we be - hold your grace;

quae sub his fi - gu - ris ve - re la - ti - tas:
Un - der - neath these forms lies your re - al - i - ty;
Through this bread you of - fer true life, rich and full.
We a - wait the day when you re - veal your face;

Ti - bi se cor me - um to - tum sub - ji - cit,
To know you com - plete - ly my heart seeks in vain;
Clean me spot - less, Je - sus, by your blood a - lone,
Then un - veiled to us your splen - dor we may see—

qui - a te con - tem - plans to - tum de - fi - cit.
Thus, my Sov - ereign, I give all un - to your reign.
That for all the world's sin can one drop a - tone.
Blessed, to view your glo - ry in hu - mil - i - ty.

J. M. Neale, previous translator of this hymn, commented that Aquinas, ". . . as if afraid to employ any pomp of words on approaching so tremendous a Mystery, has used the very simplest expressions throughout." The words have been linked to the above tune since the seventeenth century.

Tune: ADORO TE DEVOTE 11.11.11.11.
Plainsong melody from Processionalle, *Paris, 1697*
Harm. The New Century Hymnal, *1994*

Somos pueblo que camina

340

(We Are People on a Journey)

"Misa Popular Nicaragüense," 20th century; alt.
English version, Carolyn Jennings, 1993

John 6:32–35

1 So-mos pue-blo que ca - mi - na por la sen - da del do - lor.
2 Los hu - mil-des y los po - bres in - vi - ta - dos son de Dios.
1 We are peo-ple on a jour - ney; pain is with us all the way.
2 God has sent the in - vi - ta - tion to the hum-ble and the poor.

Estribillo (Refrain)

A - cu - da-mos ju - bi - lo - sos a la san - ta co - mu - nión.
Joy-ful - ly we come to - geth - er at the ho - ly feast of God.

3 Es-te pan que Dios nos brin-da
a-li-men-ta nues-tra u-nión. *(Estribillo)*

3 This is bread that God pro-vides us,
nour-ish-ing our u-ni-ty. *(Refrain)*

4 Cris-to a-quí se ha-ce pre-sen-te;
al reu-nir-nos es su a-mor. *(Estribillo)*

4 Christ is ev-er pres-ent with us
to u-nite us all in love. *(Refrain)*

5 Los se-dien-tos de jus-ti-cia
bus-can su li-be-ra-ción. *(Estribillo)*

5 All who tru-ly thirst for jus-tice
seek their lib-er-a-tion here. *(Refrain)*

The "Misa Popular Nicaragüense," in which this hymn appeared, was composed for the Eucharist liturgy by members of the "comunidades de base"—a group of laypersons who organized to deal with issues in the Latin American church and community.

Tune: SOMOS PUEBLO 8.7. with refrain (8.7.)
"Misa Popular Nicaragüense," 20th century

341

Great Spirit God

Jer. 10:12–13; Matt. 6:25–33

Dakota hymn, Joseph R. Renville, 1842
Transl. Sidney H. Byrd, 1993
For another translation, see 3

Optional hand-drum rhythm:

1 Great Spir-it God, the things which are yours are nu-mer-ous and great. The heavens a-bove you set in their place, and earth re-ceived its form by your hands. The o-cean depths re-spond to your will, for you can do all things.

2 Your will, mys-ter-i-ous and so strong, brings growth to all the earth. Food for our souls and cloth-ing to wear, are like your cup that bless-es and fills. Pro-vide for us each day of our lives suf-fi-cient for our needs.

3 You gave your law to Ad-am and Eve, fore-bears of hu-man-kind. That law I dis-o-beyed with my sin, and now I suf-fer pain and dis-grace. Je-sus, ex-press your mer-cy to me, and pay for all my sins.

4 That day you came to dwell on the earth, bring-ing us all great joy! The na-tions scat-tered o-ver the world, to them you gave the light of all life. O Je-sus, O Com-pas-sion-ate One, we of-fer praise to you.

Recollecting the accounts told by his grandfather and others, Sidney Byrd stated: "This hymn was sung by thirty-eight Dakota Indian prisoners of war as they went to the gallows at Mankato, Minnesota, on December 26, 1862, in the largest mass execution in American history."

Tune: LACQUIPARLE 9.6.9.9.9.6.
Native American melody (Dakota)
Adapt. Joseph R. Renville, 1842
Harm. J. R. Murray, 1877

5 Your sac-ra-ment en-trust-ed to us,
   Je-sus, now share with me.
   Your bread of life and drink
      for our souls,
   which you have of-fered,
      pur-i-fy now.
   Sanc-ti-fy minds and bod-ies to you;
   re-store us by your love.

6 "Take now my flesh as food
      for your soul,"
   these are your words, O Christ.
   "Take my shed blood and drink
      from my cup,
   that it may serve to strength-en
      your faith."
   En-trance in-to your door I de-sire;
   Je-sus, now hear my plea.

7 Your plan for our sal-va-tion, O God,
   grant to my sin-ful soul.
   Be-yond the heavens is your great a-bode;
   all good-ness is se-cure in your hands.
   This life di-vine which you gave to me
   is one that has no end.

Be Known to Us in Breaking Bread 342

James Montgomery, 1825; alt.   Luke 24:30–31, 35

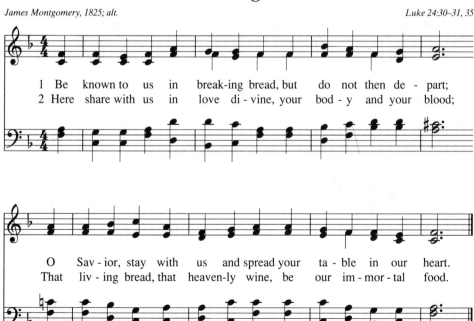

1 Be known to us in break-ing bread, but do not then de - part;
2 Here share with us in love di - vine, your bod - y and your blood;

O Sav - ior, stay with us and spread your ta - ble in our heart.
That liv - ing bread, that heaven-ly wine, be our im - mor - tal food.

This hymn is sometimes found as the second and third stanzas
of an American hymn, "Shepherd of Souls, Refresh and Bless."
Montgomery—Moravian poet, journalist, humanitarian, and author
of more than 400 hymns—titled this hymn "The Family Table."

Tune: ST. FLAVIAN C.M.
Day, The Whole Booke of Psalms, 1562

343

Jesus Took the Bread

Matt. 26:26–28; Luke 9:16; 22:19; 24:30

Ruth Duck, 1982

Ruth Duck wrote this hymn emphasizing the actions of communion—taking, blessing, breaking, and giving the bread—following a summer study of liturgy at the University of Notre Dame. It was first used at New Hope United Church of Christ in Milwaukee.

Tune: NEW HOPE 10.11.10.12.
Ruth Duck, 1982
Arr. Randall Sensmeier, 1982

The Time Was Early Evening

344

The Iona Community, 1988

Mark 14:12–25

1 The time was ear-ly eve-ning, the place a room up-stairs;
2 The com-pa-ny of Je-sus had met to share a meal;
3 "The bread and bod-y bro-ken, the wine and blood out-poured,
4 Christ Je-sus, now a-mong us, con-firm our faith's in-tent,

The guests were the dis-ci-ples, few in num-ber and few in prayers.
The One who made them wel-come had much more to re-veal.
The cross and kitch-en ta-ble are one by my sign and word."
As, with your words and ac-tions, we u-nite in this sac-ra-ment.

Refrain

Oh, the food comes from the bak-er; the drink comes from the vine;

The words come from the Sav-ior, "I will meet you in bread and wine."

In the Iona Community collection Enemy of Apathy, *this piece is titled "The Song of the Supper" and is accompanied by an instruction that it is an "effective song for a house communion, or when the sacrament is celebrated in the usual eating place."*

Tune: AFTON WATER Irr. with refrain
Traditional Scottish melody
Harm. The New Century Hymnal, *1994*

345   Let All Mortal Flesh Keep Silence

Isa. 6:1–3; 1 Tim. 6:13–15

From the Liturgy of St. James, 4th century
Transl. Gerard Moultrie, 1864; alt.

1 Let all mor - tal flesh keep si - lence, and with fear and
2 Mon-arch great, yet born of Mar - y, as of old on
3 Rank on rank the host of heav - en spreads its van-guard
4 At Christ's feet the six - winged ser - aphs, cher - u - bim with

trem - bling stand; Pon-der noth-ing earth - ly - mind - ed,
earth Christ stood, Lord of all, in hu - man ves - ture—
on the way, As the Light of light de - scend - ing
sleep - less eye, Veil their fac - es to the Pres - ence,

for with bless - ing in the hand, Christ our God to
in the bod - y and the blood— Christ will give to
from the realms of end - less day, That the powers of
as with cease-less voice they cry, Al - le - lu - ia,

This Greek hymn comes from the Liturgy of St. James of
Jerusalem. It has been paraphrased by Gerard Moultrie, a
priest of the Church of England. The French folk melody
first appeared with these words in The English Hymnal (1906).

Tune: PICARDY 8.7.8.7.8.7.
French carol melody, 17th century
Harm. Ralph Vaughan Williams, 1906

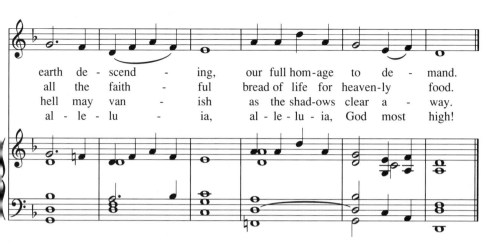

earth de - scend - ing, our full hom-age to de - mand.
all the faith - ful bread of life for heaven-ly food.
hell may van - ish as the shad-ows clear a - way.
al - le - lu - ia, al - le - lu - ia, God most high!

Bread of the World, in Mercy Broken 346

Reginald Heber, 1827; alt. *John 6:35–58*

1 Bread of the world, in mer - cy bro - ken, Wine of the soul in
2 Look on the heart by sor - row bro - ken, look on the tears by

mer - cy shed, By whom the words of life were spo-ken,
sin - ners shed, And be your feast to us the to - ken

and in whose death our sins are dead,
that by your grace our lives are fed.

Author of a number of familiar hymns, Reginald Heber published the first modern English hymnal arranged according to the church year. The musical setting for this hymn was written by Episcopal priest and hymnal editor John Sebastian Bach Hodges.

Tune: EUCHARISTIC HYMN 9.8.9.8.
J. S. B. Hodges, 1868
Alternate tune: RENDEZ À DIEU
(sung in one stanza)

347   Let Us Talents and Tongues Employ

Luke 10:1–9   *Fred Kaan, 1975; alt.*

1 Let us tal - ents and tongues em-ploy,   reach-ing out with a   shout of joy:
2 Christ is a - ble to make us one,   at his ta - ble he   set the tone,
3 Je - sus calls us in, sends us out   bear - ing fruit in a   world of doubt,

bread is bro - ken, the   wine is poured,   Christ is spo - ken and   seen and heard.
teach-ing peo - ple to   live to bless,   love in word and in   deed ex - press.
gives us love to tell,   bread to share: God (Im-man - u - el)   ev - ery-where!

*Refrain (first time **p**, second time **f**)*

Je-sus lives a-gain, earth can breathe a-gain, pass the Word a-round: loaves a-bound!

This hymn came into being when composer Doreen Potter asked poet Fred Kaan to write a text for her adaptation of a Jamaican folk melody. It was first used at the World Council of Churches Assembly in Nairobi (1975), and in Vancouver (1983).

Tune: LINSTEAD L.M. with refrain
Jamaican folk song
Adapt. Doreen Potter, 1975

Jesus Is Here Right Now

348

Leon C. Roberts, 1986; alt.

Je - sus is here right now. Je - sus is here. With this bread and wine true peace you'll find; Christ Je - sus is here right now. (right now).

Composer Leon C. Roberts is perhaps best known for his "Mass of St. Augustine" and other liturgical compositions that appear in Lead Me, Guide Me: The African-American Catholic Hymnal. His work is greatly influenced by priest and composer Clarence Joseph Rivers.

Tune: JESUS IS HERE 6.4.5.4.6.
Leon C. Roberts, 1986

349

I Come with Joy

Brian Wren, 1968; rev. 1982, 1994

Unison

1 I come with joy, a child of God, for - giv - en, loved, and
2 I come with Chris - tians far and near to find, as all are
3 As Christ breaks bread, and bids us share, each proud di - vi - sion
4 And thus we meet, and bet - ter know the Pres - ence, ev - er
5 To - geth - er met, to - geth - er bound, in friend - ship we will

free, The life of Je - sus to re - call, in
fed, The new com - mu - ni - ty of love in
ends. The love that made us, makes us one, and
near, And join our hearts and sing with joy that
stay, And go with joy to love the world and

love laid down for me, in love laid down for me.
Christ's com - mu - nion bread, in Christ's com - mu - nion bread.
strang - ers now are friends, and strang - ers now are friends.
Christ is ris - en here, that Christ is ris - en here.
live the way we pray, and live the way we pray.

One of Brian Wren's most widely published texts, this hymn was
originally written to "sum up a series of sermons on the meaning
of communion. It tries to use simple words to suggest important
theological themes."

Tune: DOVE OF PEACE 8.6.8.6.6
Southern Harmony, 183.
Arr. Austin Lovelace, 197

Words Copyright © 1971; music Copyright © 1977 by Hope Publishing Company

Now in the Days of Youth

350

Walter J. Mathams, 1913; alt.
Adapt. Sylvia G. Dunstan, 1992

Eccles. 12:1; 1 Cor. 16:13; Deut. 30:19–20

1 Now in the days of youth when life is filled with choice, when
2 Teach us to use our lives with pur - pose and with power for
3 Teach us to love in truth, to give and to re - ceive with
4 Teach-er, Cre - a - tor, God, en - fold us in your arms; be

hope and doubt touch ev - ery hour, when all thoughts find a voice,
vi - sions of a bet - ter world and for de - ci - sion's hour;
joy - ful and with o - pen hearts, with all that we be - lieve;
with us as we try our wings, and keep us safe from harm.

We turn, O God, to you for guid-ance and for grace. In
To choose the way of life, re - ject the way of death, un -
To seek an - oth - er's good, to hon - or what is right, to
All good and per - fect gifts come to us from your hand. O

all our days, in all our ways, help us to seek your face.
til the ra - diant force of God fills mind and strength and breath.
let our will and our de - sire be held in ho - ly light.
help us use them care-ful - ly and live by love's com - mand.

*When the Rev. Walter J. Mathams of London wrote this hymn
for use at Christian Endeavor and Sunday School conventions,
he did not realize it would receive wide circulation. It was
introduced in the United States in 1913 in Worship and Song.*

Tune: DIADEMATA S.M.D.
George J. Elvey, 1868

351
I Was There to Hear Your Borning Cry

John Ylvisaker, 1985; a.

1 I was there to hear your born - ing cry, I'll be
2 When you found the won - der of the Word, I was
3 In the mid - dle a - ges of your life, not too
4 I was there to hear your born - ing cry, I'll be

there when you are old. I re - joiced the day you
there to cheer you on; You were raised to praise the
old, no long - er young, I'll be there to guide you
there when you are old. I re - joiced the day you

were bap - tized, to see your life un - fold.
liv - ing God, to whom you now be - long.
through the night, com - plete what I've be - gun.
were bap - tized, to see your life un - fold. *St. 4, end*

I was there when you were but a child, with a
Should you find some - one to share your time and you
When the eve - ning gent - ly clos - es in and you

John Ylvisaker is the composer of a number of collections
of music in the "contemporary" or "folk" idiom, as well as
soundtracks for various media productions. This is perhaps
his best-known song.

Tune: BORNING CRY 9.7.9.6.D.
John Ylvisaker, 1985

faith to suit you well; I'll be there in case you
join your hearts as one, I'll be there to make your
shut your wea - ry eyes, I'll be there as I have

wan - der off and find where de - mons dwell.
vers - es rhyme from dusk till ris - ing sun.
al - ways been with just one more sur - prise.

My God, Accept My Heart This Day　　　352

Matthew Bridges, 1848; alt.　　　　　　　　　　　　*Gal. 4:5; Eph. 1:5*

1 My God, ac - cept my heart this day, and make it al - ways yours,
2 Be - fore the cross of One who died, I bow in deep re - gret.
3 A - noint me with your love and grace, a - dopt me for your own,
4 Let ev - ery thought and work and word be given, O God, to you.

That I from you no more may stray as long as life en - dures.
Let ev - ery sin be cru - ci - fied, and ev - ery wrong off - set.
That I in heaven may find my place and wor - ship at your throne.
In life and death, may I be stirred your pur - pose to pur - sue.

Influenced by the Oxford Movement, Matthew Bridges left the
Church of England and became a Roman Catholic in 1848, the
year this confirmation hymn was published. He wrote numerous
other prose and poetry works.

Tune: ST. STEPHEN C.M.
William Jones, 1789

353 Great Work Has God Begun in You

Phil. 1:6; Col. 2:6; Eph. 5:1

Carol Birkland, 1995

1 Great work has God be - gun in you, so let the Spir - it
2 In love, God calls you to this day, and gives you strength, these
3 A - round God's ta - ble cel - e - brate the end of bond - age,
4 Great work has God be - gun in you; take on God's love in

fol - low through; The mark of Christ up - on your brow, bap -
vows to say; Take up the faith that you were shown, and
sin, and hate: A feast of love and vic - to - ry, the
all you do, And may that love in you in - crease— now,

tis - mal touch re - mem - ber now.
grow, as - sured you are God's own.
gift of Christ who sets us free.
with God's bless - ing, go in peace.

*Carol Birkland has served as director of Christian education in
Lutheran and United Church of Christ congregations, and has
written and edited curriculum. William Rowan's tune first
appeared in* Together Met, Together Bound, *a collection of his
hymn settings.*

Tune: VERBUM DEI L.M.
William P. Rowan, 1993
Alternate tune: PUER NOBIS NASCITUR

God, When I Came into This Life

354

Fred Kaan, 1979

Isa. 43:1

1 God, when I came in - to this life, you
2 You give me free - dom to be - lieve; to -
3 With - in the cir - cle of the faith, as
4 In all the ten - sions of my life, be -
5 So help me in my un - be - lief and

called me by my name; To - day I come, com -
day I make my choice, And to the wor - ship
mem - ber of your cast, I take my place with
tween my faith and doubt, Let your great Spir - it
let my life be true: Feet firm - ly plant - ed

mit my - self, re - spond - ing to your claim.
of the church I add my learn - ing voice.
all the saints of fu - ture, pres - ent, past.
give me hope, sus - tain me, lead me out.
on the earth, my sights set high on you.

The musical setting for this text by contemporary poet Fred Kaan is an Appalachian folk tune of possible British origin. Annabel Morris Buchanan, an organist, music teacher, and scholar of American hymnody, collected and arranged this and other tunes in Folk Hymns of America, *1938.*

Tune: LAND OF REST C.M.
The Christian Harp, 1832
Harm. Annabel Morris Buchanan, 1938

355 God the Spirit, Guide and Guardian

Gen. 2:7; John 10:11–16

Carl P. Daw, Jr., 1987

1 God the Spir - it, guide and guard - ian, wind - sped
2 Christ our Sav - ior, sov - ereign, shep - herd, Word made
3 Great Cre - a - tor, life - be - stow - er, truth be -
4 Tri - une God, mys - te - rious be - ing, un - di -

flame and hov - ering dove, Breath of life and voice of
flesh, love cru - ci - fied, Teach - er, heal - er, suf - fering
yond all thought's re - call, Fount of wis - dom, womb of
vid - ed and di - verse, Deep - er than our minds can

proph - ets, sign of bless - ing, power of love: Give to
ser - vant, friend of sin - ners, foe of pride: In your
mer - cy, giv - ing and for - giv - ing all: As you
fath - om, great - er than our creeds re - hearse: Help us

those who lead your peo - ple fresh a - noint - ing
tend - ing may all pas - tors* learn and live a
know our strength and weak - ness, so may those the
in our var - ied call - ings your full im - age

*Where appropriate, "ministers" may be substituted for "pastors."

Words Copyright © 1989 by Hope Publishing Company
Harmonization Copyright ©, Oxford University Press. From *The English Hymnal 1906.*

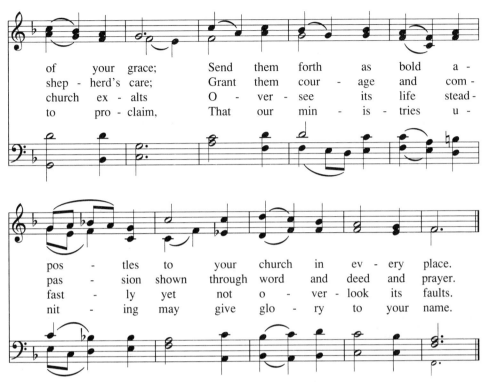

of	your	grace;	Send	them	forth	as	bold	a -
shep -	herd's	care;	Grant	them	cour -	age	and	com -
church	ex -	alts	O -	ver -	see	its	life	stead -
to	pro -	claim,	That	our	min -	is -	tries	u -

pos -	tles	to	your	church	in	ev -	ery	place.
pas -	sion	shown	through	word	and	deed	and	prayer.
fast -	ly	yet	not	o -	ver -	look	its	faults.
nit -	ing	may	give	glo -	ry	to	your	name.

A gift from Carl P. Daw, Jr., to Episcopal colleague Jeffery
Rowthorn for his consecration as bishop suffragan of the
Diocese of Connecticut, this text calls on the Triune God
to aid and bless the person being ordained in his or her ministry.

Tune: HYFRYDOL 8.7.8.7.D.
Rowland H. Prichard, 1844
Arr. Ralph Vaughan Williams, 1906
Alternate tune: JEFFERSON

356 God, Who Summons through All Ages

Eph. 4:11–12   *Edith Sinclair Downing, 1992*

1 God, who sum-mons through all   a - ges   men and wom - en to or - dain,
2 Called to   keep your   house-hold's mys-teries, guar-dian, coun - sel-or, and   friend,
3 God, E - ter - nal   Word With - in   Us,   help us   lis - ten so that   we

now   a - noint your cho - sen   ser-vant, join *her** to   the a - pos - tles' train.
blessed with gifts   u - nique and   pre-cious, may *she* these   with your grace blend.
hear   your call   to   be Christ's bod - y,   claim our gifts, serve faith - ful - ly.

*Or *him, he,* as appropriate.

Edith Sinclair Downing wrote this text "to affirm persons called to the pastoral ministry, particularly women, and to encourage believers to claim their gifts for mutual ministry." The tune by David Hurd was first published in a collection of the composer's works in 1983, and later appeared in several hymnals.

Tune: JULION 8.7.8.7.8.7.
David Hurd, 1974
Alternate tune: REGENT SQUARE

Give *her* pa-tience, cour - age, wis-dom, as *she* serves your tri-une name. *St. 1, 2, to %*
As *she* an-swers Christ's com-mis-sion, keep *her* stead - fast to life's end.
May we each in word and ac-tion join in mu - tual min-is - try! *St. 3, to Coda*

Coda

You Are Called to Tell the Story   357

Ruth Duck, 1991   *Eph. 3:14–21*

1 You are called to tell the sto-ry,
   pass-ing words of life a-long,
   Then to blend your voice with oth-ers
   as you sing the sa-cred song.
   Christ be known in all our sing-ing,
   fill-ing all with songs of love.

2 You are called to teach the rhy-thm
   of the dance that nev-er ends,
   Then to move with-in the cir-cle,
   hand in hand with strang-ers, friends.
   Christ be known in all our danc-ing,
   touch-ing all with hands of love.

3 You are called to set the ta-ble,
   bless-ing bread as Je-sus blessed,
   Then to come with thirst and hun-ger,
   need-ing care like all the rest.
   Christ be known in all our shar-ing,
   feed-ing all with signs of love.

4 May the One whose love is broad-er
   than the mea-sure of all space
   Give us words to sing the sto-ry,
   move a-mong us in this place.
   Christ be known in all our liv-ing,
   fill-ing all with gifts of love.

In this text, hymnwriter Ruth Duck sought to "set ordained ministry in the larger context of the ministry of the whole people of God." It was written for the ordination of her longtime friend, Elizabeth Caldwell.

Tune: JULION 8.7.8.7.8.7.
David Hurd, 1974
Alternate tune: REGENT SQUARE

358

God of the Prophets

2 Kings 2:9; Exod. 28:1–3; 1 Sam. 16:1, 13; Rom. 1:1–6

Denis Wortman, 1884; alt.

1 God of the proph - ets, bless the proph-et's heirs,
 E - li - jah's man - tle o'er E - li - sha cast.
 Each age for its own sol - emn tasks pre - pares:
 make each one no - bler, strong-er than the last.

2 A - noint them proph - ets! Make their ears at - tend
 to your di - vin - est speech; their hearts a - wake
 To hu - man need; their lips make el - o - quent
 for righ - teous - ness that shall all e - vil break.

3 A - noint them priests! Strong in - ter - ces - sors they
 for par - don, and for char - i - ty and peace!
 O might with them the world, though gone a - stray,
 pass in - to Christ's pure life of sac - ri - fice.

4 Make them a - pos - tles! Her - alds of your cross,
 forth may they go to tell all realms your grace.
 In - spired of you, may they count all but loss,
 and stand at last with joy be - fore your face.

Denis Wortman wrote "God of the Prophets" for the centenary of the New Brunswick Theological Seminary (Reformed) in New Jersey. A pastor of the Reformed Church in America, Wortman became president of its General Synod in 1901.

Tune: TOULON 10.10.10.10.
*Adapt. from OLD 124TH,
Trente quatre Pseaumes, Geneva, 1551*

O God, Who Teaches Us to Live 359

Tom Hunter, 1992

1 O God, who teach - es us to live and
2 For love that wel - comes chil - dren in and
3 For wis - dom, skills, and con - fi - dence where
4 For words and num - bers, hopes and dreams that
5 For all who fol - low teach - ing's call with

guides us on our way, For all the teach - ers
holds them when they stray, For knowl - edge hearts and
won - der leads to faith, For those who ask and
grow from day to day, For in - spi - ra - tion's
cour - age and with grace To build a fu - ture

in our midst, we give you thanks and praise.
souls re - ceive, we give you thanks and praise.
those who hear, we give you thanks and praise.
mes - sen - gers, we give you thanks and praise.
for us all, we give you thanks and praise.

*United Church of Christ minister Tom Hunter describes himself
as a "minstrel" for schools and churches across the United States.
This hymn was written "to celebrate and thank teachers in both
Sunday and weekday schools because their work shapes the
future for us all."*

Tune: ST. ANNE C.M.
William Croft, 1708

360

Thuma Mina
(Send Me, Lord)

Isa. 6:8

South African traditional song

Transcribed from recordings of South African worship, this
prayer-song has gained international popularity since its use
at the seventh assembly of the World Council of Churches at
Canberra, Australia, 1991, and subsequent publication.

Tune: THUMA MINA Irr.
South African traditional song

Your Love, O God, Has Called Us Here 361

Russell Schulz-Widmar, 1982   *Heb. 13:1; 1 Pet. 1:22*

1 Your love, O God, has called us here, for all love
2 O gra-cious God, you con - se - crate all that is
3 O God of love, in - spire our life, re - veal your

finds its source in you, The per - fect love that casts out
love - ly, good, and true. Bless those who in your pres - ence
will in all we do; Join ev - ery hus - band, ev - ery

fear, the love that Christ makes ev - er new.
wait, and ev - ery day their love re - new.
wife in mu - tual love and love for you.

Russell Schulz-Widmar of Austin, Texas, has been a lecturer, music director, and professor of church music. He has served as president of The Hymn Society and co-editor of A New Hymnal for Colleges and Schools, 1992.

Tune: GERMANY (GARDINER) L.M.
William Gardiner's Sacred Melodies, 1815

362

When Love Is Found

Matt. 19:6; Mark 10:8

Brian Wren, 1978; rev. 1992

Unison

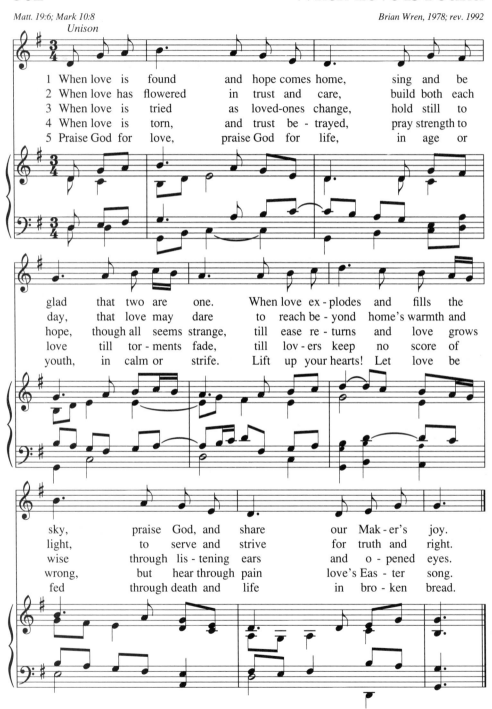

1 When love is found and hope comes home, sing and be
2 When love has flowered in trust and care, build both each
3 When love is tried as loved-ones change, hold still to
4 When love is torn, and trust be - trayed, pray strength to
5 Praise God for love, praise God for life, in age or

glad that two are one. When love ex - plodes and fills the
day, that love may dare to reach be - yond home's warmth and
hope, though all seems strange, till ease re - turns and love grows
love till tor - ments fade, till lov - ers keep no score of
youth, in calm or strife. Lift up your hearts! Let love be

sky, praise God, and share our Mak - er's joy.
light, to serve and strive for truth and right.
wise through lis - tening ears and o - pened eyes.
wrong, but hear through pain love's Eas - ter song.
fed through death and life in bro - ken bread.

*Brian Wren has noted one important hope for all committed
Christian relationships, "that love may reach out beyond the nuclear
family, rather than the more cozy and familiar theme of inviting
others into 'home's warmth and light.'"*

Tune: O WALY WALY L.M.
English folk melody
Arr. Jonathan McNair, 1993

O God of Love 363

William Vaughan Jenkins (1868–1920); alt.   *Gen. 2:24; Matt. 19:5; Mark 10:7–9*

1 O God of love, to you we bow
  and pray for these be-fore you now,
  That close-ly knit in ho-ly vow
  they may in you be-come as one.

2 What-ev-er comes to be their share
  of quick-ening joy or bur-dening care,
  In power to do and grace to bear,
  may they in you re-main as one.

3 E-ter-nal Love, with them a-bide;
  through change and chance, O be their guide,
  Let noth-ing in this life di-vide
  those whom you now have joined as one.

William Vaughan Jenkins, by profession a chartered
accountant in England, was active in mission work of
Baptist and Congregational churches and was involved
in the Adult School Movement. This hymn, written
for his wedding in 1900, was published in 1909.

Tune: O WALY WALY L.M.
English folk melody
Arr. Jonathan McNair, 1993

God, Today Bless This New Marriage 364

Marie J. Post, 1974; alt.

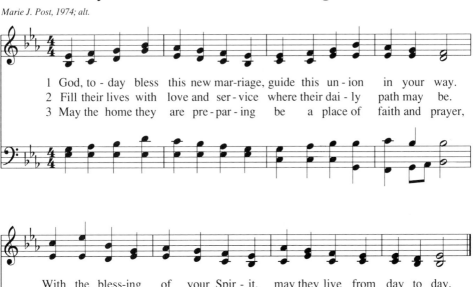

1 God, to-day bless this new mar-riage, guide this un-ion in your way.
2 Fill their lives with love and ser-vice where their dai-ly path may be.
3 May the home they are pre-par-ing be a place of faith and prayer,

With the bless-ing of your Spir-it, may they live from day to day.
Grant them hum-ble hearts when pros-pered, pa-tience in ad-ver-si-ty.
fruit-ful for this life and your do-min-ion which they glad-ly share.

Marie Post wrote poetry for the Grand Rapids Press *in*
Michigan for thirty years, and published a collection of her work
titled I Had Never Visited an Artist Before *(1977). Her text was*
inspired by a traditional wedding prayer of the Christian
Reformed Church.

Tune: SERVANT SONG 8.7.8.7.
Richard Gillard, 1977
Arr. Betty Carr Pulkingham, 1977; adapt.

365 How Blessed Are They Who Trust in Christ

John 3:13–16; Jude 1:20–21   *Fred Pratt Green, 1972*

1 How blessed are they who trust in Christ when we and
2 In rip - ened age, their har - vest reaped, or gone from
3 In Christ, who tast - ed death for us, we rise a -

those we love must part; We yield them up, for
us in youth or prime, In Christ they have e -
bove our nat - ural grief, and wit - ness to a

go they must, but do not lose them from our heart.
ter - nal life, re - leased from all the bonds of time.
strick - en world the strength and splen - dor of be - lief.

This text was one of four chosen from 457 entries for publication   Tune: MARYTON L.M.
by The Hymn Society of America in 1980. Works of this eminent   H. Percy Smith, 1874
British writer have been published in The New Yorker and in
anthologies.

God of Our Life

366

Hugh T. Kerr, 1916; alt.

1 God of our life, through all   the   cir-cling years, we trust in   you.
2 God of the past, our   times   are   in your hand; with us   a - bide.
3 God of the com - ing   years, through paths un - known we   fol - low   you;

In   all the   past, through all   our hopes and   fears, your care shines through.
Lead us by   faith   to   hope's true prom-ised   land; be   now our   guide.
When we are   strong, O   leave   us   not   a - lone, our   ref - uge   true.

With   each   new   day,   when   morn - ing   lifts   the   veil,
Bless   us   in   times   of   dark - ness   and   of   light,
Be   now   for   us   in   life   our   dai - ly   bread,

We   own   your   mer - cies,   God, which nev - er   fail.
Then   faith's   fair   vi - sion   chang - es   in - to   sight.
Our   heart's   true   home   when   all   our years have   sped.

Hugh Kerr was educated in Canada and the United States and was a pioneer in religious broadcasting. He wrote this hymn for the fiftieth anniversary of Shadyside Presbyterian Church in Pittsburgh, where he had a long tenure as pastor.

Tune: SANDON   10.4.10.4.10.10.
Charles Henry Purday, 1860
For another harmonization, see 466

367 Christ the Victorious

Gen. 1:26–27; 3:19   *Carl P. Daw, Jr., 1982*

1 Christ the Vic - to - ri - ous,   give to your ser - vants
2 On - ly Im - mor - tal One,   might - y Cre - a - tor!
3 God - spo - ken proph - e - cy,   word at cre - a - tion:
4 Christ the Vic - to - ri - ous,   give to your ser - vants

rest with your saints in the re - gions of light.
We are your crea - tures and chil - dren of earth.
"You came from dust and to dust shall re - turn."
rest with your saints in the re - gions of light.

Grief and pain end - ed, and sigh - ing no long - er,
From earth you formed us, both glo - rious and mor - tal,
Yet at the grave shall we raise up our glad song,
Grief and pain end - ed, and sigh - ing no long - er,

there may they find ev - er - last - ing life.
and to the earth shall we all re - turn.
"Al - le - lu - ia, al - le - lu - ia!"
there may they find ev - er - last - ing life.

Carl P. Daw, Jr.'s paraphrase of the "Kontakion for the Departed" from the Eastern Orthodox memorial service was written specifically for this tune to preserve some of the flavor of the original text for congregations unable to sing the traditional Kiev melody.

Tune: RUSSIAN HYMN   11.10.11.9.
Alexis F. Lvov, 1833

Sheltered by God's Loving Spirit 368

Deborah Patterson, 1993   *1 Cor. 13:4–13; Rom. 5:8*

1 Shel-tered by God's lov - ing Spir - it, gath-ered here we share our grief:
2 Giv - en breath by God's own pur-pose, back to God our breath does go.

Seek-ing so - lace, seek - ing cour-age— know-ing God does bring re - lief.
Life e - ter - nal in our pres - ent here we on - ly part - ly know.

We are free to name our sor-rows, speak our an - ger, weep our loss,
But for-give-ness, love, and cour-age show us God's a - maz - ing grace,

For our God did suf - fer al - so when Christ died up - on a cross.
Strength-en us to face the jour-ney till we know God face to face.

Reflecting on the love she had experienced while going through deep pain, Deborah Patterson wrote this text for the funeral of a parishioner at St. John's United Church of Christ in Smithton, Illinois, while serving as minister.

Tune: BEECHER 8.7.8.7.D.
John Zundel, 1855

369   Keep Your Lamps Trimmed and Burning

Matt. 25:1–13; Gal. 6:9   *African-American spiritual*

Last time, end

Refrain

By tradition, a leader may call out substitute words for the refrain,
such as "Christians don't grow weary, Christians don't grow weary, . . ."
etc., or "people," "preacher," or any others that may be appropriate.

This spiritual is possibly one of the code songs in which to keep
one's lamp "trimmed and burning" could have meant keeping a
lookout for a conductor of the underground railroad, such as
Harriet Tubman. It is often sung at church dedication services.

Tune: KEEP YOUR LAMPS   7.7.7.6.6.6.6.6
African-American spiritual
Harm. The New Century Hymnal, *1994*

What Gift Can We Bring? 370

Jane Marshall, 1980   *1 Sam. 9:7; 1 Cor. 3:8–9; 1 John 4:13–16*

1 What gift can we bring, what pres - ent, what to - ken?
2 Give thanks for the past, for those who had vi - sion,
3 Give thanks for to - mor - row, full of sur - pris - es,
4 This gift we now bring, this pres - ent, this to - ken,

What words can con - vey it, the joy of this day?
who plant - ed and wa - tered so dreams could come true.
for know - ing what - ev - er to - mor - row may bring,
these words can con - vey it, the joy of this day!

When grate - ful we come, re - mem - bering, re - joic - ing,
Give thanks for the now, for stud - y, for wor - ship,
The Word is our prom - ise al - ways, for - ev - er;
When grate - ful we come, re - mem - bering, re - joic - ing,

what song can we of - fer in hon - or and praise?
for mis - sion that bids us turn prayer in - to deed.
we rest in God's keep - ing and live in God's love.
this song we now of - fer in hon - or and praise!

Jane Marshall received the first "Woman of Achievement"
award at Perkins School of Theology, Southern Methodist
University, where she teaches. She wrote this hymn for the
twenty-fifth anniversary of her home church, Northaven United
Methodist Church in Dallas.

Tune: ANNIVERSARY SONG 11.11.11.11.
Jane Marshall, 1980

371 God, Creation's Great Designer

Gen. 1:1–2:7; 1 Pet. 2:4–9

Jane Parker Huber, 1984

1 God, cre - a - tion's great de - sign - er, ar - chi - tect, and ar - ti - san,
2 Hear our thanks for those who found - ed in this place a church for praise.
3 Sing we, too, of church - es stand - ing not a - lone in wood and stone,
4 Shape us as your con - gre - ga - tions, called to - geth - er, sent a - far,

dream - er, build - er, and re - fin - er— how we mar - vel at your plan.
Firm in Christ their faith was ground - ed as they lived their earth - ly days.
but in hu - man lives com - mand - ing con - fi - dence in you a - lone.
so as peo - ple or as na - tions we can serve you where we are.

You have formed us to re - flect you, filled us with your Spir - it's breath,
Build - ers, they, in brick and stone - work, walls sup - port - ing roof and floors,
For high arch - es, ris - ing, yearn - ing, soar - ing towers that fill with song,
O ac - cept the praise we bring you, bless the work of hu - man hands.

freed us to ac - cept, re - ject you, and in Christ, de - feat - ed death.
prais - ing you in all their own work— sol - id stee - ple, o - pen doors.
win - dows o - pened for our learn - ing— God, we praise you all day long.
Hear the hymns our voic - es sing you, ech - o - ing through years and lands.

Jane Parker Huber wrote this text specifically for the dedication of an Indiana church's rebuilding program to be sung with this twentieth-century tune, New Reformation. "It celebrates the skill and labor of human workers as well as of our creating God."

Tune: NEW REFORMATION 8.7.8.7.D.
J. T. Morrow, 1950
Alternate tunes: WEISSE FLAGGEN, HOLY MANNA

God, You Have Set Us

372

Jane Parker Huber, 1984; rev. 1993

1 Cor. 4:1; 1 Pet. 4:10–11

1 God, you have set us in this time and place,
2 We ded - i - cate this work of hu - man hand;
3 Let doors and hearts pro-vide a wel - come here.
4 Call youth and age in - to these halls for praise.
5 So may the world be-come our neigh-bor - hood,

Called us as stew - ards of your love and grace.
Built for your glo - ry, may it firm - ly stand.
Let walls and voic - es ring with songs of cheer.
Then send us out for ser - vice all our days,
Each wish - ing each the right, the true, the good,

O keep us faith - ful, set our souls a - fire,
Let truth be preached and jus - tice right - ly done.
Let win - dows speak of beau - ty and of light.
Your word of peace and chal-lenge here made real
Word, font, and ta - ble call - ing us to be

And by your Spir - it all our work in - spire.
In Christ our Sav - ior make us tru - ly one.
Let smile and ges - ture show your love a - right.
Spurs us to act with en - er - gy and zeal.
Bound up in Christ, in Christ set bold - ly free.

Commissioned to write a hymn for the dedication of a remodeled sanctuary and the twenty-fifth anniversary of the Church of Saint Andrew in Roswell, Georgia, Jane Parker Huber provided a text that could be used by others for related occasions.

Tune: NATIONAL HYMN 10.10.10.10.
George William Warren, 1892

373

They Did Not Build in Vain

Acts 2:1–4, 43–47; 1 Cor. 3:11; Eph. 2:19–22; Heb. 12:1–2

Alan Luff, 1989; alt.

1 They did not build in vain who found - ed here a church
2 Those who have loved this place, a cloud of wit - nes - ses,
3 In ev - ery place our world is storm and tem - pest tossed,
4 Make this the meet-ing place where doubt finds grounds of faith,

as wit - ness to God's love a - mid a world of pain;
sur - round and urge us on as we now run our race;
the flames of fear and hate are e - vil's flags un - furled;
where hurt finds heal-ing love, our pen - i - tence your grace;

They built up - on the rock that is the ris - en Christ,
Though the ho - ri - zon's bend con - ceals the way a - head,
Yet still the Spir-it's power in wind and fire of love
Where God in Trin - i - ty is bridge from death to life,

the one foun-da-tion laid, that stands each earth - ly shock.
the foot-prints on the road show Christ waits at the end.
pours gifts up - on the church for ser - vice in this hour.
from sin to ho - li - ness, time to e - ter - ni - ty.

Alan Luff, a graduate of the Royal College of Music, has served the Anglican Church as parish priest, precentor of Westminster Abbey, and canon of Birmingham Cathedral. He is also known as the author of Welsh Hymns and Their Tunes *(1990).*

Tune: LEONI 6.6.8.4.D.
Traditional Yigdal melody
Adapt. Meyer Lyon, 1770

O God of All Your People Past 374

Thomas H. Gill, 1868; alt. *Ps. 90:1*

1 O God of all your peo-ple past, your grace is our sal - va - tion;
2 Their joy in you, the joy we bring, rings thrill-ing in its blend - ing;
3 O saints to come, take up the strain, and bless the Bound-less Giv - er.

your arms of love, their home se - cure, re - main our hab - i - ta - tion.
the Spir - it who in them did sing to us new song is lend - ing.
Un - bro-ken be the gold-en chain! Let not di - vi-sions sev - er.

We bring to you the praise they brought, we seek you as the
That song in them, in us, is one; we raise it high, we
But safe in that dear dwell-ing place, and rich with that e -

saints have sought in ev - er - y gen - er - a - tion.
send it on, the mus - ic nev - er end - ing.
ter - nal grace, sing on, sing on for - ev - er.

Barred from studies at Oxford University because of his Unitarian heritage, Thomas Gill pursued his own study of history and theology. He wrote several volumes of poetry and historical writings. Later in life, Gill associated with the evangelical branch of the Anglican church.

Tune: NUN FREUT EUCH 8.7.8.7.8.8.7.
Melody by Martin Luther
Klug's Geistliche Lieder, *1535*

375   Christ Jesus, Please Be by Our Side

Rev. 4:8

Attrib. to Wilhelm August II, 17th century
Cantionale Sacrum, Gotha, 165.
Transl. Madeleine Forell Marshall, 199.

1 Christ Je - sus, please be by our side, your
2 Pre - pare our hearts to sing your praise, in -
3 So shall we join that faith - ful crowd, who,
4 Now hon - or God who shaped this earth; praise

Ho - ly Spir - it send as guide: With gra - cious help, your
struct our lips, re - fine each phrase, Em - power our mind, our
"Ho - ly, ho - ly," cry a - loud: E - ter - nal joy, most
Je - sus Christ of mor - tal birth; A - dore the Ho - ly

peo - ple may keep to the true and righ - teous way.
faith in - flame, that hu - man - kind may bless your name.
ho - ly light, the face of God is their de - light.
Spir - it: three in One, the bless - ed Trin - i - ty.

Wilhelm August II was severely wounded twice during the Thirty Years' War, the second time left for dead, but he recovered to devote himself to the rebuilding of his country and to poetry and music. His authorship of this hymn is uncertain.

Tune: HERR JESU CHRIST
DICH ZU UNS WEND L.M
Pensum Sacrum, *Görlitz, 164.*
Arr. J. S. Bach, c. 170.

God, We Thank You for Our People 376

Ruth Duck, 1986

1 God, we thank you for our peo-ple, roots dug deep with-in the soil,
2 Thank you, God, for gen-tle plea-sure: les-sons learned and se-crets told,
3 Still we must con-fess be-fore you, some-times, Sav-ior, we have failed;
4 By your Spir-it of cre-a-tion keep us bold for risk-ing still,

har-dy spir-its, rich in lov-ing, strong for strug-gle, bold for toil.
hopes and mem-ories saved as trea-sure, passed to young ones by the old,
though we wor-ship and a-dore you, some-times love has not pre-vailed.
ea-ger in an-ti-ci-pa-tion, ev-er strong to do your will.

Faith-ful Rock of gen-er-a-tions, you whom par-ents' par-ents praised:
Pranks and glo-ries, songs and sto-ries, food by lov-ing hands pre-pared.
Tem-pers rac-ing, dev-il chas-ing, hearts es-tranged by ice or flame
Bind us close to one an-oth-er, shar-ing life and death and birth,

Here in hope as we re-mem-ber may our song to you be raised.
God, we bless you for your pres-ence in our tears and laugh-ter shared.
You trans-form by ways for-giv-ing. Grace a-maz-ing! Grace, your name!
Wel-com-ing as sis-ter, broth-er, all your chil-dren on the earth.

Ruth Duck created this text at the request of Harold (Hal)
McSwain, Jr., for a family reunion. She found her inspiration
in the stories of Harold, Sr., and in her own family heritage.
The hymn speaks to any community that has shared life together
for a long time.

Tune: HOLY MANNA 8.7.8.7.D.
William Moore, 1825

377   Forward through the Ages

Heb. 11; 1 Cor. 12   *Frederick Lucian Hosmer, 1908; alt.*

1 For - ward through the a - ges, in un - bro - ken line,
2 Wide grows God's do - min - ion, reign of love and peace;
3 Not a - lone we con - quer, not a - lone we fall;

move the faith - ful spir - its at the call di - vine;
for it we must la - bor, till all striv - ings cease.
in each loss or tri - umph, lose or tri - umph all.

Gifts in dif - fering mea - sure, hearts of one ac - cord,
Proph-ets have pro - claimed it, teach - ers tes - ti - fied,
Bound by God's far pur - pose in one liv - ing whole,

man - i - fold in ser - vice, one the sure re - ward.
po - ets sung its glo - ry, mar - tyrs for it died.
move we on to - geth - er to the shin - ing goal.

Frederick Hosmer, educated at Harvard and ordained to the Unitarian ministry, served Congregational and Unitarian churches throughout the country. He was known for his concern for social issues, his service book for Sunday schools, and his lectures on hymnology.

Tune: ST. GERTRUDE 6.5.6.5.D. with refrain
Arthur S. Sullivan, 1871

For - ward through the a - ges, in un - bro - ken line,
Move the faith - ful spir - its at the call di - vine.

Jerusalem, My Happy Home 378

F. B. P., c. 16th century; alt.

Ps. 144:9–10; 1 Cor. 13:12; Luke 1:46–55

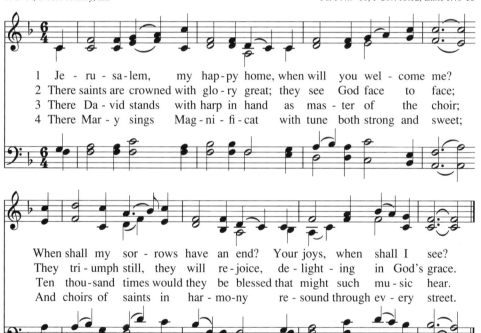

1 Je - ru - sa - lem, my hap-py home, when will you wel - come me?
2 There saints are crowned with glo - ry great; they see God face to face;
3 There Da - vid stands with harp in hand as mas - ter of the choir;
4 There Mar - y sings Mag - ni - fi - cat with tune both strong and sweet;

When shall my sor - rows have an end? Your joys, when shall I see?
They tri - umph still, they will re - joice, de - light - ing in God's grace.
Ten thou-sand times would they be blessed that might such mu - sic hear.
And choirs of saints in har - mo-ny re - sound through ev - ery street.

5 There Mag-da-len no more la-ments
   but joins the ris-ing sound;
   What tongue can tell or heart con-ceive
   the joys that there are found!

6 Je-ru-sa-lem, Je-ru-sa-lem,
   God grant that I may see
   your end-less joy, and of the same
   par-tak-er ev-er be!

*The earliest known version of this hymn (1585) is forty-four
stanzas long. A later and shorter version, found in the British
Museum, credits "F. B. P.," about whom nothing is known. The
American tune was often sung with the words "O Land of rest,
for thee I sigh."*

Tune: LAND OF REST C.M.
The Christian Harp, *1832*
Adapt. and harm. Annabel Morris Buchanan, *1938*

379 Come, We Who Love God's Name

Ps. 48:1–2; Heb. 12:22–24; Rev. 4:2–11   *Isaac Watts, 1707; alt.*

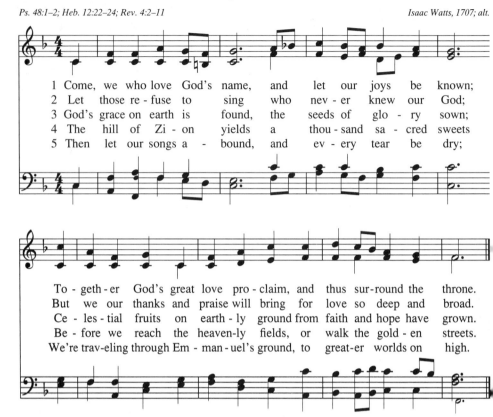

1 Come, we who love God's name, and let our joys be known;
2 Let those re-fuse to sing who nev-er knew our God;
3 God's grace on earth is found, the seeds of glo-ry sown;
4 The hill of Zi-on yields a thou-sand sa-cred sweets
5 Then let our songs a-bound, and ev-ery tear be dry;

To-geth-er God's great love pro-claim, and thus sur-round the throne.
But we our thanks and praise will bring for love so deep and broad.
Ce-les-tial fruits on earth-ly ground from faith and hope have grown.
Be-fore we reach the heaven-ly fields, or walk the gold-en streets.
We're trav-eling through Em-man-uel's ground, to great-er worlds on high.

*A story concerning this hymn holds that the pastor of a New
England church once asked the choir to lead the singing of the
second stanza on a Sunday when it threatened to "refuse to sing"
because of a disagreement in the congregation. Needless to say,
the choir acquiesced.*

Tune: ST. THOMAS S.M.
Williams' New Universal Psalmodist, 1770
Alternate setting: MARCHING TO ZION

380 O Saints in Splendor Sing

Rev. 7   *Sylvia G. Dunstan, 1991*

1 O saints in splen-dor sing
  the praise of God Most High.
  Through trib-u-la-tion you have come,
  through blood been sanc-ti-fied.

2 Robed in bap-tis-mal grace
  a-mid the world's de-spair,
  Pro-claim the glo-ry of our God
  whose love has con-quered fear.

3 Those saints who went be-fore
  pre-pared for us the way;
  The church ex-pec-tant, yet to come,
  re-lies on us to-day.

4 O wor-thy is the Lamb!
  the Lamb that once was slain!
  Of hon-or, bless-ing, thanks, and praise
  lift up the glad re-frain!

*Sylvia Dunstan wrote this hymn based on the Revelation 7 text
to accompany a sermon preached for a small struggling
congregation. It was intended to encourage them to identify
with the saints and to persevere as a community of faith.*

Tune: ST. THOMAS S.M. (see above)

Faith of the Martyrs

381

Frederick W. Faber, 1849; alt.

1 Faith of the mar - tyrs, liv - ing still in spite of
2 Mar - tyrs con - fined in pris - ons bleak were still in
3 Faith of the mar - tyrs! We will love both friend and
4 Faith of the mar - tyrs! Faith and prayer shall long out -

dun - geon, fire, and sword; O how our hearts beat high with
heart and con - science free; and no less blessed will be our
foe in peace or strife; and sow the seeds of hope and
live sin's ty - ran - ny; and through the truth that comes from

joy, when we re - call their faith's re - ward:
fate if we, like them, live faith - ful - ly:
faith by strength-ening word and fear - less life:
God all hu - man - kind shall then be free:

Refrain

Faith of the mar-tyrs, liv - ing faith! We would be true in life and death.

The Greek term *martures is translated in the New Testament as*
"witness" and forms the basis for the English word "martyr."
The hymn was written as a call for the return of the Church of
England to the Roman Catholic church, and "our fathers . . ." in
the original text referred to those faithful to Rome who had
suffered martyrdom.

Tune: ST. CATHERINE L.M. with refrain
Henri F. Hemy, 1864
Adapt. James G. Walton, 1874

382 Come, We Who Love God's Name

Ps. 48:1–2; Heb. 12:22–24; Rev. 4:2–11

Isaac Watts, 1707; alt.
Refrain by Robert Lowry, 1867; alt.

1 Come, we who love God's name, and let our joys be known; To-
2 Let those re - fuse to sing who nev - er knew our God; But
3 God's grace on earth is found, the seeds of glo - ry sown; Ce -
4 The hill of Zi - on yields a thou-sand sa - cred sweets Be -
5 Then let our songs a - bound, and ev - ery tear be dry; We're

geth - er God's great love pro - claim, to - geth - er God's great love pro -
we our thanks and praise will bring, but we our thanks and praise will
les - tial fruits on earth - ly ground, ce - les - tial fruits on earth - ly
fore we reach the heaven-ly fields, be - fore we reach the heaven-ly
trav - eling through Em - man - uel's ground, we're trav - eling through Em - man - uel's

claim, and thus sur - round the throne, and thus sur-round the throne.
bring for love so deep and broad, for love so deep and broad.
ground from faith and hope have grown, from faith and hope have grown.
fields, or walk the gold - en streets, or walk the gold - en streets.
ground to great - er worlds on high, to great-er worlds on high.

And thus sur-round the throne, and thus sur - round the throne.

Isaac Watts' joyous hymn was a favorite of the early American singing schools and was set to a variety of fuguing tunes. This gospel tune by Baptist preacher Robert Lowry incorporates a camp-meeting style refrain and is a favorite of many Christians.

Tune: MARCHING TO ZION S.M. with refrain
Robert Lowry, 1867
Alternate setting: ST. THOMAS

Refrain

We're march-ing to Zi - on, beau-ti-ful, beau-ti-ful Zi - on; We're

We're march-ing on to Zi - on,

march-ing on-ward to Zi - on, the beau-ti-ful cit-y of God.

Zi - on, Zi - on, the

Come, Let Us Join with Faithful Souls — 383

William G. Tarrant, 1892; alt. *Rev. 5:11–14*

1 Come, let us join with faith-ful souls our song of faith to raise;
2 Faith - ful are all who love the truth and per - fect truth pro - claim,
3 And faith-ful are the gen - tle hearts to whom the power is given
4 O God of hosts, our faith re-new, and grant us, in your grace,

One fam - i - ly in heart are we, and one the God we praise.
Who stead-fast stand at God's right hand and glo - ri - fy God's name.
Of ev - ery hearth to make a home, of ev-ery home a heaven.
To join the songs sung by the saints in ev-ery time and place.

A leader of the Unitarian Church in England, William Tarrant
edited a Unitarian weekly and for thirty-seven years ministered
to the Unitarian Christian Church in London. This hymn was
one of many he wrote for use by that congregation.

Tune: AZMON C.M.
Carl G. Gläser, 1828
Arr. Lowell Mason, in Modern Psalmody, *1839*

384   For the Faithful Who Have Answered

Heb. 11:4–12:2

Sylvia G. Dunstan, 1986; al.

1 For the faith - ful who have an-swered when they heard your call to serve,
2 Man-y minds have glimpsed the prom-ise; man - y hearts have yearned to see;
3 For this cloud of faith - ful wit-ness, for the com - mon life we share,

for the man - y ways you led them, test-ing will and stretch-ing nerve,
man - y souls have heard you call-ing us to great-er lib - er - ty.
for the work of peace and jus-tice, for the gos - pel that we bear,

For their work and for their wit - ness as they strove a - gainst the odds,
Some have fall - en in the strug - gle; oth - ers still are press-ing on.
For the vi - sion that our home - land is your love— deep, high, and broad—

for their cour-age and o - be-dience, we give thanks and praise, O God.
You are not a - shamed to own us; we give thanks and praise, O God.
for the dif - ferent roads we trav - el, we give thanks and praise, O God.

*In commissioning a hymn for the fiftieth anniversary of women's
ordination in 1986, the United Church of Canada specified that it
should concentrate on all people's faithful response to God's call.
Sylvia Dunstan selected Hebrews 11 and 12 as her primary reference.*

Tune: OMNI DIE 8.7.8.7.D
German melody, 1625
Trier Gesangbuch, 1695

O What Their Joy and Their Glory Must Be 385

Peter Abelard (1079–1142)
Transl. composite John M. Neale, 1841, and S. W. Duffield, 1886; alt.

Rev. 7:9–17; 21:1–6

1 O what their joy and their glo - ry must be,
2 The true Je - ru - sa - lem ho - ly is there,
3 Long - ing for home now let ev - ery heart raise
4 There in a Sab - bath of un - end - ing light,

as end - less Sab - baths the bless - ed ones see;
whose peace-ful du - ties give joy free from care;
prayers of de - vo - tion and an - thems of praise;
joy - ful - ly keep - ing that ho - ly day bright,

Crowns for the val - iant, for wea - ry ones rest;
Where dis - ap - point - ment no heart can as - sail,
From streams of sor - row we lift up our eyes,
We join in chant - ing the song with - out cease

God shall be all, and in all ev - er blessed.
where each prayer whis - pered is heard with - out fail.
to the blessed cit - y, our home and our prize.
with all the saints in that sweet realm of peace.

Peter Abelard, a brilliant and daring thinker, was a founder of
the University of Paris. His questioning and reasoning approach
to Scripture made enemies. This was one of ninety-three hymns
to the Spirit (Hymnus Paraclitensis) he wrote for the Convent of
Heloisa.

Tune: O QUANTA QUALIA 10.10.10.10.
La Feillée's Nouvelle Méthode de Plain Chant, 1808

386

The Church's One Foundation

Eph. 2:13–22; 4:4–6; 1 Cor. 3:11

Samuel J. Stone, 1866; alt.

1 The church's one foun - da - tion is Je - sus Christ our Lord;
2 E - lect from ev - ery na - tion, yet one o'er all the earth,
3 'Mid toil and trib - u - la - tion, and tu - mult of our war,
4 Yet we on earth have un - ion with God, the Three - in - One,

we are Christ's new cre - a - tion by wa - ter and the word;
one char - ter of sal - va - tion, one God, one faith, one birth,
we wait the con - sum - ma - tion of peace for - ev - er - more;
and mys - tic sweet com - mu - nion with those whose rest is won.

From heaven Christ came and sought us in love to set us free;
One name to - geth - er bless - ing, one ho - ly food we share,
Till with the vi - sion glo - rious, our long - ing eyes are blessed,
O hap - py ones and ho - ly! God, give us grace that we,

with pre - cious blood Christ bought us for all e - ter - ni - ty.
to one hope we are press - ing, at one in work and prayer.
and the great church vic - to - rious shall be the church at rest.
like them, the meek and low - ly, may live e - ter - nal - ly.

Like the writings of Ambrose many centuries earlier, this hymn was born out of a doctrinal dispute. The young priest Samuel J. Stone composed twelve hymns on the articles of the Apostles' Creed in support of those reacting against nontraditional views of biblical scholarship. This hymn is based on article nine, "the holy Catholic Church."

Tune: AURELIA 7.6.7.6.D.
Samuel S. Wesley, 1864

O Christ, the Great Foundation

387

Timothy Tingfang Lew, 1933; alt.
Transl. Frank W. Price, 1953; alt.

Acts 2:17–21; Eph. 4:4–6; Col. 1:18–20

1 O Christ, the great foun-da-tion
   on which your peo-ple stand
   to preach your true sal-va-tion
   in ev-ery age and land:
   Pour out your Ho-ly Spir-it
     to make us strong and pure,
   to keep the faith un-bro-ken
   as long as worlds en-dure.

2 Bap-tized in one con-fes-sion,
   one church in all the earth,
   we bear Christ's own im-pres-sion,
   the sign of sec-ond birth:
   One ho-ly peo-ple gath-ered
     in love be-yond our own,
   by grace we were in-vit-ed,
   by grace we make you known.

3 Where ty-rants' hold is tight-ened,
   where strong de-vour the weak,
   where in-no-cents are fright-ened,
   the righ-teous fear to speak,
   There let your church a-wak-ing
     at-tack the powers of sin
   and, all their ram-parts break-ing,
   with you the vic-tory win.

4 This is the mo-ment glo-rious
   when Christ who once was dead
   shall lead the church vic-to-rious,
   their cham-pion and their head.
   The Sov-ereign of cre-a-tion
     a new do-min-ion brings,
   the fi-nal con-sum-ma-tion,
   the glo-ry of all things.

Timothy Tingfang Lew was born in China and was educated both there and in the United States. He served as representative to the World Council of Churches from 1927 to 1939 and chaired the commission that prepared the Chinese Union hymnbook in 1936.

Tune: AURELIA 7.6.7.6.D.
Samuel S. Wesley, 1864

Help Us Accept Each Other

388

Fred Kaan, 1974; alt.

John 15:12; 17:20–23; Eph. 4:1–6, 11–16

1 Help us ac-cept each oth-er
   as Christ ac-cept-ed us;
   teach us as sis-ter, broth-er,
   each per-son to em-brace.
   Be pres-ent, God, a-mong us,
     and bring us to be-lieve
   we are our-selves ac-cept-ed
   and meant to love and live.

2 Teach us, O God, your les-sons,
   as in our dai-ly life
   we strug-gle to be hu-man
   and search for hope and faith.
   Teach us to care for peo-ple,
     for all, not just for some,
   to love them as we find them,
   or as they may be-come.

3 Let your ac-cep-tance change us,
   so that we may be moved
   in liv-ing sit-u-a-tions
   to do the truth in love;
   To prac-tice your ac-cep-tance,
     un-til we know by heart
   the ta-ble of for-give-ness
   and laugh-ter's heal-ing art.

4 God, for to-day's en-coun-ters
   with all who are in need,
   who hun-ger for ac-cep-tance,
   for righ-teous-ness and bread,
   Bring us new eyes for see-ing,
     new hands for hold-ing on;
   re-new us with your Spir-it;
   God! Free us, make us one!

Dutch theologian Fred Kaan was ordained in the United Reformed Church in England and Wales and has served as an international church administrator. Author of more than 200 hymns, Kaan frequently has addressed contemporary issues in his texts.

Tune: AURELIA 7.6.7.6.D.
Samuel S. Wesley, 1864

389

Un mandamiento nuevo

Matt. 22:34–40; Mark 12:28–34;
John 13:34–35; 14:6; 15:9–12; 1 John 4:7–21

William Loperena, 1965; rev. 1993
English version, Carolyn Jennings, 1993

Estribillo (Refrain)

Un man - da-mien-to nue - vo Je-sús nos dio
Je-sus a new com - mand-ment has giv - en us:

que nos a - me-mos siem - pre co-mo nos a - ma
that we should love each oth - er just as our God loves

1 Dios. **2** *to Stanzas* Dios. *Last time, end*
us. us.

Estrofas (Stanzas)

1 La se - ñal de cris-tian - dad
2 Quien al pró - ji - mo no a - ma,
1 The clear sign of all true Chris - tians
2 Those who do not love their neigh - bors

Originally written for a Maundy Thursday service, this hymn has received widespread use throughout Puerto Rico, where William Loperena is a Dominican priest working on the development of ecumenical liturgies.

Tune: LOPERENA 8.8. with refrain (10.7.6.)
William Loperena, 1965
Arr. Luis Olivieri and Roberto Milano, 1993

es	a -	mar	-	se en	her - man -	dad.
mien-te	si a			Dios	di - ce	que a - ma. *(Estribillo)*
is	the	way		they	love each	oth - er.
do	not	tru	-	ly	love their	Sav - ior. *(to Refrain)*

3 Cris-to, Luz, Ver-dad y Vi-da
   al per-dón y a-mor in-vi-ta.

3 Christ, the Light, the Truth, and true Life,
   bids us share our love and par-don.

4 Per-do-ne-mos los a-gra-vios
   co-mo Dios ha or-de-na-do.
   (Estribillo)

4 Let us all for-give each oth-er
   as by God we are com-mand-ed.
   (Refrain)

5 De Je-sús her-ma-nos so-mos
   si de ve-ras per-do-na-mos.

5 We are tru-ly friends of Je-sus
   if we free-ly give our par-don.

6 En la vi-da y en la muer-te
   Dios nos a-ma pa-ra siem-pre.
   (Estribillo)

6 In our liv-ing and our dy-ing,
   God is ev-er there to love us.
   (Refrain)

7 Don-de hay ca-ri-dad y a-mor.
   siem-pre es-tá pre-sen-te Dios.

7 In true char-i-ty and lov-ing,
   God is pres-ent here a-mong us.

8 Co-mul-gue-mos con fre-cuen-cia
   pa-ra a-mar-nos a con-cien-cia.
   (Estribillo)

8 Let us come to Je-sus' ta-ble
   with our love for one an-oth-er.
   (Refrain)

9 Glo-ria a Dios el Cre-a-dor
   y a Cris-to el Sal-va-dor.

9 Glo-ry be to the Cre-a-tor;
   glo-ry be to Christ, our Sav-ior;

10 Y al Es-pí-ri-tu di-vi-no
    en Tri-ni-dad han vi-vi-do.
    (Estribillo)

10 Glo-ry be to God, the Spir-it,
    Ho-ly Trin-i-ty for-ev-er.
    (Refrain)

390

Eternal Christ, Who, Kneeling

John 17:20–23

William W. Reid, Jr., 1976; alt.

1 E - ter - nal Christ, who, kneel - ing when earth-ly tasks were done,
2 But we have of - ten slight - ed the ties de-signed to hold
3 Ac - cept our deep con - tri - tion for all our sun-dering ways

turned un - to God ap - peal - ing, "That they may all be one,"
your fol-low - ers u - nit - ed with - in one com - mon fold.
which still dis - rupt your mis - sion, which mock our words of praise.

We thank you for your vi - sion of u - ni - ty un - torn,
On his - tory's tat - tered pa - ges we see, O Christ, with shame,
Christ, may your Spir - it guide us that we may find, be - yond

of faith with - out di - vi - sion with which your church was born.
the strife which through the a - ges has marred your church's name.
the things which still di - vide us, love's all - em - brac - ing bond.

William Watkins Reid, Jr., is a pastor, author, hymnwriter, and
past member of the executive committee of The Hymn Society.
He takes an active part in politics at all levels, and his hymns are
often written as responses to current events.

Tune: NYLAND 7.6.7.6.D.
Finnish hymn melody
Harm. David Evans, 1927

In the Midst of New Dimensions

391

Julian Rush, 1985; alt.

Gen. 9:12–16; Exod. 13:21–22; Num. 14:14

1 In the midst of new di - men-sions, in the face of chang-ing ways,
2 Through the flood of starv-ing peo - ple, war - ring fac-tions and de - spair,
3 As we stand a world di - vid - ed by our own self - seek - ing schemes,
4 We are man and we are wom - an, all per-sua-sions, old and young,
5 Should the threats of dire pre - dic - tions cause us to with - draw in pain,

Who will lead the pil - grim peo - ples wan-dering in their sep - arate ways?
Who will lift the ol - ive branch-es? Who will light the flame of care?
Grant that we, your glob - al vil - lage, might en - vi - sion wid - er dreams.
Each a gift in your cre - a - tion, each a love song to be sung.
May your blaz-ing phoe-nix spir - it res - ur - rect the church a - gain.

Refrain

God of rain-bow, fier - y pil - lar, lead-ing where the ea - gles soar, We your

peo-ple, ours the jour-ney now and ev - er, now and ev - er, now and ev - er - more.

Julian Rush, an ordained minister in the United Methodist Church, has spent more than a decade as director of the Colorado AIDS Project. He wrote this hymn on the theme of "diversity" for a meeting of the Rocky Mountain Conference (United Methodist).

Tune: NEW DIMENSIONS 8.7.8.7. with refrain
Julian Rush, 1985
Arr. The New Century Hymnal, 1994

392

En santa hermandad
(United by God's Love)

Eph. 3:14–21; Col. 1:11–12

William Loperena
Transcribed by Luis Olivieri
English version, Carolyn Jennings, 1994

1 En san - ta her-man - dad   va - mos a can -
2 Al Cre - a - dor can - te - mos   que nos dio su
1 U - nit - ed by God's love,   let us sing to -
2 Sing praise to our Cre - a - tor,   God of grace and

Estribillo (Refrain)

tar.   (Al) gra - cia.   Tú e - res Cris-to el
geth - er.   (Sing) mer - cy,   You are the one Re -

Re - den - tor;   llé-na - nos de a-mor.   Tú e - res nues-tro
deem-er Christ,   fill our hearts with love;   You are the Sav-ior,

Last time, end

Sal - va - dor   y Li-ber - ta - dor.
Je - sus Christ,   Lib-er - a - tor God. *(to stanzas 3, 4)*

Many of the hymns of William Loperena employ folk music and rhythms, such as the popular "guaracha" used here.

Tune: EN SANTA HERMANDAD Irr.
William Loperena
Transcribed by Luis Olivieri
Arr. Roberto Milano, 1989

3 A Cris-to en-sal-ce-mos
   por su san-ta a-lian-za.
4 Al Fiel Con-so-la-dor
   de-mos a-la-ban-za.
(Estribillo)

3 Sing praise to Christ the Sav-ior,
   Bring-er of sal-va-tion.
4 And praise the Ho-ly Spir-it,
   Com-fort-er most ho-ly.
(Refrain)

Blessed Be the Tie That Binds

393

John Fawcett, 1782; alt.

Gal. 3:28; 6:2; Col. 3:13–15

1 Blessed be   the   tie   that binds our   hearts in   Chris - tian love;
2 Be - fore   our   God   we   come and   pour   our   ar - dent prayers;
3 We   share each   oth - er's woes, each   oth - er's bur - dens bear,
4 When we   are   called to   part   it   gives   us   in - ward pain,

The   shar - ing of   a   com - mon life   is   like   to   that   a - bove.
Our   fears, our hopes, our aims are one,   our   com - forts and   our cares.
And   of - ten for   each oth - er   flows a   sym - pa - thiz - ing tear.
But   we   shall still   be   joined in heart, and hope to   meet a - gain.

An English Baptist minister, John Fawcett published a number
of poetic works. His entire ministry was spent at a church near
Hebden Bridge, Yorkshire, where he wrote most of his hymns to
follow his sermons.

Tune: DENNIS S.M.
Melody by Johann G. Nägeli (c. 1768–1836)
Adapt. Lowell Mason, 1845

394 In Christ There Is No East or West

1 Cor. 12:13; Gal. 3:28; Eph. 2:14–22

John Oxenham, 1908; alt.
St. 3, Laurence Hull Stookey, 1987

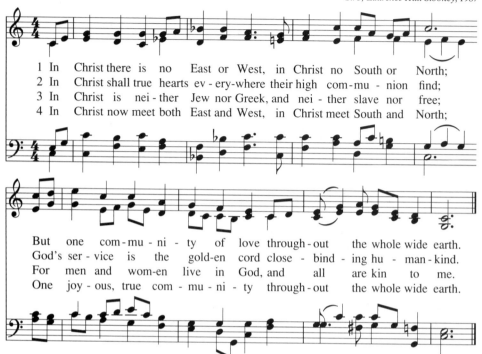

1 In Christ there is no East or West, in Christ no South or North;
2 In Christ shall true hearts ev - ery-where their high com-mu - nion find;
3 In Christ is nei - ther Jew nor Greek, and nei - ther slave nor free;
4 In Christ now meet both East and West, in Christ meet South and North;

But one com - mu - ni - ty of love through-out the whole wide earth.
God's ser - vice is the gold-en cord close - bind - ing hu - man-kind.
For men and wom-en live in God, and all are kin to me.
One joy - ous, true com - mu - ni - ty through-out the whole wide earth.

Singer and composer Harry T. Burleigh studied at the National Conservatory of Music from 1892 to 1896. He is recognized as the first African-American composer to employ spirituals in concert arrangements. This tune is named after the rector of St. George's Episcopal Church in New York City, where Burleigh served as baritone soloist for more than fifty years.

Tune: McKEE C.M.
African-American melody
Arr. Harry T. Burleigh, 1939
Alternate setting: ST. PETER

395 In Christ There Is No East or West

1 Cor. 12:13; Gal. 3:28; Eph. 2:14–22

John Oxenham, 1908; alt.
St. 3, Laurence Hull Stookey, 1987

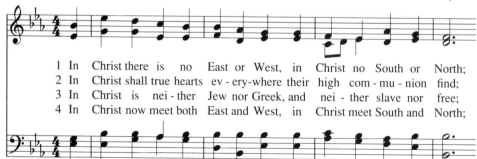

1 In Christ there is no East or West, in Christ no South or North;
2 In Christ shall true hearts ev - ery-where their high com - mu - nion find;
3 In Christ is nei - ther Jew nor Greek, and nei - ther slave nor free;
4 In Christ now meet both East and West, in Christ meet South and North;

At the beginning of the twentieth century, many hymns were written to promote the oneness of humanity. English Congregationalist John Oxenham's text is a lasting example. His great concern for those in military service led to the publication of a World War I hymnbook that exceeded eight million in circulation.

Tune: ST. PETER C.M.
Alexander R. Reinagle, 1836
Alternate setting: McKEE

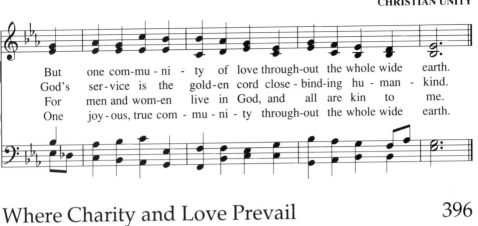

But   one com-mu-ni - ty of love through-out the whole wide   earth.
God's   ser-vice is the   gold-en cord close - bind-ing hu - man - kind.
For   men and wom-en live in God, and   all are kin to   me.
One   joy-ous, true com - mu-ni - ty through-out the whole wide   earth.

Where Charity and Love Prevail   396

Latin hymn, "Ubi caritas et amor," 9th century
Paraphr. by Omer Westendorf, 1961; alt.

John 13:34–35; 15:9–12; 2 Cor. 5:17–20; 1 John 4:7–21

With freedom

1 Where char-i - ty and love pre-vail, there God is ev - er found; Brought
2 With grate-ful joy and ho - ly fear true char-i - ty we learn; Let
3 For - give we now each oth-er's faults as we our faults con-fess; And
4 Let strife a-mong us be un-known, let all con-ten-tion cease; Be

here to-geth-er by Christ's love, by love are we thus bound.
us with heart and mind and strength now love Christ in re-turn.
let us love each oth-er well in Chris-tian ho-li-ness.
Christ the glo-ry that we seek, be ours Christ's ho-ly peace.

Believed to date from the time of Charlemagne (768–814), this hymn was, before Vatican II (1962–1965), the last and indispensable song during the Maundy Thursday foot-washing service. Benedictine priest Paul Benoit composed many organ works.

Tune: CHRISTIAN LOVE C.M.
Paul Benoit, 1961
Alternate tune: ST. FLAVIAN

397 Thank Our God for Sisters, Brothers

Roger Powell, 1948; alt.

1 Thank our God for sis-ters, broth-ers, one by grace, in har-mo-ny,
2 Praise to God for con-gre-ga-tions, keep-ing faith with Christ as guide;
3 Ho-ly is your name for-ev-er! Heal di-vi-sions that re-main;

Join-ing heart to heart with oth-ers, mak-ing strong com-mu-ni-ty,
Man-y tongues of man-y na-tions, song and ser-vice u-ni-fied.
Bless the church's new en-deav-ors; make our wit-ness one a-gain.

With the cross of Christ our stan-dard, let us sing as with one voice,
Sweet the psalm and sweet the car-ol, when our song is raised as one.
One in Christ and in Christ's gos-pel, make us one we now im-plore.

Glo-ry, glo-ry, yours the prom-ise: we who are the church re-joice.
Glo-ry, glo-ry, yours the pow-er, as in heaven your will be done.
Glo-ry, glo-ry, yours the glo-ry, then and now and ev-er-more.

This hymn was written for a Union Thanksgiving service in 1948
by the Rev. Roger Powell of Camillus, New York. It served as a
rallying song for the first meeting of the National Council of
Churches in 1952.

Tune: PLEADING SAVIOR 8.7.8.7.D.
Melody from The Christian Lyre, *1831*

Shadow and Substance

398

Dan Damon, 1989

Gen. 1:26–27

1 Shad - ow and sub - stance, won - der and mys - ter - y,
2 We are your im - age, formed in com - mu - ni - ty;
3 Nam - ing the name - less Spir - it of u - ni - ty,

spell-bind-ing spin-ner of at - oms and earth; Soul of the cos-mos,
sis - ters and broth-ers of Ad - am and Eve. You gave us col - or,
scan-ning the heav-ens for signs of your care; God of the a - ges,

per - son and en - er - gy, source of our be - ing: we sing of your worth.
cus - tom and his-to-ry; teach us to hon - or what oth - ers re - ceive.
give us hu - mil-i - ty; guide us to mys-ti - cal un - ion in prayer.

This hymn by writer and composer Dan Damon exemplifies one of the goals he has articulated about his work: "To keep things simple and singable while at the same time exploring the edges of our spoken and sung faith."

Tune: TWILIGHT 5.6.10.D.
Dan Damon, 1989

399   When Minds and Bodies Meet as One

Gal. 3:28; Eph. 4:1–16   *Brian Wren, 1980; rev. 1993*

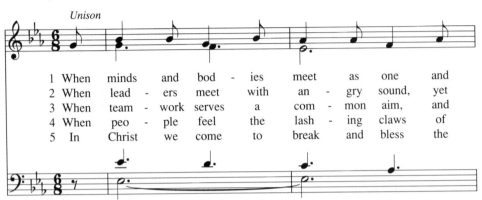

1 When minds and bod - ies meet as one and
2 When lead - ers meet with an - gry sound, yet
3 When team - work serves a com - mon aim, and
4 When peo - ple feel the lash - ing claws of
5 In Christ we come to break and bless the

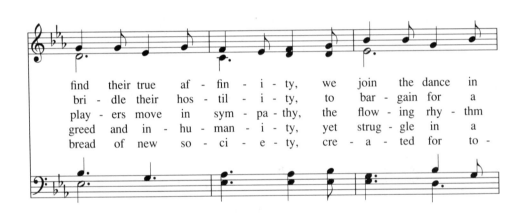

find their true af - fin - i - ty, we join the dance in
bri - dle their hos - til - i - ty, to bar - gain for a
play - ers move in sym - pa - thy, the flow - ing rhy - thm
greed and in - hu - man - i - ty, yet strug - gle in a
bread of new so - ci - e - ty, cre - a - ted for to -

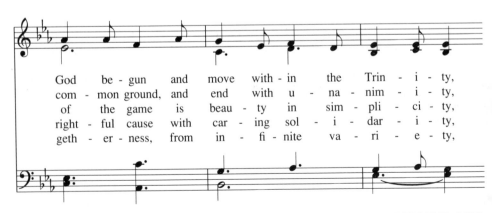

God be - gun and move with - in the Trin - i - ty,
com - mon ground, and end with u - na - nim - i - ty,
of the game is beau - ty in sim - pli - ci - ty,
right - ful cause with car - ing sol - i - dar - i - ty,
geth - er - ness, from in - fi - nite va - ri - e - ty,

*British poet Brian Wren and composer Peter Cutts were both
encouraged in their work by the renowned hymnologist Erik
Routley. They later collaborated in the 1983 collection* Faith
Looking Forward, *in which this hymn was first published.*

Tune: TRINITY CAROL L.M.D.
Peter Cutts, 1980

so praise the good that's seen and done in
be glad for all the hope that's won in
so praise the good that's seen and done in
be glad for all the hope that's won in
so praise the good that's seen and done in

lov - ing, giv - ing u - ni - ty, re - veal - ing God, for -
ev - ery gleam of u - ni - ty, re - veal - ing God, for -
swift - ly mov - ing u - ni - ty, re - veal - ing God, for -
free - dom - lov - ing u - ni - ty, re - veal - ing God, for -
Spir - it - giv - en u - ni - ty, re - veal - ing God, for -

ev - er One, whose na - ture is Com - mu - ni - ty.
ev - er One, whose na - ture is Com - mu - ni - ty.
ev - er One, whose na - ture is Com - mu - ni - ty.
ev - er One, whose na - ture is Com - mu - ni - ty.
ev - er One, whose na - ture is Com - mu - ni - ty.

400   Christ Is Made the Sure Foundation

Eph. 2:20–22; 1 Pet. 2:4–7

Latin, 6th–8th century
Transl. John Mason Neale, 1851; alt.
St. 3 adapt. Thomas H. Troeger, 1992

1 Christ is made the sure foun - da - tion, Christ the head and cor - ner-stone,
2 To this tem - ple, where we call you, come, O God of Hosts, to - day!
3 Here re - new your ser - vants' vis - ion, that by faith they may at - tain

chos - en of our God and pre - cious, bind - ing all the Church in one;
With your con-stant, lov - ing kind-ness hear your peo - ple as they pray.
peace and hope, re - newed com-pas - sion, strength to com-fort those in pain,

Ho - ly Zi - on's help for-ev - er, and our con - fi - dence a - lone.
Give your full - est ben - e - dic - tion: grace to fol - low Christ the Way.
Tears and grief trans-formed to glad-ness in your ev - er - last - ing reign.

The hymn has its origins in an early Latin poem, Urbs beata
Jerusalem, *based on passages from Ephesians, 1 Peter, and
Revelation. "Holy Zion" refers to the church transcendent, built
of "living stones"—the saints of God.*

Tune: REGENT SQUARE 8.7.8.7.8.7.
Henry T. Smart, 1867
Alternate tune: WESTMINSTER ABBEY

O God in Whom All Life Begins

401

Carl P. Daw, Jr., 1992

1 O God in whom all life be-gins, who births the seed to fruit,
2 U - nite in mu - tual min - is - try our minds and hands and hearts
3 Through tears and laugh-ter, grief and joy, en - large our trust and care;

be - stow your bless-ing on our lives; here let your love find root.
that we may have the grace to seek the power your peace im - parts.
so bind us in com - mu - ni - ty that we may risk and dare.

Bring forth in us the Spir - it's gifts of pa - tience, joy, and peace;
So let our var - ied gifts com-bine to glo - ri - fy your Name
Be with us when we gath - er here to wor - ship, sing, and pray,

de - liv - er us from numb - ing fear, and grant our faith in - crease.
that in all things by word and deed we may your love pro - claim.
then send us forth in power and faith to live the words we say.

Carl P. Daw, Jr., is an Episcopal priest who began hymnwriting while serving on the text committee for The Hymnal 1982. *He has held academic positions at the College of William and Mary and the University of Connecticut, where he was also vicar-chaplain.*

Tune: NOEL C.M.D.
Traditional English melody
Arr. Arthur S. Sullivan, 1874

402

De colores
(Sing of Colors)

Mexican folk song
Transl. The New Century Hymnal, 1995

1 De co - lo - res, de co - lo - res se vis - ten los
1 Sing of col - ors, sing of col - ors that o - ver the
2 Sing, re - joic - ing! Ev - ery crea - ture that breathes raise a

cam - pos en la pri - ma - ve - ra. De co -
hills in pro - fu - sion are spring - ing; Sing of
song to the God of cre - a - tion. Sing, re -

lo - res, de co - lo - res son los pa - ja - ri - tos que vie - nen de a -
col - ors, of the birds that fly out - side my win - dow their can - ti - cles
joic - ing! Sing to God who so ear - nest - ly cares, who has of - fered sal -

fue - ra. De co - lo - res, de co -
sing - ing; Sing of col - ors, in the
va - tion. Sing the good news! Sing the

This Mexican folk song is known by many Mexican-American churchgoers, and has also been popular among the United Farm Workers.

Tune: DE COLORES
Mexican folk song
Arr. Alfredo Morales, F.S.C.

lo - res es el ar - co i - ris que ve - mos sa - lir, Y por
rain-bow's bright col - ors God's prom-ise of hope we re - call; Sing of
love of the Sav-ior re - flect-ing the col - ors of all. Man - y

e - so los gran - des a - mo - res de mu - chos co - lo - res me gus-tan a
col-ors that make up the earth and give thanks to the God who cre - at - ed us
col-ors that shine from God's face, man - y col - ors that tell us God's love to re -

mí, Y por e - so los gran - des a - mo - res de mu - chos co -
all. Sing of col - ors that make up the earth and give thanks to the
call. Man - y col - ors that shine from God's face, man - y col - ors that

lo - res me gus - tan a mí.
God who cre - at - ed us all.
tell us God's love to re - call.

403 My Hope Is Built on Nothing Less

Matt. 7:24–27; 1 Cor. 3:11; Heb. 6:19; Rev. 11:15   *Edward Mote, c. 1834; alt.*

1 My hope is built on noth-ing less than Je - sus' love and
2 When shad - ows veil my Sav-ior's face, I rest up - on un -
3 Christ's oath and cov - e - nant and blood sup - port me in the
4 When Christ shall come with trum-pet sound, oh, may I then in

righ - teous-ness; I dare not trust this earth - ly frame, but
chang-ing grace; In ev - ery high and storm - y gale, my
ris - ing flood; When all a - round my soul gives way, Christ
Love be found, Dressed in God's righ - teous - ness a - lone, fault -

Refrain

whol-ly lean on Je - sus' name.
an - chor holds with - in the veil.
then is all my hope and stay.   On Christ, the sol - id Rock, I stand;
less to stand be - fore the throne.

all oth - er ground is sink-ing sand, all oth - er ground is sink-ing sand.

William Bradbury met great success by composing hymn tunes and religious songs in a lively, popular style. He also helped establish music programs in New York public schools, served a church, and co-founded a piano company.

Tune: SOLID ROCK L.M. with refrain
William B. Bradbury, 1863

Give Up Your Anxious Pains

404

Paul Gerhardt, 1656
Transl. Madeleine Forell Marshall, 1994

1 Give up your anx - ious pains, con - fu - sion, and re - morse,
2 All things con-form to please the faith - ful when they pray,
3 "Don't let us be dis - mayed by griev-ous so - cial wrong;

To God, who set and still main-tains cre - a - tion's com - plex course.
So fall up - on your trust-ing knees and all to - geth - er say:
Re - spon-sive, ac - tive, un - a - fraid, may we be brave and strong.

God leads what may ap - pear cha - o - tic, ran-dom, wild: So
"O faith - ful God of grace who rules the rag - ing storm, En -
Ex - tend your lov-ing care through all our live-long days; And

God has planned and will make clear a path for you, dear child.
light - en our poor mor - tal race; your prom-ised works per - form."
when we die, bring us to where bright an - gels sing your praise."

Each word of Martin Luther's German translation of Psalm 37:5 provided a beginning word for Paul Gerhardt's twelve-stanza hymn of comfort. While traveling to America, John Wesley heard Moravians sing this hymn; he later translated it into English.

Tune: ICH HALTE TREULICH STILL S.M.D.
J. S. Bach, 1736

405   There Are Some Things I May Not Know
(Yes, God Is Real)

Kenneth Morris, 1942; alt.

1 There are some things   I   may   not   know,   there are some
2 Some folks may   doubt,   some folks may scorn,   all   can de -
3 I   can - not   tell   just   how   you   felt   when Je - sus

plac - es   I   can't   go,   But   I   am sure   of   this   one
sert   and leave me a - lone,   But   as   for me   I'll   take God's
took   your sins   a - way,   But since that day,   yes, since that

thing,   that God is   real   for I can feel   God deep with - in.
part,   for God is   real   and I can feel   God   in   my heart.
hour,   God has been real   for I can feel   God's ho - ly power.

Refrain

Yes, God is   real,   real in my soul;   yes, God is   real   for God has

This gospel song by Kenneth Morris is considered his most successful composition. It has become a standard in many African-American churches, and has been translated into twenty-four languages. Morris is also known for his musical arrangements, which number more than 3,000.

Tune: YES, GOD IS REAL   8.8.8.12. with refrain
Kenneth Morris, 1942

washed and made me whole; God's love for me is like pure

gold, yes, God is real for I can feel God in my soul.

Not with Naked Eye, Not with Human Sense   406

Dan Damon, 1989   *John 1:18; 20:26–29*

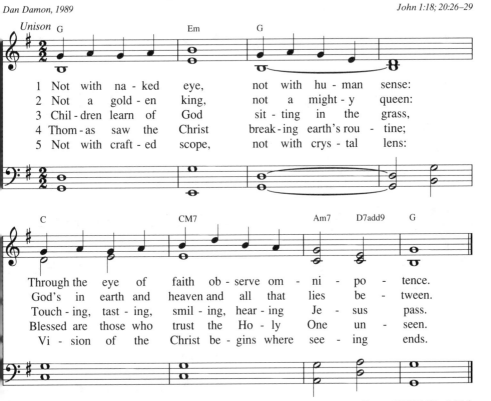

Unison   G   Em   G

1 Not with na - ked   eye,   not with hu - man   sense:
2 Not a gold - en   king,   not a might - y   queen:
3 Chil - dren learn of   God   sit - ting in the   grass,
4 Thom - as saw the   Christ   break - ing earth's rou - tine;
5 Not with craft - ed   scope,   not with crys - tal   lens:

C   CM7   Am7   D7add9   G

Through the eye of   faith ob - serve om - ni - po - tence.
God's in earth and   heaven and all that lies be - tween.
Touch - ing, tast - ing,   smil - ing, hear - ing Je - sus pass.
Blessed are those who   trust the Ho - ly One un - seen.
Vi - sion of the   Christ be - gins where see - ing ends.

Dan Damon commented about this hymn: "People who do
not see with their physical eyes learn to rely on other senses.
Sometimes faith is one of them." The tune is named for
Valerie Stiteler, a United Church of Christ minister.

Tune: STITELER 5.5.5.6.
Dan Damon, 1989

407

How Firm a Foundation

Isa. 43:2–5; 2 Tim. 2:19; Heb. 13:5

"K" in John Rippon's *Selection of Hymns, 1787; alt*

1 How firm a foun - da - tion for you has been laid,
2 "Fear not, I am with you, oh, be not dis - mayed,
3 "When through the deep wa - ters I call you to go,
4 "When through fi - ery tri - als your path - way shall lie,
5 "The soul that on Je - sus has leaned for re - pose,

by God in the Word, in the sac - ri - fice paid!
for I am your God, I will still give you aid;
the riv - ers of woe shall not o - ver you flow;
my grace all - suf - fi - cient shall be your sup - ply;
I will not, I will not de - sert to its foes;

What more can God say than to you has been said,
I'll strength - en you, help you, and cause you to stand
For I will be with you, your trou - bles to bless,
the flame shall not hurt you; for I have de - signed
That soul, though all hell should en - deav - or to shake,

to you, who for ref - uge to Je - sus have fled?
up - held by my gra - cious, om - ni - po - tent hand."
de - liv - er - ing you from your deep - est dis - tress.
your soul to make pure just as gold is re - fined."
I'll nev - er, no nev - er, no nev - er for - sake!"

In 1787, John Rippon, English Baptist clergyman, identified the author of this hymn as "K"; no one has yet verified a complete name. The pentatonic melody has been known by several names since it first appeared in Funk's Genuine Church Music (1832).

Tune: FOUNDATION 11.11.11.11
Early United States melody from Funk's Genuine Church Music, 1832
Alternate tune: ADESTE FIDELES

All My Hope on God Is Founded 408

Joachim Neander, c. 1680
Paraphr. by Robert Bridges, 1899; alt.

Ps. 62:5–8; 1 Tim. 6:17

1 All my hope on God is found - ed: who else can my hope re-new?
2 Well does the al - might-y Giv - er boun-teous gifts on us be-stow!
3 In glad hymns to God e - ter - nal sac - ri - fice of praise be done,

Still through change and chance God guides me, on - ly good and on - ly true.
With de - light our souls are nour-ished; plea-sure leads us where we go.
high a - bove all prais - es prais - ing for the love in Christ made known.

God un - known, grace a - lone, calls my heart to be God's own.
At God's hand does love stand; joy a - waits each new com - mand.
Hear Christ's call, one and all; those who fol - low shall not fall.

British composer Herbert Howells studied with Charles V.
Stanford at the Royal College of Music in London and later
taught there. The tune was composed for an English school and
was named for Howells' son who died in childhood.

Tune: MICHAEL 8.7.8.7.3.3.7.
Herbert Howells, 1930, 1977

409

I Heard My Mother Say

African-American traditional

1 I   heard my moth-er   say,   I   heard my moth-er   say,
2 At   mid-night was my   cry,   at   mid-night was my   cry,
3 Oh,   when I come to   die,   oh,   when I come to   die,
4 In   the morn-ing when I   rise,   in the   morn-ing when I   rise,

I   heard my moth-er   say,   "Give me Je - sus."
at   mid-night was my   cry,   "Give me Je - sus."
oh,   when I come to   die,   give me Je - sus.
in the   morn-ing when I   rise,   give me Je - sus.

Refrain

Give me Je - sus, give me Je - sus, you may

have all this world, give me Je - sus.

This spiritual is better known as "Give Me Jesus." The musical
arrangement was created for The New Century Hymnal by
Joyce Finch Johnson, organist and professor of music at
Spelman College, Atlanta, Georgia.

Tune: GIVE ME JESUS 6.6.10. with refrain
African-American traditional
Harm. Joyce Finch Johnson, 1992

If You But Trust in God to Guide You

Georg Neumark, 1641
Transl. Catherine Winkworth, 1863; alt.

Ps. 55:22

1 If you but trust in God to guide you, with hope-ful heart through
2 On - ly be still, and wait God's plea - sure in cheer-ful hope, with
3 Sing, pray, and keep God's ways un - swerv-ing; of - fer your ser - vice

all your ways, you will find strength, with God be - side you,
heart con - tent, trust-ing that grace which knows no mea-sure
faith - ful - ly, and trust God's word, though un - de - serv-ing,

to bear the worst of e - vil days; For those who trust God's
will by un - bound - ed Love be sent; Nor doubt our in - most
there find the truth to set you free; God will not fail to

change-less love build on the rock that will not move.
wants are clear to One who holds us al - ways near.
guide and bless those who em - brace God's faith - ful - ness.

The comforting words of Psalm 55:22 inspired this beautiful
hymn by Georg Neumark, who wrote both words and music.
Neumark was a German poet who suffered much during the
Thirty Years' War.

Tune: NEUMARK 9.8.9.8.8.8.
Georg Neumark, 1657

411   Praise the Source of Faith and Learning

Prov. 2:6   *Thomas H. Troeger, 1987, 1989*

1 Praise the Source of faith and learn - ing that has sparked and stoked the mind
2 God of wis - dom, we ac - knowl-edge that our sci - ence and our art
3 May our faith re - deem the blun - der of be - liev - ing that our thought
4 As two cur - rents in a riv - er fight each oth - er's un - der - tow

with a pas - sion for dis - cern - ing how the world has been de-signed.
and the breadth of hu - man knowl-edge on - ly par - tial truth im-part.
has dis-placed the grounds for won - der which the an - cient proph-ets taught.
till con-verg - ing they de - liv - er one co - her - ent stead - y flow,

Let the sense of won-der flow - ing from the won - ders we sur-vey
Far be-yond our cal - cu - la - tion lies a depth we can-not sound
May our learn-ing curb the er - ror which un - think - ing faith can breed
Blend, O God, our faith and learn-ing till they carve a sin - gle course,

*Thomas Troeger's text was commissioned by Duke University
to honor Waldo Beach, a retired professor of ethics who has
written about the theology conveyed by hymns. Composer
William Albright has served as professor of music at the
University of Michigan.*

Tune: PROCESSION 8.7.8.7.D.
William Albright, 1992
Alternate tune: HYFRYDOL

Words Copyright © 1987, Oxford University Press, Inc.

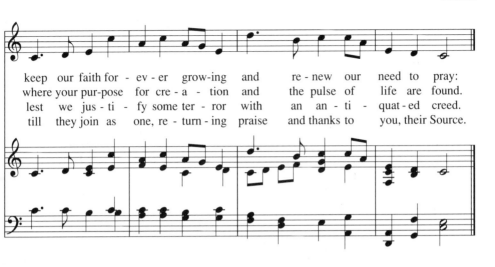

keep our faith for - ev - er grow-ing and re - new our need to pray:
where your pur-pose for cre - a - tion and the pulse of life are found.
lest we jus - ti - fy some ter - ror with an an - ti - quat - ed creed.
till they join as one, re - turn - ing praise and thanks to you, their Source.

God Moves in a Mysterious Way 412

William Cowper, 1774; alt. Ps. 77:19; Rom. 11:33–36

1 God moves in a mys - te - rious way great won - ders to per - form;
2 Deep in un - fath - om - a - ble mines of nev - er - fail - ing skill
3 O fear - ful saints, fresh cour-age take, the clouds you so much dread
4 Judge not God's way through hu - man sense, but trust un - fail - ing grace:

God plants firm foot - steps in the sea and rides up - on the storm.
God floods the earth with bright de - signs, guards with a sov-ereign will.
Are big with mer - cy and shall break in bless - ings on your head.
Be - hind a frown-ing prov - i - dence there shines a smil - ing face.

5 God's pur-pos-es will rip-en fast,
  un-fold-ing ev-ery hour;
  The bud may have a bit-ter taste,
  but sweet will be the flower.

6 Our un-be-lief is sure to err
  and scan God's work in vain;
  God is God's own in-ter-pret-er,
  whose truth shall be made plain.

This hymn by the English poet William Cowper seems to have been written a few months after his suicide attempt. It was first published in John Newton's Twenty-six Letters on Religious Subjects.

Tune: DUNDEE C.M.
The 150 Psalms of David, *Edinburgh, 1615*

413

By Gracious Powers

Dietrich Bonhoeffer, 1944
Transl. Fred Pratt Green, 1972

1 By gra-cious powers so won-der-ful-ly shel-tered,
2 Yet is this heart by its old foe tor-ment-ed,
3 And when this cup you give is filled to brim-ming
4 Yet when a-gain in this same world you give us

and con-fi-dent-ly wait-ing, come what may,
still e-vil days bring bur-dens hard to bear;
with bit-ter sor-row, hard to un-der-stand,
the joy we had, the bright-ness of your sun,

We know that God is with us night and morn-ing,
O give our fright-ened souls the sure sal-va-tion
We take it thank-ful-ly and with-out trem-bling,
We shall re-mem-ber all the days we lived through,

and nev-er fails to greet us each new day.
for which, O God, you taught us to pre-pare.
out of so good and so be-loved a hand.
and our whole life shall then be yours a-lone.

Dietrich Bonhoeffer, theologian, professor, and leader of the
German Opposition, composed the poem on which this hymn is
based, "New Year 1945," while imprisoned by the Gestapo in
Berlin. Four months later, Bonhoeffer was executed by special
order of Himmler.

Tune: BONHOEFFER 11.10.11.10.
Herbert G. Hobbs, 1976
Harm. Jan Helmut Wubbena, 1976

Incarnate God, Immortal Love 414

Alfred Tennyson, 1850; alt.

2 Cor. 5:7

1 In - car - nate God, im - mor - tal Love, whom we, that
2 You will not leave us in the dust; you gave us
3 In you meet hu - man and di - vine, the high - est,
4 Our lit - tle sys - tems have their day; they have their

have not seen your face, by faith, and faith a -
life, we know not why. We trust we were not
ho - liest un - ion known. We false - ly call our
day and cease to be; They are but fleet - ing

lone, em - brace, be - liev - ing where we can - not prove:
made to die, for you have made us, you are just.
powers our own un - til our wills with yours com - bine.
cer - tain - ty, and you, O Christ, are more than they.

5 We have but faith; we can-not know,
    for knowl-edge is of things proved true;
    And yet we trust it comes from you,
    a sign of prom-ise; let it grow.

6 Let knowl-edge grow from more to more,
    but more of rev-erence in us dwell;
    That mind and soul, ac-cord-ing well,
    may make one music as be-fore.

The English poet laureate Alfred Tennyson included an eleven-stanza prologue to his In Memoriam *(1850), written in memory of a friend, Arthur Hallam. Some stanzas of the prologue have been selected to form this hymn.*

Tune: ROCKINGHAM L.M.
Anon.
Adapt. Edward Miller, 1790

415 God's Actions, Always Good and Just

Samuel Rodigast, 1675; transl. Madeleine Forell Marshall, 199

1 God's ac-tions, al-ways good and just, pro-ceed from God's per-fec-tion; So we our world's af-fairs en-trust to god-ly just pro-tec-tion. When all I see is mis-e-ry, when rank op-pres-sion pains me, God's righ-teous-ness sus-tains me.

2 My gra-cious guide in righ-teous ways, God sets my course of ac-tion; And I may trace life's seem-ing maze as-sured of sat-is-fac-tion. For, just and fair, God shall re-pair all e-vil and dis-tor-tion, and can-cel each mis-for-tune.

3 The lamp of truth, my God dis-pels the shad-ows that a-larm me. A liv-ing shield, my God re-pels the death-beams that would harm me. The truth will win, the light break in, a-chiev-ing rev-e-la-tion, com-plet-ing my sal-va-tion.

4 God's ways are ev-er lov-ing-kind, what-ev-er our de-lu-sion, And if I taste the bit-ter wine, the cup of my con-fu-sion, Take heart, my soul, for you shall know, sweet com-fort fol-lows sad-ness. The pain shall end in glad-ness.

When Severus Gastorius suffered a serious illness in 1675, his friend Samuel Rodigast wrote this hymn to comfort him. Gastorius was a German Lutheran music director at Jena. Rodigast was a scholar and educator in Berlin.

Tune: WAS GOTT TUT 8.7.8.7.8.7.7.
Severus Gastorius, c. 1675

I Will Trust in the Lord

African-American traditional

Ps. 37:3

1 I will trust in the Lord, I will trust in the
2 I'm gon-na treat ev-ery-bod-y right, I'm gon-na treat ev-ery-bod-y

Lord, I will trust in the Lord, till I die.
right, I'm gon-na treat ev-ery-bod-y right, till I die.

I will trust in the Lord, I will trust in the
I'm gon-na treat ev-ery-bod-y right, I'm gon-na treat ev-ery-bod-y

Lord, I will trust in the Lord, till I die.
right, I'm gon-na treat ev-ery-bod-y right, till I die.

One use of this traditional song has been in African-American churches, where someone giving a testimony would raise a verse or two, and be joined by the congregation in singing. Then the person would build a testimony upon the hymn's thematic language.

Tune: TRUST IN THE LORD Irr.
African-American traditional
Arr. Jeffrey Radford, 1993

417

This Is a Day of New Beginnings

2 Cor. 5:16–17

Brian Wren, 1978; rev. 198

```
1 This is a day of new be - gin - nings, time to re -
2 For by the life and death of Je - sus, God's might - y
3 Then let us, with the Spir - it's dar - ing, step from the
4 Christ is a - live, and goes be - fore us to show and
* In faith we'll gath - er 'round the ta - ble to taste and
```

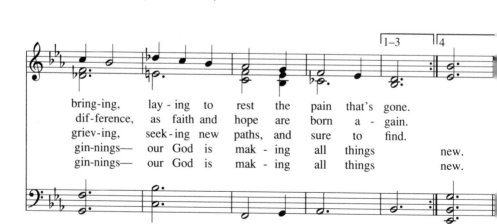

```
mem - ber and move on, time to be - lieve what love is
Spir - it, now as then, can make for us a world of
past and leave be - hind our dis - ap - point - ment, guilt, and
share what love can do. This is a day of new be -
share what love can do. This is a day of new be -
```

```
          1–3                    4
bring-ing, lay - ing to rest the pain that's gone.
dif - ference, as faith and hope are born a - gain.
griev-ing, seek - ing new paths, and sure to find.
gin-nings— our God is mak - ing all things      new.
gin-nings— our God is mak - ing all things      new.
```

*Alternate fourth stanza for Holy Communion

Brian Wren wrote this hymn in 1978 for a New Year's Day service in Oxford, England. The music is by the editor of two hymnals of the United Methodist Church and was composed for the original Wren text.

Tune: BEGINNINGS 9.8.9.8
Carlton R. Young, 1987

My Faith, It Is an Oaken Staff

Thomas T. Lynch, 1855; alt.

1 My faith, it is an oak - en staff, the trav-eler's well-loved aid;
2 My guide is Je - sus Christ whose steps, when trav-el - ers have trod,
3 My faith, it is an oak - en staff, O let me on it lean.

My faith, it is a song of trust, sus - tains me un - dis - mayed.
Wheth - er be - neath was flint - y rock or yield-ing grass - y sod,
My faith pro - vides the ground of hope, sup - ports a pur-pose keen.

I'll trav - el on and still be stirred by si - lent thought or so - cial
They car - ried on, their joy un-spent; through pain and trial they on - ward
Your Spir - it, God, up - on me send, that I may be what you in -

word; By all my per - ils un - de - terred, a pil - grim un - a - fraid.
went, Un - stayed by plea-sure, still they bent their zeal-ous course to God.
tend. With pa - tient cour-age, we'll con-tend as ra - diant saints se - rene.

A gifted Congregational minister in London, Thomas Toke Lynch was the subject of controversy within the churches upon the publication of his hymn collection, The Rivulet, *which received poor reviews. This hymn was labeled Lynch's "best" when it appeared in* Congregational Praise *(1951).*

Tune: THE STAFF OF FAITH   8.6.8.6.8.8.8.6.
Swiss folk melody
Fellowship Hymn Book, *1910*

419

Nun danket alle Gott
(Now Thank We All Our God)

Sir. 50:20–24; 39:35; Ps. 67

Martin Rinkart, 1647; transl. Catherine Winkworth, 1858; alt.

1 Nun dank-et al-le Gott, mit Herz-en, Mund und Händ - en,
1 Now thank we all our God with heart and hands and voic - es,
2 O may this boun-teous God through all our life be near us,
3 All praise and thanks to God our Mak - er now be giv - en,

der gro - sse Ding - e tut an uns und al - len End - en;
Who won-drous things has done, in whom this world re - joic - es,
With ev - er joy - ful hearts and bless - ed peace to cheer us,
To Christ, and Spir - it, too, our help in high - est heav - en,

der uns von Mut - ter - leib und Kind - es - bein - en an
Who, from our par - ents' arms, has blessed us on our way
And keep us still in grace, and guide us when per - plexed,
The one e - ter - nal God, whom earth and heaven a - dore,

un - zäh - lig viel zu gut bis hier-her hat ge - tan.
With count-less gifts of love, and still is ours to - day.
And free us from all ills in this world and the next.
For thus it was, is now, and shall be ev - er - more.

For much of his life, German Lutheran pastor and musician Martin Rinkart ministered to the walled city of Eisleben amidst the horrors of the Thirty Years' War. This hymn has become one of the most widely used hymns of the church.

Tune: NUN DANKET 6.7.6.7.6.6.6.6.
Johann Crüger, 1647
Harm. Felix Mendelssohn, 1840

We Praise You, O God

Julia C. Cory, 1902; alt.

1 We praise you, O God, our Re - deem - er, Cre - a - tor;
2 We wor - ship you, God of our moth - ers and fa - thers;
3 With voic - es u - nit - ed our prais - es we of - fer,

in grate - ful de - vo - tion our trib - ute we bring.
through life's storm and tem - pest our guide you have been.
and glad - ly our song of thanks - giv - ing we raise.

We lay it be - fore you, we kneel and a - dore you;
When per - ils o'er - take us, you nev - er will for - sake us,
Our sins now con - fess - ing, we pray for your bless - ing;

we bless your ho - ly name, glad prais - es we sing.
and with your help, O God, in life's strug - gles we win.
to you, our great Re - deem - er, for - ev - er be praise!

Julia Bulkley Cady Cory wrote this hymn for Thanksgiving in 1902 at the invitation of the organist of New York's Brick Presbyterian Church who felt that the familiar words to Kremser contained too much militaristic imagery.

Tune: KREMSER 12.11.12.11.
Valerius, Nederlandtsch Gedenkclanck, 1626

421

We Gather Together

Netherlands folk hymn, 16th century
Transl. Theodore Baker, 1894
Adapt. Lavon Bayler, 1992

1 We gath-er to-geth-er
to ask for God's bless-ing,
to live in com-mu-ni-ty,
seek-ing God's will.
We come now, as sis-ters
and broth-ers, con-fess-ing
the sins that di-vide
and the wrong in us still.

2 Be-side us, for-giv-ing,
en-a-bling, sus-tain-ing,
you call us, O Sav-ior,
to life that is new.
You draw us a-way
from self-cen-tered com-plain-ing.
You lead us and guide us
in ways that are true.

3 All praise to the Spir-it,
pro-vid-er, de-fend-er.
You of-fer us free-dom,
to fol-low or stray,
Em-pow-er-ing all by
the hope you en-gen-der.
Grant wis-dom and cour-age
to fol-low your way.

The original text of this hymn was one of thanksgiving for The Netherlands' independence from Spanish domination in the sixteenth century. It has been reinterpreted for contemporary congregations by United Church of Christ minister and writer Lavon Bayler.

Tune: KREMSER 12.11.12.11.
16th-century Dutch melody
Arr. Edward Kremser, 1877

422

Come, O Thankful People, Come

Exod. 23:16

St. 1, Henry Alford, 1844; alt.
St. 2, Anna Laetitia Aiken Barbauld, 1772; alt.
St. 3, composite of Alford and Barbauld; alt.

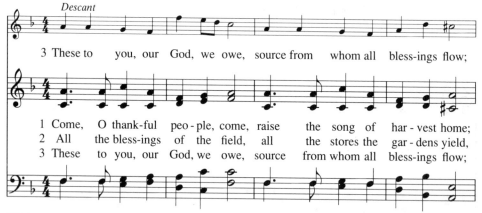

1 Come, O thank-ful peo-ple, come, raise the song of har-vest home;
2 All the bless-ings of the field, all the stores the gar-dens yield,
3 These to you, our God, we owe, source from whom all bless-ings flow;

This hymn represents the joining of two Thanksgiving hymns by nineteenth-century poet Henry Alford and eighteenth-century poet Anna Laetitia Aiken Barbauld. The creator of this combined form, which appeared early in the twentieth century, is not known.

Tune: ST. GEORGE'S WINDSOR 7.7.7.7.D.
George J. Elvey, 1858
Descant: H. A. Chambers, 1931

and for these our songs we raise, grate - ful vows and sol - emn praise.

all is safe - ly gath - ered in as the win - ter storms be - gin;
all the fruits in full sup-ply, rip-ened 'neath the sum - mer sky,
and for these our songs we raise, grate-ful vows and sol - emn praise.

Come, then, thank - ful peo - ple, come, raise the song of har-vest home;

God our Mak - er does pro - vide for our wants to be sup - plied;
All that spring with boun-teous hand scat - ters o'er the smil-ing land,
Come, then, thank - ful peo - ple, come, raise the song of har-vest home;

come to God's own tem-ple, come, raise the song of har - vest home.

come to God's own tem - ple, come, raise the song of har-vest home.
all that lib - eral au - tumn pours from its rich o'er-flow-ing stores,
come to God's own tem - ple, come, raise the song of har-vest home.

423

Great Is Your Faithfulness

Lam. 3:22–23

Thomas O. Chisholm, 1923; alt.

1 Great is your faith - ful - ness, O God, Cre - a - tor,*
2 Sum - mer and win - ter, and spring-time and har - vest,
3 Par - don for sin and a peace so en - dur - ing,

with you no shad - ow of turn - ing we see.
sun, moon, and stars in their cours - es a - bove,
your own dear pres - ence to cheer and to guide.

You do not change, your com - pas - sions they fail not;
Join with all na - ture in man - i - fold wit - ness
Strength for to - day and bright hope for to - mor - row,

all of your good - ness for - ev - er will be.
to your great faith - ful - ness, mer - cy, and love.
bless - ings all mine with ten thou - sand be - side.

*originally "my Father"

This hymn was one of a number sent by poet Thomas O. Chisholm to composer William M. Runyan for musical settings. It became a favorite of Will Houghton, president of Moody Bible Institute, whose enthusiasm helped establish its popularity.

Tune: FAITHFULNESS 11.10.11.10. with refrain
William M. Runyan, 1923

Great is your faith-ful-ness! Great is your faith-ful-ness! Morn-ing by morn-ing new mer-cies I see; All I have need-ed your hand has pro-vid-ed, Great is your faith-ful-ness, God, un-to me!

424

Praise Our God Above

Matt. 6:25–33; Deut. 8:1–3, 6–10

Tzu-chen Chao, 1931
Transl. Frank W. Price, 1953; alt.

1 Praise our God a-bove, Source of bound-less love: spring wind,
2 God's care like a cloak wraps us hum - ble folk, makes all

sum - mer rain, then the har - vest grain; Pearl - y
green things grow, rip - ens what we sow. Through God

rice and corn, fra - grant au - tumn morn.
we are strong; sing our har - vest song.

Though our work is hard, God gives us re-ward.
Sing praise, field and flower, praise God's might - y power.

Frank Price, a Presbyterian missionary to China, titled this hymn
"Harvest Song" in Chinese Christian Hymns—a collection of
English hymn translations. The tune is a Confucian chant
proclaiming peace, harmonized by W. H. Wong for the 1977
edition of Hymns of Universal Praise.

Tune: HSUAN P'ING 5.5.5.5.D.
Confucian Dacheng chant
Arr. W. H. Wong, 1973

For the Fruit of All Creation

425

Fred Pratt Green, 1970

1 For the fruit of all cre - a - tion, thanks be to God.
2 In the just re - ward of la - bor, God's will is done.
3 For the har - vests of the Spir - it, thanks be to God.

For God's gifts to ev - ery na - tion, thanks be to God.
In the help we give our neigh-bor, God's will is done.
For the good we all in - her - it, thanks be to God.

For the plow - ing, sow-ing, reap-ing, si - lent growth while we are sleep-ing,
In our world-wide task of car - ing for the hun - gry and de - spair-ing,
For the won - ders that as-tound us, for the truths that still con-found us,

Fu - ture needs in earth's safe-keep-ing, thanks be to God.
In the har - vests we are shar - ing, God's will is done.
Most of all that love has found us, thanks be to God.

This text was written in response to a request for a new harvest hymn for an existing tune. After its publication in England in 1970, it became popular in many countries and can be found set to various tunes.

Tune: AR HYD Y NOS 8.4.8.4.8.8.8.4.
Welsh traditional melody
Musical Relicks of the Welsh Bards, *Dublin, 1784*
Harm. L. O. Emerson, 1906
For another harmonization, see 82

426   O God, Whose Steadfast Love

Gen. 18:9–15; 1 Sam. 1:1–20; Luke 1:26–56; 2:1–7   *James L. Haddix, 1986; rev. 1994*

1 O God, whose stead-fast love true moth-er-hood has blessed;
2 Your prom-is-es, O God, so sure through-out the years,
3 In your great love, O God, full par-ent-hood is known:
4 May your house-hold of faith one fam-i-ly be-come,

who shields the in-fant small up-on its moth-er's breast:
have lived in moth-ers' hearts, have bloomed from moth-ers' tears.
a fa-ther mourns his child, a moth-er's strength is shown.
that love may be in-creased and none may be a-lone;

Em-brace us, too, O God, our God, and hold us in your
So Sar-ah laughed, and Han-nah wept, and sing-ing Mar-y
Let par-ents' faith-ful lives un-bind your love that through them
That moth-er's love and fa-ther's care and chil-dren's joy we

lov-ing arms, and hold us in your lov-ing arms.
se-crets kept, and sing-ing Mar-y se-crets kept.
we might find Christ's deep-er love for hu-man-kind.
all may share, and chil-dren's joy we all may share.

*United Church of Christ minister James Haddix wrote this text
for the "Festival of the Christian Home." It was dedicated and
sung to his mother, Margaret Ann Lewis Haddix, at a reception
in Missouri recognizing her thirty-year career as a first-grade
teacher.*

Tune: RHOSYMEDRE 6.6.6.6.8.8.8.
John D. Edwards, c. 1840

God Made from One Blood

427

Thomas H. Troeger, 1988

1. God made from one blood all the fam-ilies of earth,
   the cir-cles of nur-ture that raise us from birth,
   Com-pan-ions who join us to work through each stage
   of child-hood and youth and a-dult-hood and age.

2. We turn to you, God, with our thanks and our tears
   for all of the fam-ilies we've known through the years,
   The in-ti-mate net-works on whom we de-pend
   of par-ents and part-ners and chil-dren and friends.

3. Through fam-ilies we've tast-ed the val-ue of trust
   and felt what it means to be lov-ing and just,
   Yet fam-ilies have al-so be-trayed their best goals,
   mis-treat-ing their mem-bers and bruis-ing their souls.

4. Help fam-ilies in all of their var-i-ous forms
   to face with in-teg-ri-ty strug-gles and storms;
   Grant peace to our homes that will nur-ture the bud
   of peace for the fam-ilies you made from one blood.

This text was commissioned by Yale University Press for A New
Hymnal for Colleges and Schools *(1992) to provide a hymn that
recognizes the many different kinds of families that are
represented when a campus congregation gathers to worship.*

Tune: ST. DENIO 11.11.11.11.
Adapt. from a Welsh ballad in John Roberts'
Caniadaeth y Cysegr, *1839*

428 Malipayong Adlaw'ng Natawhan
(What a Glad Day)

Grace R. Tabada
Transl. Fé Nebres, 1993

Ma - li - pa - yong ad-law'ng na - taw - han ka - ni - mo a - mong ig -
What a glad day, to - day's your birth-day, our lov - ing greet-ings we

so - on, Ma - li - pa - yong ad-law'ng na - taw - han, pa - na -
say! What a glad day, to - day's your birth - day, may God's

la - ngi-nan ka sa Dios. Ma - ga - du - yog ka -
bless - ings up-on you stay! We your friends join with

mi sa i - mo nga pag-sa - u - log. Ma - li -
you in cel - e - brat - ing this day! What a

It is the custom of some churches in the Visayas provinces in
the Philippines to serenade individuals at early dawn on their
birthday. This song by Grace Tabada is a new addition to the
serenaders' repertoire.

Tune: TABADA 9.8.9.8.6.8.9.8.8.
Grace R. Tabada
Arr. Vérne de la Peña, 1994

pa - yong   ad - law'ng na - taw - han,   pa - na -
glad   day,   to - day's your birth - day,   may God's

la - ngi-nan ka   sa   Dios.   Pa - na - la - ngi-nan ka   sa   Dios.
bless - ings up-on   you   stay!   May God's bless - ings up-on you   stay!

429   God, Bless Our Homes

Frank von Christierson, 1957

1 God, bless our homes with peace and love and laugh - ter,
2 May ev - ery heart re - ceive God's lov - ing spir - it
3 For - give the hurts our self - ish - ness in - flict - ed
4 O God, in grat - i - tude for homes and loved ones,

with un - der - stand-ing and with loy - al - ty.
and know the truth that makes life tru - ly free;
on those we love and those who love us best.
we o - pen now our hearts to hu - man - kind.

May we to - geth - er fol - low Christ our Sav - ior
Then, in that spir - it may we live u - nit - ed,
Christ, heal the scars, and draw us all to - geth - er
Grant us your spir - it— love for all our neigh - bors—

Frank von Christierson was born in Finland and came to the
United States as a child. After completing degrees at Stanford
University and San Francisco Theological Seminary, he
ministered to and founded several Presbyterian congregations
in California.

Tune: CHARTERHOUSE 11.10.11.10.
David Evans, 1927

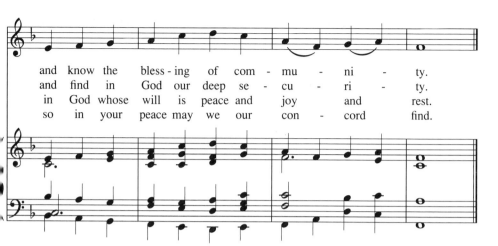

and know the bless-ing of com - mu - ni - ty.
and find in God our deep se - cu - ri - ty.
in God whose will is peace and joy and rest.
so in your peace may we our con - cord find.

Praise to God, Your Praises Bring 430

William C. Gannett, 1872; alt.

1 Praise to God, your prais-es bring; hearts bow down and voic - es sing
2 Praise God for the bud-ding green, A - pril's res - ur - rec - tion scene;
3 Praise God for the sum-mer rain, feed - ing, day and night, the grain;
4 Praise God for the gar - den root, mead-ow grass, and or - chard fruit:

Prais - es to the glo - rious One, all God's year of won - der done.
Praise God for the shin - ing hours, star-ring all the land with flowers.
Praise God for the ti - ny seed, hold-ing all the world shall need.
Praise for hills and val - leys broad, each the ta - ble of our God.

5 Praise God for the win-ter's rest,
   snow that falls on na-ture's breast;
Praise for hap-py dreams of birth,
   brood-ing in the qui-et earth.

6 For God's year of won-der done,
   praise to the all-glo-rious One!
Hearts bow down and voic-es raise
   songs of thanks for all God's days.

Most of William C. Gannett's hymns were written for special occasions, including this one for a harvest festival in St. Paul, Minnesota. Gannett and Frederick L. Hosmer, both Unitarian ministers, edited The Thought of God in Hymns and Poems.

Tune: SAVANNAH 7.7.7.7.
The Foundery Collection, *1742*

431   Now Greet the Swiftly Changing Year

Luke 2:8–14

17th-century Slovak
Transl. Jaroslav J. Vajda, 1969; alt.

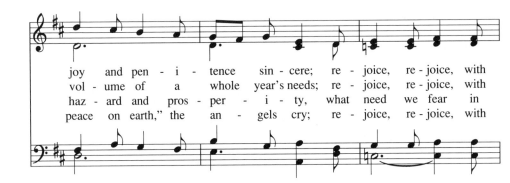

Unison

1 Now greet the swift - ly chang - ing year with
2 Christ's love a - bun - dant far ex - ceeds the
3 With such a God to lead our way in
4 "All glo - ry be to God on high and

joy and pen - i - tence sin - cere; re - joice, re - joice, with
vol - ume of a whole year's needs; re - joice, re - joice, with
haz - ard and pros - per - i - ty, what need we fear in
peace on earth," the an - gels cry; re - joice, re - joice, with

thanks em - brace an - oth - er year of grace.
thanks em - brace an - oth - er year of grace.
earth or space in this new year of grace?
thanks em - brace an - oth - er year of grace.

This seventeenth-century New Year's hymn was included in the
*Tranoscius, a collection published by the Czech Lutheran pastor
Juraj Tranovský (1591–1637). Translator Jaroslav Vajda is also
known for his original hymn texts.*

Tune: SIXTH NIGHT 8.8.8.6.
Alfred V. Fedak, 1984

'Tis Winter Now; the Fallen Snow

432

Samuel Longfellow, 1864; alt.

Unison

1 'Tis win-ter now; the fal-len snow has left the
2 And yet God's love is not with-drawn; new life with-
3 And though a-broad the sharp winds blow, and skies are
4 O God! who gives the win-ter's cold, as well as

heavens all cold-ly clear; Through leaf-less boughs the sharp winds
in the keen air breathes; God's beau-ty paints the crim-son
chill, and frosts are keen, Home clos-er draws its cir-cle
sum - mer's joy-ous rays, Us warm-ly in your love en-

blow, and all the earth lies dead and drear.
dawn, and clothes the boughs with glit-tering wreaths.
now, and warm-er glows the light with-in.
fold, and keep us through life's win-try days.

Samuel Longfellow served as a Unitarian minister in Fall River, Massachusetts, Brooklyn, New York, and finally, Germantown, Pennsylvania. Among his published works was a biography of his brother, Henry Wadsworth Longfellow. With Samuel Johnson he published Hymns of the Spirit.

Tune: DANBY L.M.
Traditional English melody
Arr. Ralph Vaughan Williams, 1925
Alternate tune: O WALY WALY

433 In the Bulb There Is a Flower

Natalie Sleeth, 1985

Unison

1 In the bulb there is a flow - er; in the seed, an ap-ple tree;
2 There's a song in ev-ery si - lence, seek-ing word and mel-o - dy;
3 In our end is our be - gin-ning; in our time, in - fin - i - ty;

in co-coons, a hid-den prom-ise: but - ter - flies will soon be free!
there's a dawn for ev-ery dark-ness, bring-ing hope to you and me.
in our doubt there is be - liev - ing; in our life, e - ter - ni - ty.

In the cold and snow of win - ter there's a spring that waits to be,
From the past will come the fu - ture; what it holds, a mys-ter - y,
In our death, a res - ur - rec - tion; at the last, a vic - to - ry,

un-re - vealed un-til its sea - son, some-thing God a-lone can see.
un-re - vealed un-til its sea - son, some-thing God a-lone can see.
un-re - vealed un-til its sea - son, some-thing God a-lone can see.

Natalie Sleeth composed her "Hymn of Promise" first as a choral anthem and then adapted it to this version for congregational singing. It was dedicated to her husband, Ronald Sleeth, who died shortly after she completed it.

Tune: PROMISE 8.7.8.7.D.
Natalie Sleeth, 1985

All Beautiful the March of Days

434

Frances W. Wile, 1910; alt.

1 All beau-ti-ful the march of days, as sea-sons come and go;
2 O'er bril-liant fields of spar - kling snow the ra - diant morns un - fold;
3 O you from whose un - fath - omed law the year in beau - ty flows,

the hand that shaped the rose has formed the crys - tal of the snow,
The sol - emn splen - dors of the night burn bright-ly through the cold.
your - self the splen - did vi - sion seen in crys - tal and in rose,

Has sent the sil - ver frost of heaven, the flow-ing wa - ters sealed,
Life mounts in ev - ery puls - ing vein, love deep-ens 'round the hearth,
The pass - ing days with grace de - clare, and pass-ing nights pro - claim,

And laid a si - lent love - li - ness on hill and wood and field.
And clear-er sounds the an - gel hymn, "Good will to all on earth."
In ev - er-chang - ing words of light, the won-der of your name.

*Frances Wile wrote this hymn extolling the beauty of winter
at the suggestion of her pastor, William Gannett, and Frederick
Hosmer, both of whom were hymnwriters.*

Tune: FOREST GREEN C.M.D.
*Traditional English melody
Harm. Ralph Vaughan Williams, 1906*

Harmonization Copyright ©, Oxford University Press. From *The English Hymnal 1906.*

435 Each Winter as the Year Grows Older

William Gay, 1969; alt.

1 Each win-ter as the year grows old-er, we all grow old-er too. The chill sets in a lit-tle cold-er; the ver-i-ties I knew seem shak-en and un-true.

2 When race and class cry out for trea-son, when si-rens call for war, They o-ver-shout the voice of rea-son, and scream till we ig-nore all we held dear be-fore.

3 But I be-lieve be-yond be-liev-ing, that life can spring from death; That growth can flow-er from our griev-ing; that we can catch our breath and turn trans-fixed by faith.

4 So e-ven as the sun is turn-ing to jour-ney to the north, The liv-ing flame, in se-cret burn-ing, can kin-dle on the earth, and bring God's love to birth.

5 O Child of ec-sta-sy and sor-rows, O Child of peace and pain, Bright-en to-day's world by to-mor-row's, re-new our lives a-gain; Christ Je-sus, come and reign!

This hymn is a collaboration between United Church of Christ minister William Gay and composer-organist Annabeth McClelland Gay. It is one of several Christmas carols the couple wrote to send to their friends during the Vietnam War era of the 1960s.

Tune: CAROL OF HOPE 9.6.9.6.6.
Annabeth McClelland Gay, 1969

God of Grace and God of Glory 436

Harry Emerson Fosdick, 1930; alt.

1 God of grace and God of glo - ry, on your peo - ple
2 From the e - vils that sur - round us and as - sail the
3 Cure your chil - dren's war - ring mad - ness; bend our pride to
4 Set our feet on loft - y plac - es; gird our lives that
5 Save us from weak res - ig - na - tion to the e - vils

pour your power; crown your an - cient church - 's sto - ry;
Sav - ior's ways, from the fears that long have bound us—
your con - trol. Shame our reck - less, self - ish glad - ness,
they may be ar - mored with all Christ - like grac - es,
we de - plore; let the search for your sal - va - tion

bring its bud to glo - rious flower. Grant us wis - dom, grant us cour - age,
free our hearts for faith and praise. Grant us wis - dom, grant us cour - age,
rich in things and poor in soul. Grant us wis - dom, grant us cour - age,
in the fight to set us free. Grant us wis - dom, grant us cour - age,
be our glo - ry ev - er - more. Grant us wis - dom, grant us cour - age,

for the fac - ing of this hour, for the fac - ing of this hour.
for the liv - ing of these days, for the liv - ing of these days.
make our bro - ken spir - its whole, make our bro - ken spir - its whole.
in the quest for lib - er - ty, in the quest for lib - er - ty.
serv - ing you whom we a - dore, serv - ing you whom we a - dore.

Harry Emerson Fosdick, a prophetic preacher and writer, taught at Union Theological Seminary from 1915 to 1946. This hymn was written for the opening service and dedication of Riverside Church, New York City, which he served for twenty years.

Tune: CWM RHONDDA 8.7.8.7.8.7.7.
John Hughes, c. 1907

437

We Shall Not Give Up the Fight

South African freedom song

This protest song of South Africa came to Europe via Tanzania. It reflects the determined faith and unity of those who fought against apartheid, and offers hope and strength to all Christians struggling against the evils of injustice.

Tune: ONLY STARTED Irr.
South African freedom song

438

When Peace, Like a River
(It Is Well with My Soul)

Ps. 146; Col. 1:19–23; 2:13–14; 3 John 1:2   *Horatio G. Spafford, 1873; alt.*

1 When peace, like a riv - er, up - holds me each day, when
2 Though e - vil should tempt me, though tri - als should come, let
3 My sin— oh, the bliss of this glo - ri - ous thought— my
4 O God, speed the day that is filled with your light, when

sor - rows like sea bil - lows roll, What - ev - er my lot, you have
this blessed as - sur - ance con - trol, That Christ has re - gard - ed my
sin— not in part, but the whole— Is nailed to the cross and I
clouds are rolled back as a scroll; The trum - pet shall sound and the

Refrain

taught me to say, "It is well, it is well with my soul."
help - less es - tate, and has paid life and blood for my soul: It is
bear it no more. Praise the Lord! Praise the Lord, O my soul!
Lord shall ap - pear, "e - ven so"— it is well with my soul.

well with my soul, it is well, it is well with my soul.
It is well with my soul.

This hymn was written out of grief over the loss of the author's four daughters in the sinking of the SS Ville du Havre. After leaving his Chicago law practice, Horatio G. Spafford and his wife settled in Jerusalem.

Tune: VILLE DU HAVRE 11.8.11.9. with refrain
Philip P. Bliss, 1876

A Mighty Fortress Is Our God

439

Martin Luther, c. 1529
Transl. Frederick H. Hedge, 1853; adapt. Ruth Duck, 1981

Ps. 46

1 A might-y for-tress is our God, a bul-wark nev-er fail-ing,
2 Did we in our own strength con-fide, our striv-ing would be los-ing,
3 And though this world with dev - ils filled should threat-en to un - do us,
4 That word be-yond all earth - ly powers for-ev-er is a-bid-ing;

Our pres-ent help a - mid the flood of mor-tal ills pre - vail - ing.
But there is one who takes our side, the One of God's own choos - ing.
We will not fear for God has willed the truth to tri - umph through us.
The Spir-it and the gifts are ours, for Christ is with us sid - ing.

For still our an-cient foe does seek to work us woe with craft and pow-er
You ask who that may be? Christ Je - sus sets us free! With might-y power to
The powers of e - vil grim, we trem-ble not for them; their rage we can en -
Let goods and kin-dred go, this mor-tal life al - so; the bod-y they may

great, and armed with cru - el hate, on earth with-out an e - qual.
save, vic - to - rious o'er the grave, Christ will pre-vail tri - um - phant.
dure, for lo, their doom is sure: one lit - tle word shall fell them.
kill; God's truth shall tri-umph still; God's reign en-dures for - ev - er.

There is speculation that this psalm paraphrase was written in 1527 when Martin Luther's friend was burned at the stake, or in 1529, when Lutheran German princes protested the revocation of their liberties. It has been translated into more than fifty languages.

Tune: EIN' FESTE BURG (isometric) 8.7.8.7.6.6.6.6.7.
Martin Luther, c. 1529
Harm. The New Hymnal for American Youth, 1930; alt.
For another version, see 440

440   A Mighty Fortress Is Our God

Ps. 46

Martin Luther, c. 1529
Transl. Madeleine Forell Marshall, 1993

1 A might-y for - tress is our God, our strong and sure pro-tec - tion;
2 These hu-man hands, for all their skill, can - not shape our sal-va - tion.
3 When e - vil pow - ers rage and swear and threat - en mass de - struc - tion,
4 God's ev - er - last - ing Word a - bides, our strong and sure sal-va - tion.

Our God, who loves us, has re - solved to free us from sub-jec - tion.
We need a cham-pion, one who will a - chieve our lib - er - a - tion.
When we are tempt - ed to de - spair, to yield to their se - duc - tion—
The Spir - it here and now pro - vides rich gifts and con - so - la - tion.

With bold Sa - tan - ic pride and ha - tred well sup - plied,
Who is there, good and brave, with strength and will to save
Then may we stand as - sured by God's most ho - ly Word,
Let wealth and fam - ily go, this bod - y be brought low.

the dead - ly force of sin has sworn to do us in.
our weak and fear - ful race? Who will our cause em - brace?
the e - vil one shall fail, God's righ - teous-ness pre - vail:
What - ev - er loss we bear God will at last re - pair.

Reformation-era psalm and hymn tunes usually did not have
regular rhythms, but combined duple and triple groupings. This
version of the tune is much as Martin Luther wrote it. Later
generations "squared up" the rhythm, as in the previous setting.

Tune: EIN' FESTE BURG
(rhythmic) 8.7.8.7.6.6.6.6.7.
Martin Luther, c. 1529
For another version, see 439

Mere hu - man strength will per - ish.
God's on - ly Child, Christ Je - sus!
Then why should we be fear - ful?
God's realm is ours for - ev - er.

Jesus, Savior, Pilot Me   441

Edward Hopper, 1871; alt.

Mark 4:35–41

1 Je - sus, Sav - ior, pi - lot me   o - ver life's tem-pes-tuous sea;
2 As a moth - er stills her child, you can hush the o - cean wild;
3 When at last I near the shore, and the fear - ful break-ers roar,

Un - known waves be - fore me roll, hid - ing rock and treach-erous shoal;
Bois-terous waves o - bey your will when you say to them, "Be still."
Keep-ing me from peace-ful rest, then, while lean-ing on your breast,

Chart and com - pass ev - er be; Je - sus, Sav - ior, pi - lot me.
Won-drous Sov - ereign of the sea, Je - sus, Sav - ior, pi - lot me.
May I hear your words so true, "Fear not, I will pi - lot you."

Inspired by the many sailors in his congregation in New York City, Edward Hopper wrote these lines. They were first sung for an anniversary service of the American Seamen's Friend Society at Broadway Tabernacle (Congregational).

Tune: PILOT 7.7.7.7.7.7.
John E. Gould, 1871

442   I'm Pressing on the Upward Way
(Higher Ground)

Johnson Oatman, Jr., 1892; alt.

1 I'm press-ing on the up-ward way, new heights I'm gain-ing ev-ery
2 My heart has no de-sire to stay where doubts a - rise and fears dis -
3 I want to live be-yond the world, though Sa - tan's darts at me are
4 I want to scale the ut-most height, and catch a gleam of glo - ry

day; Still pray-ing as I'm on - ward bound, "O plant me,
may; Though some may dwell where these a - bound, my prayer, my
hurled; For faith has caught a joy - ful sound, the song of
bright; But still I'll pray till heaven I've found, "God, lead me

Refrain

God, on high-er ground."
aim is high-er ground.
saints on high-er ground.   O lift me up, and I shall be by faith in heaven e-ter-nal - ly,
on to high-er ground."

A high-er plane than I have found, O plant me, God, on high - er ground.

Johnson Oatman, Jr., wrote hymns while in the insurance business in Mount Holly, New Jersey. Words for more than 5,000 gospel songs are credited to him. Iowa-born Charles Gabriel taught singing schools and compiled many collections of gospel and Sunday School songs.

Tune: HIGHER GROUND L.M. with refrain
Charles H. Gabriel, 1898

How Like a Gentle Spirit

443

C. Eric Lincoln, 1987; alt.

1 John 4:16

May be sung in unison

1 How like a gen - tle spir - it deep with - in
2 Let God be God wher - ev - er life may be;
3 God like a moth - er ea - gle hov - ers near
4 When in our vain pre - ten - sions we con - spire
5 Through all our fret - ful claims of sex and race

God reins our fer - vent pas - sions day by day,
let ev - ery tongue bear wit - ness to the call;
on might - y wings of pow - er man - i - fest;
to shape God's im - age as we see our own,
the un - i - ver - sal love of God shines through,

and gives us strength to chal - lenge and to win
all hu - man - kind is one by God's de - cree;
God like a gen - tle shep - herd stills our fear,
hark to the voice a - bove our base de - sire;
for God is love tran - scend - ing style and place

de - spite the per - ils of our cho - sen way.
let God be God, let God be God for all.
and com - forts us a - gainst a peace - ful breast.
God is the sculp - tor, we the fash - ioned stone.
and all the i - dle op - tions we pur - sue.

The author of this hymn has been a professor at several universities and seminaries and has received thirteen honorary degrees. C. Eric Lincoln is also known for his scholarly books on the African-American church and for his poems and novels.

Tune: SURSUM CORDA 10.10.10.10.
Alfred M. Smith, 1941

444   We Are Often Tossed and Driven
(We'll Understand It Better By and By)

Charles Albert Tindley, c. 1906; alt.

1 We are of-ten tossed and driven on the rest-less sea of time,
2 We are of-ten des-ti-tute of the things that life de-mands,
3 Tri-als harsh on ev-ery hand, and we can-not un-der-stand
4 Temp-ta-tions, hid-den snares of-ten take us un-a-wares,

Som-ber skies and howl-ing tem-pests oft suc-ceed a bright sun-shine;
Want of food and want of shel-ter, thirst-y hills and bar-ren lands;
All the ways that God would lead us to that bless-ed prom-ised land;
And our hearts are made to bleed for man-y a thought-less word or deed,

In that land of per-fect day, when the mists have rolled a-way,
In our God our trust's as-sured, and ac-cord-ing to the Word,
We are guid-ed by God's eye, and we'll fol-low till we die,
And we won-der, why the test, when we try to do our best,

to Refrain

We will un-der-stand it bet-ter by and by.
We will un-der-stand it bet-ter by and by.
For we'll un-der-stand it bet-ter by and by.
But we'll un-der-stand it bet-ter by and by.

Refrain

By and by, when the morn-ing comes, when the saints of God are gath - ered home, We'll tell the sto - ry how we've o - ver-come: for we'll un - der-stand it bet-ter by and by. (by and by.)

This is probably Charles A. Tindley's most celebrated gospel hymn of the early twentieth century. Far from being a song that merely looks heavenward, Tindley's song identifies poverty as a social problem.

Tune: BY AND BY Irr. with refrain
Charles Albert Tindley, c. 1906
Transcribed by F. A. Clark, 1906

445   Lift Your Head, O Martyrs, Weeping

Deut. 31:6; Ps. 36:7; Matt. 8:23–26

Károly Jeszensky, 1890; based on a hymn b
Pauli Joachim (1636–1708); transl. William Tóth, 193
Adapt. Theodore S. Horvath, 199

1 Lift your heads, O mar-tyrs, weep - ing, God our Mak - er
2 Though the storms may rage and roil . . . . o'er the vast and
3 Though the hills and vales be riv - en, once con-ceived by
4 Though in chains you now are griev - ing, though a tor - tured

still does reign! You are dai - ly in God's keep - ing,
fear - ful sea, Though you cry from wretch-ed toil, ...
God's own hand, Though the signs of earth and heav - en
slave you die, Mar - tyrs, if you die be - liev - ing,

God is with you in your pain. Rise and be of val - iant heart,
"O my Sav - ior, res - cue me!" Though it seems that God does sleep,
sig - nal doom in ev - ery land, Yet, O mar - tyrs, have no fear;
heav - en's path shall o - pen lie. Up - ward gaze and trust a - new,

and with cour - age bear your part; Soon a - gain God's
hope and trust in God still keep; Calm your hearts though
ev - er is your help - er near; God has sought you,
God has not for - sak - en you; You are God's own

In thge Counter-Reformation of the 1670s, Hungarian Reformed ministers were imprisoned, and forty-two who would not recant their faith were sold as galley slaves. This hymn of faith reflects the strain and rhythm of their oars. It eventually became an anthem of liberation for Hungarian Protestants.

Tune: MAGYAR 8.7.8.7.7.7.8.8.
"Hymn of the Hungarian Galley Slaves," 1674
Adapt. and harm. G. J. Neumann, 1938

arms will fold   you   to God's lov - ing   heart and hold   you.
they be quak - ing,   God   is   faith-ful,   none for-sak - ing.
God has found   you;   God's pro - tec-tive   wings sur-round   you.
peo - ple, sure - ly   God   will   fold God's own   se-cure - ly.

Jesus, Still Lead On   446

Nicolaus Ludwig von Zinzendorf, 1721; transl. Jane Borthwick, 1846; alt.

1 Je - sus, still   lead   on,   till   our   rest   be   won;
2 If   the   way   be   drear,   if   the   woe   be   near,
3 When we   seek   re - lief   from   a   long - felt   grief,
4 Je - sus, still   lead   on,   till   our   rest   be   won;

And   al-though the   way   be cheer-less,   we   will fol - low,   calm and fear-less;
Let   not faith - less   fears o'er-take   us,   let   not faith and   hope for-sake us;
When temp-ta - tions   come al - lur - ing,   make us   pa - tient   and   en-dur-ing;
Heaven-ly Lead - er   still   di - rect   us,   still sup-port, con - sole, pro-tect us,

Guide us   by   your   hand   to   the prom - ised   land.
For through man - y a   woe   to   our home   we   go.
Show us   that   bright   shore   where we   weep   no   more.
Guide us   by   your   hand   to   the prom - ised   land.

Selections from two German hymns written by Count Nicolaus
von Zinzendorf in 1721 were combined by Christian Gregor in
1778 to create this hymn. Zinzendorf, who gave the Moravian
Brethren asylum on his estate, later became a Moravian pastor.

Tune: SEELENBRÄUTIGAM 5.5.8.8.5.5.
Adam Drese in
Geistreiches Gesangbuch, Darmstadt, 1698

447   Beams of Heaven as I Go

Charles Albert Tindley, c. 1906; alt.

1 Beams of heav - en, as I go, through this wil - der - ness of woe,
2 Of - ten - times my sky is clear, joy a - bounds with - out a tear,
3 Bur - dens now may crush me down, dis - ap - point - ments all a - round,

guide my heart in peace - ful ways, turn my mid - nights in - to days;
though a day so bright be - gun, clouds may hide to - mor - row's sun.
trou - bles speak in mourn - ful sigh, sor - row through a tear-stained eye;

When in life's shad - ows I would grope, faith al - ways finds a star of hope,
There'll be a day that's al - ways bright, a day that nev - er yields to night,
There is a world where plea-sure reigns, no mourn-ing soul shall roam its plains,

And soon from all life's grief and dan - ger, I shall be free some day.
And in its light the streets of glo - ry, I shall be - hold some day.
And to that land of peace and glo - ry, I want to go some day.

I do not know how long 'twill be, nor what the fu-ture holds for me,

But this I know, if Je-sus leads me, I shall get home some day.

Composer Charles A. Tindley, a prolific writer of gospel hymns, was a highly respected African-American Methodist minister in Philadelphia. It is Rev. Tindley whom Thomas Dorsey, perhaps the most famous gospel songwriter, credited as his influential predecessor.

Tune: SOME DAY 7.7.7.7.8.8.9.6. with refrain
Charles Albert Tindley, c. 1906
Transcribed by F. A. Clark, 1906

Take My Life, God, Let It Be 448

Frances R. Havergal, 1874; alt.

Rom. 12:1

1 Take my life, God, let it be con-se-crat-ed faith-ful-ly.
2 Take my spir-it, let it move at the im-pulse of your love.
3 Take my will; your will be done! Make your will and mine be one.
4 Take my love and help it grow; let my lov-ing ov-er-flow.

Take my mo-ments and my days, let them flow in cease-less praise.
Take my in-tel-lect and use all its pow-ers as you choose.
Take my heart, and by your grace make of it your dwell-ing place.
Take me now, and help me be part of Christ's com-mu-ni-ty.

Frances R. Havergal wrote her hymn following a visit to Areley House in Worcestershire, England. Among the ten persons at the house were "some unconverted . . . some converted but not rejoicing." Before she left, "everyone had got a blessing."

Tune: VIENNA 7.7.7.7.
Justin H. Knecht, 1797
Alternate tune: HENDON

449

Softly and Tenderly

Will L. Thompson, 1880; alt.

1 Soft - ly and ten - der - ly Je - sus is call - ing, call - ing for
2 Why should we tar - ry when Je - sus is plead-ing, plead-ing for
3 Time is now fleet - ing, the mo - ments are pass - ing, pass - ing from
4 O for the won - der - ful love Je - sus prom-ised, prom-ised for

you and for me; See at the por - tals Christ wait - ing and
you and for me? Why should we lin - ger and heed not God's
you and from me; Shad - ows are gath - er - ing, death-beds are
you and for me; Though we have sinned Je - sus of - fers us

watch-ing, watch-ing for you and for me.
mer - cies, mer - cies for you and for me?
com - ing, com - ing for you and for me.
par - don, par - don for you and for me.

Refrain

Come home, come
Come home,

home, come home, All who are wea-ry, come home;

Will Thompson established publishing firms in Chicago and East
Liverpool, Ohio, the community to which he left a legacy of song.
Dwight L. Moody once remarked that he would rather have
written "Softly and Tenderly" than anything he had ever done.

Tune: SOFTLY AND TENDERLY
11.7.11.7. with refrain
Will L. Thompson, 1880

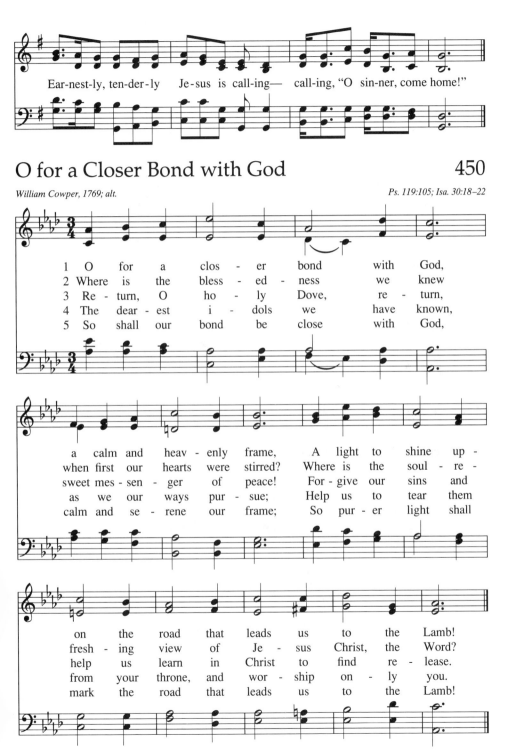

Ear-nest-ly, ten-der-ly Je-sus is call-ing— call-ing, "O sin-ner, come home!"

O for a Closer Bond with God 450

William Cowper, 1769; alt.

Ps. 119:105; Isa. 30:18–22

1 O for a clos - er bond with God,
2 Where is the bless - ed - ness we knew
3 Re - turn, O ho - ly Dove, re - turn,
4 The dear - est i - dols we have known,
5 So shall our bond be close with God,

a calm and heav - enly frame, A light to shine up -
when first our hearts were stirred? Where is the soul - re -
sweet mes - sen - ger of peace! For - give our sins and
as we our ways pur - sue; Help us to tear them
calm and se - rene our frame; So pur - er light shall

on the road that leads us to the Lamb!
fresh - ing view of Je - sus Christ, the Word?
help us learn in Christ to find re - lease.
from your throne, and wor - ship on - ly you.
mark the road that leads us to the Lamb!

This hymn was written during the illness of William Cowper's dear friend, Mary Unwin. Cowper wrote poetry and, together with John Newton, published Olney Hymns. *John B. Dykes, organist and Church of England priest, wrote many hymn tunes.*

Tune: BEATITUDO C.M.
John B. Dykes, 1875

451

Be Now My Vision

Ancient Irish text, c. 8th century; transl. Mary E. Byrne, 1905
Versified by Eleanor H. Hull, 1912; adapt.

Unison

1 Be now my vi - sion, O God of my heart;
2 Be now my wis - dom, and be my true word;
3 Rich - es I need not, nor life's emp - ty praise,
4 Sov - ereign of heav - en, my vic - to - ry won,

noth - ing sur - pass - es the love you im - part—
ev - er with - in me, my soul is as - sured;
you, my in - her - i - tance, now and al - ways;
may I reach heaven's joys, O bright heav - en's Sun!

You my best thought, by day or by night,
Moth - er and Fa - ther, you are both to me,
You and you on - ly are first in my heart,
Heart of my own heart, what - ev - er be - fall,

wak - ing or sleep - ing, your pres - ence my light.
now and for - ev - er your child I will be.
great God, my trea - sure, may we nev - er part.
still be my vi - sion, O Rul - er of all.

Dating from the eighth century or earlier, this Irish hymn was translated into prose by Mary Byrne. It was then versified by Eleanor Hull, author of several books on Irish literature and history. David Evans arranged the Irish melody for this text in 1927.

Tune: SLANE 10.10.9.10.
Traditional Irish melody
Harm. David Evans, 1927

Savior, Who Dying Gave

452

Sylvanus Dryden Phelps, 1862
Adapt. Thomas H. Troeger, 1992

Rom. 5:6–11; Gal. 5:22–24

1 Sav - ior, who dy - ing gave your love to me,
2 Give me a faith - ful heart guid - ed by you,
3 All that I am and have is yours a - lone,

that all God made me for might come to be—
that ev - ery day may bring your love to view
my love for you the fruit your love has sown.

I make this sol - emn vow: my heart will al - ways bow
through some small kind - ness done, some work of love be - gun,
Not doubt, nor fear, nor wrong, nor death can still this song:

when I re - mem - ber how you died for me.
some thread of jus - tice spun, some life made new.
my gifts of love be - long to you a - lone.

Both author and composer of this hymn were ministers. Sylvanus
Phelps' text first appeared in a denominational journal and was
later altered to be used in the collection Pure Gold by Robert
Lowry, music editor for Biglow Publishing Company.

Tune: SOMETHING FOR JESUS 6.4.6.4.6.6.6.4.
Robert Lowry, 1872

453 When the Morning Stars Together

Ps. 150; Job 38:7; 2 Chron. 5:13–14

Albert F. Bayly, 1969; alt.

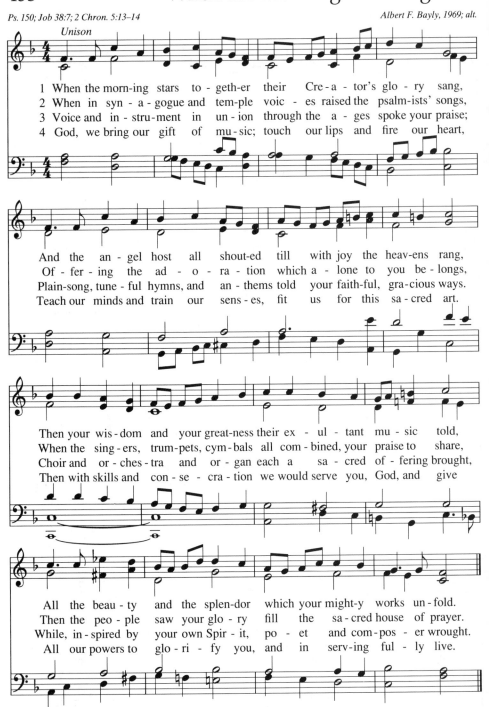

Unison

1 When the morn-ing stars to - geth-er their Cre - a - tor's glo - ry sang,
2 When in syn - a - gogue and tem-ple voic - es raised the psalm-ists' songs,
3 Voice and in - stru-ment in un - ion through the a - ges spoke your praise;
4 God, we bring our gift of mu - sic; touch our lips and fire our heart,

And the an - gel host all shout-ed till with joy the heav-ens rang,
Of - fer - ing the ad - o - ra - tion which a - lone to you be - longs,
Plain-song, tune - ful hymns, and an - thems told your faith-ful, gra-cious ways.
Teach our minds and train our sens - es, fit us for this sa - cred art.

Then your wis - dom and your great-ness their ex - ul - tant mu - sic told,
When the sing - ers, trum-pets, cym - bals all com - bined, your praise to share,
Choir and or - ches - tra and or - gan each a sa - cred of - fering brought,
Then with skills and con - se - cra - tion we would serve you, God, and give

All the beau - ty and the splen-dor which your might-y works un - fold.
Then the peo - ple saw your glo - ry fill the sa - cred house of prayer.
While, in - spired by your own Spir - it, po - et and com - pos - er wrought.
All our powers to glo - ri - fy you, and in serv-ing ful - ly live.

Albert Bayly, a British shipbuilder and, later, minister of the
United Reformed Church, was an outstanding twentieth-century
hymnwriter. He also produced books of verse, missionary pageants,
and librettos for some of W. L. Lloyd Webber's cantatas.

Tune: OFFERING 8.7.8.7.D.
Jean Slates Hawk, 1991
Alternate tune: WEISSE FLAGGEN

Lord, I Want To Be a Christian

454

African-American spiritual

Deut. 6:5–6; 10:12–16

1 Lord, I want to be a Chris-tian in my heart, in my heart;
2 Lord, I want to be more lov - ing in my heart, in my heart,
3 Lord, I want to be more ho - ly in my heart, in my heart;
4 Lord, I want to be like Je - sus in my heart, in my heart;

Lord, I want to be a Chris-tian in my heart.
Lord, I want to be more lov - ing in my heart.
Lord, I want to be more ho - ly in my heart.
Lord, I want to be like Je - sus in my heart.

Refrain

In my heart, in my heart,
In my heart, in my heart,

Lord, I want to be a Chris-tian in my heart.
Lord, I want to be more lov - ing in my heart.
Lord, I want to be more ho - ly in my heart.
Lord, I want to be like Je - sus in my heart.

Many of the enslaved of antebellum America did not want to become Christians because they did not want to adopt the religion of their captors. But this spiritual attests that the Christian faith was an internal strength and aim for many.

Tune: I WANT TO BE A CHRISTIAN
8.6.8.3. with refrain
African-American spiritual
Arr. Joyce Finch Johnson, 1992

455

I Am Yours, O Lord

Ps. 119:94

Fanny Crosby, 1874; alt.

1 I am yours, O Lord, I have heard your voice, and it
2 O the pure de - light of a sin - gle hour that be -
3 Con - se - crate me now to your ho - ly work by the
4 There are depths of love that I can - not know till I

told your love to me; But I long to rise in the
fore your throne I spend, When I kneel in prayer, and with
power of grace di - vine; Let my soul look up with a
cross the nar - row sea; There are heights of joy that I

Refrain

arms of faith, drawn to you e - ter - nal - ly.
you, my God, I com - mune as friend with friend!
stead - fast hope; let your will be done, not mine.
may not reach till I rest e - ter - nal - ly.

Draw me

near - er, near - er, bless-ed Lord, to the cross where you have died;
near - er, near - er

Fanny Crosby, blind from infancy, wrote more than 8,500 gospel hymns. On a speaking tour, she composed this hymn while she was a guest in the Cincinnati home of William Doane, a wealthy manufacturer, amateur musician, and gospel songwriter.

Tune: I AM YOURS 10.7.10.7. with refrain
William H. Doane, 1874

Draw me near-er, near-er, near-er, bless-ed Lord, to your pre-cious, bleed-ing side.

More Love to You, O Christ 456

Elizabeth P. Prentiss, c. 1856; alt.

1 More love to you, O Christ, more love to you! Hear now the
2 Once earth-ly joy I craved, sought peace and rest; Now you a-
3 Then shall my lat-est breath whis-per your praise; This be the

Refrain

prayer I make faith to re - new.
lone I seek, give what is best: In all I say and do,
part - ing cry my heart shall raise:

more love, O Christ, to you, more love to you, more love to you!

Elizabeth Prentiss, a teacher and author of numerous books, wrote this hymn at a time of grief and physical illness. It was published some fifteen years later, together with William H. Doane's tune.

Tune: MORE LOVE TO YOU 6.4.6.4.6.6.4.4.
William H. Doane, 1870

457

Jesus, I Live to You

Rom. 14:8; Phil. 1:21

Henry Harbaugh, c. 1850; alt.

1 Je - sus, I live to you, the love - li - est and best;
2 Je - sus, I die to you, when - ev - er death shall come;
3 Wheth - er to live or die, I know not which is best;
4 Liv - ing or dy - ing, Lord, I ask to be your own;

My life will be your life in me, in your blessed love I rest.
Un - ceas - ing - ly, you'll live in me in my e - ter - nal home.
To live will be your bliss in me, to die is end - less rest.
My life will be your life in me, and heaven on earth be known.

This is the most famous of all hymns from the German Reformed tradition of the United Church of Christ. Henry Harbaugh, a noted educator and clergyman, was associated with institutions that became Franklin and Marshall College, Lancaster Theological Seminary, and The Mercersberg Academy.

Tune: LAKE ENON S.M.
Isaac B. Woodbury, 1856

458

I've Got a Feeling

In a relaxed, "swing" style

African-American traditional; alt.

Leader (Unison)

1 I've got a feel - ing, ev - ery -

Leader (Unison)

2 Je - sus al - read - y told me, ev - ery -
3 The Spir - it has con - firmed it, ev - ery -

All (Harmony; see st. 2–3)

thing is gon-na be all right. O .... I've got a

All (Harmony)

thing is gon-na be all right. O .... Je - sus al - read-y
thing is gon-na be all right. O the Spir - it has con -

feel - ing, ev - ery - thing is gon-na be all right. O ....

told me, ev - ery - thing is gon-na be all right. O ....
firmed it, ev - ery - thing is gon-na be all right. O the

I've got a feel - ing, ev - ery - thing is gon-na be all right,

Je - sus al - read-y told me, ev - ery - thing is gon-na be all right,
Spir - it has con - firmed it, ev - ery - thing is gon-na be all right,

(1–3) be all right, be all right, be all right.

This traditional song is often sung in churches that have a devotional service prior to the worship service. A worshiper might raise this song to encourage another whose testimony indicated he or she is going through difficult times.

Tune: I'VE GOT A FEELING Irr.
African-American traditional
Arr. Jeffrey Radford, 1993

459   Come, O Fount of Every Blessing

Robert Robinson, 1758; alt.

Ps. 36:7–9

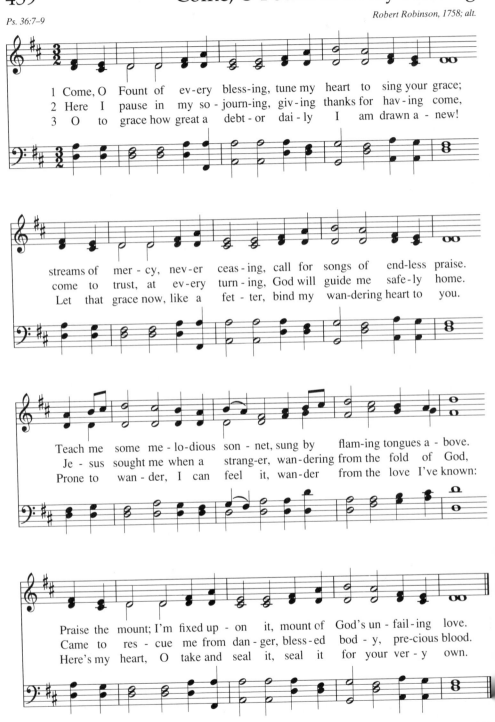

1 Come, O Fount of ev-ery bless-ing, tune my heart to sing your grace;
2 Here I pause in my so-journ-ing, giv-ing thanks for hav-ing come,
3 O to grace how great a debt-or dai-ly I am drawn a-new!

streams of mer-cy, nev-er ceas-ing, call for songs of end-less praise.
come to trust, at ev-ery turn-ing, God will guide me safe-ly home.
Let that grace now, like a fet-ter, bind my wan-dering heart to you.

Teach me some me-lo-dious son-net, sung by flam-ing tongues a-bove.
Je-sus sought me when a strang-er, wan-dering from the fold of God,
Prone to wan-der, I can feel it, wan-der from the love I've known:

Praise the mount; I'm fixed up-on it, mount of God's un-fail-ing love.
Came to res-cue me from dan-ger, bless-ed bod-y, pre-cious blood.
Here's my heart, O take and seal it, seal it for your ver-y own.

*Converted to Methodism at age twenty, Robert Robinson soon
became a Calvinistic Methodist preacher and later gained great
popularity. The melody, associated with this text since 1813, is
an American folk tune.*

Tune: NETTLETON 8.7.8.7.D
John Wyeth's Repository of Sacred Music, 1813

Be Not Dismayed
(God Will Take Care of You)

460

Civilla D. Martin, 1904; alt.

Ps. 91

1 Be not dis-mayed what-e'er be - tide, God will take care of you;
2 Through days of toil when heart grows frail, God will take care of you;
3 All you may need God will pro - vide, God will take care of you;
4 No mat - ter what may be the test, God will take care of you;

Be - neath God's wings of love a - bide, God will take care of you.
When dan - gers fierce your path as - sail, God will take care of you.
Noth - ing you ask will be de - nied, God will take care of you.
Lean, wea - ry one, up - on God's breast, God will take care of you.

Refrain

God will take care of you, through ev - ery day, o'er all the way;

God will take care of you, God will take care of you.
take care of you

This early hymn by Civilla Martin was written in 1904 and set to music by her husband, a Baptist minister, as a contribution to a songbook he was compiling for a school. This is one of several such collaborations.

Tune: MARTIN C.M. with refrain
W. Stillman Martin, 1905

461   Let Us Hope when Hope Seems Hopeless

Ps. 126:5–6; Rom. 4:18; 1 Cor. 13   David Beebe, 1989

1 Let us hope when hope seems hope - less, when the
2 Faith and hope in love's com - pas - sion will sur -
3 Like a child out - grow - ing child - hood, set - ting

dreams we dreamed have died. When the morn - ing
vive though knowl - edge cease, though the tongues of
child - hood things a - way, we will learn to

breaks in bright - ness, hun - ger shall be sat - is - fied.
joy fall si - lent, dull the words of proph - e - cies.
live in free - dom, in the life of God's new day.

Emma Lou Diemer, organist since the age of thirteen, studied
composition at Yale University and Eastman School of Music,
and has published orchestra, chamber, choral, and organ works.
David Beebe wrote this text while teaching a course on creative
writing. A minister of the United Church of Christ, Beebe has
served on the staff of the denomination's Stewardship Council.

Tune: LET US HOPE 8.7.8.7.D.
Emma Lou Diemer, 1994
Alternate tune: *HYFRYDOL*

One who sows the fields with weep - ing shall re - trace the
Faith shall see and trust its ob - ject; hope shall set its
Now we see as in a mir - ror. Then we shall see

sor-row - ing way and re - joice in har - vest
an - chor sure; love shall bloom in Love e -
face to face, un - der - stand how love's com -

boun - ty at the break - ing of the day.
ter - nal. Faith and hope and love en - dure.
pas - sion blos - soms through a - maz - ing Grace.

462 Creating God, Your Fingers Trace

Ps. 148   *Jeffery Rowthorn, 1979*

1 Cre - at - ing God, your fin - gers trace the bold de - signs of
2 Sus-tain - ing God, your hands up - hold earth's mys-teries known or
3 Re-deem-ing God, your arms em-brace all now de - spised for
4 In-dwell-ing God, your gos - pel claims one fam - ily with a

far - thest space; . . . . . Let sun and moon and stars and light
yet un - told; . . . . . . Let wa - ter's frag - ile blend with air,
creed or race; . . . . . . Let peace, de - scend - ing like a dove,
bil - lion names; . . . . . Let ev - ery life be touched by grace

and what lies hid - den praise . . . . your might.
en - a - bling life, pro - claim . . . . your care.
make known on earth your heal - ing love.
un - til we praise you face . . . . to face.

Jeffery Rowthorn's paraphrase of Psalm 148 was one of two winning texts in the 1979 Hymn Society competition seeking "New Psalms for Today." It is set to the first published tune by composer Eugene Hancock and appears in The Presbyterian Hymnal, 1990.

Tune: HANCOCK L.M.
Eugene W. Hancock, 1989
Alternate tunes: *DEO GRACIAS,*
DICKINSON COLLEGE

I Look to You in Every Need

Samuel Longfellow, 1864; alt.

1 I look to you in ev - ery need, and nev - er look in vain; I
2 Dis - cour-aged in the work of life, dis - heart-ened by its load, Shamed
3 Se - rene and calm, you cir - cle me, my rest - less - ness to still; A -
4 En - fold - ed deep in your dear love, held in your law, I stand; Your

feel your strong and ten - der love, and all is well a - gain: The
by its fail - ures or its fears, I sink be - side the road; But
round me flows your quick-ening life, to nerve my fal-tering will: Your
hand in all things I be - hold, and all things in your hand; You

thought of you is might-ier far than sin and pain and sor - row are.
let me on - ly think of you and all my strength re - turns a - new.
pres - ence fills my sol - i - tude; your prov - i - dence turns all to good.
lead me in sur - pris - ing ways, and turn my mourn-ing in - to praise.

Samuel Longfellow—poet, hymnwriter, and Unitarian minister—was the brother of Henry Wadsworth Longfellow. The German organist Reimann was a contemporary of J. S. Bach and traveled to Leipzig to hear Bach perform.

Tune: O JESU 8.6.8.6.8.8.
Reimann's Sammlung Alter und Neuer
Melodien, *1747*

464

The Weaver's Shuttle Swiftly Flies

Job 7:6

James Gertmenian, 1990

1 The weav-er's shut-tle swift-ly flies a-cross the tap-es-
2 The Weav-er's shut-tle swift-ly flies a-cross the earth-ly
3 Who knows the pat-terns of our lives be-fore our days are
4 When will we find the true de-sign in-tend-ed for our
5 O gen-tle Weav-er, lov-ing God, we are your works of

try; then pat-terns, tex-tures, var-ied hues e-merge for
loom. Our sto-ries all too quick-ly pass from cra-dle
spun? Who knows the rea-son why, and how, be-fore it's
days? In heaven to come, when life is done and noth-ing's
art, and so we see e-ter-ni-ty with-in each

all to see. And so our lives are wo-ven fine as
to the tomb. Day fol-lows day and year on year; they
all be-gun? The One whose hand weaves all with love and
left but praise? Or shall we see in glimps-es now the
hu-man heart. In all we think and do and say, in

Developing an image from Job 7:6, United Church of Christ
minister James Gertmenian reminds us of the swift passage of
our days and invites us to seek glimpses of God, the Eternal
Weaver, in them.

Tune: ST. MATTHEW C.M.D.
William Croft, 1708

in that weav - er's hand, a fair de - sign and
fade as in a dream. And none can hold the
mys - ter - y and care; The One whose thread and
pat - tern God re - veals, and here em - brace this
all we hope and fear, give us the eyes to

rich - er still than we can un - der - stand.
shut - tle still or stop the flow - ing stream.
warp and weft are flesh and earth and air!
earth - ly race that wounds us and that heals?
rec - og - nize the heav - en al - ways here.

465   Teach Me, O Lord, Your Holy Way

William Matson, 1866; alt.

1 Teach me, O Lord, your ho-ly way, and give me an o-be-dient mind, That in your ser-vice I may find my heart's de-light from day to day.

2 Help me, O Sav-ior, here to trace the sa-cred foot-steps you have trod; and ful-ly trust-ing in my God, to grow in good-ness, truth, and grace.

3 Guard me, O Christ, that I may ne'er for-sake the right, or do the wrong; A-gainst temp-ta-tion make me strong, and keep me in your shel-tering care.

4 Bless me in ev-ery task I face, be-gun, con-tin-ued, done for you; Ful-fill your will in all I do, and grant me your a-bun-dant grace.

*William Matson, English poet and Congregational minister,
wrote a poem of 321 four-line stanzas titled "The Inner Life"
(1866). This hymn of obedience to Christ has been drawn from
that extended poem.*

Tune: ROCKINGHAM L.M.
*Anon
Adapt. Edward Miller, 1790*

Unto the Hills We Lift Our Longing Eyes   466

John Campbell, Duke of Argyll, 1877; alt.   *Ps. 121*

1 Un - to the hills we lift our long - ing eyes with yearn-ing sighs.
2 God will not let our ser - vant feet be moved; safe we will be.
3 God is our keep - er, change-less through the years, a shel - ter strong.
4 From ev - ery e - vil, God will keep our lives, from ev - ery sin.

Who will pro - vide the help we sore - ly need? Who hears our cries?
God will sup - ply, for all our nights and days, se - cu - ri - ty.
God is our shade, pro - tect - ing ev - ery hand, through a - ges long.
God will pre - serve and guard our go - ing out, our com - ing in.

From our Cre - a - tor comes our cer - tain aid.
God does not sleep when we are tak - ing rest.
Sun will not strike or harm through-out the day,
Ev - er a - round, with - in, we will a - dore

Our help is from our God, who all things made.
God's cov - e - nant en - dures through ev - ery test.
Nor moon by night, those liv - ing by God's way.
our God who holds and guides for - ev - er - more.

John Campbell's paraphrase of Psalm 121 was a favorite with
Canadian soldiers during World War II. Campbell, a member of
Parliament, was married to Queen Victoria's daughter, Princess
Louise. For six years he was governor-general of Canada.

Tune: SANDON 10.4.10.4.10.10.
Charles Henry Purday, 1860
For another harmonization, see 366

467   Mothering God, You Gave Me Birth

Gen. 1:1–5; Matt. 26:26–29;   *Jean Janzen, 1991*
Mark 14:22–25; Luke 22:15–20   *Based on the writings of Julian of Norwich*

1 Moth - er - ing God, you gave me birth in the bright
2 Moth - er - ing Christ, you took my form, of - fer - ing
3 Moth - er - ing Spir - it, nur - turing One, in arms of

morn - ing of this world. Cre - a - tor,
me your food of light, Grain . . . of
pa - tience hold me close, So that in

Source of ev - ery breath, you are my rain, my wind, my
life, and grape of love, your ver - y bod - y for my
faith I root and grow un - til I flower, un - til I

In the late fourteenth century in Norwich, England, a
well-educated Christian woman, Julian of Norwich, devoted her
life to God through the study and contemplation of scripture.
This hymn by Jean Janzen is based on some of the ideas from
Julian's important theological treatise, Showings.

Tune: ANDREW 8.8.8.8.8
Jonathan McNair, 1994

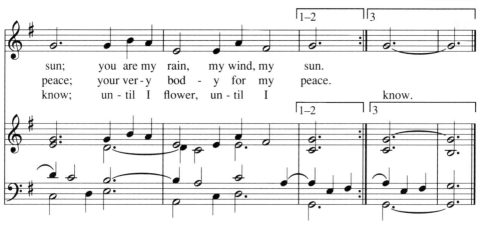

	1–2		3

sun;   you are my rain,   my wind, my   sun.
peace;   your ver - y bod - y for my   peace.
know;   un - til I flower, un - til I   know.

The Care the Eagle Gives Her Young   468

R. Deane Postlethwaite, 1980   Deut. 32:11–12a; Exod. 19:4

1 The care the ea - gle gives her young, safe in   her
2 As when the time to ven - ture comes, she stirs them
3 And if we flut - ter help - less - ly, as fledg - ling

loft - y nest, Is like the ten - der
out to flight, So we are pressed to
ea - gles fall, Be - neath us lift God's

love of God for us made man - i - fest.
bold - ly try, to strive for dar - ing height.
might - y wings to bear us, one and all.

This text was originally titled "For a Recognition of God's Feminine Attributes." The author explains: "I find a deep meaning and power in the image of a God who, like a mother eagle, pushes me from her nest, but who catches me, bears me up, when I fall."

Tune: CRIMOND C.M.
Jesse Seymour Irvine, 1872
Harm. T. C. L. Pritchard, 1929

469

O Grant Us Light

Ps. 43:3

Lawrence Tuttiett, 1864; alt.

1 O grant us light, that we may know wis-dom that you a -
2 O grant us light that we may find where er - ror lurks in
3 O grant us light, that we may learn how dead is life from
4 O grant us light, when soon or late, all earth-ly scenes shall

lone can give, That truth may guide us as we go,
hu - man lore, And turn to you our seek - ing minds,
you a - part, How sure is joy for all who turn
pass a - way, In you to find the o - pen gate,

and vir - tue bless the lives we live.
and love your ho - ly Word the more.
to you an un - di - vid - ed heart.
to death - less home and end - less day.

Ordained a priest of the Church of England, Lawrence Tuttiett
served a parish at Warwickshire. His last two appointments were
in Scotland. Henry W. Baker, an important English hymnal
editor, wrote this tune while an undergraduate at Oxford.

Tune: HESPERUS L.M.
(QUEBEC)
Henry W. Baker, 1854

Golden Breaks the Dawn

470

Tzu-chen Chao (b. 1888)
Paraphr. by Frank W. Price (b. 1895); alt.

Ps. 50:1–2; Matt. 6:11–12

1 Gold-en breaks the dawn, comes the east-ern sun
2 Give me dai - ly bread, while I do my part;

o - ver lake and lawn, new day has be - gun.
bright skies o - ver - head, glad - ness in my heart.

Birds a - bove me fly, flow-ers bloom be - low;
Sim-ple wants pro - vide, e - vil let me shun;

through the earth and sky God's great mer-cies flow.
Je - sus at my side, till the day is done.

Tzu-chen Chao was a prominent Chinese Christian leader, theologian, and dean of the School of Religion of Yenching University. He was elected one of the first vice presidents of the World Council of Churches at its inaugural meeting in 1948.

Tune: LE P'ING 10.10.10.10.
Chinese folk tune; adapt. Te-ngai Hu
Harm. Bliss Wiant, 1936

471

What a Covenant

Deut. 33:27

Elisha A. Hoffman, 1887; alt.

1 What a *cov-e-nant, what a joy di-vine, lean-ing on the ev-er-
2 Oh, how sweet to walk in this pil-grim way, lean-ing on the ev-er-
3 What have I to dread, what have I to fear, lean-ing on the ev-er-

last-ing arms. What a bless-ed-ness, what a peace is mine, lean-ing
last-ing arms. Oh, how bright the path grows from day to day, lean-ing
last-ing arms? I have bless-ed peace with my Sav-ior near, lean-ing

Refrain

on the ev-er-last-ing arms.
on the ev-er-last-ing arms. Lean-ing, lean-ing, safe and se-cure from
on the ev-er-last-ing arms.

all a-larms; lean-ing, lean-ing, lean-ing on the ev-er-last-ing arms.

Or, "fellowship"

*In a letter to two grieving friends, A. J. Showalter quoted
Deuteronomy 33:27, " . . . underneath are the everlasting arms."
Showalter then wrote this music and the refrain and sent them to
E. A. Hoffman to provide the stanzas.*

Tune: LEANING 5.5.9.D. with refrai
Anthony J. Showalter, 188

Precious Lord, Take My Hand

472

Thomas A. Dorsey, 1932; alt.

1 Pre - cious Lord, take my hand, lead me on, let me stand,
2 When my way grows drear, pre-cious Lord, lin - ger near,
3 When the shad - ows ap - pear and the night draws near,

I am tired, I am weak, I am worn;
when my life is al - most gone,
and the day is past and gone,

Through the storm, through the night, lead me on to the light:
Hear me cry, hear my call, hold my hand, lest I fall:
At the riv - er I stand, guide my feet, hold my hand:

Refrain

Take my hand, pre - cious Lord, lead me home.

Thomas A. Dorsey was known as "Georgia Tom" when he played piano for blues singer Ma Rainey. He started writing gospel songs after what he called "a definite spiritual change." This inspirational song, composed following the deaths of his wife, Nettie, and a newborn child, derives from the tune Maitland.

Tune: PRECIOUS LORD Irr. with refrain
Thomas A. Dorsey, 1932

473 Blessed Assurance

Acts 17:30–31; Rev. 7:9–14   *Fanny Crosby, 1873; alt.*

1 Bless-ed as - sur - ance, Je - sus is mine! O what a
2 Per - fect sub - mis - sion, per - fect de - light! Vi - sions of
3 Per - fect sub - mis - sion, all is at rest, I in my

fore - taste of glo - ry di - vine! Heir of sal - va - tion, pur - chase of
rap - ture now burst on my sight; An - gels de - scend-ing, bring from a -
Sav - ior am hap - py and blessed; Watch-ing and wait - ing, look - ing a -

God, born of the Spir - it, washed in Christ's blood.
bove ech - oes of mer - cy, whis - pers of love.
bove, filled with God's good - ness, lost in Christ's love.

Refrain

This is my sto - ry, this is my song, prais-ing my Sav - ior all the day long;

After hearing Phoebe Knapp play this tune on the piano, Fanny
Crosby composed the poem on the spot. In her almost 95 years,
Crosby wrote more than 8,500 gospel hymns and songs.

Tune: ASSURANCE Irr.
Phoebe P. Knapp, 1873

This is my sto - ry, this is my song, prais-ing my Sav-ior all the day long.

I'm So Glad, Jesus Lifted Me

African-American spiritual

474

1 I'm so glad, Je-sus lift-ed me, I'm so glad,
2 Sa - tan had me bound, Je-sus lift-ed me, Sa - tan had me bound,
3 When I was in trou - ble, Je-sus lift-ed me, when I was in trou - ble,

Je - sus lift - ed me, I'm so glad,
Je - sus lift - ed me, Sa - tan had me bound,
Je - sus lift - ed me, when I was in trou - ble,

Je-sus lift-ed me, sing-ing glo-ry, hal - le - lu - jah, Je-sus lift-ed me.

Just as the spirituals were adapted to be sung in a folk-song style during the 1960s music festivals and civil rights marches, so have they been adapted in a gospel style. This is a spiritual that especially lends itself to gospel rendering.

Tune: I'M SO GLAD Irr.
African-American spiritual

475 God's Eye Is on the Sparrow

Matt. 10:26–30; Luke 12:4–7 *Civilla D. Martin, c. 1905; alt.*

Stanzas, in unison

1 Why should I feel dis-cour-aged, why should the shad-ows come,
2 "Let not your heart be trou-bled," Christ's ten-der word I hear,
3 When-ev-er I am tempt-ed, when-ev-er clouds a-rise,

Why should my heart be lone-ly and long for heaven and
And rest-ing on God's good-ness, I lose my doubts and
When song gives place to sigh-ing, when hope with-in me

home, When God is ev-er my por-tion? My
fears; Though by the path . . . God leads me but
dies, I then draw close to my Sav-ior, from

con-stant friend will be: God's eye is on the spar-row, and I
one step I may see: God's eye is on the spar-row, and I
care I am set free: God's eye is on the spar-row, and I

Civilla Martin, a native of Nova Scotia, assisted her husband in his evangelistic campaigns. Charles Gabriel was editor for Rodeheaver Publishing Company, Chicago, and one of the most popular gospel songwriters of the early 1900s.

Tune: SPARROW Irr.
Charles H. Gabriel, 1905

know God watch-es   me;   God's eye is on   the   spar-row,   and I
know God watch-es   me;   God's eye is on   the   spar-row,   and I
know God watch-es   me;   God's eye is on   the   spar-row,   and I

Refrain, in harmony

know   God watch-es   me.
know   God watch-es   me.   I   sing   be - cause   I'm
know   God watch-es   me.

hap - py,   I   sing   be - cause   I'm   free,   God's
I'm   hap - py,   I'm   free,

eye   is   on   the   spar - row,   and I   know God watch-es   me.

476 My Life Flows on in Endless Song
(How Can I Keep from Singing)

Ps. 46:1–7; 1 Cor. 3:21–23; 2 Cor. 5:17

Anon. in Bright Jewels for the Sunday School,
ed. Robert Lowry, 1869; alt.
St. 3, Doris Plenn, c. 1957

1 My life flows on in end-less song; a-bove earth's lam-en-
2 What though my joys and com-forts die? My Sav-ior still is
3 When ty-rants trem-ble, sick with fear, and hear their death knells
4 I lift my eyes; the cloud grows thin; I see the blue a-

ta-tion, I hear the sweet, though far-off hymn that
liv-ing. What though the shad-ows gath-er 'round? A
ring-ing; When friends re-joice both far and near, how
bove it; And day by day this path-way smooths, since

hails a new cre-a-tion. Through all the tu-mult
new song Christ is giv-ing. No storm can shake my
can I keep from sing-ing? In pris-on cell and
first I learned to love it. The peace of Christ makes

and the strife, I hear the mu-sic ring-ing; It
in-most calm, while to that Rock I'm cling-ing; Since
dun-geon vile, our thoughts to them are wing-ing; When
fresh my heart, a foun-tain ev-er spring-ing; All

In various nineteenth-century hymnals this hymn was attributed to different poets, including Anna Warner. The earliest published source credits Robert Lowry as the composer, although Silas Vail later claimed the music. The third stanza was written by Doris Plenn in the 1950s when her friends were imprisoned during the McCarthy era.

Tune: ENDLESS SONG 8.7.8.7.D.
Attrib. to Robert Lowry in Bright Jewels
for the Sunday School, *New York, 1869*

finds an ech - o in my soul— how can I keep from sing-ing?
Love com-mands both heaven and earth, how can I keep from sing-ing?
friends by shame are un - de - filed, how can I keep from sing-ing?
things are mine since I am Christ's— how can I keep from sing-ing?

Though Falsely Some Revile or Hate Me 477

1 Kings 17:1–16; Matt. 28:20

Chi-pi Ni, 1929
Transl. Frank W. Price; alt.

1 Though false - ly some re - vile or hate me, friends for-sake me, too,
2 My path may be hedged up with briars, fierce foes my life sur - round;
3 Though parched my pas-ture - land be - come and fears of fam-ine haunt,
4 The brook of Cher-ith may dry up, the rav - ens hun-gry cry,
5 In ev - ery cir-cum-stance of life God's pow - er will pre - vail;

I will re - mem-ber Christ's own word: "I'll al - ways be with you."
God's mer - cy is for - ev - er sure, it makes God's love a - bound.
My Shep-herd leads me all the way; I shall not suf - fer want.
The Shep-herd will God's ser - vants feed, their ev - ery need sup - ply.
The jar of meal and cruse of oil will nev - er, nev - er fail.

With echoes of the psalms and a direct reference to 1 Kings 17,
this moving hymn from the East Asia Christian Council hymnal
blends imagery from both the Hebrew Scriptures and the New
Testament, assuring us of God's eternal presence and provision.

Tune: THE BROOK CHERITH C.M.
Maryette H. Lum, 1936

478 I've Got Peace Like a River

Isa. 66:12; 1 Pet. 1:8–9; 1 John 4:7–12

African-American spiritual

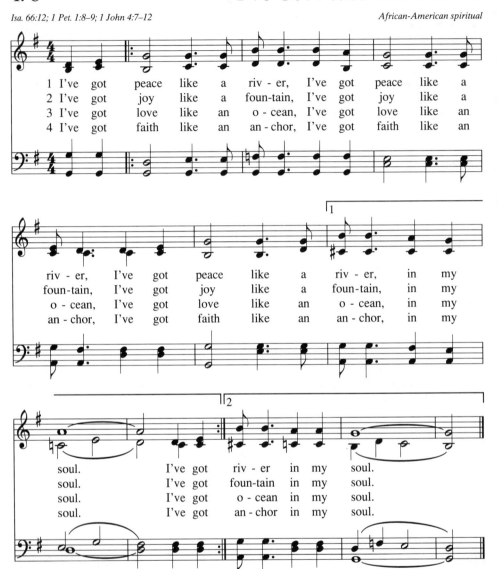

1 I've got peace like a riv-er, I've got peace like a
2 I've got joy like a foun-tain, I've got joy like a
3 I've got love like an o-cean, I've got love like an
4 I've got faith like an an-chor, I've got faith like an

1

riv-er, I've got peace like a riv-er, in my
foun-tain, I've got joy like a foun-tain, in my
o-cean, I've got love like an o-cean, in my
an-chor, I've got faith like an an-chor, in my

2

soul. I've got riv-er in my soul.
soul. I've got foun-tain in my soul.
soul. I've got o-cean in my soul.
soul. I've got an-chor in my soul.

Congregations or individuals may wish to add additional verses of their own making.

Most of the spirituals that drew from biblical stories and images used the Hebrew scriptures, rather than the New Testament, as their inspiration. The imagery of "peace like a river" derives from the book of Isaiah.

Tune: PEACE LIKE A RIVER 7.7.10.D.
African-American spiritual

God Is My Shepherd 479

Scottish Psalter, *1650*
Adapt. Lavon Bayler, 1992

Ps. 23

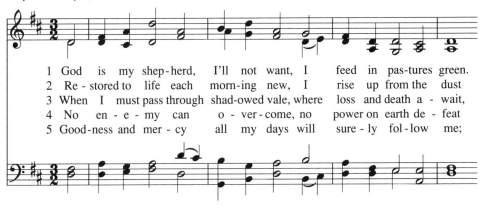

1 God is my shep-herd, I'll not want, I feed in pas-tures green.
2 Re - stored to life each morn-ing new, I rise up from the dust
3 When I must pass through shad-owed vale, where loss and death a - wait,
4 No en - e - my can o - ver - come, no power on earth de - feat
5 Good-ness and mer - cy all my days will sure - ly fol - low me;

God grants me rest and bids me drink from wa - ters calm and clean.
to fol - low God whose pres - ence gives me con - fi - dence and trust.
I will not fear for God is there, my shep-herd strong and great,
the ones a - noint - ed by God's grace and fed with man - na sweet.
and where God reigns in heaven and earth, my dwell-ing place will be.

Through dai - ly tasks, I'm blessed and led by One I have not seen.
I praise the name of God to - day; in God I put my trust.
Whose rod and staff will com - fort me and all my fears a - bate.
My cup is filled and o - ver-flows as I my Sav - ior greet.
My shep-herd bless - es, cares, and leads through all e - ter - ni - ty.

The Scottish Psalter of 1650, developed over a span of 100 years, is still in use today. Its metrical version of Psalm 23 is the most popular entry in this classic work of Protestantism.

Tune: BROTHER JAMES' AIR 8.6.8.6.8.6.
James Leith Macbeth Bain, c. 1840–1925
Arr. Gordon Jacob, 1934

Arrangement Copyright © 1934, Oxford University Press.

480   Jesus, Priceless Treasure

John 15:15; 1 Pet. 1:19

Johann Franck, 1653
Trans. Catherine Winkworth, 1863; alt.

1 Je - sus, price - less trea - sure, source of pur - est plea - sure,
2 Let your arms en - fold me: those who try to wound me
3 Ban-ish thoughts of sad - ness, for the source of glad - ness,

friend most sure and true: Long my heart was burn - ing,
can - not reach me here. Though the earth be shak - ing,
Je - sus, en - ters in; Though the clouds may gath - er,

faint - ing much and yearn - ing, thirst-ing af - ter you.
ev - ery heart be quak - ing, Je - sus calms my fear.
those who love the Sav - ior still have peace with - in.

Yours I am, O spot - less Lamb, so will I let
Fires may flash and thun - der crash; yet, though sin and
Though I bear much sor - row here, still in you lies

A contemporary of German pietist Paul Gerhardt, Johann
Franck was a lawyer and a poet. Modeled on a love song by
Heinrich Albert, "Flora, meine Freude," this hymn has had
many translations, including one in Russian attributed to Peter
the Great in 1724.

Tune: JESU, MEINE FREUDE 6.6.5.6.6.5.7.8.6.
Johann Crüger, 1653
Arr. J. S. Bach (1685–1750)

noth - ing hide   you,   seek no   joy   be - side   you.
hell as - sail   me,   Je - sus   will   not fail   me.
pur - est plea -   sure,   Je - sus   price - less trea - sure!

As Pants the Hart for Cooling Streams 481

A New Version of the Psalms of David,
ed. Nahum Tate and Nicholas Brady, 1696; alt.

Ps. 42

1 As   pants   the   hart   for   cool - ing   streams when
2 Why   rest - less, why   cast   down, my   soul?   Trust
3 God   of   my   strength, how   long   shall   I,   like
4 Why   rest - less, why   cast   down, my   soul?   Hope

heat - ed   in   the   chase, So   longs   my   soul, O
God,   who   will   em - ploy   All   grace   for   you,   and
one   for - got - ten,   mourn,   For - lorn,   for - sak - en,
still, and   you   shall sing   The   praise of   One   who

God,   for   you,   and   your   re - fresh - ing   grace.
change your   sighs   to   thank - ful   hymns   of   joy.
and   ex - posed to   my   op - pres - sor's   scorn?
is   your   God,   your   health's e - ter - nal   spring.

*Both Nahum Tate and Nicholas Brady were Irish. Brady, a
priest, held various posts, including that of royal chaplain. Tate
made his living writing for the state. This is one of the most
enduring paraphrases from their* A New Version of the Psalms
of David. *(A "hart" is a deer.)*

Tune: MARTYRDOM C.M.
(AVON)
Hugh Wilson, 1825

482

I Will Lift the Cloud of Night

Charles P. Jones, 1916; alt.

1 I will lift the cloud of night be - fore you, what is
2 With an ev - er - last - ing love I'll love you, though with
3 Al-though Sa - tan in a rage would tear you, and with
4 I will lift the cloud of night be - fore you, I will

wrong I'll make it right be - fore you, all your bat - tles I will
tri - als I will test and prove you, still there's noth - ing that can
ev - ery win-ning art would snare you, yet from youth to your old
make the crook-ed straight be - fore you, I will spread my wings pro -

fight be - fore you, and the high place I'll bring down.
hurt or move you; and the high place I'll bring down.
age I'll bear you and the high place I'll bring down.
tect - ing o'er you; and the high place I'll bring down.

Refrain

When you walk and lose the way I'll lead you; on the

African-American hymnwriter Charles P. Jones was the founder and
first bishop of the Church of Christ (Holiness) U.S.A. He composed
more than 1,000 gospel hymns, texts and music, which appeared in
numerous hymnbooks Jones published beginning in 1899.

Tune: JONES 10.10.10.7. with refrain
Charles P. Jones, 1916

pro-duce of the land I'll feed you; And a home with-in my heart I'll

deed you; and the high place I'll bring down.

Out of the Depths I Call 483

A New Version of the Psalms of David,
ed. Nahum Tate and Nicholas Brady, 1696; alt.

Ps. 130

1 Out of the depths I call, to God I send my cry: Oh,
2 For you my soul still waits with pa-tience un - de - terred; My
3 My faint-ing spir - it longs for your en - liv - ening ray, More
4 Let Is - rael trust in God, whose mer - cy bound-less grows, The

hear my sup - pli - ca - ting voice and gra - cious-ly re - ply.
hopes are on your prom - ise built, your nev - er - fail - ing word.
ea - ger than the morn - ing watch to greet the dawn-ing day.
plen-teous source and spring from whom re - demp-tion ev - er flows.

In seventeenth-century England, the "old" Sternhold and Hopkins psalter was being displaced by the "new" Tate and Brady version, while in America, the Bay Psalm Book was gaining great popularity. All this preceded the outpouring of psalm hymns by the prolific Congregationalist Isaac Watts.

Tune: ST. BRIDE S.M.
Samuel Howard, 1762

484   O Come to Me, You Weary

Matt. 11:28–30; John 6:35–40; 11:25–26   *William C. Dix, 1867; alt.*

1 "O come to me, you wea-ry, and I will give you rest."
2 "O come to me, you wan-derers, and I will give you light."
3 "O come to me, you faint-ing, and I will give you life!"
4 "All you who come and seek me will nev-er be cast out."

The bless-ed voice of Je-sus, which comes to hearts op-pressed!
The lov-ing voice of Je-sus, which comes to cheer the night!
The cheer-ing voice of Je-sus, which stills our in-ner strife!
The wel-come voice of Je-sus, which drives a-way our doubt!

It tells of ben-e-dic-tion, of par-don, grace, and peace,
Our hearts were filled with sad-ness, and we had lost our way;
The e-vil one sur-rounds us and would our faith sub-due,
And though we are un-wor-thy of love so free and true,

of joy that has no end-ing, of love which does not cease.
but morn-ing brings us glad-ness and songs for each new day.
but you are strong with-in us, our cour-age brave and true.
we hear your call to sin-ners; in trust we come to you.

William C. Dix, manager of a marine insurance company, wrote this hymn after many weeks of illness. Shortly thereafter, he began to recover. William Lloyd, a Welsh farmer and cattle drover, had a good voice and conducted singing classes.

Tune: MEIRIONYDD 7.6.7.6.D.
Welsh hymn tune
Attrib. to William Lloyd, 1840

O Love That Will Not Let Me Go 485

George Matheson, 1882; alt.   *Rom. 8:38–39; John 8:12*

1 O Love that will not let me go,
2 O Light that fol - lows all my way,
3 O Joy that seeks me through my pain,
4 O Cross that rais - es up my head,

I rest my wea - ry soul in you;
to you I yield my flick - ering flame;
to you I can - not close my heart;
from you I dare not seek to flee;

I give you back the life I owe, that
Re - new my spir - it's fee - ble ray, that
I trace the rain - bow through the rain, and
Life's glo - ries with - er and are dead, but

in your o - cean depths its flow may swell with ar - dor true.
from your bril - liant sun - lit day it may new bright - ness claim.
know the prom - ise is not vain that you will ne'er de - part.
from the ground there blos - soms red, life that shall end - less be.

Although he was nearly blind, George Matheson studied for the Church of Scotland ministry, assisted by his sisters, who learned Latin, Greek, and Hebrew to help him. Matheson wrote this hymn in five minutes on June 6, 1882, at his parsonage.

Tune: ST. MARGARET 8.8.8.8.6.
Albert L. Peace, 1885

486

I Must Tell Jesus

Heb. 2:18

Elisha A. Hoffman, 1894; alt.

1 I must tell Je - sus all of my tri - als, I can - not
2 I must tell Je - sus all of my trou - bles, Je - sus my
3 Tempt-ed and tried, I need a great Sav - ior, One who can
4 Oh, how the world to e - vil al - lures me! Oh, how my

bear these bur-dens a - lone; In my dis - tress my Je - sus will
kind, com - pas-sion-ate Friend; If I but ask, my Sav - ior will
help my bur-dens to bear; I must tell Je - sus, I must tell
heart is tempt-ed to sin! I must tell Je - sus, my Friend who

help me, who ev - er loves and cares for God's own.
an - swer, all of my trou - bles quick - ly will end.
Je - sus, who all my cares and sor - rows will share.
helps me o - ver the world the vic - tory to win.

Refrain

I must tell Je - sus! I must tell Je - sus! I can - not

An Evangelical minister, Elisha Hoffman also served the
Evangelical Publications House in Cleveland, Ohio, for eleven
years. This hymn was inspired by a parishioner in Lebanon,
Pennsylvania. Orwigsburg (Pennsylvania) was the place of
Hoffman's birth.

Tune: ORWIGSBURG 10.9.10.9. with refrain
Elisha A. Hoffman, 1894

bear my bur-dens a - lone; I must tell Je - sus! I must tell

Je - sus! Je - sus can help me, Je - sus a - lone.

Surely No One Can Be Safer

487

Lina Sandell, 1855
Transl. The New Century Hymnal, 1994

Rom. 8:38–39

1 Sure - ly no one can be saf - er than God's chil - dren, held in fa - vor,
2 With the flock God is a - bid-ing, heav-en's plen - ty all pro - vid-ing,
3 None shall ev - er meet re - jec-tion, be de - nied God's own pro - tec-tion;
4 Wheth-er tak - ing, wheth-er giv-ing, God a - lone re - mains for - giv-ing,

Not the stars so bright - ly burn-ing, not the birds to nests re - turn-ing.
Rich in mer - cy, nev - er spar-ing, like a fa - ther, gent - ly car - ing.
Has there been a friend who bet - ter knows our hopes, our fears that fet - ter?
And with one true pur - pose ho - ly to pre - serve our wel - fare sole - ly.

Lina Sandell endured many hardships in her early years,
including illness, the death of a child, and the drowning of her
father, who was a Swedish Lutheran pastor. She maintained a
deep piety and strong commitment to mission, and wrote more
than 650 hymns and poems.

Tune: TRYGGARE KAN INGEN VARA L.M.
Swedish folk melody
Harm. Song Book for Sunday School, 1871

488

Be Still, My Soul

Ps. 37:7; Ps. 46:10; 1 Tim. 4:10

Katharina von Schlegel, 1752
Transl. Jane Laurie Borthwick, 1855; alt.

1 Be still, my soul: for God is on your side; bear pa-tient-ly the cross of grief or pain; Leave to your God to or - der and pro - vide; in ev - ery change God faith-ful will re - main. Be still, my soul: your best e - ter - nal

2 Be still, my soul: for God will un - der - take to guide in fu - ture days as in the past. Your hope, your con - fi - dence let noth - ing shake; all now mys - te - rious shall be clear at last. Be still, my soul: the waves and winds still

3 Be still, my soul: the hour will soon be here when we shall be with God whom we a - dore, with dis - ap - point - ment gone, no grief nor fear, sor - row re - placed with joy for - ev - er - more. Be still, my soul: when change and tears are

Little is known about Katharina von Schlegel, the author of twenty-six hymns, except that she seems to have been a member of the duke's court at Cöthen, Germany. The tune is adapted from an orchestral work by Finland's great composer Jean Sibelius.

Tune: FINLANDIA 10.10.10.10.10.10.
Jean Sibelius, 1899
Arr. The Hymnal, 1933

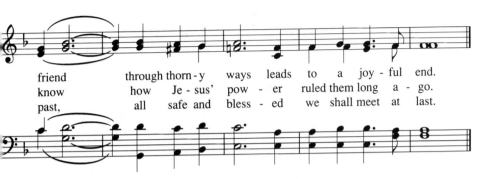

friend	through thorn-y	ways	leads	to	a	joy - ful	end.
know	how	Je - sus'	pow - er	ruled them long	a - go.		
past,	all	safe and	bless - ed	we shall meet	at	last.	

I Heard the Voice of Jesus Say   489

Horatius Bonar, 1846; alt.   *Matt. 11:28–30; John 4:7–15; 8:12*

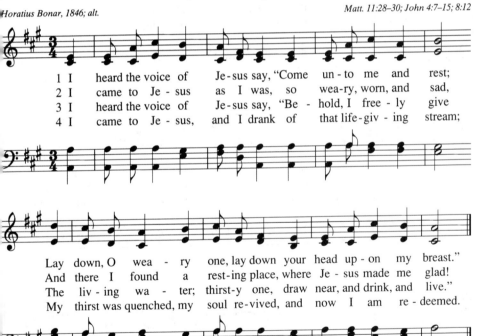

1 I	heard the voice of	Je-sus say, "Come	un - to me and	rest;
2 I	came to Je - sus	as I was, so	wea-ry, worn, and	sad,
3 I	heard the voice of	Je-sus say, "Be -	hold, I free - ly	give
4 I	came to Je - sus,	and I drank of	that life-giv - ing	stream;

Lay down, O wea - ry	one, lay down your head up - on	my breast."
And there I found a	rest-ing place, where Je - sus made me	glad!
The liv - ing wa - ter;	thirst-y one, draw near, and drink, and	live."
My thirst was quenched, my	soul re-vived, and now I am	re - deemed.

5 I heard the voice of Je-sus say,
   "I am this lost world's Light,
   Look un-to me; your morn shall rise,
   and all your day be bright."

6 I looked to Je-sus, and I found
   my guid-ing Star, my Sun;
   And in that light of life I'll go
   till trav-eling days are done.

Horatius Bonar was one of the founders of the Free Church of Scotland. A man of wide scholarship and great devotion to his ministry, he wrote nearly one book a year, as well as some 600 hymns.

Tune: EVAN C.M.
William H. Havergal, 1847
Arr. Lowell Mason, 1850
Alternate tune: KINGSFOLD
(Pair stanzas 1–2, 3–4, 5–6)

490

I Want Jesus to Go with Me

African-American spiritual; al

Unison

1 I want Je - sus to go with me;
2 In my tri - als, O com - fort me;
3 When I'm in trou - ble, O stay with me;

I want Je - sus to go with me;
In my tri - als, O com - fort me;
When I'm in trou - ble, O stay with me;

All a - long my pil - grim jour - ney,
When my heart is al - most break - ing,
When my head is bowed in sor - row,

O I want Je - sus to go with me.
O I want Je - sus to com-fort me.
O I want Je - sus to stay with me.

Most spirituals were congregational songs, but such "sorrow songs" as this convey the image of a lone person singing prayerfully to God. The solemnity of this particular spiritual reminds us of the oppression and tragedy with which slavery afflicted so many lives.

Tune: African-American spiritual 8.8.8.9.
*Harm. J. Jefferson Clevelana
and Verolga Nix, 1981*

Awake, My Soul, Stretch Every Nerve

491

Philip Doddridge (1702–1751); alt.

2 Tim. 4:7–8; Phil. 3:12–14

1 A - wake, my soul, stretch ev - ery nerve, and
2 A cloud of wit - ness - es a - round holds
3 For God's all - an - i - mat - ing voice still
4 O Sav - ior, shown the way by you, I

press with vig - or on; A heaven - ly race de - mands your zeal,
you in full sur - vey; For - get the steps al - read - y trod,
calls us to the race; And God's own hand still gives the prize
have my race be - gun; And, crowned with vic - tory, at your feet

and an im - mor - tal crown, and an im - mor - tal crown.
and on - ward urge your way, and on - ward urge your way.
with nev - er - end - ing grace, with nev - er - end - ing grace.
I'll lay my hon - ors down, I'll lay my hon - ors down.

This hymn is one of more than 400 written by a Congregational minister, Philip Doddridge, but none of them were published in his lifetime. Pressing on in the heavenly race is a theme found in several New Testament passages.

Tune: CHRISTMAS C.M.
G. F. Handel, 1728

492

I Would Be True

Phil. 4:8–9

St. 1, 2, Howard Arnold Walter, 1917
St. 3, anon.; alt.

1 I would be true, for there are those who trust me; I would be
2 I would be friend of all, the foe, the friend-less; I would be
3 I would be prayer-ful through each bus-y mo-ment; I would be

pure, for there are those who care; I would be strong, for
giv-ing, and for-get the gift; I would be hum-ble,
con-stant-ly in touch with God; I would be tuned to

there is much to suf-fer; I would be brave, for
for I know my weak-ness; I would look up, and
sense God's slight-est whis-per; I would have faith to

there is much to dare, I would be brave, for there is much to dare.
laugh, and love, and live, I would look up, and laugh, and love, and live.
keep the path Christ trod, I would have faith to keep the path Christ trod.

The first two stanzas of this hymn are from "My Creed," a poem
that Howard Walter sent to his mother from Japan, where he
taught English before becoming a Congregational minister.
Walter died at the age of thirty-five while working for the
Y.M.C.A. in India.

Tune: PEEK 11.10.11.10.10.
Joseph Y. Peek, 1911

O Jesus, I Have Promised

John E. Bode, 1868; alt.

Luke 9:57; John 14:1–4

1 O Je - sus, I have prom - ised to serve you to the end;
2 O let me hear you speak - ing in ac - cents clear and still,
3 O Je - sus, you have prom - ised to all who fol - low you

re - main for - ev - er near me, my Sav - ior and my Friend:
a - bove the storms of pas - sion, the mur - murs of self - will!
that where you are in glo - ry your ser - vant shall be, too;

I shall not fear life's strug - gles if you are by my side,
O speak to re - as - sure me, to has - ten or con - trol!
And, Je - sus, I have prom - ised to serve you to the end;

nor wan - der from the path - way if you will be my guide.
O speak, and make me lis - ten, O guar - dian of my soul!
O give me grace to fol - low my Sav - ior and my Friend!

John Ernest Bode wrote these words when his daughter and two sons were confirmed. Although the Oxford scholar and rector wrote books of hymns, this is the only one to achieve lasting fame.

Tune: ANGEL'S STORY 7.6.7.6.D.
A. H. Mann, 1883
Alternate tune: MUNICH

494

We Who Would Valiant Be

John Bunyan, 1684; alt

1 We who would val - iant be: let us not wa - ver,
2 Those who may us sur-round with dis - mal sto - ries,
3 Since, Sav - ior, you de - fend us with your Spir - it,

but in true con - stan-cy fol - low the Sav - ior.
on - ly them - selves con-found; our strength the more is.
we know we at the end shall life in - her - it.

There's no dis - cour - age-ment shall make us once re - lent
No foes shall give us fright, ours is the one true Light;
Cruel ru - mors, flee a - way! We'll fear not what they say;

our first a - vowed in - tent to live as pil - grims.
we will make good our right to live as pil - grims.
we'll la - bor night and day to live as pil - grims.

The English author John Bunyan became an influential Congregational and Baptist preacher, for which he was imprisoned for many years. Part One of his Pilgrim's Progress *was written in prison. Lines from* Pilgrim's Progress, *Part Two, have been recast as this hymn.*

Tune: ST. DUNSTAN'S 6.5.6.5.6.6.6.5.
C. Winfred Douglas, 1917

Called as Partners in Christ's Service 495

Jane Parker Huber, 1981

John 15:12–17; Gal. 6:2; Eph. 2:14–22

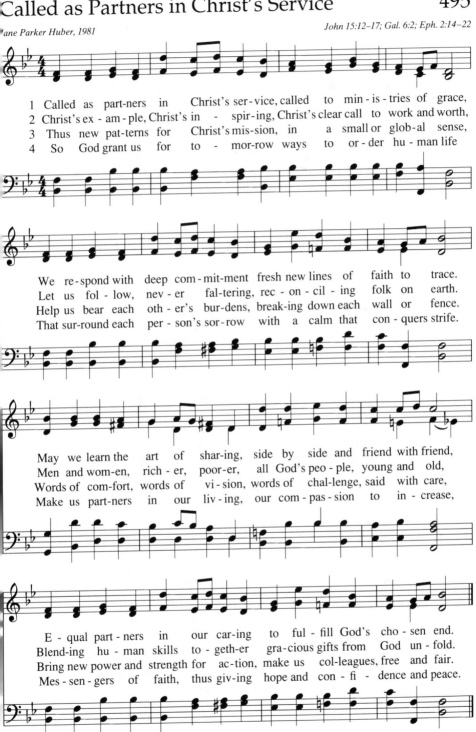

1 Called as part-ners in Christ's ser-vice, called to min - is - tries of grace,
2 Christ's ex - am - ple, Christ's in - spir-ing, Christ's clear call to work and worth,
3 Thus new pat-terns for Christ's mis-sion, in a small or glob-al sense,
4 So God grant us for to - mor-row ways to or - der hu - man life

We re-spond with deep com - mit-ment fresh new lines of faith to trace.
Let us fol - low, nev - er fal-tering, rec - on - cil - ing folk on earth.
Help us bear each oth - er's bur-dens, break-ing down each wall or fence.
That sur-round each per - son's sor-row with a calm that con - quers strife.

May we learn the art of shar-ing, side by side and friend with friend,
Men and wom-en, rich - er, poor-er, all God's peo - ple, young and old,
Words of com-fort, words of vi - sion, words of chal-lenge, said with care,
Make us part-ners in our liv - ing, our com - pas - sion to in - crease,

E - qual part - ners in our car-ing to ful - fill God's cho - sen end.
Blend-ing hu - man skills to - geth-er gra-cious gifts from God un - fold.
Bring new power and strength for ac-tion, make us col-leagues, free and fair.
Mes - sen - gers of faith, thus giv-ing hope and con - fi - dence and peace.

One of Jane Parker Huber's most widely sung texts, this hymn was originally written for a women's breakfast at the 1981 Presbyterian General Assembly meeting to celebrate the partnership of women and men in service of the church.

Tune: BEECHER 8.7.8.7.D.
John Zundel, 1855
For another key, see 43, 368

496

Ekolu Mea Nui
(Three Greatest Things)

1 Cor. 13:13

Robert Nawahine (1868–1951)

1 E - ko-lu me-a nu - i ma ka ho - nu - a,
2 E na ma - ku - a, na ke - i - ki,

ho - nu - a,

O ka ma-na-'o - i - 'o, ka ma-na-'o - la - na,
Na ma-mo a Iu - da me E - pe - lai - ma,

e - pe - lai - ma,

a me ke - a - lo - ha. Ke - a - lo - ha kai oi a - 'e,
E pa'a ka ma - na - 'o i ka po - no i oi a - e.

Po-mai-ka'i na mea a - pau, po-mai-ka'i na mea a - pau.
Po-mai-ka'i na mea a - pau, po-mai-ka'i na mea a - pau.

This translation is not intended to be sung.

1 Three important things in the world, faith, hope, and aloha, aloha is the best, and everything is blessed, and everything is blessed.

2 O parents, children, descendants of Judah and Ephraim, think always that righteousness is best, and everything is blessed, and everything is blessed.

Composed by Robert Nawahine, the "Three Greatest Things" are from 1 Corinthians 13, which ends "And now faith, hope, and love abide, these three; and the greatest of these is love." Nawahine was a leader among the churches of Maui.

Tune: NAWAHINE Irr.
Robert Nawahine (1868–1951)
Arr. Martha Hohu, 1971

Guide My Feet

African-American traditional; alt.

Heb. 12:1–15

1 Guide my feet while I run this race, guide my feet
2 Hold my hand while I run this race, hold my hand
3 I'm your child while I run this race, I'm your child
4 Stand by me while I run this race, stand by me

Yes, my God.

while I run this race, guide my feet while I run this race,
while I run this race, hold my hand while I run this race,
while I run this race, I'm your child while I run this race,
while I run this race, stand by me while I run this race,

Yes, my God.

For I don't want to run this race in vain.

This stanza may be added following stanza 1:
Wheel with me while I run this race . . .

The words and music of some African-American spirituals have been widely adapted during the twentieth century, especially in the civil rights movement of the 1960s. The alternate words were suggested by a fifth-grade church school class to include those who must "run this race" in a wheelchair.

Tune: GUIDE MY FEET 8.8.8.10.
African-American traditional
Arr. Joyce Finch Johnson, 1992

498

Jesu, Jesu, Fill Us with Your Love

John 13:1–20; Gal. 5:13–14

Tom Colvin, 1969; rev. 199

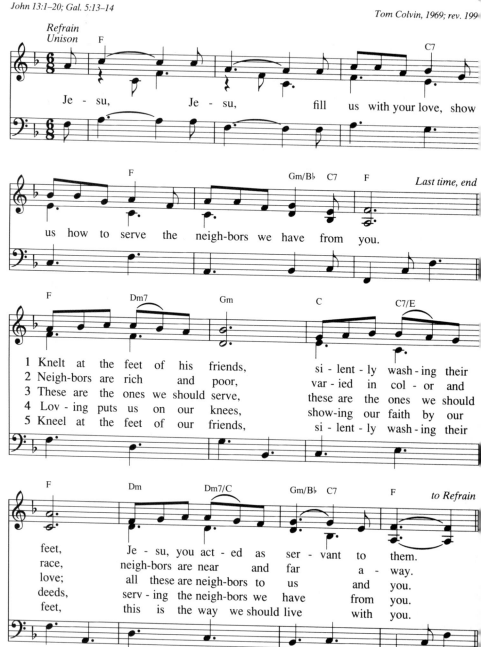

Refrain
Unison

Je - su, Je - su, fill us with your love, show
us how to serve the neigh-bors we have from you.

1 Knelt at the feet of his friends, si - lent - ly wash-ing their
2 Neigh-bors are rich and poor, var - ied in col - or and
3 These are the ones we should serve, these are the ones we should
4 Lov - ing puts us on our knees, show-ing our faith by our
5 Kneel at the feet of our friends, si - lent - ly wash-ing their

feet, Je - su, you act - ed as ser - vant to them.
race, neigh-bors are near and far a - way.
love; all these are neigh-bors to us and you.
deeds, serv - ing the neigh-bors we have from you.
feet, this is the way we should live with you.

This African folk melody was presented to the Church at
Cherenoni, Northern Ghana, by Ghanaian musicologist, A. A.
Mensah, when United Church of Christ missionaries, Al and
Sue Krass were serving there. Like Tom Colvin, a Scottish
missionary in neighboring Tamale, Al Krass was encouraging
the making of hymns to indigenous melodies. Tom Colvin wrote
these words to this adapted form of the melody in dedication to
the Church at Chereponi.

Tune: CHEREPONI Irr. with refrain
Ghanaian folk song; adapt. Tom Colvin, 1969
Arr. Jane Marshall, 1982

Pues si vivimos

499

(In All Our Living)

St. 1, Mexican folk hymn; transl. anon.
St. 2, Elise S. Eslinger, 1983

1 Pues si vi - vi - mos, pa-ra Dios vi - vi - mos
1 In all our liv - ing, we be-long to God;
2 God sent Christ Je - sus to be our sha-lom,

y si mo - ri - mos, pa-ra Dios mo - ri - mos.
and in our dy - ing, we are still with God;
to show us mer - cy and heal - ing love;

Se-a que vi - va - mos o que mu - ra - mos,
So, wheth-er liv - ing, or wheth-er dy - ing,
So in our liv - ing, and in our dy - ing,

so - mos del buen Dios, so - mos del buen Dios.
we be-long to God; we be-long to God.
Christ is our sha - lom; Christ is our sha - lom.

This anonymous Mexican folk hymn was transcribed by hymnologist Gertrude Suppe after she first heard it sung by two church women visiting California from Mexico. It was published in Celebremos II *(1983).*

Tune: PUES SI VIVIMOS Irr.
Anon.; arr. B. C. M., 1988

500   We Are Climbing Jacob's Ladder

Gen. 28:10–17

African-American spiritual

1 We are climb-ing Ja-cob's lad-der, we are climb-ing Ja-cob's lad-der,
2 Ev-ery round goes high-er, high-er, ev-ery round goes high-er, high-er,
3 Rise, shine, give God glo-ry, rise, shine, give God glo-ry,

we are climb-ing Ja-cob's lad-der, bear-ers of the cross.
ev-ery round goes high-er, high-er, bear-ers of the cross.
rise, shine, give God glo-ry, bear-ers of the cross.

Like many spirituals, this one uses a story from the Hebrew scriptures as its starting point and the element of the ladder as a creative device to draw us into the narrative. In like manner, the following twentieth-century adaption of the song by Carole Etzler employs the story of Sarah, the matriarch of the Hebrew people, and extends the direction of the pilgrimage from the upward climb of the ladder to the outward embrace of a circle.

Tune: JACOB'S LADDER 8.8.8.5.
African-American spiritual

501   We Are Dancing Sarah's Circle

Gen. 17:15–19; 18:9–15

Carole A. Etzler, 1975

1 We are danc-ing Sar-ah's cir-cle, . . . sis-ters, broth-ers, all.
2 Here we seek and find our sto-ry, . . . sis-ters, broth-ers, all.
3 We will all do our own nam-ing, . . . sis-ters, broth-ers, all.
4 Ev-ery round a gen-er-a-tion, . . . sis-ters, broth-ers, all.
5 On and on the cir-cle's mov-ing, . . . sis-ters, broth-ers, all.

Tune: JACOB'S LADDER 8.8.8.5.
African-American spiritual

Dear God, Embracing Humankind   502

John Greenleaf Whittier, 1872; alt.   *Mark 1:16–20; Matt. 14:22–23; 1 Kings 19:11–12*

1 Dear God, em-brac-ing hu-man-kind, for-give our fool-ish
2 In sim-ple trust like theirs who heard, be-side the Syr-ian
3 O sab-bath rest by Gal-i-lee! O calm of hills a-
4 Drop your still dews of qui-et-ness, till all our striv-ings
5 Breathe through the puls-es of de-sire your cool-ness and your

ways;   Re-clothe us in our right-ful mind, in
sea,   The gra-cious call-ing of your word, let
bove!   There Je-sus met you prayer-ful-ly: the
cease;   Take from our souls the strain and stress, and
balm;   Let sense be numb, let flesh re-tire; speak

pur-er lives your ser-vice find, in deep-er rev-erence, praise.
us, like them, by spir-it stirred, rise up and fol-lowers be.
si-lence of e-ter-ni-ty, in-ter-pret-ed by love.
let our or-dered lives con-fess the beau-ty of your peace.
through the earth-quake, wind, and fire, O still, small voice of calm.

In his poem "The Brewing of Soma," New England poet John
Greenleaf Whittier compares frenzied ecstasies of a sect of
Hindu priests to the noisy Christian revivals he found so
offensive. This hymn of quiet worship is from the final stanzas.

Tune: REST 8.6.8.8.6.
Frederick C. Maker, 1887
Alternate tune: REPTON
(repeating last phrase)

503 O Savior, Let Me Walk with You

Washington Gladden, 1879; al

1 O Sav - ior, let me walk with you in earth - ly
2 Help me the slow of heart to move by some clear
3 Teach me your pa - tience; let me be in clos - er,
4 In hope that sends a shin - ing ray far down the

paths of ser - vice true; Tell me your se - cret,
win - ning word of love. Teach me the way - ward
dear - er com - pa - ny, In work that keeps faith
fu - ture's broad - ening way, In peace that on - ly

help me bear the strain of toil, the fret of care.
feet to stay, and guide them in the home - ward way.
sweet and strong, in trust that tri - umphs o - ver wrong.
you can give, with you, O Sav - ior, let me live.

Washington Gladden was a Congregational minister,
distinguished preacher and lecturer, and author of over thirty
works. Gladden wrote extensively on civic and social affairs of
his day. This hymn was penned in 1879 and published in his
periodical, The Sunday Afternoon.

Tune: MARYTON L.M
H. Percy Smith, 187

You Walk along Our Shoreline 504

Sylvia G. Dunstan, 1984; alt.

Mark 1:16–20; John 17:20–26

1 You walk a - long our shore - line where land meets un - known sea.
2 You call us, Christ, to gath - er the peo - ple of the earth.
3 We cast our net, O Je - sus; we seek your prom - ised reign;

We hear your voice of pow - er, "Now come and fol - low me. And
We can - not fish for on - ly those lives we think have worth. We
We work for love and jus - tice; we learn to hope through pain. You

if you still will fol - low through storm and wave and shoal,
spread your net of gos - pel a - cross the wa - ter's face,
call on us to gath - er God's daugh - ters and God's sons,

Then I will make you fish - ers, but of the hu - man soul."
Our boat a com - mon shel - ter for all found by your grace.
To let your judg - ment heal us so that all may be one.

Hymnwriter Sylvia Dunstan credited an article by Michael
Steinhauser in the March 1984 issue of *Practice of Ministry*
in Canada *entitled "Fishing: A Metaphor for Ministry" as the
inspiration for her text. Dunstan was an ordained minister of
the United Church of Canada.*

Tune: SALLEY GARDENS 7.6.7.6.D.
Traditional Irish melody
Harm. *The New Century Hymnal, 1994*

Words Copyright © 1991 by G.I.A. Publications, Inc.

505

Sweet Hour of Prayer

William Walford, 1845; alt.

1 Sweet hour of prayer! Sweet hour of prayer! that calls me from a world of care,
2 Sweet hour of prayer! Sweet hour of prayer! the joys I feel, the bliss I share
3 Sweet hour of prayer! Sweet hour of prayer! whose wings shall my pe - ti - tion bear

and bids me at my Ma-ker's throne let all my needs and wants be known.
of those whose anx-ious spir-its burn with strong de-sires for your re-turn!
to One whose truth and faith-ful - ness en - gage the wait - ing soul to bless.

In sea-sons of dis-tress and grief, my soul has of - ten found re - lief,
With them I has-ten to the place where I would know my Sav-ior's face,
And since I'm bid to seek God's face, be-lieve God's word, and trust God's grace,

and oft es-caped the tempt-er's snare by your re - turn, sweet hour of prayer!
And glad - ly take my sta - tion there, and wait for you, sweet hour of prayer!
I'll cast a - way my ev - ery care, and wait for you, sweet hour of prayer!

Although credited to a different poet when first published in 1845, researchers believe this hymn was written by William Walford. William Bradbury, a highly trained musician, sang under Lowell Mason in Boston and also wrote "Jesus Loves Me."

Tune: SWEET HOUR L.M.D.
William B. Bradbury, 1861

What a Friend We Have in Jesus

Joseph Scriven, 1855; alt.

Phil. 4:6–7

1 What a friend we have in Je - sus, all our sins and griefs to bear!
2 Have we tri - als and temp - ta - tions? Is there trou-ble an - y - where?
3 Are we weak and heav-y lad - en, bur-dened with a load of care?

What a priv-i-lege to car - ry ev - ery-thing to God in prayer!
We should nev-er be dis - cour - aged; take it to our God in prayer!
Pre - cious Sav-ior, still our ref - uge, take it to our God in prayer!

Oh, what peace we of - ten for - feit, oh, what need-less pain we bear,
Can we find a friend so faith - ful, who will all our sor-rows share?
Do your friends de-spise, for - sake you? Take it to our God in prayer!

All be - cause we do not car - ry ev - ery-thing to God in prayer.
Je - sus knows our ev - ery weak - ness; take it to our God in prayer!
Je - sus' arms will take and shield you; you will find a sol-ace there.

No stranger to sorrow himself, Joseph Scriven wrote this hymn to comfort his mother in Ireland. Scriven, who moved to Canada as a young man, attempted to follow literally the teachings of the Sermon on the Mount.

Tune: ERIE 8.7.8.7.D.
Charles C. Converse, 1868

507

Jesus—The Very Thought to Me

Phil. 2:1–11; 1 Pet. 1:1–9

Latin, possibly 12th century
Transl. Edward B. Caswall, 1849; alt

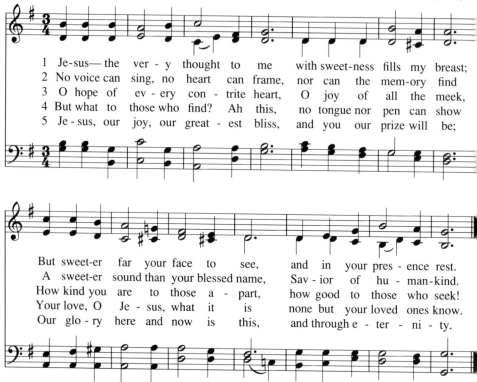

1 Je-sus— the ver - y thought to me with sweet-ness fills my breast;
2 No voice can sing, no heart can frame, nor can the mem-ory find
3 O hope of ev - ery con - trite heart, O joy of all the meek,
4 But what to those who find? Ah this, no tongue nor pen can show
5 Je - sus, our joy, our great - est bliss, and you our prize will be;

But sweet-er far your face to see, and in your pres - ence rest.
A sweet-er sound than your blessed name, Sav - ior of hu - man-kind.
How kind you are to those a - part, how good to those who seek!
Your love, O Je - sus, what it is none but your loved ones know.
Our glo - ry here and now is this, and through e - ter - ni - ty.

"Jesus dulcis memoria" was an anonymous medieval poem originally
forty-two stanzas long. Several hymns have been derived from it,
including this one set to John B. Dykes' tune named for a young
Roman girl, Christian by birth, who was martyred in 304 C.E.

Tune: ST. AGNES C.M.
John B. Dykes, 1866

508

Prayer Is the Soul's Sincere Desire

Luke 11:1; Rom. 8:26–28

James Montgomery, 1818; alt.

1 Prayer is the soul's sin-cere de-sire,
   ut-tered or un-ex-pressed;
   The mo-tion of a hid-den fire
   that trem-bles in the breast.

2 Prayer is the sim-plest form of speech
   that in-fant lips can try;
   Prayer, the sub-lim-est strains that reach
   the Maj-es-ty so nigh.

3 Prayer is the con-trite sin-ner's voice,
   turn-ing from thought-less ways,
   While an-gels in their songs re-joice
   and cry, "Be-hold, one prays!"

4 No prayers do hu-mans make a-lone;
   the Ho-ly Spir-it pleads,
   And Je-sus on the e-ter-nal throne
   for sin-ners in-ter-cedes.

5 O Christ, by whom we come to God,
   the Life, the Truth, the Way,
   The path of prayer you too have trod:
   Christ, teach us how to pray.

This hymn by Moravian journalist and hymnwriter James
Montgomery was written for Edward Bickersteth's Treatise
on Prayer to answer the question, "What is prayer?" The hymn
closes with the disciples' request of Jesus, "Teach us to pray."

Tune: ST. AGNES C.M.
John B. Dykes, 1866

How Deep the Silence of the Soul

Sylvia G. Dunstan, 1989

1 How deep the si - lence of the soul that lives with - in your grace.
2 Like un - seen chimes on mov-ing air, like warm and morn-ing sun,

How full the grat - i - tude of heart in your a - bid - ing place.
Like glad-dening, green - ing, grow-ing things, like trees with blooms be - gun.

What rich se - ren - i - ty is found, what cour - age and re - lease
Such is your pres - ence in our lives, you touch with-out a trace,

when wis - dom teach - es us to seek the gen-tle path to peace.
un - til we turn and find our-selves held fast in your em - brace.

This hymn by Sylvia Dunstan, entitled "Morning Meditation,"
recounts the Canadian writer's experience one February when
she left cold, snowy Toronto to visit her mother in California.
There she enjoyed meditating in the garden that was abloom
with camellias.

Tune: TALLIS' THIRD TUNE C.M.D.
Thomas Tallis, c. 1557
For another key, see 178

510

Grant Us Wisdom to Perceive You

Rae Whitney, 1991; rev. 199

1 Grant us wis-dom to per-ceive you, hearts a-
2 Grant us faith-ful-ness in pray-ing, strength to
3 Grant us dil-i-gence in do-ing, pa-tience
4 Grant us cour-age to pro-claim you; Sav-ior

wak-ened to re-ceive you, minds a-lert to
keep our souls from stray-ing, sense to cease from
when your truth pur-su-ing, ea-ger to re-
of our lives we name you! May our ac-tions

thoughts that grieve you, God of mer-cy, hear us.
dis-o-bey-ing, God of mer-cy, hear us.
ceive re-new-ing, God of mer-cy, hear us.
nev-er shame you; God of mer-cy, hear us.

This text was inspired by a prayer of St. Benedict, the founder of the Benedictine monastic order, c. 529 C.E. Rae Whitney grew up in England, but settled in Nebraska with her American husband in 1960. She is the author of some 300 hymns.

Tune: QUEM PASTORES 8.8.8.6
German carol, 14th century
Harm. Ralph Vaughan Williams, 190

511

I Love My God, Who Heard My Cry

Ps. 116:1–2

Isaac Watts, 1719; alt.

1 I love my God, who heard my cry and pit-ied
2 I love my God, who heard my cry and chased my

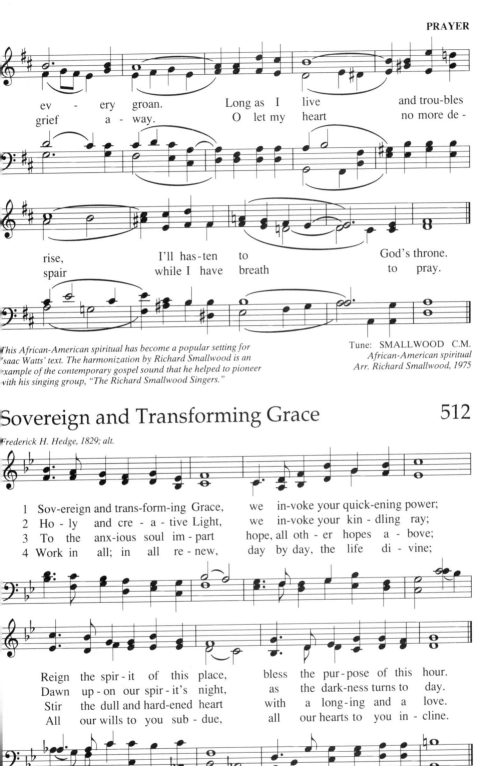

ev - ery groan.   Long as I live   and trou-bles
grief   a - way.   O let my heart   no more de -

rise,   I'll has-ten to   God's throne.
spair   while I have breath   to pray.

This African-American spiritual has become a popular setting for Isaac Watts' text. The harmonization by Richard Smallwood is an example of the contemporary gospel sound that he helped to pioneer with his singing group, "The Richard Smallwood Singers."

Tune: SMALLWOOD C.M.
African-American spiritual
Arr. Richard Smallwood, 1975

Sovereign and Transforming Grace   512

Frederick H. Hedge, 1829; alt.

1 Sov-ereign and trans-form-ing Grace,   we in-voke your quick-ening power;
2 Ho - ly and cre - a - tive Light,   we in-voke your kin - dling ray;
3 To the anx-ious soul im - part   hope, all oth - er hopes a - bove;
4 Work in all; in all re - new,   day by day, the life di - vine;

Reign the spir - it of this place,   bless the pur-pose of this hour.
Dawn up - on our spir - it's night,   as the dark-ness turns to day.
Stir the dull and hard-ened heart   with a long-ing and a love.
All our wills to you sub - due,   all our hearts to you in - cline.

Frederick Henry Hedge, a professor and Unitarian minister, was perhaps best known for his translations of German hymns. He was also a hymnwriter, and contributed this text to Hymns for the Church of Christ, a Unitarian hymnal, which he co-edited in 1853.

Tune: MANTON 7.7.7.7.
Jane Marshall, 1992
Alternate tune: MERCY

513

O Source of All That Is

Johann Heermann, 16?

Transl. Madeleine Forell Marshall, 199

1 O   Source of   all   that   is,   most   good-ly Fount of   fa - vor,
2 Help me   to Christ-like   speech,   my   care-less tongue re - strain - ing.
3 Let   me   en - joy,   with   friends,   a   life of   mu - tual   car - ing,
4 Re - mind me,   as   I   die,   of   Je - sus' cru - ci - fix - ion.

Al - low me health and   strength, and   bless my   dai - ly   la - bor.
Pre - vent the   i - dle   vow   and   si - lence dull com - plain - ing.
Com - mu - ni - ty   in   Christ,   each   oth - er's bur-dens bear - ing.
Be - stow on   me,   that   hour,   your   fi - nal ben - e - dic - tion.

Grant   that   I   may com - plete   the   good works you   as - signed,
But   should in - jus - tice   rage,   the   strong op - press the   weak,
If   I   find wealth or   fame,   if   I   live man - y   years,
Then   wel - come my   glad   soul   in - to   that glo - rious   place,

My   con-science clear and   sweet,   my   words   both true and   kind.
My   el - o - quence en - gage,   and   teach   me how to   speak.
Save   me from   sin   and   shame,   and   calm   my mor - tal   fears.
Where   I   shall, pure and   whole,   a - dore   you face to   face.

Amid the fighting of the Thirty Years' War, Lutheran pastor Johann Heermann wrote this hymn of faith. The chorale tune is one of several sometimes referred to as O Gott, du frommer Gott through association with this text.

Tune: O GOTT, DU FROMMER GOT?
(DARMSTADT) 6.7.6.7.6.6.6.6
Neuvermehrtes Gesangbuch, *Meiningen,* 169?

Over My Head

514

African-American traditional

1 O-ver my head   I hear mu-sic in the   air.
2 O-ver my head   I hear sing-ing in the   air.
3 O-ver my head   I see trou-ble in the   air.
4 O-ver my head   I see Je-sus in the   air.

O-ver my head   I hear mu-sic in the   air.
O-ver my head   I hear sing-ing in the   air.
O-ver my head   I see trou-ble in the   air.
O-ver my head   I see Je-sus in the   air.

O-ver my head   I hear mu-sic in the   air,
O-ver my head   I hear sing-ing in the   air,
O-ver my head   I see trou-ble in the   air,
O-ver my head   I see Je-sus in the   air,

there must be a God some-where.

This African-American spiritual was widely sung during the 1960s folk-song movement. It was also a freedom song for the civil rights struggle and sometimes included the stanza: "Over my head I see freedom in the air."

Tune: African-American traditional
Arr. J. Jefferson Cleveland and Verolga Nix, 1981

515

O God, My God

Ps. 22:1–2

The Iona Community, 1988; al.

Refrain
Not too fast

O God, my God, O gra - cious God, why do you seem so

Last time, end

far from me, O God, my God, O gra - cious God?

O gra - cious God, O gra - cious God?

O gra - cious God, O gra - cious God?

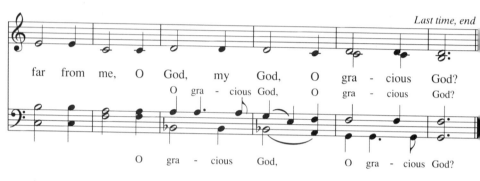

1 Night and morn - ing I make my prayer: Peace for
2 Pain and suf - fering un - bound and blind Plague the
3 Why, oh, why do the wick - ed thrive, Poor folk
4 Turn a - gain as you hear my plea; Tend the

this place and help for there; Wait - ing and won - dering,
prog - ress of hu - man - kind, Al - ways de - mand - ing,
per - ish, the rich sur - vive; Beg - ging the ques - tion,
tor - ment in all I see: Lov - ing and heal - ing,

In the Iona Community collection Enemy of Apathy, *this hymn
is described as a "protest song or a complaint." It exhibits the
kind of "stark honesty before God" characteristic of many of the
psalms.*

Tune: O GOD MY GOD 8.8.5.5.3.3. with refrain
*John Bell, 1988
The Iona Community*

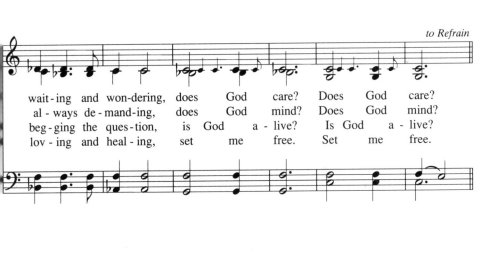

to Refrain

wait-ing and won-dering,	does	God	care?	Does	God	care?
al - ways de - mand-ing,	does	God	mind?	Does	God	mind?
beg-ging the ques-tion,	is	God	a - live?	Is	God	a - live?
lov - ing and heal - ing,	set	me	free.	Set	me	free.

O Grant Us, God, a Little Space   516

John Ellerton, 1870; alt.

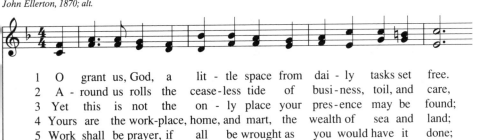

1	O	grant us, God,	a	lit - tle space from	dai - ly	tasks set	free.
2	A - round us rolls	the	cease-less tide	of	busi-ness,	toil, and	care,
3	Yet	this	is not	the	on - ly place your	pres-ence	may be	found;
4	Yours	are	the work-place, home, and mart,	the	wealth of	sea and	land;
5	Work	shall	be prayer, if	all	be wrought as	you would have it	done;

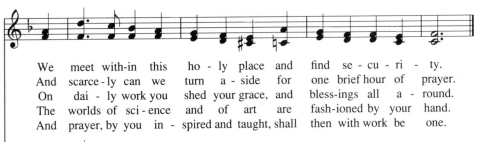

We	meet with-in this	ho - ly place and	find se - cu - ri - ty.
And	scarce - ly can we	turn a - side for	one brief hour of prayer.
On	dai - ly work you	shed your grace, and	bless-ings all a - round.
The	worlds of sci - ence	and of art are	fash-ioned by your hand.
And	prayer, by you in -	spired and taught, shall	then with work be one.

John Ellerton's hymn, written for a noonday service in a city church, is one of the earliest to speak of science and art as part of God's creation. Thomas Este was a famous English printer and music publisher.

Tune: WINCHESTER OLD C.M.
Este's Whole Book of Psalmes, *1592*

517

I Need You Every Hour

Annie S. Hawks, 1872; alt.
Refrain added by Robert Lowry, 1872; alt.

1 I need you ev-ery hour, O God of grace;
2 I need you ev-ery hour, in faith or fear;
3 I need you ev-ery hour, in joy or pain;
4 I need you ev-ery hour; teach me your will,

the peace your voice af - fords, I now em - brace.
temp - ta - tions lose their power when you are near.
come quick - ly and a - bide or life is vain.
and your rich prom-is - es in me ful - fill.

Refrain

I need you, how I need you! Ev - ery hour I need you;

O bless me now, my Sav - ior; I come to you.

First sung at a convention of the National Baptist Sunday School Association, this hymn was used by Dwight Moody and Ira Sankey in both England and the United States. Annie S. Hawks, a Baptist, was the author of some 400 hymns.

Tune: NEED 6.4.6.4. with refrain
Robert Lowry, 1872

Father Almighty, Bless Us

518

L. J. W., in The Sunny Side, *1875; alt.*

Ps. 23

1 Fa - ther al - might - y, bless us with your bless - ing;
2 Christ of com - pas - sion, car - ry all who seek you
3 Moth - er of mer - cy, from your watch and keep - ing

an - swer in love your chil - dren's sup - pli - ca - tion;
to pas - tures green be - side the peace-ful wa - ters;
no space can part, nor hour of time re - move us;

Hear now our prayer, the spo - ken and un -
Most ten - der guide, in ways of cheer - ful
Give us your good, and save us from our

spo - ken; hear us, E - ter - nal God.
du - ty lead us, good Shep - herd.
e - vil, In - fi - nite Spir - it.

Credited to the Rev. L. J. W.—possibly the Rev. Loammi J.
Ware—this hymn appeared in The Sunny Side, *a Unitarian*
collection. Berlin physician Friedrich F. Flemming wrote the
music as a male chorus setting of an ode by Horace.

Tune: INTEGER VITAE 11.11.11.5.
Friedrich F. Flemming (1778–1813)

519

Not My Brother, nor My Sister
(Standing in the Need of Prayer)

African-American spiritual; alt

Leader

1 Not my broth-er, nor my sis-ter, but it's me, O God,
2 Not the preach-er, nor the dea-con, but it's me, O God,
3 Not my fa-ther, nor my moth-er, but it's me, O God,
4 Not the strang-er, nor my neigh-bor, but it's me, O God,

All   **Leader**

stand-ing in the need of prayer; Not my broth-er, nor my sis-ter, but it's
stand-ing in the need of prayer; Not the preach-er, nor the dea-con, but it's
stand-ing in the need of prayer; Not my fa-ther, nor my moth-er, but it's
stand-ing in the need of prayer; Not the strang-er, nor my neigh-bor, but it's

All   **Refrain**

me, O God, stand-ing in the need of prayer.
me, O God, stand-ing in the need of prayer.
me, O God, stand-ing in the need of prayer.   It's
me, O God, stand-ing in the need of prayer.

me,   it's me, O God, stand-ing in the need of prayer;
it's me,

James Weldon Johnson included this African-American spiritual in his historic collection of 1925, The Book of American Negro Spirituals. *It was popularized by Mahalia Jackson, who specialized in such spirituals when she began her public singing career.*

Tune: NEED OF PRAYER 13.7.13.7. with refrain
African-American spiritual

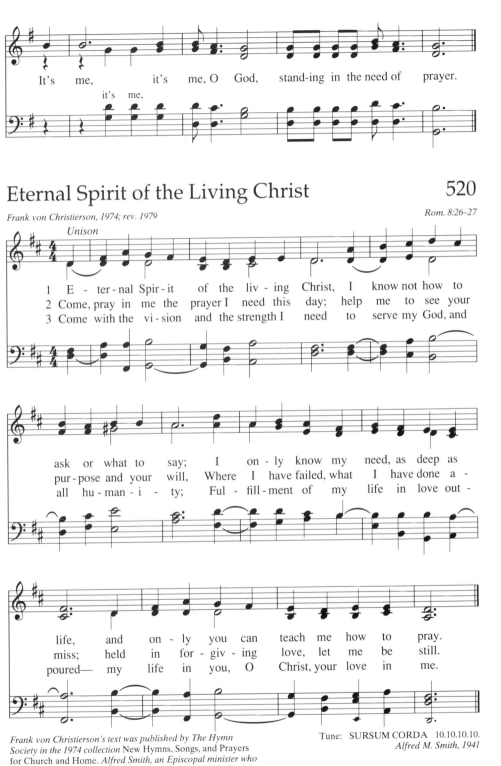

It's me, it's me, O God, stand-ing in the need of prayer.
it's me,

Eternal Spirit of the Living Christ 520

Frank von Christierson, 1974; rev. 1979

Rom. 8:26–27

Unison

1 E - ter - nal Spir - it of the liv - ing Christ, I know not how to
2 Come, pray in me the prayer I need this day; help me to see your
3 Come with the vi - sion and the strength I need to serve my God, and

ask or what to say; I on - ly know my need, as deep as
pur - pose and your will, Where I have failed, what I have done a -
all hu - man - i - ty; Ful - fill - ment of my life in love out -

life, and on - ly you can teach me how to pray.
miss; held in for - giv - ing love, let me be still.
poured— my life in you, O Christ, your love in me.

Frank von Christierson's text was published by The Hymn Society in the 1974 collection New Hymns, Songs, and Prayers for Church and Home. *Alfred Smith, an Episcopal minister who first studied music as an adult, composed* Sursum Corda *for a hymn, "Lift up your hearts. . . ."*

Tune: SURSUM CORDA 10.10.10.10.
Alfred M. Smith, 1941

521 In Solitude

Rom. 8:26–27; Eph. 5:18–20

Ruth Duck, 1983

1 In sol - i - tude, in sol - i - tude, I come to God in prayer.
2 When-e'er the world is troub-ling me, and stress is all a - round,
3 In sea - sons of per - plex - i - ty, in times of deep de - spair,
4 And when my heart is bur - dened down with cares for those I love,
5 With psalms and hymns and songs of praise be - fore my God I'll come,

In si - lence and sim - plic - i - ty, my spir - it blos - soms there.
I seek the pres - ence of my God, and heal - ing light is found.
I light a can - dle in the night and turn to God in prayer.
too deep for words, with groans and sighs, de - scends the ho - ly dove.
till death it - self is past and gone, and I ar - rive at home.

Ruth Duck has commented that "these words were inspired by a pentatonic melody which came to me as I taught myself to play the mandolin." They are an expression of her "deep-rooted southern spirituality."

Tune: LAND OF REST C.M.
Traditional United States melody
Harm. Annabel Morris Buchanan, 1938

522 I Love to Tell the Story

Katherine Hankey, 1866; alt.

1 I love to tell the sto - ry of un - seen things a - bove.
2 I love to tell the sto - ry; more won - der - ful it seems
3 I love to tell the sto - ry; it's pleas - ant to re - peat
4 I love to tell the sto - ry, for those who know it best

Born in Clapham, England, Katherine Hankey belonged to the Clapham Sect of Evangelicals and established a Bible class for girls in London's West End. This hymn is drawn from her extended poem on the life of Jesus, which also contains "Tell me the old, old story."

Tune: HANKEY 7.6.7.6.D. with refrain
William G. Fischer, 1869

Of Je - sus' ra - diant glo - ry, of Je - sus' end - less love.
than all the gold - en vi - sions of all our gold - en dreams.
what seems, each time I tell it, more won - der - ful - ly sweet.
seem hun - ger - ing and thirst-ing to hear it, like the rest.

I love to tell the sto - ry, be - cause I know it's true;
I love to tell the sto - ry, I tell it now to you
I love to tell the sto - ry, for some have nev - er heard
And when I sing in glo - ry, I know the new, new song

it sat - is - fies my long-ings as noth - ing else can do.
be - cause I want to share it, be - cause I know it's true.
the mes - sage of sal - va - tion from God's own ho - ly Word.
will be the old, old sto - ry that I have loved so long.

Refrain

I love to tell the sto - ry; and when I am in glo - ry

I'll tell the old, old sto - ry of Je - sus' end - less love.

523   Someone Asked the Question
(Why We Sing)

Matt. 10:26–31; Luke 12:4–7   *Kirk Franklin, 1993*

1. Some-one asked the ques-tion, "Why do we sing? When we
   Some-one may be won-dering when we sing our song, at
2. When the song is o - ver, we've all said "A - men," in your heart
   if some-bod - y asks you, "Was it just a show," lift your
3. When we cross that riv - er to stu - dy war no more, we will

lift our hands to Je - sus what do we real - ly mean?"
times we may be cry-ing and noth-ing's real - ly wrong.
just keep on sing-ing and the song will nev - er end. And
hands and be a wit-ness and tell the whole world, "No!"
sing our song to Je - sus, the One whom we a - dore! *(to Refrain)*

St. 3, 2nd ending only

Refrain
I sing be-cause I'm hap-py! I sing be-cause I'm free!

Kirk Franklin began to compose and arrange gospel music at the age of eleven, when he was appointed Minister of Music at Mt. Rose Baptist Church in Ft. Worth, Texas. The recording of "Why We Sing" by Kirk Franklin and the Family became immediately popular.

Tune: WHY WE SING Irr.
Kirk Franklin, 1993

God's eye is on the spar-row— That's the rea-son why I sing.

(Harmony)

Glo-ry hal - le - lu - jah! You're the rea-son why I sing.

Glo-ry hal - le - lu - jah! I give the prais - es to you.

Glo-ry hal - le - lu - jah! You're the rea-son why I sing.

524 This Little Light/This Joy I Have

Matt. 5:14-16

African-American spiritual

1 This lit-tle light of mine, I'm gon-na let it shine. . . . . .
1 This . . . joy I have, the world did-n't give to me. . . . . . .

I am gon - na let it, let it shine,
oh, the world did not give to me,

This lit - tle light of mine, I'm gon-na let it shine.
This joy . . . . I have, the world did-n't give to me.

This lit - tle light of mine, I'm gon-na let it shine,
This . . . joy I have, the world did-n't give to me.

Hal - le-lu - jah,
Hal - le-lu, the

let it shine, ... let it shine, ... let it shine, (oh let it shine.)
No, the world did-n't give it, the world can't take it a - way.

*The texts of these two spirituals may be used interchangeably
with the tune This Joy. For an alternate version, this melody may
be sung with the accompaniment of "Glory, Glory Hallelujah."
A more traditional setting of "This Little Light" is provided with
the tune Lattimer.*

Tune: THIS JOY Irr.
*African-American spiritual
Arr. Jeffrey Radford, 1993
See also LATTIMER*

"This Little Light" continued:
2 Ev-ery-where I go . . .
3 All--through the night . . .

"This Joy I Have" continued:
2 This love I have . . .
3 This hope I have . . .
4 This faith I have . . .
5 This peace I have . . .

This Little Light of Mine 525

African-American spiritual *Matt. 5:14–16*

1 This lit-tle light of mine, I'm gon-na let it shine,

this lit-tle light of mine, I'm gon-na let it shine,

This lit-tle light of mine, I'm gon-na let it shine, let it

shine, let it shine, let it shine. (let it shine.)

2 Ev-ery-where I go, I'm gon-na let it shine . . .
3 All--through the night, I'm gon-na let it shine . . .

This was the favorite song of civil rights activist Fannie Lou Hamer, who could sing as well as she could give powerful speeches. During that era this spiritual was sometimes modified and sung as "This little light of freedom."

Tune: LATTIMER Irr.
African-American spiritual
Adapt. William Farley Smith, 1987

526   Siyahamb' ekukhanyen' kwenkhos'
(We Are Marching in the Light of God)

Ps. 89:15   *South African freedom song; transl.* Freedom Is Coming, *1984*

This South African song and fourteen others were first recorded
and published in 1980 by the Church of Sweden Mission and the
singing group "Fjedur" after a visit they made to South Africa.
The subsequent 1984 collection Freedom Is Coming *brought the*
songs to a worldwide audience.

Tune: SIYAHAMBA Irr.
South African song

We Offer Christ

Brian Wren, 1986

1 We of-fer Christ to all the world a-round us, born in-to faith,
2 We of-fer Christ from all our best tra-di-tions, by grace a-lone,
3 We of-fer Christ the bar-ri-er-be-strid-er, whose full-ness far
4 We of-fer Christ and, God-be-loved, our Sav-ior now of-fers us,

re-leased from pride and shame; Em-braced by love, we show how
a-mazed and strange-ly warmed, Cre-a-ted e-qual, stirred by
ex-ceeds our lo-cal view, Whose Spir-it, breath-ing deep in
born of the Spir-it's kiss, to love cre-a-tion and cre-

love has found us; at peace with God, we speak our Sav-ior's name.
free-dom-vi-sions, self-crit-i-cal, pre-pared to be re-formed.
ev-ery cul-ture, brings Christ to us, the same, yet strange-ly new.
a-tion's Lov-er, with skill, com-pas-sion, jus-tice, care and peace.

"We Offer Christ" was commissioned by St. Paul's United Methodist Church, Orangeburg, South Carolina, for its 150th anniversary. The opening phrase derives from John Wesley's advice to Thomas Coke as he departed for America: "Offer them Christ."

Tune: CHARTERHOUSE 11.10.11.10.
David Evans, 1927

528

Sois la Semilla
(You Are the Seed)

Matt. 13:24–30, 33, 36–43; 5:13–16; 28:18–20

Cesáreo Gabaraín, 1979; alt.
Transl. Raquel Gutiérrez-Achon and Skinner Chávez-Melo, 1987; alt.

Unison

1. Sois la se - mi - lla que ha de cre - cer, sois es -
   Sois la ma - ña - na que vuel - ve a na - cer sois es -

1. You are the seed that will grow a new sprout; you're a
   You are the dawn that will bring a new day; you're the

tre - lla que ha de bri - llar. Sois le - va - du - ra, sois
pi - ga que em-pie - za a gra - nar. Sois a - gui - jón y ca -
star that will shine through the day; You are the yeast and a
wheat that will bear gold - en grain; You are a sting and a

gra - no de sal, an - tor - cha que de - be a-lum - brar.
ri - cia a la vez, tes - ti - gos que voy a en - viar.
small grain of salt, a bea - con to glow in the night.
soft, gen - tle touch, my wit - ness - es wher - e'er you go.

Estribillo (Refrain)

Id, a - mi - gas, por el mun - do, a - nun-cian - do el a -
Sed, a - mi - gos, mis tes - ti - gos de mi re - su - rrec -
Go, my friends, go to the world, pro - claim - ing love to
Be, my friends, a loy - al wit - ness, from the dead I a -

mor,   men - sa - je - ras de la vi - da,
ción.   Id lle - van - do mi pre - sen - cia;
all,   mes - sen - gers of my for - giv - ing peace,
rose;   "Lo, I'll be with you for - ev - er,

de   la paz y el per - dón.

e - ter - nal love.

con   u - ste - des es - toy.

till   the end of the world."

2   Sois u-na lla-ma
     que ha de en-cen-der
       res-plan-do-res de fe y ca-ri-dad.
     Sois los pas-to-res que han de lle-var
     al mun-do por sen-das de paz.
     Sois los a-mi-gos que qui-se es-co-ger,
       sois pa-la-bra que in-ten-to es-par-cir.
     Sois rei-no nue-vo
     que em-pie-za a en-gen-drar
       jus-ti-cia, a-mor y ver-dad.
     Estribillo

3   Sois fue-go y sa-bia
     que vi-ne a tra-er,
       sois la o-la que a-gi-ta la mar.
     La le-va-du-ra pe-que-ña de a-yer
     fer-men-ta la ma-sa del pan.
     U-na ciu-dad no se pue-de es-con-der,
       ni los mon-tes se han de o-cul-tar,
     en es-tas o-bras que bus-can el bien,
     el mun-do a Dios ha de ver.
     Estribillo

2   You are the flame that will bright-en
     the way,
     send-ing spar-kles of hope, faith,
     and love;
     you are the shep-herds
     to lead the whole world
     through val-leys and pas-tures of peace.
     You are the friends that I chose for my-self,
     the word that I want to pro-claim.
     You are the cit-y that's built on a rock
     where jus-tice and truth al-ways reign.
     Refrain

3   You are the life that will nur-ture the plant;
     you're the waves in a tur-bu-lent sea;
     yes-ter-day's yeast is be-gin-ning to rise,
     a new loaf of bread it will yield.
     There is no place for a cit-y to hide,
     nor a moun-tain can cov-er its might;
     may your good deeds
     show a world in de-spair
     a path that will lead all to God.
     Refrain

This hymn by Spanish theologian Cesáreo Gabaraín first appeared in the collection Dios con nosotros, *published in Madrid. The tune, which can be translated in English as "Go and Teach," was arranged by Mexican organist and choral director Skinner Chávez-Melo.*

Tune: ID Y ENSEÑAD   10.9.10.8.D. with refrain
Cesáreo Gabaraín, 1979
Harm. Skinner Chávez-Melo, 1987

529 Now Let Us All, in Hymns of Praise

Fred Pratt Green, 1982

Unison

1 Now let us all, in hymns of praise, bear wit - ness with one voice
2 What chang - es, chal - leng - es, and tests the church of Christ sur - vives!
3 Of all our la - bors, who can say what har - vest there shall be,

to God's re - deem - ing work in Christ, and bid the world re - joice.
How rich the rec - ords left to us of ded - i - cat - ed lives!
when time, that lim - its and dis - torts, be - comes e - ter - ni - ty?

To - day we call to mind the things that time can - not e - rode:
Still must the church pro - claim to all that now, and ev - er - more,
Then shall our hymns, re - hearsed be - low, be per - fect praise a - bove,

what God, Cre - a - tor of the world, is do - ing for our good.
the house of God is o - pen house, and Christ the O - pen Door.
as, face to face, we ful - ly know what this means: God is love!

This setting of Fred Pratt Green's 1982 text appears in the composer's collection of thirty-five hymns, The Roy Hopp Hymnary (1990). Hopp holds master's degrees in both choral conducting and composition, and has served as a director of music in Michigan.

Tune: OPEN DOOR C.M.D.
Roy Hopp, 1990
Alternate tune: ELLACOMBE

God Our Author and Creator

530

Carl P. Daw, Jr., 1985   *Gen. 1:1–2:3; Acts 17:22–31; Rom. 12:2; John 3:16–17*

Unison

1 God our Au-thor and Cre-a-tor, in whose life we find our own,
2 Like those first a-pos-tles, Sav-ior, give us strength to love and serve:
3 Keep us faith-ful, Ho-ly Spir-it, help us bear the mes-sage true,

make our dai-ly wit-ness great-er, by our lives make your love known.
when our faint-ing spir-its wa-ver, fire our hearts and steel our nerve.
that at last all lands may hear it: "God is love; Christ died for you."

Help us show how love em-brac-es those whom fear and greed down-trod;
Teach us wis-dom and com-pas-sion: bid our rest-less thoughts be still;
Join our lives in might-y cho-rus till we come from ev-ery place,

in all yearn-ing hearts and fac-es let us see a child of God.
by your guid-ance help us fash-ion lives con-formed un-to your will.
with all those who went be-fore us, to the full-ness of God's grace.

In 1985, a hymn competition was held to commemorate the centennial of the Women's Missionary Union of the Southern Baptist Convention. This winning text by Carl P. Daw, Jr., fulfilled the guideline that the hymn address mission in the context of daily life.

Tune: JEFFERSON 8.7.8.7.D.
Southern Harmony, 1835
Harm. John Ferguson, 1973

531 God, Speak to Me, That I May Speak

Frances Ridley Havergal, 1872; alt.

1 God, speak to me, that I may speak in
2 O lead me, God, that I may lead some
3 O fill me with your full - ness, God, your
4 O use me, God, use ev - en me just

liv - ing ech - oes of your tone; as you have sought, so
wan - der - ers a - long life's way; O feed me so that
ov - er - flow - ing love to know; In glow - ing word and
as you will, and when, and where, un - til your bless - ed

let me seek your err - ing chil - dren lost and lone.
I may feed your hun - gry ones with - out de - lay.
kin - dling thought, your love to tell, your praise to show.
face I see, your rest, your joy, your glo - ry share.

*Daughter of the English hymnwriter William H. Havergal,
Frances Ridley Havergal was a gifted poet and student of several
languages, including Hebrew and Greek. She also composed
several hymn tunes. Canonbury was adapted from one of Robert
Schumann's piano pieces.*

Tune: CANONBURY L.M.
Arr. from Robert Schumann, 1872

Come, Labor On

532

Jane Laurie Borthwick, 1859, rev. 1863; alt.

Matt. 9:37–38; 20:1–7

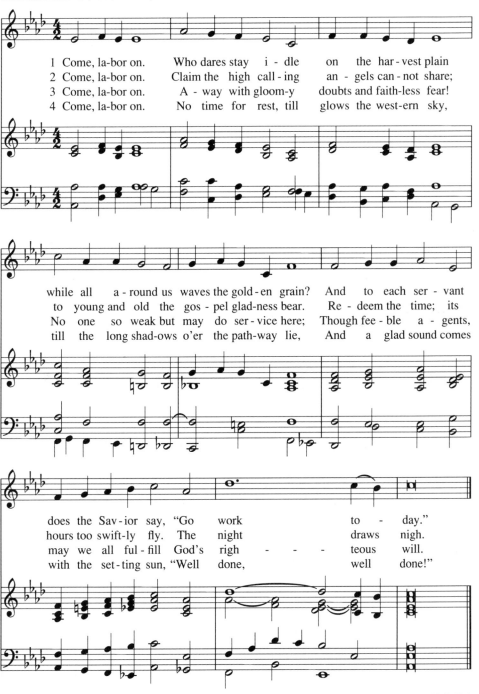

1 Come, la-bor on. Who dares stay i - dle on the har - vest plain
2 Come, la-bor on. Claim the high call - ing an - gels can - not share;
3 Come, la-bor on. A - way with gloom-y doubts and faith-less fear!
4 Come, la-bor on. No time for rest, till glows the west-ern sky,

while all a - round us waves the gold - en grain? And to each ser - vant
to young and old the gos - pel glad-ness bear. Re - deem the time; its
No one so weak but may do ser - vice here; Though fee - ble a - gents,
till the long shad-ows o'er the path-way lie, And a glad sound comes

does the Sav - ior say, "Go work to - day."
hours too swift-ly fly. The night draws nigh.
may we all ful - fill God's righ - - - teous will.
with the set - ting sun, "Well done, well done!"

Jane Laurie Borthwick, along with her sister, Sarah, was a member of the Scottish Free Church and translated many German hymns. English-born Thomas Tertius Noble was organist-choirmaster at St. Thomas' Church, New York City, for thirty-five years.

Tune: ORA LABORA 4.10.10.10.4.
Thomas Tertius Noble, 1918

533

Children of God

Eph. 4:31–5:2

John Greenleaf Whittier, 1848; alt.

1 Chil - dren of God, lift hearts to one an - oth - er;
2 For God whom Je - sus loved has tru - ly spo - ken:
3 Fol - low with rev - erent steps the great ex - am - ple
4 Then shall all shack - les fall; the storm - y clan - gor

where pit - y dwells, the peace of God is there;
the ho - lier wor - ship which Christ deigns to bless
of Christ whose ho - ly work was do - ing good;
of wild war mu - sic o'er the earth shall cease;

To wor - ship right - ly is to love each oth - er,
Re - stores the lost, and binds the spir - it bro - ken,
So shall the wide earth seem a ho - ly tem - ple,
Love shall tread out the bale - ful fire of an - ger,

each smile a hymn, each kind - ly deed a prayer.
and feeds the wid - ow and the par - ent - less.
each lov - ing life a psalm of grat - i - tude.
and in its ash - es plant the tree of peace.

Of Puritan ancestry and Quaker parentage, the American poet and journalist John Greenleaf Whittier was a strong supporter of the abolition of slavery. This hymn is comprised of the final stanzas of "Worship," a poem expressing his views on the life of faith.

Tune: WELWYN 11.10.11.10.
Alfred Scott-Gatty, 1900

O God of Strength 534

Shepherd Knapp, 1907; alt.

1 O God of strength, whose
 pur-pose, nev-er swerv-ing,
shall make com-plete the
 work Christ has be-gun,
Grant us to join and__
 work with all dis-ci-ples,
filled with your strength
 to see your will is done.

2 O Word Made Flesh, whose
 work God's work con-tin-ued,
one with the Spir-it's thought
 and deed and word,
Now make us one,
 com--pan-ions in your ser-vice,
your liv-ing bod-y
 by the Spir-it stirred.

3 O Power of Peace,
 who brings to us good tid-ings,
teach us to speak your word
 of hope and cheer:
Rest for the soul, and__ strength
 for all our striv-ing,
light for the path of life,
 your truth brought near.

4 O God, whose grace
 has called us to your ser-vice,
how good your thoughts toward us,
 how great their sum!
We work with you, we__ go
 where you will lead us,
un-til in all the earth
 your reign shall come.

This hymn was written for a meeting of the Men's Association of the Brick Presbyterian Church, New York, while Shepherd Knapp was assistant minister there. It later became very popular among the students at Eden Seminary, St. Louis.

Tune: WELWYN 11.10.11.10.
Alfred Scott-Gatty, 1900

O Holy God, Whose Gracious Power 535

Jane Parker Huber, 1978 *Matt. 28:19–20; Acts 1:8*

1 O ho-ly God, whose
 gra-cious power re-deems us,
Make us by faith, true
 stew-ards of your grace.
Help us to hear and__ heed
 Christ's great com-mis-sion,
Shar-ing good news in this
 our time and place.

2 Go we to all the world
 as Christ com-mand-ed
To be your wit-ness-es
 both far and near,
To feed the flock and to
 nour-ish flesh and spir-it,
Sens-ing in sac-ra-ment,
 Christ's pres-ence here.

3 Spir-it di-vine, we need
 your lov-ing fa-vor,
For we con-fess we
 can-not stand a-lone.
May we re-ceive and__ give
 with e-qual plea-sure,
Thus build-ing strong
 your church in flesh, not stone.

4 So may we face the fu-ture
 with-out swerv-ing,
Al-ways em-powered to
 wit-ness to your grace,
In thank-ful-ness for__
 gifts re-ceived and giv-en,
And for those mo-ments
 when we glimpse your face.

Jane Parker Huber has commented: "This hymn was written early in my time of experimenting with new words for familiar tunes." Huber wanted to provide an alternative for the original Whittier text.

Tune: WELWYN 11.10.11.10.
Alfred Scott-Gatty, 1900

536   Savior, an Offering Costly and Sweet

John 12:1–3; Eph. 5:1–2   *Edwin Parker, 1888; alt.*

1 Sav - ior, an   of - fer - ing   cost - ly and   sweet
2 Dai - ly our   lives would show   weak - ness made   strong,
3 Some word of   hope for hearts   bur - dened with   fears,
4 Thus, ev - er   serv - ing you,   till   e - ven - tide

Mar - y of   Beth - an - y   laid   at your   feet;
toil - some and   gloom - y ways   bright - ened with   song,
some balm of   peace for eyes   swol - len with   tears,
clos - es the   day of life,   may   we a - bide;

May our love's   in - cense rise   sweet - er than   sac - ri - fice,
Some deeds of   kind - ness done,   some souls by   pa - tience won,
Some dews of   mer - cy shed,   some way - ward   foot - steps led,
And when earth's   la - bors cease,   bid   us de - part   in peace,

Sav - ior to   you,   dear   Sav - ior to   you.
Sav - ior to   you,   dear   Sav - ior to   you.
Sav - ior to   you,   dear   Sav - ior to   you.
Sav - ior to   you,   dear   Sav - ior to   you.

Edwin P. Parker served as the minister of the First Church of Christ (Center Church, Congregational) in Hartford, Connecticut, for fifty years. Parker was also a choir director, composer, and arranger. He wrote this hymn to summarize a sermon.

Tune: LOVE'S OFFERING 6.4.6.4.6.6.4.5
Edwin Parker, 1888

Christian, Rise and Act Your Creed

537

Francis Albert Rollo Russell, 1893; alt.

1 Chris - tian, rise and act your creed; let your
2 Hearts a - round you sink with care; you can
3 Of - fer oth - ers hope and joy, and God's
4 Come then, law di - vine, and reign: faith that

prayer be in your deed; Seek the right, per - form the
help their load to bear; You can bring in - spir - ing
wor - ship your em - ploy; Giv - ing thanks in hum - ble
doubt as - sails in vain, Per - fect love be - reft of

true, raise your work and life a - new.
light, strength - en them to do the right.
zeal, learn - ing all God's will to feel.
fear, born in heaven and ra - diant here.

*Francis Albert Rollo Russell was a writer on scientific subjects
and a Fellow of the Royal Meteorological Society. This hymn
was first published in the Pilgrim Hymnal (1904). The tune
originated with a text used for the Feast of the Holy Innocents.*

Tune: INNOCENTS 7.7.7.7.
The Parish Choir, *1850*

538   Standing at the Future's Threshold

Matt. 25:31–40   *Paul R. Gregory, 1985; rev. 1994*

1 Stand-ing at the fu-ture's thresh-old, grate-ful for God's guid-ing hand,
2 Midst the teem-ing cit-ies' mil-lions, wit-ness to God's bound-less love,
3 O-pen-heart-ed in ex-chang-es with the faith-ful not our own,
4 Build-ing jus-tice as the bul-wark of the peace that God would give,
5 Je-sus Christ, e-ter-nal Sav-ior, Source of life and truth and grace,

Ask-ing no pro-tect-ed strong-hold, called to be a pil-grim band,
Reach-ing for each sys-tem's lost ones, seek-ing jus-tice with each move;
Trust-ing God's way with these strang-ers not to leave the truth un-known,
Mak-ing sac-ri-fice the hall-mark of the life we're called to live:
We would ask no spe-cial fa-vor, with the low-liest seek our place,

Seek-ing ev-er for new vi-sion of the gos-pel for our day,
Grant us cour-age, strength, and pa-tience to con-tend with vi-cious power,
Join-ing them in shared en-deav-or where we have Christ's clear com-mand,
Grant us, God, to bear our wit-ness to this peace in Christ, and move
Know the in-as-much of serv-ing, have your cross as our com-mand:

Paul Gregory served as East and Southeast Asia secretary of the United Church Board for World Ministries from 1957 to 1986. This hymn was written for the conclusion of the 175th anniversary of that board, and looked to the mission challenges of the future. "Inasmuch" in stanza five is a reference to the command Jesus gives in Matthew 25:40.

Tune: LUX EOI 8.7.8.7.D.
Arthur S. Sullivan (1842–1900)

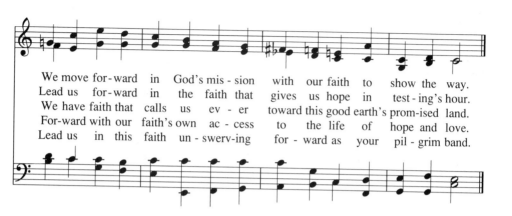

We move for-ward in God's mis - sion with our faith to show the way.
Lead us for-ward in the faith that gives us hope in test - ing's hour.
We have faith that calls us ev - er toward this good earth's prom-ised land.
For-ward with our faith's own ac - cess to the life of hope and love.
Lead us in this faith un - swerv-ing for - ward as your pil - grim band.

Won't You Let Me Be Your Servant? 539

Richard Gillard, 1977; alt.

Rom. 12:9–18; Col. 1:24–29

1 & 6 Won't you let me be your ser - vant, let me be as Christ to you?
2 We are pil - grims on a jour-ney, we are trav - elers on the road;
3 I will hold the Christ-light for you in the shad - ow of your fear;
4 I will weep when you are weep-ing; when you laugh, I'll laugh with you.
5 When we sing to God in heav - en we shall find such har - mo - ny,

Pray that I may have the grace to let you be my ser - vant, too.
We are here to help each oth - er go the mile and bear the load.
I will hold my hand out to you, speak the peace you long to hear.
I will share your joy and sor-row till we've seen this jour-ney through.
Born of all we've known to-geth - er of Christ's love and ag - o - ny.

(repeat stanza 1)

Richard Gillard was born in England and later made his home in New Zealand. Largely self-taught, Gillard has described his musical style as "folk." This is the best known of his many songs in the United States.

Tune: SERVANT SONG 8.7.8.7.
Richard Gillard, 1977
Arr. Betty Carr Pulkingham, 1977; adapt.

540   We Plant a Grain of Mustard Seed

Matt. 13:31–32; Mark 4:30–32; Luke 13:18–19;   *Mary Bryan Matney, 1990*
John 13:34–35; 15:12–17

1 We plant a grain of mus - tard seed, and in our faith we find
2 Our ac - tions, more than words, de - fine how love's ex - am - ple feeds
3 When stooped to lend a help - ing hand, we find a touch that heals,
4 Make love our pur - pose, love our aim, for love en - dures all things,

the proof of God is love, in - deed, which blos - soms from its kind;
a great - er love, for love di - vine bursts forth from small-est seeds;
for love in - vest - ed will ex - pand to bear the fruit love yields;
and choos - ing love our lives will claim the peace for - give-ness brings;

the proof of God is love, in - deed, which blos-soms from its kind.
a great - er love, for love di - vine bursts forth from small - est seeds.
for love in - vest - ed will ex - pand to bear the fruit love yields.
and choos - ing love our lives will claim the peace for - give - ness brings.

5 So may our new be-gin-nings prove,
    like liv-ing bread and wine,
  that through our com-mon hu-man love
    we taste what is di-vine;
  that through our com-mon hu-man love
    we taste what is di-vine.

6 Our lives will be ful-filled and blessed
    if through the seeds we've sown
  and by the love that we pro-fess
    the love of Christ is known;
  and by the love that we pro-fess
    the love of Christ is known.

Mary Bryan Matney and Sally Ann Morris wrote this hymn in
1990 for the marriage of friends. In 1992, it won first prize
in its category in a hymnwriting competition sponsored by
the Charlotte, North Carolina, chapter of the American Guild
of Organists.

Tune: NEW BEGINNINGS 8.6.8.6.8.6.
Sally Ann Morris, 1990

They Asked, "Who's My Neighbor?" 541

Jan Wesson, 1981; alt. Luke 10:29–37

Unison

1 They asked, "Who's my neigh - bor and whom should I love; for
2 There once was a trav - el - er set on by thieves who
3 A cer - tain Sa - mar - i - tan then came a - long to
4 I know who's my neigh - bor and whom I should love, for

whom should I do a good deed?" Then Je - sus re - lat - ed a
beat him and left him to die; A priest and a Le - vite each
bind up his wounds and give aid; He took him to stay at an
whom I should do a good deed; For Je - sus made clear in the

sto - ry and said, "It's an - y - one who has a
saw him in pain; but they turned a - way and walked
inn un - til well, and for all the ser - vice he
sto - ry he told, it's an - y - one who has a

need, yes, an - y - one who has a need."
by, yes, they turned a - way and walked by.
paid, yes, for all the ser - vice he paid.
need, yes, an - y - one who has a need.

Ruth Janelle (Jan) Wesson wrote this hymn for the dedication of her church in Nashville, Tennessee, and was encouraged to submit it to a Hymn Society competition. It was published at the society's national conference in 1982.

Tune: NEIGHBOR 11.8.11.8.8.8.
Jan Wesson, 1981

542   Born of God, Eternal Savior

1 Pet. 4:8–11; John 17:11; Matt. 6:10

Somerset T. C. Lowry, 1893; alt.

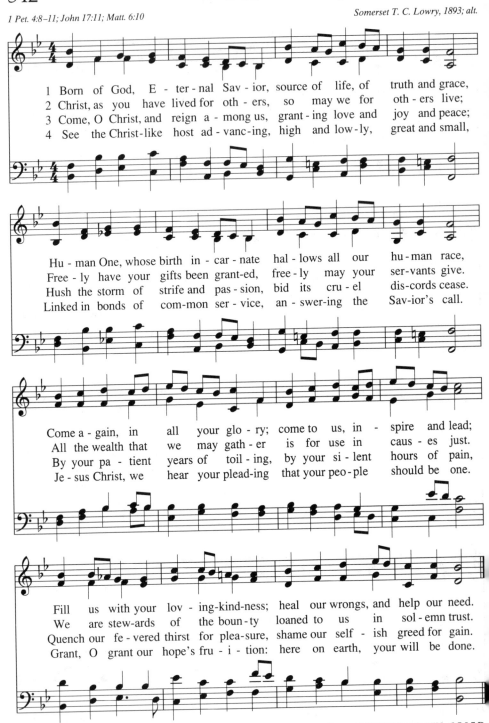

1 Born of God, E - ter - nal Sav - ior, source of life, of truth and grace,
2 Christ, as you have lived for oth - ers, so may we for oth - ers live;
3 Come, O Christ, and reign a - mong us, grant - ing love and joy and peace;
4 See the Christ-like host ad - vanc - ing, high and low - ly, great and small,

Hu - man One, whose birth in - car - nate hal - lows all our hu - man race,
Free - ly have your gifts been grant - ed, free - ly may your ser - vants give.
Hush the storm of strife and pas - sion, bid its cru - el dis-cords cease.
Linked in bonds of com-mon ser - vice, an - swer-ing the Sav-ior's call.

Come a - gain, in all your glo - ry; come to us, in - spire and lead;
All the wealth that we may gath - er is for use in caus - es just.
By your pa - tient years of toil - ing, by your si - lent hours of pain,
Je - sus Christ, we hear your plead-ing that your peo-ple should be one.

Fill us with your lov - ing-kind-ness; heal our wrongs, and help our need.
We are stew-ards of the boun-ty loaned to us in sol - emn trust.
Quench our fe - vered thirst for plea-sure, shame our self - ish greed for gain.
Grant, O grant our hope's fru - i - tion: here on earth, your will be done.

Born in Dublin, Ireland, Somerset T. C. Lowry was a priest of the Church of England and author of several prose and poetic works. This hymn, originally titled "For Unity," was written while he served in North Holmwood, Surrey.

Tune: WEISSE FLAGGEN 8.7.8.7.D
Tochter Sion, Cologne, 1741
Alternate tune: BEECHER

Where Cross the Crowded Ways of Life 543

Frank Mason North, 1903; alt.   *Luke 19:41; Matt. 10:42; Rev. 22:20*

1 Where cross the crowd-ed ways of life, where sound the
2 In haunts of wretch-ed - ness and need, on shad-owed
3 From ten - der child - hood's help - less - ness, from hu - man
4 The cup of wa - ter given for you still holds the

cries of clan and race, A - bove the noise of self - ish
thresh-olds framed with fears, From paths where hide the lures of
griefs and bur - dened toil, From fam - ished souls, from sor - rows'
fresh - ness of your grace; Yet long these mul - ti - tudes to

strife, O Christ, we hear your voice of grace.
greed, we catch the vi - sion of your tears.
stress, we know your heart does not re - coil.
view the deep com - pas - sion of your face.

5 O Sav-ior, from
       the moun-tain-side,
    Make haste to heal
       these hearts of pain;
    A-mong these rest-less
       throngs a-bide,
    O tread the cit-y's streets a-gain:

6 Till all shall learn
       com-pas-sion's might,
    And fol-low where
       your feet have trod,
    Till glo-rious from
       your realm of light,
    Shall come the cit-y of our God.

This hymn was written for the 1905 Methodist Hymnal by Frank Mason North, a Methodist minister who was deeply committed to the role of the church in urban life. North later served as president of the Federal Council of Churches of Christ in America.

Tune: GERMANY (GARDINER) L.M.
William Gardiner's Sacred Melodies, *1815*

544 Si Fui Motivo de Dolor, Oh Dios
(If I Have Been the Source of Pain, O God)

Spanish text, Sara M. de Hall; based on a text by C. M. Battersby
English transl., Janet W. May, 1992

(capo 1st fret)

Unison
Em D C Bm Em
To be sung freely

1 Si fui mo - ti - vo de do - lor, oh Dios; si por mi
2 Si va - na y fú - til mi pa - la - bra fue; si al que su -
1 If I have been the source of pain, O God; If to the
2 If I have spo-ken words of cru - el - ty; If I have

D C Bm Em D

cau-sa el dé - bil tro - pe - zó; si en tus ca - mi - nos
frí - a en su do - lor de - jé; no me con - de - nes,
weak I have re - fused my strength; If, in re - bel - lion,
left some suf-fering un - re - lieved; Con-demn not my in -

C Em Am6 Bm C [1-3] E [4]

yo no qui - se an - dar, ¡per - dón, oh Dios!
tú, por mi mal - dad, ¡per - dón, oh Dios!
I have strayed a - way; For - give me, God.
sen - si - tiv - i - ty; For - give me, God.
(Stanza 4) A - mén, A - mén.

3 Si por la vi-da qui-se an-dar en paz,
   tran-qui-lo, li-bre y sin lu-char por ti
   cuan-do an-he-la-bas ver-me en la lid,
   ¡per-dón, oh Dios!

4 Es-cu-cha oh Dios, mi hu-mil-de
   con-fe-sión
   y lí-bra-me de ten-ta-ción su-til;
   pre-ser-va siem-pre mi al-ma en
   tu re-dil.
   A-mén, A-mén.

3 If I've in-sist-ed on a peace-ful life,
   Far from the strug-gles that the
   gos-pel brings,
   When you pre-fer to guide me to the strife,
   For-give me, God.

4 Re-ceive, O God, this ar-dent word of prayer,
   And free me from temp-ta-tion's
   sub-tle snare,
   With ten-der pa-tience, lead me to your care.
   A-men, A-men.

Tune: CAMACUA 10.10.10.4.
Pablo D. Sosa (b. 1933)

The gospel hymn "If I Have Wounded Any Soul Today"
was translated into Spanish and set to a new tune. This new
setting and its English re-translation provide a strikingly fresh
understanding of the poetic intent. Pablo Sosa is an international
composer and leader in church music.

There Was Jesus by the Water

545

Versified by Gracia Grindal, 1983; alt.

Matt. 9:18–25; Mark 5:21–42; Luke 8:40–56

Unison

1 There was Je - sus by the wa - ter speak - ing to the press - ing
2 As the Sav - ior healed an - oth - er, news was brought that she was
3 Je - sus went back with the rul - er where they heard the mourn-ers
4 Je - sus touched the lit - tle daugh-ter, say - ing, "Lit - tle girl, a -

crowd, when, be - hold, there came a rul - er from the syn - a - gogue, who
dead. "Do not trou - ble Je - sus fur-ther." Je - sus heard the news and
weep. Je - sus said un - to the wail-ers, "Why this tu - mult— she's a -
rise!" And she rose to see her fa-ther's and her moth-er's stunned sur -

bowed, say - ing, "Come and heal my daugh - ter, lay your
said, "I will come and see your daugh - ter, I will
sleep. I will go un - to his daugh - ter, and will
prise. They then held their lit - tle daugh - ter and they

heal - ing hands up - on her, heal her, please, that she may live."
lay my hands up - on her, do not fear, she yet may live."
lay my hands up - on her, do not laugh, on - ly be - lieve."
laid their hands up - on her, trust-ing how he made her live.

Hymnwriter Gracia Grindal is also a teacher, poet, and published hymnologist. Her text first appeared with Rusty Edwards' tune in Songs of Rejoicing *(1989). Talitha Cumi is an Aramaic command that means "little girl, arise."*

Tune: TALITHA CUMI 8.7.8.7.8.8.7.
Rusty Edwards, 1983

546 Jesus, Lover of My Soul

Charles Wesley, 1740; alt.

1 Je - sus, lov - er of my soul, let me to your bos - om fly,
2 Oth - er ref - uge have I none; in your hands, my des - ti - ny;
3 Plen-teous grace in you is found, grace to cov - er all my sin;

While the near - er wa - ters roll, while the tem - pest still is high;
Leave, O leave me not a - lone, still sup-port and com - fort me.
Let the heal - ing streams a-bound, make and keep me pure with - in.

Hide me, O my Sav - ior, hide, till the storm of life is past;
All my trust on you is stayed, all my help from you I bring;
Fount of life, your love im - part, fill my cup a - bun - dant - ly;

Safe in - to the ha - ven guide, O re-ceive my soul at last!
Cov - er my de - fense-less head with the shad - ow of your wing.
Spring up now with - in my heart, rise to all e - ter - ni - ty.

Tune: MARTYN 7.7.7.7.D.
Simeon B. Marsh, 1834
Alternate tune: ABERYSTWYTH

Charles Wesley wrote this hymn soon after his 1738 conversion and titled it "In Temptation." Once considered so intimate that it was omitted from many eighteenth-century hymnals, it is presently found in many languages in collections around the world.

Amazing Grace, How Sweet the Sound 547

St. 1–4, John Newton, 1779; alt.
St. 5, A Collection of Sacred Ballads, 1790

1 A - maz - ing grace, how sweet the sound, that
2 'Twas grace that taught my heart to fear, and
3 Through man - y dan - gers, toils, and snares, I
4 My God has prom - ised good to me, whose
5 When we've been there ten thou - sand years, bright

saved a wretch like me! I once was lost, but
grace my fears re - lieved; How pre - cious did that
have al - read - y come; 'Tis grace has brought me
word my hope se - cures; God will my shield and
shin - ing as the sun, We've no less days to

now am found, was blind but now I see.
grace ap - pear the hour I first be - lieved!
safe thus far, and grace will lead me home.
por - tion be as long as life en - dures.
sing God's praise than when we'd first be - gun.

John Newton's autobiographical hymn reflects his conversion from his earlier existence as a slave trader. While serving as curate in the English village of Olney, Newton met William Cowper, and together they published Olney Hymns, which included this hymn.

Tune: AMAZING GRACE C.M.
(NEW BRITAIN)
Columbia Harmony, *Cincinnati, 1829*
Arr. Edwin O. Excell, 1900

548

Onuniyan tehanl waun
(Amazing Grace, How Sweet the Sound)

St. 1–4, John Newton, 1779; alt.; st. 5, A Collection of Sacred Ballads, 1790
Lakota transl. Stephen W. Holmes, 1987

1 O-nu-ni-yan te-hanl wa-un,
  Ma-shi-cha tke wa-ni,
  Wo-wash-te kin i-ye-wa-ye,
  wi-cho-ni wan-bla-ke.

2 Wo-wash-te he chan-te ma-hel,
  wash-ag-ma-ya-yin kte,
  Wo-wi cha-ke kin un le-hanl,
  o-a-pe kin wan-na.

3 O-ta kig-le te-ke wan el,
  eg-na i-ma-cha-ge,
  Wo-wash-te kin hel ma-wa-ni,
  Wash-te o-ma-ju-la.

4 O-to-ka-he-ya chi-ya-tan,
  o-hin-ni-yan ya-un,
  Wa-kan-tan-ka wo-wi-tan kin,
  yu-ha ma-wa-ni kte.

5 Wa-kan-tan-ka ya-tan un-we,
  Wa-kan-tan-ka ya-tan,
  Wa-kan-tan-ka ya-tan un-we,
  wa-kan-tan-ka a-men.

United Church of Christ minister Stephen Holmes developed this translation in collaboration with Lakota members of a church he served in South Dakota. "Amazing Grace" has long been a favorite hymn among the Lakota people, but it does not appear in Dakota Odowan, the hymnbook published by the Dakota Mission.

Tune: AMAZING GRACE C.M.
(NEW BRITAIN)
Columbia Harmony, Cincinnati, 1829
Arr. Edwin O. Excell, 1900

549

Bless God, O My Soul
Russell E. Sonafrank II, 1987; rev. 1993

Ps. 103

Response, Unison

(1–4) Bless God, O my soul! All with-in me bless God's name!
(5) Bless God, hosts of heaven, ev-ery-one who does God's will!

Last time, end
Cue notes, last time only

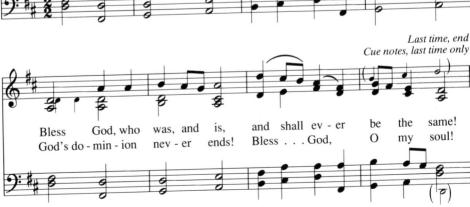

Bless God, who was, and is, and shall ev-er be the same!
God's do-min-ion nev-er ends! Bless . . . God, O my soul!

1 When we suf - fer, God sends heal - ing; when we sin, our
2 With com - pas - sion God works jus - tice when op - pres - sion
3 God will not be al - ways chid - ing, nor for - ev - er
4 As a par - ent's love is end - less, so God's mer - cy
5 God re - moves all our trans - gres - sions far as east is

God for - gives; From the grave our God re - deems us,
shac - kles truth; Like the phoen - ix, God re - stores us
an - gry be; God will deal with us in mer - cy,
fol - lows us; For the One who framed our be - ing
from the west; For the grace of God is great as

to Response

and by grace, we rise to live!
to the vig - or of our youth.
not ac - cord - ing to our sin.
well re - calls that we are dust!
heaven stands high a - bove the earth!

This paraphrase of Psalm 103 by Russell E. Sonafrank II and
Stephen J. Morris was awarded first place among fifty-nine
unsolicited new hymns submitted to The Hymn Society in 1988.
It was subsequently published in that organization's journal, The
Hymn.

Tune: SPRING WOODS 8.7.8.7. with response
Stephen J. Morris, 1987

550 O God, as with a Potter's Hand

Herman G. Stuempfle, Jr., 1991; rev. 1994

Gen. 2:4b–8; 1 Cor. 15:21–22; 2 Cor. 4:7–12

1 O God, as with a pot-ter's hand, when earth was morn-ing
2 Can clay de-fy the pot-ter's touch, a-lone its form de-
3 But once you shaped from hu-man clay a life whose truth and
4 O God, you hold our earth-en lives with-in your shap-ing

bright, you shaped from clay a hu-man form that
fine, or spoil with wild, re-bel-lious will the
grace re-vealed an im-age pure and whole that
hand and turn our form-ing clay to show the

gave your eye de-light; You breathed in love your
art-ist's true de-sign? Yet we, in whom your
sin could not de-face. And when we seized your
im-age you have planned. For-give the sin that

Composer Sally Ann Morris has frequently collaborated with hymnwriter Herman Stuempfle, Jr., who dedicated this text to his son, David, a potter. Morris named the tune Winston-Salem for her hometown in North Carolina.

Tune: WINSTON-SALEM C.M.D.
Sally Ann Morris, 1993

Spir - it's breath: a liv - ing crea - ture stirred and
hand has formed an im - age good and fair, dis -
choic - est work and broke its frag - ile clay, your
mars your work and strives a - gainst your will. Con -

stood with-in the gar - den green, a - wake to hear your Word.
fig - ure what you meant to be a work be - yond com - pare.
hands re-stored the shat-tered shards on earth's first Eas - ter day.
form our lives to Je - sus Christ with wis - dom, love, and skill.

551   Pass Me Not, O Gentle Savior

Luke 18:35–43   *Fanny Crosby (1820–1915); alt.*

1 Pass me not, O gen - tle Sav - ior, hear my hum - ble cry;
2 Let me at your throne of mer - cy find a sweet re - lief;
3 Trust - ing on - ly in your mer - it, would I seek your face;
4 Be the Spring of all my com - fort, more than life to me;

While on oth - ers you are call - ing, do not pass me by.
Kneel - ing there in deep con - tri - tion, help my un - be - lief.
Heal my wound - ed, bro - ken spir - it, save me by your grace.
Not just here on earth be - side me, but e - ter - nal - ly.

Refrain

Sav - ior, Sav - ior, hear my hum - ble cry;

While on oth - ers you are call - ing, do not pass me by.

Fanny Crosby was already a successful writer when she became associated with gospel hymnists Sankey, Sweney, Root, and others. She directed her talent to gospel songs in her early forties, and collaborated with William Doane on many hymns.

Tune: PASS ME NOT 8.5.8.5. with refrain
William H. Doane (1832–1915)

From the Crush of Wealth and Power

552

Kendyl L. R. Gibbons, 1992

Luke 10:34; James 5:14–16

1 From the crush of wealth and pow-er some-thing bro-ken in us
2 E-ven now our hearts are wa-ry of the friend we need so
3 When our love for one an-oth-er makes our bur-dens light to
4 Ev-ery time our spir-its lan-guish, ter-ri-fied to draw too

all waits the Spir-it's si-lent hour . . . . plead-ing
much. When I see the pain you car-ry, shall I,
bear, find the sis-ter and the broth-er, hun-gry
near, may we know each oth-er's an-guish and, with

with a poi-gnant call, bind all my wounds a - gain.
with a gen-tle touch, bind all your wounds a - gain?
for the feast we share; bind all their wounds a - gain.
love that casts out fear, bind all our wounds a - gain.

This text was commissioned by the Unitarian Universalist Association for the 1993 hymnal Singing the Living Tradition. *It was written for Peter Cutts' tune* Bridegroom *by Kendyl Gibbons, a Unitarian Universalist minister serving churches in Illinois.*

Tune: BRIDEGROOM 8.7.8.7.6.
Peter Cutts, 1969

There Is a Balm in Gilead

553

Jer. 8:18–22; 46:11; Acts 10:34–43

African-American spiritual; alt.

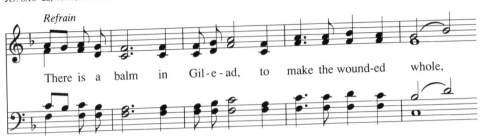

Refrain

There is a balm in Gil-e-ad, to make the wound-ed whole,

Last time, end

there is a balm in Gil-e-ad, to heal the sin-sick soul.

1 Some - times I feel dis - cour-aged, and think my work's in vain,
2 Don't ev - er feel dis - cour-aged, for Je - sus is your friend,
3 If you can - not preach like Pe - ter, if you can - not pray like Paul,

to Refrain

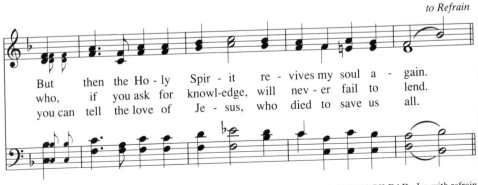

But then the Ho - ly Spir - it re - vives my soul a - gain.
who, if you ask for knowl-edge, will nev - er fail to lend.
you can tell the love of Je - sus, who died to save us all.

This is one of the most moving of the African-American
spirituals because it illustrates the way in which the enslaved tried
to encourage those who were feeling especially weighed down by
the burden of their captivity.

Tune: BALM IN GILEAD Irr. with refrain
African-American spiritual

Out of the Depths, O God, We Call

554

Ruth Duck, 1988

Ps. 130:1–8

Unison

1 Out of the depths, O God, we call to you.
2 Out of the depths of fear, O God, we speak.
3 God of the lov - ing heart, we praise your name.

*Wounds of the past re - main, af - fect - ing all we do.
Break - ing the si - lenc - es, the sear - ing truth we seek.
Dance through our lives and loves; a - noint with Spir - it flame.

Fac - ing our lives, we need your love so much.
Safe a - mong friends, our grief and rage we share.
Your light il - lu - mines each fa - mil - iar face.

1, 2
Here in this com-mu - ni-ty, heal us by your touch.
Here in this com-mu - ni-ty, hold us in your care.
Here in this com-mu - ni-ty,

3
meet us with your grace.

*Ruth Duck has provided the following words that may be
substituted for those who are seriously ill:*
Free us from fear of death, our faith and hope re-new. . . .
or, for those who have been abused:
Wounds of a-buse re-main, af-fect-ing all we do. . . .

Tune: FENNVILLE 10.12.10.12.
Robert J. Batastini, 1994

555

Here, Savior, in this Quiet Place

James 5:13–16; Mark 9:14–29

Fred Pratt Green, 1974; alt.

1 Here, Sav - ior, in this qui - et place, where
2 If pain of bod - y, stress of mind, de -
3 If self up - on its sick - ness feeds and
4 You nev - er said, "You ask too much," to

an - y - one may kneel, I al - so come to ask for
stroys my in - ward peace, In prayer for oth - ers may I
turns my life to gall, Let me not brood up - on my
an - y trou - bled soul. I long to feel your heal - ing

grace, be - liev - ing you can heal.
find the se - cret of re - lease.
needs, but sim - ply tell you all.
touch— will you not make me whole?

5 But if the thing I most de-sire
   is not your way for me,
   May faith, when test-ed in the fire,
   prove its in-teg-ri-ty.

6 Of all my prayers, may this be chief:
   till faith is ful-ly grown,
   Christ, dis-be-lieve my un-be-lief,
   and claim me as your own.

Tune: CHATHAM C.M.
Peter Cutts, 1994

Peter Cutts, Director of Music and Associate Dean of Chapel at Andover Newton Theological School, was commissioned to provide a musical setting for this text especially for The New Century Hymnal. *Cutts' work appears in numerous hymnals in the United States and his native Great Britain.*

God, Who Stretched the Spangled Heavens 556

Catherine Cameron, 1967

Gen. 5:1–2; Isa. 42:5–9

1 God, who stretched the span-gled heav-ens in-fi-nite in time and place,
2 We have ven-tured worlds un-dreamed of since the child-hood of our race;
3 As each far hor-i-zon beck-ons, may it chal-lenge us a-new,

Flung the suns in burn-ing ra-diance through the si-lent fields of space;
Known the ec-sta-sy of wing-ing through un-trav-eled realms of space;
Chil-dren of cre-a-tive pur-pose, serv-ing oth-ers, hon-oring you.

We, your chil-dren, in your like-ness, share in-ven-tive powers with you;
Probed the se-crets of the at-om, yield-ing un-i-mag-ined power,
May our dreams prove rich with prom-ise, each en-deav-or, well be-gun;

Great Cre-a-tor, still cre-a-ting, show us what we yet may do.
Fac-ing us with life's de-struc-tion or our most tri-um-phant hour.
Great Cre-a-tor, give us guid-ance till our goals and yours are one.

*Catherine Cameron, a professor of social psychology in
California, wrote this text in 1967 with Haydn's* Austrian
Hymn *in mind. This tune,* Holy Manna, *appeared in* The
Columbian Harmony *(1825), and was attributed to the compiler
of that volume, William Moore.*

Tune: HOLY MANNA 8.7.8.7.D.
William Moore, 1825

557

Pray for the Wilderness

Dan Damon, 1989; rev. 1994

1 Pray for the wil - der - ness, van - ish - ing fast,
2 Learn from the el - e - phant, ea - gle, and whale,
3 Work for the jus - tice cre - at - ed things need,
4 Trust that God's Christ o - ver - came nails and wood,
5 Pray for the at - mos-phere, pray for the sea,

pray for the rain for - est, o - pen and vast;
learn from the drag - on - fly, spi - der, and snail;
work for the health of each plant and its seed;
trust that earth's peo - ple will turn to the good;
learn from the riv - er, the rock, and the tree;

Pray for the wa - ter - falls, pray for the trees,
Learn from the peo - ple in neigh - bor - ing lands,
Work for the crea - tures a - buse has be - trayed,
Trust that cre - a - tion for - ev - er will grow,
Work till sha - lom in full har - mo - ny rings.

pray for the plan - et brought down by de - grees.
learn from the chil - dren who play in their sands.
work for the gar - den God's wis - dom once made.
trust that God's good - ness to us o - ver - flows.
Trust the con - nec - tion of all liv - ing things.

*Hymnwriter Dan Damon tried for several months to write a
hymn for the earth. A movie about the vanishing rain forest
finally provided the inspiration he needed, along with his
seven-year-old daughter, Heather, who suggested including
"waterfalls."*

Tune: WILDERNESS 10.10.10.10.
Lee Yu San, 1967

O How Glorious, Full of Wonder

558

Curtis Beach, 1958, rev. 1980; alt.

Ps. 8

1 O how glo-rious, full of won-der is your name o'er all the earth,
2 When we see your lights of heav-en, moon and stars, your power dis-played,
3 You have set us in com-mu-nion with the won-ders of your hand,
4 O how won-drous, O how glo-rious is your name in ev-ery land,

God, who wrought cre-a-tion's splen-dor, bring-ing suns and stars to birth!
Who are we that you should love us, crea-tures that your hand has made?
Made us fly with ea-gle pin-ion, pil-grims o-ver sea and land.
God, whose pur-pose shines be-fore us toward the goal that you have planned!

Rapt in rev-erence we a-dore you, mar-veling at your mys-tic ways.
Born of earth, yet full of yearn-ing, mix-ture strange of good and ill,
Soar-ing spire and ru-ined cit-y, these our hopes and fail-ures show.
Yours the will our hearts are seek-ing, con-scious of our hu-man need.

Hum-bly now we bow be-fore you, lift-ing up our hearts in praise.
From your ways so of-ten turn-ing, yet your love does seek us still.
Teach us more of hu-man pit-y, that we in your im-age grow.
Spir-it in our spir-it speak-ing, make us yours, O God, in-deed.

*United Church of Christ minister Curtis Beach submitted this
hymn to the editorial committee of the* Pilgrim Hymnal *(1958). It
was one of two psalm paraphrases by Beach to be accepted. The
hymn was also included in* The Hymnal of the United Church
of Christ *(1974).*

Tune: IN BABILONE 8.7.8.7.D.
*Traditional Dutch melody
Arr. Julius Röntgen, c. 1906
Alternate tune: HYMN TO JOY*

Thank You, God

Brian Wren, 1973

1 Thank you, God, for wa - ter, soil, and air, large gifts sup-port-ing the ba - sis of all ev - ery-thing that lives. For - give our spoil - ing and a - buse of them. Help us re - new the face of the earth.

2 Thank you, God, for min - er - als and ores, the ba - sis of all build-ing, wealth, and speed. For - give our reck - less plun-der - ing and waste. Help us re - new the face of the earth.

3 Thank you, God, for price-less en - er - gy, stored in each at - om, gath-ered from the sun. For - give our greed and care-less - ness of power. Help us re - new the face of the earth.

4 Thank you, God, for weav-ing na - ture's life in - to a seam-less robe, a frag - ile whole. For - give our haste that tam-pers un - a - ware. Help us re - new the face of the earth.

5 Thank you, God, for mak - ing plan - et earth a home for us and a - ges yet un - born. Help us to share, con - sid - er, save, and store. Come and re - new the face of the earth.

John Weaver composed the tune Amstein for Brian Wren's text for The Presbyterian Hymnal (1990). It is named for Charles A. Amstein, associate pastor of Madison Avenue Presbyterian Church in New York, where Weaver was named music director in 1970.

Tune: AMSTEIN 9.10.10.9.
John Weaver, 1988

By Whatever Name We Call You

560

Dosia Carlson, 1990

1 Pet. 4:10; Job 11:7–9

Unison

1 By what-ev-er name we call you Fash-ion-er of spheres,
2 In what-ev-er way we wor-ship, Mys-ter-y di-vine,
3 In what-ev-er gifts we of-fer, All-in-clu-sive One,

you are grand-er, so much wis - er than our minds per - ceive.
you are on-ly dim-ly known through ri-tu-al and creed.
you ac-cept your own cre-a - tion, frag-ments we re - turn.

La - bels lim-it un-der-stand-ing, God, you have no peers.
Though we try to cap-ture you in sym-bol or in sign,
Not as own-ers but as stew-ards is our giv-ing done.

So, we ques-tion— chang-ing, grow - ing— want-ing to be - lieve.
on - ly as we let you be can long-ing hearts be freed.
In true won-der we re-ceive the love we can-not earn.

Dosia Carlson credits "sermons preached by Culver Nelson when he was senior pastor at Church of the Beatitudes, United Church of Christ, in Phoenix, Arizona," as her inspiration for this text. Peter Niedmann, a composer and church music director, provided this musical setting especially for The New Century Hymnal.

Tune: OGONTZ 8.5.8.5.D.
Peter Niedmann, 1994

561 When in Our Music God Is Glorified

2 Chron. 5:11–14

Fred Pratt Green, 1972

1 When in our mu - sic God is glo - ri - fied, and ad - o - ra - tion leaves no room for pride, It is as though the whole cre - a - tion cried: Al - le - lu - ia!

2 How of - ten, mak - ing mu - sic, we have found a new di - men - sion in the world of sound, As wor-ship moved us to a more pro-found Al - le - lu - ia!

3 So has the church, in lit - ur - gy and song, in faith and love, through cen - tu - ries of wrong, Borne wit-ness to the truth in ev - ery tongue: Al - le - lu - ia!

4 Let ev - ery in - stru-ment be tuned for praise! Let all re - joice who have a voice to raise! And may God give us faith to sing al - ways: Al - le - lu - ia!

Fred Pratt Green wrote this text at the request of British editor and composer John Wilson, who asked for a "festival" hymn to be set with Engelberg. *Charles Villiers Stanford originally composed the tune for the text "For All the Saints" in* Hymns Ancient and Modern *of 1904.*

Tune: ENGELBERG 10.10.10.4.
Charles V. Stanford, 1904

Take My Gifts

Shirley Erena Murray, 1991

1 Take my gifts and let me love you, God who first of all loved me,
2 Take the fruit that I have gath - ered from the tree your Spir-it sowed,
3 Take what-ev - er I can of - fer— gifts that I have yet to find,

gave me light and food and shel - ter, gave me life and set me free,
har - vest of your own com-pas - sion, juice that makes the wine of God,
skills that I am slow to sharp - en, tal - ents of the hand and mind,

now be - cause your love has touched me, I have love to give a - way,
spiced with hu - mor, laced with laugh - ter— fla-vor of the Je - sus life,
things made beau - ti - ful for oth - ers in the place where I must be:

now the bread of love is ris - ing, loaves of love to mul - ti - ply!
tang of risk and new ad - ven - ture, taste and zest be - yond be - lief.
take my gifts and let me love you, God who first of all loved me.

Shirley Erena Murray recounted that Colin Gibson composed this tune for her stewardship text "almost instantaneously." Gibson has served as professor at the University of Ortago, as well as organist and choir director in nearby Dunedin, New Zealand.

Tune: TALAVERA TERRACE 8.7.8.7.D.
Colin Gibson, 1991
Alternate tune: HOLY MANNA

563   We Cannot Own the Sunlit Sky

Ruth Duck, 1984; rev. 1989

John 10:10

1 We can-not own the sun-lit sky, the moon, the wild-flowers grow-ing, for we are part of all that is with-in life's riv - er flow-ing. With o - pen hands re-ceive and share the gifts of God's cre - a - tion, that

2 When bod - ies shiv - er in the night and, wea - ry, wait for morn-ing, when chil - dren have no bread but tears, and war - horns sound their warn-ing, God calls hu - man - i - ty to wake, to join in com - mon la - bor, that

3 God calls hu - man - i - ty to join as part - ners in cre - a - ting a fu - ture free from want or fear, life's good-ness cel - e - brat-ing. That new world beck - ons from a - far, in - vites our shared en - deav - or, that

Ruth Duck wrote this text while she was serving as a corporate member of the United Church Board for World Ministries. In it, she wanted to "emphasize humanity's shared partnership with God in caring for one another and the whole creation."

Tune: ENDLESS SONG 8.7.8.7.D.
Attrib. to Robert Lowry in Bright Jewels
for the Sunday School, New York, 1869

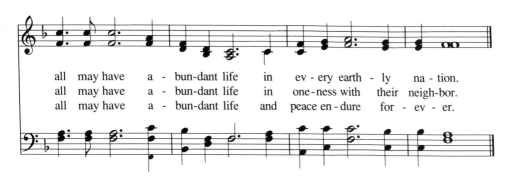

all may have a - bun-dant life in ev - ery earth - ly na - tion.
all may have a - bun-dant life in one-ness with their neigh-bor.
all may have a - bun-dant life and peace en - dure for - ev - er.

We Are Not Our Own   564

Brian Wren, 1987

Unison

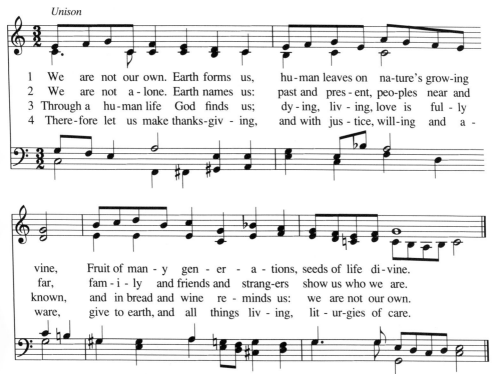

1 We are not our own. Earth forms us, hu-man leaves on na-ture's grow-ing
2 We are not a - lone. Earth names us: past and pres - ent, peo-ples near and
3 Through a hu-man life God finds us; dy - ing, liv - ing, love is ful - ly
4 There-fore let us make thanks-giv - ing, and with jus - tice, will-ing and a -

vine, Fruit of man - y gen - er - a - tions, seeds of life di-vine.
far, fam - i - ly and friends and strang-ers show us who we are.
known, and in bread and wine re - minds us: we are not our own.
ware, give to earth, and all things liv - ing, lit - ur-gies of care.

5 And if love's en-coun-ters lead us
   on a way un-cer-tain and un-known,
   All the saints with prayer sur-round us:
   we are not a-lone.

6 Let us be a house of wel-come,
   liv-ing stone up-hold-ing liv-ing stone,
   Glad-ly show-ing all our neigh-bors
   we are not our own!

This hymn was commissioned for the tenth anniversary of the Liturgical Studies Program of Drew University, New Jersey, in 1987. Brian Wren's melody came to him early on in the writing process and was helpful in the creation of the final hymn text.

Tune: YARNTON 8.9.8.5.
Brian Wren, 1987
Arr. Fred Graham, 1987

565 God, Whose Giving Knows No Ending

Robert L. Edwards, 1961; alt.

1 God, whose giv-ing knows no end-ing, from your rich and
2 Skills and time are ours for serv-ing, that your will on
3 Trea-sure, too, you have en-trust-ed, gain through powers your
4 Lend your joy to all our giv-ing, let it light our

end-less store, Na-ture's won-der, Je-sus' wis-dom, cost-ly cross, grave's
earth be done: All at peace in health and free-dom, rac-es joined, the
grace con-ferred; Ours to use for home and kin-dred, and to spread the
pil-grim way; From the night of anx-ious keep-ing, loose us in-to

shat-tered door: Gift-ed by you, we turn to you
Church made one. Now di-rect our dai-ly la-bor,
gos-pel Word. O-pen wide our hands in shar-ing
gen-erous day. Then when years on earth are o-ver,

of-fering up our-selves in praise; Thank-ful song shall
lest we strive for self a-lone; born with tal-ents,
as we heed Christ's age-less call, Heal-ing, teach-ing,
and we've lived our hu-man span, God, ful-fill be-

Robert L. Edwards, an ordained United Church of Christ minister,
has served several churches in Connecticut. He wrote this text for a
competition of The Hymn Society, and it was subsequently
published in Ten New Stewardship Hymns *in 1961.*

Tune: AUSTRIAN HYMN 8.7.8.7.D.
Franz Joseph Haydn, 1797
Alternate tune: HYFRYDOL

rise for - ev - er, gra - cious do - nor of our days.
make us ser - vants fit to an - swer at your throne.
and re - claim - ing, hon - oring you by lov - ing all.
yond our dream - ing, all our stew - ard - ship be - gan.

Heaven and Earth, and Sea and Air 566

Joachim Neander, 1680   Ps. 57:7–11; 108:1–5
Transl. Madeleine Forell Marshall, 1993

1 Heaven and earth, and sea and air all their Mak - er's praise de - clare.
2 See, at dawn, the ris - ing sun, show the won - ders God has done!
3 Look a - round this earth - ly ball, God has rich - ly dressed it all,
4 Wa - ters surge and wind-storms blow, thun - der, light-ning, hail, and snow:
5 All these things with cu - rious force, find them drawn to praise their source:

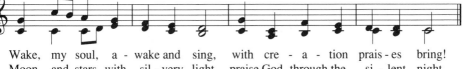

Wake, my soul, a - wake and sing, with cre - a - tion prais - es bring!
Moon and stars with sil - very light praise God through the si - lent night.
Ur - ban lights and can - yons deep, for - ests, fields, with cows and sheep.
Through their fren - zy, e - ven these, God would praise and God would please.
Wake, my soul, a - wake and sing, to your Mak - er prais - es bring.

Words and music of this hymn come to us from two German Pietists: Joachim Neander, writer of both hymns and tunes, and Johann Freylinghausen, known especially as editor and compiler of the most important Pietist hymnbook.

Tune: GOTT SEI DANK 7.7.7.7.
Freylinghausen's Geistreiches Gesangbuch
Halle, 1704

567   Stars and Planets Flung in Orbit

Ps. 148   *Herman G. Stuempfle, Jr., 1989*

1 Stars and plan - ets flung in or - bit, gal - ax - ies that swirl through space, Pow - ers hid with - in the at - om, cells that form an in - fant's face: These, O God, in si - lence praise you; by your wis - dom they are made.

2 Skies a - dorned with sun - set splen - dor, si - lent peaks in calm re - pose, Gold - en fields a - wait - ing har - vest, foam - ing surf and fra - grant rose: Earth, its boun - ty clothed with beau - ty, ech - oes all cre - a - tion's praise.

3 Life in won - drous, wild pro - fu - sion, seed and fruit, each flower and tree, Beast and fish and swarm-ing in - sect, soar - ing bird, re - joic - ing, free: These, your crea - tures, join in cho - rus, prais - ing you in word-less song.

4 Hu - man - kind, earth's deep-est mys - tery, born of dust but touched by grace, Torn a - part by tongue and col - or, yet a sin - gle, striv - ing race: We, in whom you trace your im - age, add our words to na - ture's song.

Herman G. Stuempfle, Jr., began his ministry as a parish pastor.
His long association with Lutheran Theological Seminary in
Gettysburg began in 1962 when he joined the faculty as professor
of preaching, and continued until 1989 when he retired as
president emeritus.

Tune: LAUDA ANIMA 8.7.8.7.8.7
John Goss, 1869

5 Gra-cious God, we bring be-fore you
  gifts of hu-man life a-lone,
  Truth that throbs through song and sto-ry,
  vi-sions caught in paint and stone:
  These, O God, we glad-ly of-fer,
  gifts to praise the Giv-er's name.

6 Christ, the Word be-fore cre-a-tion
  as cre-a-tion's fin-al goal,
  Once you came for earth's re-demp-tion;
  by your Spir-it make earth whole.
  Then, O God, the new cre-a-tion
  will your praise for-ev-er sing.

God Marked a Line and Told the Sea   568

Thomas H. Troeger, 1986   Job 38:1–11; Gen. 2:15–17; 3:1–7

1 God marked a line and told the sea its
2 God set one lim - it in the glade where
3 The line, the lim - it, and the law are
4 But, dis - con - tent with fi - nite powers, we
5 We are not free when we're con - fined to

surg - ing tides and waves were free To trav - el up the
tempt - ing, fruit - ed branch - es swayed. And that first lim - it
pat - terns meant to help us draw A bound be - tween what
reach to take what is not ours And then de - fend our
ev - ery wish that sweeps the mind. But free when free - ly

slop - ing strand but not to o - ver - take the land.
stands be - hind the lim - its that the law de - fined.
life re - quires and all the things our heart de - sires.
claim by force and swerve from life's in - tend - ed course.
we ac - cept the sa - cred bounds that must be kept.

Thomas Troeger has provided the following commentary on this text: "It was written as a polemical poem to counter spurious ideas of freedom as undisciplined license, and to affirm how the profoundest liberty involves a sense of boundaries and structure."

Tune: KEDRON L.M.
Attrib. to Elkanah Kelsay Dare in Amos Pilsbury's United States Harmony, 1799

569

Touch the Earth Lightly

Unison
Brightly

Shirley Erena Murray, 1992

1 Touch the earth light - ly, use the earth gent - ly,
*2 We who en - dan - ger, who cre - ate hun - ger,
3 Let there be green - ing, birth from the burn - ing,
4 God of all liv - ing, God of all lov - ing,

*The second verse only may be sung in A minor, omitting the sharps except where indicated in parentheses.

nour-ish the life of the world in our care:
a - gents of death for all crea - tures that live,
wa - ter that bless - es, and air that is sweet,
God of the seed - ling, the snow, and the sun,

Gift of great won - der, ours to sur - ren - der,
We who would fos - ter clouds of dis - as - ter—
Health in God's gar - den, hope in God's chil - dren,
Teach us, de - flect us, Christ re - con - nect us,

trust for the chil - dren to - mor - row will bear.
God of our plan - et, fore - stall and for - give!
re - gen - er - a - tion that peace will com - plete.
us - ing us gent - ly, and mak - ing us one.

Shirley Erena Murray's notes on this hymn state that the title line
is borrowed from an Australian Aboriginal saying. The "clouds
of disaster" mentioned in stanza 2 refer to nuclear testing by
France, which New Zealand has protested at the United Nations
many times.

Tune: TENDERNESS 5.5.10.D.
Colin Gibson, 1992

We Shall Overcome

570

United States traditional

John 8:31–32; Rom. 12:21; 2 Cor. 13:11

1 We shall o - ver - come,   we shall o - ver -
2 We'll go hand in hand,   we'll go hand in
3 We are not a - fraid,   we are not a -
4 Our God will see us through,   our God will see us

come,   we shall o - ver - come some day;
hand,   we'll go hand in hand some day;
fraid,   we are not a - fraid to - day;
through,   our God will see us through some day;

(1–6) Oh, deep in my heart, I do be - lieve,

we shall o - ver - come some day.
we'll go hand in hand some day.
we are not a - fraid to - day.
our God will see us through some day.

5 The truth shall make us free . . . some day.
6 We shall live in peace . . . some day.

This anthem of the 1960s civil rights movement was frequently sung at mass meetings and marches. Several sources have been cited as its origins, including the spiritual "No more auction block for me" based on the tune known as Sicilian Mariners; an old Baptist hymn "I'll Be All Right"; and part of the text from C. A. Tindley's gospel hymn "I'll Overcome Someday."

Tune: WE SHALL OVERCOME Irr.
United States traditional
Harm. J. Jefferson Cleveland, 1981

571   O God of Love, O God of Peace

Isa. 2:2–4

Henry W. Baker, 1861; alt

1 O God of love, O God of peace, make wars through-out the world to cease; The wrath of hu - man wrong re - strain: Give peace, O God, give peace a - gain!

2 Re - mem-ber, God, your works of old, the won - ders that our peo - ple told; Heal ev - ery mal - ice, harm, and pain:

3 Whom shall we trust, O God, but you? For you are con - stant, strong, and true. None ev - er called on you in vain:

Both words and music of this hymn were composed by Henry W. Baker. A priest of the Church of England, Baker was the first committee chair for Hymns Ancient and Modern, *which sold sixty million copies in fifty years.*

Tune: HESPERUS L.M.
(QUEBEC)
Henry W. Baker, 1854

When Israel Was in Egypt's Land 572

African-American spiritual; alt. *Exod. 3:7–12; 7:16; 8:1, 20; 9:1, 13; 10:3*

Unison

1 When Is - rael was in E - gypt's land, Let my peo-ple go,
2 "Thus spoke our God," bold Mo - ses said, "Let my peo-ple go;
3 No more in bond - age shall they toil, Let my peo-ple go,
4 Oh, let us all from bond-age flee, Let my peo-ple go,

Op - pressed so hard they could not stand, Let my peo-ple go.
If not I'll smite your first-born dead, Let my peo-ple go."
Nor spill their blood on E - gypt's soil, Let my peo-ple go.
And let us all in Christ be free, Let my peo-ple go.

Refrain

Go down, Mo - ses, way down in E - gypt's land,

Tell old Pha - raoh to let my peo-ple go.

According to historian Jon Michael Spencer, this is the most famous of the spirituals to speak subtly of the desire the enslaved had for freedom, believing that God would set them free just as God had set the Hebrew people free from captivity in Egypt.

Tune: GO DOWN, MOSES 8.5.8.5. with refrain
African-American spiritual

573 — Lead On Eternal Sovereign

Ernest W. Shurtleff, 1887; alt.

1 Lead on e-ter-nal Sov-ereign, we fol-low in your way;
2 Lead on e-ter-nal Sov-ereign, we fol-low not with fear,
3 Lead on e-ter-nal Sov-ereign, till sin's fierce war shall cease,

loud rings your cry for jus - tice, your call for peace this day:
for in each hu - man con - flict your words of strength we hear:
and all your saints to - geth - er will sing a hymn of peace;

Through prayer-ful prep - a - ra - tion, your grace will make us strong,
That when we serve with glad - ness, you will not let us fall,
Then all in your do - min - ion will live with hearts set free,

to car - ry on the strug - gle to tri - umph o - ver wrong.
our trust is in your prom - ise that love will con - quer all.
to love and serve each oth - er for all e - ter - ni - ty.

At Andover Seminary, fellow students asked Ernest W. Shurtleff
to write a hymn for their graduation. This is the result. Shurtleff
became a Congregational minister and in his last years
established churches in Europe and did relief work during
World War I.

Tune: LANCASHIRE 7.6.7.6.D
Henry T. Smart, 1836

In Egypt under Pharaoh 574

Dosia Carlson, 1989   *Exod. 1:1–14; 7:8–11:10; 14:21–31*

1. In E-gypt un-der Pha-raoh the Is-rael-ites were bound,
   from plagues and trib-u-la-tions no re-spite could be found.
   Praise God who in sur-pris-ing ways gave pas-sage through the waves.
   Our Lib-er-a-tor res-cues, our Lib-er-a-tor saves.

2. From Af-ri-ca to gang-planks, a-cross a friend-less sea,
   black cap-tives harsh-ly treat-ed all strug-gled to be free.
   Praise God who strength-ened ad-vo-cates with power that does and dares.
   Our Lib-er-a-tor res-cues, our Lib-er-a-tor cares.

3. Wher-ev-er hurt-ing hu-mans un-just-ly live in pain,
   the hun-gry, home-less, hope-less, cry out for growth and gain.
   Praise God whose great re-deem-ing love each ser-vant free-ly gives.
   Our Lib-er-a-tor res-cues, our Lib-er-a-tor lives!

Dosia Carlson wrote this text in 1989 for the United Church of   Tune: LANCASHIRE 7.6.7.6.D.
Christ celebration of the 150th anniversary of the Amistad event.   *Henry T. Smart, 1836*

O for a World 575

Miriam Therese Winter, 1987   *Acts 4:32–35; 1 Cor. 1:26–31; 1 Pet. 3:8–12*

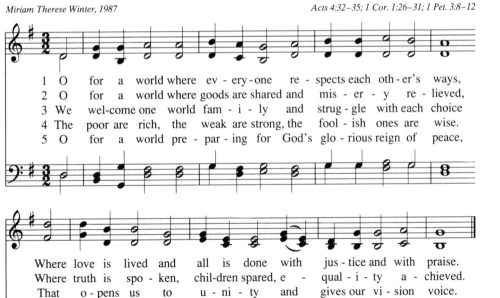

1 O for a world where ev - ery - one re - spects each oth - er's ways,
2 O for a world where goods are shared and mis - er - y re - lieved,
3 We wel-come one world fam - i - ly and strug - gle with each choice
4 The poor are rich, the weak are strong, the fool - ish ones are wise.
5 O for a world pre - par - ing for God's glo - rious reign of peace,

Where love is lived and all is done with jus - tice and with praise.
Where truth is spo - ken, chil-dren spared, e - qual - i - ty a - chieved.
That o - pens us to u - ni - ty and gives our vi - sion voice.
Tell all who mourn: out - casts be - long, who per - ish - es will rise.
Where time and tears will be no more, and all but love will cease.

Inspired by Charles Wesley's phrase "O for a thousand tongues"   Tune: AZMON C.M.
and the familiar tune Azmon, *Miriam Therese Winter wrote this*   *Carl G. Gläser, 1828*
hymn envisioning a new world order for the Presbyterian   *Adapt. Lowell Mason in* Modern Psalmody, *1839*
Women's Triennial Conference in 1982. It was later recrafted
and recorded by the Medical Mission Sisters.

576 For the Healing of the Nations

Fred Kaan, 1965

1 For the heal - ing of the na - tions, God, we pray with
2 Lead us for - ward in - to free-dom; from de - spair your
3 All that kills a - bun - dant liv - ing, let it from the
4 You, Cre - a - tor God, have writ-ten your great name on

one ac - cord; for a just and e - qual shar - ing
world re - lease, that, re - deemed from war and ha - tred,
earth be banned; pride of sta - tus, race, or school-ing,
hu - man - kind; for our grow - ing in your like - ness

of the things that earth af - fords; to a life of
all may come and go in peace. Show us how through
dog - mas that ob - scure your plan. In our com - mon
bring the life of Christ to mind, that by our re -

love in ac - tion help us rise and pledge our word.
care and good - ness fear will die and hope in - crease.
quest for jus - tice may we hal - low life's brief span.
sponse and ser - vice earth its des - ti - ny may find.

Fred Kaan's most widely published text was first sung at
Pilgrim Church in Plymouth, England, at a service of worship
marking Human Rights Day in 1965. It has been used for many
subsequent occasions, including the twenty-fifth anniversary of
the United Nations.

Tune: WESTMINSTER ABBEY 8.7.8.7.8.7.
Henry Purcell, c. 1680
Arr. Ernest Hawkins, 1842

Words Copyright © 1968 by Hope Publishing Company

God the Omnipotent! 577

St. 1–2, Henry F. Chorley, 1842; alt.
St. 3–4, John Ellerton, 1870; alt.

1 God the Om - ni - po - tent! bold - ly or - dain - ing
2 God the All - mer - ci - ful! earth has for - sak - en
3 God the All - righ - teous One! earth has de - fied you,
4 God the All - prov - i - dent! by your great chas - tening

thun - der and light - ning your strength to dis - play,
all you make ho - ly, and slight - ed your way;
yet to e - ter - ni - ty stands what you say;
earth shall see free - dom and truth hold - ing sway;

Bring forth com - pas - sion where vi - o-lence is reign - ing;
Bid not your wrath in its ter - rors a - wak - en:
False - hood and wrong shall not tar - ry be - side you:
Through the thick cha - os your reign is still has - tening:

give to us peace in our time, we pray.
give to us peace in our time, we pray.
give to us peace in our time, we pray.
you will give peace in your time, we pray.

Two English hymns, one by Henry F. Chorley, a friend of
Charles Dickens, and another by Church of England priest John
Ellerton, are combined in this text. The tune was originally
written for the Russian national anthem.

Tune: RUSSIAN HYMN 11.10.11.9.
Alexis F. Lvov, 1833

578

Profetiza, Pueblo mío
(You Shall Prophesy, All My People)

Acts 2:17–21; Rev. 10:11

Rosa Martha Zárate Macías, 1989; rev. 1994
Transl. The New Century Hymnal, 1994

Estribillo (Refrain)

Pro - fe - ti - za, Pue-blo mí - o, pro - fe - ti - za u-na vez más.
You shall proph - e - sy, all my peo - ple, you shall proph - e - sy once more,

Que tu voz sea el e - co del cla-mor de los Pue-blos en o - pre - sión.
That your voice may ech - o all the cries of the peo-ple who are op - pressed.

Pro - fe - ti - za, Pue-blo mí - o, pro - fe - ti - za u-na vez más,
You shall proph - e - sy, my peo - ple, you shall proph-e - sy once more,

a-nun-cián - do-le a los po - bres u-na nue-va so-cie - dad.
to the poor an-nounce the com - ing of a new so-ci - e - ty.

to Stanzas

Last time, end

Rosa Martha Zárate Macías wrote this hymn for her Mexican
People and other Pueblos deprived of their homeland, whom the
Great Spirit calls to be prophets, men and women of courage,
responsible for constructing the new society based in justice and love.

Tune: PROPHESY Irr. with refrain
Rosa Martha Zárate Macías, 1989
Harm. Raquel Gutiérrez-Achon, 1993

1 Pro - fe - ta te con - sa - gro, no ha-ya du-da y te - mor
2 A - nún - cia-le a los Pue - blos que se re - no - va - rá
1 "I con - se-crate you proph-ets!" Ban - ish all doubt and fear;
2 An-nounce to all the peo - ples the cov - e - nant re - newed:

to Refrain

en tu an-dar por la his - to - ria; sé fiel a tu mi - sión.
el pac - to en la jus - ti - cia; la paz flo - re - ce - rá.
be faith - ful to your mis - sion, lead-ing through his - to - ry.
the prom-ise of God's jus - tice, blos-som - ing forth in peace.

3 De-nun-cia a quie-nes cau-san
  el llan-to y la o-pre-sión
  la ver-dad sea tu es-cu-do
  sé luz de un nue-vo sol.
  Estribillo

4 Es-ta sea tu es-pe-ran-za,
  es-te sea tu lu-char,
  cons-tru-ir en la jus-ti-cia
  la nue-va so-cie-dad.
  Estribillo

3 De-nounce those who are caus-ing,
  all those op-pressed to cry,
  Truth will be your pro-tec-tion,
  the light of a new sun.
  Refrain

4 Let this hope be your mis-sion,
  let hope be-come your fight,
  To build a so-cial or-der
  with jus-tice at its base.
  Refrain

579 Great God of Earth and Heaven

Shirley Erena Murray, 1986

Unison

1 Great God of earth and heav - en whose Spir - it is our breath,
2 While ref - u - gees go home - less and die be - fore they live,
3 Where hun - ger kills your peo - ple, in - jus - tice cries a - loud,

at Christ-mas-time born hu - man, at Eas - ter shared our death:
while chil - dren have no fu - ture— our ap - a - thy for - give!
while weap - ons grow more le - thal and on - ly power stands proud—

All - gen - er - ous, all - lov - ing, in whom all beau - ty thrives—
Where hope fades to de - pres - sion, de - spair e - rodes the soul,
God of our flesh and fi - ber, whose mer - cy does not cease,

for - give your sons and daugh - ters the com - fort of our lives!
re - store in us a pas - sion to make the bro - ken whole.
im - plant your mind with - in us, cre - ate a world for peace!

This text by New Zealand writer Shirley Erena Murray was first used for a Refugee Sunday at the inner-city parish of St. Andrew's-on-the-Terrace, Wellington. It was intended as "a protest against apathy and 'the comfortable pew.'"

Tune: KING'S LYNN 7.6.7.6.D.
Traditional English melody
Arr. Ralph Vaughan Williams, 1906

O Kou Aloha No

580

(The Queen's Prayer)

Queen Liliuokalani, 1893

1 O kou a-lo-ha no A i-a i ka La - ni,
2 Kou no - ho mi - hi a - na A pa - 'a - ha - o la,
3 Mai na - na 'i - no - 'i - no Na he - wa o ka - na - ka,
4 No - lai - la e ka Ha - ku Ma - la - lo okou e - he - u

A o kou oi - a - i' - o, He he - mo - le - le ho'i.
O o - e ku - 'u la - ma kou na - ni, ko - 'u ko'o.
A - ka, e hu - i - ka - la, a ma - 'e - ma - 'e no.
Ko ma - kou ma - lu - hi - a, a mau loa a - ku no.

This translation is not intended to be sung.

Your love is in heaven and your truth so perfect. I live in sorrow
imprisoned; you are my light, your glory my support. Behold not
with malevolence the sins of humankind, but forgive and cleanse.
And so, O Lord, beneath your wings be our peace forever more.

*In June 1893, after having been deposed from her throne in
Hawaii, the imprisoned Queen Liliuokalani wrote a hymn to tell
of her love of God, so great that she asked that even the sins of
those who imprisoned her be forgiven.*

Tune: LILIUOKALANI 6.7.7.6.
*Queen Liliuokalani (1838–1917)
Arr. Emerson C. Smith, 1954*

581   Lead Us from Death to Life

2 John 1:3; Isa. 2:2–4

Refrain, Satish Kumar
Stanzas, Marty Haugen, 1985

Lead us from death to life, from false-hood to truth, from de-spair to hope, from fear to trust. Lead us from hate to love, from war to peace; let peace fill our hearts, let peace fill our world, let peace fill our u - ni - verse.

to Stanzas

Last time, end

1 Still all the an-gry cries, still all the an-gry guns, still now your
2 So man-y lone-ly hearts, so man-y bro-ken lives, long-ing for
3 Let jus-tice ev-er roll, let mer-cy fill the earth, let us be-

peo-ple die, earth's sons and daugh-ters. Let jus-tice roll, let
love to break in-to their an-guish. Come, teach us love,
gin to grow in-to your peo-ple. We can be love,

mer-cy pour down, come and teach us your way of com-pas-sion.
come, teach us peace, come and teach us your way of com-pas-sion.
we can bring peace, we can still be your way of com-pas-sion.

The text for the refrain of this hymn is known as the "World Peace Prayer." It is a paraphrase of a verse from the Upanishads, *the most ancient scriptures of Hinduism. Since its introduction at a service in Westminster Abbey on Hiroshima Day, 1981, the prayer has been translated into numerous languages and circulated around the world. The musical setting and additional stanzas were composed by Marty Haugen, composer-in-residence at Mayflower United Church of Christ, Minneapolis, Minnesota.*

Tune: WORLD PEACE PRAYER
12.11.9.10. with refrain
Marty Haugen, 1985

582 O God of Earth and Altar

St. 1–2, Gilbert K. Chesterton, 1906; alt.
St. 2, alt. Jane Parker Huber, 1985
St. 3, Jane Parker Huber, 1985

1 O God of earth and al - tar, bow down and hear our cry;
2 From all that ter - ror teach - es, from lies of pen and voice,
3 A - wak - en us to ac - tion and forge us in - to one,

Our earth-ly rul - ers fal - ter, our peo - ple drift and die;
From all the eas - y speech - es that make our hearts re - joice,
de - fy - ing sect and fac - tion; O God, your will be done!

The walls of gold en - tomb us, the swords of scorn di - vide;
From val - ue's pro - fan - a - tion, from hon - or sac - ri - ficed,
Op - pres-sive sys-tems snare us; our ap - a - thies in - crease.

Take not your thun - der from us, but take a - way our pride.
From sleep and from dam - na - tion, de - liv - er us, O Christ!
Great God, in mer - cy spare us for jus - tice and for peace!

*G. K. Chesterton of England was a prolific journalist,
lecturer, and author of some one hundred literary works. This
hymn has been updated by Jane Parker Huber to "incorporate
contemporary concerns for the church's mission."*

Tune: LLANGLOFFAN 7.6.7.6.D.
*Traditional Welsh melody
Harm. David Evans, 1927*

Like a Mother Who Has Borne Us 583

Daniel Bechtel, 1986

Hos. 11:1–9; 2 Tim. 1:8–10

1 Like a moth - er who has borne us, held us
2 Like a fa - ther who has taught us, grasped our
3 Though as chil - dren we have wan - dered, placed our
4 When we of - fer food and com - fort, grasp our

close in her de - light, Fed us free - ly from her
hand and been our guide, Lift - ed us and healed our
trust in power and might, Left be - hind our broth - ers,
neigh - bor's hand in love, Tread the path of peace and

bod - y, God has called us in - to life.
sor - rows, God has walked with us in life.
sis - ters, God still calls us in - to life.
jus - tice, God still walks with us in life.

This hymn was inspired by Hosea's depiction of the parental aspects of God's relationship with Israel. It was first sung at a chapel service at Dickinson College, where Daniel Bechtel, an ordained minister in the United Church of Christ, began his tenure as professor of religion in 1964.

Tune: AUSTIN 8.7.8.7.
William P. Rowan, 1992
Alternate tune: STUTTGART

584

I Am the Light of the World

John 8:12

Jim Strathdee, 1969; rev. 1981
In response to a Christmas poem by Howard Thurman

1 When the song of the an-gels is stilled, when the
2 ⁊ To find the lost and lone-ly one, ⁊ to
3 ⁊ To free the pris-oner from all chains, ⁊ to
4 To bring hope to ev-ery task you do, ⁊ to

This text is based on a Christmas poem by Howard Thurman,
a prolific twentieth-century writer, theologian, and teacher.
The song grew out of Jim Strathdee's music ministry at an
intercultural, bilingual congregation in Los Angeles.

Tune: LIGHT OF THE WORLD Irr.
Jim Strathdee, 1969

star in the sky is gone,   When the
heal the bro - ken soul with love,   ꞈ To
make the pow - er - ful care,   To re -
dance at a ba - by's new birth,   ꞈ To

sag - es and the shep - herds have found their way home,   the
feed the hun - gry chil - dren with warmth and good food,   To
build the na - tions with strength of good will,   to
make mu - sic in . . . . an old per - son's heart,   and

Return to 𝄋

work of Christ-mas is be - gun:
feel the earth be - low, the sky a - bove!
see all God's chil - dren ev - ery - where!
sing to the col - ors of the earth!

585   O God, We Bear the Imprint of Your Face

Shirley Erena Murray, 1981; rev. 1994

1 O God, we bear the im-print of your face: the col-ors of our
2 Where we are torn and pulled a-part by hate be-cause our race, our
3 O God, we share the im-age of the One whose flesh and blood are

skin are your de-sign, and what we have of beau-ty in our race as
skin is not the same, while we are judged un-e-qual by the state and
ours, what-ev-er skin; in Christ's hu-man-i-ty we find our own, and

man or wom-an, you a-lone de-fine, who stretched a liv-ing fab-ric
vic-tims made be-cause we own our name, hu-man-i-ty re-duced to
in your fam-i-ly our prop-er kin: Je-sus our broth-er we still

on our frame and gave to each a lan-guage and a name.
lit-tle worth, dis-hon-ored is your liv-ing face on earth.
cru-ci-fy; love is the lan-guage we must learn, or die.

Composer Bruce Neswick provided this setting at the request of The New Century Hymnal. Neswick, Organist-Choirmaster of Christ Church Episcopal Cathedral, Lexington, Kentucky, is a graduate of the Institute of Sacred Music of Yale University Divinity School.

Tune: ROSEBERRY 10.10.10.10.10.10.
Bruce Neswick, 1994

Come to Tend God's Garden

586

John A. Dalles, 1992

Luke 13:6–9; Gal. 5:22–26

*Whenever this repeated figure appears in the bass,
the organist should tie the eighth notes in the bass part.*

1 Come to tend God's gar - den, seeds of hope to sow, plant-ing fields of
2 As we tend God's gar - den, from its fur-rows rise stems of fresh be -
3 May God's gar - den flour - ish, may our toil suc - ceed, may God bless our

jus - tice, watch-ing mer - cy grow! In an ar - id waste - land,
gin - nings, stretch-ing toward the skies! Gra-cious-ness, our mead - ow,
ac - tions, ev - ery word and deed! Serv-ing Christ each sea - son,

spread a ver - dant heath! In a land of tu-mult, cul - ti - vate God's peace!
joy - ful - ness, our root, u - ni - ty, our fo-liage, righ-teous-ness, our fruit!
with God's di - a - gram, chart-ed by the Spir-it, for the task at hand!

*John Dalles is the author of more than 200 hymn texts. This one
was written for the 275th anniversary of the Synod of the Trinity
(Pennsylvania), where Dalles has served as a pastor at Fox
Chapel Presbyterian Church, Pittsburgh.*

Tune: KING'S WESTON 6.5.6.5.D.
Ralph Vaughan Williams, 1925
For another setting see 255

587   Through All the World, a Hungry Christ

Mark 1:40–42; Luke 4:16–20; 16:19–22   *Shirley Erena Murray, 1992; alt.*

1 Through all the world, a hun-gry Christ   must
2 Be - yond the church, a lep - er Christ   takes
3 In tor - ture cell, a pris-oner Christ   for
4 We do not know you, beg-gar Christ,   we

scav - enge far for dai - ly bread,   Must beg the
each un - touch-a - ble by hand,   Gives hope to
jus - tice and for truth must cry   To free the
do not rec - og - nize your sores,   We do not

rich for crumb and crust—   we are the
those who have no trust,   whose stig - ma
in - no - cent op - pressed   while we at
see, for we are blind: for - give us,

The small notes in the right hand of the accompaniment may be played on the keyboard by an assistant or by a solo instrument.
Play this note for st. 2, 3, 4 only.

rich, the dai - ly fed.
is our so - cial brand.
lib - er - ty pass by.
touch us, make us yours.

Shirley Erena Murray's text addresses "the Christ presence in the victims of the world, including the differently abled and AIDS sufferers." Calvin Hampton's innovative tune is named for Vernon De Tar, organist and retired faculty member of The Juilliard School of Music. Hampton served as music director at Calvary/St. George's Episcopal Parish in New York City.

Tune: DE TAR L.M.
Calvin Hampton, 1973
Alternate tune: GERMANY

Let Justice Flow like Streams 588

Jane Parker Huber, 1984   *Amos 5:14–15, 24; 7:7–8*

1 Let jus - tice flow like streams of spark-ling wa - ter, pure,
2 Let righ-teous - ness roll on as oth - ers' cares we heed,
3 So may God's plumb line, straight, de - fine our mea - sure true,

En - a - bling growth, re - fresh-ing life, a - bun - dant, cleans-ing, sure.
An ev - er - flow - ing stream of faith trans - lat - ed in - to deed.
And jus - tice, right, and peace per-vade this world our whole life through.

This is one of two hymns Jane Parker Huber wrote for special events emphasizing economic justice for women at the time of the reunification of two Presbyterian denominations in 1983. The text's brevity underscores the urgency of Amos' pronouncements against injustice.

Tune: ST. THOMAS S.M.
Aaron Williams' New Universal Psalmodist, 1770

589   Let There Be Light, O God of Hosts

William M. Vories, 1908; alt.

1 Let there be light, O God of hosts!
2 With-in our pas-sioned hearts in-still
3 Give us the peace of sens-es clear
4 Let woe and waste of war-fare cease,

Let there be wis-dom on the earth!
the calm that ends all strain and strife;
to know our neigh-bors' good our own;
that use-ful la-bor yet may build

Let broad hu-man-i-ty have birth!
Make us your min-is-ters of life;
To hope and suf-fer not a-lone,
Its homes with love and laugh-ter filled!

Let there be deeds, in-stead of boasts!
purge us from lusts that curse and kill!
bond-ed in love that con-quers fear!
God, give your way-ward chil-dren peace!

*William Vories, founder of the vast, interdenominational Omi
Mission in Japan, wrote this hymn as a response to the rising
threat of German militarism in 1908. It exemplifies the vision of
world peace and unity Vories strove to promote through his
lifelong missionary work.*

Tune: PENTECOST L.M.
William Boyd, 1864

Spirit of Jesus, If I Love My Neighbor 590

Brian Wren, 1973; rev. 1994   *Rom. 13:8–14*

1 Spir - it of Je - sus, if I love my neigh - bor,
2 And if, when I have an - swered need with kind - ness,
3 If I am hug - ging safe - ty or pos - ses - sions,

out of my knowl - edge, lei - sure, power or wealth,
my neigh - bor ris - es, wak-ened from de - spair,
un - curl my spir - it, as your love pre - vails,

o - pen my mind to un - der-stand the an - ger of
o - pen my heart to hear the cry for jus - tice that
to join my neigh - bors, work for lib - er - a - tion, and

help - less-ness that hates my power to help.
strug-gles for the chang - es that I fear.
find . . . my free - dom at the mark of nails.

Brian Wren gave this poem the subtitle "Pilgrimage of   Tune: BENJAMIN 11.10.11.10.
Confession" when it was first written, referring in part to the   *Jonathan McNair, 1994*
walk made by nine white South Africans in 1972 to draw
other whites' attention to the injustice of migrant labor laws.

591

This Is My Song

Ps. 82:8

Lloyd Stone, 1934

1 This is my song, O God of all the na - tions, a song of
2 My coun-try's skies are blu - er than the o - cean, and sun-light

peace for lands a - far and mine. This is my home, the
beams on clo - ver - leaf and pine; But oth - er lands have

coun - try where my heart is; here are my hopes, my
sun - light, too, and clo - ver, and skies are ev - ery -

dreams, my ho - ly shrine; But oth - er hearts in oth - er lands are
where as blue as mine. O hear my song, O God of all the

beat - ing with hopes and dreams as true and high as mine.
na - tions, a song of peace for their land and for mine.

These stanzas, published during the period between the two
world wars, express a hope for lasting peace among all nations,
races, and cultures. Finlandia is derived from a "tone poem" of
the same name by Finnish composer Jean Sibelius.

Tune: FINLANDIA 10.10.10.10.10.10.
Jean Sibelius, 1899
Arr. for The Hymnal, 1933

God of the Ages, Who with Sure Command 592

Daniel Crane Roberts, 1876; alt.

1 God of the a - ges, who with sure com-mand
2 Your pur - pose, just, en - vi - sions mor-tals free;
3 From war's a - larms, from dead-ly pes - ti - lence,
4 Re - fresh your peo - ple on life's toil-some way;

brought forth in beau - ty all the star - ry band
God, set our path toward hu - man lib - er - ty.
with stead - fast care be ev - er our de - fense;
lead us from night to nev - er - end - ing day;

of shin - ing worlds in splen-dor through the skies,
Still be our rul - er, guard-ian, guide, and stay—
Your love and faith with - in our hearts in - crease;
With truth and love guide us through er - ror's maze,

our grate - ful songs be - fore your throne a - rise.
your Word our law, your paths our cho - sen way.
with boun-teous good - ness nour - ish us in peace.
and we shall give you glo - ry, laud, and praise.

Episcopal priest Daniel Crane Roberts wrote this hymn for a July 4, 1876, centennial celebration at Brandon, Vermont. George W. Warren, composer of the tune, was organist at St. Thomas' Church in New York City for thirty years.

Tune: NATIONAL HYMN 10.10.10.10.
George William Warren, 1892

593 Lift Every Voice and Sing

James Weldon Johnson, 1921; alt.

1 Lift ev-ery voice and sing, till earth and heav - en ring, ring with the
2 Ston-y the road we trod, bit-ter the chas-tening rod, felt in the
3 God of our wea - ry years, God of our si - lent tears, God who has

har - mo - nies of lib - er - ty; Let our re - joic - ing
days when hope un - born had died; Yet with a stead - y
brought us thus far on the way; God, who by your

rise, high as the lis - tening skies, let it re - sound loud as the
beat, have not our wea - ry feet, come to the place for which our
might, led us in - to the light, keep us for - ev - er in the

roll - ing sea. Sing a song full of the
peo - ple sighed? We have come o - ver a
path, we pray. Lest our feet stray from the

Poet James Weldon Johnson was the first African-American to pass the bar examination in the state of Florida, and served as U.S. consul in Venezuela and Nicaragua. He collaborated with his composer brother, John Rosamond Johnson, to write Broadway operettas and edit song collections. John appeared in vaudeville, directed London musicals, and headed the Music School Settlement in New York.

Tune: LIFT EVERY VOICE Irr.
J. Rosamond Johnson, 1921

faith that the harsh past has taught us,
way that with tears has been wa - tered,
plac - es, our God, where we met you,

Sing a song full of the
We have come, tread - ing our
Lest our hearts, drunk with the

hope that the pres - ent has brought us;
path through the blood of the slaugh - tered,
wine of the world, for - get you;

Fac - ing the
Out from the
Shad-owed be -

ris - ing sun of our new day be - gun, let us march
gloom - y past, till now we stand at last where the white
neath your hand, may we for - ev - er stand, true to our

on till vic - to - ry is won.
gleam of our bright star is cast.
God, true to our na - tive land.

594 How Beautiful, Our Spacious Skies

St. 1, Katharine Lee Bates, 1893; alt.
St. 2, 3, 4, Miriam Therese Winter, 1993

1 How beau-ti-ful, our spa-cious skies, our am - ber waves of grain;
2 In - dig - e-nous and im - mi - grant, our daugh-ters and our sons:
3 How beau-ti-ful, sin - cere la - ment, the wis - dom born of tears,
4 How beau-ti-ful, two con - ti - nents, and is - lands in the sea

our pur - ple moun-tains as they rise a - bove the fruit - ful plain.
O may we nev - er rest con-tent till all are tru - ly one.
the cour-age called for to re - pent the blood-shed through the years.
that dream of peace, non - vi - o - lence, all peo - ple liv - ing free.

A - mer - i - ca! A - mer - i - ca! God's gra-cious gifts a - bound,
A - mer - i - ca! A - mer - i - ca! God grant that we may be
A - mer - i - ca! A - mer - i - ca! God grant that we may be
A - mer - i - cas! A - mer - i - cas! God grant that we may be

and more and more we're grate-ful for life's boun-ty all a - round.
a sis - ter-hood and broth-er-hood from sea to shin-ing sea.
a na - tion blessed with none op-pressed, true land of lib - er - ty.
a hem - i - sphere where peo - ple here all live in har-mo - ny.

On her first trip west in the summer of 1893 the distinguished
New England educator Katharine Lee Bates was inspired to
write "O Beautiful for Spacious Skies." One hundred years later
Miriam Therese Winter wrote new stanzas to clearly include all
of the Americas.

Tune: MATERNA C.M.D.
Samuel A. Ward, 1882

Some Glad Morning
(I'll Fly Away)

595

Albert E. Brumley, 1932   *Ps. 55:6*

1 Some glad morn-ing when this life is o'er, I'll fly a - way;
2 When the shad-ows of this life have gone, fly a-way, fly a-way;
3 Just a few more wea - ry days and then,

to a home on God's ce - les-tial shore, I'll fly a - way.
Like a bird from pris - on bars has flown, fly a-way, fly a-way.
To a land where joys shall nev - er end,

Refrain
I'll fly a - way, O glo - ry, I'll fly a - way;
fly a-way, fly a-way, in the morn-ing;

When I die, hal-le - lu - jah, by and by, I'll fly a - way.
fly a-way, fly a-way.

This is a favorite song of the golden age of gospel music, in which heaven is vividly described and highly desired. Albert E. Brumley's musical style grew out of his Ozark mountain roots. He wrote this song while working in a cotton field.

Tune: I'LL FLY AWAY 9.4.9.4. with refrain
Albert E. Brumley, 1932

596

Rock of Ages, Cleft for Me

Isa. 26:4; John 19:34

Augustus M. Toplady, 1776; alt.

1 Rock of a - ges, cleft for me, let me hide; my shel - ter be!
2 Not the la - bors of my hands can ful - fill your law's de - mands;
3 Noth-ing in my hand I bring, sim - ply to your cross I cling;
4 While I draw this fleet-ing breath, when my eyes shall close in death,

Let the wat - er and the blood, from your wound-ed side which flowed,
Could my zeal no re - spite know, could my tears for - ev - er flow,
Na - ked, come to you for dress; help-less, look to you for grace;
When I soar to worlds un - known, meet you at your judg-ment throne,

Be of sin the dou - ble cure, cleanse me from its guilt and power.
All for sin could not a - tone; you must save, and you a - lone.
Stained, I to the foun-tain fly; wash me, Sav - ior, or I die!
Rock of a - ges, cleft for me, let me hide; my shel - ter be!

Augustus Toplady first published this poem as part of an
extensive article in which he likened the English national debt to
the burden of sin. The present form is a hybrid of the original
and revisions in 1815 by Thomas Cotterill.

Tune: TOPLADY 7.7.7.7.7.7.
Thomas Hastings, 1830
Alternate tune: REDHEAD NO. 76

Shall We Gather at the River

597

Robert Lowry, 1864; alt.

Rev. 22:1–5

1 Shall we gath-er at the riv - er, where bright an - gel feet have trod,
2 On the mar-gin of the riv - er, wash - ing up its sil - ver spray,
3 As we reach the shin-ing riv - er, lay we ev - ery bur-den down;
4 Soon we'll reach the shin-ing riv - er, soon our pil-grim-age will cease;

with its crys-tal tide for - ev - er flow-ing by the throne of God?
we will walk and wor - ship ev - er, all the hap - py gold - en day.
grace our spir - its will de - liv - er, and pro - vide a robe and crown.
soon our hap - py hearts will quiv - er with the mel - o - dy of peace.

Refrain

Yes, we'll gath-er at the riv - er, the beau-ti-ful, the beau-ti-ful riv - er,

Gath-er with the saints at the riv - er that flows by the throne of God.

Written during a time when an epidemic was claiming many lives in New York, Robert Lowry's hymn raised the question "Shall we meet again?" Lowry was pastor at Hanson Place Baptist Church in Brooklyn from 1861 to 1869, and collaborated on numerous hymn collections with William H. Doane.

Tune: HANSON PLACE 8.7.8.7. with refrain
Robert Lowry, 1864

598 On River Jordan's Banks I Stand

Samuel Stennett, 1787; alt.

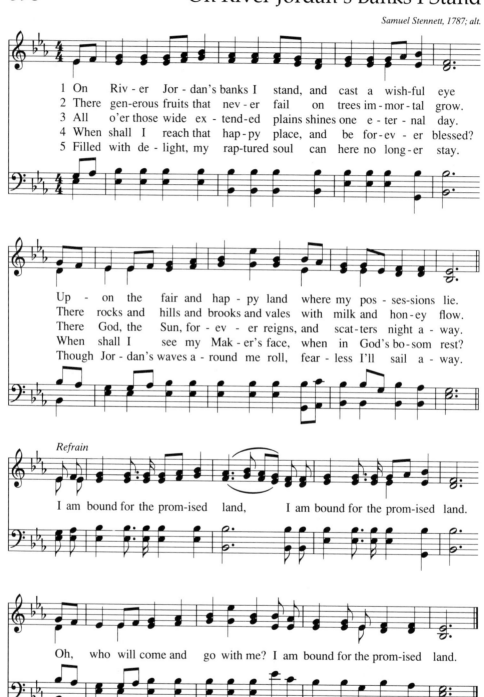

1 On Riv-er Jor-dan's banks I stand, and cast a wish-ful eye
2 There gen-erous fruits that nev-er fail on trees im-mor-tal grow.
3 All o'er those wide ex-tend-ed plains shines one e-ter-nal day.
4 When shall I reach that hap-py place, and be for-ev-er blessed?
5 Filled with de-light, my rap-tured soul can here no long-er stay.

Up - on the fair and hap-py land where my pos-ses-sions lie.
There rocks and hills and brooks and vales with milk and hon-ey flow.
There God, the Sun, for-ev-er reigns, and scat-ters night a-way.
When shall I see my Mak-er's face, when in God's bo-som rest?
Though Jor-dan's waves a-round me roll, fear-less I'll sail a-way.

Refrain

I am bound for the prom-ised land, I am bound for the prom-ised land.

Oh, who will come and go with me? I am bound for the prom-ised land.

Born into an English family that had been active for generations in Seventh Day Baptist churches, Samuel Stennett became an outstanding Baptist preacher. He was a personal friend of King George III. The hymn originally had no refrain.

Tune: PROMISED LAND C.M. with refrain
Southern Harmony, 1835; alt.
Arr. Rigdon M. McIntosh, 1875

Steal Away

599

African-American spiritual; alt.

Matt. 24:27; 27:52–53; 1 Cor. 15:51–52; 1 Thess. 4:13–18

Slowly, with feeling

Refrain

Steal a-way, steal a-way, steal a-way to Je-sus!

Last time, end

Steal a-way, steal a-way home, I don't have long to stay here!

1 I hear God call-ing, God calls me by the thun-der; the
2 Green trees are bend-ing, poor sin-ner stands a-trem-bling; the
3 I hear God call-ing, God calls me by the light-ning; the
4 Tomb-stones are burst-ing, poor sin-ner stands a-trem-bling; the

to Refrain

trum-pet sounds with-in my soul, I don't have long to stay here.
trum-pet sounds with-in my soul, I don't have long to stay here.
trum-pet sounds with-in my soul, I don't have long to stay here.
trum-pet sounds with-in my soul, I don't have long to stay here.

This is an example of the spiritual with coded meaning that Frederick Douglass spoke of in his narrative of 1855, My Bondage and My Freedom. To "steal away home" could have meant to run away to freedom.

Tune: STEAL AWAY 5.7.8.7. with refrain
African-American spiritual

600 How Lovely Is Your Dwelling

Ps. 84

Jean Janzen, 1991

1 How love - ly is your dwell-ing, O God, my hope and strength.
2 How blessed are those whose trav - els are strength-ened by your hand,
3 Look on me, God of good-ness, you are my sun and shield.

My spir - it longs for shel - ter, my flesh cries out for
who pass through shad-owed val - leys and find re - fresh - ing
One day with - in your house - hold is what I most de -

home, where ev - en swal-lows nest - ing be - side your al - tar
springs. Your rains fall soft as kind - ness on all your faith - ful
sire. O guide me in your mer - cy a - long my lone - ly

rest - ing are ev - er prais - ing you.
pil - grims un - til they come to you.
path - way; O bring me safe - ly home.

Jean Wiebe Janzen is a published poet who also teaches poetry writing at Fresno Pacific College and Eastern Mennonite College. She began writing hymns at the invitation of the Mennonite Church for their Hymnal: A Worship Book *(1992) where this text appears with the setting by Heinrich Schütz.*

Tune: ES IST EIN' ROS'
altered to 7.6.7.6.7.7.6.
Catholische Geistliche Kirchengesäng, *Cologne, 1599*

How Lovely Is Your Dwelling

601

Jean Janzen, 1991

Ps. 84

1 How love - ly   is   your dwell-ing,   O   God,   my   hope and strength.
2 How blessed are those whose trav - els   are strength-ened by   your hand,
3 Look   on   me, God   of   good-ness,   you   are   my   sun   and shield.

My   spir - it   longs for shel - ter,   my   flesh cries out   for home,
who   pass through shad-owed val - leys   and   find   re - fresh-ing springs.
One   day   with - in   your house-hold   is   what   I   most de - sire.

where   ev - en   swal - lows nest - ing   be - side your al - tar rest - ing
Your   rains   fall   soft   as   kind-ness   on   all your faith - ful   pil - grims
O   guide   me   in   your mer - cy   a - long my   lone - ly   path-way;

are   ev - er   prais   -   ing   you.
un - til   they   come   to   you.
O   bring   me   safe   -   ly   home.

Some performing editions show G natural in soprano.

Tune: PSALM 84   7.6.7.6.7.7.6.
Heinrich Schütz, Psalter, 1628

602

Savior God Above

Ps. 108:5–6; Rom. 13:9–12; Rev. 1:4–6

Duke Ellington, 1943; alt.

Refrain

Sav-ior God a-bove, God al-might-y, God of love,

please look down and see my peo-ple through.

Last time, end

1 I be-lieve that God put sun and moon up in the sky.
2 Heav-en is a good-ness time, a bright-er light on high.
3 I be-lieve God is now, was then, and al-ways will be.

This song is part of the jazz suite Black, Brown and Beige *by African-American jazz classicist Duke Ellington. The suite had its premiere in Carnegie Hall in 1943 as a musical portrait of African-American social history.*

Tune: COME SUNDAY Irr. with refrain
Duke Ellington, 1943

to Refrain

I don't mind the gray skies, 'cause they're just clouds pass-ing by.
Love your neigh-bor as your-self, and have a bright-er by and by.
With God's bless-ing we can make it through e - ter - ni - ty.

to Refrain

Giver of Life, Where'er They Be 603

Frederick Lucian Hosmer, 1888; alt.

1 Giv - er of life, wher - e'er they be, safe in your own e -
2 All souls you call, both here and there, do rest with - in your
3 Your word is true, your ways are just; a - bove the chant - ed
4 Hap - py are they in God who rest, no more by fear and

ter - ni - ty, now live your chil - dren glo - rious - ly.
shel - ter - ing care; one prov - i - dence a - like they share:
"Dust to dust" shall rise our song of grate - ful trust:
doubt op - pressed; liv - ing or dy - ing they are blessed:

Al - le - lu - ia! Al - le - lu - ia! Al - le - lu - ia!

Frederick Hosmer wrote this hymn for Easter services at the
Church of Unity in Cleveland, Ohio, where he served as minister
for many years. Hosmer wrote more than fifty hymns.

Tune: GELOBT SEI GOTT 8.8.8. with alleluias
Melchior Vulpius, 1609

604 Hush, Hush, Somebody's Calling My Name

African-American spiritual

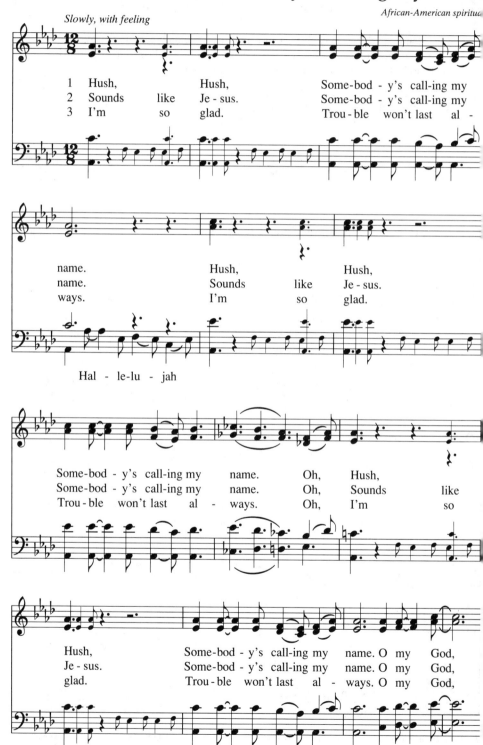

Slowly, with feeling

1 Hush, Hush, Some-bod-y's call-ing my
2 Sounds like Je-sus. Some-bod-y's call-ing my
3 I'm so glad. Trou-ble won't last al -

name. Hush, Hush,
name. Sounds like Je-sus.
ways. I'm so glad.

Hal - le-lu - jah

Some-bod-y's call-ing my name. Oh, Hush,
Some-bod-y's call-ing my name. Oh, Sounds like
Trou-ble won't last al - ways. Oh, I'm so

Hush, Some-bod-y's call-ing my name. O my God,
Je-sus. Some-bod-y's call-ing my name. O my God,
glad. Trou-ble won't last al - ways. O my God,

O my God, what shall I do? What shall I do?
O my God, what shall I do? What shall I do?
O my God, what shall I do? What shall I do?

This spiritual is an example of the call to personhood that Jesus was able to evoke within the hearts of the enslaved. It suggests that the inward "call" also anticipated physical freedom. Jeffrey Radford has served as Director of Music at Trinity United Church of Christ, Chicago.

Tune: African-American spiritual
Arr. Jeffrey Radford, 1993

As Moses Raised the Serpent Up　　605

Versification The New Century Hymnal, *1993*　　　　　　*John 3:14–17*

1 As Mo - ses raised the ser - pent up, God's
2 For God so loved the world that God, all
3 That Child was sent in - to the world not

Child is lift - ed high; And all who in that
hu - man life to free, Gave to the world God's
to con - demn but save; Now through Christ's name all

Child be - lieve shall nev - er, nev - er die.
Child that all might live e - ter - nal - ly.
are re - deemed— what won - drous love God gave.

This hymn is a paraphrase of the gospel for Holy Cross Day, traditionally a time for reflection on faith and the meaning of the cross. In this reading, the image of Christ on the cross as the way to eternal life is related to the story of redemption of God's rebellious people in the wilderness.

Tune: MORNING SONG C.M.
Melody from Sixteen Tune Settings, *1812*
Harm. C. Winfred Douglas, 1940

606 Nearer, My God, to You

Gen. 28:10–22; Matt. 16:24

Sarah Flower Adams, 1841
Adapt. Thomas H. Troeger

1 Near - er, my God, to you, near - er to you. I'll bear the
2 When I am wan - der-ing as Ja - cob did, and in the
3 Let Ja-cob's lad - der fill the sky a - bove, and an - gels
4 Then, wak-ing from the night to morn-ing air by Beth-el's

cross as Christ calls me to do and pray each day a - new:
deep - est night the path is hid, my dreams will bring me, too,
car - ry down the faith and love to keep this goal in view:
stone, I'll know you heard my prayer, and how my yearn-ing grew:

1–4 Near - er my God, to you, near - er my God, to you, near - er to you.

*Sarah Flower Adams, daughter of a well-known English editor,
was a successful actress in London. During her short life she
wrote prose and poetry for religious publications, a five-act
drama, and a children's catechism.*

Tune: BETHANY 6.4.6.4.6.6.6.4.
Lowell Mason, 1856

607 We Would Be Building

Matt. 7:24–27; Luke 6:47–49; 1 Esd. 5:56–7:15

Purd E. Deitz, 1935; alt.

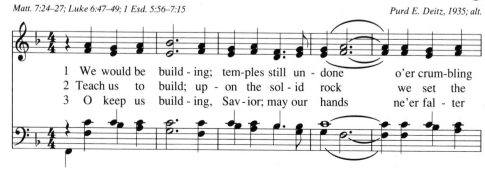

1 We would be build - ing; tem-ples still un - done o'er crum-bling
2 Teach us to build; up - on the sol - id rock we set the
3 O keep us build - ing, Sav-ior; may our hands ne'er fal - ter

walls their cross-es scarce-ly lift, wait-ing till love can
dream that hard-ens in - to deed, ribbed with fine steel, both
when the dream is in our hearts, when to our ears there

raise the bro - ken stone, and hearts cre - a - tive
time and change to mock, the un-fail - ing pur - pose
come di - vine com - mands and all the pride of

bridge the hu - man rift. We would be build - ing,
of our no - blest creed. Teach us to build; O
sin - ful will de - parts. We build with you; O

Ar - chi-tect Di - vine, re-veal the shape of life in your de-sign.
Mak-er, lend us sight to see the tow - ers gleam-ing in the light.
grant en-dur-ing worth un-til your prom-ised realm shall come on earth.

*Purd Deitz, pastor of Trinity Evangelical and Reformed Church
in Philadelphia, wrote this hymn to express the youth conference
theme, "Christian Youth Building a New World." Set to one of
his favorite tunes, Finlandia, it became popular around the
world.*

Tune: FINLANDIA 10.10.10.10.10.10.
Jean Sibelius, 1899
Arr. for The Hymnal, *1933*

608 Christ Will Come Again

Matt. 13:24–30; John 14:3

Brian Wren, 1987

Unison

1 Christ will come a - gain, God's jus - tice to com - plete, to
2 Christ will come a - gain and life shall be com - plete. The
3 Christ will come a - gain, and joy shall be com - plete as

reap the fields of time and sift the weeds from wheat: then
wa - ters from the throne shall wash the na - tions' feet: then
flames of light-ning love be - deck the judg - ment seat: then

let us pas-sion-ate-ly care for peace and jus - tice here on earth,
let us pas-sion-ate-ly care for health and whole-ness here on earth,
let us pas-sion-ate-ly share the whole great gos - pel here on earth,

and e - vil's rage re - strain with love, till Christ shall come a - gain.
and ease our neigh-bor's pain with love, till Christ shall come a - gain.
un - til all things at - tain their end, when Christ shall come a - gain.

*This hymn was written during a Seventh Day Adventist
Musicians Convention in 1987. Brian Wren wanted to honor his
hosts with "a hymn on the Second Advent which, whether
understood literally or symbolically, would connect ultimate
hope with present action."*

Tune: IDA 5.6.6.6.8.8.8.6.
Joan Collier Fogg, 1987

Now Is the Time Approaching

609

Jane Laurie Borthwick, 1859; alt.

Jer. 33:14–16; Isa. 11:6–9; 61:11

1 Now is the time ap - proach - ing, by proph-ets long fore - told,
2 Let all that now di - vides us re - move and pass a - way,
3 O long - ex - pect - ed dawn - ing, come with your cheer-ing ray!

when all shall dwell to - geth - er, se - cure and man - i - fold.
like mists of ear - ly morn - ing be - fore the blaze of day.
Yet shall the prom-ise beck - on and lead us not a - stray.

Let war be learned no long - er, let strife and tu - mult cease,
Let all that now u - nites us more sweet and last - ing prove,
O sweet an - tic - i - pa - tion! It cheers the watch-ers on

all earth a bless - ed gar - den that God shall tend in peace.
a clos - er bond of un - ion, in bless - ed lands of love.
to pray, and hope, and la - bor till Christ's new realm is come.

Jane Laurie Borthwick's text titled "Anticipation of Heaven" was
published in her Thoughts for Thoughtful Hours (1859). George
J. Webb, American organist and music publisher, originally wrote
this music for a secular song, "'Tis dawn, the lark is singing."

Tune: WEBB 7.6.7.6.D.
George J. Webb, 1837

610
My Eyes Have Seen the Glory

Acts 7:55–59; 2 Cor. 5:1–10   *Julia Ward Howe, 1861; alt.*

1 My eyes have seen the glo - ry of the com - ing of the Lord,
2 God has been there in the watch-fires of a hun - dred cir - cling camps,
3 God has sound-ed forth the trum - pet that shall nev - er call re - treat;
4 In the beau - ty of the lil - ies Christ was born a - cross the sea,

who is tram - pling out the vin - tage where the grapes of wrath are stored,
where they built a sa - cred al - tar in the eve - ning dews and damps;
and is sift - ing out the hearts of all be - fore the judg - ment seat;
with a glo - ry in whose bo - som that trans - fig - ures you and me;

And has loosed the fate - ful light - ning of a ter - ri - ble swift sword;
I can read the righ - teous sen - tence by the dim and flar - ing lamps;
O be swift, my soul, to an - swer and be ju - bi - lant, my feet!
As Christ died to make us ho - ly, let us die to make all free;

Refrain

God's truth is march-ing on.
God's day is march-ing on.
Our God is march-ing on.
While God is march-ing on.

Glo - ry, glo - ry, hal - le - lu - jah!

Julia Ward Howe, an early leader in the movement for women's suffrage and an abolitionist, wrote this text specifically for a familiar camp-meeting tune one night after reviewing Union troops near Washington, D.C. It was published on the front page of the Atlantic Monthly, *which added the title "Battle Hymn of the Republic."*

Tune: BATTLE HYMN OF THE REPUBLIC Irr.
United States camp-meeting tune, 19th century

Glo - ry, glo - ry, hal - le - lu - jah! Glo - ry, glo - ry, hal - le - lu - jah! God's truth is march - ing on.

O Day of God, Draw Near 611

R. B. Y. Scott, 1937; alt.   Ps. 105:7; 2 Pet. 3:8–15

1 O Day of God, draw near in beau - ty and in power,
2 Bring to our trou - bled minds, un - cer - tain and a - fraid,
3 Bring jus - tice to our land, that all may dwell se - cure,
4 Bring to our world of strife your sov - ereign word of peace,
5 O Day of God, draw near as at cre - a - tion's birth;

Come with your time - less judg - ment now to match our pres - ent hour.
The qui - et of a stead - fast faith, calm of a call o - beyed.
And fine - ly build for days to come foun - da - tions that en - dure.
That war may haunt the earth no more and des - o - la - tion cease.
Let there be light a - gain, and let your reign be - gin on earth.

R. B. Y. Scott was a theologian, Old Testament scholar, and
social reformer who taught at McGill University, Montreal, and
at Princeton University. A minister in the United Church of
Canada, he wrote this text in 1937 for the Fellowship for a
Christian Social Order.

Tune: ST. MICHAEL S.M.
Trente quatre Pseaumes, Geneva, 1551
Adapt. William Crotch, 1836

612 Strengthen All the Weary Hands

Isa. 35

Martie McMane, 1991; rev. 1993

1 Strength-en all the wea - ry hands, stead - y all the
2 Wa - ters flow in the wil - der - ness, streams break forth a -
3 Then the ran - somed shall re - turn, they shall come to
4 Let the wil - der - ness be glad, and the des - ert

trem - bling knees, and say to all faint hearts:
mid ar - id des - erts, burn - ing sands turn to pools.
Zi - on with sing - ing. Joy shall crown their heads.
burst in - to blos - som, dance and sing for joy!

"Cour - age, cour - age, do not be a - fraid.
Be strong, fear not, for your God is near.
Sor - row, sigh - ing, all shall flee a - way.
Hal - le - lu - jah! Hal - le - lu - jah!

(1–4) Look, your God is com - ing. God comes, comes to save you.

Martie McMane, an ordained United Church of Christ minister,
wrote many songs for worship as a pastor-evangelist in local
church and national settings. This one first appeared in Worship
Comes Alive, a resource developed for a denominational
program, "The Evangelism Institutes."

Tune: SONG OF REJOICING Irr.
Martie McMane, 1991
Harm. Don Brandon, 1991

Cour - age, cour - age, do not be a - fraid."
Be strong, fear not, for your God is near.
Sor - row, sigh - ing, all shall flee a - way.
Hal - le - lu - jah! Hal - le - lu - jah!

O Holy City, Seen of John 613

Walter Russell Bowie, 1910; alt. *Rev. 21:1–22:5; Heb. 11:16*

1 O ho - ly cit - y, seen of John, where Christ, the Lamb, does reign,
2 O shame to us who rest con-tent while lust and greed for gain
3 Give us, O God, the strength to build the cit - y that has stayed
4 Al - read - y in the mind of God that cit - y is pre - pared:

with-in whose four - square walls shall come no night, nor need, nor pain,
in street and shop and ten - e - ment wring gold from hu - man pain,
too long a dream, whose laws are love, whose ways are your own ways,
oh, how its splen - dor chal - leng - es the souls that great - ly dare,

And where the tears are wiped from eyes that shall not weep a - gain.
And bit - ter lips in deep de - spair cry, "Christ has died in vain!"
And where the sun that blaz - es is your grace for all our days.
Yes, bids us seize the whole of life and build its glo - ry there.

Walter Russell Bowie, Episcopal priest and seminary professor, was a member of the committee that prepared the Revised Standard Version of the Bible. This hymn expresses a hope for a realm of God beginning here and now.

Tune: MORNING SONG 8.6.8.6.8.6.
Melody from Sixteen Tune Settings, 1812
Harm. C. Winfred Douglas, 1940

614

Camina, Pueblo de Dios
(Go Forth, O People of God)

Rom. 7:5–8:4; 2 Cor. 5:14–19; Rev. 21:1–7

Cesáreo Gabaraín, 1979
Transl. George Lockwood, 1987; alt.

Unison

Cesáreo Gabaraín was a Roman Catholic priest who was very active as a congregational composer and head of a liturgical music association. He also served as the Spanish chaplain to Pope Paul VI, and was given the title "emeritus" shortly before his death in 1991.

Tune: NUEVA CREACION 7.8.8.7.D. with refrain
Cesáreo Gabaraín, 1979
Harm. Juan Luis García, 1987

muer - te que en-gen-dra la vi - da, nue-vos se - res, nue - va luz.
Al des - tru - ir - los, nos tra - e u - na nue-va ple - ni - tud.
death that gives birth to new liv - ing, a new peo-ple, a new light.
Crush-ing all e - vil, Christ brings us life's a - bun-dance, life's new joy.

Cris - to nos ha sal - va - do con su muer-te y re - su-rrec - ción.
Po - ne en paz a los pue-blos, a las co - sas y al Cre - a - dor.
Christ has brought us sal - va - tion, dy-ing there and ris-ing a - gain.
Christ brings rec - on-cil - ia - tion to all things and peo-ple with God.

to Refrain
(Estribillo)

To-das las co - sas re - na - cen en la nue-va cre-a - ción.
To-do re - na - ce a la vi - da en la nue-va cre-a - ción.
Ev-ery-thing comes to new birth-ing, all cre - a - tion is re - born.
Na-ture bursts in - to new flow-ering, all cre - a - tion is re - born.

3 Cie-lo y tie-rra se a-bra-zan,
   nues-tra al-ma ha-lla el per-dón.
   Vuel-ven a a-brir-se los cie-los
   pa-ra el mun-do pe-ca-dor.
   Is-ra-el pe-re-gri-no,
   vi-ve y can-ta tu re-den-ción.
   Hay nue-vos mun-dos a-bier-tos
   en la nue-va cre-a-ción.
   Estribillo

3 Heav-en and earth are em-brac-ing,
   and our souls find par-don at last.
   Now heav-en's gates are re-o-pened
   to the sin-ner, to us all.
   This is Is-ra-el's jour-ney;
   now we live, sal-va-tion's our song;
   Christ's re-sur-rec-tion has freed us.
   There are new worlds to ex-plore.
   Refrain

615   Enter in the Realm of God

Mark 4:26–32; 10:13–16; 1 John 4:7–12   *Lavon Bayler, 1994*

1 En - ter in the realm of God.
2 In com - mu - ni - ties that serve,
3 God has loved, and so we love,
4 Come a - gain, O Christ, to rule

It has come, and yet will be.
and a - mong the saints who care,
and we give that all may share
in that realm that has no end.

It is known, and yet un - known.
There is jus - tice for the poor,
In the heal - ing God sup - plies,
May your chil - dren ev - ery - where

Christ re - vealed its mys - ter - y.
and new free - dom from de - spair.
in good news that we de - clare.
hear your greet - ing: "Wel - come, friend!"

Hymnwriter Lavon Bayler referred to Jesus' teachings about the realm of God in the Gospel of Mark when asked to provide a text on this theme. Contemporary Philippine composer Vérne de la Peña provided the arrangement of the traditional Visayan folk melody.

Tune: DANDANSOY 7.7.7.7.
Visayan folk melody, Philippines
Arr. Vérne de la Peña, 1994

I Want to Be Ready

616

African-American spiritual

Rev. 21:1–4, 10–27; John 11:1–44; Acts 2:14, 36–41

I want to be read - y, I want to be read - y,

Last time, end

I want to be read - y to walk in Je - ru - sa - lem just like John.

Leader   *All*

1 Oh, John, oh, John, what do you say?
2 When Mar - tha spoke the Sav - ior's name,
3 When Pe - ter was preach-ing at Pen - te - cost, walk in Je-ru-sa-lem just like John.
4 When Mar-y asked Je - sus to "come and see,"
5 John said the cit - y was just four-square,

All   *to Refrain*

That I'll be there at the com-ing day,
She knew she'd nev - er be the same,
He was en - dowed with the Ho - ly Ghost, walk in Je-ru-sa-lem just like John.
Her faith gave Laz - a - rus vic - to - ry,
And he de - clared he'd meet me there,

Leader

This African-American spiritual is one of a small number based not on the Hebrew Scriptures but the New Testament, specifically the book of Revelation. Stanzas two and four are additions to the traditional text and include some of the female followers of Jesus.

Tune: I WANT TO BE READY Irr.
African-American spiritual
Arr. J. Jefferson Cleveland and Verolga Nix, 1981

617   Unite and Join Your Cheerful Songs

Rev. 5:9–14

Hymns and Spiritual Songs,
ed. James O'Kelly, 1816; alt.

1 U - nite and join your cheer - ful songs, with
2 This is the way the church should strive, in
3 Wor - thy the Lamb, the an - gels say, to
4 As - sist us, all a - bove the sky, on

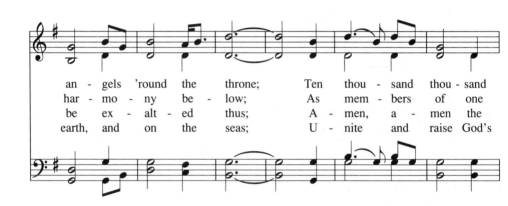

an - gels 'round the throne; Ten thou - sand thou - sand
har - mo - ny be - low; As mem - bers of one
be ex - alt - ed thus; A - men, a - men the
earth, and on the seas; U - nite and raise God's

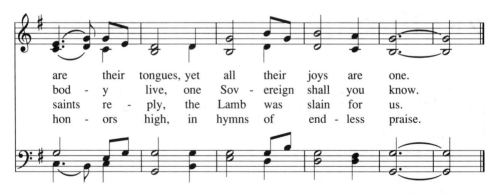

are their tongues, yet all their joys are one.
bod - y live, one Sov - ereign shall you know.
saints re - ply, the Lamb was slain for us.
hon - ors high, in hymns of end - less praise.

This hymn appears in Hymns and Spiritual Songs, *a collection
of hymn texts (without tunes), published in 1816 in Raleigh,
North Carolina. It may have been written by the book's editor,
James O'Kelly, an itinerant preacher who broke away from the
Methodist Church because of its hierarchical government.
O'Kelly founded the Christian Church in the southern United
States in 1794. In 1931, the Christian Church merged with the
Congregational Church to form a predecessor denomination of
the United Church of Christ. The themes of unity and freedom
appear throughout O'Kelly's collection of hymns.*

Tune: AMAZING GRACE (NEW BRITAIN) C.M.
from Columbia Harmony, *Cincinnati, 1829*
Arr. Edwin O. Excell, 1900
Alternate tune: LAND OF REST

PSALMS AND CANTICLES

PSALMS AND CANTICLES

The psalms and canticles of Judeo-Christian worship heritage link Christians of today with their earliest roots. The Israelites sang psalms in worship and for other religious occasions. Early Christians continued the practice, and in one form or another the saying or singing of psalms has been a thread through centuries of Christian worship. During a long period of Reformed history, psalms were sung in meter, for example, the *Bay Psalm Book*. In early times, however, they were sung antiphonally, leader and congregation alternating verses, or with the congregation singing a response. Although exact performance practices and tunes are not known, it is clear that corporate participation in the singing of the psalms was the common practice.

Psalms were originally intended for singing, and this century has seen a revival in this ancient custom. This section of *The New Century Hymnal* presents the Psalms in their biblical form, with verses arranged in balance for antiphonal use. They are pointed to be sung to simple tunes, or tones. The format also allows for their use as readings for private or corporate meditation. The same is true for the canticles, Bible texts that were traditionally sung, but taken from sources other than the Book of Psalms.

The translation used for this adaptation is the New Revised Standard Version of the Bible, 1990. In addition to adjustments in the verses for musical flow, the text has been rendered using the same language standards found throughout the hymnal. The selection of psalms and verses is based on the *Revised Common Lectionary*, 1992, and psalms have been added for use in morning and evening prayer. When the lectionary designates varied selections of verses on different days, directions are given following the psalm. At the end of this section are several psalms set in Anglican-style chant, and two hymns, "Phos Hilaron" and "O Wisdom," for use in evening prayer.

USING THE PSALMS AND CANTICLES IN WORSHIP

The psalms and canticles in this section of the book may be used in a variety of ways:

They may be read by an individual for private devotions.

They may be sung responsively:

a solo voice (*cantor*) alternating with congregation;

choir alternating with congregation;

one part of the congregation alternating with another part of the congregation.

They may be sung through entirely by congregation, without alternating.

They may be read responsively (when reading, the points ['] are ignored):

leader alternating with congregation;

two sides of congregation alternating;

alternating by half couplet or whole couplet.

SINGING THE PSALMS AND CANTICLES
USING A PSALM TONE AND POINTS

The psalms and canticles have been arranged into couplets, each with an A phrase and a B phrase (indented), to match the melody of a *tone*. The point (´) in the text is positioned to indicate exactly where the melody note changes. If the choice is to have a cantor alternate with congregation, the cantor sings the first couplet as follows:

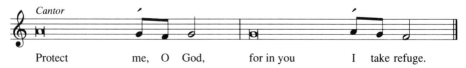

Protect me, O God, for in you I take refuge.

The congregation then answers with the indented couplet, repeating the same melody (tone) "by ear," and observing the point as the place to change the note.

Congregation

I say to God, "You are my God; I have no good a - part from you."

This alternating continues for the desired number of verses.

USING THE RESPONSE (℟)

The symbol ℟ indicates the singing, by all, of the response. If the psalm or canticle is read responsively, instead of being sung, the response may be spoken or sung by all at the designated places.

ONE WAY TO USE A PSALM OR CANTICLE IN WORSHIP

1. The response is played through once.
2. The response is sung by all.
3. The tone is played.
4. The first couplet is sung by the cantor or choir, accompanied by the tone.
5. The second couplet is sung by the congregation, accompanied by the tone.
6. Continue alternating couplets. Where indicated, the response is played and sung (with no musical introduction).
7. The singing of the psalm or canticle continues as before.
8. The response is sung by all at the end (with no introduction).

ADDITIONAL HELPS

1. The points are always placed so that an accented syllable will fall on the last note of musical phrase A or B in the tone. If there are extra syllables, they are also sung on the last note.

2. The psalms and canticle texts are to be sung in a natural speech rhythm, at a comfortable pace, and with minimal (if any) pause for punctuation.

3. Several tones have been provided here. These, plus additional tones, will be found in the accompanist edition in various transpositions.

4. This form of psalm singing can be learned with little difficulty, and the same tone may be used for any psalm.

5. Double tones are designed to carry the text of two couplets. The above guidelines for singing will apply, except that two couplets will be matched with phrases A, B, C, and D of the tone. Thus, alternating may be accomplished by having the cantor sing the first *two* couplets, with the congregation responding with the next *two* couplets. Or the congregation, by itself, may sing the entire selection to the double tone, and with the designated response.

Psalm tones

Tones 1, 8: May Schwarz; tones 2, 3, 4, 7, 9, 10: Jonathan McNair; tone 5: Jeffrey Radford; tones 6, 11: Arthur G. Clyde.

620

Psalm 1

Response

Antiphon: Judy Hunnicutt, 1994

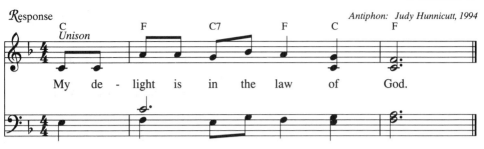

My de - light is in the law of God.

R

¹Happy are those who do not follow
  the advice óf the wicked,
    or take the path that sinners tread,
    or sit in the šeat of scoffers;

²but their delight is in the láw of God,
  and on God's law they meditate dáy
  and night.

³They are like trees planted by štreams
  of water,
    which yield their fruit ín its season,
    and their leaves dó not wither.
    In all that they dó they prosper.

⁴The wicked áre not so,
  but are like chaff that the wind
  dŕives away.

⁵Therefore the wicked will not stand ín
  the judgment,
    nor sinners in the congregation óf
    the righteous;

⁶for God watches over the way óf the
  righteous,
    but the way of the wickéd will
    perish. *R*

Psalm 2

Response

Antiphon: Carolyn Jennings, 1994

Hap - py are all who take ref - uge in God.

R

¹Why do the naťions conspire,
  and the peoples plót in vain?

²The rulers of the earth set themselves,
  and the leaders take counšel together,

against God and those God has
anointed, saying,

³"Let us burst their bonds asunder,
and cast their cords from us."

⁴The one who sits in the heavens
laughs;
God has them in derision. ℟

⁵Then God will speak to them in
wrath,
and terrify them in fury, saying,

⁶"I have set my ruler on Zion,
my holy hill."

⁷I will tell of the decree of God:
God said to me, "You are my child;
today I have begotten you.

⁸"Ask of me, and I will make the
nations your heritage,

and the ends of the earth your
possession. ℟

⁹"You shall break them with a rod of
iron,
and dash them in pieces like a
potter's vessel."

¹⁰Now therefore, O rulers, be wise;
be warned, O leaders of the earth.

¹¹Serve God with fear, with trembling
¹²kiss God's feet,
or God will be angry, and you will
perish in the way;

for God's wrath is quickly kindled.
Happy are all who take refuge in
God. ℟

(May be sung with double tone.)

Psalm 4

℟esponse

Antiphon: Peter Niedmann, 1994

Let the light of your face shine on us, O God.

℟
¹Answer me when I call,
O God of my right!

You gave me room when I was in
distress.
Be gracious to me, and hear my
prayer.

²How long, you people, shall my
honor suffer shame?

How long will you love vain
words, and seek after lies?

³But know that God has set apart the
faithful for God;
God hears when I call. ℟

⁴When you are disturbed, do not sin;
ponder it on your beds, and be
silent.

⁵Offer right sacrifices, and put your trust in God.
⁶There are many who say, "O that we might see some good!

Let the light of your face shine on us, O God!"

⁷You have put gladness in my heart more than when their grain and wine abound.

⁸I will both lie down and sleep in peace;
for you alone, O God, make me lie down in safety. ℛ

(May be sung with double tone.)

Psalm 5

ℛesponse

Antiphon: *Martie McMane, 1994*

Lead me, O God, in your righteous-ness.

ℛ

¹Give ear to my words, O God;
give heed to my sighing.

²Listen to the sound of my cry,
my Sovereign and my God, for to you I pray.

³O God, in the morning you hear my voice;
in the morning I plead my case to you, and watch.

⁴For you are not a God who delights in wickedness;
evil will not sojourn with you. ℛ

⁵The boastful will not stand before your eyes;
you hate all evildoers.

⁶You destroy those who speak lies;
God abhors the bloodthirsty and deceitful.

⁷But I, through the abundance of your steadfast love, will enter your house,
I will bow down toward your holy temple in awe of you.

⁸Lead me, O God, in your righteousness because of my enemies;
make your way straight before me. ℛ

(May be sung with double tone.)

Psalm 8

Response

(capo 1)EM7

Unison

Antiphon: Lee Dengler, 1994

How ma - jes - tic is your name in all the earth.

R

¹O God, our Sovereign, how majestic
is your name in áll the earth!
  You have set your glory abóve the
  heavens.

²Out of the mouths of babes and
infants you have founded a bulwark
because óf your foes,
  to silence the enemy and thé
  avenger.

³When I look at your heavens, the
work óf your fingers,
  the moon and the stars that you
  háve established;

⁴what are human beings that you are
mindful of them,
  mortals thát you care for them? **R**

⁵Yet you have made them a little
lowér than God,
  and crowned them with glorý and
  honor.

⁶You have given them dominion over
the works óf your hands;
  you have put all things undér their
  feet,

⁷all sheep and oxen, and also the beasts
óf the field,
  ⁸the birds of the air, and the fish of
  the sea, whatever passes along the
  paths óf the seas.

⁹O Gód, our Sovereign,
  how majestic is your name in áll
  the earth! **R**

(May be sung with double tone.)

Psalm 9

Antiphon: Elaine Kirkland, 1994

Response

You, O God, have not for-sak-en those who seek you.

℟
⁹God is a stronghold for the oppressed,
a stronghold in times of trouble.

¹⁰And those who know your name put
their trust in you,
for you, O God, have not forsaken
those who seek you.

¹¹Sing praises to God, who dwells in
Zion.
Declare God's deeds among the
peoples.

¹²For God who avenges blood is
mindful of them;
God does not forget the cry of the
afflicted. ℟

¹³Be gracious to me, O God.
See what I suffer from those who
hate me;

you are the one who lifts me up from
the gates of death,
¹⁴so that I may recount all your
praises, and, in the gates of
daughter Zion, rejoice in your
deliverance.

¹⁵The nations have sunk in the pit that
they have made;
in the net that they hid has their
own foot been caught.

¹⁶God has made God known,
God has executed judgment; the
wicked are snared in the work of
their own hands. ℟

¹⁷The wicked shall depart to Sheol,
all the nations that forget God.

¹⁸For the needy shall not always be
forgotten,
nor the hope of the poor perish
forever.

¹⁹Rise up, O God! Do not let mortals
prevail;
let the nations be judged before
you.

²⁰Put them in fear, O God;
let the nations know that they are
only human. ℟

(May be sung with double tone.)

Psalm 13

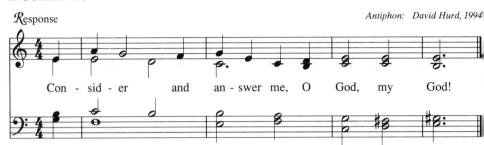

Antiphon: David Hurd, 1994

℟

[1]How long, O God? Will you forget me forever?
  How long will you hide your face from me?

[2]How long must I bear pain in my soul, and have sorrow in my heart áll day long?
  How long shall my enemy be exálted over me?

[3]Consider and answer me, O Gód, my God!
  Give light to my eyes, or I will sleep the śleep of death,

[4]and my enemy will say, "I háve prevailed";
  my foes will rejoice because Í am shaken.

[5]But I trusted in your śteadfast love; my heart shall rejoice in ýour salvation.

[6]I will śing to God,
  because God has dealt bountifullý with me. ℟

Psalm 14

Antiphon: Hyeon Jeong, 1994

℟

[1]Fools say in their hearts, "There ís no God."
  They are corrupt, they do abominable deeds; there is no one who does good.

[2]God looks down from heaven on húmankind
  to see if there are any who are wise, who seek áfter God.

³They have all gone astray, they are all alíke perverse;
  there is no one who does good, ño, not one.

⁴Have they no knowledge, all the evildoers who eat up my people as th̀ey eat bread,
  and do not call úpon God? ℟

⁵There they shall be ín great terror, for God is with the company óf the righteous.

⁶You would confound the plans óf the poor,
  but God ís their refuge.

⁷O that deliveránce for Israel would ćome from Zion!

When God restores the fortunes óf God's people,
  Jacob will rejoice; Israel wíll be glad. ℟

(May be sung with double tone.)

Psalm 15

℟esponse

Antiphon: *Emma Lou Diemer, 1994*

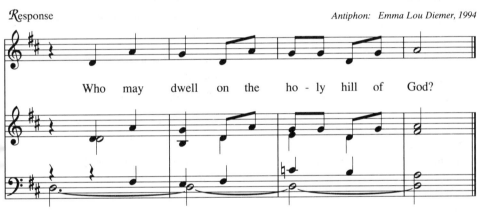

Who may dwell on the ho - ly hill of God?

℟
¹O God, who may abide ín your tent?
  Who may dwell on your hóly hill?

²Those wĥo walk blamelessly,
  and do wĥat is right,

who speak the truth f̀rom their heart,
³and do not slander wíth their tongue,

who do no evil t̀o their friends,
  nor take up a reproach agáinst their neighbors; ℟

⁴in whose eyes the wicked áre despised,
  but wἠo honor those wĥo fear God;

who stand bý their oath
  even t̀o their hurt;

⁵who do not lend mońey at interest,
  and do not take a bribe agáinst the innocent.

Those who dó these things
  shall nev́er be moved. ℟

(May be sung with double tone.)

627

Psalm 16

℟

¹Protect me, O God,
  for in you I take refuge.

²I say to God, "You are my God;
  I have no good apart from you."

³As for the holy ones in the land,
  they are the noble, in whom is all
  my delight.

⁴Those who choose another god
  multiply their sorrows; ℟

their drink offerings of blood I will
  not pour out
    or take their names upon my lips.

⁵God is my chosen portion and my
  cup;
    you hold my lot.

⁶The boundary lines have fallen for me
  in pleasant places;
    I have a goodly heritage.

⁷I bless God who gives me counsel;
  in the night also my heart instructs
  me. ℟

⁸I keep God always before me;
  because God is at my right hand,
    I shall not be moved.

⁹Therefore my heart is glad, and my
  soul rejoices;
    my body also rests secure.

¹⁰For you do not give me up to Sheol,
  or let your faithful one see the Pit.

¹¹You show me the path of life. In
  your presence there is fullness of joy;
    in your right hand are pleasures
    forevermore. ℟

(May be sung with double tone.)

Psalm 17

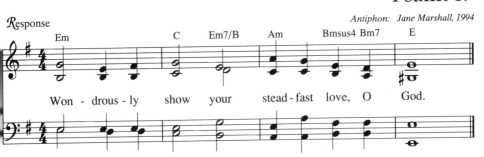

Antiphon: *Jane Marshall, 1994*

R

¹Hear a just cause, O God; attend to
my cry;
give ear to my prayer from lips
free óf deceit.

²From you let my vindićation come;
let your eyes śee the right.

³If you try my heart, if you visit me
by night, if you test me, you will
find no wickedness in me;
my mouth does ńot transgress.

⁴As for what óthers do,
by the word of your lips I have
avoided the ways óf the violent.

R

⁵My steps have held fast to your paths;
my feet háve not slipped.

⁶I call upon you, for you will answer
me, O God;
incline your ear to me, hear my
words.

⁷Wondrously show your śteadfast love,
O savior of those who seek refuge
from their adversaries at your
mighty hand.

⁸Guard me as the apple of the eye; hide
me in the shadow óf your wings,
⁹from the wicked who despoil me,
my deadly enemies who surround
me.

¹⁵As for me, I shall behold your face in
righteousness;
when I awake I shall be satisfied,
beholding your likeness. **R**

Proper 13 [18] A vs. 1–7, 15; Proper 27 [32] C vs. 1–9.

Psalm 19

℟esponse

Antiphon: Jean Slates Hawk, 1994

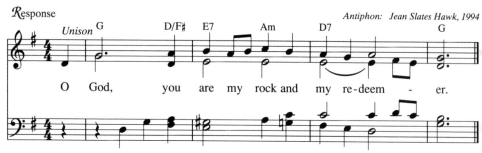

O God, you are my rock and my re-deem - er.

℟

¹The heavens are telling the glóry of God;
  and the firmament procláims God's handiwork.

²Day to day póurs forth speech,
  and night to night déclares knowledge.

³There is no speech, nor áre there words;
  their voice ís not heard;

⁴yet their voice goes out through áll the earth,
  and their words to the end óf the world.

In the heavens God has set a tent fór the sun,
  ⁵which comes out like a beloved from a wedding canopy, and like an athlete runs its cóurse with joy.

⁶Its rising is from the end óf the heavens,
  and its circuit to the end of them,
  and nothing is hid fróm its heat. ℟

⁷The law of God is perfect, revíving the soul;
  the decrees of God are sure, making wíse the simple;

⁸the precepts of God are right,
  rejoícing the heart;

the commandment of God is clear,
  enlighteñing the eyes;

⁹the fear of God is pure, enduríng forever;
  the ordinances of God are true and righteous áltogether.

¹⁰More to be desired are they than gold, even múch fine gold;
  sweeter also than honey, and drippings óf the honeycomb.

¹¹Moreover by them is your śervant warned;
  in keeping them there is gŕeat reward.

¹²But who can detéct their errors?
  Clear me from hídden faults.

¹³Keep back your servant also fŕom the insolent;
  do not let them have domínion over me.

Then I śhall be blameless,
  and innocent of gŕeat transgression.

¹⁴Let the words of my mouth and the meditation of my heart be acceptaˊble to you,
  O God, my rock and m´y redeemer.
℟

Proper 21 [26] B vs. 7–14.

Psalm 20

Antiphon: *Vérne de la Peña, 1994*

Response

An-swer us,   O   God,   when we   call.

R
[1]May God answer you in the day of
trouble!
   The name of the God of Jacob
   protect you!

[2]May God send you help from the
sanctuary,
   and give you support from Zion.

[3]May God remember all your
offerings,
   and regard with favor your burnt
sacrifices.

[4]May God grant you your heart's
desire,
   and fulfill all your plans. *R*

[5]May we shout for joy over your
victory, and in the name of our God
set up our banners.
   May God fulfill all your petitions.

[6]Now I know that God will help God's
anointed,
   and will answer them from God's
holy heaven with mighty victories
by God's strong hand.

[7]Some take pride in chariots, and some
in horses,
   but our pride is in the name of the
Sovereign our God.

[8]They will collapse and fall, but we
shall rise and stand upright.
[9]Give victory to the ruler, O God;
   answer us when we call. *R*

(May be sung with double tone.)

Psalm 22

Response   Antiphon: Marty Haugen, 1994

O God, do not be far a-way; O God, do not be far a-way.

R

¹My God, my God, why have you forsaken me?
    Why are you so far from helping me, from the words óf my groaning?

²O my God, I cry by day, but you do not answer;
    and by night, but find no rest.

³Yet you are holy, enthroned on the praisés of Israel.
    ⁴In you our ancestors trusted; they trusted, and you delivered them.

⁵To you they cried, ánd were saved;
    in you they trusted, and were not put to shame. R

⁶But I am a worm, ánd not human;
    scorned by others, and despised by the people.

⁷All who see me mock at me;
    they make mouths at me, they shake their heads;

⁸"Commit your cause to God;
    let God deliver — let God rescue the one in whom God delights!" R

⁹Yet it was you who took me from the womb;
    you kept me safe on my mother's breast.

¹⁰On you I was cast from my birth,
    and since my mother bore me you have been my God.

¹¹Do not be far from me,
    for trouble is near and there is no óne to help.

¹²Many bulls encircle me, strong bulls of Bashan surround me;
    ¹³they open wide their mouths at me, like a ravening and roaring lion.

¹⁴I am poured out like water, and all my bones are óut of joint;
    my heart is like wax; it is melted within my breast;

¹⁵my mouth is dried up like a potsherd,
    and my tongue sticks to my jaws; you lay me in the dust of death. R

¹⁹O God, do not be far away!
    O my help, come quickly to my aid!

²⁰Deliver my soul from the sword,
    my life from the power óf the dog!

²¹Save me from the mouth óf the lion!
    From the horns of the wild oxen you have rescued me.

²²I will tell of your name to my brothers and sisters;

in the midst of the congregation
I will praise you: ℟

²³You who fear God, praise God!
All you offspring of Jacob, glorify
God;

stand in áwe of God,
all you offspring of Israel!

²⁴For God did not despise or abhor
the affliction of the afflicted;
God did not hide God's face from
me, but heard when I cried to God.
℟

²⁵From you comes my praise in the
great congregation;
my vows I will pay before those
who fear God.

²⁶The poor shall eat ánd be satisfied;
those who seek God shall praise
God. May your hearts live forever!

²⁷All the ends of the earth shall
remember and turn to God;
and all the families of the nations
shall worship before God.

²⁸For dominion belongs to God,
and God rules over the nations. ℟

²⁹To God, indeed, shall all who sleep in
the éarth bow down;
before God shall bow all who go
down to the dust, and I shall live
for God.

³⁰Posterity will serve God;
future generations will be told
ábout God,

³¹and proclaim God's deliverance to a
people yet unborn,
saying that God has done it. ℟

Good Friday ABC, the entire Psalm; Lent 2 B vs. 23–31;
Easter 5 B vs. 25–31; Proper 23 [28] B vs. 1–15; Proper 7
[12] C vs. 19–28.

Psalm 23

℟esponse

Antiphon: *Carolyn Jennings, 1994*

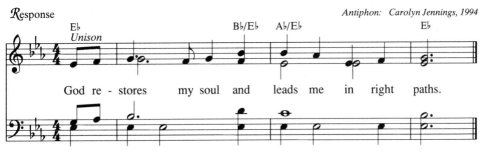

God re - stores my soul and leads me in right paths.

℟

¹God is my shepherd, I shall not want.
²God makes me lie down in green
pastures, and leads me beside still
waters;

³God restores my soul,
and leads me in right paths for the
sake óf God's name.

⁴Even though I walk through the
darkest valley, I fear no evil;
for you are with me; your rod and
your staff — they comfort me.

⁵You prepare a table before me in the
presence óf my enemies;
you anoint my head with oil; my
cup óverflows.

633

℟ *God restores my soul and leads me in right paths.*

⁶Surely goodness and mercy shall
follow me all the days óf my life,
and I shall dwell in the house of
God my whole life long. ℟

Psalm 24

℟esponse

Unison

Antiphon: *Peter Niedmann, 1994*

Vs. 1–6 Who shall as - cend the hill of God?
Vs. 7–10 God is the Rul - er of glo - ry.

℟

¹The earth is God's and all that is in it,
the world, and those who live in it;

²for God has founded it ón the seas,
and established it ón the rivers.

³Who shall ascend the hill of God?
And who shall stand in God's
holy place?

⁴Those who have clean hands ánd
pure hearts,
who do not lift up their souls to
what is false, and do not swear
deceitfully.

⁵They will receive blessing from God,
and vindication from the God of
their salvation.

⁶Such is the company of those who
seek God,

who seek the face of the God of
Jacob. ℟

⁷Lift up your heads, O gates! and be
lifted up, O áncient doors!
that the Ruler of glory may
come in.

⁸Who is the Ruler of glory?
God, strong and mighty, God,
mighty in battle.

⁹Lift up your heads, O gates! and be
lifted up, O áncient doors!
that the Ruler of glory may
come in.

¹⁰Who is this Ruler of glory?
The Sovereign of hosts — God is
the Ruler of glory. ℟

Presentation ABC vs. 7–10 (Alt.).

Psalm 25

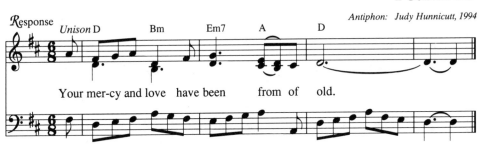

Your mer-cy and love have been   from of   old.

Antiphon: Judy Hunnicutt, 1994

ℛ

¹To you, O God,
  I lift úp my soul.

²O my God, in you I trust; do not let
  me be pút to shame;
    do not let my enemies exult óver
    me.

³Do not let those who wait for you be
  pút to shame;
    let them be ashamed who are
    wantonly treacherous.

⁴Make me to know your ẃays, O God;
  teach mé your paths. ℛ

⁵Lead me in your truth, and teach me,
  for you are the God of mý salvation;
    for you I wait áll day long.

⁶Be mindful of your mercy, O God,
  and of your steadfast love,
    for they have been from of old.

⁷Do not remember the sins óf my
  youth
    or mý transgressions;
  according to your steadfast love
  remember me,
    for your goodness' sake, O God! ℛ

⁸Good and upright is God;
  therefore God instructs sinners ín
    the way.

⁹God leads the humble in ẃhat is
  right,
    and teaches the humble God's way.

¹⁰All the paths of God are steadfast love
  and faithfulness,
    for those who keep God's covenant
    and God's decrees. ℛ

Proper 21 [26] A vs. 1–9.

Psalm 26

Response
Antiphon: *Elaine Kirkland, 1994*

Your stead - fast love is be - fore my eyes.

ℛ

¹Vindicate me, O God, for I have
walked in my integrity,
and I have trusted in God without
wavering.

²Prove me, O God, and try me;
test my heart and mind.

³For your steadfast love is before my
eyes,
and I walk in faithfulness to you.

⁴I do not sit with the worthless,
nor do I consort with hypocrites; ℛ

⁵I hate the company of evildoers,
and will not sit with the wicked.

⁶I wash my hands in innocence,
and go around your altar, O God,

⁷singing aloud a song of thanksgiving,
and telling all your wondrous deeds.

⁸O God, I love the house in which you
dwell,
and the place where your glory
abides. ℛ

⁹Do not sweep me away with sinners,
nor my life with the bloodthirsty,

¹⁰those in whose hands are evil devices,
and whose right hands are full of
bribes.

¹¹But as for me, I walk in my integrity;
redeem me, and be gracious to me.

¹²My foot stands on level ground;
in the great congregation I will
bless God. ℛ

Proper 17 [22] A vs. 1–8. (May be sung with double tone.)

Psalm 27

Antiphon: *Lee Dengler, 1994*

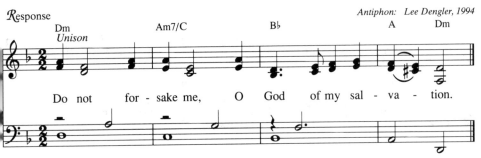

Do not for - sake me, O God of my sal - va - tion.

R

¹God is my light and my salvation;
whom shall I fear?

God is the stronghold of my life; of
whom shall I be afraid?

²When evildoers assail me to devour
my flesh —

my adversaries and foes — they
shall stumble and fall.

³Though an army encamp against me,
my heart shall not fear.

Though war rise up against me, yet
I will be confident.

⁴One thing I asked of God, that will
I seek after:

to live in the house of God all the
days of my life, **R**

to behold the beauty of God, and to
inquire in God's temple.

⁵For God will hide me in God's
shelter in the day of trouble;

God will conceal me under the cover
of God's tent;

God will set me high on a rock.

⁶Now my head is lifted up above my
enemies all around me,

and I will offer in God's tent
sacrifices with shouts of joy;

I will sing and make melody to God.

⁷Hear, O God, when I cry aloud, be
gracious to me and answer me! **R**

⁸"Come," my heart says, "seek God's
face!"

Your face, O God, do I seek.

⁹Do not hide your face from me.

Do not turn your servant away in
anger, you who have been my help.

Do not cast me off, do not forsake
me,

O God of my salvation!

¹⁰If my father and mother forsake me,
God will take me up. **R**

¹¹Teach me your way, O God,

and lead me on a level path because
of my enemies.

¹²Do not give me up to the will of my
adversaries, for false witnesses have
risen against me,

and they are breathing out violence.

¹³I believe that I shall see the goodness
of God
in the land of the living.

¹⁴Wait for God, be strong;

let your heart take courage, wait for
God! **R**

Epiphany 3 [3] A vs. 1, 4–9.

(May be sung with double tone.)

Psalm 29

Response　　　　　　　　　　　　　　　　　　　　　*Antiphon: David Hurd, 1994*

The voice of God is full of maj - es - ty.

℟

[1] Ascribe to God, O heavenly beings,
ascribe to God glory and strength.

[2] Ascribe to God the glory of God's
name;
worship God in holy splendor.

[3] The voice of God is over the waters;
the God of glory thunders, God,
over mighty waters.

[4] The voice of God is powerful;
the voice of God is full of majesty.
℟

[5] The voice of God breaks the cedars;
God breaks the cedars of Lebanon.

[6] God makes Lebanon skip like a calf,
and Sirion like a young wild ox.

[7] The voice of God flashes forth
in flames of fire.

[8] The voice of God shakes the
wilderness;
God shakes the wilderness of
Kadesh. ℟

[9] The voice of God causes the oaks to
whirl, and strips the forest bare;
and in God's temple all say,
"Glory!"

[10] God sits enthroned over the flood;
God sits enthroned as ruler forever.

[11] May God give strength to the people!
May God bless the people with
peace! ℟

Psalm 30

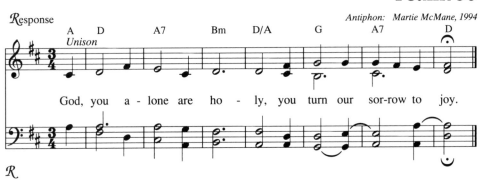

Response   Antiphon: *Martie McMane, 1994*

God, you a - lone are ho - ly, you turn our sor-row to joy.

ℛ

¹I will extol you, O God, for you
have drawn me up,
   and did not let my foes rejoice
over me.

²O God my God, I cried to you for
help,
   and you have healed me.

³O God, you brought up my soul from
Sheol,
   restored me to life from among
those gone down to the Pit.

⁴Sing praises to God, O you God's
faithful ones,
   and give thanks to God's holy
name. ℛ

⁵For God's anger is but for a moment;
God's favor is for a lifetime.
   Weeping may linger for the night,
but joy comes with the morning.

⁶As for me, I said in my prosperity,
   "I shall never be moved."

⁷By your favor, O God, you had
established me as a strong mountain;
   you hid your face; I was dismayed.

⁸To you, O God, I cried,
   and to you I made supplication: ℛ

⁹"What profit is there in my death, if I
go down to the Pit?
   Will the dust praise you? Will it
tell of your faithfulness?

¹⁰"Hear, O God, and be gracious to me!
O God, be my helper!"

¹¹You have turned my mourning into
dancing;
   you have taken off my sackcloth
and clothed me with joy,

¹²so that my soul may praise you and
not be silent.
   O God, my God, I will give thanks
to you forever. ℛ

(May be sung with double tone.)

Psalm 31a

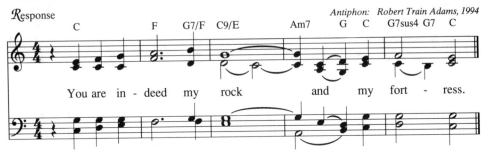

Response · Antiphon: *Robert Train Adams, 1994*

You are in - deed my rock and my fort - ress.

ℛ

¹In you, O God, I seek refuge; do not
  let me ever be put to shame;
    in your righteousness deliver me.

²Incline your ear to me; rescue me
  speedily.
    Be a rock of refuge for me, a strong
    fortress to save me.

³You are indeed my rock and my
  fortress;
    for your name's sake lead me and
    guide me,

⁴take me out of the net that is hidden
  for me,
    for you are my refuge.

⁵Into your hand I commit my spirit;
  you have redeemed me, O God,
  O faithful God.

¹⁵My times are in your hand;
  deliver me from the hand of my
  enemies and persecutors.

¹⁶Let your face shine upon your
  servant;
    save me in your steadfast love. ℛ

¹⁹O how abundant is your goodness that
  you have laid up for those who fear
  you,

and accomplished for those who
  take refuge in you, in the sight of
  everyone!

²⁰In the shelter of your presence you
  hide them from human plots;
    you hold them safe under your
    shelter from contentious tongues.

²¹Blessed be God, who has wondrously
  shown steadfast love to me
    when I was beset as a city under
    siege.

²²I had said in my alarm, "I am driven
  far from your sight."
    But you heard my supplications
    when I cried out to you for help.

²³Love God, all you God's saints.
  God preserves the faithful, but
  abundantly repays the one who acts
  haughtily.

²⁴Be strong, and let your heart take
  courage,
    all you who wait for God. ℛ

Holy Saturday ABC vs. 1–4, 15–16; Easter 5 A vs. 1–5,
15–16; Proper 4 [9] A vs. 1–5, 19–24.

Psalm 31b

Antiphon: Robert Train Adams, 1994

Let your face shine up-on your ser - vant.

(Selection for Palm/Passion Sunday)

℟

⁹Be gracious to me, O God, for I am in distress;
  my eye wastes away from grief, my soul and body also.

¹⁰For my life is spent with sorrow, and my years with sighing;
  my strength fails because of my misery, and my bones waste away.

¹¹I am the scorn of all my adversaries, a horror to my neighbors, an object of dread to my acquaintances;
  those who see me in the street flee from me.

¹²I have passed out of mind like one who is dead;
  I have become like a broken vessel. ℟

¹³For I hear the whispering of many — terror all around! —
  as they scheme together against me, as they plot to take my life.

¹⁴But I trust in you, O God;
  I say, "You are my God."

¹⁵My times are in your hand;
  deliver me from the hand of my enemies and persecutors.

¹⁶Let your face shine upon your servant;
  save me in your steadfast love. ℟

(May be sung with double tone.)

Psalm 32

R̶esponse   *Antiphon: Emma Lou Diemer, 1994*

Stead - fast love sur - rounds those who trust in God.

R̶

¹Happy are those whose transgression is forgiven,
   whose śin is covered.

²Happy are those to whom God imputes ńo iniquity,
   and in whose spirit there is ńo deceit.

³While I kept silence, my body wasted away
   through my groaning áll day long.

⁴For day and night your hand was heavý upon me;
   my strength was dried up as by the heat of summer. R̶

⁵Then I acknowledged my śin to you,
   and I did not hide mý iniquity;

I said, "I will confess my transgresśions to God,"
   and you forgave the guilt óf my sin.

⁶Therefore let all who are faithful offer prayer to you;

at a time of distress, the rush of mighty waters śhall not reach them.

⁷You are a hiding place for me; you preserve mé from trouble;
   you surround me with glad cries óf deliverance. R̶

⁸I will instruct you and teach you the way ýou should go;
   I will counsel you with my éye upon you.

⁹Do not be like a horse or a mule, without únderstanding,
   whose temper must be curbed with bit and bridle, else it will ńot stay near you.

¹⁰Many are the torments óf the wicked,
   but steadfast love surrounds those who trust in God.

¹¹Be glad in God and rejoice, O righteous,
   and shout for joy, all you upright in heart. R̶

*Proper 26 [31] C vs. 1–7. (If all verses are used, may be
sung with double tone.)*

Psalm 33

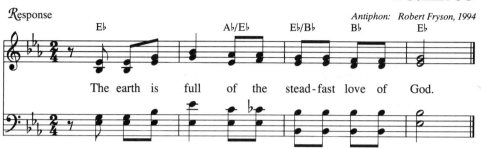

R̆esponse

E♭   A♭/E♭   E♭/B♭   B♭   E♭

The earth is full of the stead-fast love of God.

R̆

¹Rejoice in God, O you righteous.
Praise befits the upright.

²Praise God with the lyre;
make melody to God with the harp
of ten strings.

³Sing to God a new song;
play skillfully on the strings, with
loud shouts.

⁴For the word of God is upright,
and all God's work is done in
faithfulness. R̆

⁵God loves righteousness and justice;
the earth is full of the steadfast love
of God.

⁶By the word of God the heavens
were made,
and all their host by the breath of
God's mouth.

⁷God gathered the waters of the sea as
in a bottle;
God put the deeps in storehouses.

⁸Let all the earth fear God;
let all the inhabitants of the world
stand in awe of God. R̆

⁹For God spoke, and it came to be;
God commanded, and it stood firm.

¹⁰God brings the counsel of the nations
to nothing;

God frustrates the plans of the
peoples.

¹¹The counsel of God stands forever,
the thoughts of God's heart to all
generations.

¹²Happy is the nation whose God is the
Sovereign,
the people whom God has chosen
as God's own heritage.

¹³God looks out from heaven;
God sees all humankind.

¹⁴From where God sits enthroned, God
watches all the inhabitants of the
earth —
¹⁵God who fashions the hearts of
them all, and observes all their
deeds.

¹⁶A ruler is not saved by a great army;
a warrior is not delivered by great
strength.

¹⁷The war horse is a vain hope for
victory,
and by its great might it cannot
save. R̆

¹⁸Truly the eye of God is on those who
fear God,
on those who hope in God's
steadfast love,

R The earth is full of the steadfast love of God.

¹⁹to deliver their soul from death,
and to keep them alive in famine.

²⁰Our soul waits for God,
who is our help and shield.

²¹Our heart is glad in God,

because we trust in God's holy
name.

²²Let your steadfast love, O God,
be upon us,
even as we hope in you. *R*

Proper 5 [10] A vs. 1–12; Proper 14 [19] C vs. 12–22.

Psalm 34

*R*esponse   Antiphon: Jane Marshall, 1994

O let us ex - alt God's name for - ev - er.

*R*esponse *(To be sung on All Saints Day)*   Antiphon: Jane Marshall, 1994

Hap - py are those who take ref - uge in God.

R

¹I will bless God at all times;
God's praise shall continually be in
my mouth.

²My soul makes its boast in God;
let the humble hear and be glad.

³O magnify God with me,
and let us exalt God's name
together.

⁴I sought God, and God answered me,
and delivered me from all my fears.
R

⁵Look to God, and be radiant;
so your faces shall never be
ashamed.

⁶This poor soul cried, and was heard by
God,
and was saved from every trouble.

⁷The angel of God encamps around
those who fear God;
God's angel delivers them.

⁸O taste and see that God is good;
  happy are those who take refúge in
  God. ℛ

⁹O fear God, all you holy ónes of God,
  for those who fear God háve no
  want.

¹⁰The young lions suffer wánt and
  hunger,
  but those who seek God lack ńo
  good thing.

¹¹Come, O children, listén to me;
  I will teach you the fear of God.

¹²Which of you desires life, and covets
  many days to énjoy good?
¹³Keep your tongue from evil, and
  your lips from speakíng deceit. ℛ

¹⁴Depart from evil, ánd do good;
  seek peace, ánd pursue it.

¹⁵The eyes of God are ón the righteous,
  God's ears are open ío their cry.

¹⁶The face of God is against évildoers,
  to cut off the remembrance of them
  from the earth.

¹⁷When the righteous cry for help, God
  hears,
  and rescues them from áll their
  troubles. ℛ

¹⁸God is near to the brokenhearted,
  and saves the crushed in spirit.

¹⁹Many are the afflictions óf the
  righteous,
  but God rescues them from them
  all.

²⁰God keeps áll their bones;
  not one of them will be broken.

²¹Evil brings death ío the wicked,
  and those who hate the righteous
  will be condemned.

²²God redeems the life of those who
  serve God;
  none of those who take refuge in
  God will be condemned.

All Saints A vs. 1–10, 22; Proper 14 [19] B vs. 1–8;
Proper 15 [20] B vs. 9–14; Proper 16 [21] B vs. 15–22;
Proper 25 [30] B vs. 1–8, (19–22).

Psalm 36

ℛesponse   *Antiphon: Jean Slates Hawk, 1994*

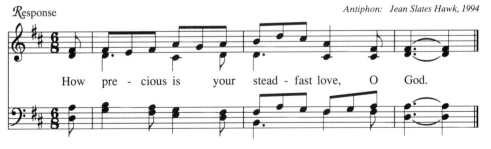

How pre - cious is your stead - fast love, O God.

ℛ
⁵Your steadfast love, O God, extends
  ío the heavens,
  your faithfulness ío the clouds.

⁶Your righteousness is like the mighty
  mountains, your judgments are like
  íhe great deep;

645

you save humans and animals alíke,
O God.

⁷How precious is your steadfast lóve,
O God!
All people may take refuge in the
shadow óf your wings.

⁸They feast on the abundance óf your
house,
and you give them drink from the
river of ýour delights. ℟

⁹For with you is the fountain of life;
in your light we see light.

¹⁰O continue your steadfast love to
thóse who know you,
and your salvation to the upright
of heart!

¹¹Do not let the foot of the arrogant
tread on me,
or the hand of the wicked drive me
away. ℟

*Monday in Holy Week ABC vs. 5–11; Epiphany 2 [2] C vs.
5–10.*

Psalm 37

℟esponse   *Antiphon: Vérne de la Peña, 1994*

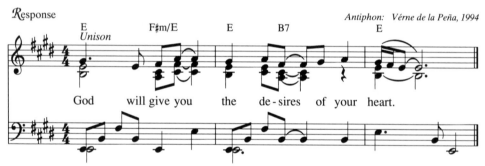

God   will give you   the   de - sires   of your   heart.

℟

¹Do not fret because of the wicked; do
not be envióus of wrongdoers,
²for they will soon fade like the
grass, and wither like the green
herb.

³Trust in God, ánd do good;
so you will live in the land, and
enjoy security.

⁴Take delíght in God,
who will give you the desires óf
your heart.

⁵Commit your way to God;
trust in God, and God will act. ℟

⁶God will make your vindication shine
like the light,
and the justice of your cause like
the day at noon.

⁷Be still before God, ánd wait
patiently;
do not fret over those who prosper
in their way, over those who carry
out evil devices.

⁸Refrain from anger, and forsake wrath.
Do not fret — it leads only to evil.

⁹For the wicked shall be cut off,
but those who wait for God shall
inherit the land. ℟

646

¹⁰Yet a little while, and the wicked will
be no more;
though you look diligently for their
place, they will not be there.

¹¹But the meek shall inherit the land,
and delight themselves in abundant
prosperity.

³⁹The salvation of the righteous is from
God,

who is their refuge in the time of
trouble.

⁴⁰God helps them and rescues them;
God rescues them from the wicked,
and saves them, because they take
refuge in God. ℟

Epiphany 7 [7] C all verses; Proper 22 [27] C vs. 1–9.
(May be sung with double tone.)

Psalm 40

Antiphon: Marty Haugen, 1994

I de-light to do your will, O my God, I de-light to do your will.

℟

¹I waited patiently for God,
who inclined to me and heard my
cry.

²God drew me up from the desolate pit,
out of the miry bog;
God set my feet upon a rock,
making my steps secure.

³God put a new song in my mouth, a
song of praise to our God.
Many will see and fear, and put
their trust in God.

⁴Happy are those who make God their
trust,
who do not turn to the proud, to
those who go astray after false
gods. ℟

⁵You have multiplied, O God my God,
your wondrous deeds and your
thoughts toward us;
none can compare with you.

Were I to proclaim and tell of them,
they would be more than can be
counted.

⁶Sacrifice and offering you do not
desire, but you have given me an
open ear.
Burnt offering and sin offering you
have not required.

⁷Then I said, "Here I am;
in the scroll of the book it is
written of me. ℟

℟ I delight to do your will, O my God, I delight to do your will.

⁸"I delight to do your will, Ó my God;
your law is withín my heart."

⁹I have told the glad news of
deliverance in the great cóngregation;
see, I have not restrained my lips,
as you know, O God.

¹⁰I have not hidden your saving help
withín my heart,
I have spoken of your faithfulness
and ýour salvation;

I have not concealed your steadfast
love ánd your faithfulness,
I have not concealed them from the
great cóngregation.

¹¹Do not, O God, withhold your mercý
from me;
let your steadfast love and your
faithfulness keep me sáfe forever. ℟

*Epiphany 2 [2] A vs. 1–11; Annunciation ABC vs. 5–10
(Alt.).*

Psalm 41

℟esponse   Antiphon: Peter Niedmann, 1994

O set me in your pres-ence for-ev-er.

℟

¹Happy are those who considér the
poor;
God delivers them in the dáy of
trouble.

²God protects them and keeps them
alive; they are called happy ín the
land.
You do not give them up to the
will óf their enemies.

³God sustains them ón their sickbed;
in their illness you heal all their
infirmities.

⁴As for me, I said, "O God, be
gracíous to me;
heal me, for I have sínned against
you." ℟

⁵My enemies wonder in malice when Í
will die,
and when my náme will perish.

⁶And when they come to see me, they
utter empty words, while their hearts
gáther mischief;
when they go out, they tell ít
abroad.

⁷All who hate me whisper together
about me; they imagine the wórst for
me.
⁸They think that a deadly thing has
fastened on me, that I will not rise
again from whére I lie.

⁹Even my friend in whom I trusted,
who ate óf my bread,
has exalted at mý misfortune. ℟

¹⁰But you, O God, be gracious to me,
and raise me up, that I may repay
them.

¹¹By this I know that you are pleased
with me;
because my enemy has not
triumphed over me.

¹²But you have upheld me because of
my integrity,
and set me in your presence forever.

¹³Blessed be the Sovereign, the God of
Israel,
from everlasting to everlasting.
Amen and Amen. ℟

(May be sung with double tone.)

Psalm 42, 43

Antiphon: Carolyn Jennings, 1994

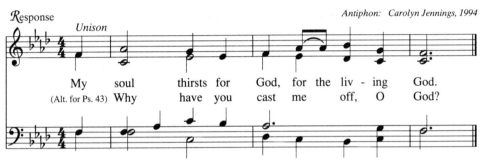

℟esponse

My soul thirsts for God, for the liv - ing God.

(Alt. for Ps. 43) Why have you cast me off, O God?

℟

¹As a deer longs for flowing streams,
so my soul longs for you, O God.

²My soul thirsts for God, for the
living God.
When shall I come and behold the
face of God?

³My tears have been my food day and
night,
while people say to me continually,
"Where is your God?"

⁴These things I remember,
as I pour out my soul:

how I went with the throng, and led
them in procession to the house of
God,
with glad shouts and songs of
thanksgiving, a multitude keeping
festival. ℟

⁵Why are you cast down, O my soul,
and why are you disquieted within
me?
Hope in God; for I shall again
praise God, my help ⁶and my God.

My soul is cast down within me;
therefore I remember you from the
land of Jordan and of Hermon, from
Mount Mizar.

⁷Deep calls to deep at the thunder of
your cataracts;
all your waves and your billows
have gone over me.

⁸By day God commands God's steadfast
love,
and at night God's song is with me,
a prayer to the God of my life. ℟

R̖ My soul thirsts for God, for the living God.

⁹I say to God, my rock, "Why have
    ýou forgotten me?
    Why must I walk about mournfully
    because the eneḿy oppresses me?"

¹⁰As with a deadly wound in my body,
    my adverśaries taunt me,

while they say to me continually,
    "Where ís your God?"

¹¹Why are you cast down, Ó my soul?
    Why are you disquieťed within me?

Hope in God; for I shall again ṕraise
    the one,
    who is my help ánd my God. *R̖*

(Psalm 43)

R̖ Why have you cast me off, O God?

R̖

¹Vindicate me, O God, and defend my
    cause against an unǵodly people;
    from those who are deceitful and
    unjust deliver me!

²For you are the God in whom Í take
    refuge;
    why have you ćast me off?

Why must I walk ábout mournfully
    because of the oppression óf the
    enemy?

³O send out your light and your truth;
    lét them lead me;

let them bring me to your holy hill
    and ťo your dwelling.

⁴Then I will go to the altar of God, to
    God my exćeeding joy;
    and I will praise you with the harp,
    O God, my God.

⁵Why are you cast down, Ó my soul,
    and why are you disquieťed within
    me?

Hope in God; for I shall again ṕraise
    the one,
    who is my help ánd my God. *R̖*

Psalms 42 and 43 Easter Vigil ABC and Proper 7 [12] C;
Psalm 43 Proper 26 [31] A.

Psalm 45

*R̖*esponse

Antiphon: Judy Hunnicutt, 1994

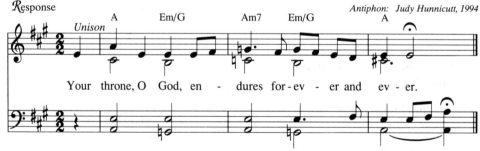

Your throne, O God, en - dures for-ev - er and ev - er.

R̖

¹My heart overflows with a goodly
    theme; I address my verses ťo the
    king;
    my tongue is like the pen of a ŕeady
    scribe.

²You are the most handsome of men;
    grace is poured uṕon your lips;
    therefore God has blessed ýou
    forever.

³Gird your sword on your thigh, O
mighty one,
  in your glory and majesty.

⁴In your majesty ride on victoriously
for the cause of truth and to defend the
right;
  let your right hand teach you dread
  deeds. ℟

⁵Your arrows are sharp in the heart of
the king's enemies;
  the peoples fall under you.

⁶Your throne, O God, endures forever
and ever.
  Your royal scepter is a scepter of
  equity;

⁷you love righteousness and hate
wickedness.
  Therefore God, your God, has
  anointed you with the oil of
  gladness beyond your companions;

⁸your robes are all fragrant with myrrh
and aloes and cassia.
  From ivory palaces stringed
  instruments make you glad; ℟

⁹daughters of kings are among those
who serve you,
  at your right hand stands the queen
  in gold of Ophir.

¹⁰Hear, O daughter, consider and incline
your ear;

forget your people and your parents'
house,

¹¹and the king will desire your beauty.
  Since he is your lord, bow to him;

¹²the people of Tyre will seek your
favor with gifts,
  the richest of the people ¹³with all
  kinds of wealth. ℟

The princess is clothed in her chamber
with gold-woven robes;
  ¹⁴in many-colored robes she is led
  to the king;

behind her the virgins, her
companions, follow.
  ¹⁵With joy and gladness they are led
  along as they enter the palace of the
  king.

¹⁶In the place of ancestors you, O king,
shall have descendants;
  you will make them nobles in all
  the earth.

¹⁷I will cause your name to be
celebrated in all generations;
  therefore the peoples will praise
  you forever and ever. ℟

Annunciation ABC (Alt.) all verses; Proper 9 [14] A vs.
10–17; Proper 17 [22] B vs. 1–2, 6–9. (If all verses are
used, may be sung with double tone.)

Psalm 46

R̂esponse   Antiphon: Lee Dengler, 1994

The God of hosts is with us, there - fore we will not fear.

℞

¹God is our refuge and strength,
  a very present help in trouble.

²Therefore we will not fear, though the
  earth should change,
    though the mountains shake in the
    heart of the sea;

³though its waters roar and foam,
  though the mountains tremble with
  its tumult.

⁴There is a river whose streams make
  glad the city of God,
    the holy habitation of the Most
    High. ℞

⁵God is in the midst of the city; it
  shall not be moved;
    God will help it when the morning
    dawns.

⁶The nations are in an uproar, the
  empires totter;
    God's voice resounds and the earth
    melts.

⁷The God of hosts is with us;
  the God of Jacob is our refuge.

⁸Come, behold the works of God;
  see what desolations God has
  brought on the earth. ℞

⁹God makes wars cease to the end of
  the earth;
    God breaks the bow, and shatters
    the spear; God burns the shields
    with fire.

¹⁰"Be still, and know that I am God!
  I am exalted among the nations, I
  am exalted in the earth."

¹¹The God of hosts is with us;
  the God of Jacob is our refuge. ℞

Psalm 47

Antiphon: Elaine Kirkland, 1994

Response

Sing prais-es to God, sing prais - es to our Rul - er.

R

¹Clap your hands, áll you peoples;
shout to God with loud šongs of joy.

²For God, the Most Hígh, is awesome,
a great ruler over áll the earth.

³God subdued peoples under us, and
nations undér our feet.
⁴God chose our heritage for us, the
pride of Jacob whom God loves.

⁵God has gone up wíth a shout,
God has gone up with the sound óf
a trumpet. R

⁶Sing praises to Gód, sing praises;
sing praises to our Rulér, sing
praises.

⁷For God is the ruler of áll the earth;
sing praises wíth a psalm.

⁸God is ruler over the nations;
God sits on God's hóly throne.

⁹The nobles of the péoples gather
as the people of the God of Saŕah
and Abraham.

For the shields of the earth belong to
God;
God is highlý exalted. R

653

Psalm 48

Response

Antiphon: Martie McMane, 1994

We pon-der your stead-fast love, O God.

℟.

¹Great is God and greatly to be praised
in the city óf our God.

God's holy mountain, ²beautiful in
élevation,
is the joy of áll the earth,

Mount Zion, in the far north,
the city of the great Ruler.
  ³Within its citadels God is a
  śure defense. ℟

⁴Then the rulers assembled,
they came ón together.
  ⁵As soon as they saw it, they
  were astounded; they were in
  panic, they took to flight;

⁶trembling took hold of them there,
pains as of a womán in labor,
  ⁷as when an east wind
  shatters the śhips of
  Tarshish.

⁸As we have heard, so have we
seen in the city of the God of hosts,
in the city of our God, which
God estabĺishes forever.

⁹We ponder your steadfast love, O
God,
in the midst óf your temple. ℟

¹⁰Your name, O God, like your praise,
reaches to the ends óf the earth.
Your right hand is filled with
victory.

¹¹Let Mount Zión be glad,
let the towns of Judah rejoice
because óf your judgments.

¹²Walk about Zion, go all around
it, ćount its towers,
  ¹³consider well its ramparts;
  go through its citadels,

that you may tell the next
generation¹⁴that this is God,
our God forevér and ever.
God will be our ǵuide forever. ℟

654

Psalm 49

Antiphon: David Hurd, 1994

Response
Unison

The med - i - ta - tion of my heart shall be my un - der - stand - ing.

℟

¹Hear this, all you peoples; give ear,
all inhabitants of the world,
²both low and high, rich and
poor together.

³My mouth shall speak wisdom;
the meditation of my heart
shall be understanding.

⁴I will incline my ear to a proverb;
I will solve my riddle to the
music of the harp. ℟

⁵Why should I fear in times of trouble,
when the iniquity of my persecutors
surrounds me,

⁶those who trust in their wealth
and boast of the abundance of
their riches?

⁷Truly, no ransom avails for one's life,
there is no price one can give
to God for it.

⁸For the ransom of life is costly,
and can never suffice
⁹that one should live on forever
and never see the grave. ℟

¹⁰When we look at the wise, they die;
the foolish and stupid perish
together and leave their wealth to
others.

¹¹Their graves are their homes forever,
their dwelling places to all
generations, though they named
lands their own.

¹²Mortals cannot abide in their pomp;
they are like the animals that
perish. ℟

Psalm 50

𝓡esponse

Antiphon: Hyeon Jeong, 1994

Our God comes and does not keep si - lence.

𝓡

¹The mighty one, God the Sovereign,
speaks and summons the earth:
from the rising of the sun to
its setting.

²Out of Zion, the perfection of beauty,
God shines forth.
³Our God comes and does not
keep silence,

before God is a devouring fire,
and a mighty tempest all around. 𝓡

⁴God calls to the heavens above
and to the earth,
that God may judge God's
people:

⁵"Gather to me my faithful ones,
who made a covenant with me
by sacrifice!"

⁶The heavens declare God's
righteousness,
for God indeed is judge. 𝓡

⁷"Hear, O my people, and I will speak,
O Israel, I will testify against
you for I am God, your God.

⁸"Not for your sacrifices do I
rebuke you;
your burnt offerings
are continually before me. 𝓡

⁹"I will not accept a bull from your
house, or goats from your folds.

¹⁰For every animal of the forest is
mine, the cattle on a thousand hills.

¹¹"I know all the birds of the air,
and all that moves in the field
is mine.

¹²"If I were hungry,
I would not tell you,
for the world and all that is
in it is mine. 𝓡

¹³"Do I eat the flesh of bulls,
or drink the blood of goats?

¹⁴"Offer to God a sacrifice of
thanksgiving,
and pay your vows to
the Most High.

¹⁵"Call on me in the day of trouble;
I will deliver you,
and you shall glorify me." 𝓡

²²"Mark this, then, you who forget
God,
or I will tear you apart, and there
will be no one to deliver.

²³"Those who bring thanksgiving
as their sacrifice honor me;
to those who go the right way I
will show the salvation of God." 𝓡

Proper 5 [10] A vs. 7–15; Epiphany Last and Trans-
figuration B vs. 1–6; Proper 14 [19] C vs. 1–8, 22–23.

Psalm 51

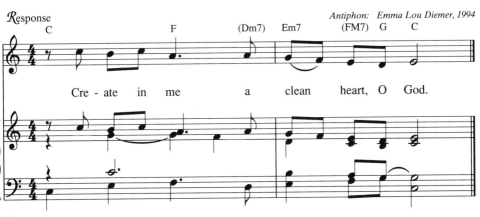

Response
C   F   (Dm7) Em7   (FM7) G   C

Antiphon: Emma Lou Diemer, 1994

Cre - ate in me a clean heart, O God.

℟

¹Have mercy on me, O God,
according to your steadfast love;
according to your abundant mercy
blot out my transgressions.

²Wash me thoroughly from my
iniquity, and cleanse me from my sin.
³For I know my transgressions,
and my sin is ever before me.

⁴Against you, you alone, have I
sinned, and done what is evil
in your sight,
so that you are justified in your
sentence and blameless when you
pass judgment.

⁵Indeed, I was born guilty,
a sinner when my mother
conceived me. ℟

⁶You desire truth in the inward being;
therefore teach me wisdom in
my secret heart.

⁷Purge me with hyssop,
and I shall be clean;
wash me, and I shall be
purer than snow.

⁸Let me hear joy and gladness;
let the bones that you have
crushed rejoice.

⁹Hide your face from my sins,
and blot out all my iniquities. ℟

¹⁰Create in me a clean heart, O God,
and put a new and right spirit
within me.

¹¹Do not cast me away from
your presence,
and do not take your
holy spirit from me.

¹²Restore to me the joy of your
salvation,
and sustain in me a willing spirit.

¹³Then I will teach transgressors
your ways,
and sinners will return to you. ℟

¹⁴Deliver me from bloodshed, O God,
O God of my salvation,
and my tongue will sing aloud
of your deliverance.

657

℟ Create in me a clean heart, O God

¹⁵O God, opén my lips,
and my mouth will decláre
your praise.

¹⁶For you have no delíght in sacrifice;
if I were to give a burnt offering,
you would nót be pleased.

¹⁷The sacrifice acceptable to God
is a tróubled spirit;
a broken and contrite heart, O God,
you will nót despise. ℟

Ash Wednesday ABC vs. 1–17; Lent 5 B vs. 1–12 (Alt.);
Proper 13 [18] B vs. 1–12; Proper 19 [24] C vs. 1–10.
(If all verses are used, may be sung with double tone.)

Psalm 52

℟esponse
Unison

Antiphon: Jane Marshall, 1994

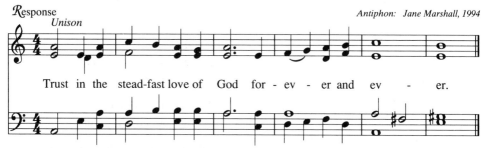

Trust in the stead-fast love of God for - ev - er and ev - er.

℟

¹Why do you boast, O míghty one,
of mischief done agáinst the godly?

All day long ²you are plottíng
destruction.
Your tongue is like a sharp razor,
you workér of treachery.

³You love evil more than good, and
lying more than speakíng the truth.
⁴You love all words that devour,
O decéitful tongue.

⁵But God will break you dówn forever;
God will snatch and tear you from
your tent and uproot you from the
land óf the living. ℟

⁶The righteous will see, and fear,
and will laugh at the evildóer, saying,
⁷"See the one who would not take
refuge in God, but trusted in
abundant riches, and sought refúge
in wealth!"

⁸But I am like a green olive tree
in the hóuse of God.
I trust in the steadfast love of God
forevér and ever.

⁹I will thank you forever,
because of what ýou have done.
In the presence of the faithful I will
proclaim your name,
for your náme is good. ℟

Psalm 54

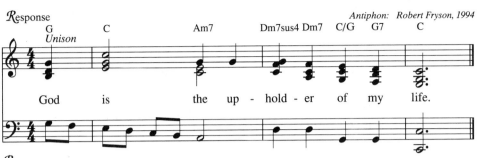

Antiphon: Robert Fryson, 1994

God is the up - hold - er of my life.

R

¹Save me, O God, by your name,
and vindicate me by your might.

²Hear my prayer, O God;
give ear to the words of my
mouth.

³For the insolent have risen
against me,
the ruthless seek my life;
they do not set God before them.

⁴But surely, God is my helper;
God is the upholder of my life. R

⁵God will repay my enemies
for their evil.
In your faithfulness,
put an end to them.

⁶With a freewill offering I will
sacrifice to you;
I will give thanks to your name,
O God, for it is good.

⁷For God has delivered me from
every trouble,
and my eye has looked in triumph
on my enemies. R

Psalm 62

Antiphon: Jean Slates Hawk, 1994

Trust God at all times, O peo - ple.

R

⁵For God alone my soul waits in
silence,
for my hope is from God.

⁶God alone is my rock
and my salvation, my fortress;

I shall not be shaken.

⁷On God rests my deliverance
and my honor;
my mighty rock, my refuge is
in God.

℟ Trust God at all times, O people.

⁸Trust in God at all times, O people;
  pour out your heart before God
  who is a refuge for us. ℟

⁹Those of low estate are but a breath,
  those of high estate are á delusion;
  in the balances they go up; they
  are together lighter than a breath.

¹⁰Put no confidence in extortion,
  and set no vain hopes on robbery;

if riches increase, do not set
  your heart on them.

¹¹Once God has spoken;
  twice have I heard this:

that power belongs to God,
  ¹²and steadfast love belongs to you,
  O God.

For you repay to all
  according to their work. ℟

Psalm 63

℟esponse

Antiphon: *Vérne de la Peña, 1994*

I will bless God as long as I live.

℟

¹O God, you áre my God.
  I seek you, my soul thirsts for you;

my flesh faints for you,
  as in a dry and weary land where
  there is no water.

²So I have looked upon you in the
sanctuary,
  beholding your power and glory.

³Because your steadfast love is better
than life,
  my lips will praise you.

⁴So I will bless you as long ás I live;
  I will lift up my hands and call ón
  your name. ℟

⁵My soul is satisfied as with á rich
feast,
  and my mouth praises you with
  joyful lips

⁶when I think of you ón my bed,
  and meditate on you in the watches
  óf the night;

⁷for you have been my help,
  and in the shadow of your wings I
  sing for joy.

⁸My soul clings to you;
  your mighty hand upholds me. ℟

Psalm 65

Antiphon: *Marty Haugen, 1994*

God is the hope of all the ends of the earth.

℟

¹Praise is due to you, O Gód, in Zion;
and to you shall vows
be performed,

²O you who ánswer prayer!
To you all flesh shall come.

³When deeds of iniquity óverwhelm us,
you forgive óur transgressions.

⁴Happy are those whom you choose
and bring near to live ín your courts.
We shall be satisfied with the
goodness of your house, your
holy temple. ℟

⁵By awesome deeds you answer us
with deliverance,
O God of óur salvation;

you are the hope of all
the ends óf the earth
and of the fárthest seas.

⁶By your strength you estabĺished the
mountains;
you are girded with might.

⁷You silence the roaring of the seas,
the roaring óf their waves,
the tumult óf the peoples. ℟

⁸Those who live at earth's farthest
bounds are awed by your signs;

you make the gateways of the
morning and the evening
shout for joy.

⁹You visit the earth and water it,
you greatĺy enrich it;
the river of God is full of water;

you provide the peopĺe with grain,
for so you have prepared it.

¹⁰You water its furrows abundantly,
and settle its ridges; ℟

you soften the éarth with showers,
and you bless its growth.

¹¹You crown the year with
your bounty;
your wagon tracks overflow
with richness.

¹²The pastures of the wilderness
óverflow,
the hills gird themśelves with joy,

¹³the meadows clothe themselves with
flocks, the valleys deck themśelves
with grain,
they shout and sing togéther
for joy. ℟

Proper 10 [15] A vs. (1–8), 9–13.

661

Psalm 66

Response   Antiphon: *Carolyn Jennings, 1994*

Let the sound of God's praise be heard.

℟

¹Make a joyful noise to God, áll
the earth;
  ²sing the glory of God's name;
  give to God gloríous praise.

³Say to God, "How awesome áre
your deeds!
  Because of your great power,
  your enemies cringe before you.

⁴"All the earth worships you;
  they sing praises to you,
  sing praises to your name."

⁵Come and see what God has done:
  God is awesome in deeds
  ámong mortals. ℟

⁶God turned the sea ínto dry land;
  they passed through the ríver
  on foot.

There we rejoiced in God, ⁷who
rules by God's míght forever,
  whose eyes keep watch on the
  nations — let the rebellious
  not exált themselves.

⁸Bless our God, O peoples, let the
sound of God's práise be heard,
  ⁹who has kept us among the
  living, and has not let our feet slip.

¹⁰For you, O Gód, have tested us;
  you have tried us as silver is tried.
℟

¹¹You brought us into the net;
  you laid burdens ón our backs;
  ¹²you let people ride óver our heads;

we went through fire
ánd through water;
  yet you have brought us out to
  a spacious place.

¹³I will come into your house
with burnt offerings;
  I will pay you my vows ¹⁴that my
  lips uttered and my mouth promised
  when I was in trouble.

¹⁵I will offer to you burnt offerings of
fatlings, with the smoke of the
sacrifice of rams;
  I will make an offering
  of bulls and goats. ℟

[16]Come and hear, all you who fear God,
and I will tell what God
has done for me.
[17]I cried aloud to God,
and extolled God with my tongue.

[18]If I had cherished iniquity in my heart,
God would not have listened.

[19]But truly God has listened;

God has given heed to the words
of my prayer.

[20]Blessed be God, because God
has not rejected my prayer
or removed God's steadfast
love from me. ℞

Easter 6 A vs. 8–20; Proper 9 [14] C vs. 1–9; Proper 23
[28] C vs. 1–12. (If all verses are used, may be sung with
double tone.)

Psalm 67

℞esponse

Antiphon: *Peter Niedmann, 1994*

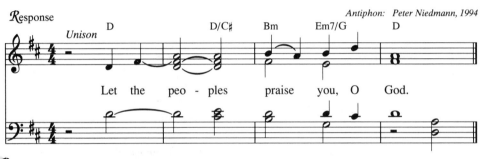

Let the peo - ples praise you, O God.

℞

May God be gracious to us and
bless us
and make God's face to shine
upon us,

that your way may be known
upon earth,
your saving power
among all nations.

Let the peoples praise you, O God;
let all the peoples praise you.

Let the nations be glad and
sing for joy,

for you judge the peoples with
equity and guide the nations
upon earth. ℞

[5]Let the peoples praise you, O God;
let all the peoples praise you.

[6]The earth has yielded its increase;
God, our God, has blessed us.

[7]May God continue to bless us;
let all the ends of the earth
revere God. ℞

663

Psalm 68

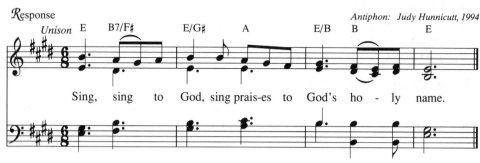

R

¹Let God rise up, let God's enemies
be scattered;
  let those who hate God
  flee before God.

²As smoke is driven away,
so drive them away;
  as wax melts before the fire,
  let the wicked perish before God.

³But let the righteous be joyful;
  let them exult before God;
  let them be jubilant with joy. **R**

⁴Sing to God, sing praises
to God's name;
  lift up a song to the one who rides
  upon the clouds;

be exultant before God
  whose name is the Sovereign.

⁵Father-Mother of orphans and
protector of widows
  is God in God's holy habitation.

⁶God gives the desolate a home to
live in; God leads out the prisoners
to prosperity,
  but the rebellious live in
  a desolate land. **R**

⁷O God, when you went out before
your people,

when you marched through the
wilderness, ⁸the earth quaked,

the heavens poured down rain at the
presence of God, the God of Sinai,
  at the presence of God,
  the God of Israel.

⁹Rain in abundance, O God, you
showered abroad;
  you restored your heritage
  when it languished;

¹⁰your flock found a dwelling in it;
  in your goodness, O God, you
  provided for the needy. **R**

³²Sing to God, O nations of the earth;
  sing praises to God,

³³O rider in the heavens,
  the ancient heavens;
  listen, God sends out a voice,
  a mighty voice.

³⁴Ascribe power to God, whose
majesty is over Israel;
  and whose power is in the skies.

³⁵Awesome is God in God's sanctuary;
  the God of Israel gives power
  and strength to God's people.
  Blessed be God! **R**

Psalm 69

Antiphon: *Lee Dengler, 1994*

Response *Unison*

An - swer me, O God, for your stead-fast love is good.

℟

⁷It is for your sake that I have
borne reproach,
   that shame has covered my face.

⁸I have become a stranger to my
kindred,
   an alien to my mother's children.

⁹It is zeal for your house that has
consumed me;
   the insults of those who insult you have
   fallen on me. ℟

¹⁰When I humbled my soul with
fasting, they insulted me for doing so.
   ¹¹When I made sackcloth my
   clothing, I became a
   byword to them.

¹²I am the subject of gossip for those
who sit in the gate,
   and the drunkards make songs
   about me.

¹³But as for me, my prayer is to
you, O God.

At an acceptable time, O God,
in the abundance of your
steadfast love, answer me.

With your faithful help ¹⁴rescue me
from sinking in the mire;
   let me be delivered from my
   enemies and from the deep waters.
℟

¹⁵Do not let the flood sweep over me,
or the deep swallow me up,
   or the Pit close its mouth over me.

¹⁶Answer me, O God, for your
steadfast love is good;
   according to your abundant mercy,
   turn to me.

¹⁷Do not hide your face from your
servant, for I am in distress–
   make haste to answer me.

¹⁸Draw near to me, redeem me,
set me free because of my enemies.
℟

Psalm 70

℟esponse

Antiphon: *Elaine Kirkland, 1994*

Has - ten to help me, O God.

℟
¹Be pleased, O God, to deliver me.
  O God, make haste to help me!

²Let those be put to shame and
confusion who seek my life.
  Let those be turned back and
  brought to dishonor who
  desire to hurt me.

³Let those who say, "Aha, Aha!"
  turn back because of their shame.

⁴Let all who seek you rejoice and
  be glad in you.
  Let those who love your
  salvation say evermore,
  "God is great!"

⁵But I am poor and needy;
  hasten to me, O God!
  You are my help and my
  deliverer; O God, do not delay! ℟

Psalm 71

℟esponse
Unison

Antiphon: *David Hurd, 1994*

You, O God, are my hope, my trust, O God from my youth.

℟
¹In you, O God, I take refuge;
  let me never be put to shame.

²In your righteousness deliver me
and rescue me;
  incline your ear to me and save me.

³Be to me a rock of refuge,
  a strong fortress, to save me,

for you are my rock and my
  fortress.

⁴Rescue me, O my God, from the
  hand of the wicked,
  from the grasp of the unjust
  and cruel.

⁵For you, O God, are my hope,
my trust, O God, from my youth.
⁶Upon you I have leaned from
my birth;

it was you who took me from my
mother's womb.
My praise is continually of you. ℟

⁷I have been like a portent to many,
but you are my strong refuge.

⁸My mouth is filled with your praise,
and with your glory all day long.

⁹Do not cast me off in the
time of old age;
do not forsake me when my
strength is spent.

¹⁰For my enemies speak
concerning me,

and those who watch for my
life consult together.

¹¹They say, "Pursue and seize that
person whom God has forsaken,
for there is no one to deliver." ℟

¹²O God, do not be far from me;
O my God, make haste to help me!

¹³Let my accusers be put to shame
and consumed;
let those who seek to hurt me be
covered with scorn and disgrace.

¹⁴But I will hope continually,
and will praise you yet more
and more. ℟

Tuesday in Holy Week ABC vs. 1–14; Epiphany 4 [4] C;
Proper 16 [21] C vs. 1–6.

Psalm 72

℟esponse   Antiphon: Hyeon Jeong, 1994

Give the rul - er your jus - tice, O God.

℟

¹Give the ruler your justice, O God,
and your righteousness
to a ruler's heir.

²May the ruler judge your people
with righteousness,
and your poor with justice.

³May the mountains yield prosperity
for the people,
and the hills, in righteousness. ℟

⁴May the ruler defend the cause of the
poor of the people,
give deliverance to the needy,
and crush the oppressor.

⁵May the ruler live while
the sun endures,
and as long as the moon,
throughout all generations.

℟ *Give the ruler your justice, O God.*

⁶May the ruler be like rain
that falls on the mown grass,
like showers that water the earth.

⁷In the ruler's days may
righteousness flourish
and peace abound, until the
moon is no more. ℟

¹⁰May the monarchs of Tarshish and of
the isles render the ruler tribute,
may the monarchs of Sheba
and Seba bring gifts.

¹¹May all monarchs fall down
before the ruler,
all nations give the ruler service.

¹²For the ruler delivers the needy
when they call,
the poor and those who have
no helper.

¹³The ruler has pity on the weak
and the needy,
and saves the lives of the needy.

¹⁴From oppression and violence
the ruler redeems their life;
and precious is their blood in
the ruler's sight. ℟

¹⁸Blessed be the Sovereign,
the God of Israel,
who alone does wondrous things.

¹⁹Blessed be God's glorious name
forever;
may the whole earth be filled
with God's glory.

Amen and Amen.
Amen and Amen. ℟

Epiphany ABC, end with vs. 14; Advent 2 A, omit vs. 10–14.

Psalm 77

℟esponse   Antiphon: Emma Lou Diemer, 1994

I   will   call   to   mind   the   deeds   of   God.

℟
¹I cry aloud to God,
aloud to God, that God may
hear me.

²In the day of my trouble I seek God;
in the night my hand is stretched
out without wearying;
my soul is not comforted.

¹¹I will call to mind the deeds of God;
I will remember your
wonders of old.

¹²I will meditate on all your work;
I will muse on your mighty deeds.
℟

¹³Your way, O God, is holy.
What god is so great as our God?

¹⁴You are the God who works wonders;
 you have displayed your might
 among the peoples.

¹⁵With your strong arm you
 redeemed your people,
 you redeemed the descendants
 of Jacob and Joseph.

¹⁶When the waters saw you, O God,
 when the waters saw you,
 they were afraid;
 the very deep trembled. ℛ

¹⁷The clouds poured out water;

the skies thundered; your arrows
 flashed on every side.

¹⁸The crash of your thunder was
 in the whirlwind;
 your lightnings lit up the world;
 the earth trembled and shook.

¹⁹Your way was through the sea,
 your path, through the mighty waters;
 yet your footprints were unseen.

²⁰You led your people like a flock
 by the hand of Moses and Aaron. ℛ

Psalm 78

ℛesponse

Antiphon: Robert Fryson, 1994

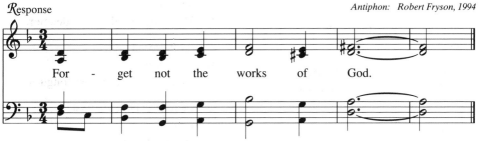

For - get not the works of God.

ℛ

¹Give ear, O my people,
 to my teaching;
 incline your ears to the words
 of my mouth.

²I will open my mouth in a parable;
 I will utter dark sayings
 from of old,

³things that we have heard and known,
 that our ancestors have told us.

⁴We will not hide them
 from their children;
 we will tell to the coming
 generation the glorious deeds
 of God,

we will tell of God's might,
 and the wonders that God has done.
ℛ

⁵God established a decree in Jacob,
 and appointed a law in Israel,
 which God commanded our
 ancestors to teach to their children;

⁶that the next generation might
 know them, the children yet unborn,
 that they might rise up and tell
 them to their children,

⁷so that they should set their
 hope in God,
 and not forget God's works,
 but keep God's commandments. ℛ

ℛ *Forget not the works of God.*

¹²In the sight of their ancestors
God worked marvels in the land
of Egypt, in the fields of Zoan.
 ¹³God divided the sea and let them
   pass through it, and made the
   waters stand like a heap.

¹⁴In the daytime God led them
with a cloud,
   and all night long with
   a fiery light.

¹⁵God split rocks open
in the wilderness,
   and gave them drink abundantly
   as from the deep.

¹⁶God made streams come out of
the rock,
   and caused waters to flow
   down like rivers. ℛ

²³Yet God commanded the skies above,
   and opened the doors of heaven;

²⁴God rained down on them manna
to eat,
   and gave them the grain of heaven.

²⁵Mortals ate of the bread of angels;
   God sent them food in abundance.
ℛ

²⁶God caused the east wind to blow
in the heavens,
   and by God's power led out
   the south wind;

²⁷God rained flesh upon them like dust,
   winged birds like the sand
   of the seas;

²⁸God let them fall within their camp, and
   all around their dwellings.

²⁹And they ate and were well filled,
   for God gave them
   what they craved. ℛ

³²In spite of all this they still sinned;
   they did not believe
   in God's wonders.

³³So God made their days vanish
like a breath,
   and their years in terror. ℛ

³⁴When God killed them,
   they sought for God;
   they repented and sought God
   earnestly.

³⁵They remembered that God
was their rock,
   the Most High God their redeemer.

³⁶But they flattered God
with their mouths;
   they lied to God with their tongues.

³⁷Their heart was not steadfast
   toward God;
   they were not true
   to God's covenant.

³⁸Yet God, being compassionate,
   forgave their iniquity,
   and did not destroy them;
   often God was restrained in anger,
   and did not stir up all God's wrath.
ℛ

Proper 21 [26] A vs. 1–4, 12–16; Proper 27 [32] A vs. 1–7;
Proper 13 [18] B vs. 23–29; Holy Cross ABC vs. 1–2,
34–38 (Alt.).
(Verses 32 and 33 have been added here to the lectionary
verses.)

Psalm 79

Antiphon: *Jane Marshall, 1994*

How long, O God? Will you be an-gry for-ev-er?

℟

¹O God, the nations have come
into your inheritance;
they have defiled your holy temple;
they have laid Jerusalem in ruins.

²They have given the bodies
of your servants to the birds
of the air for food,
the flesh of your faithful
to the wild animals of the earth.

³They have poured out their blood like
water all around Jerusalem,
and there was no one to bury them.

⁴We have become a taunt
to our neighbors,
mocked and derided by those
around us.

⁵How long, O God? Will you
be angry forever?

Will your jealous wrath burn
like fire? ℟

⁶Pour out your anger on the nations
that do not know you,
and on the nations that do not
call on your name.

⁷For they have devoured Jacob
and laid waste his habitation.

⁸Do not remember against us the
iniquities of our ancestors;
let your compassion come speedily
to meet us, for we are brought
very low.

⁹Help us, O God of our salvation,
for the glory of your name;
deliver us, and forgive our sins,
for your name's sake. ℟

Psalm 80

℟espone   *Antiphon: Vérne de la Peña, 1994*

Stir up your might and come to save us.

℟

¹Give ear, O Shepherd of Israel,
you who lead Joseph like a flock!
  You who are enthroned upón
  the cherubim,

shine forth ²before Ephraim
and Benjamin ánd Manasseh.
  Stir up your might, and come
  to save us!

³Restore ús, O God;
  let your face shine, that
  we máy be saved.

⁴O Sovereign God of hosts, how long
will you be angry with your
péople's prayers?
  ⁵You have fed them with the
  bread of tears, and given them tears
  to drink ín full measure.

⁶You make us the scorn
óf our neighbors;
  our enemies laugh
  amóng themselves.

⁷Restore us, O Gód of hosts;
  let your face shine,
  that we máy be saved. ℟

⁸You brought a vine óut of Egypt;
you drove out the natíons
and planted it.

⁹You cléared the ground for it;
it took deep root and fílled the land.

¹⁰The mountains were covered
with its shade,
  the mighty cedars wíth its branches;

¹¹it sent out its branches ío the sea,
  and its shoots ío the River.

¹²Why then have you broken dówn
its walls,
  so that all who pass along the
  way plúck its fruit?

¹³The boar from the forest raváges it,
  and all that move in the field
  feed upon it. ℟

¹⁴Turn again, O God of hosts; look
down from heáven, and see;
  have regard for this vine,
  ¹⁵the stock that your
  strong hand planted.

¹⁶They have burned it with fire,
  they have cút it down;
  may they perish at the rebuke
  óf your countenance.

¹⁷But let your hand be upon the
one at your right hand,
  the one whom you made strong
  for yourself.

¹⁸Then we will never turn back
from you;
    give us life, and we will
    call on your name.

¹⁹Restore us, O Sovereign
God of hosts;

    let your face shine,
    that we may be saved. ℛ

*Advent 4 A and 1 B vs. 1–7, 17–19; Proper 22 [27] A vs.
7–15; Advent 4 C vs. 1–7 (Alt.); Proper 15 [20] C vs. 1–2,
8–19.*

Psalm 81

ℛesponse

Antiphon: Jean Slates Hawk, 1994

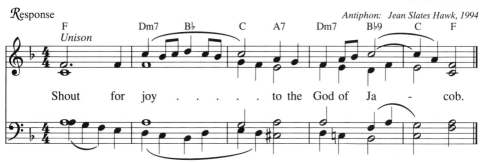

Shout for joy . . . . . to the God of Ja - cob.

ℛ

¹Sing aloud to God our strength;
    shout for joy to the God of Jacob.

²Raise a song, sound the tambourine,
    the sweet lyre with the harp.

³Blow the trumpet at the new moon,
    at the full moon, on our festal day.

⁴For it is a statute for Israel,
    an ordinance of the God of Jacob. ℛ

⁵God made it a decree in Joseph, when
he went out over the land of Egypt.
    I hear a voice I had not known:

⁶"I relieved your shoulder
of the burden;
    your hands were freed
    from the basket.

⁷"In distress you called,
and I rescued you;
    I answered you in the secret place
    of thunder; I tested you at the
    waters of Meribah.

⁸"Hear, O my people, while I
admonish you;
    O Israel, if you would but
    listen to me! ℛ

⁹"There shall be no strange god
among you;
    you shall not bow down to a
    foreign god.

¹⁰"I am the Sovereign your God,
who brought you up out of the
land of Egypt.
    Open your mouth wide and I
    will fill it.

¹¹"But my people did not listen to
my voice;
    Israel would not submit to me.

¹²"So I gave them over to their
stubborn hearts,
    to follow their own counsels. ℛ

¹³"O that my people would
listen to me,
    that Israel would walk in my ways!

¹⁴"Then I would quickly subdúe
their enemies,
and turn my hand agáinst their foes.

¹⁵"Those who hate God would
cringe befóre God,
and their doom would lást forever.

¹⁶"I would feed you with the finest
óf the wheat,
and with honey from the rock
I would satisfy you." ℟

*Epiphany 9 [9] B, Proper 4 [9] B vs. 1–10; Proper 17 [22]
C vs. 10–16. (If all verses are used, may be sung with
double tone.)*

Psalm 82

℟esponse   *Antiphon: Marty Haugen, 1994*

Rise up, O God,   judge the earth; for   all   na-tions be - long to   you.

℟

¹In the divine council God has
takén God's place;
God holds judgment in the
midst óf the gods:

²"How long will ýou judge unjustly
and show partiality tó the wicked?

³"Give justice to the weak
ánd the orphan;
maintain the right of the
lowly ánd the destitute.

⁴"Rescue the weak ánd the needy;
deliver them from the hand óf
the wicked." ℟

⁵They have neither knowledge
nor understanding, they walk
aróund in shadows;

all the foundations of the
éarth are shaken.

⁶I say, "Yóu are gods,
children of the Móst High,
all of you;

⁷"nevertheless, you shall díe
like mortals,
and fall like ány noble."

⁸Rise up, O God, júdge the earth;
for all the nations belóng to you! ℟

(May be sung with double tone.)

Psalm 84

Response
Antiphon: Peter Niedmann, 1994

Hap-py are those who live in your house, ev - er sing-ing your praise.

℟

¹How lovely is your dwelling place,
  O God of hosts!

²My soul longs, indeed it faints
  for the courts of God;
    my heart and my flesh sing
    for joy to the living God.

³Even the sparrow finds a home,
    and the swallow a nest for herself,

  where she may lay her young,
  at your altars,
    O God of hosts, my Ruler
    and my God. ℟

⁴Happy are those who live
  in your house,
    ever singing your praise.

⁵Happy are those whose strength
  is in you,
    in whose heart are the
    highways to Zion.

⁶As they go through the valley of Baca
  they make it a place of springs;
    the early rain also covers it
    with pools.

⁷They go from strength to strength;
  the God of gods will be seen
  in Zion. ℟

⁸O Sovereign God of hosts, hear
  my prayer;
    give ear, O God of Jacob!

⁹Behold our shield, O God;
    look on the face of your anointed.

¹⁰For a day in your courts is better than
  a thousand elsewhere.
    I would rather be a doorkeeper
    in the house of my God than live
    in the tents of wickedness.

¹¹For the Sovereign God is a sun
  and shield;
    God bestows favor and honor.

  No good thing does God withhold
    from those who walk uprightly.

¹²O God of hosts,
  happy is everyone who trusts
  in you. ℟

Proper 25 [30] C vs. 1–7.

675

Psalm 85

Response   Antiphon: *Carolyn Jennings, 1994*

Show us your stead-fast love, O God, and grant us your sal - va - tion.

℟

¹O God, you were favorable
to your land;
you restored the fortunes of Jacob.

²You forgave the iniquity
of your people;
you pardoned all their sin.

³You withdrew all your wrath;
you turned from your hot anger.

⁴Restore us again, O God of our
salvation,
and put away your indignation
toward us. ℟

⁵Will you be angry with us forever?
Will you prolong your anger
to all generations?

⁶Will you not revive us again,
so that your people may
rejoice in you?

⁷Show us your steadfast love, O God,
and grant us your salvation. ℟

⁸Let me hear what God the
Sovereign will speak,
for God will speak peace
to the people;

God will speak to the faithful,
to those who turn to God in
their hearts.

⁹Surely God's salvation is at hand for
those who fear God,
that God's glory may dwell in
our land. ℟

¹⁰Steadfast love and faithfulness
will meet;
righteousness and peace will
kiss each other.

¹¹Faithfulness will spring up
from the ground,
and righteousness will look
down from the sky.

¹²God will give what is good,
and our land will yield its increase.

¹³Righteousness will go before God,
and will make a path
for God's steps. ℟

*Proper 10 [15] B and Proper 14 [19] A vs. 8–13; Advent 2
B omit vs. 3–7.*

Psalm 86

Antiphon: *Judy Hunnicutt, 1994*

Response

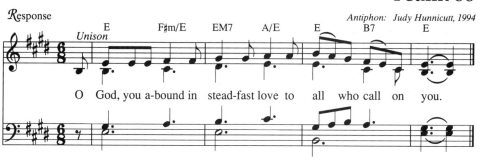

O God, you a-bound in stead-fast love to all who call on you.

℟

¹Incline your ear, O God,
and ánswer me,
  for I am póor and needy.

²Preserve my life, for I am
devoted to you;
  save your servant
  who trusts in you.

You áre my God;
  ³be gracious to me, O God,
  for to you do I cry áll day long.

⁴Gladden the soul óf your servant,
  for to you, O God,
  I lift úp my soul. ℟

⁵For you, O God, are good ánd
forgiving,
  abounding in steadfast love to
  all who cáll on you.

⁶Give ear, O God, to my prayer;
  listen to my cry of súpplication.

⁷In the day of my trouble
I cáll on you,
  for you will ánswer me.

⁸There is none like you among
the góds, O God,
  nor are there any wórks like yours.
℟

⁹All the nations you have made
  shall come and bow down
  before ýou, O God,
  and shall glorífy your name.

¹⁰For you are great and do
  wóndrous things;
  you alóne are God.

¹¹Teach me your way, O God,
  that I may walk ín your truth;
  give me an undivided heart to
  revére your name.

¹²I give thanks to you, O God my God,
  with áll my heart,
  and I will glorify your náme
  forever. ℟

¹³For great is your steadfast lóve
  toward me;
  you have delivered my soul
  from the dépths of Sheol.

¹⁴O God, the insolent rise úp
  against me;
  a band of ruffians seeks my life,
  and they do not set ýou
  before them.

¹⁵But you, O God, are a God
  mercíful and gracious,
  slow to anger and abounding
  in steadfast lóve and faithfulness.

℟ *O God, you abound in steadfast love to all who call on you.*

¹⁶Turn to me and be gracious to me;
give your strength to your servant;
save the child of your servant.

¹⁷Show me a sign of your favor, so
that those who hate me may see it

and be put to shame, because you,
O God, have helped me and
comforted me. ℟

Proper 7 [12] A vs. 1–10, 16–17; Proper 11 [16] A vs. 11–17.

Psalm 89

℟esponse

Antiphon: Lee Dengler, 1994

Unison

Your stead - fast love is es - tab - lished for - ev - er.

℟

¹I will sing of your steadfast love,
O God, forever;
with my mouth I will proclaim
your faithfulness to all generations.

²I declare that your steadfast love
is established forever;
your faithfulness is as firm
as the heavens.

³You said, "I have made a
covenant with my chosen one,
I have sworn to my servant David:

⁴"I will establish your descendants
forever,
and build your throne for all
generations.'" ℟

¹⁵Happy are the people who know
the festal shout,
who walk, O God, in the light
of your countenance;

¹⁶they exult in your name all day long, and
extol your righteousness.

¹⁷For you are the glory
of their strength;
by your favor our horn is exalted.

¹⁸For our shield belongs to God,
our ruler to the Holy One of Israel.
℟

¹⁹Then you spoke in a vision to
your faithful one, and said:
"I have set the crown on one
who is mighty, I have exalted
one chosen from the people.

²⁰"I have found my servant David;
with my holy oil
I have anointed him;

²¹"my hand shall always remain
with him;
my arm also shall strengthen him.

²²"The enemy shall not outwit him,
the wicked shall not humble him.
℟

²³"I will crush his foes before him
and strike down those
who hate him.

²⁴"My faithfulness and steadfast love
shall be with him;
and in my name his horn
shall be exalted.

²⁵"I will set his hand on the sea
and his right hand on the rivers.

²⁶"He shall cry to me, 'You are my
Father and Mother,
my God, and the Rock
of my salvation!' ℟

²⁷"I will make him the firstborn,
the highest of the rulers
of the earth.

²⁸"Forever I will keep my steadfast
love for him,
and my covenant with him
will stand firm.

²⁹"I will establish his line forever,
and his throne as long as the
heavens endure. ℟

³⁰"If his children forsake my law
and do not walk according to
my ordinances,

³¹"if they violate my statutes
and do not keep my
commandments,

³²"then I will punish their transgression
with the rod
and their iniquity with scourges;

³³"but I will not remove from him
my steadfast love,
or be false to my faithfulness. ℟

³⁴"I will not violate my covenant,
or alter the word that went forth
from my lips.

³⁵"Once and for all I have sworn
by my holiness;
I will not lie to David.

³⁶"His line shall continue forever,
and his throne endure before me
like the sun.

³⁷"It shall be established forever
like the moon,
an enduring witness in the skies."
℟

Proper 8 [13] A vs. 1–4, 15–18; Advent 4 B vs. 1–4, 19–26
(Alt.); Proper 11 [16] B vs. 20–37.

Psalm 90

Response *Unison*

Antiphon: *Elaine Kirkland, 1994*

From ev - er - last-ing to ev - er - last - ing, you are God.

℟

¹O God, you have been
our dwelling place
in all generations.

²Before the mountains were brought
forth, or ever you had formed the earth
and the world,
from everlasting to everlasting
you are God.

³You turn us back to dust,
and say, "Turn back, you mortals."

⁴For a thousand years in your sight are
like yesterday when it is past,
or like a watch in the night. ℟

⁵You sweep them away;
they are like a dream,
like grass that is renewed in
the morning;

⁶in the morning it flourishes
and is renewed;
in the evening it fades and withers.

⁷For we are consumed by your anger;
by your wrath we are overwhelmed.

⁸You have set our iniquities
before you,
our secret sins in the light of
your countenance. ℟

⁹For all our days pass away
under your wrath;
our years come to an end
like a sigh.

¹⁰The days of our life are seventy years,
or perhaps eighty, if we are strong;

even then their span is only toil
and trouble;
they are soon gone,
and we fly away.

¹¹Who considers the power
of your anger?
Your wrath is as great as the
fear that is due you.

¹²So teach us to count our days
that we may gain a wise heart. ℟

¹³Turn, O God! How long?
Have compassion on your servants!

¹⁴Satisfy us in the morning
with your steadfast love,
so that we may rejoice
and be glad all our days.

¹⁵Make us glad as many days as
you have afflicted us,
and as many years as
we have seen evil.

¹⁶Let your work be manifest
ïo your servants,
    and your glorious power
    ïo their children.

¹⁷Let the favor of the Sovereign our
God be upon us, and prosper for us
    the work óf our hands —
    O prosper the work óf our hands! ℛ

*Proper 25 [30] A vs. 1–6, 13–17; Proper 28 [33] A vs. 1–8,
(9–11), 12; Proper 23 [28] B vs. 12–17.*

Psalm 91

ℛesponse

Antiphon: David Hurd, 1994

My ref - uge and my for - tress, my God in whom I trust.

ℛ

¹You who live in the shelter of
ïhe Most High,
    who abide in the shadow of
    the Almighty, ²will śay to God,

"My refuge ánd my fortress;
my God, in whóm I trust."

³For God will deliver you from
the snare óf the fowler
    and from the déadly pestilence;

⁴God will cover you with God's
pinions, and under God's wings
you will find refuge;
    God's faithfulness is a śhield
    and buckler. ℛ

⁵You will not fear the terror
óf the night,
    or the arrow that flíes by day,

⁶or the pestilence that stalks ín
the nighttime,
    or the destruction that wástes
    at noonday.

⁹Because you have made Gód
your refuge,
    the Most High your dwélling place,

¹⁰no evil śhall befall you,
    no scourge come néar your tent. ℛ

¹¹For God will command God's angels
concérning you
    to guard you in áll your ways.

¹²On their hands they will béar you up,
    so that you will not dash your foot
    agáinst a stone.

¹³You will tread on the lion
ánd the adder,
    the young lion and the serpent
    you will trample únder foot.

¹⁴Those who love me, I wíll deliver;
    I will protect those who know
    my name.

R My refuge and my fortress, my God in whom I trust.

¹⁵When they call to me,
  I will ánswer them;
  I will be with them in trouble,
  I will rescue them and hónor them.

¹⁶With long life I will satisfy them,
  and show them mý salvation. *R*

*Proper 24 [29] B omit vs. 1–8; Lent 1 C omit vs. 3–8;
Proper 21 [26] C omit vs. 7–13.*

Psalm 92

*R*esponse

Antiphon: Robert Train Adams, 1994

The righ - teous flour - ish like the palm tree.

R

¹It is good to give thanks to God,
  to sing praises to your name,
  Ó Most High;

²to declare your steadfast love ín
  the morning,
  and your faithfulñess by night,

³to the music of the lute ánd the harp,
  to the melody óf the lyre.

⁴For you, O God, have made me glad
  bý your work;
  at the works of your hands
  I śing for joy. *R*

¹²The righteous flourish líke the
  palm tree,
  and grow like a cedár in Lebanon.

¹³They are planted in the house of God;
  they flourish in the courts
  óf our God.

¹⁴In old age they still próduce fruit;
  they are always green
  and fúll of sap,

¹⁵showing that God is upright;
  God is my rock, and has
  ño unrighteousness. *R*

(May be sung with double tone.)

Psalm 93

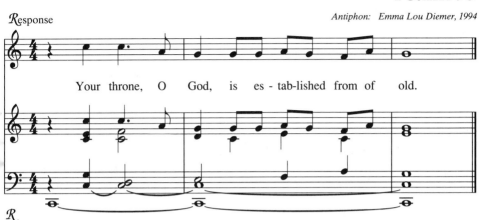

Response

Antiphon: *Emma Lou Diemer, 1994*

Your throne, O God, is es - tab-lished from of old.

℟

¹God is ruler, God is robed in majesty;
the Sovereign is robed,
and is girded with strength.

God has established the world;
it shall never be moved;

²your throne is established from
of old;
you are from everlasting. ℟

³The floods have lifted up, O God,
the floods have lifted up their voice;
the floods lift up their roaring.

⁴More majestic than the thunders
of mighty waters,
more majestic than the waves
of the sea, majestic on high is God!

⁵Your decrees are very sure;
holiness befits your house,
O God, forevermore. ℟

Psalm 95

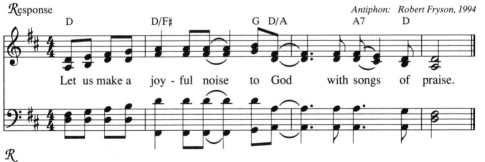

Response

Antiphon: *Robert Fryson, 1994*

D   D/F♯   G D/A   A7   D

Let us make a joy - ful noise to God with songs of praise.

℟

¹O come, let us sing to God;
let us make a joyful noise to
the rock of our salvation!

²Let us come into God's presence
with thanksgiving;

let us make a joyful noise to
God with songs of praise!

³For God is a great God,
and a great Ruler above all gods.

⁴In God's hand are the depths of the
earth;

℟ *Let us make a joyful noise to God with songs of praise.*

the heights of the mountains
are álso God's. ℟

⁵The sea is God's, for God made it,
and the dry land, which God's hands
have formed.

⁶O come, let us worship ánd bow
down,
let us kneel before God, our Maker!

⁷For God ís our God,
and we are the people of God's
pasture, and the sheep óf God's hand.

O that today you would listen to
God's voice!

⁸Do not harden your hearts,
as at Meribah, as on the day at
Massah ín the wilderness, ℟

⁹when your ancestors tested me,
and put me to the proof, though
they had séen my work.

¹⁰For forty years I loathed
that generation and said,
"They are a people whose hearts go
astray, and they do not regárd my
ways."

¹¹Therefore in my anger I swore,
"They shall not enter my rest." ℟

Proper 29 [34] A vs. 1–7a.

Psalm 96

℟esponse   *Antiphon: Jane Marshall, 1994*

Sing   to   God   and   bless   God's   name.

℟

¹O sing to God á new song;
sing to God, áll the earth.

²Sing to God, bless God's name;
tell of God's salvation
from dáy to day.

³Declare God's glory amóng
the nations,
God's marvelous works among
áll the peoples. ℟

⁴For great is God, and greatly
to be praised;

God is to be revered abóve all gods.

⁵For all the gods of the peoples
are idols,
but God máde the heavens.

⁶Honor and majesty áre before God;
strength and beauty are ín
God's sanctuary.

⁷Ascribe to God, O families óf
the peoples,
ascribe to God glorý and strength. ℟

⁸Ascribe to God the glory
  due God's name;
    bring an offering,
    and come into God's courts.

⁹Worship God in holy splendor;
    tremble before God, all the earth.

¹⁰Say among the nations, "God is ruler!
    The world is firmly established;
    it shall never be moved.

"God will judge the peoples;
    God will judge the peoples
    with equity." ℛ

¹¹Let the heavens be glad,
    and let the earth rejoice;

let the sea roar, and all that fills it;

¹²let the field exult,
    and everything in it.
    Then shall all the trees of the forest
    sing for joy ¹³before God;

for God is coming,
    for God is coming
    to judge the earth.

God will judge the world
    with righteousness,
    and the peoples with God's truth. ℛ

Proper 24 [29] A vs. 1–9 (10–13); Epiphany 9 [9] C and
Proper 4 [9] C vs. 1–9.

Psalm 97

Response — Antiphon: Vérne de la Peña, 1994

F Cm7 F Cm7 F Cm7 Dsus4 D

Re - joice in God, O you righ-teous! Give thanks to God's ho - ly name!

ℛ

¹God is ruler! Let the earth rejoice;
    let the many coastlands be glad!

²Clouds and thick darkness
  are all around God;
    righteousness and justice are
    the foundation of God's throne.

³Fire goes before God,
    and consumes God's adversaries
    on every side.

⁴God's lightnings light up the world;
    the earth sees and trembles. ℛ

⁵The mountains melt like wax
  before God,
    before the God of all the earth.

⁶The heavens proclaim
  God's righteousness;
    and all the peoples behold
    God's glory.

⁷All worshipers of images are
  put to shame, those who make their
  boast in worthless idols;
    all gods bow down before God.

℟ Rejoice in God, O you righteous! Give thanks to God's holy name!

⁸Zion hears ánd is glad,
and the towns of Judah rejoice,
because of your judgménts, O God.
℟

⁹For you, O God, are most high
over áll the earth;
you are exalted far abóve all gods.

¹⁰God loves those whó hate evil;
God guards the lives of God's

faithful; God rescues them
from the hand óf the wicked.

¹¹Light dawns fór the righteous,
and joy for the upríght in heart.

¹²Rejoice in God, Ó you righteous,
and give thanks to God's
hóly name! ℟

(May be sung with double tone.)

Psalm 98

℟esponse   Antiphon: Marty Haugen, 1994

Make a joy-ful noise, a   joy-ful noise, un-to God,   all the   earth.

℟

¹O sing to God á new song,
for God has done marvélous things.

God's strong hand and hóly arm
have given Gód the victory.

²God has made knówn God's victory,
and has revealed God's vindication
in the sight óf the nations.

³God has remembered having steadfast
love and faithfulness to the hóuse
of Israel.
All the ends of the earth have
seen the victory óf our God.

⁴Make a joyful noise to God,
áll the earth;
break forth into joyous song
ánd sing praises.

⁵Sing praises to God wíth the lyre,

with the lyre and the sóund
of melody. ℟

⁶With trumpets and the sound óf
the horn
make a joyful noise before the
Ruler, the Sovereign.

⁷Let the sea roar, and áll that fills it;
the world and thóse who live in it.

⁸Let the floods cláp their hands;
let the hills sing together for
joy ⁹at the presence of God;
for God is coming to júdge
the earth.

God will judge the wórld
with righteousness,
and the peóples with equity. ℟

Holy Cross ABC vs. 1–5 (Alt.).

686

Psalm 99

Antiphon: Carolyn Jennings, 1994

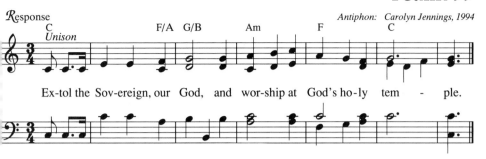

Ex-tol the Sov-ereign, our God, and wor-ship at God's ho-ly tem - ple.

ℛ

¹God is ruler; let the peoples tremble!
God sits enthroned upon the
cherubim; let the earth quake!

²God is great in Zion;
God is exalted over all the peoples.

³Let them praise your great and
awesome name.
Holy is God!

⁴Mighty Ruler, lover of justice,
you have established equity;
you have executed justice and
righteousness in Jacob.

⁵Extol the Sovereign our God;
worship at God's footstool.
Holy is God! ℛ

⁶Moses and Aaron were
among God's priests,

Samuel also was among those
who called on God's name.

They cried to God,
and God answered them.

⁷God spoke to them
in the pillar of cloud;
they kept God's decrees, and
the statutes that God gave them.

⁸O Sovereign our God,
you answered them;
you were a forgiving God to them,
but an avenger of
their wrongdoings.

⁹Extol the Sovereign our God, and
worship at God's holy mountain;
for the Sovereign our God is holy.
ℛ

Psalm 100

Response
Antiphon: Peter Niedmann, 1994

Unison

It is God that made us, and we are God's peo - ple.

℟

¹Make a joyful noise to God,
áll the earth.
  ²Worship God with gladness; come
  into God's présence with singing.

³Know that the Sovereign is God. It
is Gód that made us,
  and we are God's; we are God's
  people, and the sheep óf God's
  pasture.

⁴Enter God's gates with thanksgiving,
and enter God's ćourts with praise.
  Give thanks to God, and bléss
  God's name.

⁵For God is good; God's steadfast love
endúres forever,
  and God's faithfulness to all
  génerations. ℟

(May be sung with double tone.)

Psalm 103

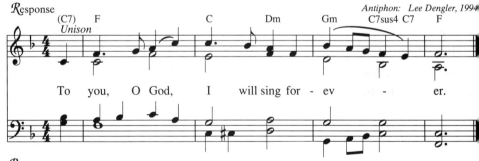

Response
Antiphon: Lee Dengler, 1994

(C7)   F   C   Dm   Gm   C7sus4 C7   F

Unison

To you, O God, I will sing for - ev - er.

℟

¹Bless God, Ó my soul,
  and all that is within me, bless God's
  hóly name.

²Bless God, Ó my soul,
  and do not forget áll God's benefits —

³who forgives all ýour iniquity,
  who heals all ýour diseases,

⁴who redeems your life fróm the Pit,
  who crowns you with steadfast lóve
  and mercy,

⁵who satisfies you with good as long ás
  you live
    so that your youth is renewed líke
    the eagle's. ℟

[6]God works vindication and justice
for all who áre oppressed.

[7]God made known God's ways to Moses,
and God's acts to the people of Israel.

[8]God is merciful and gracious,
slow to anger and abounding in
steadfast love. ℛ

[9]God will not always accuse,
nor will God be angry forever.

[10]God does not deal with us according to
our sins,
nor repay us according to óur
iniquities.

[11]For as the heavens are high above the
earth,

so great is God's steadfast love
toward those who fear God;

[12]as far as the east is from the west,
so far God removes our
transgressions from us. ℛ

[13]As a father and mother have compassion
for their children,
so God has compassion for those
who fear God.

[22]Bless God, all God's works, in all places
of God's dominion.
Bless God, O my soul. ℛ

Proper 19 [24] A vs. (1–7), 8–13; Epiphany 8 [8] B vs.
1–13, 22; Proper 16 [21] C vs. 1–8.

Psalm 104

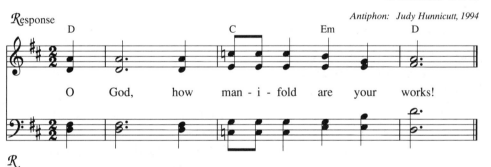

Antiphon: Judy Hunnicutt, 1994

ℛesponse

O God, how man-i-fold are your works!

ℛ
[1]Bless God, O my soul.
O God my God, you are véry great.

You are clothed with honor and majesty,
[2]wrapped in light as with a garment.

You stretch out the heavens like a tent,
[3]you set the beams of your chambers
ón the waters,

you make the clouds your chariot,
you ride on the wings óf the wind, ℛ

[4]you make the winds your messengers,
fire and flame áre your ministers.

[5]You set the earth on íts foundations,
so that it shall never be shaken.

[6]You cover it with the deep as with a
garment;
the waters stood above the
mountains.

[7]At your rebuke they flee;
at the sound of your thunder they
take to flight. ℛ

℟ *O God, how manifold are your works!*

⁸They rose up to the mountains;
   they ran down to the valleys to the
   place that you appointed for them.

⁹You set a boundary that they may not
pass,
   so that they might not again cover
   the earth.

²⁴O God, how manifold áre your works!
   In wisdom you have made them all;
   the earth is full óf your creatures.

³⁵ᶜBless God, O my soul.
   Praise be to God! ℟

Proper 24 [29] B. (May be sung with double tone.)

Psalm 104

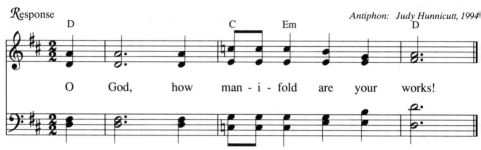

℟esponse   *Antiphon: Judy Hunnicutt, 1994*

O God, how man-i-fold are your works!

(Selection for Pentecost Day)

℟

²⁴O God, how manifold áre your works!
   In wisdom you have made them all;
   the earth is full óf your creatures.

²⁵Yonder is the sea, great and wide;
   it is teeming with countless
   creatures, living things both small
   and great.

²⁶There go the ships,
   and Leviathan that you formed to
   sport in it.

²⁷These all look to you
   to give them their food in due
   season; ℟

²⁸when you give to them, they gather it
up;
   when you open your hand, they are
   filled with good things.

²⁹When you hide your face, they áre
dismayed;
   when you take away their breath,
   they die and return to their dust.

³⁰When you send forth your spirit, they
   áre created;
   and you renew the face óf the ground.

³¹May the glory of God endure forever;
   may God rejoice in God's works —
   ℟

³²God who looks on the earth ánd it
   trembles,
   God who touches the mountains ánd
   they smoke.

³³I will sing to God as long ás I live;
   I will sing praise to my God while I
   have being.

³⁴May my meditation be pleasing to God,
   for in God do I rejoice.

³⁵Let sinners be consumed from the earth,
   and let the wicked be no more.
   Bless God, O my soul. Praise be to
   God! ℟

(May be sung with double tone.)

Psalm 105

Antiphon: Elaine Kirkland, 1994

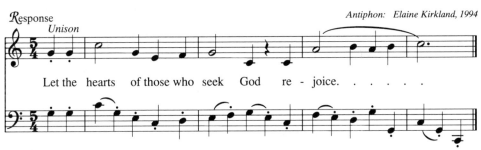

Let the hearts of those who seek God re - joice. . . . . .

℟

¹O give thanks to God, call ón God's name,
make known God's deeds amóng the peoples.

²Sing to God, sing praíses to God;
tell of all God's wonderful works.

³Glory in God's hóly name;
let the hearts of those who seek God rejoice.

⁴Seek God ánd God's strength;
seek God's preśence continually.

⁵Remember the wonderful works God has done,
God's miracles, and the judgménts God uttered,

⁶O offspring of God's servants Abraham and Sarah,
children of Jacob, God's chosen ones. ℟

⁷God is the Sovereign our God,
whose judgments are in áll the earth.

⁸God is mindful of the covénant forever,
of the word that God commanded, for a thousand génerations,

⁹the covenant máde with Abraham,
God's sworn promíse to Isaac,

¹⁰which was confirmed to Jacob ás a statute,

to Israel as an everlasting covenant,

¹¹saying, "To you I will give the land of Canaan
as your portion for án inheritance." ℟

¹⁶When God summoned famine against the land, and broke every staff of bread,

¹⁷God had sent a man ahead of them,
Joseph, who was sold ás a slave.

¹⁸His feet were hurt with fetters, his neck was put in a collar of iron;

¹⁹until what he had said came to pass, the word of God kept testing him.

²⁰The king sent ánd released him;
the ruler of the peoples śet him free.

²¹He made Joseph lord of his house, and ruler of all his possessions,

²²to instruct his officials at his pleasure, and to teach his élders wisdom. ℟

²³Then Israel came to Egypt,
and Jacob lived as an alien in the land of Ham.

²⁴And God made the people very fruitful,
and made them stronger than their foes,

²⁵whose hearts God then turned to hate God's people,
to deal craftily with God's servants.

691

℞ *Let the hearts of those who seek God rejoice.*

²⁶God sent God's servant Moses,
and Aaron whom God had chosen. ℞

³⁷Then God brought Israel out with silver and gold,
and there was no one among their tribes who stumbled.

³⁸Egypt was glad when they departed,
for dread of them had fallen upon Egypt.

³⁹God spread a cloud for a covering,
and fire to give light by night.

⁴⁰They asked, and God brought quails,
and gave them food from heaven in abundance.

⁴¹God opened the rock, and water gushed out;
it flowed through the desert like a river.

⁴²For God remembered God's holy promise,
and Abraham and Sarah, God's servants. ℞

⁴³So God brought God's people out with joy,
God's chosen ones with singing.

⁴⁴God gave them the lands of the nations,
and they took possession of the wealth of the peoples,

⁴⁵that they might keep God's statutes and observe God's laws.
Praise be to God! ℞

Proper 12 [17] A vs. 1–11, 45b (Alt.); Proper 14 [19] A vs. 1–6, 16–22, 45b; Proper 17 [22] A vs. 1–6, 23–26, 45c; Proper 20 [25] A vs. 1–6, 37–45.

Psalm 106

℞esponse   *Unison*   *Antiphon: David Hurd, 1994*

Re - mem-ber me, O God, when you show fa - vor to your peo-ple.

℞

¹Praise God! O give thanks to God, for God is good;
for God's steadfast love endures forever.

²Who can utter the mighty doings of God,
or declare all God's praise?

³Happy are those who observe justice always,
who do righteousness at all times.

⁴Remember me, O God, when you show favor to your people;
help me when you deliver them;

⁵that I may see the prosperity of your chosen ones,
that I may rejoice in the gladness of your nation, and glory in your heritage. ℞

⁶Both we and our ancestors have sinned; we have committed iniquity, and have done wickedly.
¹⁹They made a calf at Horeb and worshiped á cast image.
²⁰They exchanged the glory of God for the image of an ox that eats grass.

²¹They forgot God, their Savior, who had done great things in Egypt,
²²wondrous works in the land of Ham, and awesome deeds by the Red Sea.

²³Therefore God said God would destroy them —
had not Moses, God's chosen one, stood in the breach before God,
to turn away God's wrath, that it not destroy them. ℞

Psalm 107

℞esponse

Antiphon: Marty Haugen, 1994

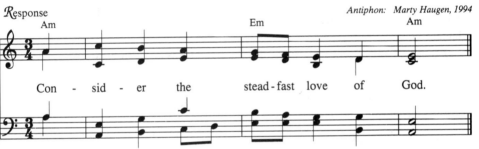

Con - sid - er the stead - fast love of God.

℞
¹O give thanks to God, for God is good; for God's steadfast love endures forever.

²Let the redeemed of God say so, those whom God redeemed from trouble

³and gathered in from the lands, from the east and the west, from the north ánd the south. ℞

⁴Some wandered in desert wastes, finding no way to an inhabited town;
⁵hungry and thirsty, their soul fainted within them.

⁶Then they cried to God in their trouble, and God delivered them from their distress;

⁷God led them by á straight way, until they reached an inhabited town.

⁸Let them thank God for God's steadfast love,
for God's wonderful works to humankind.

⁹For God satisfies the thirsty, and the hungry God fills with good things. ℞

¹⁷Some were sick through their sinful ways,

℟ *Consider the steadfast love of God.*

and because of their iniquities endured affliction;

¹⁸they loathed any kind of food,
and they drew near to the gates of death.

¹⁹Then they cried to God in their trouble,
and God saved them from their distress;

²⁰God sent out God's word and healed them,
and delivered them from destruction.

²¹Let them thank God for God's steadfast love,
for God's wonderful works to humankind.

²²And let them offer sacrifices of thanksgiving,
and tell of God's deeds with songs of joy. ℟

²³Some went down to the sea in ships,
doing business on the mighty waters;

²⁴they saw the deeds of God,
God's wondrous works in the deep.

²⁵For God commanded and raised the stormy wind,
which lifted up the waves of the sea.

²⁶They mounted up to heaven, they went down to the depths;
their courage melted away in their calamity;

²⁷they reeled and staggered like drunkards,
and were at their wits' end. ℟

²⁸Then they cried to God in their trouble,
and God brought them out from their distress;

²⁹God made the storm be still,
and the waves of the sea were hushed.

³⁰Then they were glad because they had quiet,
and God brought them to the haven they desired.

³¹Let them thank God for God's steadfast love,
for God's wonderful works to humankind.

³²Let them extol God in the congregation of the people,
and praise God in the assembly of the elders. ℟

³³God turns rivers into a desert,
and springs of water into thirsty ground;

³⁴God turns a fruitful land into a salty waste,
because of the wickedness of its inhabitants.

³⁵God turns a desert into pools of water,
a parched land into springs of water.

³⁶And there God lets the hungry live,
and they establish a town to live in;

³⁷they sow fields, and plant vineyards,
and they get a fruitful yield.

⁴³Let those who are wise give heed to these things,
and consider the steadfast love of God. ℟

Proper 26 [31] A vs. 1–7, 33–37; Lent 4 B vs. 1–3, 17–22;

Proper 7 [12] B vs. 1–3, 23–32; Proper 13 [18] C vs. 1–9, 43.

Psalm 110

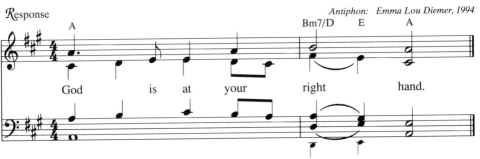

Antiphon: *Emma Lou Diemer, 1994*

℟ ¹God says to my sovereign,
 "Sit at my right hand until I
 make your enemies your
 footstool."

²God sends out from Zion your
 mighty scepter.
 You shall rule in the midst of
 your foes.

³Your people will offer themselves
 willingly
 on the day you lead your forces on
 the holy mountains.

From the womb of the morning,
 like dew,
 your youth will come to you. ℟

⁴God has sworn and will not regret it,
 "You are a priest forever according
 to the order of Melchizedek."

⁵God is at your mighty hand;
 God will shatter rulers on the day
 of God's wrath.

⁶God will execute judgment among the
 nations, filling them with corpses;
 God will shatter heads over the
 wide earth.

⁷My sovereign will drink from the
 stream by the path;
 and therefore will lift up the head.
 ℟

(May be sung with double tone.)

Psalm 111

Response

Great, great, great are the works of God.

℞

¹Praise God! I will give thanks to God with my whole heart,
in the company of the upright, in the congregation.

²Great are the works of God,
studied by all who delight in them.

³Full of honor and majesty is God's work,
and God's righteousness endures forever.

⁴God has gained renown by wonderful deeds;
God is gracious and merciful. ℞

⁵God provides food for those who fear God;
God is ever mindful of God's covenant.

⁶God has shown God's people the power of God's works,

in giving them the heritage of the nations.

⁷The works of God's hands are faithful and just;
all God's precepts are trustworthy.

⁸They are established forever and ever,
to be performed with faithfulness and uprightness. ℞

⁹God sent redemption to God's people;
God has commanded God's covenant forever. Holy and awesome is God's name.

¹⁰The fear of God is the beginning of wisdom;
all those who practice it have a good understanding. God's praise endures forever. ℞

Psalm 112

Antiphon: Jane Marshall, 1994

Response
Unison

Hap - py are those who fear God.

℟

¹Praise be to God!
Happy are those who fear God, who greatly delight in God's commandments.

²Their descendants will be mighty in the land;
the generation of the upright will be blessed.

³Wealth and riches are in their houses, and their righteousness endures forever.

⁴They rise in the night as a light for the upright;
they are gracious, merciful, and righteous.

⁵It is well with those who deal generously and lend,
who conduct their affairs with justice. ℟

⁶For the righteous will never be moved;
they will be remembered forever.

⁷They are not afraid of evil tidings;
their hearts are firm, secure in God.

⁸Their hearts are steady, they will not be afraid;
in the end they will look in triumph on their foes.

⁹They have distributed freely, they have given to the poor;
their righteousness endures forever;
their horn is exalted in honor.

¹⁰The wicked see it and are angry; they gnash their teeth and melt away;
the desire of the wicked comes to nothing. ℟

Epiphany 5 [5] A vs. 1–9, (10).

Psalm 113

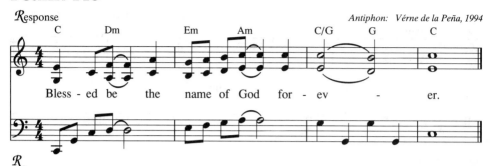

Response   *Antiphon: Vérne de la Peña, 1994*

Bless - ed be the name of God for - ev - er.

R

¹Praise be to God!
  Praise, O servants of God; praise the
  name of God.

²Blessed be the name of God from this
time on and forevermore.
  ³From the rising of the sun to its
  setting the name of God is to be
  praised.

⁴God is high above all nations,
  and God's glory above the heavens. R

⁵Who is like God our God, who is seated
on high,
  ⁶who looks far down on the heavens
  and the earth?

⁷God raises the poor from the dust, and
lifts the needy from the ash heap,
  ⁸to make them sit with nobles, with
  the leaders of God's people.

⁹God gives the childless woman a home,
  making her the joyous mother of
  children. Praise be to God! R

Psalm 114

Response   *Antiphon: Hyeon Jeong, 1994*

trem - ble,
Trem - ble, O earth, at the pre - sence of God.

R

¹When Israel went out from Egypt,
  the house of Jacob from a people of
  strange language,

²Judah became God's sanctuary,
  Israel became God's dominion.

³The sea looked and fled; Jordan turned
back.
  ⁴The mountains skipped like rams,
  the hills like lambs. R

⁵Why is it, O sea, that you flee? O
Jordan, that you turn back?

⁶O mountains, that you skip like rams? O hills, like lambs?

⁷Tremble, O earth, at the presence of God,
at the presence of the God of Jacob,

⁸who turns the rock into a pool of water, who turns the flint into a spring of water. ℛ

Psalm 116

ℛesponse

Antiphon: *Judy Hunnicutt, 1994*

I will call on God as long as I live (as long as I live).

ℛ

¹I love God, because God has heard my voice
and has heard my supplications.

²Because God inclined an ear to me,
therefore I will call on God as long as I live. ℛ

³The snares of death encompassed me;
the pangs of Sheol laid hold on me;
I suffered distress and anguish.

⁴Then I called on the name of God:
"O God, I pray, save my life!"

⁵Gracious is God, and righteous;
our God is merciful.

⁶God protects the simple;
when I was brought low, God saved me. ℛ

⁷Return, O my soul, to your rest,
for God has dealt bountifully with you.

⁸For you have delivered my soul from death,
and my eyes from tears, and my feet from stumbling.

⁹I walk before God
in the land of the living. ℛ

¹²What shall I return to God for all God's bounty to me?
¹³I will lift up the cup of salvation
and call on the name of God,

¹⁴I will pay my vows to God,
I will pay them in the presence of all God's people.

¹⁵Precious in the sight of God
is the death of God's faithful ones.

¹⁶O God, I am your servant, and the child of your servant.
You have loosed my bonds.

R I will call on God as long as I live (as long as I live).

[17]I will offer to you a thanksgiving
  sacrifice;
  I will call on the name of God.

[18]I will pay my vows to God
  in the presence of all God's people,

[19]in the courts of the house of God,
  in your midst, O Jerusalem. Praise
  be to God! *R*

Holy Thursday ABC and Proper 6 [11] A omit vs. 3–9;
Easter 3A omit vs. 5–9; Proper 19 [24] B vs. 1–9.

Psalm 118

*R*esponse

Antiphon: Carolyn Jennings, 1994

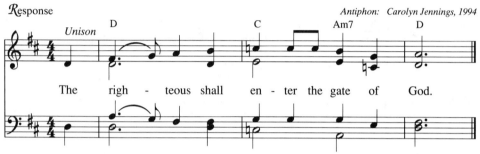

(Selection for Easter Sunday)

R

[1]O give thanks to God, for God is good;
  God's steadfast love endures forever!

[2]Let all Israel say,
  "God's steadfast love endures
  forever."

[14]God is my strength and my might;
  God has become my salvation.

[15]There are glad songs of victory in the
  tents of the righteous: "The strong hand
  of God does valiantly;

  [16]the mighty hand of God is exalted;
  the strong hand of God does valiantly."

R

[17]I shall not die, but I shall live,
  and recount the deeds of God.

[18]God has punished me severely,
  but God did not give me over to
  death.

[19]Open to me the gates of righteousness,
  that I may enter through them and
  give thanks to God.

[20]This is the gate of God;
  the righteous shall enter through it.

R

[21]I thank you that you have answered me
  and have become my salvation.

[22]The stone that the builders rejected
  has become the chief cornerstone.

[23]This is God's doing;
  it is marvelous in our eyes.

[24]This is the day that God has made;
  let us rejoice and be glad in it. *R*

Easter 2 C vs. 14–29 (Alt.); vs. 25–29 are on following page.
(May be sung with double tone.)

℟ *The righteous shall enter the gate of God.*

(Selection for Palm/Passion Sunday)

℟

¹O give thanks to God, for Gód is good;
God's steadfast love endúres forever!

²Let all Isŕael say,
"God's steadfast love endúres
forever."

¹⁹Open to me the gátes of righteousness,
that I may enter through them and
give t́hanks to God.

²⁰This is the gáte of God;
the righteous shall ent́er through it.
℟

²¹I thank you that you have ánswered me
and have become ḿy salvation.

²²The stone that the builders rejected has
become t́he chief cornerstone.
²³This is God's doing; it is
marvelous ín our eyes.

²⁴This is the day that Gód has made;
let us rejoice ánd be glad in it.

²⁵Save us, we beseech ́you, O God!
O God, we beseech you, give ús
success! ℟

²⁶Blessed is the one who comes in the
ńame of God.
We bless you from the h́ouse of God.

²⁷The Sovereign is God, and God has
gív́en us light.
Bind the festal procession with
branches, up to the horns óf the altar.

²⁸You are my God, and I will give t́hanks
to you;
you are my God, I ẃill extol you.

²⁹O give thanks to God, for Gód is good,
for God's steadfast love endúres
forever. ℟

(May be sung with double tone.)

Psalm 119

℟esponse

Antiphon: Elaine Kirkland, 1994

Teach me, O God, the way of your stat-utes.

(First selection)

℟

¹Happy are those whose ẃay is
blameless,
who walk in the ĺaw of God.

²Happy are those who keep Gód's
decrees,
who seek God with t́heir whole heart,

³who also d́o no wrong,
but walk ín God's ways.

⁴You have commanded that áll your
precepts
shall be képt with diligence. ℟

℟ *Teach me, O God, the way of your statutes.*

⁵O that my ways máy be steadfast
  in keepíng your statutes!

⁶Then I shall not be pút to shame,
  having my eyes fixed on all ýour
  commandments.

⁷I will praise you with an úpright heart,
  when I learn your ríghteous
  ordinances.

⁸I will obsérve your statutes;
  do not utterly forsake me. ℟

⁹How can young people keep their way
  pure?
  By guarding it according to your
  word.

¹⁰With my whole heart I seek you;
  do not let me stray from ýour
  commandments.

¹¹I treasure your word ín my heart,
  so that I may not sín against you.

¹²Blessed are ýou, O God;
  teach me your statutes. ℟

¹³With my lips I shall declare
  all the ordinances of ýour mouth.

¹⁴I delight in the way of ýour decrees
  as much as ín all riches.

¹⁵I will meditate ón your precepts,
  and fix my eyes ón your ways.

¹⁶I will delight ín your statutes;
  I will not forget your word. ℟

³³Teach me, O God, the way óf your
  statutes,
  and I will observe it to the end.

³⁴Give me understanding, that I may keep
  your law,
  and observe it with mý whole heart.

³⁵Lead me in the path of ýour
  commandments,
  for I delight ín your way.

³⁶Turn my heart to ýour decrees,
  and not to selfish gain. ℟

³⁷Turn my eyes from looking at vanities;
  give me life ín your ways.

³⁸Confirm to your servant your promise,
  which is for those who fear you.

³⁹Turn away the disgrace that I dread,
  for your ordinances are good.

⁴⁰See, I have longed for your precepts;
  in your righteousness give me life.
℟

Epiphany 6 [6] A vs. 1–8; Epiphany 7 [7] A vs. 33–40;
Proper 18 [23] A vs. 33–40; Lent 5 B vs. 9–16 (Alt.);
Proper 26 [31] B vs. 1–8. (May be sung with double tone.)

℟ *Teach me, O God, the way of your statutes.*

(Second selection)
℟
⁹⁷O God, how I love your law!
  It is my meditation áll day long.

⁹⁸Your commandment makes me wiser
  than my enemies,
  for it is alwáys with me.

⁹⁹I have more understanding than áll my
  teachers,
  for your decrees are my meditation.

¹⁰⁰I understand more than the aged,
  for I keep your precepts. ℟

¹⁰¹I hold back my feet from every évil way,
  in order to keep your word.

¹⁰²I do not turn away from your ordinances,
  for you have taught me.

¹⁰³How sweet are your words to my taste,
  sweeter than honey to my mouth!

¹⁰⁴Through your precepts I get understanding;
  therefore I hate every way that is false. ℟

¹⁰⁵Your word is a lamp to my feet,
  and a light to my path.

¹⁰⁶I have sworn an oath ánd confirmed it,
  to observe your righteous ordinances.

¹⁰⁷I am severely afflicted;
  give me life, O God, according to your word.

¹⁰⁸Accept my offerings of práise, O God,
  and teach me your ordinances. ℟

¹⁰⁹I hold my life in my hand continually,
  but I do not forget your law.

¹¹⁰The wicked have laid a snare for me,
  but I do not stray from your precepts.

¹¹¹Your decrees are my heritage forever;
  they are the joy óf my heart.

¹¹²I incline my heart to perform your statutes
  forever, to the end. ℟

Proper 10 [15] A vs. 105–112; Proper 24 [29] C vs. 97–104.
(May be sung with double tone.)

(Psalm 119)

(Third selection)

℟

¹²⁹Your decrees are wonderful;
  therefore my soul keeps them.

¹³⁰The unfolding of your words gives light;
  it imparts understanding to the simple.

¹³¹With open mouth I pant,
  because I long for your commandments.

¹³²Turn to me and be grácious to me,
  as is your custom toward those who love your name. ℟

¹³³Keep my steps steady according to your promise,
  and never let iniquity have dominion over me.

¹³⁴Redeem me from human oppression,
  that I may keep your precepts.

℟ *Teach me, O God, the way of your statutes.*

¹³⁵Make your face shine upón your
servant,
and teach mé your statutes.

¹³⁶My eyes shed streams of tears
because your law ís not kept. ℟

¹³⁷You are righteous, O God,
and your judgménts are right.

¹³⁸You have appointed your decrees in
righteousness
and ín all faithfulness.

¹³⁹My zeal consumes me
because my foes forget your words.

¹⁴⁰Your promise ís well tried,
and your servant loves it. ℟

¹⁴¹I am small ánd despised,
yet I do not forget your precepts.

¹⁴²Your righteousness is an everlasting
righteousness,
and your law ís the truth.

¹⁴³Trouble and anguish have cóme upon
me,
but your commandments are mý
delight.

¹⁴⁴Your decrees are righteous forever;
give me understanding that Í may
live. ℟

Proper 12 [17] A vs. 129–136; Proper 26 [31] C vs.
137–144. (May be sung with double tone.)

Psalm 121

℟esponse   *Antiphon: David Hurd, 1994*

My   help comes from   God   who made   heav - en   and   earth.

℟

¹I lift up my eyes to the hills —
from where will mý help come?

²My help cómes from God,
who made heaven and earth.

³God will not let your foot be moved;
God who keeps you will not
slumber.

⁴God who keeps Israel
will neither slumber nor sleep. ℟

⁵God ís your keeper;
God is your shade át your side.

⁶The sun shall not strike ýou by day,
nor the moon by night.

⁷God will keep you from all evil;
God will keep your life.

⁸God will keep your going out and your
cóming in
from this time on and forévermore. ℟

(May be sung with double tone.)

704

Psalm 122

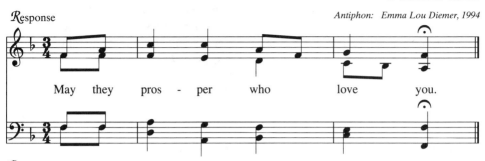

Antiphon: Emma Lou Diemer, 1994

Response

May they pros - per who love you.

℟

¹I was glad when they said to me,
   "Let us go to the house of God!"

²Our feet are standing within your gates,
 O Jerusalem.
   ³Jerusalem — built as a city that is
   bound firmly together.

⁴To it the tribes go up, the tribes of God,
 as was decreed for Israel,
   to give thanks to the name of God.

⁵For there the thrones for judgment were
 set up,
   the thrones of the house of David. ℟

⁶Pray for the peace of Jerusalem:
   "May they prosper who love you.

⁷"Peace be within your walls,
   and security within your towers."

⁸For the sake of my relatives and friends
 I will say,
   "Peace be within you."

⁹For the sake of the house of the
 Sovereign our God,
   I will seek your good. ℟

(May be sung with double tone.)

Psalm 123

Response

Antiphon: Robert Train Adams, 1994

Em   CM7   Am9   Em

Unison

Have mer - cy on us, O God; have mer - cy on us, O God.

℟

¹To you I lift up my eyes,
   O you who are enthroned in
   the heavens!

²As the eyes of subjects look to the hand
 of their ruler,
   so our eyes look to the Sovereign
   our God, until God has mercy upon
   us.

℟ Have mercy on us, O God; have mercy on us, O God.

³Have mercy upon us, O God, have mercy upon us,
for we have had more than enough óf contempt.

⁴Our soul has had more than its fill of the scorn of those who áre at ease,
and its fill of the contempt óf the proud. ℟

(May be sung with double tone.)

Psalm 124

℟esponse

Antiphon: Jane Marshall, 1994

Our help is in the name of God.

℟

¹If it had not been God who was ón our side
— let Israél now say —

²if it had not been God who was ón our side,
when our enemíes attacked us,

³then they would have swallowed us úp alive,
when their anger was kindled against us;

⁴then the flood would have swept ús away,

the torrent would have gone over us;
⁵then over us would have gone the raging waters. ℟

⁶Blessed be the Sovereign, our God,
who has not given us as prey tó their teeth.

⁷We have escaped like a bird from the snare óf the fowlers;
the snare is broken, and we háve escaped.

⁸Our help is in the name of God,
who made heaven and earth. ℟

Psalm 125

Antiphon: *Vérne de la Peña, 1994*

Do good, O God, to those who are good.

℟

¹Those who trust in God are like Mount Zion,
which cannot be moved, but abides forever.

²As the mountains surround Jerusalem,
so God surrounds the people, from this time on and forevermore.

³For the scepter of wickedness shall not rest on the land allotted to the righteous,
so that the righteous might not stretch out their hands to do wrong.

⁴Do good, O God, to those who are good,
and to those who are upright in their hearts.

⁵But those who turn aside to their own crooked ways,
God will lead them away with evildoers. Peace be upon Israel! ℟

Psalm 126

Antiphon: *Martie McMane, 1994*

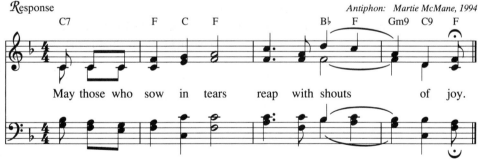

May those who sow in tears reap with shouts of joy.

℟

¹When God restored the fortunes of Zion,
we were like those who dream.

²Then our mouth was filled with laughter,
and our tongue with shouts of joy;

then it was said among the nations,
"God has done great things for them."

³God has done great things for us,
and we rejoiced. ℟

⁴Restore our fortunes, O God,
   like the watercourses ín the Negeb.

⁵May those who śow in tears
   reap with śhouts of joy.

⁶Those who go out weeping, bearing the
   śeed for sowing,
      shall come home with shouts of joy,
   carrýing their sheaves. *R̩*

Psalm 127

R̩esponse   *Antiphon: Robert Fryson, 1994*

We shall not be put to shame.

R̩

¹Unless God búilds the house,
   those who build it labór in vain.

Unless God gúards the city,
   the guard keeps ẃatch in vain.

²It is in vain that you rise up early and
go late to rest, eating the bread of
ánxious toil;
   for God gives sleep to Gód's beloved.
R̩

³Sons and daughters are indeed a herítage
from God,
   the fruit of the womb is á reward.

⁴Like arrows in the hand óf a warrior
are the offspring óf one's youth.

⁵Happy is the person whose quíver is full
of them,
   who shall not be put to shame
   speaking with enemies ín the gate.
R̩

Psalm 128

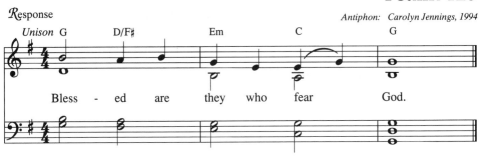

Antiphon: Carolyn Jennings, 1994

Response

Bless - ed are they who fear God.

R

¹Happy is everyone who fears God,
and who walks in God's ways.

²You shall eat the fruit of the labor of
your hands;
you shall be happy, and it shall go
well with you.

³Your spouse will be like a fruitful vine
within your house;
your children will be like olive
shoots around your table. *R*

⁴Thus shall the one be blessed who fears
God.
⁵May God bless you from Zion.

May you see the prosperity of Jerusalem
all the days of your life.
⁶May you see your children's
children. Peace be upon Israel! *R*

Psalm 130

Response

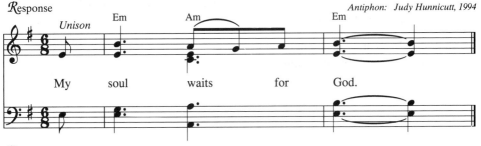

Antiphon: Judy Hunnicutt, 1994

My soul waits for God.

R

¹Out of the depths I cry to you, O God.
²O God, hear my voice!

Let your ears be attentive to the voice of
my supplications!
³If you, O God, should mark
iniquities, who could stand? *R*

⁴But there is forgiveness with you, so
that you may be revered.
⁵I wait for God, my soul waits, and
in God's word I hope;

⁶my soul waits for God more than those
who watch for the morning,

℟ My soul waits for God.

more than those who watch for the morning.

⁷O Israel, hope in God!
For with God there is steadfast love.

With God is great power to redeem;
⁸It is God who will redeem Israel
from all its iniquities. ℟

Psalm 131

℟esponse

Antiphon: Elaine Kirkland, 1994

May be sung as a round the last time.

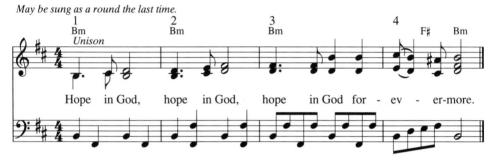

Hope in God, hope in God, hope in God for - ev - er-more.

℟
¹O God, my heart is not lifted up,
my eyes are not raised too high;

I do not occupy myself with things too great
or things too marvelous for me.

²But I have calmed and quieted my soul,
like a weaned child with its mother;

my soul is like the weaned child
that stays with me.

³O Israel, hope in God
from this time on and forevermore. ℟

Psalm 132

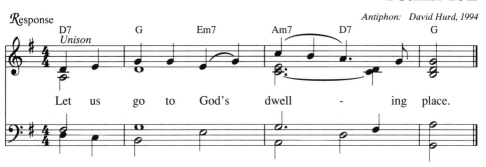

Response

Antiphon: David Hurd, 1994

D7   G   Em7   Am7   D7   G

Unison

Let us go to God's dwell - ing place.

℟

¹O God, remember in David's favor
  all the hardships he endured;

²how David swore to God
  and vowed to the Mighty One of
  Jacob,

³"I will not enter my house or get into
my bed;
  ⁴I will not give sleep to my eyes or
  slumber to my eyelids,

⁵"until I find a place for God,
  a dwelling place for the Mighty One
  of Jacob." ℟

⁶We heard of it in Ephrathah;
  we found it in the fields of Jaar.

⁷"Let us go to God's dwelling place;
  let us worship at God's footstool."

⁸Rise up, O God, and go to your resting
place,
  you and the ark of your might.

⁹Let your priests be clothed with
righteousness,
  and let your faithful shout for joy. ℟

¹⁰For your servant David's sake
  do not turn away the face of your
  anointed one.

¹¹God swore to David a sure oath and will
not turn back on it:
  "One of the offspring of your body I
  will set on your throne.

¹²"If your offspring keep my covenant and
my decrees that I shall teach them,
  their offspring also shall sit on your
  throne forevermore." ℟

¹³For God has chosen Zion;
  God has desired it for a habitation:

¹⁴"This is my resting place forever;
  here I will reside, for I have desired
  it.

¹⁵"I will abundantly bless its provisions;
  I will satisfy its poor with bread.

¹⁶"Its priests I will clothe with salvation,
  and its faithful will shout for joy. ℟

¹⁷"There I will cause a horn to sprout up
for David;
  I have prepared a lamp for my
  anointed one,

¹⁸"whose enemies I will clothe with
disgrace,
  but upon my anointed a crown will
  gleam."
              ℟

Psalm 133

℟esponse   *Antiphon: Hyeon Jeong, 1994*

How plea - sant to live in u - ni - ty.

℟

[1]How very good and pleásant it is
    when kindred live togéther in unity!

[2]It is like the precious oil ón the head,
    running down upón the beard,

    upon the béard of Aaron,
    running down over the collar óf his
    robes.

[3]It is like the déw of Hermon,
    which falls on the mountains of
    Zion.

    For there God ordáined the blessing,
    the blessing of life forévermore. ℟

Psalm 136

℟esponse   *Antiphon: Emma Lou Diemer, 1994*

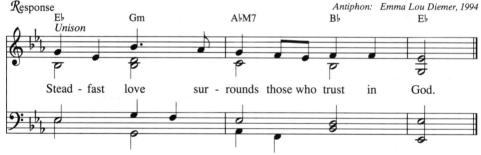

Stead - fast love sur - rounds those who trust in God.

℟

[1]O give thanks to God, for Gód is good,
    for God's steadfast love endúres
    forever.

[2]O give thanks to the Gód of gods,
    for God's steadfast love endúres
    forever.

[3]O give thanks to the Soveréign of
    sovereigns,
    for God's steadfast love endúres
    forever;

[4]who alone dóes great wonders,
    for God's steadfast love endúres
    forever; ℟

[5]who by understanding máde the heavens,
    for God's steadfast love endúres
    forever;

[6]who spread out the earth ón the waters,
    for God's steadfast love endúres
    forever;

[7]who made the great lights,
for God's steadfast love endures
forever;

[8]the sun to rule over the day,
for God's steadfast love endures
forever; ℛ

[9]the moon and stars to rule over the
night,
for God's steadfast love endures
forever.

[23]It is God who remembered us in our low
estate,

for God's steadfast love endures
forever;

[24]and rescued us from our foes,
for God's steadfast love endures
forever;

[25]who gives food to all flesh,
for God's steadfast love endures
forever;

[26]O give thanks to the God of heaven,
for God's steadfast love endures
forever. ℛ

Psalm 137

ℛesponse

Antiphon: Jonathan McNair, 1994

By the riv-ers of Bab-y-lon, there we wept.

ℛ

[1]By the rivers of Babylon — there we sat
down
and we wept when we
remembered Zion.

[2]And so we hung up our harps,
there upon the willows.

[3]For there our captors asked us for songs,
and our tormentors asked for mirth,
saying, "Sing us one of the songs of
Zion!"

[4]How could we sing God's song in a
foreign land?
[5]If I forget you, O Jerusalem, let my
right hand wither! ℛ

[6]Let my tongue cling to the roof of my
mouth, if I do not remember you,
if I do not set Jerusalem above my
highest joy.

[7]Remember, O God, against the
Edomites the day of Jerusalem's fall,
how they said, "Tear it down!
Tear it down to its foundations!"

[8]O city of Babylon, you devastator!
Happy shall they be who pay you
back what you have done to us!

[9]Happy shall they be who take your little
ones
and dash them against the rock! ℛ

(May be sung with double tone.)

Psalm 138

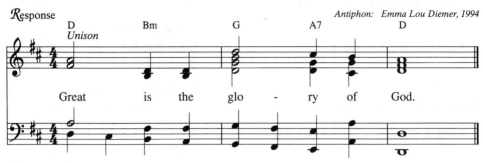

Response

Antiphon: Emma Lou Diemer, 1994

Great is the glo - ry of God.

℟

¹I give you thanks, O God, with my
whole heart;
  before the gods I sing your praise;

²I bow down toward your holy temple
and give thanks to your name
  for your steadfast love and your
  faithfulness;

for you have exalted your name
  and your word above everything.

³On the day I called, you answered me,
  you increased my strength of soul. ℟

⁴All the rulers of the earth shall praise
you, O God,
  for they have heard the words of your
  mouth.

⁵They shall sing of the ways of God,
  for great is the glory of God.

⁶For though God is high, God regards the
lowly;
  but the haughty, God perceives from
  far away.

⁷Though I walk in the midst of trouble,
  you preserve me against the wrath of
  my enemies;

you stretch out your hand,
  and your right hand delivers me.

⁸God will fulfill God's purpose for me;
  your steadfast love, O God, endures
  forever. Do not forsake the work of
  your hands. ℟

Psalm 139

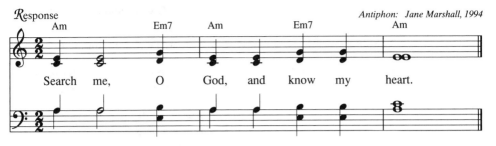

Search me, O God, and know my heart.

Antiphon: Jane Marshall, 1994

℟

¹O God, you have searched me and known me.
  ²You know when I sit down and when I rise up; you discern my thoughts from far away.

³You search out my path and my lying down,
  and are acquainted with áll my ways. ℟

⁴Even before a word is ón my tongue, O God, you know ít completely.

⁵You hem me in, behind ánd before, and lay your hand upon me.

⁶Such knowledge is too wonderful for me;
  it is so high that I cannot attain it. ℟

⁷Where can I go from your spirit? Or where can I flee from your presence?

⁸If I ascend to heaven, you are there; if I make my bed in Sheol, you are there. ℟

⁹If I take the wings óf the morning and settle at the farthest limits óf the sea,

¹⁰even there your hand shall lead me, and your right hand shall hold me fast.

¹¹If I say, "Surely the shadows shall cover me,
  and the light around me become night,"

¹²even the night is not without light to you; the night is as bright ás the day,
  for the night is as líght to you. ℟

¹³For it was you who formed my inward parts;
  you knit me together in my mother's womb.

¹⁴I praise you, for I am fearfully and wonderfully made.
  Wonderful are your works; that I know véry well. ℟

¹⁵My frame was not hidden from you, when I was being made in secret, intricately woven in the depths óf the earth.

¹⁶Your eyes beheld my únformed substance.
  In your book were written all the days that were formed for me before they existed.

R̃ Search me, O God, and know my heart.

¹⁷How weighty to me are your
thoughts, O God!
  How vast is the sum of them!

¹⁸I try to count them — they are more
than the sand;
  I come to the end — I am still
  with you. *R̃*

²³Search me, O God, and know my
heart;
  test me and know my thoughts.

²⁴See if there is in me any wicked way,
  and lead me in the way everlasting. *R̃*

*Proper 11 [16] A vs. 1–12, 23–24; Epiphany 2 [2] B vs.
1–6, 13–18; Proper 4 [9] B and Proper 18 [23] C vs. 1–6,
13–18.*

Psalm 141

*R̃*esponse

Antiphon: Jonathan McNair, 1994

May the lift-ing of my hands be as an eve-ning sac-ri-fice.

R̃

¹I call upon you, O God; come quickly
to me;
  give ear to my voice when I call to
  you.

²Let my prayer be counted as incense
before you,
  and the lifting up of my hands as an
  evening sacrifice.

³Set a guard over my mouth, O God;
  keep watch over the door of my lips.

⁴Do not turn my heart to any evil, to
busy myself with wicked deeds with
those who work iniquity;
  do not let me eat of their delicacies. *R̃*

⁵Let the righteous strike me;
  let the faithful correct me.

Never let the oil of the wicked anoint
my head,
  for my prayer is continually against
  their wicked deeds.

⁶When they are given over to those who
shall condemn them,
  then they shall learn that my words
  were pleasant.

⁷Like a rock that one breaks apart and
shatters on the land,
  so shall their bones be strewn at the
  mouth of Sheol. *R̃*

⁸But my eyes are turned toward you, O
God, my God;
  in you I seek refuge; do not leave me
  defenseless.

⁹Keep me from the trap that they have laid for me,
and from the snares of évildoers.

¹⁰Let the wicked fall into their own nets,
while I alone escape. ℟

Psalm 143

Antiphon: Marty Haugen, 1994

℟esponse

My soul thirsts for you, my soul thirsts for you like a parched land.

℟

¹Hear my prayer, O God; give ear to my supplications in your faithfulness;
answer me in your righteousness.

²Do not enter into judgment with your servant,
for no one living is righteous before you.

³For the enemy has pursued me, crushing my life to the ground,
making me sit in the shadows like those long dead.

⁴Therefore my spirit faints within me;
my heart within me is appalled. ℟

⁵I remember the days of old, I think about áll your deeds,
I meditate on the works óf your hands.

⁶I stretch out my hands to you;
my soul thirsts for you like á parched land.

⁷Answer me quickly, O God; my spirit fails.

Do not hide your face from me, or I shall be like those who go down to the Pit.

⁸Let me hear of your steadfast love in the morning, for in you I put my trust.
Teach me the way I should go, for to you I lift úp my soul. ℟

⁹Save me, O God, from my enemies;
I have fled to you for refuge.

¹⁰Teach me to do your will, for you áre my God.
Let your good spirit lead me on a level path.

¹¹For your name's sake, O God, preserve my life.
In your righteousness bring me óut of trouble.

¹²In your steadfast love cut off my enemies, and destroy áll my adversaries,
for I ám your servant. ℟

(May be sung with double tone.)

Psalm 145

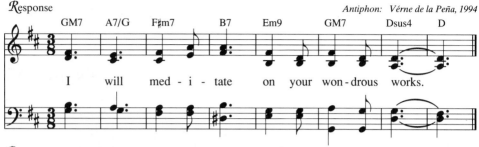

𝓡espone   *Antiphon: Vérne de la Peña, 1994*

I will med - i - tate on your won - drous works.

𝓡

¹I will extol you, my God and Ruler,
and bless your name forever and ever.

²Every day I will bless you,
and praise your name forever and
ever.

³Great is God, and greatly to be praised;
God's greatness is unsearchable.

⁴One generation shall laud your works to
another,
and shall declare your mighty acts. 𝓡

⁵On the glorious splendor of your
majesty,
and on your wondrous works, I will
meditate.

⁶The might of your awesome deeds shall
be proclaimed,
and I will declare your greatness.

⁷They shall celebrate the fame of your
abundant goodness,
and shall sing aloud of your
righteousness.

⁸God is gracious and merciful,
slow to anger and abounding in
steadfast love. 𝓡

⁹God is good to all,
and God's compassion is over all that
God has made.

¹⁰All your works shall give thanks to
you, O God,
and all your faithful shall bless you.

¹¹They shall speak of the glory of your
dominion,
and tell of your power,

¹²to make known to all people your
mighty deeds,
and the glorious splendor of your
dominion. 𝓡

¹³Your reign is an everlasting reign,
and your dominion endures
throughout all generations.

God is faithful in every word,
and gracious in every deed.

¹⁴God upholds all who are falling,
and raises up all who are bowed
down.

¹⁵The eyes of all look to you,
and you give them their food in due
season.

¹⁶You open your hand to all,
satisfying the desire of every living
thing. 𝓡

¹⁷In every way God is just,
and kind in every action.

[18]God is near to all who call,
  to all who call on God in truth.

[19]God fulfills the desire of all who fear God;
  God also hears their cry, and saves them.

[20]God watches over all who love God,
  but will destroy all the wicked.

[21]My mouth will speak the praise of God,
  and all flesh will bless God's holy name forever and ever. ℟

Proper 9 [14] A vs. 8–14; Proper 13 [18] A vs. 8–9, 14–21;
Proper 20 [25] A vs. 1–8; Proper 12 [17] B vs. 10–18;
Proper 27 [32] C vs. 1–5, 17–21 (Alt.).

Psalm 146

℟esponse

Antiphon: Judy Hunnicutt, 1994

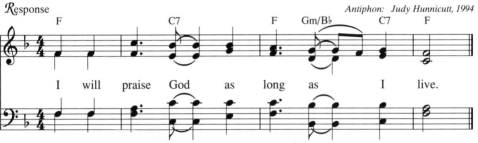

I will praise God as long as I live.

℟

[1]Praise be to God!
  Praise God, O my soul!

[2]I will praise God as long as I live;
  I will sing praises to my God all my life long.

[3]Do not put your trust in nobles, in mortals,
  in whom there is no help.

[4]When their breath departs, they return to the earth;
  on that very day their plans shall perish. ℟

[5]Happy are those whose help is the God of Jacob,
  whose hope is in the Sovereign their God,

[6]who made heaven and earth, the sea, and all that is in them;
  who keeps faith forever;

[7]who executes justice for the oppressed;
  who gives food to the hungry. ℟

God sets the prisoners free;
  [8]God opens the eyes of those who cannot see.

God lifts up those who are bowed down;
  God loves those who are righteous.

[9]God watches over the strangers, and upholds the orphan and the widow,
  but the way of the wicked God brings to ruin.

[10]The Sovereign will reign forever, your God, O Zion, for all generations.
  Praise be to God! ℟

Advent 3 A vs. 5–10 (Alt.).

719

Psalm 147

Response   *Antiphon: Elaine Kirkland, 1994*

Great is our God, and a - bun - dant in power.

℟

¹Praise God! How good it is to sing praises to our God;
for God is gracious, and a song of praise is fitting.

²God builds up Jerusalem;
God gathers the outcasts of Israel.

³God heals the brokenhearted,
and binds up their wounds.

⁴God determines the number of the stars;
God gives to all of them their names.

⁵Great is our God, and abundant in power,
whose understanding is beyond measure. ℟

⁶God lifts up the downtrodden;
God casts the wicked to the ground.

⁷Sing to God with thanksgiving;
make melody to our God on the lyre.

⁸God covers the heavens with clouds,
prepares rain for the earth,
and makes grass grow on the hills.

⁹God gives to the animals their food,
and to the young ravens when they cry.

¹⁰God has no delight in the strength of the horse,
nor pleasure in the speed of a runner;

¹¹but God takes pleasure in those who fear God,
in those who hope in God's steadfast love. ℟

¹²Praise God, O Jerusalem!
Praise your God, O Zion!

¹³For God strengthens the bars of your gates;
God blesses your children within you.

¹⁴God grants peace within your borders;
God fills you with the finest of wheat.

¹⁵God sends out a command to the earth;
God's word runs swiftly. ℟

¹⁶God gives snow like wool;
God scatters frost like ashes.

¹⁷God hurls down hail like crumbs —
who can stand before God's cold?

¹⁸God sends out a word, and melts them;
God makes a wind blow, and the waters flow.

¹⁹God declares the word to Jacob,
 and declares God's statutes and
 ordinances to Israel.

²⁰God has not dealt thus with any other
 nation; they do not know God's
 ordinances.
   Praise be to God! ℛ

Christmas 2 ABC vs. 12–20 (Alt.); Epiphany 5 [5] B vs. 1–11, 20c.

Psalm 148

Antiphon: David Hurd, 1994

ℛesponse
Unison

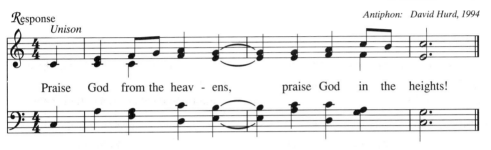

Praise God from the heav - ens, praise God in the heights!

ℛ

¹Praise God! Praise God from the
 heavens;
   praise God in the heights!

²Praise God, all you angels of God;
   praise God, all you host of heaven!

³Praise God, you sun and moon;
   praise God, all you shining stars!

⁴Praise God, you highest heavens,
   and you waters above the heavens! ℛ

⁵Let them praise the name of God,
   for God commanded and they were
   created.

⁶God established them forever and ever;
   God fixed their bounds, which cannot
   be passed.

⁷Praise God from the earth, you sea
 monsters and all deeps,

⁸fire and hail, snow and frost, stormy
 wind fulfilling God's command!

⁹Mountains and all hills, fruit trees and
 all cedars!
   ¹⁰Beasts of the forest and all cattle,
   crawling things and flying birds! ℛ

¹¹Rulers of the earth and all peoples,
   nobles and all leaders of the earth!

¹²Young men and women alike,
   old and young together!

¹³Let them praise the name of the
 Sovereign,
   whose name alone is exalted, whose
   glory is above earth and heaven.

¹⁴God has raised up a horn for the people,
   and praise for all the faithful,
   for the people of Israel who are close
   to God. Praise be to God! ℛ

(May be sung with double tone.)

Psalm 149

Antiphon: *Robert Train Adams, 1994*

Response

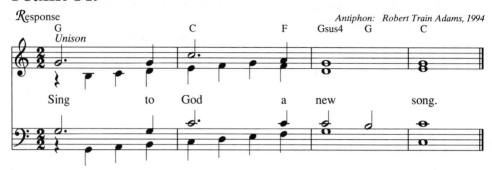

Sing to God a new song.

℟

¹Praise God! Sing to God á new song;
  sing God's praise in the assembly óf
  the faithful.

²Let Israel be glad ín its Maker;
  let the children of Zion rejoice ín
  their Ruler.

³Let them praise God's ńame with
 dancing,
  making melody to God with
  tambouŕine and lyre.

⁴For God takes pleasure ín the people;
  God adorns the humb́le with victory. ℟

⁵Let the faithful exúlt in glory;
  let them sing for joy ón their
  couches.

⁶Let the high praises of God be ín their
 throats,
  and two-edged swords ín their hands,

⁷to execute vengeance ón the nations
  and punishment ón the peoples,

⁸to bind their rulers with fetters and their
 nobles with ćhains of iron,
  ⁹to execute on them the judgḿent
  decreed.

This is glory for all God's faithful ones.
  Praise b́e to God! ℟

Psalm 150

Antiphon: Emma Lou Diemer, 1994

Response

Let ev - ery - thing that breathes praise God.

R

¹Praise be to God! Praise God in God's own sanctuary;
  praise God in the mighty firmament!

²Praise God for God's mighty deeds;
  praise God according to God's surpassing greatness! R

³Praise God with trumpet sound;
  praise God with lute and harp!

⁴Praise God with tambourine and dance;
  praise God with strings and pipe!

⁵Praise God with clanging cymbals;
  praise God with loud clashing cymbals!

⁶Let everything that breathes praise God!
  Praise be to God! R

Psalm 51A

Chant setting: Henry Purcell (1659–1695)

1 Have mercy
on me, O God,
according to your stead-fast love; according to your abundant mercy blot out my trans-gressions.

2 Wash me
thoroughly from my in - iquity, and cleanse me from my sin.

3 For I know ᴵmy transᵎgressions, ᴵᴵand my ᴵsin is ᴵever be - ᴵfore me.

4 Against you,
you alone, have I sinned, and done what is e - vil in your sight,

so that you
are justified ᴵin your ᴵsentence ᴵᴵand blame-less ᴵwhen you ᴵpass . . . ᴵjudgment.

5 Indeed, I was born guilty, a sinner when my mother con - ceived me.

6 You desire
truth in the ᴵin - ward ᴵbeing; ᴵᴵtherefore teach me ᴵwisdom in my ᴵse - cret ᴵheart.

7 Purge me with
hyssop, and I shall be clean; wash me, and I shall be purer than snow.

8 Let me hear ᴵjoy and ᴵgladness; ᴵᴵlet the bones that ᴵyou have ᴵcrushed re - ᴵjoice.

9 Hide your face from my sins, and blot out all my in - iquities.

10 Create in
me a clean ᴵheart, O ᴵGod, ᴵᴵand put a ᴵnew and right ᴵspirit with - ᴵin me.

11 Do not
cast me a - way from your presence, and do not take your ho - ly spir - it from me.

12 Restore
to me the ᴵjoy of your sal-ᴵvation, ᴵᴵand sus- ᴵtain in me a ᴵwill - ing ᴵspirit.

13 Then I will
teach trans - gressors your ways, and sinners will re-turn to you.

14 Deliver me
from bloodshed, ᴵᴵand my tongue

O God, O ᴵGod of my sal-ᴵvation, will sing a - ᴵloud of ᴵyour de - ᴵliverance.

15 O God, open my lips, and my mouth will de-clare your praise.

16 For you
have no de - ᴵlight in ᴵsacrifice; ᴵᴵif I were to give a burnt offering, ᴵyou would ᴵnot be ᴵpleased.

17 The sacrifice
acceptable
to God is a trou - bled spirit; a broken and contrite heart, O God, you will not de - spise.

(May be sung as a double chant. See next page.)

Psalm 63A

Chant setting: Thomas Morley (c. 1557–1603)

I seek
¹O God,   you are my God,   you, my   soul . . . .   thirsts   for   you;

as in a dry
my flesh   faints for you,   and weary land   where   there is no   water.

²So I have
looked upon   ˡyou in the ˡsanctuary, ˡˡbe - ˡholding your ˡpower and ˡglory.

³Because your
steadfast love is better than life,   my   lips   will   praise . . .   you.

⁴So I will   ˡˡI will
bless you as   ˡlong as I ˡlive;   lift up my ˡhands and ˡcall on your ˡname.

⁵My soul is   and
satisfied as   with a rich feast, my mouth praises you with joy - ful lips

                           ˡˡand
⁶when I think of ˡyou on my ˡbed, meditate on ˡyou   in the ˡwatches of the ˡnight;

and in
the shadow
⁷for you have   been my help, of your   wings   I   sing   for joy.
⁸My soul   ˡclings to ˡyou; ˡˡyour   ˡmight - y ˡhand up - ˡholds me.

I seek
O God,   you are my God,   you, my   soul . . . .   thirsts   for   you.

(May be sung as a double chant. See below.)

Cambridge Chant

Daniel Hathaway, 1994

Psalm 67A

Chant setting: Vincent Novello (1781–1861)

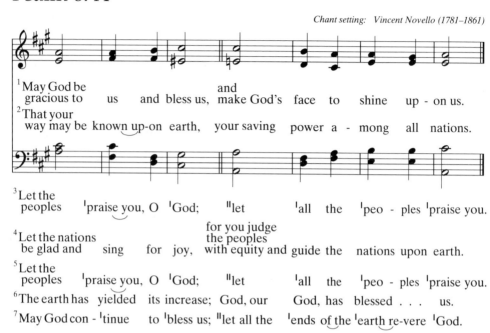

1 May God be gracious to us and bless us, and make God's face to shine up - on us.

2 That your way may be known up-on earth, your saving power a - mong all nations.

3 Let the peoples ˈpraise you, O ˈGod; ˈˈlet ˈall the ˈpeo - ples ˈpraise you.

4 Let the nations be glad and sing for joy, for you judge the peoples with equity and guide the nations upon earth.

5 Let the peoples ˈpraise you, O ˈGod; ˈˈlet ˈall the ˈpeo - ples ˈpraise you.

6 The earth has yielded its increase; God, our God, has blessed . . . us.

7 May God con - ˈtinue to ˈbless us; ˈˈlet all the ˈends of the ˈearth re-vere ˈGod.

Joseph Barnby (1838–1896)

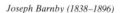

Jonathan McNair, 1994

Psalm 95A

Chant setting: Richard Farrant (c. 1530–1580)

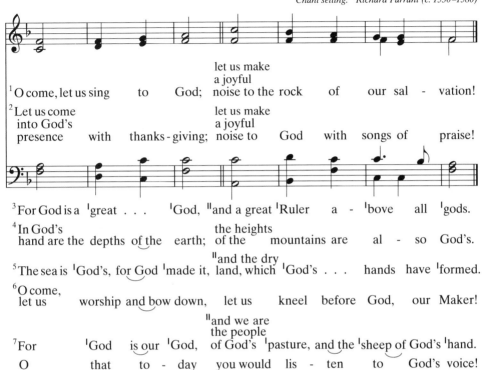

¹O come, let us sing to God; let us make / a joyful / noise to the rock of our sal - vation!

²Let us come into God's presence with thanks - giving; let us make / a joyful / noise to God with songs of praise!

³For God is a ¹great . . . ¹God, ⁿand a great ¹Ruler a - ¹bove all ¹gods.

⁴In God's hand are the depths of the earth; the heights / of the / mountains are al - so God's.

⁵The sea is ¹God's, for God ¹made it, ⁿand the dry / land, which ¹God's . . . hands have ¹formed.

⁶O come, let us worship and bow down, let us kneel before God, our Maker!

⁷For ¹God is our ¹God, ⁿand we are / the people / of God's ¹pasture, and the ¹sheep of God's ¹hand.

O that to - day you would lis - ten to God's voice!

(May be sung as a double chant. See below.)

James Turle (1802–1882)

Daniel Hathaway, 1994

Psalm 100A

Chant setting: William Byrd (1538–1623)

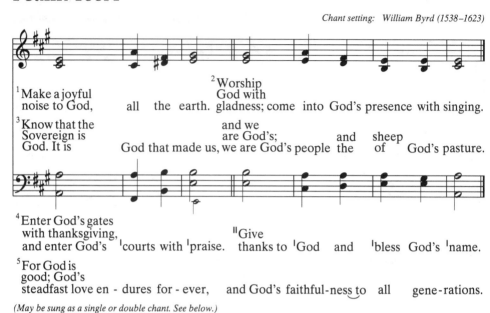

²Worship

¹Make a joyful   God with
noise to God,   all   the   earth.   gladness; come   into   God's   presence with singing.

³Know that the   and we
Sovereign is   are God's;   and   sheep
God. It is   God that made us, we are God's people   the   of   God's pasture.

⁴Enter God's gates
with thanksgiving,   ‖Give
and enter God's   ¹courts with ¹praise.   thanks to ¹God   and   ¹bless God's ¹name.
⁵For God is
good; God's
steadfast love en - dures for - ever,   and God's faithful-ness to   all   gene-rations.

(May be sung as a single or double chant. See below.)

Daniel Hathaway, 1994   *Bruce Neswick, 1994*

Bruce Neswick, 1994

Psalm 121A

Chant setting: James Turle (1802–1882)

¹I lift up my eyes to the hills— from where will my help come?
²My help comes from God, the God who made heaven and earth.

³God will
not let your ˈfoot be ˈmoved; ‖God who ˈkeeps you ˈwill not ˈslumber.
⁴God who keeps Israel will nei - ther slumber nor sleep.
⁵God ˈis your ˈkeeper; ‖God is your ˈshade . . . ˈat your ˈside.
⁶The sun
shall not strike you by day, nor shall the moon by night.
⁷God will ˈkeep you from all ˈevil; ‖and ˈGod will ˈkeep your ˈlife.
⁸God will keep
your going from
out and your com - ing in this time on and for - ev - er - more.

(May be sung as a double chant. See below.)

John Robinson (1682–1762)

Bruce Neswick, 1994

Psalm 141A

Chant setting: William Croft (1678–1727)

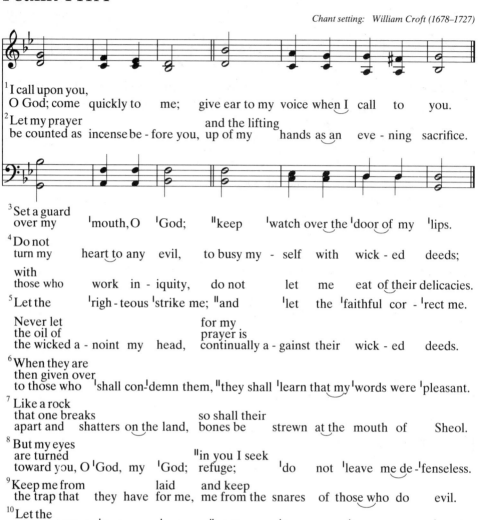

¹ I call upon you,
O God; come quickly to me; give ear to my voice when I call to you.
² Let my prayer and the lifting
be counted as incense be-fore you, up of my hands as an eve - ning sacrifice.

³ Set a guard
over my ᴵmouth, O ᴵGod; ᴵᴵkeep ᴵwatch over the ᴵdoor of my ᴵlips.
⁴ Do not
turn my heart to any evil, to busy my - self with wick - ed deeds;
with
those who work in - iquity, do not let me eat of their delicacies.
⁵ Let the ᴵrigh - teous ᴵstrike me; ᴵᴵand ᴵlet the ᴵfaithful cor - ᴵrect me.
Never let for my
the oil of prayer is
the wicked a - noint my head, continually a - gainst their wick - ed deeds.
⁶ When they are
then given over
to those who ᴵshall con-ᴵdemn them, ᴵᴵthey shall ᴵlearn that my ᴵwords were ᴵpleasant.
⁷ Like a rock
that one breaks so shall their
apart and shatters on the land, bones be strewn at the mouth of Sheol.
⁸ But my eyes
are turned ᴵᴵin you I seek
toward you, O ᴵGod, my ᴵGod; refuge; ᴵdo not ᴵleave me de -ᴵfenseless.
⁹ Keep me from laid and keep
the trap that they have for me, me from the snares of those who do evil.
¹⁰ Let the
wicked fall into ᴵtheir own ᴵnets, ᴵᴵwhile ᴵI a - ᴵlone es - ᴵcape.

(May be sung as a double chant. See below.)

Henry Purcell (1659–1695)
Arr. James Turle (1802–1882)

Psalm 141B
Let My Prayer Rise Up

Adaptation and musical setting by
Arthur G. Clyde, 1993

Let my prayer rise up like in-cense; let the

lift - ing of my hands be as an eve - ning sac - ri - fice

to you, O God.   1 Watch   o - ver all   I   do,   watch
   2 On   you, O God, I   call   to

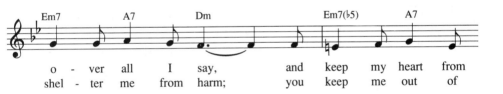

o - ver all   I   say,   and   keep   my   heart   from
shel - ter me from harm;   you   keep   me   out   of

e - vil thoughts, my hands from e - vil ways.
dan - ger's grasp, sup - port me with your arm.

A leader may sing the refrain once, followed by the congregation. Following each verse, the congregation should sing the refrain.

731

Canticle of Mary

(Magnificat)

Response

Antiphon: Carolyn Jennings, 1994

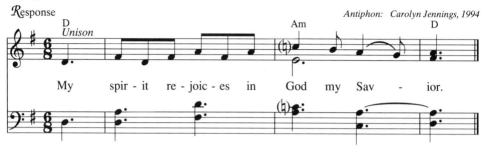

My spir - it re - joic - es in God my Sav - ior.

Luke 1:46–55

℟

My soul magnifies the
Sovereign,
   and my spirit rejoices in God
   my Savior;

for God has looked with favor on
the lowliness óf God's servant.
   Surely, from now on all
   generations will ćall me
   blessed;

for the Mighty One has done great
things for me,
   the Mighty One whose ńame is
   holy. ℟

God's mercy is for those who fear
God
   from generation to ǵeneration.

God has shown great strength;
   and has scattered the proud in
   the thoughts óf their hearts.

God has brought down the
powerful from their thrones,
   and lifted úp the lowly;

God has filled the hungry with
good things,
   and sent the rich áway empty. ℟

God has helped God's servant
Israel,
   in remembrance óf God's
   mercy,

according to the promise made ío
our ancestors,
   to Abraham and Sarah and to
   their descendants forever. ℟

732

Canticle of Zechariah
(Benedictus)

Response

Antiphon: Robert Fryson, 1994

You will have joy and glad - ness.

Luke 1:68–79

℟

Blessed be the Sovereign God of Israel,
who has looked favorably on
the people ánd redeemed them.

God has raised up a mighty
savior for us
in the house of God's servant
David;

as God spoke through the mouth
of the holy prophets from of old,
that we would be saved from our
enemies and from the hand of
áll who hate us. ℟

Thus God has shown the mercy
promised to our ancestors,

and has remembered God's holy
covenant,
the oath that God swore to our
ancestor Abraham,

to grant us that we, being rescued
from the hands óf our enemies,
might serve God without fear,
in holiness and righteousness
before God áll our days. ℟

And you, child, will be called the
prophet of the Most High,
for you will go before God
to prepare God's ways;

to give knowledge of salvation to
the people
by the forgiveness óf their sins.

By the tender mercy óf our God,
the dawn from on high will
break upon us,

to give light to those who sit in
night and in the shadow of death,
to guide our feet into the way
of peace. ℟

733

Canticle of Simeon
(Nunc Dimittis)

Response · *Antiphon: Arthur G. Clyde, 1994*

Your sal - va - tion is in the pres-ence of all peo - ples.

Luke 2:29–32

℟

O God, now you are dismissing your servant in peace,
   according to your word;

for my eyes have seen your salvation,

which you have prepared in the presence of all peoples,

a light for revelation to the Gentiles
   and for glory to your people Israel. ℟

Second Canticle of Isaiah

Response · *Antiphon: Vérne de la Peña, 1994*

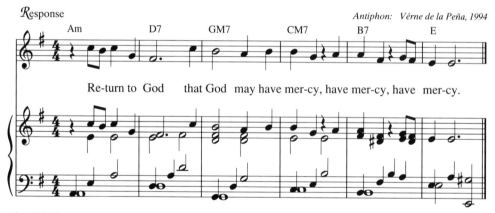

Re-turn to God that God may have mer-cy, have mer-cy, have mer-cy.

Isa. 55:6–11

℟

Seek God while God may be found,
   call upon God while God is near;

let the wicked forsake their way,
   and the unrighteous their thoughts;

let them return to God, that God may have mercy on them,
   and to our God, for God will abundantly pardon. ℟

For my thoughts are not your thoughts,
   nor are your ways my ways, says God.

734

For as the heavens are higher
than the earth,
 so are my ways higher than
 your ways and my thoughts than
 your thoughts.

For as the rain and the snow come
down from heaven,
 and do not return there until
 they have watered the earth,

making it bring forth and sprout,
 giving seed to the sower and
 bread to the eater,

so shall my word be that goes out
from my mouth;
 it shall not return to me empty,

but it shall accomplish that which
I purpose,
 and succeed in the thing for
 which I sent it. ℛ

Canticle to the Lamb

Antiphon: Robert Train Adams, 1994

Response

To the Lamb be bless-ing and hon - or.

Rev. 4:11; 5:9–10, 12, 13

ℛ
You are worthy, our Sovereign
and God,
 to receive glory and honor and
 power,

for you created all things,
 and by your will they existed
 and were created. ℛ

You are worthy, O Christ, for you
were slaughtered,
 and by your blood you
 ransomed saints for God

from every tribe and language
 and from every people and
 nation;

you have made them to be a
dominion and priests serving
our God,
 and they will reign on earth. ℛ

Worthy is the Lamb that was
slaughtered to receive power and
wealth and wisdom,
 and might and honor and glory
 and blessing!

To the one seated on the throne
and to the Lamb be blessing and
honor,
 and glory and might forever and
 ever! ℛ

Canticle to Christ

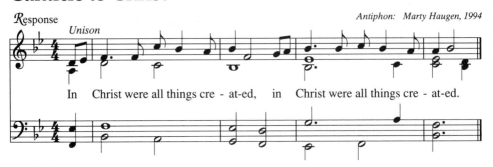

Response — Unison

Antiphon: *Marty Haugen, 1994*

In Christ were all things cre - at-ed, in Christ were all things cre - at-ed.

Col. 1:15–20

℟

Christ is the image of the
invisible God,
  the firstborn of áll creation;

for in Christ all things in
heaven and on earth wére created,
  things visible ánd invisible,

whether thrones or dominions or
rulers or powers —
  all things have been created
  through Christ ánd for
  Christ.

Christ, indeed, is beföre all
things,
  and in Christ all things hóld
  together. ℟

Christ is the head óf the body,
  which ís the church;

Christ is the beginning, the
firstborn fróm the dead,
  so that Christ might come to
  have first pláce in everything.

For in Christ all the fullńess of
God
  was pléased to dwell,

and through Christ God was
pleased to reconcile to God all
things,
  whether on earth or in heaven,
  by making peace through the
  blood óf the cross. ℟

Canticle of the Mystery Revealed in Flesh

Response   *Antiphon: Hyeon Jeong, 1994*

The   mys - tery   of   our   faith   is   great.

1 Tim. 3:16; 6:15, 16

℟

Christ was revealed in flesh,
vindicáted in spirit,
 seen by angels, proclaimed
 ámong Gentiles,

believed in throughóut the world,
 taken úp in glory.

At the right time God will bring
about the manifestátion of Christ—
 God who is the blessed and
 only Sovereign, the Ruler of

rulers and Soveŕeign of
sovereigns.

It is God alone who has
ímmortality
 and dwells in unapproacháble
 light,

whom no one has ever seen ór can
see—
 to God be honor and
 eternal dominíon. Amen. ℟

Canticle of the Three
(Benedicte omnia opera)

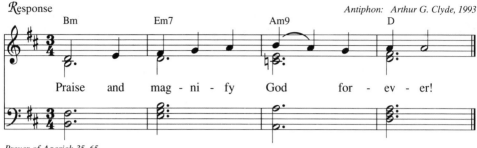

Response   Antiphon: Arthur G. Clyde, 1993

Praise and mag-ni-fy God for-ev-er!

Prayer of Azariah 35–65

℟

All you works of God, bless your
God;
    you angels of God, bless your
    God;

you heavens, bless your God;
    all the waters above the
    heavens, bless your God; ℟

You powers of God, bless your
God;
    you sun and moon, bless your
    God;

stars of the heaven, bless your
God;
    all rain and dew, bless your
    God; ℟

All the winds, bless your God;
    you fire and heat, bless your
    God;

you winter cold and summer
heat, bless your God;
    you dews and falling snow,
    bless your God; ℟

You ice and cold, bless your God;
    you frosts and snows, bless
    your God;

nights and days, bless your
God;
    you light and darkness, bless
    your God; ℟

Lightnings and clouds, bless
your God;
    let the earth bless God;

you mountains and hills, bless
your God;
    all that grows in the ground,
    bless your God; ℟

You running waters, bless your
God;
    you seas and rivers, bless
    your God;

you whales and all that move in
the waters, bless your God;
    all you birds of the air, bless
    your God; ℟

All you animals and cattle,
bless your God;
    all you people on earth, bless
    your God;

O Israel, bless your God;
    you priests of God, bless your
    God; ℟

all you who serve God, bless
your God;
 you spirits and souls of the
 righteous, bless your God;

you holy and humble in heart,
bless your God;
 Blessed are you, O God in the
 dome of heaven. ℟

(May be sung with double tone.)

O Holy Radiance, Joyous Light
(Phos Hilaron)

Col. 3:16–17; Isa. 60:19–20; John 1:1–5

Greek, 2nd–4th century C.E.
Transl. The New Century Hymnal, 1994

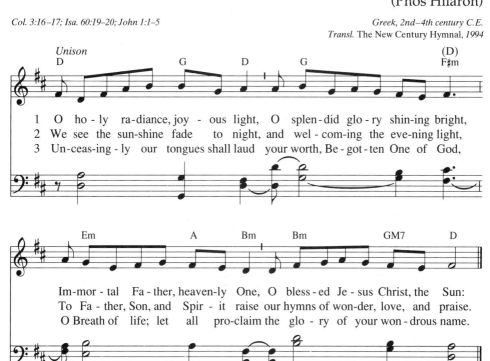

1 O ho-ly ra-diance, joy-ous light, O splen-did glo-ry shin-ing bright,
2 We see the sun-shine fade to night, and wel-com-ing the eve-ning light,
3 Un-ceas-ing-ly our tongues shall laud your worth, Be-got-ten One of God,

Im-mor-tal Fa-ther, heaven-ly One, O bless-ed Je-sus Christ, the Sun:
To Fa-ther, Son, and Spir-it raise our hymns of won-der, love, and praise.
O Breath of life; let all pro-claim the glo-ry of your won-drous name.

Known as "The Candlelight Hymn" or "Phos Hilaron," this
hymn was sung in the ancient church at the Lighting of Lamps
for Vespers. St. Basil, who died in 379 C.E., referred to it as
being of uncertain date and authorship. Its original tune is also
unknown.

Tune: CONDITOR ALME SIDERUM L.M.
ancient Sarum plainsong, Mode IV
Harm. The New Century Hymnal, *1994*
Alternate tune: TALLIS' CANON

O Wisdom, Breathed from God
(O Sapientia)

St. 1, 2, "O Antiphons," Latin, 6th–7th century,
Transl. The New Century Hymnal, 1994
St. 3, The New Century Hymnal, 1994

Sir. 24:1–6; Wisd. 7:25, 8:1, 7; Luke 1:78–79;
John 8:12; Mal. 4:2

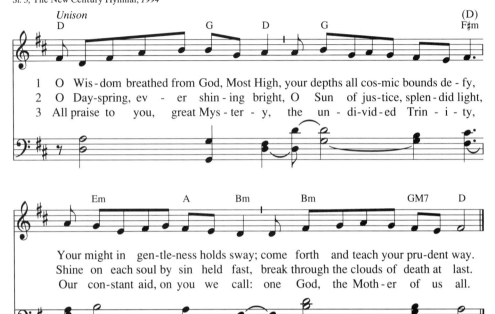

1 O Wis-dom breathed from God, Most High, your depths all cos-mic bounds de - fy,
2 O Day-spring, ev - er shin - ing bright, O Sun of jus-tice, splen-did light,
3 All praise to you, great Mys - ter - y, the un - di-vid-ed Trin - i - ty,

Your might in gen-tle-ness holds sway; come forth and teach your pru-dent way.
Shine on each soul by sin held fast, break through the clouds of death at last.
Our con-stant aid, on you we call: one God, the Moth-er of us all.

"Sophia" may be substituted for "O Wisdom" in stanza 1.

The first two stanzas of this hymn are a translation of two of the
seven ancient "O Antiphons" used at vespers, one for each of the
seven days before Christmas. The first of these is "O Sapientia"
(O Wisdom). The third stanza includes ideas from the writings
of Julian of Norwich and phrases from the early prayer services
of the Western church.

Tune: CONDITOR ALME SIDERUM L.M.
ancient Sarum plainsong, Mode IV
Harm. The New Century Hymnal, 1994
Alternate tune: TALLIS' CANON

SERVICE MUSIC

Text and music: Robert Wooten, Sr., 1982; alt.

I was glad when they said un-to me, I was glad when they said un-to me: Let us go in-to the house of our God; you'll find peace, joy, hap-pi-ness, a great re-ward. Won't you come, come, come.

742

Text and music: Phil Porter, 1990

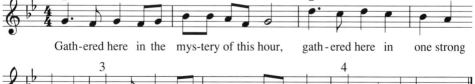

Gath-ered here in the mys-tery of this hour, gath-ered here in one strong bod-y, gath-ered here in the strug-gle and the power, Spir-it draw near.

This chant may be sung as a round.

743

Ps. 46:10

Music: Anon.

Be still and know that I am God. Be still and know that

I am God. Be still and know that I am God.

744

Opening Sentence

Ps. 70:1

Music: Thomas Tallis, c. 1564

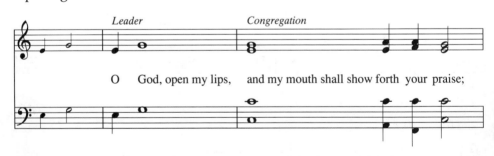

Leader   *Congregation*

O God, open my lips, and my mouth shall show forth your praise;

Leader   *Congregation*

Make haste, O God, to deliver me. Make haste to help me, O God.

745

Trisagion

Music: Ronald A. Nelson, 1986

Ho - ly God, Ho - ly and might - y One,

Ho - ly Im - mor - tal One, have mer - cy up - on us.

746

Trisagion

Music: Alice Jordan, 1986

Ho - ly God, Ho - ly and might - y,

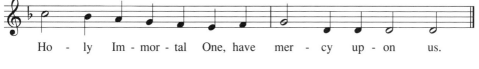

Ho - ly Im - mor - tal One, have mer - cy up - on us.

747

Agios O Theos (Trisagion)

Text: Ancient Greek

Music: Russian Orthodox tradition

A - gi - os O The - os, a - gi - os is - chi - ros,
Ho - ly, ho - ly, ho - ly God, ho - ly and might - y,

a - gi - os a - tha - na - tos, e - le - i - son i - mas.
ho - ly and e - ter - nal, have mer - cy on us.

748
Trisagion

Music: Francisco F. Feliciano

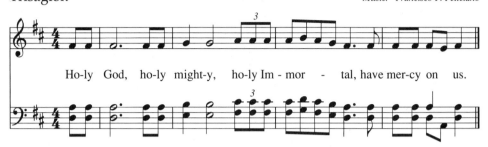

Ho-ly God, ho-ly might-y, ho-ly Im - mor - tal, have mer-cy on us.

749
Kyrie

Music: John Merbecke, 1550

Unison

Lord, have mer-cy up-on us; Christ, have mer-cy up-on us; Lord, have mer-cy up-on us.

750
Kyrie

Text: Traditional, 6th century

Music: The American Lutheran Hymnal

Congregation or choir

Leader
Lord, have mercy upon us.

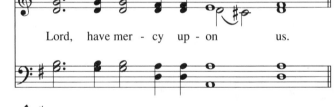

Lord,   have mer - cy up - on   us.

Christ, have mercy upon us.

Christ, have mer - cy up - on   us.

Lord, have mercy upon us.

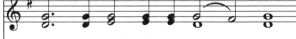

Lord,   have mer - cy up - on   us.

Text: Ancient Greek

Music: Russian Orthodox tradition

751

Kyrie

752

Music: Leon Roberts, 1981

753

Kyrie

Music: Emma Lou Diemer, 1995

754

Music: Ronald A. Nelson, 1986

Glo-ry to God the Cre - a - tor, and to the Christ, and to the Ho - ly Spir - it: as it was in the be - gin-ning, is now, and will be for ev - er. A - men. A - men.

755

Music: Alice Jordan, 1986

Glo - ry to God the Cre - a - tor, and to the Christ, and to the Ho - ly Spir - it: as it was in the be - gin - ning, is now, and will be for ev - er. A - men.

756

Music: Jacques Berthier, 1982

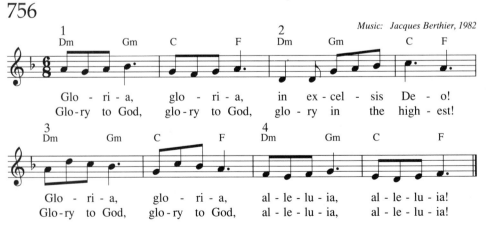

Glo - ri - a, glo - ri - a, in ex - cel - sis De - o!
Glo-ry to God, glo-ry to God, glo - ry in the high - est!

Glo - ri - a, glo - ri - a, al - le - lu - ia, al - le - lu - ia!
Glo-ry to God, glo-ry to God, al - le - lu - ia, al - le - lu - ia!

This Gloria may be sung as a round.

Music: Ancient Scottish chant

1 Glory to God in the highest, and peace to God's
2 We praise you, we bless you, we worship you, ⌈ we glorify you,
⌊ we give thanks to you for

people on earth. 3 ⌈ Holy One,
your great glory, ⌊ heavenly God, the Cre-ator and the sov-ereign God.

4 O Jesus Christ, only Child of God, O Sovereign God, Lamb of God,
5 You take away the sin of the world: have mer - cy on us;
6 ⌈ You are seated
⌊ at the right hand of Majesty: re - ceive our prayer.

7 For you alone are the Mes-siah, you alone are the Ho-ly One,
8 ⌈ You alone are ⌈ with the Holy
⌊ the Most High, Je-sus Christ, ⌊ Spirit, in the glory of the tri-une God. A-men.

758

Music: Pablo Sosa, 1988 (Cueca dance rhythm)

¡Glo - ria, glo - ria,   glo - ria   en las al - tu - ras a   Dios!
Glo - ry, glo - ry,   glo - ry!   Glo - ry to God in the   high - est,

Y en la tie - rra   paz pa-ra a-que-llos   que a - ma Dios. . . .
And on earth be   peace to all peo-ple   with whom God is   pleased.

759

Music: Henry W. Greatorex, 1851

Glo - ry to the Cre - a - tor,   the   Christ, the   Ho - ly Spir - it,

Three - in - One;   as it was in the be - gin - ning, is

now, and ev - er shall be,   world with-out end. A - men. A - men.

Or:
Glo-ry be to the Fa-ther, and to the Son, and to the Ho-ly Ghost; . . .

760

S.C. Molefe, South Africa
Arr. Dave Dargie
From the Lumko Songbook

(Ma - si - thi:) A - men, si - ya - ku - du - mi - sa. (Ma - si - thi:)
(Sing a - men:) A - men, we praise your name, O God. (Sing a - men:)

A - men, si - ya - ku - du - mi - sa. (Ma - si - thi:) A - men, Ba - wo,
A - men, we praise your name, O God. (Sing a - men:) A - men, a - men,

A - men, Ba - wo, A - men, si - ya - ku - du - mi - sa.
a - men, a - men, A - men, we praise your name, O God.

SCRIPTURE RESPONSE

761

Music: John L. Playford (1674–1730)

Before the Gospel   *After the Gospel*

Glo-ry be to you, O Christ.   Praise be to you, O Christ.

762

Music: *Daniel L. Johnson, 1994*

Before the Gospel   *After the Gospel*

Glo - ry to you, O   Christ. Praise to   you, O   Christ.

763

Music: *Jonathan McNair, 1994*

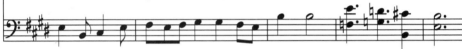

This is what the Spir-it is say-ing to the church-es: Thanks be to   God!

764

Music: *Emma Lou Diemer, 1994*

This is what the Spir-it is   say-ing to the church-es: Thanks be to   God!

765

Text and music: *Jerry Sinclair, 1972; alt.*

1 Al-le - lu - ia,   al-le - lu - ia,   al-le - lu - ia,   al-le - lu - ia,

Al - le - lu - ia, al - le - lu - ia, al - le - lu - ia, al - le - lu - ia!

2 You're my Sav-ior, al-le-lu-ia, . . .
3 You are wor-thy, al-le-lu-ia, . . .
4 I will praise you, al-le-lu-ia, . . .

766

Music: Abraham Maraire, Zimbabwe

Hal-le-lu - jah, hal-le-lu - jah, hal-le-lu - jah, hal-le-lu - jah!

Hal-le-lu - jah, hal-le-lu, hal-le-lu - jah, hal-le-lu - jah!

Hal-le-lu - jah, hal-le-lu - jah, hal-le-lu - jah, hal-le-lu - jah!

767

Music: Jacques Berthier, 1978

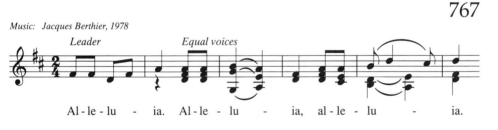

Leader *Equal voices*

Al - le - lu - ia. Al - le - lu - ia, al - le - lu - ia.

Mixed voices

Al - le - lu - ia, al - le - lu - ia!

ALLELUIA

768

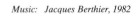

This may be used as an alternative method of chanting psalms. A cantor chants the psalm verses as the congregation hums; at appropriate moments, the congregation repeats the "Alleluia."

PRAYER RESPONSE, MEDITATION

769

Ps. 134:1

Music: George Whelpton, 1897

Ps. 19:4

Music: Eli Wilson, Jr., 1989

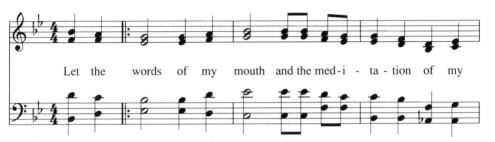

Let the words of my mouth and the med-i - ta-tion of my

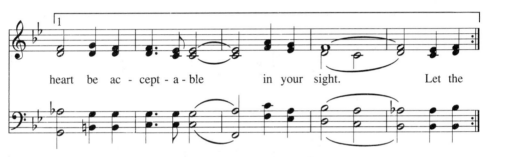

heart be ac - cept-a-ble in your sight. Let the

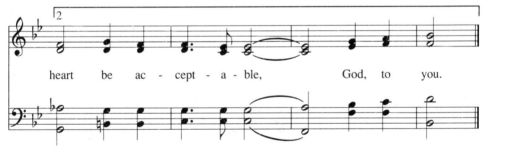

heart be ac - cept - a - ble, God, to you.

Ps. 19:4

Music: Joseph Barnby (1838–1896)

⎡ Let the words of ⎤   ⎡ be acceptable in ⎤
| my mouth and | of my   heart | your sight, O God, | my Re - deem - er.
⎣ the meditation ⎦   ⎣ my strength and ⎦

772

Text: The Taizé Community, 1991

Music: Jacques Berthier, 1991

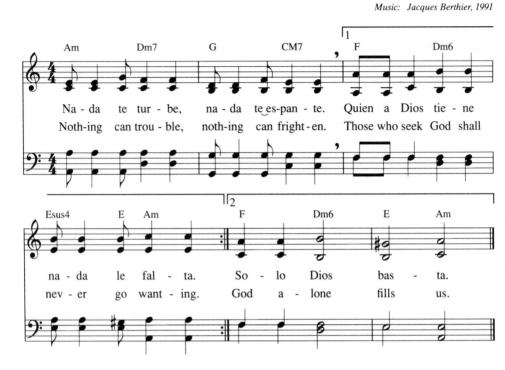

Na - da te tur - be, na - da te es-pan - te. Quien a Dios tie - ne
Noth-ing can trou - ble, noth-ing can fright - en. Those who seek God shall

na - da le fal - ta. So - lo Dios bas - ta.
nev - er go want - ing. God a - lone fills us.

773

Luke 23:42

Music: Traditional; harm. J. Jefferson Cleveland, 1981

Re - mem - ber me, re - mem - ber me,

O Je - sus, re - mem - ber me.

Ps. 5:8; 4:8

774

Text and music: Samuel S. Wesley, 1861; alt.

Shep - herd, lead, lead me in your righ - teous-ness,

make your way plain be - fore my face. For it is you, God,

you, God on - ly, who makes me to lie down in safe - ty.

775

Text: Exod. 19:4; paraphr. by Michael Joncas; alt.

Music: Michael Joncas, 1979; arr. Carlton R. Young, 1988

And God will raise you up on ea - gle's wings,

bear you on the breath of dawn, make you to shine like the

sun, and hold you in the palm of God's hand.

DOXOLOGY

776

Text: Thomas Ken, 1674; adapt.

Music: Ronald A. Nelson, 1986

Praise God from whom all bless-ings flow; Praise Christ, all crea - tures

here be - low; Praise Ho - ly Spir - it, Com-fort-er; One God, Tri - une, whom

we a - dore. A - men, A - men.

777

Text: Thomas Ken, 1674; adapt.

Music: Alice Jordan, 1986

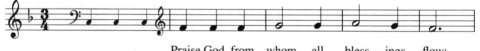

Praise God from whom all bless - ings flow;

Praise Christ, all crea - tures here be - low; Praise Ho - ly Spir - it, the

Com-fort-er; One God, Tri - une, whom we a - dore. A - men.

778

Text: Thomas Ken, 1674;
adapt. William B. Abernethy

(This and other Doxology texts that follow may be sung to musical settings 776, 779, and 780)

Praise God from whom all blessings flow;
Praise God, all creatures here below;
Praise God for all that love has done;
Creator, Christ, and Spirit, One.

779

Text: *Thomas Ken, 1674; alt.*

Music: *John Hatton (d. 1793);*
adapt. George Coles; harm. Roberta Martin, 1968

Praise God from whom all bless - ings flow; Praise Christ, all crea - tures here be - low; Praise Ho - ly Spir - it, Com - fort - er; One God, Tri - une, whom we a - dore. A - men.

780

Text: *Thomas Ken, 1674; alt.*

Music: *Louis Bourgeois, 1551*

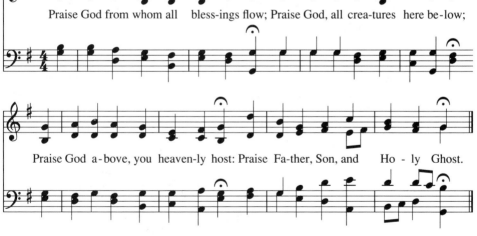

Praise God from whom all bless-ings flow; Praise God, all crea-tures here be-low;

Praise God a-bove, you heaven-ly host: Praise Fa-ther, Son, and Ho - ly Ghost.

781

Text: *Thomas Ken, 1674;*
adapt. Book of Worship, *United Church of Christ*

Praise God from whom all blessings flow;
Praise Christ the Word in flesh born low;
Praise Holy Spirit evermore;
One God, Triune, whom we adore.

782

Text: Charles Coffin, 1736; transl. John Chandler, 1837; alt.

(May be used at Advent, Christmas, and other times)

To God, all glorious heavenly Light,
to Christ revealed in earthly night,
to God the Spirit now we raise
our joyful songs of thankful praise.

783

Text and music: Marty Haugen, 1990

As the grains of wheat once

scat-tered on the hill   were gath-ered in - to one   to be - come our bread;

so may all your peo-ple   from   all the ends of earth   be   gath-ered in - to

one   in   you.   you.   1 As this cup of bless-ing   is
2 Let this be   a   fore-taste   of

shared with-in our midst,   may we share the pres - ence of   your love.
all   that is to come when all cre - a - tion shares this feast with you.

Ps. 51:10–12

784

Music: Emma Lou Diemer, 1990

Cre-ate in me a clean heart, O God, and re - new a right spir - it with-in me.

Cast me not a - way from your pres - ence, and

take not your Ho - ly Spir - it from me. Re - store in me the

joy of your sal - va - tion, and up - hold me with your free Spir - it.

Text: William W. How, 1864; alt.

785

Music: Cantica Laudis, Lowell Mason and G. J. Webb, 1850

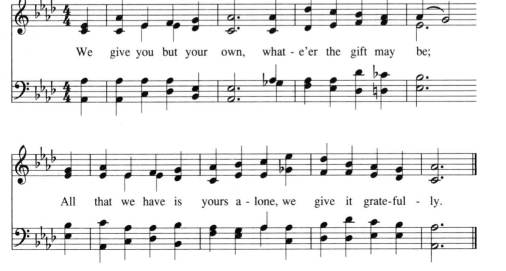

We give you but your own, what - e'er the gift may be;

All that we have is yours a - lone, we give it grate-ful - ly.

786

Music: *Ronald A. Nelson, 1986*

This is the joy - ful feast of the peo - ple of God.

Men and wom - en, youth and chil - dren, come from the east and the

west, from the north and the south, and gath - er a - bout Christ's ta - ble.

787

Music: *Alice Jordan, 1986*

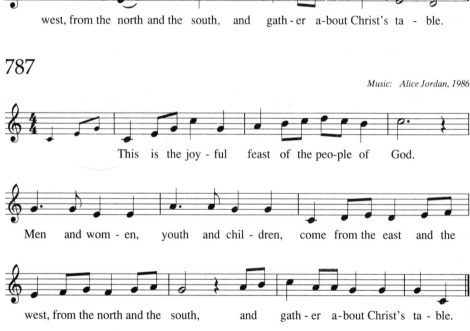

This is the joy - ful feast of the peo-ple of God.

Men and wom - en, youth and chil - dren, come from the east and the

west, from the north and the south, and gath - er a - bout Christ's ta - ble.

788

Text: *The Taizé Community, 1983*

Music: *Jacques Berthier, 1983*

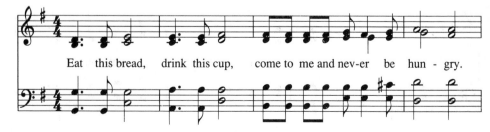

Eat this bread, drink this cup, come to me and nev-er be hun - gry.

Eat this bread, drink this cup, trust in me and you will not thirst.

HOLY, HOLY, HOLY (SANCTUS)

789

Music: Ronald A. Nelson, 1986

Ho - ly, ho - ly, ho - ly God of love and maj - es - ty, the

whole u - ni - verse speaks of your glo - ry, O God Most High.

Bless - ed is the one who comes in the name of our

God! Ho - san - na! Ho - san - na in the high - est!

790

Music: Alice Jordan, 1986

Ho - ly, ho - ly, ho - ly God of love and maj - es - ty,

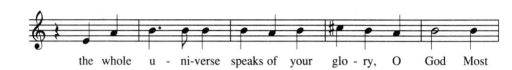

the whole u - ni-verse speaks of your glo - ry, O God Most

High. Bless - ed is the one who comes in the

name of our God! Ho - san - na in the high - est!

791

Music: Healey Willan, 1928

Unison

Ho - ly, ho - ly, ho - - - ly, O God of hosts,

Heav - en and earth are full of your glo - ry: Glo - - - ry be to

you, O God Most High. A - - - - men.

792

Music: Martie McMane, 1991

Ho - ly, ho - ly, ho - ly God, Rul-er Al - might - y;

heaven and earth are full of your glo-ry. Glo - ry be to you, O God.

Bless-ed is the one who comes, who comes in the name of God.

Ho - san - na, ho - san - na, ho - san - na in the high - est!

793

Text and music: Anon., Argentina

¡San - to, san - to, san - to, mi cor - a - zón te␣a - do - ra! Mi
Ho - ly, ho - ly, ho - ly, my heart, my heart a - dores you! My

cor - a - zón te sa - be de - cir: san - to e - res Dios.
heart is glad to say the words: you are ho - ly, God.

794

Music: Ronald A. Nelson, 1978

Ho - ly, ho - ly, ho - ly God of all power and might:

Heaven and earth are full of your glo - ry. Ho - san - na in the

high - est! Blessed is the one who comes in the name

of our God! Ho - san - na in the high - est!

795
Seraphic Hymn

Music: Alonzo P. Howard (1838–1902)

Ho - ly, ho - ly, ho - ly, God of the heaven-ly host;

Heav-en and earth are full, are full of the maj-es-ty of your glo - ry,

Ho - san - na, ho - san - na, ho - san - na in the high - est!

Bless-ed the one who comes in the name of our God,

Ho - san - na, ho - san - na, ho - san-na in the high - est!

796

Music: Ronald A. Nelson, 1986

Christ's death, O God, we pro - claim. Christ's res - ur - rec - tion we de - clare. Christ's com - ing we a - wait. Glo - ry be to you, O God.

797

Music: Ronald A. Nelson, 1986

Christ's death, O God, we pro - claim. Christ's res - ur - rec - tion we de - clare. Christ's com - ing we a - wait. Glo - ry be to you, O God.

798

Music: Alice Jordan, 1986

Christ's death, O God, we pro - claim. Christ's res - ur - rec - tion we de - clare. Christ's

com-ing we a - wait. Glo - ry be to you, O God.

799

Music: Timothy Gibson, 1987

Christ has died. Christ is ris - en. Christ will come a - gain.

800

Music: Ronald A. Nelson, 1986

Je - sus, Lamb of God: have mer-cy on us.

Je - sus, bear - er of our sins: have mer-cy on us.

Je - sus, re - deem-er of the world: give us your peace.

801

Music: Alice Jordan, 1986

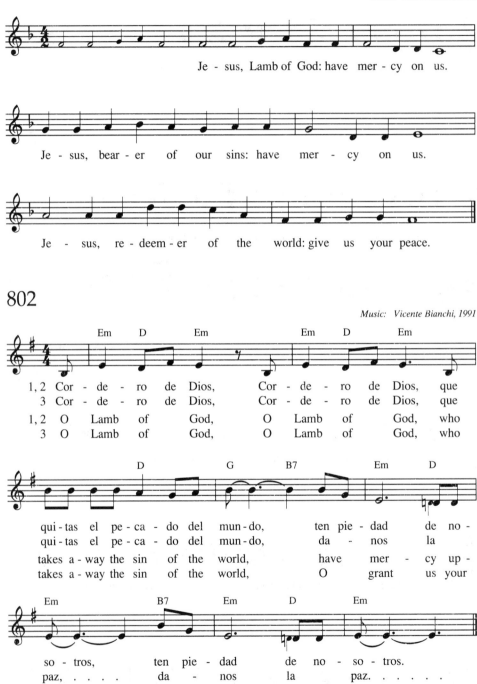

Je - sus, Lamb of God: have mer - cy on us.

Je - sus, bear - er of our sins: have mer - cy on us.

Je - sus, re - deem - er of the world: give us your peace.

802

Music: Vicente Bianchi, 1991

1, 2 Cor - de - ro de Dios, Cor - de - ro de Dios, que
3 Cor - de - ro de Dios, Cor - de - ro de Dios, que
1, 2 O Lamb of God, O Lamb of God, who
3 O Lamb of God, O Lamb of God, who

qui - tas el pe - ca - do del mun - do, ten pie - dad de no -
qui - tas el pe - ca - do del mun - do, da - nos la
takes a - way the sin of the world, have mer - cy up -
takes a - way the sin of the world, O grant us your

so - tros, ten pie - dad de no - so - tros.
paz, ... da - nos la paz. . . . . .
on us, have mer - cy up - on us.
peace, ... O grant us your peace. . . . . . .

Music: Kirchenordnung, *Braunschweig, 1528*

O Christ, the Lamb of God, you take a-way the sin of the world; have mer-cy up-on us. O Christ, the Lamb of God, you take a-way the sin of the world; have mer-cy up-on us. O Christ, the Lamb of God, you take a-way the sin of the world; grant us your peace. A—men.

LAMB OF GOD (AGNUS DEI)

804

Music: Grayson Warren Brown, 1987;
arr. Val Parker, 1987

O Lamb of God, you take a - way the sin of the world; have mer - cy on us, have mer - cy on us.

Grant us peace.

BLESSING, CLOSING SONG

805

Song of Simeon (Nunc Dimittis)

Music: Ronald A. Nelson, 1986

Ho - ly One, now let your ser - vant go in peace; your word has been ful - filled: my own eyes have seen the sal - va-tion which you have pre-pared in the sight of ev - ery peo - ple: a light to re-veal you to the na-tions and the glo-ry of your peo-ple Is - ra - el.

806

Music: Alice Jordan, 1986

Song of Simeon (Nunc Dimittis)

Ho - ly One, now let your ser-vant go in peace; your

word has been ful - filled: my own eyes have seen the sal - va - tion which

you have pre-pared in the sight of ev - ery peo-ple: a light to re -

veal you to the na - tions and the glo-ry of your peo-ple Is - ra - el.

807

Music: Richard Farrant (c. 1530–1580)

Song of Simeon (Nunc Dimittis)

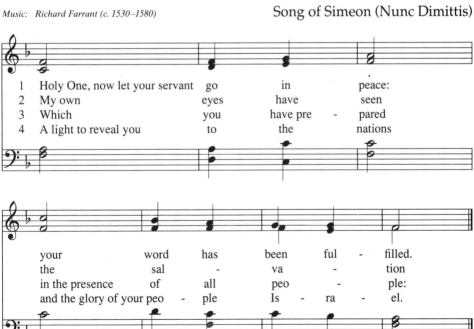

1 Holy One, now let your servant go in peace:
2 My own eyes have seen
3 Which you have pre - pared
4 A light to reveal you to the nations

your word has been ful - filled.
the sal - va - tion
in the presence of all peo - ple:
and the glory of your peo - ple Is - ra - el.

808

Song of Simeon (Nunc Dimittis)

Music: Luis Olivieri, 1992

A - ho - ra, oh Dios des - pi - de a tu sier - vo en paz con -
O God, now let your ser - vant go in peace, your

for - me a tu pa - la - bra; por - que han vis - to mis o - jos tu sal - va -
word has been ful - filled; my own eyes your sal - va - tion have

ción, la cual pre - pa - ras - te en pre - sen - cia de to - dos los
seen, pre - pared by you in the pres - ence of all

pue - blos, luz pa - ra re - ve - la - ción a los gen -
peo - ple: a light ... to re - veal you to the

ti - les, y la glo - ria de tu pue - blo Is - ra - el.
na - tions, and the glo - ry of your peo - ple Is - ra - el.

809

Text and music: Thomas A. Dorsey and Artelia W. Hutchins, 1940

God be with you, God be with you,

God be with you till we meet a - gain. O

God be with you, God be with you,

God be with you till we meet a - gain.

AMEN

810

Twofold

Music: Vincent Persichetti, 1956

A - men, a - men.

811

"Dresden"

A-men, a - men.

"Danish"

812

Threefold

A - men, a - men, a - men.

WORSHIP RESOURCES

Prayers before Worship

816

Gracious God, oil the hinges of our hearts' doors
that they may swing gently and easily to welcome your coming.

Prayer from New Guinea

817

Almighty God, who has given us grace at this time with one accord to make
our common supplications unto you, and does promise that where two or
three are gathered together in your name, you will grant their requests: fulfill
now the desires and petitions of your servants, as may be most expedient for
them, granting us in this world knowledge of your truth, and in the world to
come, life everlasting. Amen.

John Chrysostom, Bishop of Constantinople

818

O God, we give you hearty thanks for the rest of the past night and for the gift
of a new day, with its opportunities of pleasing you. Grant that we may so
pass its hours in the perfect freedom of your service, that at eventide we may
again give thanks unto you; through Jesus Christ our Sovereign. Amen.

Daybreak Office of the Eastern Church

Opening Words

819

I lift up my eyes to the hills—from where will my help come?
My help comes from God, who made heaven and earth.

from Psalm 121

820

God is Spirit, and those who worship God
must worship in spirit and in truth.

John 4:24

821

LEADER: This is the day that God has made;
PEOPLE: **let us rejoice and be glad in it.**
LEADER: O come, let us worship and bow down;
PEOPLE: **let us kneel before God, our Maker.**

from Psalms 118 and 95

822

LEADER: Blessed be the name of God
from this time on and forevermore.

PEOPLE: **From the rising of the sun to its setting
the name of God is to be praised.**

LEADER: It is good to give thanks to God,
to sing praises to your name, O Most High;

PEOPLE: **to declare your steadfast love in the morning,
and your faithfulness by night.**

from Psalms 113 and 92

823

LEADER: ¡Mi corazón está listo, oh Dios, mi corazón listo está!

PEOPLE: **¡Cantaré, cantaré alabanzas! ¡Despierta mi alma!**

LEADER: ¡Despierta, oh arpa y lira! ¡Despertaré la aurora!

PEOPLE: **¡Te daré gracias a ti, oh Dios, entre todas las gentes!**

ALL: **¡Alabemos y adoremos al Dios de la creación!**

LEADER: My heart is ready, O God, my heart is ready!

PEOPLE: **I will sing, I will sing praises! Wake up, my soul!**

LEADER: Wake up, O harp and lyre! I will awake the dawn!

PEOPLE: **I will thank you, O God, among all people!**

ALL: **Let us praise and adore the God of Creation!**

Vilma M. Machín; transl. by Rose M. Grijalva

824

LEADER: Beautiful are the works of God!

PEOPLE: **Beautiful also are the skins of God's people!**

LEADER: Beautiful is the mind of God!

PEOPLE: **Beautiful also are the hopes of God's people!**

LEADER: Beautiful is the heart of God!

PEOPLE: **Beautiful also are the souls of God's people!**

LEADER: God made the heavens and the earth!

PEOPLE: **To God be the glory for the things God has done.**

adapted, Trinity United Church of Christ, Chicago

825

LEADER: Blessed is the One who spoke and the world came into being.

PEOPLE: **Blessed is the One who creates the world.**

LEADER: Blessed is the One who speaks and does.

PEOPLE: **Blessed is the One who decrees and fulfills.**

LEADER: Blessed is the One who has compassion for the earth.

PEOPLE: **Blessed is the One who has compassion for all creatures.**

LEADER: Blessed is the One who rewards those who fear God.

PEOPLE:	**Blessed is the One who lives eternally and exists forever.**
LEADER:	Blessed is the One who redeems and saves.
ALL:	**Blessed is the Holy One.**

Congregation Beth El of the Sudbury River Valley

INVOCATIONS

826

Come, O Creator, O Immensity of love, O Eternity of mercy. Come, and be
with us and in us and beside us and over us. Be as hands upon us, and fashion
us for shining. Be as warmth within us, and fire us for caring. Be as strength
beside us, and shape our lives for healing. Abide in our prayers, the spoken
and the unspoken; and make your Word come true in our flesh; through Jesus
Christ our Redeemer. Amen.

Arnold Kenseth

827

Spirit of Love, Spirit of Truth,
Guide us as we pray,
To think and wish and praise the best,
And mean the words we say.

Hushed is our quiet room,
Still is this place of prayer;
Silent, we bow our heads and feel
Your presence everywhere.

from Children Worship

828

Almighty and everlasting God, our Sovereign, who has safely brought us to
the beginning of this day: defend us in the same with your mighty power; and
grant that this day we fall into no sin, nor run into any kind of danger, but that
all our doings, being ordered by your governance, may be righteous in your
sight; through Jesus Christ our Savior. Amen.

829

O God of the morning and of the evening hours,
let your Spirit come on us here gathered.
This is the holy place where we, your people, call on you in faith,
joining heart and voice in thanksgiving and praise to your name. Amen.

Book of Worship, United Church of Christ

830

LEADER: O God, all-powerful, true and incomparable,
present in all things, yet limited by none,
untouched by place,
unaged by time,
unhurried by the years,
undeceived by words,
not subject to birth
nor in need of protection:
you are above all corruption,
you are beyond all change,
you are by nature immutable,
living in light that none can approach,
invisible, yet you make yourself known to me
and you are found by all who seek you with their whole heart;
you are the God of Israel
and of all who hope in Christ.
LEADER: You are our God.
PEOPLE: **We adore you.**

The Joint Liturgical Group

831

Holy God, we come before you with awe, for you are great in love and power.
Some of us come with reluctance and some with joy; some with sadness and
others full of fear, yet we know you receive us as we are. Mighty God, stay
with us always, as we worship and as we share the risk and challenge of living
our faith. By your powerful Spirit, turn our fear to courage and our confusion
to confidence. Touch us, God, with your healing fire. Speak to us through your
Word. Send us back into the world renewed and eager to do your will. We
pray in the name of Jesus the Christ. Amen.

Ronald S. Beebe

CONFESSIONS

Calls to Confession

832

The Word became flesh and dwelt among us, full of grace and truth; but we
esteemed it not and turned away. Let us confess our unfaithfulness and the
limits of our trust.

Lavon Bayler

833

Examinemos ahora nuestras vidas en frente a Dios, confesando humildemente nuestros pecados y abriendo nuestros corazones, no sea que engañándonos, hasta a nosotros mismos, nos excluyamos de tu presencia.

Let us examine our lives in the presence of God, humbly confessing our sins and opening our hearts, so that we do not deceive even ourselves, and exclude ourselves from your presence.

Selva Lehman

Prayers of Confession

834

Almighty and everlasting God, always more ready to hear than we are to pray, always willing to give more than we either desire or deserve: pour upon us the abundance of your mercy; forgiving those things of which our conscience is afraid, and giving us those good things which we are not worthy to ask, except through the merits and mediation of Jesus Christ, your Begotten One, our Sovereign. Amen.

A Book of Worship for Free Churches

835

Gentle and holy God, we acknowledge to you, to one another, and to ourselves that we are not what you have called us to be. We hàve stifled our gifts and wasted our time. We have avoided opportunities to offer kindness, but have been quick to take offense. We have pretended that we could make no contribution to peace and justice in our world and have excused ourselves from risk-taking in our own community. Have mercy on us, forgive us our sins, and help us to live our lives differently, we pray in the name of Jesus Christ, whose call to follow haunts our every prayer. Amen.

Maren Tirabassi

836

God of love and justice, we long for peace within and peace without. We long for harmony in our families, for serenity in the midst of struggle, and for commitment to each other's growth. We long for the day when our homes will be a dwelling place for your love. Yet we confess that we are often anxious; we do not trust each other, and we harbor violence. We are not willing to take the risks and make the hard choices that love requires. Look upon us with kindness and grace. Rule in our homes and in all the world; show us how to walk in your paths, through the mercy of our Savior. Amen.

Ruth Duck

837

Almighty God,
> Whose breath quickened us,
> Whose tongue named us,
> Whose language we are:

Grant us grace to be true words—
> Not gentle when it is in anger that we live,
> Not smooth when it is desperation that we know,
> Not patient when time has narrowed down to now,
> Not wise, not neat, not all our fences mended,
> But words, broken yet honest words, and lost,
> Stumbling their way toward silence.

Take us back. Recall us. Then speak us once again.
> Set us in order. Mend our shattered syntax. Set all our commas straight.
> Imbue in us a power that keeps company with pain,
> Then march us across the pages of this beautiful, fragile, tormented,
> and perishable earth to sing the songs of Zion.

In the name of the Word made flesh, made dead, and made alive again. Amen.

Barbara Sargent

838

LEADER:	Help us, O God our Savior;
PEOPLE:	**Deliver us and forgive us our sins.**
LEADER:	Look upon your congregation;
PEOPLE:	**Give to your people the blessing of peace;**
LEADER:	Declare your glory among the nations;
PEOPLE:	**And your wonders among all peoples.**
LEADER:	Let not the oppressed be shamed and turned away;
PEOPLE:	**Never forget the lives of the poor.**
LEADER:	Continue your lovingkindness to those who know you;
PEOPLE:	**And your favor to those who are true of heart.**
LEADER:	Satisfy us by your lovingkindness in the morning;
PEOPLE:	**So shall we rejoice and be glad all the days of our life.**

Standing Liturgical Commission

Words of Assurance or Assurance of Pardon

839

One fact remains that does not change: God has loved you, loves you now, and will love you always. This is the good news that brings us new life.

Women and Worship

840

Escucha estas palabras de la Escritura: la misericordia y el amor de Dios son inmensos, su ira lenta y su amor es eterno.

Listen to the words of the scriptures: the mercy and the love of God are endless; God's wrath is slow, and God's love is eternal.

Vilma M. Machín; transl. by Rose M. Grijalva

841

The almighty and merciful God grant us pardon and remission of all our sins, time for amendment of life, and the grace and comfort of the Holy Spirit. Amen.

The Joint Liturgical Group

Offertory Sentences and Prayers

842

Having received new life through the generosity of God and the hope Christ brings, let us give thankfully and abundantly that we may be called God's generous people.

June Christine Goudey

843

LEADER: Let us present with joy our offerings of commitment and support for the work of Christ's church.

PEOPLE: **Let us prepare Christ's table with the offerings of our life and labor.**

The United Congregational Church of South Africa

844

All good gifts around us come from you, O God. You have given us life, and new life in Christ. As you have given us gifts, so we offer our gifts that we may be gifts to one another, even as Jesus so taught and lived. Amen.

845

O God, most merciful and gracious, of whose bounty we have all received: accept, we pray, this offering of your people. Remember in your love those who have brought it and those for whom it is given; and so follow it with your blessing that it may promote peace and goodwill among all people and advance the realm of our Savior Jesus Christ. Amen.

PRAYERS

Preparation

846

Almighty God, unto whom all hearts are open, all desires known, and from whom no secrets are hid: cleanse the thoughts of our hearts by the inspiration of your Holy Spirit, that we may perfectly love you and worthily magnify your holy name; through Christ our Sovereign. Amen.

847

Eternal One, Silence from whom my words come; Questioner from whom my questions arise; Lover of whom all my loves are hints; Disturber in whom alone I find my rest; Mystery in whose depths I find healing and myself: enfold me now in your presence; restore to me your peace; renew me through your power; and ground me in your grace. Amen.

Ted Loder

Post Communion

848

Gracious and loving God, you have made us one in the body of Christ, and nourished us at your table with holy food and drink. Now send us forth to be your people in the world. Grant us strength to persevere in resisting evil, and to proclaim in all we say and do your Good News in Christ Jesus our Savior. Amen.

849

O God, who is eternal salvation and inestimable blessedness: grant to all your servants, we pray you, that we who have received things holy and blessed may be enabled to be holy and blessed evermore. Amen.

Henry Harbaugh

Intercession

850

To God be glory;
To the angels honor;
To Satan confusion;

To the cross reverence;
To the church exaltation;
To the departed quickening;
To the penitent acceptance;
To the sick and infirm recovery and healing;
And to the four quarters of the world great peace and tranquillity;
And on us who are weak and sinful may the compassion and mercies of
our God come, and may they overshadow us continually. Amen.

from the Old Syriac used by Christians in Turkey, Iran, and
South India

Guidance

851

My spirit is one with you, Great Spirit.
You strengthen me day and night to share my very best
with my brothers and sisters.
You, whom my people see in all of creation and in all people,
show your love for us.
Help me to know, like the soaring eagle, the heights of knowledge.
From the Four Directions, fill me with the four virtues of fortitude, generosity,
respect, and wisdom;
so that I will help my people walk in the path of understanding and peace.

Lakota prayer

Serenity

852

God, give us
grace to accept with serenity the things that cannot be changed,
courage to change the things that should be changed,
and the wisdom to distinguish the one from the other.

Reinhold Niebuhr -1943

Peace

853

O God, it is your will to hold both heaven and earth in a single peace. Let the
design of your great love shine on the waste of our wraths and sorrows, and
give peace to your church, peace among nations, peace in our homes, and
peace in our hearts. Amen.

854

O God of many names, Lover of all nations: we pray for peace in our hearts, in our homes, in our nation, in our world; the peace of your will; the peace of our need. Amen.

For the Church

855

We beseech you, O God, for your church throughout the world. May it grow in the faith of the cross and the power of the resurrection. May your spirit minister to it continually the redemption and reconciliation of all things. Keep it in your eternal unity, in great humility, in godly fear, and in your own pure and peaceable wisdom so easy to be entreated. Make it swift and mighty in the cause of the dominion of heaven. Cover, establish, and enlighten it, that it may see through all that obscures the time, and that it may move in the shadow of your wing, with faith, obedience, sacrifice, and godly power, through Jesus Christ our Sovereign. Amen.

P. T. Forsyth

Eternal Life

856

Bring us, O God, at our last awakening into the house and gate of heaven, to enter into that gate and dwell in that house, where there shall be no night nor burning sun, but one equal light; no voice nor silence, but one equal music; no fears nor hopes, but one equal possession; no ends nor beginnings, but one equal eternity in the habitation of your glory and dominion, world without end. Amen.

John Donne

Renewal of Mission

857

Come, Holy Spirit, renew the whole creation. Send the wind and flame of your transforming life to lift up the church in this day. Give wisdom and faith that we may know the great hope to which we are called. Come, Holy Spirit, renew the whole creation. Amen.

Providence of God

858

O God, giver of all good, who continually pours your benefits upon us, age after age the living wait upon you and find that of your faithfulness there is no end and that your care is unfailing. We praise you that the mystery of our life is a mystery of infinite goodness. We praise you for the order and constancy of nature; for the beauty and bounty of the earth; for day and night, summer and winter, seed time and harvest; for the varied gifts of loveliness and usefulness which every season brings. We give you thanks for all the comfort and joy of life, for our homes, for our friends, and for all the love and sympathy and goodwill of all people. Amen.

A Book of Worship for Free Churches

Thankfulness and Hope

859

We thank you, for you are our God, and God of our fathers and mothers forever. You are the Refuge of our life, the Shield of our help. From generation to generation may we thank you and count your praises—evening, morning, and noon—for our lives which are committed into your hand, for our souls which are entrusted to you, for your miracles which are with us every day, for your wonders and goodness at all times. O Good One, your compassion does not fail. O Merciful One, your lovingkindness never ceases. Forever we hope in you.

Congregation Beth El of the Sudbury River Valley

Those in Need

860

We bring before you, O God, the troubles and perils of people and nations, the sighing of prisoners and captives, the sorrows of the bereaved, the necessities of strangers, the helplessness of the weak, the despondency of the weary, the failing powers of the aged. O God, draw near to each, for the sake of Jesus Christ our Strength. Amen.

Saint Anselm (1033–1109)

861

Let us remember tonight those who are in the bonds of poverty, who have neither sufficient food nor drink, the beauty of home, or the love of beauty. Bring us the day, O God, when the world shall no longer know such poverty as stunts growth and feeds crime, and teach us to realize that such things are not necessary to earth but are the result of our greed and selfishness, our wastefulness and willful forgetting. Amen.

W. E. B. DuBois

862

Make us worthy, Blessed One, to serve those throughout the world who live and die in poverty or hunger. Give them, through our hands, this day their daily bread; and by our understanding love, give peace and joy. Amen.

Mother Teresa of Calcutta

Justice

863

Show me the suffering of the most miserable
      so I will know my people's plight.
Free me to pray for others
      for you are present in every person.
Help me to take responsibility for my own life
      so that I can be free at last.
Grant me courage to serve others
      for in service there is true life.
Give me honesty and patience
      so that I can work with other workers.
Bring forth song and celebration
      so that the spirit will be alive among us.
Let the spirit flourish and grow
      so that we will never tire of the struggle.
Let us remember those who have died for justice
      for they have given us life.
Help us love even those who hate us,
      so that we can change the world. Amen.

United Farm Workers

God's World

864

Almighty God, your word of creation caused the water to be filled with many kinds of living beings and the air to be filled with birds. With

those who live in this world's small islands we rejoice in the richness
of your creation, and we pray for your wisdom for all who live on this
earth, that we may wisely manage and not destroy what you have
made for us and for our descendants. In Jesus' name we pray. Amen.

Prayer from Samoa

Endeavors of the Day

865

O God, we thank you for the sweet refreshment of sleep and for the glory and
vigor of the new day. As we set our faces once more toward our daily work,
we pray for the strength sufficient for our tasks. May Christ's spirit of duty
and service ennoble all we do. Uphold us by the consciousness that our work
is useful and a blessing to all. If there has been anything in our work harmful
to others and dishonorable to ourselves, reveal it to our inner eye with such
clearness that we shall hate it and put it away, though it be at a loss to ourselves. When we work with others, help us to regard them, not as servants to
our will, but as brothers and sisters equal to us in human dignity, and equally
worthy of their full reward. May there be nothing in this day's work of which
we shall be ashamed when the sun has set, nor in the eventide of life when our
task is done and we go to our eternal home to meet your face.

Walter Rauschenbusch

Evening

866

At last, O God, the sun's heat has given way to the cool evening.
Take, we pray, the heat out of our desires and our tempers,
and in this evening hour calm us,
that we may experience the peace and serenity which come from you.
At last, O God, the sun's brightness has given way
to the rich colors of the evening.
Prevent us, we pray, from being dazzled by the apparent brilliance
of human achievement.
And, in this evening hour, help us to rediscover the varied beauty of your creation, and appreciate afresh, in the stillness, the value of your abiding presence.
For the sake of Jesus Christ. Amen.

Prayers for Today, for African congregations

Prayers for Home Use

Before a Meal

867

O God, you are the final source of all our comforts and to you we give thanks for this food. But we also remember in gratitude the many men and women whose labor was necessary to produce it, and who gathered it from the land and from the sea for our sustenance. Grant that they too may enjoy the fruit of their labor without want, and may be bound up with us in a communion of thankful hearts.

Walter Rauschenbusch

868

Jesus of the wedding feast, of breakfast by the lake,
(bless this food we have prepared for you and all our friends.)*
Be with us now and at all our meals give us appetite and joy in eating together.
Blessed be God for daily bread.

(*optional)

Evening Prayer

869

We thank you, loving God, for the day you have given us, and for all the pleasure we have had. Guard us while we sleep, and bless all those we love, this night and forever.

Evening Prayer with Young Children

870

Dear God, thank you for today. We are sorry if we have been unkind to anyone. Help us to forgive each other. Thank you for our family and for our friends. Please be with us tonight. Amen.

Forgiveness

871

God of mercy, we are sorry that we have not always done what you wanted us to do. We have not loved you with all our heart, and we have not cared enough for other people. Forgive us, for Jesus' sake. Amen.

Prayers of Benediction

872

May the God who shakes heaven and earth,
whom death could not contain,
who lives to disturb and heal us,
bless you with power to go forth
and proclaim the gospel. Amen.

Janet Morley

873

May the blessing of the God of Abraham and Sarah,
and of Jesus Christ born of our sister Mary,
and of the Holy Spirit, who broods over the world
        as a mother over her children,
be upon you and remain with you always. Amen.

874

May you love God so much that you love nothing else too much;
May you fear God enough that you need fear nothing else at all.

875

Jesus said, "You ought always to pray and not to faint."
Do not pray for easy lives;
        pray to be stronger women and men.
Do not pray for tasks equal to your powers,
        but for power equal to your tasks.
Then, the doing of your work will be no miracle—
        you will be the miracle.
Every day you will wonder at yourself and the richness of life
        which has come to you by the grace of God.

876

O Jesus,
Be the canoe that holds me up in the sea of life;
Be the rudder that keeps me in the straight road;
Be the outrigger that supports me in times of temptation.
Let your Spirit be my sail that carries me through each day.
Keep my body strong, so that I can paddle steadfastly on in the voyage of life.
Amen.

An Islander's prayer from Melanesia

877

May the great Ruler of all high places,
God of many names,
touch you with a wind that keeps you strong,
for all the days to come. Amen.

Litanies

A Litany of Intercession

878

LEADER: Gracious God, who loves all and forgets none, we bring to you our prayers for all your children.
For all whom we love, watch over, and care for;

PEOPLE: **Hear us, O God.**

LEADER: For all prisoners and captives, and all who suffer from oppression, that you will manifest your mercy toward them, and make all hearts as merciful as your own;

PEOPLE: **Hear us, O God.**

LEADER: For all who bear the cross of suffering, the sick in body or mind;

PEOPLE: **Hear us, O God.**

LEADER: For all those who are troubled by the sin or suffering of those they love;

PEOPLE: **Hear us, O God.**

LEADER: For all who are absorbed in their own grief, that they may be raised to share the sorrows of others, and know the saving grace of the cross;

PEOPLE: **Hear us, O God.**

LEADER: For all perplexed by the deeper questions of life and overshadowed with doubt, that your light may guide them;

PEOPLE: **Hear us, O God.**

LEADER: For all who are tried by temptations or weakness, that your mercy may be their strength;

PEOPLE: **Hear us, O God.**

LEADER: For all who are lonely and sad in the midst of others' joy, that they may know you as their friend and comforter;

PEOPLE: **Hear us, O God.**

LEADER: For the infirm and aged and for all who are dying, that they may find their strength in you and light at evening time;

PEOPLE: **Hear us, O God.**

LEADER: For all forgotten by us, but dear to you;

PEOPLE: **Hear us, O God.**

LEADER: O compassionate God, hear our prayers, answer them according to your will, and make us channels of your infinite grace; through Jesus Christ we pray.

ALL: **Amen.**

A Litany for Evening

879

LEADER: In faith let us offer our prayer, saying, "Christ, have mercy." For the peace of the whole world, and for our salvation, we pray to you, O Christ;

PEOPLE: **Christ, have mercy.**

LEADER: For your church, and for all who minister in it, we pray to you, O Christ;

PEOPLE: **Christ, have mercy.**

LEADER: For the leaders of nations, that they may ever seek justice and peace, we pray to you, O Christ;

PEOPLE: **Christ, have mercy.**

LEADER: For all who are traveling, and for those in danger, we pray to you, O Christ;

PEOPLE: **Christ, have mercy.**

LEADER:	For those who are in need, especially those who are hungry, sick, and dying, we pray to you, O Christ;
PEOPLE:	**Christ, have mercy.**
LEADER:	For those who are frightened and alone, we pray to you, O Christ;
PEOPLE:	**Christ, have mercy.**
LEADER:	For those who are oppressed and suffer injustice, we pray to you, O Christ;
PEOPLE:	**Christ, have mercy.**
LEADER:	For rest and refreshment for our minds and bodies, we pray to you, O Christ;
PEOPLE:	**Christ, have mercy.**
LEADER:	Remembering all who have died, (*especially <u>Name(s)</u>*) and all the faithful saints, grant us eternal life with you, we pray to you, O Christ;
PEOPLE:	**Christ, have mercy.**
LEADER:	Grant us your protection as we sleep, and guide us in all that we do when we awaken. For all these things, and for whatever may be best for us, we pray in your holy name.
ALL:	**Amen.**

A Litany of Darkness and Light

880

I:*	We wait in the darkness, expectantly, longingly, anxiously, thoughtfully.
II:	The darkness is our friend. In the darkness of the womb, we have all been nurtured and protected. In the darkness of the womb, the Christ-child was made ready for the journey into light.
ALL:	**You are with us, O God, in darkness and in light.**
I:	It is only in the darkness that we can see the splendor of the universe—blankets of stars, the solitary glowings of distant planets.
II:	It was the darkness that allowed the Magi to find the star that guided them to where the Christ-child lay.

ALL: **You are with us, O God, in darkness and in light.**

I: In the darkness of night, desert peoples find relief from the cruel, relentless heat of the sun.

II: In the blessed desert darkness, Mary and Joseph were able to flee with the infant Jesus to safety in Egypt.

ALL: **You are with us, O God, in darkness and in light.**

I: In the darkness of sleep, we are soothed and restored, healed and renewed.

II: In the darkness of sleep, dreams rise up. God spoke to Jacob and Joseph through dreams. God is speaking still.

ALL: **You are with us, O God, in darkness and in light.**

I: In the solitude of darkness, we sometimes remember those who need God's presence in a special way—the sick, the unemployed, the bereaved, the persecuted, the homeless, those who are demoralized and discouraged, those whose fear has turned to cynicism, those whose vulnerability has become bitterness.

II: Sometimes in the darkness, we remember those who are near to our hearts—colleagues, partners, parents, children, neighbors, friends. We thank God for their presence and ask God to bless and protect them in all that they do—at home, at school, as they travel, as they work, as they play.

ALL   **You are with us, O God, in darkness and in light.**

I: Sometimes, in the solitude of darkness, our fears and concerns, our hopes and our visions rise to the surface. We come face to face with ourselves and with the road that lies ahead of us. And in that same darkness, we find companionship for the journey.

II: In that same darkness, we sometimes allow ourselves to wonder and worry whether the human race is going to survive.

ALL: **We know you are with us, O God, yet we still await your coming. In the darkness that contains both our hopelessness and our expectancy, we watch for a sign of God's hope.**

Department of Parish Development and Mission, New Zealand

*This litany may be said in various ways: parts I and II may be spoken by individuals, by groups, or by a worship leader, with all responding.

CREEDS, AFFIRMATIONS OF FAITH

881

The Apostles' Creed

I believe in God, the Father almighty,
  creator of heaven and earth.

I believe in Jesus Christ, God's only Son, our Lord,
  who was conceived by the Holy Spirit,
  born of the Virgin Mary,
  suffered under Pontius Pilate,
  was crucified, died, and was buried;
  he descended to the dead.
  On the third day he rose again;
  he ascended into heaven,
  he is seated at the right hand of the Father,
  and he will come to judge the living and the dead.

I believe in the Holy Spirit,
  the holy catholic Church,
  the communion of saints,
  the forgiveness of sins,
  the resurrection of the body,
  and the life everlasting. Amen.

882

The Apostles' Creed,
an alternate version

I believe in God
  the Father-Mother almighty,
  creator of heaven and earth.

I believe in Jesus Christ, God's only Child, our Sovereign,
  who was conceived by the Holy Spirit,
  born of the Virgin Mary,
  suffered under Pontius Pilate,
  was crucified, dead, and buried.
  Having descended to the dead and having risen on the third day,
  Christ ascended into heaven,
  sits at the right hand of the Father-Mother,
  and from there will come to judge the living and the dead.

I believe in the Holy Spirit,
  the holy catholic church,
  the communion of saints,
  the forgiveness of sins,
  the resurrection of the body,
  and the life everlasting. Amen.

883

The Nicene Creed

We believe in one God,
    the Father, the Almighty,
    maker of heaven and earth,
    of all that is, seen and unseen.

We believe in one Lord, Jesus Christ,
    the only Son of God,
    eternally begotten of the Father,
    God from God, Light from Light,
    true God from true God,
    begotten, not made,
    of one Being with the Father;
    through him all things were made.
    For us and for our salvation
        he came down from heaven,
        was incarnate of the Holy Spirit and the Virgin Mary
        and became truly human.
        For our sake he was crucified under Pontius Pilate;
        he suffered death and was buried.
        On the third day he rose again
        in accordance with the Scriptures;
        he ascended into heaven
        and is seated at the right hand of the Father.
        He will come again in glory to judge the living and the dead,
        and his kingdom will have no end.

We believe in the Holy Spirit, the Lord, the giver of life,
    who proceeds from the Father and the Son,
    who with the Father and the Son is worshiped and glorified,
    who has spoken through the prophets.
    We believe in one holy catholic and apostolic Church.
    We acknowledge one baptism for the forgiveness of sins.
    We look for the resurrection of the dead,
        and the life of the world to come. Amen.

884

The Nicene Creed,
an alternate version

We believe in one God, the Father-Mother, the Almighty
    maker of heaven and earth,
    and of all things visible and invisible.

We believe in one Sovereign, Jesus Christ,
    the only Child of God,
    begotten from the Father-Mother before all worlds —
    God from God, Light from Light, true God from true God;
    begotten, not made;
    of one Being with the Father-Mother;
    through whom all things were made;
    who because of us human beings and for our salvation,
    came down from heaven,
    being made flesh by the Holy Spirit and the Virgin Mary,
    and became a human being;
    who was crucified for us under Pontius Pilate,
    and suffered and was buried,
    and rose again the third day in accordance with the scriptures,
    and ascended into heaven,
    and sits at the right hand of the Father-Mother;
    who will come again with glory to judge the living and the dead;
    whose dominion will have no end.

We believe in the Holy Spirit, the Sovereign, the giver of life,
    who proceeds from the Father-Mother, and from the Child;
    who with the Father-Mother and the Child is worshiped and glorified;
    who spoke by the prophets.
    And we believe in one holy catholic and apostolic church;
    we acknowledge one baptism for the forgiveness of sins;
    we look for the resurrection of the dead,
    and the life of the world to come. Amen.

885

United Church of Christ Statement of Faith
in the Form of a Doxology

We believe in you, O God, Eternal Spirit,
God of our Savior Jesus Christ and our God,
    and to your deeds we testify:
You call the worlds into being,
      create persons in your own image,
      and set before each one the ways of life and death.

You seek in holy love to save all people from aimlessness
and sin.
You judge people and nations by your righteous will
declared through prophets and apostles.
In Jesus Christ, the man of Nazareth, our crucified and
risen Savior,
you have come to us
and shared our common lot,
conquering sin and death
and reconciling the world to yourself.

You bestow upon us your Holy Spirit,
creating and renewing the church of Jesus Christ,
binding in covenant faithful people of all ages,
tongues, and races.

You call us into your church
to accept the cost and joy of discipleship,
to be your servants in the service of others,
to proclaim the gospel to all the world
and resist the powers of evil,
to share in Christ's baptism and eat at his table,
to join him in his passion and victory.

You promise to all who trust you
forgiveness of sins and fullness of grace,
courage in the struggle for justice and peace,
your presence in trial and rejoicing,
and eternal life in your realm which has no end.

Blessing and honor, glory and power be unto you. Amen.

886

Affirmation of Faith

You, O God, are supreme and holy.
You create our world and give us life.
Your purpose overarches everything we do.
You have always been with us.
You are God.
You, O God, are infinitely generous,
good beyond all measure.
You came to us before we came to you.

You have revealed and proved
your love for us in Jesus Christ,
who lived and died and rose again.
You are with us now.
You are God.

You, O God, are Holy Spirit.
You empower us to be your gospel in the world.
You reconcile and heal; you overcome death.

You are our God. We worship you.

A New Zealand Prayer Book

887

A New Creed

LEADER: We are not alone, we live in God's world.
PEOPLE: **We believe in God:**
   who has created and is creating,
   who has come in Jesus,
     the Word made flesh,
     to reconcile and make new,
   who works in us and others by the Spirit.
We trust in God.
We are called to be the Church:
   to celebrate God's presence,
   to love and serve others,
   to seek justice and resist evil,
   to proclaim Jesus,
     crucified and risen,
     our judge and our hope.
In life, in death, in life beyond death,
   God is with us.
We are not alone. Thanks be to God.

United Church of Canada, 1980

INDEXES

888

COPYRIGHT ACKNOWLEDGMENTS

Divider page artwork by Joan Menocal Copyright © 1995 *The New Century Hymnal.*

Orders for Worship

See acknowledgments following Orders for Worship.

Hymns

2 Arrangement Copyright © 1992 The Pilgrim Press.

5 Words Copyright © 1983 Nobuaki Hanaoka. Translation Copyright © 1983 Abingdon Press. Harmonization Copyright © 1993 The Pilgrim Press.

6 Translation Copyright © 1993 by Madeleine Forell Marshall. Harmonization Copyright © , Oxford University Press. From THE ENGLISH HYMNAL, 1906.

8 Words Copyright © 1966 by the Estate of Curtis Beach.

9 Words Copyright © 1992 by Gracia Grindal. Music Copyright © 1980 by G.I.A. Publications, Inc.

11 Copyright © 1989 by Hope Publishing Co., Carol Stream, IL 60188. All rights reserved. Used by permission.

12 Descant Copyright © 1993 The Pilgrim Press.

13 Words reprinted from "THE PRESBYTERIAN HYMNAL" Copyright © 1990 Westminster/John Knox Press. Alt.

14 Copyright © 1971 Bud John Songs, Inc.

15 Words Copyright © 1993 Medical Mission Sisters. Music Copyright © 1978 LUTHERAN BOOK OF WORSHIP. Reprinted by permission of Augsburg Fortress.

17 Word adaptations Copyright © 1993 Medical Mission Sisters. Harmonization Copyright © , Oxford University Press. From THE ENGLISH HYMNAL, 1906. Descant Copyright © 1993 The Pilgrim Press.

20 Copyright © 1986 James Gertmenian. Harmonization Copyright © 1986 Ronald Huntington. Used by permission.

21 Words Copyright © 1987 Jane Parker Huber from A SINGING FAITH. Used by permission of Westminster/John Knox Press.

22 Translation Copyright © 1993 Madeleine Forell Marshall.

26 Word alterations Copyright © 1993 The Pilgrim Press.

27 Harmonization Copyright © , Oxford University Press. From THE ENGLISH HYMNAL, 1906.

28 Words stanza 4 Copyright © 1993 Medical Mission Sisters.

29 Words and arrangement Copyright © 1991 The Iona Community. Used by permission of G.I.A. Publications, Inc. Music Copyright © 1989 Salvador T. Martinez.

30 Copyright © 1993 by Hope Publishing Co., Carol Stream, IL 60188. All rights reserved. Used by permission.

32 Words Copyright © 1983 Jaroslav J. Vajda. Music Copyright © 1983 by G.I.A. Publications, Inc.

33 Translation Copyright © 1983 Boris and Clare Anderson. Harmonization Copyright © 1983 I-to Loh.

34 Copyright © 1983 Discipleship Resources.

35 Translation and harmonization Copyright © 1994 The Pilgrim Press.

36 Words Copyright © 1986 by G.I.A. Publications, Inc.

37 Words Copyright © 1986 London Yearly Meeting of the Religious Society of Friends (Quakers).

38 Word alterations Copyright © 1993 The Pilgrim Press. Music Copyright © , Oxford University Press.

39 Words and music Copyright © 1976 by Resource Publications, Inc., 160 E. Virginia St., #290, San Jose, CA 95112. English translation Copyright © 1989 Augsburg Fortress. Reprinted by permission. Harmonization Copyright © 1993 The Pilgrim Press.

40 Word alterations Copyright © 1992 The Pilgrim Press.

41 Words and music by Kenneth Morris. Copyright © 1948 by Martin & Morris; Copyright renewed. All rights administered by UniChappell Music, Inc. International copyright secured. All rights reserved. Arrangement Copyright © 1992 The Pilgrim Press.

43 Word alterations Copyright © 1992 The Pilgrim Press.

44 Translation Copyright © 1993 Madeleine Forell Marshall.

45 Translation Copyright © 1993 The Pilgrim Press. Arrangement Copyright © 1993 Luis Olivieri.

46 Words Copyright © 1954, renewal 1982 by The Hymn Society, Texas Christian University, Fort Worth, TX 76129. All rights reserved. Used by permission.

47 Words Copyright © 1994 The Pilgrim Press.

48 Words Copyright © , Methodist Church Division of Education and Youth. Harmonization Copyright © , Oxford University Press.

50 Translation Copyright © 1993 Madeleine Forell Marshall.

51 Music arrangement and harmonization Copyright © , Oxford University Press. From THE ENGLISH HYMNAL, 1906.

52 Word alterations Copyright © 1993 The Pilgrim Press.

53 Copyright © 1982 Bob Jay Publishers.

54 Copyright © 1985, Oxford University Press, Inc. From NEW HYMNS FOR THE LECTIONARY.

55 Word adaptations Copyright © 1981 Ruth C. Duck.

56 Spanish Copyright © Osvaldo Catena. Translation Copyright © 1993 The Pilgrim Press. Arrangement Copyright © 1991 Concordia Publishing House.

57 Words Copyright © 1991 Jean Wiebe Janzen.

58 Words Copyright © 1992 by Hope Publishing Co., Carol Stream, IL 60188. All rights reserved. Used by permission.

59 Words Copyright © , The Community of Resurrection.

60 Translation Copyright © 1993 Madeleine Forell Marshall.

61 Music Copyright © 1985 by Hope Publishing Co., Carol Stream, IL 60188. All rights reserved. Used by permission.

62 Copyright © 1987 Vicki Vogel Schmidt.

64 Words Copyright © 1988, Oxford University Press.

65 Copyright © 1983 Pablo Sosa. English translation Copyright © 1983 Discipleship Resources. Arrangement Copyright ©1984 Roberto Milano.

66 Words stanza 3 Copyright © 1982 Charles P. Price. Words stanza 4 Copyright © 1982 The Church Pension Fund. Used by permission.

67 Translation Copyright © 1993 Madeleine Forell Marshall.

69 Copyright © 1992 Marion M. Meyer. Harmonization Copyright © 1994 The Pilgrim Press.

70 Words Copyright © 1979; Music Copyright © 1942, renewed 1970 by Hope Publishing Co., Carol Stream, IL 60188. All rights reserved. Used by permission.

71 Word adaptations Copyright © 1981 Ruth C. Duck. Music Copyright © 1974 by Shawnee Press, Inc. (ASCAP). All rights reserved. Used by permission.

72 Words Copyright © 1958; Phonetic transcription Copyright © 1989 The United Methodist Publishing House. Music: JASRAC; 1-7-13 Nishishimbashi, Minato-ku, Tokyo 105, Japan.

73 Words and music Copyright © 1992 Louise Ruspini. Harmonization Copyright © 1993 The Pilgrim Press.

74 Translation Copyright © 1993 Madeleine Forell Marshall.

76 Words Copyright © 1964 by World Library Publications (A Div. of J. S. Paluch Company, Inc.). All rights reserved. Used by permission. Music Copyright © 1972 CONTEMPORARY WORSHIP 4: Hymns for Baptism and Holy Communion. Reprinted by permission of Augsburg Fortress. Descant Copyright © 1993 The Pilgrim Press.

78 Harmonization Copyright © 1965 Abingdon Press.

79 Copyright © 1989 by Hope Publishing Co., Carol Stream, IL 60188. All rights reserved. Used by permission.

80 Word alterations Copyright © 1992 The Pilgrim Press.

82 Words stanza 1 and 3 Copyright © 1983; Words stanza 2 Copyright © 1990 Jaroslav J. Vajda.

Psalms and Canticles

Service Music

Worship Resources

Author, Composer, and Source Index

Abe, Seigi (1890–1974) 162
Abelard, Peter (1079–1142) 385
Adams, Sarah Flower (1805–1848) 78, 606
The Agincourt Song, England, c. 1415 ....184, 209, 259
Ahle, Johann R. (1625–1673) 74
Ainger, Geoffrey (b. 1925) 152
Airs sur les hymnes sacrez, Paris, 1623 244
Akers, Doris M. (b. 1923) 293
Albright, William H. (b. 1944) 411
Alexander, Cecil F. (1818–1895) 31, 145, 171, 172
Alexander, James W. (1804–1859) 226
Alford, Henry (1810–1871) 256, 422
Alford, Janie (1887–1986) 267
Ambrose of Milan (340–397) 87
Anderson, Boris (20th cent.) 33
Anderson, Clare (20th cent.) 33
Anglo-Genevan Psalter, 1556 316
Aquinas, Thomas (c. 1225–1274) 339
Arias, Mortimer (b. 1924) 246
Arnatt, Ronald (b. 1930) 274
Atkinson, Frederick C. (1841–1896) 290, 336
Auza, Antonio (1915–1981) 246
Avila, Rubén Ruíz (b. 1945) 214
B. C. M. (20th cent.) 499
Bach, J. S. (1685–1750) 37, 60, 112, 140, 158, 179,
                                  202, 226, 375, 404, 480
Badillo, Pablo Fernández (b. 1919) 34
Bain, James Leith Macbeth (c. 1840–1925) 479
Baker, Henry W. (1821–1877) 248, 329, 469, 571
Baker, Theodore (1851–1934) 127, 421
Bancroft, Henry Hugh (1904–1988) 120
Barbauld, Anna Laetitia Aiken (1743–1825) 422
Baring-Gould, Sabine (1834–1924) 98
Barnby, Joseph (1838–1896) 58, 86, 98, 261
Barnes, Edward Shippen (1887–1958) 139
Batastini, Robert J. (b. 1942) 554
Bates, Katharine Lee (1859–1929) 594
Battersby, C. Maud (19th–20th cent.) 544
Bayler, Lavon (b. 1933) 170, 174, 215, 312, 421, 479, 615
Bayly, Albert F. (1901–1984) 64, 453
Beach, Curtis (1914–1993) 8, 558
Bechtel, Daniel (b. 1932) 583
Bede, The Venerable (673–735) 259
Beebe, David (b. 1931) 461
Beethoven, Ludwig van (1770–1827) 4
Bell, John (b. 1949) 150, 153, 515
Bell, Maurice F. (1862–1947) 6
Bello, Lois (b. 20th cent.) 142
Bennard, George (1873–1958) 195
Bennett, William S. (1816–1875) 22
Benoit, Paul (1893–1979) 396
Benson, Louis F. (1855–1930) 51
Bernard of Clairvaux (1090–1153) 226, 329
Biggs, E. Power (1906–1977) 259
Billings, William (1746–1800) 192
Birkland, Carol (b. 1946) 105, 353
Blanchard, Ferdinand Q. (1876–1968) 191
Bliss, Philip P. (1838–1876) 319, 438
Boberg, Carl (1859–1940) 35
Bode, John E. (1816–1874) 493
Bohemian Brethren's Kirchengesäng, 1566 6
Bonar, Horatius (1808–1889) 336, 489
Bonhoeffer, Dietrich (1906–1945) 413
Borthwick, Jane Laurie (1813–1897) 446, 488, 532, 609
Bortniansky, Dimitri (1752–1825) 50
Bourgeois, Louis (c. 1510–c. 1561) 7, 167
Bourne, George Hugh (1840–1925) 258

Bowie, Walter Russell (1882–1969) 613
Bowring, John (1792–1872) 103, 193, 194
Boyd, William (1847–1928) 328, 589
Bradbury, William B. (1816–1868) 207, 252, 327, 403, 505
Brandon, Don (b. 1956) 612
Brébeuf, Jean de (d. 1649) 151
Bridges, Matthew (1800–1894) 301, 352
Bridges, Robert (1844–1930) 218, 408
Bristol, Lee Hastings, Jr. (1923–1979) 168, 268
Brooks, Phillips (1835–1893) 133
Brorson, Hans A. (1694–1764) 296
Brumley, Albert E. (1905–1977) 595
Buchanan, Annabel Morris (1888–1983) 354, 378, 521
Buck, Percy C. (1871–1947) 221
Budry, Edmond L. (1854–1932) 253
Bunyan, John (1628–1688) 494
Burleigh, Harry T. (1866–1949) 394
Butler, Henry M. (1833–1918) 38
Byrd, Sidney H. (b. 1918) 341
Byrne, Mary E. (1880–1931) 451

Cameron, Catherine (b. 1927) 556
Campbell, John, Duke of Argyll (1845–1914) 466
Canitz, Friedrich R. L. von (1654–1699) 91
Cantate Domino, 1980 279
Cantionale Sacrum, Gotha, 1651 375
Carlson, Dosia (b. 1930) 179, 560, 574
Carmines, Al (b. 1936) 177
Carols Old and Carols New, Boston, 1916 125
Carr, Benjamin (1768–1831) 185
Carter, Sydney (b. 1915) 108, 210
Caswall, Edward (1814–1878) 86, 507
Catena, Osvaldo (20th cent.) 56
Catholische Geistliche Kirchengesäng, Cologne, 1559 ....127, 600
Cawood, John (1775–1852) 318
Chambers, H. A. (1880–1946) 129, 422
Chao, Tzu-chen (1888–1979) 424, 470
Charles, Elizabeth R. (1828–1896) 259
Chávez-Melo, Skinner (1944–1992) 121, 173, 174, 338, 528
Chesterton, Gilbert K. (1874–1936) 582
Chisholm, Thomas O. (1866–1960) 423
Chorley, Henry F. (1808–1872) 577
The Christian Harp, 1832 ....354, 378
The Christian Lyre, 1831 397
Christierson, Frank von (b. 1900) 429, 520
Christmas Carols New and Old, 1871 139
Clark, Francis A. (1851–1933) 444, 447
Clausnitzer, Tobias (1618–1684) 74
Clephane, Elizabeth C. (1830–1869) 190
Cleveland, J. Jefferson (1937–1986) 284, 490, 514, 570, 616
Clyde, Arthur G. (b. 1940) 112, 206, 280, 287
Cober, Kenneth L. (b. 1902) 311
Coffin, Charles (1676–1749) 115
Coffin, Henry Sloane (1877–1954) 116
Cole-Turner, Ronald S. (b. 1948) 325
A Collection of Sacred Ballads, 1790 ....547, 548
Collections of Motets or Antiphons, 1792 135
Colom M., Alfredo (1904–1971) 88
Columbia Harmony, Cincinnati, 1829 .....547, 548, 617
Colvin, Thomas S. (b. 1925) 498
Conkey, Ithamar (1815–1867) 193
Converse, Charles C. (1832–1918) 506
Copes, V. Earle (b. 1921) 264
Corbett, Cecil (b. 20th cent.) 291
Cory, Julia C. (1882–1963) 420
Cowper, William (1731–1800) 250, 412, 450
Crawford, James W. (b. 1936) 47

Croft, William (1678–1727) 25, 263, 278, 305, 359, 464
Croly, George (1780–1860) 290
Crosby, Fanny (1820–1915) 146, 197, 455, 473, 551
Crossman, Samuel (c. 1624–1684) 222
Crotch, William (1775–1847) 611
Crouch, Andraé (b. 1945) 14
Crown of Jesus Music II, 1862 125
Crüger, Johann (1598–1622) 40, 218, 334, 419, 480
Crull, August (1845–1923) 208
Crum, John M. C. (1872–1958) 238
Cummings, William H. (1831–1915) .144
Cutts, Peter (b. 1937) .270, 399, 552, 555
Cyprian of Carthage (d. 258) 163

Dakota Odowan, 1842 327
Dalles, John A. (b. 1954) 265, 586
Damon, Dan (b. 1955) 201, 302, 398, 406, 557
Dare, Elkanah Kelsay (1782–1826) .568
Darwall, John (1731–1789) 303
Das grosse Cantional, Darmstadt, 1687 74
Daw, Carl P., Jr. (b. 1944) 100, 167, 182, 270, 332, 355,
                                                         367, 401, 530
Day's The Whole Booke of Psalms, 1562 . . . . .211, 318, 342
Dearmer, Percy (1867–1936) 337
Deitz, Purd E. (1897–1987) 607
Diemer, Emma Lou (b. 1927) 227, 461
Dirksen, Richard Wayne (b. 1921) 71
Dix, William C. (1837–1898) 148, 159, 257, 484
Doane, George W. (1799–1859) 40
Doane, William H. (1832–1915) 197, 455, 456, 551
Doddridge, Philip (1702–1751) 491
Doran, Carol (b. 1936) 54, 176, 271
Dorsey, Thomas A. (1899–1993) 472
Douglas, C. Winfred (1867–1944) 89, 118, 119, 494, 605, 613
Douroux, Margaret J. (b. 1941) 188
Doving, Carl (1867–1937) 296
Downing, Edith Sinclair (b. 1922) 196, 356
Drese, Adam (1620–1701) 446
Duck, Ruth (b. 1947) 30, 36, 106, 110, 164, 168, 274, 343,
                                                357, 376, 439, 521, 554, 563
Duffield, S. W. (1843–1887) 385
Dunstan, Sylvia G. (1955–1993) 326, 350, 380, 384, 504, 509
Dwight, Timothy (1725–1817) 312
Dykes, John B. (1823–1876) . . .215, 248, 277, 281, 450, 507, 508

Edwards, Howard M., III (Rusty) (b. 1955) 180, 545
Edwards, John D. (1806–1885) 222, 426
Edwards, Robert L. (b. 1915) 565
Elderkin, George D. 160
Ellerton, John (1826–1893) 80, 95, 516, 577
Ellington, "Duke" (1899–1974) 602
Elliott, Charlotte (1789–1871) 207
Elvey, George J. (1816–1893) 8, 301, 350, 422
Emerson, Luther O. (1820–1915) 425
The English Hymnal, 1906 . . . . .334, 582
Erneuerten Gesangbuch, Stralsund, 1665 22
Escamilla, Roberto (b. 1931) 34, 65, 246
Eschbach, Douglas C. (b. 1960) 280
Eslinger, Elise S. (b. 1942) 34, 65, 246, 499
Este's Whole Book of Psalmes, 1592 516
Etzler, Carole A. (b. 1944) 501
The European Magazine and Review, 1792 77
Evans, David (1874–1948) 212, 390, 429, 451, 527
Everest, Charles W. (1814–1877) 204
Excell, Edwin O. (1851–1921) 547, 548, 617

F. B. P. (c. 16th cent.) 378
Faber, Frederick William (1814–1863) 23, 381
Fawcett, John (1739/40–1817) 77, 393
Fedak, Alfred V. (b. 1953) 431

Fellowship Hymn Book, 1910 418
Ferguson, John (b. 1941) 530
Ferguson, Manie Payne (b. 1850) 284
Fischer, William G. (1835–1912) 522
Fleischaker, Mary Frances (b. 1945) .123
Flemming, Friedrich F. (1778–1813) .518
Floríndez, Lorraine (b. 1926) 56
Fogg, Joan Collier (b. 1949) 608
Foley, Brian (b. 1919) 264
Fortunatus, Venantius Honorius (c. 535–c. 600) . .220, 221, 262
Fosdick, Harry Emerson (1878–1969) 436
Foster, Frederick W. (1760–1835) 68
The Foundery Collection, 1742 430
Francis of Assisi (1182–1226) 17
Franck, Johann (1618–1677) 334, 480
Franklin, Kirk (b. 20th cent.) 523
Frazier, R. Philip (1892–1964) 3
Freedom Is Coming, 1984 526
Freylinghausen's Geistreiches Gesangbuch, Halle, 1704 566
French "Processional," 15th century 116
Friedell, Harold (1905–1958) 337
Frostenson, Anders (b. 1906) 163
Fryson, Robert J. (1944–1994) 53
Funk's Genuine Church Music, 1832 .407

Gabaraín, Cesáreo (1936–1991) 173, 338, 528, 614
Gabriel, Charles H. (1856–1932) 442, 475
Gannett, William C. (1840–1923) 430
García, Juan Luis (b. 1935) 614
William Gardiner's Sacred Melodies, 1815 . . . . .361, 543
Garrett, Les (b. 1943) 84
Gastorius, Severus (fl. 1675) 415
Gauntlett, Henry J. (1805–1876) 145
Gay, Annabeth McClelland (b. 1925) 320, 435
Gay, William (b. 1920) 435
Geistliche Gesangbuchlein, Wittenberg, 1524 64
Geistliche Kirchengesäng, Cologne, 1623 . . . . .17, 27, 60
Geistreiches Gesangbuch, Darmstadt, 1698 446
Gerhardt, Paul (1607–1676) 94, 102, 226, 269, 404
Gertmenian, James (b. 1947) 20, 464
Gesangbuch der herzoglichen Wirtembergischen katholischen
     Hofkapelle, 1784 . . . . .12, 104, 213
Giardini, Felice de (1716–1796) 275
Gibbons, Kendyl L. R. (b. 1955) 552
Gibson, Colin (b. 1933) .141, 562, 569
Gieseke, Richard (b. 1952) 175
Gill, Thomas H. (1819–1906) 374
Gillard, Richard (b. 1953) 364, 539
Gladden, Washington (1836–1918) 503
Gläser, Carl G. (1784–1829) 42, 383, 575
Glaubund Liebesübung, Bremen, 1680 .68
Goss, John (1800–1880) 273, 567
Gottheil, Gustave (1827–1903) 10
Gottschalk, Louis Moreau (1829–1869) 63
Gould, John E. (1822–1875) 441
Graham, Fred (20th cent.) 564
Grant, Robert (1779–1838) 26, 185
Greatorex, Walter (1877–1949) 38
Green, Fred Pratt (b. 1903) 70, 140, 175, 261, 306, 323, 365,
                                                413, 425, 529, 555, 561
Gregory, Paul R. (b. 1920) 317, 538
Gregory the Great (540–604) 90, 187
Grenoble Antiphoner, 1753 204
Grieg, Edvard (1843–1907) 296
Grindal, Gracia (b. 1943) 9, 545
Grubb, Edward (1854–1939) 37
Gruber, Franz (1787–1863) 134
Gutiérrez–Achon, Raquel (b. 1927) 528, 578

Haddix, James L. (b. 1946) 426

Haile, Elizabeth (b. 20th cent.) 291
Hall, Sara M. de 544
Hampton, Calvin (1938–1984) 587
Hanaoka, Nobuaki (b. 1944) 5
Hancock, Eugene W. (b. 1929) 462
Handel, G. F. (1685–1759) 253, 491
Hankey, Katherine (1834–1911) 522
Harbaugh, Henry (1817–1867) 457
Harding, James P. (1850–1911) 157
Harkness, Georgia (1891–1974) 46
Hartunian, Vartan (b. 1915) 327
Hassler, Hans Leo (1564–1612) 130, 179, 202, 226
Hastings, Thomas (1784–1872) 19, 596
Hatch, Edwin (1835–1889) 292
Hatton, John (d. 1793) 300
Haugen, Marty (b. 1950) 107, 181, 581
Havergal, Frances Ridley (1836–1879) 448, 531
Havergal, William H. (1793–1870) .489
Haweis, Thomas (1734–1820) 36
Hawk, Jean Slates (b. 1925) 453
Hawkins, Ernest (1802–1868) 47, 308, 576
Hawks, Annie S. (1835–1918) 517
Haydn, Franz Joseph (1732–1809) 91, 307, 565
Haydn, J. Michael (1737–1806) 26
Heber, Reginald (1783–1826) 156, 157, 277, 346
Hedge, Frederick H. (1805–1890) 439, 512
Heermann, Johann (1585–1647) 513
Heiliges Lippen und Herzens Opfer, Stettin, 1778 208
Helmore, Thomas (1811–1890) 116
Hemy, Henri F. (1818–1888) 381
Herbert, George (1593–1633) 331
Herbst, Martin (1654–1681) 205
Hernaman, Claudia F. I. (1838–1898) 211
Hibbard, Esther (b. 1903) 203
Hildegard, Abbess of Bingen (12th cent.) 57
Himnario Metodista, 1968 327
Hobbs, Herbert G. (b. 1934) 413
Hodges, Edward (1796–1867) 4
Hodges, J. S. B. (1830–1915) 346
Hoffman, Elisha A. (1839–1929) 189, 471, 486
Hohu, Martha (b. 1907) 496
Holden, Oliver (1765–1844) 304
Holmes, Stephen W. (b. 20th cent.) .548
Holst, Gustav (1874–1934) 128
Hopkins, Edward J. (1818–1901) 80
Hopkins, John H. (1861–1945) 295
Hopp, Roy (b.1951) 313, 323, 529
Hopper, Edward (1818–1888) 441
Hopson, Hal H. (b. 1933) 186
Horvath, Theodore S. (b. 1919) 445
Hosmer, Frederick Lucian (1840–1929) 377, 603
How, William W. (1823–1897) 299, 315
Howard, Samuel (1710–1782) 483
Howe, Julia Ward (1819–1910) 610
Howells, Herbert (1892–1983) 408
Hu, Te-ngai (b. c. 1900) 470
Huber, Jane Parker (b. 1926) 21, 272, 278, 328, 371, 372,
                                         495, 535, 582, 588
Hudson, Ralph E. (1843–1901) 199
Hughes, John (1873–1932) 18, 436
Hull, Eleanor H. (1860–1935) 451
Hunter, Tom (b. 1946) 359
Huntington, Ronald (1929–1994) 20
Hurd, David (b. 1950) 93, 169, 171, 330, 356, 357
Hussey, Jennie Evelyn (1874–1958) 228
Hymn of the Hungarian Galley Slaves, 1674 445
The Hymnal, 1933 . . . . 488, 591, 607
The Hymnal 1982 66
Hymnal: A Worship Book, 1992 327
Hymns for the Young, 1836 252

Imakoma, Yasushige (b. 1926) 317
The Iona Community 29, 150, 273, 344, 515
Irvine, Jesse Seymour (1836–1887) 468
Isaak, Heinrich (c. 1450–1517) 94
Iverson, Daniel (1890–1977) 283

Jackson, Robert (1840–1914) 292
Jacob, Gordon (1895–1984) 479
Janzen, Jean (b. 1933) 57, 467, 600, 601
Jastrow, Marcus (20th cent.) 10
Jeffrey, J. Albert (1855–1929) 46
Jenkins, William Vaughan (1868–1920) 363
Jennings, Carolyn (b. 1936) 88, 155, 235, 340, 389, 392
Jeszensky, Károly (b. c. 1674) 445
Joachim, Pauli (1636–1708) 445
John of Damascus (c. 696–c. 754) 230, 245
Johnson, J. Rosamond (1873–1954) 593
Johnson, James Weldon (1871–1938) 593
Johnson, Joyce Finch (b. 1935) 2, 41, 154, 229, 282, 409,
                                         454, 497
Johnson, Nelsie T. (b. 1912) 161
Jones, Charles P. (1865–1949) 482
Jones, Joseph David (1827–1870) 260
Jones, William (1726–1800) 352
Judah, Daniel ben (b. c. 1400) 24
Jude, William H. (1851–1922) 172
Julian of Norwich (d. c. 1417) 467
Juncos, Manuel Fernández (1846–1928) 155

"K" in John Rippon's Selection of Hymns, 1787 407
Kaan, Fred (b. 1929) 347, 354, 388, 576
Katholisches Gesangbuch, 1828 86
Katholisches Gesangbuch, Vienna, c. 1774 . . . . .96, 276
Kawashima, Mas (20th cent.) 327
Keble, John (1792–1866) 96
Ken, Thomas (1637–1711) 100
Kennedy, Benjamin H. (1804–1889) 49
Kentucky Harmony, 1816 . . . . .89, 119
Kerr, Hugh T. (1872–1950) 366
Kethe, William (d. 1608) 7
Kirchengesäng, Psalmen und Geistlich Lieder,
    Nürnberg, 1608 130
Kirkland, Elaine (b. 1946) 335
Kirkland, Patrick M. (1857–1943) 255
Kirkpatrick, William J. (1838–1921) 228
Kitchin, George William (1827–1912) 198
Klug's Geistliche Lieder, 1535 374
Klug's Geistliche Lieder, 1543 187
Knapp, Phoebe P. (1839–1908) 473
Knapp, Shepherd (1873–1946) 534
Knapp, William (c. 1698–1768) 306
Knecht, Justin H. (1752–1817) 448
Kocher, Conrad (1786–1872) 28, 159
Koizumi, Isao (b. 1907) 72
Johann B. König, Harmonischer Liederschatz, 1738 324
Koyama, Shōzō (b. 1930) 317
Kremser, Edward (1838–1914) 421
Kumar, Satish 581

La Feillée's Méthode de plain chant, 1782 90
La Feillée's Nouvelle Méthode de Plain Chant, 1808 385
Laiana (Lorenzo Lyons) (1807–1886) 146, 252, 327
Landsberg, Max (1845–1928) 24
Lathbury, Mary A. (1841–1913) 321
Latin 111, 129, 135, 209, 241, 242, 268, 396, 400, 507
Leach, Richard D. (b. 1953) 201, 206
LeCroy, Anne (b. 1930) 93
Leech, Bryan Jeffery (b. 1931) 285
Lew, Timothy Tingfang (1892–1947) 333, 387
Lewis, David (b. 1916) 163

Lewis, Freeman (1780–1859) 225
Lewis-Butts, Magnolia (d. 1949) 288
Liliuokalani, Queen (1838–1917) 580
Lincoln, C. Eric (b. 1924) 443
Lindsley, Phil V. S. 239
Littledale, Richard F. (1833–1890) 289
Liturgy of St. James, 4th cent 345
Lloyd, William (1786–1852) 484
Lockwood, George (b. 1946) .338, 614
Loh, I-to (b. 1936) 33, 72
Longfellow, Samuel (1819–1892) 63, 432, 463
Loperena, William (b. 1935) 389, 392
Lovelace, Austin (b. 1919) 349
Robert Lowry's Bright Jewels for the Sunday School, 1869 . . .476
Lowry, Robert (1826–1899) 146, 382, 452, 476, 517, 563, 597
Lowry, Somerset T. C. (1855–1932) .542
Luce, Allena (19th cent.) 149
Luff, Alan (b. 1928) 373
Lum, Maryette H. 477
Luther, Martin (1483–1546) 130, 374, 439, 440
The Lutheran Book of Worship, 1978 . . . . .94, 130
Lvov, Alexis F. (1798–1870) 367, 577
Lynch, Thomas T. (1818–1871) 418
Lyon, Meyer (1751–1797) .24, 314, 373
Lyra Davidica, London, 1708 . . . . .233, 240
Lyte, Henry F. (1793–1847) 99

Macías, Rosa Martha Zárate (b. 20th cent.) 578
Maimonides, Moses (1130–1205) 24
Maker, Frederick C. (1844–1927) 190, 191, 502
Malan, H. A. César (1787–1864) 49
Manley, James K. (b. 1940) 286
Mann, A. H. (1850–1929) 145, 493
Mann, Newton (1836–1926) 24
Mant, Richard (1776–1848) 298
Maquiso, Elena G. (b. 1914) 97, 279
Marsh, Simeon B. (1798–1875) 546
Marshall, Jane (b. 1924) 61, 180, 370, 498, 512
Marshall, Madeleine Forell (b. 1946) 6, 22, 44, 50, 60, 67, 74,
91, 173, 269, 375, 404, 415, 440, 513, 566
Marshall, W. S. 284
Martin, Civilla D. (1869–1948) 460, 475
Martin, James F. D. (b. 1953) 114, 313
Martin, W. Stillman (1862–1935) 460
Martínez, Nicolás (1917–1972) 235
Martinez, Salvador T. (b. 1939) 29
Mason and Webb's Cantica Laudis, 1850 170
Mason, Lowell (1792–1872) 132, 224, 393, 489, 606
Lowell Mason's Modern Psalmody, 1839 . . . . .42, 383, 575
Mathams, Walter J. (1853–1932) 350
Matheson, George (1842–1906) 485
Matney, Mary Bryan (b. 1955) 540
Matsumoto, Sogo (1840–1903) 203
Matson, William (1833–1906) 465
Maule, Graham (b. 1958) 153
Maurus, Rhabanus (d. 856) 268
May, Janet W. (b. 20th cent.) 544
McAllister, Louise (1913–1960) 225
McDougall, Alan (1895–1964) 93
McFarland, Samuel (fl. 1816) 256
McGuire, David Rutherford (1929–1971) 327
McIntosh, Rigdon M. (1836–1899) 598
McKinstry, Anne (b. 1937) 109
McMane, Martie (b. 1943) 612
McNair, Jonathan (b. 1959) 5, 143, 151, 156, 254, 362, 363,
467, 590
Memmingen manuscript, 17th century 66
Mendelssohn, Felix (1809–1847) 144, 272, 315, 419
Mercer's Cluster, 1836 223
Messiter, Arthur H. (1834–1916) 55

Meyer, Marion M. (b. 1923) 69
Middleton, Jesse Edgar (1872–1960) 151
Milano, Roberto (b. 1936) 65, 389, 392
Miles, C. Austin (1868–1946) 237
Miller, Anabel S. (b. 1921) 227
Miller, Edward (1731–1807) 208, 414, 465
Milligan, J. Lewis (1876–1961) 120
Milman, Henry H. (1791–1868) 215
Milton, John (1608–1674) 16
"Misa Popular Nicaragüense," 20th century 340
Miwa, Genzō (b. 19th cent.) 137
Mohr, Joseph (1792–1848) 134
Monk, William H. (1823–1889) 28, 99, 159, 242
Montgomery, James (1771–1854) 104, 126, 219, 342, 508
Moore, William (19th cent.) 376, 556
Morales, F.S.C., Alfredo (20th cent.) 402
Morris, Kenneth (1917–1988) 41, 405
Morris, Sally Ann (b. 1952) 269, 540, 550
Morris, Stephen J. (b. 1956) 549
Morrow, J. T. 371
Moss, John (b. 1925) 137
Mote, Edward (1797–1874) 403
Moultrie, Gerard (1829–1885) 345
Münster Gesangbuch, 1677 44
Murray, James R. (1841–1905) 3, 124, 341
Murray, Shirley Erena (b. 1931) 58, 141, 231, 287, 297, 314,
562, 569, 579, 585, 587
Musical Relicks of the Welsh Bards, Dublin, 1784 425
Musikalisches Handbuch, Hamburg, 1690 115

Nägeli, Johann G. (1773–1836) 393
Nawahine, Robert (1868–1951) 496
Neale, John Mason (1818–1866) 116, 129, 184, 216, 217, 230,
241, 244, 245, 385, 400
Neander, Joachim (1650–1680) 22, 67, 68, 408, 566
Nebres, Fé (b. 1938) 97, 428
Neswick, Bruce (b. 1956) 194, 585
Neu Ordentlich Gesangbuch, 1646 37
Neumann, Gustav J. (b. 1888) 445
Neumark, Georg (1621–1681) 410
Neuvermehrtes Gesangbuch, Meiningen, 1693 . . . . . .272, 315, 513
The New Century Hymnal, 1995 . . . . .12, 17, 35, 39, 45, 46, 56, 62,
69, 73, 76, 87, 90, 105, 111, 115, 118, 149, 187, 209, 220, 221,
223, 240, 249, 253, 262, 268, 286, 332, 339, 344, 369, 391, 402,
487, 504, 578, 605, 739, 740
New England Psalm Singer 192
The New Hymnal for American Youth, 1930 439
The New Psalms and Hymns, 1901 157
Newbolt, Michael Robert (1874–1956) 198
Newton, John (1725–1807) 307, 547, 548
Ng, Greer Anne Wenh-In (b. 20th cent.) 333
Ni, Chi-pi (b. 1909) 477
Nichols, Kevin (b. 1929) 202
Nicholson, Sydney Hugo (1875–1947) 198
Nicolai, Philipp (1556–1608) .112, 158
Niedling, Johann (1602–1668) 60
Niedmann, Peter (b. 1960) 560
Niles, D. T. (1908–1970) 279
Nix-Allen, Verolga (b. 1933) 284, 490, 514, 616
Nixon, Darryl 163, 333
Noble, Thomas Tertius (1867–1953) 532
North, Frank Mason (1850–1935) 543

"O Antiphons," Latin, 6th–7th century 740
James O'Kelly's (1735–1826) Hymns and
Spiritual Songs, 1816 617
Oakeley, Frederick (1802–1880) 135
Oatman, Johnson, Jr. (1856–1922) 442
Olearius, Johannes (1611–1684) 101
Olivieri, Luis (b. 1937) 45, 389, 392

The 150 Psalms of David, Edinburgh, 1615 412
J. Oudaen's *David's Psalmen*, 1685 ....231, 232
Owen, William (1813–1883) 258
Oxenham, John (1852–1941) 394, 395

Palestrina, Giovanni Perluigi da (c. 1525–1594) 242
Palmer, Ray (1808–1887) 329
The Parish Choir, 1850 ....16, 537
Parker, Edwin (1836–1925) 63, 536
Parry, C. Hubert H. (1848–1918) 114
Parry, Joseph (1841–1903) 103
Patterson, Deborah (b. 1956) 368
Patterson, Joy F. (b. 1931) 108, 291
Peace, Albert L. (1844–1912) 485
Peacey, John R. (1896–1971) 266
Peek, Joseph Y. (1843–1911) 492
Peña, Vérne de la (b. 1959) 142, 217, 428, 615
Pensum Sacrum, Görlitz, 1648 375
Perera, Homero (20th cent.) 246
Perronet, Edward (1726–1792) 304
Petri's *Piae Cantiones*, 1582 ....57, 118
Phelps, Sylvanus Dryden (1816–1895) 452
Pierpoint, Folliott S. (1835–1917) 28
Amos Pilsbury's *United States Harmony*, 1799 568
Plainsong melody 64
Plainsong melody from *Processionalle*, Paris, 1697 339
Planas-Belfort, Dimas 39
Plenn, Doris (b. 20th cent.) 476
Plumptre, Edward H. (1821–1891) 55, 71
Porter, Phil (b. 1956) 335
Post, Marie J. (1919–1990) 364
Postlethwaite, R. Deane (20th cent.) 468
Pott, Francis (1832–1909) 242
Potter, Doreen (1925–1980) 347
Powell, Roger (b. 1914) 397
Praetorius, Michael (1571–1621) 57, 127, 241
Prentiss, Elizabeth P. (1818–1869) 456
Price, Charles P. (b. 1920) 66
Price, Frank W. (1895–1974) 387, 424, 470, 477
Prichard, Rowland H. (1811–1887) 182, 257, 355
Pritchard, T. C. L. (1885–1960) 468
Proulx, Richard (b. 1938) 9, 256, 259
Prudentius, Marcus Aurelius Clemens (348–410) 118
Psalmen und Geistliche Lieder, Nürnberg, 1608 130
Psalmodia Sacra, Gotha, 1715 .... 13, 122, 325, 326
Psalter und Harfe, 1876 327
Psalteriolum Cantionum Catholicarum, 1710 116
Pulkingham, Betty Carr (b. 1928) 364, 539
Purcell, Henry (1659–1695) 47, 308, 576
Purday, Charles Henry (1799–1885) 366, 466

Quinn, James, S.J. (b. 1919) 92

Radford, Jeffrey (b. 1953) ... 85, 136, 160, 322, 416, 458, 524, 604
Rambach, Johann J. (1694–1735) 324
Rankin, Jeremiah E. (1828–1904) 81
Rawson, George (1807–1889) 316
Redhead, Richard (1820–1901) 219, 250, 294
Redner, Lewis H. (1831–1908) 133
Rees, Timothy (1874–1939) 59
Reid, William W., Jr. (b. 1923) 390
Reimann's *Sammlung Alter und Neuer Melodien*, 1747 463
Reinagle, Alexander R. (1799–1877) 395
René, Nancy M. (b. 1942) 297
Joseph R. Renville's (1779–1846) *Dakota Hymn* 3, 341
Repp, Ray (b. 1942) 249
Rinkart, Martin (1586–1649) 419
Rippon, John (1751–1836) 304
Rist, Johann (1607–1667) 140
John Roberts' *Caniadaeth y Cysegr*, 1839 ....1, 427

Roberts, Daniel Crane (1841–1907) 592
Roberts, John (1807–1876) 240
Roberts, Leon C. (b. 20th cent.) 348
Robinson, Robert (1735–1790) 459
Rodigast, Samuel (1649–1708) 415
Röntgen, Julius (1855–1932) 23, 558
Rosas, Carlos (b. 1939) 39
Rossetti, Christina G. (1830–1894) 128, 165
Rossman, Vern 162
Routley, Erik (1917–1982) 247
Rowan, William P. (b. 1951) 83, 353, 583
Rowthorn, Jeffery (b. 1934) 308, 462
Rufty, Hilton (b. 1909) 265
Runyan, William M. (1870–1957) 423
Rush, Julian (b. 1936) 391
Ruspini, Louise 73
Russell, Francis Albert Rollo (1849–1914) 537

The Sacred Harp, 1844 ....254, 332
St. Francis of Assisi (1182–1226) 17
St. Patrick (372–466) 83
San, Lee Yu 557
Sandell, Lina (1832–1903) 487
Sarum Breviary, 1495 184
Sarum plainsong, mode I 87
Sarum plainsong, mode IV 111, 739, 740
Sateren, Leland (b. 1913) 76
Scagnelli, Peter J. (b. 1949) 187
Schalk, Carl F. (b. 1929) 32, 183, 220
Schicht, Johann Gottfried (1753–1823) 276
Schlegel, Katharina von (1697–?) 488
Schmidt, Vicki Vogel (b. 1945) 62
Schmolck, Benjamin (1672–1737) 67
Scholefield, Clement E. (1839–1904) 95
Schop, Johann (c. 1595–1667) 140
Schulz-Widmar, Russell (b. 1944) 361
Schumann, Robert (1810–1856) 531
Valentin Schumann's *Geistliche Lieder*, 1539 130
Schutmaat, Alvin (b. 1921) 214
Schütz, Johann J. (1640–1690) 6
Heinrich Schütz, (1585–1672) *Psalter*, 1628 601
Schwedler, Johann C. (1672–1730) 49
Scott, Lesbia (1898–1986) 295
Scott, R. B. Y. (1899–1987) 611
Scott-Gatty, Alfred (1847–1918) 533, 534, 535
Scottish Psalter, 1650 479
Scriven, Joseph (1819–1886) 506
Sears, Edmund H. (1810–1876) 131
Seerveld, Calvin (b. 1930) 113
Sensmeier, Randall (b. 1948) 343
Shaw, Martin F. (1875–1958) 31, 113, 238
Sheppard, Franklin L. (1852–1930) 21
Sherwin, William F. (1826–1888) 321
Showalter, Anthony J. (1858–1924) 471
Shurtleff, Ernest W. (1862–1917) 573
Sibelius, Jean (1865–1957) 488, 591, 607
Siena, Bianco da (d. 1434) 289
Sixteen Tune Settings, 1812 ....605, 613
Sleeth, Natalie (1930–1992) 433
Smallwood, Richard (b. 1948) 511
Smart, Henry T. (1813–1879) 126, 245, 400, 573, 574
Smith, Alfred M. (1879–1971) 443, 520
Smith, Elizabeth L. (1817–1898) 251
Smith, Emerson C. (20th cent.) 580
Smith, H. Percy (1825–1898) 365, 503
Smith, Walter C. (1824–1908) 1
Smith, William Farley (b. 1941) 525
Smyttan, George Hunt (1822–1870) 205
Sonafrank, Russell E., II (b. 1947) 549
Song Book for Sunday School, 1871 487

Sosa, Pablo D. (b. 1933) 65, 235, 544
Sotto, Angel 142
Southern Harmony, 1835 . . . . .78, 156, 223, 247, 349, 530, 598
Spafford, Horatio G. (1828–1888) 438
Stainer, John (1840–1901) 129
Stanford, Charles V. (1852–1924) 109, 561
Stennett, Samuel (1727–1795) 598
Sternhold, Thomas (d. 1549) 247
Stockton, John H. (1813–1877) 189
Stone, Lloyd (b. 1912) 591
Stone, Samuel J. (1839–1900) 386
Stookey, Laurence Hull (b. 1937) 394, 395
Stowe, Everett M. (20th cent.) 72
Strasbourg Psalter, 1545 251
Strathdee, Jim (b. 1941) 584
Studdert-Kennedy, Geoffrey A. (1883–1929) 89
Stuempfle, Herman G., Jr. (b. 1923) 550, 567
Su, Yin-Lan (1915–1937) 333
Sullivan, Arthur S. (1842–1900) 230, 377, 401, 538
Suppe, Gertrude C. (b. 1911) 121, 214
Swift, Donald (b. 1952) 147

Tabada, Grace R. (b. 1942) 428
Tabayoyong, Wesley Tactay (b. 1925) 234
Tallis, Thomas (c. 1505–1585) 100, 178, 509
Tarrant, William G. (1853–1928) 383
Nahum Tate and Nicholas Brady's *A New Version of the Psalms
    of David*, 1696 . . . . .481, 483
Taulé, Alberto V. (b. 1932) 121
Taylor, Cyril V. (1907–1991) 70, 266
Tennyson, Alfred (1809–1892) 414
Tersteegen, Gerhard (1697–1769) .50, 68
Teschner, Melchior (1584–1635) .102, 216
Tessier, Albert D. 188
Theodulph of Orléans (d. 821) 216, 217
Thompson, Mikkel (b. 20th cent.) 79
Thompson, Will L. (1847–1909) 449
Threlfall, Jennette (1821–1880) 213
Thring, Godfrey (1823–1903) 301
Thrupp, Dorothy A. (1779–1847) 252
Thurman, Howard (1899–1981) 584
Tindley, Charles Albert (1851–1933) 444, 447
Tisserand, Jean (d. 1494) 244
Tochter Sion, Cologne, 1741 . . . . .243, 542
Tollefson, Paulette (b. 1950) 15
Tomer, William G. (1833–1896) 81
Toplady, Augustus M. (1740–1778) 596
Torii, Chûgorô (b. 1898) 137
Tóth, William (1905–1963) 445
Traditional
    African-American . . .2, 75, 85, 136, 154, 161, 229, 239, 282,
            310, 322, 330, 369, 394, 409, 416, 454, 458, 474,
            478, 490, 497, 500, 501, 511, 514, 519, 524, 525,
                                553, 572, 599, 604, 616
    Caribbean 236
    Chinese 470
    Confucian Dacheng 424
    Dutch 23, 421, 558
    English 21, 31, 51, 110, 135, 139, 143, 148, 153, 275,
            311, 362, 363, 401, 432, 434, 579
    Finnish 390
    French 125, 138, 151, 238, 250, 294, 345
    German 105, 123, 127, 129, 241, 276, 384, 510
    Ghanaian 498
    Greek 739
    Hebrew 10, 314
    Irish 109, 206, 451, 504
    Jamaican 347
    Japanese 5, 72, 203
    Mexican 402, 499

Mozarabic 94
Native American 3, 341
Netherlands 421
Norwegian 56, 296
Philippine 234
Pi-po 33
Puerto Rican 45, 149, 155
Scottish 200, 344
Sicilian 77
Silesian 44
Slovak 431
South African 360, 437, 526
Swedish 35, 106, 487
Swiss 418
Taiwanese 33
United States 52, 124, 223, 407, 521, 570, 610
Urdu 48
Visayan 615
Welsh 1, 76, 82, 92, 425, 484, 582
Yigdal 24, 373
Trente quatre Pseaumes, Geneva, 1551 . . . . .7, 101, 167, 251,
                                                                                    358, 611
Trier Gesangbuch, 1695 384
Troeger, Thomas H. (b. 1945) 7, 16, 54, 169, 176, 178, 254,
                                                            271, 301, 400, 411, 427, 568
Troutbeck, John (1832–1899) 140
Turner, Jet (1928–1984) 337
Tuttiett, Lawrence (1825–1897) 469
Tweedy, Henry Hallam (1868–1953) .263

Union Harmony, 1836 265
United Presbyterian Book of Psalms, 1871 13

Vajda, Jaroslav J. (b. 1919) 32, 82, 183, 431
Valerius, *Nederlandtsch Gedenkclanck*, 1626 420
van Dyke, Henry (1852–1933) 4
Vaughan Williams, Ralph (1872–1958) 17, 27, 51, 110, 123,
                                        138, 182, 255, 257, 262, 289, 299, 331, 345,
                                        355, 432, 434, 510, 579, 586
Victor, János (1860–1937) 327
Vinluan, Vivencio L. (b. 1937) 234
Vories, William M. (1880–1964) 589
Vulpius, Melchior (c. 1560–1615) 64, 603

L. J. W., in *The Sunny Side*, 1875 518
John Francis Wade's *Cantus Diversi*, c. 1743 135
Walford, William (1772–1850) 505
Wallace, William V. (1812–1865) 166
Walter, Howard Arnold (1883–1918) .492
Walter, William (1825–1893) 164, 298
Walther, Johann (1496–1570) 64
Walton, James G. (1821–1905) 381
Walworth, Clarence Alphonsus (1820–1900) 276
Ward, Samuel A. (1847–1903) 594
Warner, Anna B. (1820–1915) 327
Warren, George W. (1828–1902) .372, 592
Watts, Isaac (1674–1748) 12, 25, 27, 132, 199, 200, 224, 225,
                                                    247, 281, 300, 379, 382, 511
Weaver, John (b. 1937) 559
Webb, Benjamin (1819–1885) 259
Webb, George J. (1803–1887) 609
Webster, Bradford Gray (1898–1991) 212
Weissel, Georg (1590–1635) 117
Welch, Celene (b. 1949) 196
Wesley, Charles (1707–1788) 42, 43, 122, 144, 160, 233, 260,
                                                                    303, 305, 546
Wesley, Samuel S. (1810–1876) 386, 387, 388
Wesson, Jan (b. 1925) 541
Westbrook, Francis B. (1903–1975) 48
Westendorf, Omer (b. 1916) 76, 396

Wetzel, Richard D. (b. 1935) 152
Whitfield, Frederick (1829–1904) 52
Whitney, Maurice C. (1909–1984) 165
Whitney, Rae (b. 1927) 510
Whittier, John Greenleaf (1807–1892) 166, 502, 533
Wiant, Bliss (1895–1975) 470
Widestrand, Olle (b. 1906) 163
Wile, Frances W. (1878–1939) 434
Wilhelm, August, II 375
Williams, David McK. (1887–1978) 277
Williams, Peter (1722–1796) 18, 19
Williams, Robert (1781–1821) 240
Williams, Thomas J. (1869–1944) 267
Williams, William (1717–1791) 18, 19
Aaron Williams' New Universal Psalmodist, 1770 . . . . . .312, 379,
588
Thomas Williams' Psalmodia Evangelica, 1789 117
Willis, Richard S. (1819–1900) 44, 131
Wilson, Hugh (1766–1824) 481
Wilson, John W. (1905–1991) 309
Winkworth, Catherine (1827–1878) 101, 102, 117, 130, 158,
324, 334, 410, 419, 480

Winter, Miriam Therese (b. 1938) 15, 17, 28, 119, 575, 594
Witt, Christian F. (c. 1660–1716) 13, 122, 325, 326
Wong, W. H. (b. 1917) 424
Woodbury, Isaac B. (1819–1858) 457
Woodward, George R. (1848–1934) 66, 232, 241
Wordsworth, Christopher (1807–1885) 61, 66, 243
Work, John W., II (b. 1901) 154
Wortman, Denis (1835–1922) 358
Wren, Brian (b. 1936) . . .11, 79, 186, 294, 309, 320, 349, 362, 399,
417, 527, 559, 564, 590, 608
Wubbena, Jan Helmut (b. 1947) 413
Wyeth's Repository of Sacred Music, 1813 . . . . 59, 459

Y Perl Cerddoral, 1852 258
Yamaguchi, Tokuo (20th cent.) 72
Ylvisaker, John (b. 1937) 351
Young, Carlton R. (b. 1926) 11, 30, 78, 417
Young, John F. (1820–1885) 134
Yūki, Kō (b. 1896) 162

Zinzendorf, Nicolaus Ludwig von (1700–1760) 446
Zundel, John (1815–1882) 43, 368, 495

METRICAL INDEX

Short Meter
S.M. (6.6.8.6.)
DENNIS 393
FESTAL SONG 164, 298
LAKE ENON 457
ST. BRIDE 483
ST. MICHAEL 611
ST. THOMAS 312, 379, 380, 588
SCHUMANN 170
TRENTHAM 292

Short Meter with Refrain
S.M. with Refrain (6.6.8.6. with refrain)
CHRISTPRAISE RAY 54
MARCHING TO ZION 382
MARION 55
VINEYARD HAVEN 71

Short Meter Double
S.M.D. (6.6.8.6.D.)
DIADEMATA 8, 301, 350
ICH HALTE TREULICH STILL 404
TERRA BEATA 21

Common Meter
C.M. (8.6.8.6.)
AMAZING GRACE (NEW BRITAIN) 547, 548, 617
ANTIOCH 132
AZMON 42, 383, 575
BEATITUDO 450
CHATHAM 555
CHRISTIAN LOVE 396
CHRISTMAS 491
CORONATION 304
CRAVEN 196
CRIMOND 468

DUNDEE 412
DUNLAP'S CREEK 256
EVAN 489
GRÄFENBERG 40
LAND OF REST 354, 378, 521
MARTYRDOM 200, 481
MCKEE 394
MORNING SONG 119, 605
NEW BRITAIN 547, 548, 617

NUN DANKET ALL' (GRÄFEN-BERG) 40
RICHMOND 36
ST. AGNES 281, 507, 508
ST. ANNE 25, 278, 359
ST. COLUMBA 109
ST. FLAVIAN 211, 318, 342
ST. PETER 395
ST. STEPHEN 352
SERENITY 166
SMALLWOOD 511
THE BROOK CHERITH 477
WINCHESTER OLD 516

Common Meter Extended
C.M. Extended (8.6.8.6. extended)
MURRAY 287

Common Meter with Refrain
C.M. with Refrain (8.6.8.6. with refrain)
DUNCANNON 228
HUDSON 199
MARTIN 460
O HOW I LOVE JESUS 52
PROMISED LAND 598
WATER OF BAPTISM 169
WORDS OF LIFE 319

Common Meter Double
C.M.D. (8.6.8.6.D.)
CAROL 131
CONSOLATION 247
ELLACOMBE 12, 104, 213
FOREST GREEN 110, 434
KINGSFOLD 51
MARIAS LOVSÅNG 106
MATERNA 594
NOEL 401
OLD 22ND 316
OPEN DOOR 529
ST. MATTHEW 263, 464
SHEPHERDS' PIPES 320
TALLIS' THIRD TUNE 178, 509
WINSTON-SALEM 550

Long Meter
L.M. (8.8.8.8.)
BAHAY KUBO 234
BOURBON 225
CANONBURY 531
CONDITOR ALME SIDERUM 111, 739, 740
DANBY 432
DE TAR 587
DEO GRACIAS 184, 209, 259
DEUS TUORUM MILITUM 204
DICKINSON COLLEGE 168, 268
DISTRESS 254
DUKE STREET 300
ERHALT UNS, HERR 187
GATHER 335
GERMANY (GARDINER) 361, 543
GONFALON ROYAL 221
HAMBURG 224
HANCOCK 462

HERR JESU CHRIST, DICH ZU
UNS WEND 375
HESPERUS 329, 469, 571
HURSLEY 96
KEDRON 568
KENTRIDGE 175
MARYTON 365, 503
O WALY WALY 362, 363
OLD FIRST 69
OLD HUNDREDTH 7
PENTECOST 328, 589
PUER NOBIS NASCITUR 57, 241
RELIANCE 280
ROCKINGHAM 208, 414, 465
ST. DROSTANE 215
SEED OF LIFE 83
SPLENDOR PATERNAE 87
TALLIS' CANON 100
TRURO 117
TRYGGARE KAN INGEN VARA
487
VERBUM DEI 353
VOM HIMMEL HOCH 130
WAREHAM 306
WHEN JESUS WEPT 192
WINCHESTER NEW 115
WOODWORTH 207

Long Meter with Refrain
L.M. with Refrain (8.8.8.8. with refrain)
HIGHER GROUND 442
LINSTEAD 347
SOLID ROCK 403
ST. CATHERINE 381
VENI EMMANUEL 116

Long Meter Double
L.M.D. (8.8.8.8.D.)
SCHMÜCKE DICH 334
SWEET HOUR 505
TRINITY CAROL 399
WEXFORD CAROL 206

4.10.10.10.4.
ORA LABORA 532

5.4.6.7.7.
ROEDER 32

5.5.5.5.
HALAD 279

5.5.5.5.D.
HSUAN P'ING 424

5.5.5.6.
STITELER 406

5.5.6.5.6.5.6.5. with refrain
JUDAS MACCABEUS 253

5.5.8.8.5.5.
SEELENBRÄUTIGAM 446

5.5.9.D. with refrain
LEANING 471

5.5.10.D.
TENDERNESS 569

5.6.6.6.8.8.8.6.
IDA 608

5.6.8.5.5.8.
SCHÖNSTER HERR JESU 44

5.6.10.D.
TWILIGHT 398

5.7.8.7. with refrain
STEAL AWAY 599

6.4.5.5.4.6.
JESUS IS HERE 348

6.4.6.4. with refrain
NEED 517

6.4.6.4.D.
BREAD OF LIFE 321

6.4.6.4.6.6.4.
MORE LOVE TO YOU 456

6.4.6.4.6.6.4.4.
SOMETHING FOR JESUS 452

6.4.6.4.6.6.4.5.
LOVE'S OFFERING 536

6.4.6.4.6.6.6.4.
BETHANY 606

6.5.6.5.
MERRIAL 98

6.5.6.5.D.
KING'S WESTON 255, 586

6.5.6.5.D. with refrain
ST. GERTRUDE 377

6.5.6.5.6.6.6.5.
ST. DUNSTAN'S 494

6.5.6.5.7.7.
KATHERINE 177

6.6.4.6.6.6.4.
ITALIAN HYMN 275

6.5.6.5.6.6.5.7.8.6.
JESU, MEINE FREUDE 480

6.6.6.6.
SAIPAN 323

6.6.6.6.D. with refrain
ALABANZA 34

6.6.6.6.4.4.4.4.
CAMANO 9

6.6.6.6.6.5.6.5.
MONING 97

6.6.6.6.6.6.
LAUDES DOMINI 86, 261
LORD, MAKE ME MORE HOLY 75

6.6.6.6.8.8.
DARWALL'S 148TH 303

6.6.6.6.8.8.8.
RHOSYMEDRE 222, 426

6.6.7.7.7.8.5.5.
IN DULCI JUBILO 129

6.6.8.4.D.
LEONI 24, 314, 373

6.6.8.6.6.8.3.3.6.6.
WUNDERBARER KÖNIG 68

6.6.10. with refrain
GIVE ME JESUS 409

6.6.11.D.
DOWN AMPNEY 289

6.6.11.6.6.11.D.
THE ASH GROVE 76

6.7.6.6.
THROCKMORTON 302

6.7.6.7.
WHITNEY 165

6.7.6.7.D.
VRUECHTEN 231, 232

6.7.6.7.6.6.6.6.
DARMSTADT 513
NUN DANKET 419
O GOTT, DU FROMMER GOTT
(DARMSTADT) 513
STEADFAST 37

6.7.6.8.D. with refrain
ROSAS 39

6.7.7.6.
LILIUOKALANI 580

6.7.7.7.7.6.6.
SAKURA 5

7.5.7.5.
IMAYO 203

7.5.7.5.D.
TOKYO 72

7.5.7.5.8.7.5.
IVERSON 283

7.6.7.6.
MARY'S CHILD 152

7.6.7.6. with refrain
NEAR THE CROSS 197
ROYAL OAK 31

7.6.7.6.D.
ANGEL'S STORY 493
AURELIA 386, 387, 388
BOUNDLESS MERCY 265

ES FLOG EIN KLEINS WALD
VÖGELEIN 66
EULOGIA 217
KING'S LYNN 579
LANCASHIRE 245, 573, 574
LLANGLOFFAN 582
MEIRIONYDD 484
MUNICH 272, 315
NYLAND 390
PASSION CHORALE 179, 202, 226
POST STREET 201
ST. KEVIN 230
ST. THEODULPH 102, 216
SALLEY GARDENS 504
WEBB 609

7.6.7.6.D. with refrain
HANKEY 522

7.6.7.6.6.6.3.3.6.
MAOZ TSUR 10

7.6.7.6.6.6.7.6.
TOLLEFSON 15

7.6.7.6.6.7.6.
ES IST EIN' ROS 127

7.6.7.6.7.6.9. with refrain
ASCENSIUS 239

7.6.7.6.7.7.6.
ES IST EIN' ROS' 600
PSALM 84 601

7.6.8.6.8.6.8.6.
ST. CHRISTOPHER 190, 191

7.7.6.7.7.8.
INNSBRUCK 94
(NUN RUHEN ALLE WÄLDER)

7.7.7.5.
ANDERSON 61

7.7.7.5.5.
MAUNDY THURSDAY 227

7.7.7.6.6.6.6.6.
KEEP YOUR LAMPS 369

7.7.7.7.
DANDANSOY 615
GOTT SEI DANK 566
HEINLEIN 205
INNOCENTS 16, 537
MANTON 512
MERCY 63
NUN KOMM DER HEIDEN
HEILAND 64
ORIENTIS PARTIBUS 138, 250, 294
SAVANNAH 430
THE CALL 331
TŌA-SĪA 33
VIENNA 448

7.7.7.7. with alleluias
EASTER HYMN 233
GWALCHMAI 260
LLANFAIR 240

7.7.7.7. with refrain
DIX 28
ELDERKIN 160
GLORIA (LES ANGES DANS NOS
CAMPAGNES)125
JESUS LOVES ME 327
LES ANGES DANS NOS
CAMPAGNES 125

7.7.7.7.D.
ABERYSTWYTH 103
FALCONE 271
MABUNE 162
MARTYN 546
ST. GEORGE'S WINDSOR 422
SPANISH HYMN 185

7.7.7.7.D. with refrain
MENDELSSOHN 144

7.7.7.7.6.7.8.7.
ANNIKA'S DANCE 180

7.7.7.7.7.
HENDON 49

7.7.7.7.7.7.
DIX 159
PILOT 441
REDHEAD NO. 76 219
TOPLADY 596

7.7.7.7.8.8.9.6. with refrain
SOME DAY 447

7.7.8.7.
ENTER, REJOICE 73

7.7.10.D.
PEACE LIKE A RIVER 478

7.8.7.8.7.7.
GROSSER GOTT, WIR LOBEN
DICH 276

7.8.7.8.8.8.
LIEBSTER JESU 74

7.8.8.7.D. with refrain
NUEVA CREACION 614

7.8.8.11.
JOSEPH LIEBER, JOSEPH MEIN
105

8.4.7.8.4.7.
HAYDN 91

8.4.8.4.8.8.8.4.
AR HYD Y NOS 82, 92, 425

8.5.8.3.
WESTRIDGE 113

8.5.8.5. with refrain
GO DOWN, MOSES 572
PASS ME NOT 551

8.5.8.5.D.
OGONTZ 560

8.6.8.3. with refrain
I WANT TO BE A CHRISTIAN 454

8.6.8.6.6.
DOVE OF PEACE 349

8.6.8.6.7.6.8.6.
ST. LOUIS 133

8.6.8.6.8.6.
BROTHER JAMES' AIR 479
MORNING SONG 89, 613
NEW BEGINNINGS 540

8.6.8.6.8.8.
O JESU 463

8.6.8.6.8.8. with refrain
UNE JEUNE PUCELLE 151

8.6.8.6.8.8.8.6.
THE STAFF OF FAITH 418

8.6.8.8.6.
REST 502

8.6.8.8.6.6.
REPTON 114

8.7. with refrain (8.7.)
SOMOS PUEBLO 340

8.7.8.7.
AUSTIN 583
CHARLESTOWN 78
DOMINUS REGIT ME 248
FOR THE BREAD 264
GALILEE 172
GLORY, GLORY 2
QUEM PASTORES 123
RATHBUN 193
SERVANT SONG 364, 539
STUTTGART 13, 122, 325, 326
TOMTER 194

8.7.8.7.D.
ABBOT'S LEIGH 70
AUSTRIAN HYMN 307, 565
AUTHORITY 176
BEACH SPRING 332
BEECHER 43, 368, 495
BRADBURY 252
CENTRAL 235
CONSTANTINE 20
EBENEZER (TON-Y-BOTEL) 267
ENDLESS SONG 476, 563
ERIE 506
ESPERANZA 122
HOLY MANNA 376, 556
HYFRYDOL 182, 257, 355
HYMN TO JOY 4
IN BABILONE 23, 558
JEFFERSON 530
JOEL 269
LADUE CHAPEL 274
LET US HOPE 461
LUX EOI 538
NETTLETON 59, 459
NEW REFORMATION 371
OFFERING 453
OMNI DIE 384

PLEADING SAVIOR 397
PROCESSION 411
PROMISE 433
RAQUEL 174
SCARLET RIBBONS 153
SILVER CREEK 313
TALAVERA TERRACE 562
WEISSE FLAGGEN 243, 542

8.7.8.7. with refrain
BLESSED QUIETNESS 284
HANSON PLACE 597
NEW DIMENSIONS 391

8.7.8.7. with response
SPRING WOODS 549

8.7.8.7.3.3.7.
MICHAEL 408

8.7.8.7.4.4.7.
UNION SEMINARY 337

8.7.8.7.4.7.
BRYN CALFARIA 258

8.7.8.7.4.7.4.7.
ZION 19

8.7.8.7.6.
BRIDEGROOM 270, 552

8.7.8.7.6.6.6.6.7.
EIN' FESTE BURG (ISOMETRIC) 439
EIN' FESTE BURG (RHYTHMIC) 440

8.7.8.7.6.8.6.7.
GREENSLEEVES 148

8.7.8.7.7.
ST. ANDREW 171

8.7.8.7.7.7.
IRBY 145
SILVER SPRING 183
UNSER HERRSCHER 67

8.7.8.7.7.7.8.8.
MAGYAR 445
PSALM 42 101

8.7.8.7.8.7.
FORTUNATUS NEW 220
JULION 356, 357
LAUDA ANIMA (PRAISE MY SOUL) 273, 567
PICARDY 345
REGENT SQUARE 126, 400
SICILIAN MARINERS 77
WESTMINSTER ABBEY 47, 308, 576

8.7.8.7.8.7.7.
CWM RHONDDA 18, 436
DIVINUM MYSTERIUM 118
WAS GOTT TUT 415

8.7.8.7.8.7.8.6.
KÔRIN 137

8.7.8.7.8.8.7.
MIT FREUDEN ZART 6
NUN FREUT EUCH 374
TALITHA CUMI 545

8.7.8.7.8.8.7.7.
ERMUNTRE DICH 140

8.8. with refrain (10.7.6.)
LOPERENA 389

8.8.4.4.6. Triple
DEN STORE HVIDE FLOK 296

8.8.4.4.8.8. with alleluias
LASST UNS ERFREUEN 17, 27

8.8.5.5.3.3. with refrain
O GOD MY GOD 515

8.8.7.8.8.7.4.8.4.8.
WIE SCHÖN LEUCHTET 158

8.8.8. with alleluias
GELOBT SEI GOTT 603
O FILII ET FILIAE 244
VICTORY 242

8.8.8.5.
JACOB'S LADDER 500, 501

8.8.8.6.
QUEM PASTORES 510
SIXTH NIGHT 431

8.8.8.6. with refrain
OLD SHIP OF ZION 310

8.8.8.7.D. with refrain
CHUQUISACA 246

8.8.8.8.6.
ST. MARGARET 485

8.8.8.8.8.
ANDREW 467

8.8.8.8.8.8.
SUSSEX CAROL 143

8.8.8.9.
African-American spiritual 490
ROLLINGBAY 79

8.8.8.9. with refrain
MARTINEZ 29

8.8.8.10.
GUIDE MY FEET 497

8.8.8.12. with refrain
YES, GOD IS REAL 405

8.9.5.5.7. with refrain
GARDEN 237

8.9.8.5.
YARNTON 564

8.9.8.8.9.8.6.6.4.8.8.
WACHET AUF 112

8.10.10. with refrain
PESCADOR DE HOMBRES 173

8.11.6.7.7.7.7.
MIKOTOBA 317

9.4.9.4. with refrain
I'LL FLY AWAY 595

9.6.9.6.6.
CAROL OF HOPE 435

9.6.9.9.9.6.
LACQUIPARLE 3, 341

9.7.9.6.D.
BORNING CRY 351

9.8.8.9. with refrain
GOD BE WITH YOU 81

9.8.9.8.
BEGINNINGS 417
EUCHARISTIC HYMN 346
ST. CLEMENT 95

9.8.9.8.D.
RENDEZ À DIEU 167

9.8.9.8.6.8.9.8.8.
TABADA 428

9.8.9.8.8.7.8.9.
REJOICE, REJOICE 107

9.8.9.8.8.8.
NEUMARK 410
O DASS ICH TAUSEND ZUNGEN HÄTTE 324

9.8.9.8.9.9.
ST. PETERSBURG 50

9.9.9.5. with refrain
DOWN AT THE CROSS 189

9.9.9.6.
O HOLY DOVE 285

9.9.9.9.
SHENG EN 333

9.9.9.9.9.9.
YISU NE KAHA 48

9.10.10.9.
AMSTEIN 559

9.10.11.9.
WESTCHASE 11

9.11.9.11. with refrain
SWEET, SWEET SPIRIT 293

10.4.10.4.10.10.
SANDON 366, 466

10.6.10.6.8.8.8.6.
ALL IS WELL 311

10.7.10.7. with refrain
I AM YOURS 455

10.8.8.8.10.
O HEILIGER GEIST (O JESULEIN
SÜSS) 60
O JESULEIN SÜSS 60

10.9.10.8.D. with refrain
ID Y ENSEÑAD 528

10.9.10.9. with refrain
ORWIGSBURG 486

10.10. with refrain
CRUCIFER 198
LET US BREAK BREAD 330

10.10.6.6.10.
DIFFERENT SONG 150

10.10.9.10.
SLANE 451

10.10.10. with alleluias
ROBINSON 297

10.10.10.4.
CAMACUA 544
ENGELBERG 561
SINE NOMINE 299

10.10.10.7. with refrain
JONES 482

10.10.10.10.
ELLERS 80
EVENTIDE 99
LE P'ING 470
MORECAMBE 290, 336
NATIONAL HYMN 372, 592
O QUANTA QUALIA 385
SHELDONIAN 266
SURSUM CORDA 443, 520
TOULON 251, 358
WILDERNESS 557
WOODLANDS 38

10.10.10.10. with refrain
HOSANNA 214

10.10.10.10.10.10.
FINLANDIA 488, 591, 607
ROSEBERRY 585

10.10.11.7.7.
MANGLAKAT 142

10.10.11.11.
HANOVER 305
LYONS 26

10.11.10.12.
NEW HOPE 343

10.12.10.10.
DOUROUX 188

10.12.10.12.
FENNVILLE 554

11.7.11.7. with refrain
SOFTLY AND TENDERLY 449

11.8.11.8.8.
NEIGHBOR 541

11.8.11.9. with refrain
VILLE DU HAVRE 438

11.10.8.7.11.
WONDERFUL CHILD 136

11.10.10.11.
NOËL NOUVELET 238

11.10.11.9.
RUSSIAN HYMN 367, 577

11.10.11.10.
ANCIENT OF DAYS 46
BENJAMIN 590
BONHOEFFER 413
CHARTERHOUSE 212, 429, 527
MORNING STAR 157
PERFECT LOVE 58
REVERSI 141
WALKER 156
WELWYN 533, 534, 535

11.10.11.10. with refrain
ESTE ES EL DIA 65
FAITHFULNESS 423
O STORE GUD 35

11.10.11.10.10.
PEEK 492

11.11.11.5.
HERZLIEBSTER JESU 218
INTEGER VITAE 518
MIGHTY SAVIOR 93

11.11.11.11.
ADORO TE DEVOTE 339
ANNIVERSARY SONG 370
AWAY IN A MANGER (MÜLLER)
124
FOUNDATION 407
HOUGHTON 30
ST. DENIO 1, 427

11.11.11.11. with refrain
GLAD TIDINGS 146
NU OLI (GLAD TIDINGS) 146

11.11.12.6.
CHRISTE SANCTORUM 90

11.11.12.12.
TAULE 121

11.12.12.10.
NICAEA 277

12.9.12.12.9.
WONDROUS LOVE 223

12.11.9.10. with refrain
WORLD PEACE PRAYER 581

12.11.12.11.
KREMSER 420, 421

12.12. with refrain
LOS MAGOS 155

12.12.12.12.D.
CRISTO ES LA PEÑA 45

13.7.13.7. with refrain
NEED OF PRAYER 519

13.13.D.11.11.D.
POR LA MAÑANA 88

14.14.4.7.8.
LOBE DEN HERREN 22

Irregular
(Irr.)
AMEN 161
ASCENSION 120
ASSURANCE 473
BATTLE HYMN OF THE
REPUBLIC 610
CRANHAM 128
EN SANTA HERMANDAD 392
GLORIOUS IS YOUR NAME 53
GRAND ISLE 295
I WANT TO BE READY 616
I'M SO GLAD 474
I'VE GOT A FEELING 458
JUDAS AND MARY 108, 210
KASTAAK 291
LATTIMER 525
LET IT BREATHE 288
LIFT EVERY VOICE 593
LIGHT OF THE WORLD 584
LIGHTBEAMS 163
NAWAHINE 496
ONLY STARTED 437
PASTORES A BELEN 149
PUES SI VIVIMOS 499
SHARE THE SPIRIT 62
SIYAHAMBA 526
SONG OF REJOICING 612
SPARROW 475
SPIRIT 286
STILLE NACHT 134
THANK YOU, JESUS 41
THE OLD RUGGED CROSS 195
THIS IS THE DAY 84
THIS JOY 524
THUMA MINA 360
TRUST IN THE LORD 416
UNA ESPIGA 338
WE SHALL OVERCOME 570
WERE YOU THERE 229
WHITFIELD 309
WHY WE SING 523
WOKE UP THIS MORNING 85

Irregular with Refrain
(Irr. with refrain)
ADESTE FIDELES 135
AFTON WATER 344

BALM IN GILEAD 553
BRING FORTH 181
BY AND BY 444
CHEREPONI 498
COME SUNDAY 602

DUST AND ASHES 186
FLORINDEZ 56
LITTLE BABY 147
MY TRIBUTE 14
PEACE, MY FRIENDS 249

PRECIOUS LORD 472
PROPHESY 578
SALVE FESTA DIES 262
THE FIRST NOWELL 139

TUNE INDEX

ABBOT'S LEIGH 70
ABERYSTWYTH 103
ADESTE FIDELES 135
ADORO TE DEVOTE 339
AFTON WATER 344
ALABANZA 34
ALL IS WELL 311
AMAZING GRACE (NEW BRITAIN) 547, 548, 617
AMEN 161
AMSTEIN 559
ANCIENT OF DAYS 46
ANDERSON 61
ANDREW 467
ANGEL'S STORY 493
ANNIKA'S DANCE 180
ANNIVERSARY SONG 370
ANTIOCH 132
AR HYD Y NOS 82, 92, 425
ASCENSION 120
ASCENSIUS 239
ASSURANCE 473
AURELIA 386, 387, 388
AUSTIN 583
AUSTRIAN HYMN 307, 565
AUTHORITY 176
AVON 200
AWAY IN A MANGER (MÜLLER) 124
AZMON 42, 383, 575

BAHAY KUBO 234
BALM IN GILEAD 553
BATTLE HYMN OF THE REPUBLIC 610
BEACH SPRING 332
BEATITUDO 450
BEECHER 43, 368, 495
BEGINNINGS 417
BENJAMIN 590
BETHANY 606
BLESSED QUIETNESS 284
BONHOEFFER 413
BORNING CRY 351
BOUNDLESS MERCY 265
BOURBON 225
BRADBURY 252
BREAD OF LIFE 321
BRIDEGROOM 270, 552
BRING FORTH 181
BROTHER JAMES' AIR 479
BRYN CALFARIA 258
BY AND BY 444

CAMACUA 544
CAMANO 9
CANONBURY 531
CAROL 131
CAROL OF HOPE 435

CENTRAL 235
CHARLESTOWN 78
CHARTERHOUSE 212, 429, 527
CHATHAM 555
CHEREPONI 498
CHRISTE SANCTORUM 90
CHRISTIAN LOVE 396
CHRISTMAS 491
CHRISTOPHER 223
CHRISTPRAISE RAY 54
CHUQUISACA 246
COME SUNDAY 602
CONDITOR ALME SIDERUM 111, 739, 740
CONSOLATION 247
CONSTANTINE 20
CORONATION 304
CRANHAM 128
CRAVEN 196
CRIMOND 468
CRISTO ES LA PEÑA 45
CRUCIFER 198
CWM RHONDDA 18, 436

DANBY 432
DANDANSOY 615
DARMSTADT 513
DARWALL'S 148TH 303
DE COLORES 402
DE TAR 587
DEN STORE HVIDE FLOK 296
DENNIS 393
DEO GRACIAS 184, 209, 259
DEUS TUORUM MILITUM 204
DIADEMATA 8, 301, 350
DICKINSON COLLEGE 168, 268
DIFFERENT SONG 150
DISTRESS 254
DIVINUM MYSTERIUM 118
DIX 28, 159
DOMINUS REGIT ME 248
DOUROUX 188
DOVE OF PEACE 349
DOWN AMPNEY 289
DOWN AT THE CROSS 189
DUKE STREET 300
DUNCANNON 228
DUNDEE 412
DUNLAP'S CREEK 256
DUST AND ASHES 186

EASTER HYMN 233
EBENEZER (TON-Y-BOTEL) 267
EIN' FESTE BURG (ISOMETRIC) 439
EIN' FESTE BURG (RHYTHMIC) 440
ELDERKIN 160
ELLACOMBE 12, 104, 213

ELLERS 80
EN SANTA HERMANDAD 392
ENDLESS SONG 476, 563
ENGELBERG 561
ENTER, REJOICE 73
ERHALT UNS, HERR 187
ERIE 506
ERMUNTRE DICH 140
ES FLOG EIN KLEINS WALDVÖGELEIN 66
ES IST EIN' ROS 127, 600
ESTE ES EL DIA 65
EUCHARISTIC HYMN 346
EULOGIA 217
EVAN 489
EVENTIDE 99

FAITHFULNESS 423
FALCONE 271
FENNVILLE 554
FESTAL SONG 164, 298
FINLANDIA 488, 591, 607
FLORINDEZ 56
FOR THE BREAD 264
FOREST GREEN 110, 434
FORTUNATUS NEW 220
FOUNDATION 407

GALILEE 172
GARDEN 237
GATHER 335
GELOBT SEI GOTT 603
GERMANY (GARDINER) 361, 543
GIVE ME JESUS 409
GLAD TIDINGS 146
GLORIA (LES ANGES DANS NOS CAMPAGNES) 125
GLORIOUS IS YOUR NAME 53
GLORY, GLORY 2
GO DOWN, MOSES 572
GOD BE WITH YOU 81
GONFALON ROYAL 221
GOTT SEI DANK 566
GRÄFENBERG 40
GRAND ISLE 295
GREENSLEEVES 148
GROSSER GOTT, WIR LOBEN DICH 276
GUIDE MY FEET 497
GWALCHMAI 260

HALAD 279
HALLELUJA 236
HAMBURG 224
HANCOCK 462
HANKEY 522
HANOVER 305
HANSON PLACE 597
HAYDN 91

HEINLEIN 205
HENDON 49
HERR JESU CHRIST, DICH ZU UNS
    WEND 375
HERZLICH TUT MICH VERLANGEN
    179, 202, 226
HERZLIEBSTER JESU 218
HESPERUS 329, 469, 571
HIGHER GROUND 442
HOLY MANNA 376, 556
HOSANNA 214
HOUGHTON 30
HSUAN P'ING 424
HUDSON 199
HURSLEY 96
HYFRYDOL 182, 257, 355
HYMN TO JOY 4

I AM YOURS 455
I WANT TO BE A CHRISTIAN 454
I WANT TO BE READY 616
ICH HALTE TREULICH STILL 404
ID Y ENSEÑAD 528
IDA 608
I'LL FLY AWAY 595
I'M SO GLAD 474
IMAYO 203
IN BABILONE 23, 558
IN DULCI JUBILO 129
INNOCENTS 16, 537
INNSBRUCK 94
INTEGER VITAE 518
IRBY 145
ITALIAN HYMN 275
I'VE GOT A FEELING 458
IVERSON 283

JACOB'S LADDER 500, 501
JEFFERSON 530
JESU, MEINE FREUDE 480
JESUS IS HERE 348
JESUS LOVES ME 327
JOEL 269
JONES 482
JOSEPH LIEBER, JOSEPH MEIN 105
JUDAS AND MARY 108, 210
JUDAS MACCABEUS 253
JULION 356, 357

KASTAAK 291
KATHERINE 177
KEDRON 568
KEEP YOUR LAMPS 369
KENTRIDGE 175
KING'S LYNN 579
KING'S WESTON 255, 586
KINGSFOLD 51
KŌRIN 137
KREMSER 420, 421

LACQUIPARLE 3, 341
LADUE CHAPEL 274
LAKE ENON 457
LANCASHIRE 245, 573, 574
LAND OF REST 354, 378, 521
LASST UNS ERFREUEN 17, 27
LATTIMER 525
LAUDA ANIMA (PRAISE MY SOUL) 273,
    567
LAUDES DOMINI 86, 261

LE P'ING 470
LEANING 471
LEONI 24, 314, 373
LES ANGES DANS NOS CAMPAGNES
    125
LET IT BREATHE 288
LET US BREAK BREAD 330
LET US HOPE 461
LIEBSTER JESU 74
LIFT EVERY VOICE 593
LIGHT OF THE WORLD 584
LIGHTBEAMS 163
LILIUOKALANI 580
LINSTEAD 347
LITTLE BABY 147
LLANFAIR 240
LLANGLOFFAN 582
LOBE DEN HERREN 22
LOPERENA 389
LORD, MAKE ME MORE HOLY 75
LOS MAGOS 155
LOVE'S OFFERING 536
LUX EOI 538
LYONS 26

MABUNE 162
MAGYAR 445
MANGLAKAT 142
MANTON 512
MAOZ TSUR 10
MARCHING TO ZION 382
MARIAS LOVSÅNG 106
MARION 55
MARTIN 460
MARTINEZ 29
MARTYN 546
MARTYRDOM (AVON) 200, 481
MARY'S CHILD 152
MARYTON 365, 503
MATERNA 594
MAUNDY THURSDAY 227
MCKEE 394
MEIRIONYDD 484
MENDELSSOHN 144
MERCY 63
MERRIAL 98
MICHAEL 408
MIGHTY SAVIOR 93
MIKOTOBA 317
MIT FREUDEN ZART 6
MONING 97
MORE LOVE TO YOU 456
MORECAMBE 290, 336
MORNING SONG 89, 119, 605, 613
MORNING STAR 157
MUNICH 272, 315
MURRAY 287
MY TRIBUTE 14

NATIONAL HYMN 372, 592
NAWAHINE 496
NEAR THE CROSS 197
NEED 517
NEED OF PRAYER 519
NEIGHBOR 541
NETTLETON 59, 459
NEUMARK 410
NEW BEGINNINGS 540
NEW BRITAIN 547, 548, 617
NEW DIMENSIONS 391

NEW HOPE 343
NEW REFORMATION 371
NICAEA 277
NOËL 401
NOËL NOUVELET 238
NU OLI (GLAD TIDINGS) 146
NUEVA CREACION 614
NUN DANKET 419
NUN DANKET ALL' (GRÄFENBERG) 40
NUN FREUT EUCH 374
NUN KOMM DER HEIDEN HEILAND 64
NUN RUHEN ALLE WÄLDER (INNS-
    BRUCK) 94
NYLAND 390

O DASS ICH TAUSEND ZUNGEN
    HÄTTE 324
O FILII ET FILIAE 244
O GOD MY GOD 515
O GOTT, DU FROMMER GOTT (DARM-
    STADT) 513
O HEILIGER GEIST (O JESULEIN SÜSS)
    60
O HOLY DOVE 285
O HOW I LOVE JESUS 52
O JESU 463
O JESULEIN SÜSS 60
O QUANTA QUALIA 385
O STORE GUD 35
O WALY WALY 362, 363
OFFERING 453
OGONTZ 560
OLD FIRST 69
OLD HUNDREDTH 7
OLD SHIP OF ZION 310
OLD 22ND 316
OMNI DIE 384
ONLY STARTED 437
OPEN DOOR 529
ORA LABORA 532
ORIENTIS PARTIBUS 138, 250, 294
ORWIGSBURG 486

PASS ME NOT 551
PASSION CHORALE (HERZLICH TUT
    MICH VERLANGEN) 179, 202, 226
PASTORES A BELEN 149
PEACE LIKE A RIVER 478
PEACE, MY FRIENDS 249
PEEK 492
PENTECOST 328, 589
PERFECT LOVE 58
PESCADOR DE HOMBRES 173
PICARDY 345
PILOT 441
PLEADING SAVIOR 397
POR LA MAÑANA 88
POST STREET 201
PRAISE MY SOUL 273, 567
PRECIOUS LORD 472
PROCESSION 411
PROMISE 433
PROMISED LAND 598
PROPHESY 578
PSALM 42 101
PSALM 84 601
PUER NOBIS NASCITUR 57, 241
PUES SI VIVIMOS 499

QUEM PASTORES 123, 510

RAQUEL 174
RATHBUN 193
REDHEAD NO. 76 219
REGENT SQUARE 126, 400
REJOICE, REJOICE 107
RELIANCE 280
RENDEZ À DIEU 167
REPTON 114
REST 502
REVERSI 141
RHOSYMEDRE 222, 426
RICHMOND 36
ROBINSON 297
ROCKINGHAM 208, 414, 465
ROEDER 32
ROLLINGBAY 79
ROSAS 39
ROSEBERRY 585
ROYAL OAK 31
RUSSIAN HYMN 367, 577

ST. AGNES 281, 507, 508
ST. ANDREW 171
ST. ANNE 25, 278, 359
ST. BRIDE 483
ST. CATHERINE 381
ST. CHRISTOPHER 190, 191
ST. CLEMENT 95
ST. COLUMBA 109
ST. DENIO 1, 427
ST. DROSTANE 215
ST. DUNSTAN'S 494
ST. FLAVIAN 211, 318, 342
ST. GEORGE'S WINDSOR 422
ST. GERTRUDE 377
ST. KEVIN 230
ST. LOUIS 133
ST. MARGARET 485
ST. MATTHEW 263, 464
ST. MICHAEL 611
ST. PETER 395
ST. PETERSBURG 50
ST. STEPHEN 352
ST. THEODULPH (VALET WILL ICH
    DIR GEBEN) 102, 216
ST. THOMAS 312, 379, 380, 588
SAIPAN 323
SAKURA 5
SALLEY GARDENS 504
SALVE FESTA DIES 262
SANDON 366, 466
SAVANNAH 430
SCARLET RIBBONS 153
SCHMÜCKE DICH 334
SCHÖNSTER HERR JESU 44
SCHUMANN 170
SEED OF LIFE 83
SEELENBRÄUTIGAM 446
SERENITY 166

SERVANT SONG 364, 539
SHARE THE SPIRIT 62
SHELDONIAN 266
SHENG EN 333
SHEPHERDS' PIPES 320
SICILIAN MARINERS 77
SILVER CREEK 313
SILVER SPRING 183
SINE NOMINE 299
SIXTH NIGHT 431
SIYAHAMBA 526
SLANE 451
SMALLWOOD 511
SOFTLY AND TENDERLY 449
SOLID ROCK 403
SOME DAY 447
SOMETHING FOR JESUS 452
SOMOS PUEBLO 340
SONG OF REJOICING 612
SPANISH HYMN 185
SPARROW 475
SPIRIT 286
SPLENDOR PATERNAE 87
SPRING WOODS 549
STEADFAST 37
STEAL AWAY 599
STILLE NACHT 134
STITELER 406
STUTTGART 13, 122, 325, 326
SURSUM CORDA 443, 520
SUSSEX CAROL 143
SWEET HOUR 505
SWEET, SWEET SPIRIT 293

TABADA 428
TALAVERA TERRACE 562
TALITHA CUMI 545
TALLIS' CANON 100
TALLIS' THIRD TUNE 178, 509
TAULE 121
TENDERNESS 569
TERRA BEATA 21
THANK YOU, JESUS 41
THE ASH GROVE 76
THE BROOK CHERITH 477
THE CALL 331
THE FIRST NOWELL 139
THE OLD RUGGED CROSS 195
THE STAFF OF FAITH 418
THIS IS THE DAY 84
THIS JOY 524
THROCKMORTON 302
THUMA MINA 360
TÔA-SĨA 33
TOKYO 72
TOLLEFSON 15
TOMTER 194
TOPLADY 596
TOULON 251, 358

TRENTHAM 292
TRINITY CAROL 399
TRURO 117
TRUST IN THE LORD 416
TRYGGARE KAN INGEN VARA 487
TWILIGHT 398

UNA ESPIGA 338
UNE JEUNE PUCELLE 151
UNION SEMINARY 337
UNSER HERRSCHER 67

VENI EMMANUEL 116
VERBUM DEI 353
VICTORY 242
VIENNA 448
VILLE DU HAVRE 438
VINEYARD HAVEN 71
VOM HIMMEL HOCH 130
VRUECHTEN 231, 232

WACHET AUF 112
WALKER 156
WAREHAM 306
WAS GOTT TUT 415
WATER OF BAPTISM 169
WE SHALL OVERCOME 570
WEBB 609
WEISSE FLAGGEN 243, 542
WELWYN 533, 534, 535
WERE YOU THERE 229
WESTCHASE 11
WESTMINSTER ABBEY 47, 308, 576
WESTRIDGE 113
WEXFORD CAROL 206
WHEN JESUS WEPT 192
WHITFIELD 309
WHITNEY 165
WHY WE SING 523
WIE SCHÖN LEUCHTET 158
WILDERNESS 557
WINCHESTER NEW 115
WINCHESTER OLD 516
WINSTON-SALEM 550
WOKE UP THIS MORNING 85
WONDERFUL CHILD 136
WONDROUS LOVE (CHRISTOPHER)
    223
WOODLANDS 38
WOODWORTH 207
WORDS OF LIFE 319
WORLD PEACE PRAYER 581
WUNDERBARER KÖNIG 68

YARNTON 564
YES, GOD IS REAL 405
YISU NE KAHA 48

ZION 19

SCRIPTURAL INDEX

GENESIS
1:1–2:7   371
1:1–2:3   530
1:1–5   33, 326, 467
1:26–27   367, 398, 585
1:27   11
2:4b–8   550
2:7   355
2:15–17   568
2:24   363
2:46–48   550
3:1–7   568
3:17–19   186
3:19   367
5:1–2   556
9:8–17   402
9:12–16   391
12:1   24
17:15–16   24
17:15–19   501
18:9–15   426, 501
28:10–17   500
28:10–22   606
28:12   2

EXODUS
1:1–14   574
3:7–12   572
3:14   24
7:8–11:10   574
7:16   572
8:1, 20   572
9:1, 13   572
10:3   572
13:18–22   267
13:21   18, 19
13:21–22   391
13:22   307
14:21–22   326
14:21–31   574
15   230
15:20   2
16:4   18, 19
17:6   18, 19, 45
19–20:17   116
19:4   468
23:16   422
28:1–3   358

NUMBERS
14:14   391

DEUTERONOMY
6:5–6   454
8:1–3, 6–10   424
10:12–16   454
30:19–20   350
31:6   445
32:1–2   317
32:11–12a   468
33:27   471

1 SAMUEL
1:1–20   426
2:1–10   15, 119
9:7   370
16:1, 13   358

2 SAMUEL
22:9   282

1 KINGS
17:1–16   477
19:11–12   502

2 KINGS
2:9   358

1 CHRONICLES
16:9   6

2 CHRONICLES
5:11–14   561
5:13–14   453

JOB
7:6   464
11:7–9   560
33:4   288
38:1–11   568
38:7   453

PSALMS
5:3   86
8   558
18:1–3   110
18:8   282
20:5   55, 71
22:1–2   515
23   247, 248, 479, 518
24:7–10   117
26:8   312
30:4–5, 11–12   91
36:6   1
36:7   445
36:7–9   459
37:3   416
37:7   488
42   481
43:3   469
46   439, 440
46:1–7   476
46:4   284
46:10   488
48:1–2   379, 382
50:1–2   470
51:1–12   186, 188
55:6   595
55:22   410
57:7–11   566
59:16–17   86
62:5–8   408
67   419
68:4, 32   5, 22, 39
72   104, 300
77:19   412
81:6   2
82:8   591
84   600, 601
84:1–2   8
84:8–12   69
87:3   307
89:1–2, 8–17   29
89:15   526
90:1   374
90:1–2, 4–5   25
91   460
96   34
98   36
98:4–9   132
100   7, 73

103   13, 174, 549
103:15–17   120
104:2–6, 10–13   26
104:24–25   3
104:24–30   291
105   6, 22
105:7   611
105:39–44   18, 19
108:1–5   566
108:5–6   602
115:1   14
116:1–2   511
117   27
118:19–29   65, 267
118:24   84
119:94   455
119:105   315, 450
121   466
126:5–6   461
130   483
130:1–8   554
136   16, 32
136:5–9   12
139:11–12   80
141:3–4a   80
144:9–10   378
145:10   4
146   438
148   17, 33, 462, 567
150   453

PROVERBS
2:6   411

ECCLESIASTES
12:1   350

**SONG OF
SOLOMON**
2:1–2   45

ISAIAH
2:1–5   112
2:2–4   571, 581
6:1–3   345
6:1–8   277
6:8   360
9:2–7   110
9:2, 6–7   150
11:1   127
11:1–6   153
11:1–10   109
11:1–12   114, 116
11:6–9   108, 609
12:2–6   109
12:6   107
18:3   154
21:11–12   103
26:4   307, 596
26:9   107
30:18–22   450
32:2   190
33:20–21   307
35   612
35:6   107
38:14   270
40:1–8   101
40:3–5   121
40:3–11   120
42:5–9   556

42:10–11   150
43:1   354
43:2–5   407
44:6   24
49:13   4
52:7   154
52:7–10   21
52:13   221
53   226
53:3–5   218
53:4–5   221
55:10–13   108
60:1   164
60:1–3   112
60:18   307
60:19–20   144, 158, 168, 739
61   62
61:1–2   164
61:10   334
61:11   609
64:1–9   112
66:12   478

JEREMIAH
8:18–22   553
10:12–13   3, 341
17:7–8   313
33:14–16   609
46:11   553

LAMENTATIONS
3:22–23   423

EZEKIEL
37:1–14   288

HOSEA
11:1–9   583

JOEL
2:12–23   114
2:28   265

AMOS
5:14–15, 24   588
7:7–8   588
8:11   317

MICAH
5:2   133
5:2–4   113

ZECHARIAH
9:9   215

MALACHI
3:1   43
4:2   740

**WISDOM OF
SOLOMON**
7:25; 8:1, 7   740

SIRACH
24:1–6   740
39:35   419
50:20–24   419

1 ESDRAS
5:56–7:15   607

2 ESDRAS
16:56–60   3

MATTHEW
1:18–25   105
1:23   68, 121, 137, 138, 150, 151
2:1–2, 9–11   126, 137, 147
2:1–11   153, 165
2:1–12   139, 155, 159
2:9–11   156, 157
2:11   148
3:1–6, 11–12   115
3:13–17   167, 168, 169
4:1–2   167
4:1–11   205, 209
4:18–22   171, 172, 173
5:3–12   180
5:13–15   181
5:13–16   311, 528
5:14–16   524, 525
6:1–6, 16–21   187
6:10   542
6:11–12   470
6:25–33   341, 424
7:24–27   403, 607
8:5–13   175
8:8   317
8:20   162
8:23–26   445
8:26   284
9:18–25   545
9:37–38   532
10:26–30   475
10:26–31   523
10:42   543
11:5   107
11:28   98
11:28–30   484, 489
13:1–9, 18–23   318
13:24–30   608
13:24–30, 33, 36–43   528
13:31–32   540
14:13–21   321
14:22–23   502
14:22–33   51
15:21–28   175
16:24   606
17:1–5   184
17:1–8   182, 183
18:20   337
19:5   363
19:6   362
20:1–7   532
21:6–9   214
21:8–9   216, 217
21:15   213
22:1–10   332
22:34–40   389
22:37   290
23:37–39   212
24:27   599
24:36–44   112
25:1–13   369
25:31–40   538
26:26–28   343
26:26–29   467
26:36–39   228
26:39   227

27:50–54   183
27:52–53   599
27:57–28:7   238
28:1–10   240, 253
28:2–6   239
28:5–8   233, 243
28:5–10   229
28:18–20   528
28:19   280, 324
28:19–20   535
28:20   477

MARK
1:1–8   115
1:9–11   168, 169, 326
1:9–13   167
1:12–13   211
1:16–20   171, 172,
    173, 502, 504
1:21–28   176
1:40–42   587
2:1–12   178
2:21–22   174
3:7–10   161
4:26–32   615
4:30–32   540
4:35–41   441
4:39   51
5:21–42   545
5:25–29   166
5:25–34   175
6:30–44   321
6:47–52   51
8:34   191, 204
9:2–7   184
9:2–8   182, 183
9:14–29   555
10:7–9   363
10:8   362
10:13–16   615
10:18   152
11:7   214
11:8–10   213
12:28–34   311, 389
14:3–9   206
14:12–25   344
14:22–25   225, 467
14:32–36   228
14:36   227
15:24   229
15:32   201
15:37–39   183
16:1–2   228
16:1–6   245
16:1–7   244
16:1–8   240
16:6–7   229

LUKE
1:26–35   145
1:26–56   426
1:30–35   136
1:39–55   123
1:46–55   106
1:46b–55   119
1:46–55   378
1:68–79   110
1:78–79   740
2:1–7   111, 138, 145,
    152, 426
2:1–14   130
2:1–20   134

2:4–7   133
2:7   124
2:7–14   147
2:7–14, 25–32   148
2:7, 46–47   161
2:8–14   131, 136, 137,
    140, 143, 153, 431
2:8–18   165
2:8–20   126, 139, 154
2:8–20, 25–32   51
2:10–11   146
2:10–14   156, 157
2:10–11, 25–32   144
2:11   151
2:11–15   132, 135
2:15   125, 142
2:29   77
3:2–6, 15–18   115
3:4–6   121
3:21–22   167, 169
4:1–13   209, 211
4:14–21   164
4:16–20   587
4:18–19   62
4:33–37   176
5:1–11   173
6:17–38   170
6:20–23   180
6:47–49   607
7:1–10   175
8:40–56   545
9:16   343
9:28–36   182, 183, 184
9:37–43a   175
9:57   493
10:1–9   347
10:29–37   541
10:34   552
11:1   508
11:1–4   311
12:4–7   475, 523
13:6–9   586
13:18–19   540
13:34–35   212
14:16–24   332
15:11–19   203
15:11–32   202
16:19–22   587
17:11–19   201
18:35–43   551
19:35–38   214
19:36–38   215
19:41   543
22:15–20   467
22:19   343
22:42   227
23:33   229
23:50–24:12   238
24   230
24:1–7   84
24:1–10   228, 231,
    235, 240
24:1–12   262
24:5b–6   229
24:13–48   255
24:29   96, 99
24:30 343
24:30–31, 35   342
24:36–37   241
24:46–51   144

JOHN
1:1–5   111, 739
1:1–5, 14   118, 143,
    152
1:6–8, 19–28   115
1:11   218
1:14   135, 148, 274
1:14–18   142
1:18   406
1:29–34   198
1:32   281, 290
3:13–16   365
3:13–17   220
3:14–17   605
3:16   5
3:16–17   208, 530
4:5–42   196
4:7–14   45
4:7–15   489
4:13–14   326
6:16–21   51
6:20–29   339
6:24–35, 51–58   294
6:32–35   340
6:35   333
6:35–40   484
6:35–58   334, 346
6:37   207
6:47–51   227
6:48   48
6:51   258
6:52–58   329
8:12   48, 160, 163,
    331, 485, 489, 584,
    1001
8:31–32   570
9:5   48, 160, 163
10:1–29   252
10:10   563
10:11–16   355
10:11, 27–30   247
11:1–44   616
11:25   48
11:25–26   484
11:25–27   251
11:35   192
12:1–3   536
12:1–8   210
12:12–15   214
13:1–20   498
13:34–35   389, 396,
    540
14:1–4   493
14:1–7   331
14:3   608
14:6   40, 48, 72, 389
14:15–19, 25–27   279
14:16   260, 284
14:16–17, 25–27   268
14:18–29   249
14:25–27   264
14:27   80
15:1–5   163, 270
15:4–5   96
15:9–12   389, 396
15:11   331
15:12 388
15:12–17 495, 540
15:15   480
15:26–16:15   264
16:13   280

17:1–26   209
17:11   542
17:17–23   47
17:20–23   388, 390
17:20–26   504
18:1–20:18   219
18:15–17   218
19:1–3   226
19:1–3, 16–18   209
19:2   228
19:5   162
19:16b–18   152
19:16–18   229, 239
19:16b–18, 34   148
19:17   223
19:17–18, 31–34   221
19:30   183
19:34   596
19:38–20:18   239
20:11–13   228
20:11–17   229
20:14–18   237
20:19–23   255, 274,
    288
20:19–29   244, 253
20:19–31   254
20:24–29   256
20:26–29   406
20:29   180
21:15   171, 172
21:15–16   250

**ACTS OF THE
APOSTLES**
1:6–11   260, 262
1:8   535
2   261
2:1–4   84, 262, 289
2:1–21   64, 263, 271
2:1–36   267
2:1–24, 32–47   265,
    266, 272
2:1–4, 43–47   373
2:14, 36–41   616
2:17–21   387, 578
2:38–42   167
2:42   330
3:12–21   262
4:32–35   291, 575
5:30–31   51
7:55–59   610
8:36–39   322
10:34–38   167
10:34–43   553
10:36–43   308
10:39–43   51
10:47–48   322
11:15   283
13:38–39   143
17:22–31   530
17:30–31   473

ROMANS
1:1–6   358
1:16   77
4:18   461
5:1–5   278
5:6–11   198, 452
5:8   368
5:12–21   235
5:21   243

6:1–3, 10–11   324
6:3–8   198
6:4–11   243
6:5–11   234
6:6–10   161
7:5–8:4   614
8:1–2, 9–17   60
8:26   270
8:26–27   520, 521
8:26–28   508
8:31–39   413
8:38–39   485, 487
10:6–7   166
10:12–13   72
11:33–36   412
12:1   448
12:2   530
12:4–5   270
12:9–18   539
12:9–21   170
12:21   570
13:8–14   590
13:9–12   602
13:11–14   112
14:7–9   298
14:8   457
14:11   5
15:7–13   158
16:1–16   297

1 CORINTHIANS
1:3–9   112
1:18–24   220
1:26–31   575
2:2 49
2:9–16   294
3:8–9   370
3:11   373, 386, 403
3:21–23   476
4:1   372
10:4   258
11:23–25   227
11:23–26   225
12   377
12:4–27   163, 177
12:13   394, 395
13   461
13:1–14   61
13:4–13   368
13:12   339, 378
13:13   496
15:20–22   233, 243
15:21–22   550
15:51–52   599
15:53–57   242
15:54–55   253
15:54–57   233, 235
15:55   99
16:13   350

2 CORINTHIANS
3:1–6   283
3:17–5:5   293
3:18   43
4:7–12   550
5:1–10   610
5:7   414
5:14–19   614
5:15–19   222
5:16–17   417
5:16–20   202
5:17   43, 476

5:17–18   180
5:17–20   396
9:8   68
13:11   570

GALATIANS
2:20   189, 199, 200
3:28   163, 393, 394,
  395, 399
4:5   352
5:13–14   498
5:22–24   452
5:22–26   586
5:25   283, 290
6:2   393, 495
6:9   369
6:14   49, 190, 191,
  193, 194, 197, 199,
  200, 224

EPHESIANS
1:5   352
1:7–14   72
1:15–16   297
1:15–23   257, 259, 302
2:11–22   54
2:13–22   386
2:14   207
2:14–22   394, 395, 495
2:19–22   373
2:20–22   400
3:14–21   357, 392
4:1–6, 11–16   388
4:1–16   399
4:4–6   386, 387

4:11–12   356
4:31–5:2   533
5:1   353
5:1–2   302, 536
5:16–20   5
5:18–20   521
5:27   43

PHILIPPIANS
1:6   353
1:21   457
1:27   191
2:1–11   259, 507
2:2–12   199, 200
2:5–11   111, 162, 209
2:9–11   166, 304
3:7–8   224
3:7–10   191
3:12–14   491
4:4   55, 71, 303
4:6–7   506
4:8–9   492

COLOSSIANS
1:11–12   392
1:15–17   118
1:15–20   235
1:18–20   387
1:19–20   339
1:19–23   438
1:24–29   539
2:6   353
2:9–12   169
2:13–14   438
3:12–17   402

3:13–15   393
3:15   308
3:16–17   739

1 THESSALONIANS
3:9–13   112
4:13–18   144, 145, 599
5:18   32
5:18   297

1 TIMOTHY
1:17   1
4:10   488
6:13–15   345
6:17   408

2 TIMOTHY
1:8–10   583
2:19   407
4:7–8   491

HEBREWS
2:10–18   585
2:18   205, 486
5:1–11   162
5:7–10   222
6:19   403
9:11–14   257
9:26   258
11   377
11:4–12:2   384
11:16   613
12:1   299, 491
12:1–2   373
12:1–3   199, 200
12:1–15   497

12:2   195
12:22–24   379, 382
12:28   91
13:1   361
13:5   407
13:8   329

JAMES
1:12   195
1:17   12
5:13–16   555
5:14–16   552

1 PETER
1:1–9   507
1:3–7   6
1:8–9   478
1:19   480
1:22   361
2:4–7   400
2:4–9   371
3:8–12   575
4:8–11   542
4:10   560
4:10–11   372

2 PETER
3:8–15   611

1 JOHN
4   294
4:7–12   478, 615
4:7–21   389, 396
4:9–12   402
4:13–16   370
4:16   443

2 JOHN
1:3   581

3 JOHN
1:2   438

JUDE
1:20–21   365

REVELATION
1:4–6   602
1:4b–8   300
3:7   303
4:2–11   379, 382
4:8   24, 375
4:8–11   68, 276, 277
4:9–11   305
5:9–14   617
5:11–14   305, 383
5:13   223
7   380
7:9–10   301
7:9–14   473
7:9–17   198, 296, 385
10:11   578
11:15   403
19   304
19:6–7   303
21:1–6   385
21:1–7   614
21:1–4, 10–27   616
21:1–22:5   613
22:1–2   18, 19
22:1–5   197, 198, 597
22:20   543

LECTIONARY INDEX

(Based on the *Revised Common Lectionary*)

The relationship of a hymn to a specific reading from the lectionary is designated by the following letters: G = Gospel; E = Epistle, Other Early Christian Scripture (Other New Testament); P = Psalm; H = Hebrew Scripture (Old Testament); A = Apocrypha.

Year A

Advent 1
(*See also* ADVENT, 101–123)
G: Keep awake, be always   112
H: O God of love   571

Advent 2
G: The Baptist shouts on   115
E: O Morning Star, how   158
H: Isaiah the prophet has   108
H: Now is the time   609
H: Return, my people   114
H: With joy draw water   109

Advent 3
G: Canticle of Mary   p. 732
G: Mary, woman of the   123
G: My heart is overflowing   15
G: My heart sings out   106
G: My soul gives glory   119
H: Awake! Awake and   107
H: Strengthen all the weary   612

Advent 4
G: "Gentle Joseph,   105
G: Hitsuji wa nemureri   137
G: Jesus, our brother, strong   138
G: O come, O come   116

Christmas Day 1
(*See also* CHRISTMAS, 124–153)
G: Break forth,   140
G: Brightest and best   156, 157
G: "I am the light"   584
G: Love came down at   165
G: Now greet the swiftly   431
H: Now bless the God   110

Christmas Day 2
(*See* Christmas Day 1)

Christmas Day 3
(*See also* CHRISTMAS, 124–153)
G: Beautiful Jesus   44
G: Christ, mighty Savior   93
G: O holy radiance, joyous   739
G: O Holy Spirit, Root   57
G: O splendor of God's   87
G: O Wisdom breathed   740
P: To God compose a   36
H: God reigns o'er all   21

Christmas 1
G: Amen, Amen   161
G: O sing a song   51
E: In a lowly manger   162
E: O love, how vast   209
E: What child is this   148

Holy Name
G: Angels, from the realms   126
G: Pastores a Belén   149

E: A hymn of glory   259
E: All hail the power   304
E: Jesus—the very thought   507
E: O loving founder of   111

New Year
G: Like a mother who   583
G: Standing at the future's   538
E: By gracious powers   413
E: For the healing of   576
E: I want to be   616
E: O holy city, seen   613
E: This is a day   417
H: In the bulb there   433

Christmas 2
G: Born in the night   152
G: Christ, mighty Savior   93
G: Go tell it on   154
G: Manglakat na kita sa   142
G: O holy radiance, joyous   739
G: O splendor of God's   87
G: Of the Parent's heart   118
A: O Wisdom breathed   740

(Year A continued)

Epiphany
(See also EPIPHANY, 154–166)
G: Angels, from the realms 126
G: Brightest and best 156, 157
G: "I am the light" 584
G: Los magos que llegaron 155
G: Love came down at 165
G: The first Nowell 139
G: 'Twas in the moon 151
G: What child is this 148
G: Who would think that 153
H: Let there be light 589
H: O radiant Christ 168

Baptism of Jesus [1]
G: Mark how the Lamb 167
G: O holy Dove of 285
G: O radiant Christ, 168
G: What ruler wades 169
E: At the font we 308
E: Soplo de Dios viviente 56

Epiphany 2 [2]
G: Come, Holy Spirit 281
G: Mark how the Lamb 167
E: O Source of all 513

Epiphany 3 [3]
G: Dear God, embracing 502
G: Jesus calls us, o'er 171, 172
G: O Jesus, I have 493
G: O Savior, let me 503
G: Tú has venido a 173

Epiphany 4 [4]
G: Blessed are the poor 180
E: God of grace and 436
E: In the cross of 193, 194
E: O for a world 575

Epiphany 5 [5]
G: Renew your church 311
G: Sois la semilla 528
G: This little light of 524, 525
G: You are salt for 181
E: There's a spirit in 294
H: Lead on eternal Sovereign 573

Epiphany 6 [6]
G: If I have been 544
E: What gift can we 370
E: Where charity and love 396

Epiphany 7 [7]
G: I would be true 492
G: Your ways are not 170
E: Christ is made the 400
E: How firm a foundation 407
E: My hope is built 403
E: The church's one 386

Epiphany 8 [8]
G: Be not dismayed 460
G: I've got a feeling 458
G: Someone asked 523
G: Why should I feel 475
H: I'm pressing on the 442

Epiphany 9 [9]
G: How firm a foundation 407

G: My hope is built 403
G: We would be building 607

Epiphany Last/Transfiguration
G: Jesus, take us to 183
G: O wondrous sight, O 184
G: We have come at 182

Ash Wednesday
(See also LENT, 189–212)
G: Again we keep this 187
G: Savior, when in tears 185
E: Christ, make me more 75
E: Dust and ashes touch 186
P: Give me a clean 188
H: Lead on eternal 573
H: Return, my people 114

Lent 1
G: Again we keep this 187
G: Forty days and forty 205
G: Lord Jesus, who 211
G: Mark how the Lamb 167
G: O love, how vast 209
E: Ekolu mea nui 496
H: God marked a line 568

Lent 2
G: As Moses raised the 605
G: Jesus, take us to 183
P: Unto the hills we 466
H: God made from one 427
H: The God of Abraham 24

Lent 3
G: Crashing waters 326
G: I heard the voice 489
G: When, the woman 196
H: Cristo es la peña 45
H: Guide me, O my 18, 19

Lent 4
G: Amazing grace 547, 548
G: Jesus the Christ says 48
G: Just as I am 207
G: There are some things 405
P: God is my shepherd 479
P: My shepherd is the 247
P: Such perfect love my 248

Lent 5
G: I want to be 616
G: Jesus the Christ says 48
G: "O come to me" 484
G: When Jesus wept 192
G: You are the way 40
P: Out of the depths 483
H: Spirit, spirit 286

Palm Sunday
G: All glory, laud, and 216, 217
G: "Hosanna, loud hosanna"
  213
G: Mantos y ramos 214
G: Ride on! Ride on 215
E: All hail the power 304
P: Este es el día 65

Passion Sunday *(See also* HOLY
WEEK, 218–229)

G: Come, my Way, my 331
G: Come, you faithful, raise 230
G: Steal away 599
G: Wonder of wonders 328
E: Alas! and did my 199, 200
E: In a lowly manger 162
E: O love, how vast 209
E: O loving founder of 111

Monday in Holy Week
G: A woman came who 206
G: Said Judas to Mary 210
G: Savior, an offering 536
P: Come, O Fount of 459
P: I will lift the 482
P: Immortal, invisible, God 1

Tuesday in Holy Week
G: Born of God, Eternal 542
G: "Take up your cross" 204
E: In the cross of 193, 194
E: Sing, my tongue 220

Wednesday in Holy Week
G: It was a sad 225
E: Awake, my soul, stretch 491
E: Guide my feet 497
E: O what their joy 385

Holy Thursday
G: Jesu, Jesu, fill us 498
G: Where charity and love 396
E: Adoro te devote 339
E: Be known to us 342
E: Bread of the world 346
E: Christ at table there 227
E: It was a sad 225
E: O Bread of life 333
P: I love my God 511

Good Friday
G: Ah, holy Jesus 218
G: Beneath the cross of 190
G: Down at the cross 189
G: Journey to Gethsemane 219
G: My song is love 222
G: O sacred Head, now 226
G: On a hill far 195
G: Ruler of life, we 228
G: Sing, my tongue 220
G: Were you there 229
G: What wondrous love is 223
G: When I survey the 224
P: O God, my God 515
H: The royal banners 221

Holy Saturday *(See* Good Friday)

Easter Vigil
(See EASTER, 230–245. For hymns
related to specific readings, see
Scriptural Index. See Psalter section, pp. 621–731; for additional
psalms; see also Second Canticle
of Isaiah, p. 734; Canticle of the
Three, p. 738; Christ, mighty Savior, no. 93, and O Holy Radiance,
p. 739. Also see MORNING,
83–91; HOLY BAPTISM, 322–328;
HOLY COMMUNION, 329–349.)

Easter *(See* EASTER, 230–245)
G: Yours is the glory 253
G: Hail, O festal day! 262
G: On a hill far 195
G: Ruler of life, we 228
G: This is the day 84
G: Were you there 229
E: At the font we 308

Easter Evening
G: Jesus is here right 348
G: Jesus, Sovereign Savior 255
G: Jesus took the bread 343
G: Joy dawned again on 241
G: Somos pueblo que camina 340

Easter 2 *(For additional Easter
Season hymns, see 246–256)*
G: Yours is the glory 253
G: Christ rose up from 239
G: Jesus, Sovereign Savior 255
G: Not with naked eye 406
G: O sons and daughters 244
G: These things did Thomas
  254
G: We live by faith 256

Easter 3
G: Be known to us 342
G: Jesus is here right 348
G: Jesus took the bread 343
G: Jesus, Sovereign Savior 255
E: The church's one 386
P: I love my God 511

Easter 4
G: Savior, like a shepherd 252
E: Draw us in the 337
E: God is here! As 70
E: Spirit of love 58
E: They did not build 373
E: When minds and bodies 399
P: God is my shepherd 479
P: My shepherd is the 247
P: Such perfect love my 248

Easter 5
G: Christ will come again 608
G: Come, my Way, my 331
G: Sekai no tomo 72
E: Christ is made the 400
E: O praise the gracious 54

Easter 6
G: Come forth, O Love 289
G: Holy Spirit, truth divine 63
E: Beams of heaven, as 447
E: Blessed assurance 473
E: God our Author and 530

Ascension
G: Hail, O festal day! 262
G: Hail the day that 260
E: A hymn of glory 259
E: Alleluia! 257
E: Christ, enthroned 258

Easter 7
(See also ASCENSION, 257–260)
G: Born of God, Eternal 542

(Year A continued)

G: Eternal Christ, 390
E: By gracious powers 413
P: Cantemos al Creador 39
P: Praise to God 5

Pentecost
(See PENTECOST, 261–272)
E: Come forth, O Love 289
E: Fire of God, undying 64
E: God of change and 177
E: Holy Spirit, ever dwelling 59
E: Joys are flowing like 284
E: Many are the lightbeams 163
E: Profetiza, Pueblo mío 578
E: They did not build 373
E: This is the day 84
P: Wakantanka taku nitawa 3

Trinity Sunday (See TRINITY
SUNDAY, 273–280)
G: O holy God, whose 535
G: Sois la semilla 528
H: God created heaven and 33
H: I sing the mighty 12
H: O mighty God, when 35
H: Soplo de Dios viviente 56

Proper 4 [9]
(See Epiphany 9, Year A)

Proper 5 [10]
G: Immortal Love, forever 166
G: There was Jesus who 545
E: Let us hope when 461
H: God made from one 427
H: The God of Abraham 24

Proper 6 [11]
G: Come to tend God's 586
G: Come, labor on 532
G: We would be building 607
H: O God, whose steadfast 426
H: The care the eagle 468
H: We are dancing Sarah's 501
H: We sing to you 9

Proper 7 [12]
G: O Savior, let me 503
G: Someone asked 523
G: Why should I feel 475
E: I'll shout the name 234

Proper 8 [13]
G: Jesu, Jesu, fill us 498
G: Where cross the 543
G: Won't you let me 539
P: Let heaven your wonders 29
P: Siyahamb' ekukhanyen' 526

Proper 9 [14]
G: I heard the voice 489
G: I must tell Jesus 486
G: Jesus—the very thought 507
G: "O come to me" 484
G: Softly and tenderly 449
G: What a friend we 506
E: Come, O Fount of 459

Proper 10 [15]
G: Almighty God, your 318

G: You are salt for 181
E: Camina, pueblo de Dios 614
E: O Spirit of God 60
H: Isaiah the prophet has 108
H: Mikotoba o kudasai 317

Proper 11 [16]
G: Christ will come again 608
G: Sois la semilla 528
E: Baptized into your name 324
E: Touch the earth lightly 569
E: We shall overcome 570
H: Glory, glory hallelujah 2
H: Nearer, my God, to 606
H: We are climbing Jacob's 500

Proper 12 [17]
G: We plant a grain 540
E: By gracious powers 413
E: Eternal Spirit of the 520
E: In solitude, in solitude 521
E: O Love that will 485
E: Prayer is the soul's 508
E: Surely no one can 487

Proper 13 [18]
G: Break now the bread 321
G: Let us talents and 347
G: Take my gifts 562
E: Dear God, embracing 502

Proper 14 [19]
G: Give up your anxious 404
G: Incarnate God 414
G: O sing a song 51
E: Immortal Love, forever 166
E: Sekai no tomo 72

Proper 15 [20]
G: Eternal Christ, you rule 302
G: O Christ, the healer 175
G: We yearn, O Christ 179
P: God of Abraham and 20
P: Now thank we all 419

Proper 16 [21]
G: The church of Christ 306
G: We offer Christ 527
E: God our Author and 530
E: Take my life, God 448
E: We are your people 309
H: In Egypt under Pharaoh 574

Proper 17 [22]
G: Before your cross, O 191
G: Jesus, I live to 457
G: More love to you 456
G: "Take up your cross" 204
E: I would be true 492
E: Your ways are not 170

Proper 18 [23]
G: Draw us in the 337
G: God is here! As 70
G: We love your realm 312
G: Where charity and love 396
E: Savior God above 602
E: Spirit of Jesus, if 590

Proper 19 [24]
G: If I have been 544
E: Jesus, I live to 457
E: Pues si vivimos 499
H: Crashing waters 326
H: Guide me, O my 18, 19
H: In Egypt under Pharaoh 574

Proper 20 [25]
G: Come, labor on 532
G: There's a wideness in 23
E: Jesus, I live to 457
P: Sing praise to God 6, 22

Proper 21 [26]
G: All hail the power 304
E: A hymn of glory 259
E: O for a thousand 42
E: O love, how vast 209
E: There is a name 52
E: What wondrous love is 223
H: Cristo es la peña 45

Proper 22 [27]
G: Christ is made the 400
E: Awake, my soul, stretch 491
E: My song is love 222
H: God of Abraham and 20

Proper 23 [28]
G: As we gather at 332
E: Come to tend God's 586
E: I would be true 492
E: Por la mañana 88
E: Rejoice, give thanks and 303
E: What a friend we 506

Proper 24 [29]
G: God, whose giving 565
G: O God of earth 582
G: Take my gifts 562
G: Take my life, God 448
E: Come, share the Spirit 62
E: Soplo de Dios viviente 56

Proper 25 [30]
G: I woke up this 85
G: Lord, I want to 454
G: More love to you 456
G: Spirit of God, descend 290
G: Un mandamiento nuevo 389
P: O God, our help 25

Proper 26 [31]
G: Ask me what great 49
G: O Savior, let me 503
G: Won't you let me 539

All Saints (See also ALL
SAINTS DAY, 295–299)
G: Blessed are the poor 180
G: God our Author and 530
E: Behold the host all 296
E: Bring many names 11
E: Crown with your richest 301
E: Lead on eternal 573
E: O saints in splendor 380
E: Rising in darkness 90

Proper 27 [32]
G: I want to be 616
G: Keep awake, be always 112
G: Keep your lamps 369
E: Steal away 599
H: Let justice flow like 588
A: O Wisdom breathed 740

Proper 28 [33]
G: Awake, my soul, stretch 491
G: My eyes have seen 610
G: O Day of God 611
E: God of grace and 436
E: We who would valiant 494
P: O God, our help 25

Reign of Christ (See REIGN OF
CHRIST, 300–305)
G: Christ will come again 608
G: Eternal Christ, you rule 302
G: God, speak to me 531
G: Like a mother who 583
G: Standing at the future's 538
E: A hymn of glory 259
E: Alleluia! 257
P: Enter, rejoice, and come 73

Thanksgiving (See also
THANKSGIVING, 419–425)
G: An outcast among 201
E: God is truly with 68
E: God, whose giving 565
E: Take my gifts 562
H: Praise to God, your 430

Year B

Advent 1
(See also ADVENT, 101–123)
G: O mighty God, when 35
G: Watcher, tell us of 103
E: Wake, my soul 91
H: Keep awake, be always 112

Advent 2
G: There's a voice in 120
E: O Day of God 611
P: Lead us from death 581
H: "Comfort, comfort 101
H: Great God of earth 579
H: Incarnate God 414
H: Toda la tierra 121

Advent 3
G: O loving founder of 111
G: Of the Parent's heart 118
E: Give thanks for life 297
E: God of the sparrow 32
P: Let us hope when 461
H: Arise, your light is 164
H: Now is the time 609

Advent 4
G: Canticle of Mary p. 732
G: Jesus, Jesus, oh, what 136
G: Mary, woman of the 123
G: My heart is overflowing 15
G: My heart sings out 106
G: My soul gives glory 119
G: Once in royal David's 145

(Year B continued)

Christmas Day 1 (*See* Year A)

Christmas Day 2 (*See* Year A)

Christmas Day 3 (*See* Year A)

Christmas 1
G: Canticle of Simeon   p. 734
G: Hark! the herald angels   144
G: Jesus the Light   160
G: Lord, dismiss us with   77
G: What child is this   148
E: My God, accept my   352
P: To you, O God   17

Holy Name (*See* Year A)

New Year (*See* Year A)

Christmas 2 (*See* Year A)

Epiphany (*See* Year A)

Baptism of Jesus [1]
G: Mark how the Lamb   167
G: O radiant Christ   168
G: What ruler wades   169
H: Crashing waters   326
H: Mothering God   467
H: Wakantanka taku nitawa   3

Epiphany 2 [2]
G: As with gladness those   159
G: Little Bethlehem   113
G: Los magos que llegaron   155
H: Like a mother who   583
H: O God of strength   534
H: Take my life, God   448

Epiphany 3 [3]
G: Dear God, embracing   502
G: Jesus calls us, o'er   171, 172
G: Tú has venido a   173
G: You walk along our   504

Epiphany 4 [4]
G: Amen, Amen   161
G: Glorious is your name   53
G: "Silence! Frenzied   176

Epiphany 5 [5]
G: Precious Lord, take my   472
G: We yearn, O Christ   179
P: God of the ages   592
H: By whatever name we   560
H: O God, the Creator   291

Epiphany 6 [6]
G: Immortal Love, forever   166
G: Through all the world   587
G: Wake, my soul   91
E: I'm pressing on the   442

Epiphany 7 [7]
G: O Christ, the healer   175
G: Pass me not, O   551
G: We have the strength   178
E: O for a thousand   42

Epiphany 8 [8]
G: Hear the voice of   174

E: Spirit of the living   283
E: The God of Abraham   24
P: Bless God, O my   549
P: O my soul, bless   13

Epiphany 9 [9]
G: O Christ, the healer   175
E: Let all mortal flesh   345
E: O God, as with   550
P: Glory, glory hallelujah   2

Epiphany Last/Transfiguration
G: Jesus, take us to   183
G: O wondrous sight, O   184
G: We have come at   182

Ash Wednesday (*See* Year A)

Lent 1
G: Forty days and forty   205
G: Jesus, still lead on   446
G: Lord Jesus, who through   211
G: Mark how the Lamb   167
G: We are often tossed   444
H: In the midst of   391

Lent 2
G: Jesus, take us to   183
G: O wondrous sight, O   184
G: "Take up your cross"   204
G: We have come at   182
P: Let us hope when   461
H: We are dancing Sarah's   501
H: The God of Abraham   24

Lent 3
G: O God of earth   582
E: God of grace and   436
E: In the cross of   193, 194
E: Sing, my tongue   220

Lent 4
G: As Moses raised the   605
G: God loved the world   208
G: My song is love   222
G: What wondrous love is   223
E: Amazing grace   547, 548

Lent 5
G: Before your cross, O   191
G: Beneath the cross of   190
G: Lift high the cross   198
E: In a lowly manger   162
E: My song is love   222
P: Give me a clean   188

Palm Sunday
G: All glory, laud, and   216, 217
G: "Hosanna, loud hosanna"   213
G: Mantos y ramos   214
G: Ride on! Ride on   215
E: All hail the power   304
P: Este es el día   65
P: This is the day   84

Passion Sunday (*See also* HOLY
WEEK, 218–229)
G: A woman came who   206

G: An outcast among   201
G: The time was early   344
E: Alas! and did my   199, 200
E: In a lowly manger   162
E: O love, how vast   209
E: O loving founder of   111

Monday in Holy Week
(*See* Year A)

Tuesday in Holy Week
(*See* Year A)

Wednesday in Holy Week
(*See* Year A)

Holy Thursday (*See* Year A)

Good Friday (*See* Year A)

Holy Saturday (*See* Good
Friday, Year A)

Easter Vigil (*See* Year A)

Easter (*See* Year A)

Easter Evening (*See* Year A)

Easter 2
(*For additional Easter Season
hymns, see* 246–256)
G: Yours is the glory   253
G: Adoro te devote   339
G: Let it breathe on   288
G: Not with naked eye   406
G: O sons and daughters   244
G: These things did Thomas   254
G: We live by faith   256
E: Draw us in the   337

Easter 3
G: Yours is the glory   253
G: I greet you, sure   251
G: Joy dawned again on   241
G: The strife is o'er   242

Easter 4
G: My shepherd is the   247
G: Savior, like a shepherd   252
E: Come, O Spirit, dwell   267
P: Father almighty, bless us   518
P: God is my shepherd   479
P: Such perfect love my   248

Easter 5
G: Many are the lightbeams   163
G: Un mandamiento nuevo   389
E: De colores   402
E: God of the sparrow   32
E: Joyful, joyful, we adore   4

Easter 6
G: Called as partners in   495
G: Come, my Way, my   331
G: Help us accept each   388
G: I sing the praise   50
G: We plant a grain   540
G: Where charity and love   396

Ascension (*See* Year A)

Easter 7
(*See also* ASCENSION, 257–260)
G: Born of God, Eternal   542
G: O Christ Jesus, sent   47
G: O love, how vast   209

Pentecost
(*See* PENTECOST, 261–272)
E: Come forth, O Love   289
E: Fire of God, undying   64
E: Hail, O festal day!   262
E: Holy Spirit, ever dwelling   59
E: Joys are flowing like   284
E: O Christ, the great   387
E: Soplo de Dios viviente   56
E: They did not build   373
E: This is the day   84
H: Let it breathe on   288

Trinity Sunday (*See* TRINITY
SUNDAY, 273–280)
G: As Moses raised the   605
G: God our Author and   530
E: Baptized into your name   324
E: I sing as I   83
E: O Spirit of God   60
H: Holy, holy, holy   277
H: Let all mortal flesh   345
H: Send Me, Lord   360

Proper 4 [9]
(*See* Epiphany 9, Year B)

Proper 5 [10]
G: I'm so glad, Jesus   474
G: In Christ there is   394, 395
G: O Christ, the great   387
E: We love your realm   312
P: Out of the depths   483

Proper 6 [11]
G: Come, O thankful people   422
G: We plant a grain   540
E: Camina, pueblo de Dios   614
E: Incarnate God,   414
E: This is a day   417
E: We live by faith   256

Proper 7 [12]
G: Be still, my soul   488
G: Jesus, lover of my   546
G: Jesus, Savior, pilot me   441
G: Joys are flowing like   284
H: God marked a line   568
H: When the morning stars   453

Proper 8 [13]
G: Immortal Love,   166
G: O Christ, the healer   175
G: There was Jesus by   545
P: Out of the depths   483
P: Out of the depths   554
P: Wake, my soul   91

Proper 9 [14]
G: O holy God, whose   535
G: Sent forth by God's   76
G: Teach me, O Lord   465

(Year B continued)
G: Send Me, Lord   360
G: We are your people   309

Proper 10 [15]
G: Faith of the martyrs   381
G: Forward through the   377
G: O saints in splendor   380
E: Great work has God   353
E: My God, accept my   352
E: O God in heaven   279
P: Lead us from death   581
H: Let justice flow like   588

Proper 11 [16]
G: O Jesus Christ, may   212
E: Christ is made the   400
E: Community of Christ   314
E: O praise the gracious   54
P: Savior, like a shepherd   252

Proper 12 [17]
G: Let us talents and   347
G: O sing a song   51
E: O love, how vast   209
E: Por la mañana   88
P: Joyful, joyful, we adore   4

Proper 13 [18]
G: Hope of the world   46
G: Jesus the Christ says   48
G: Somos pueblo que   340
E: The church's one   386
E: When minds and bodies   399
H: Guide me, O my   18, 19

Proper 14 [19]
G: Bread of the world   346
G: Christ, enthroned in   258
G: Graced with garments   334
G: O Bread of life   333
E: Children of God   533

Proper 15 [20]
G: Come, my Way, my   331
G: Great Spirit God   341
G: Jesus, the joy of   329
E: Colorful Creator   30
E: Praise to God   5
E: Rejoice, you pure in   55, 71

Proper 16 [21]
G: Blessed assurance   473
G: You are the way   40
E: Faith of the martyrs   381
E: We who would rather   494
P: Come, God, Creator, be   69
H: O God of all   374

Proper 17 [22]
G: Just as I am   207
E: Give up your anxious   404
E: Great is your faithfulness   423
E: I sing the mighty   12

Proper 18 [23]
G: God's actions, always   415
G: I heard my mother   409
G: If you but trust   410
G: My faith, it is   418

Proper 19 [24]
G: Before your cross, O   191
G: Nearer, my God, to   606
P: I love my God   511
A: O Wisdom breathed   740

Proper 20 [25]
G: Children of God   533
G: Little children, welcome!   323
G: Surely no one can   487
G: Won't you let me   539
G: Be now my vision   451

Proper 21 [26]
G: God of grace and   436
G: Sois la semilla   528
G: We love your realm   312
G: You are salt for   181
E: From the crush of   552
E: Here, Savior, in this   555
E: Let me enter God's   67

Proper 22 [27]
G: Great work has God   353
G: Jesus loves me!   327
E: A hymn of glory   259
E: O God, we bear   585
P: God reigns o'er all   21
P: O how glorious, full   558

Proper 23 [28]
G: God, speak to me   531
G: O Jesus, I have   493
G: Take my life, God   448
E: I greet you, sure   251
E: O God, my God   515
H: Let justice flow like   588

Proper 24 [29]
G: Jesu, Jesu, fill us   498
G: You servants of God   305
E: In a lowly manger   162
E: Womb of life, and   274
P: Be not dismayed   460
P: We worship you, God   26

Proper 25 [30]
G: I'm so glad, Jesus   474
G: If you but trust   410
G: Pass me not, O   551
G: There is a name   52
P: Let us hope when   461
H: Cristo es la peña   45

Proper 26 [31]
G: I woke up this   85
G: More love to you   456
G: Renew your church   311
G: Un mandamiento nuevo   389
E: Alleluia!   257
E: Where charity and love   396

All Saints *(See also* ALL
SAINTS DAY, 295–299)
G: I want to be   616
E: Camina, pueblo de Dios   614

E: Christian, rise and act   537
H: Strengthen all the weary   612

E: For the healing of   576
E: O holy city, seen   613
E: O what their joy   385
E: This is a day   417

Proper 27 [32]
G: God, whose giving   565
G: What gift can we   370
E: Born of God, Eternal   542
E: Christ, enthroned   258
H: Though falsely some   477

Proper 28 [33]
G: O Day of God   611
G: O loving founder of   111
H: My heart is overflowing   15
H: My soul gives glory   119
H: O God, whose steadfast   426

Reign of Christ *(See also*
REIGN OF CHRIST, 300–305)
G: Eternal Christ, you rule   302
G: O love, how vast   209
E: Jesus shall reign   300
E: Of the Parent's heart   118
E: We hail you God's   104

Thanksgiving *(See also*
THANKSGIVING, 419–425)
G: Great Spirit God   341

Year C

Advent 1
(See also ADVENT, 101–123)
G: Let all mortal flesh   345
G: O mighty God, when   35
G: Watcher, tell us of   103
E: Keep awake, be always   112
H: Now is the time   609

Advent 2
G: Canticle of Zechariah   p. 733
G: Now bless the God   110
G: The Baptist shouts on   115
G: There's a voice in   120
G: Toda la tierra   121
H: Love divine, all loves   43
A: O Wisdom breathed   740

Advent 3
E: Come to tend God's   586
E: Give up your anxious   404
E: Por la mañana   88
E: Rejoice, you pure in   55, 71
E: What a friend we   506
H: With joy draw water   109

Advent 4
G: Canticle of Mary   p. 732
G: Mary, woman of the   123
G: My heart is overflowing   15
G: My heart sings out   106
G: My soul gives glory   119
H: Come, O long-expected   122
H: Little Bethlehem   113
H: O little town of   133

Christmas Day 1 *(See* Year A)

Christmas Day 2 *(See* Year A)

Christmas Day 3 *(See* Year A)

Christmas 1
G: Amen, Amen   161
E: Colorful Creator   30
E: My life flows on   476
E: O God of love   571
E: O holy radiance, joyous   739
P: To you, O God   17

Holy Name *(See* Year A)

New Year *(See* Year A)

Christmas *(See* Year A)

Epiphany *(See* Year A)

Baptism of Jesus [1]
G: Mark how the Lamb   167
G: O holy Dove of   285
G: What ruler wades   169
H: Go, my children, with   82
H: God, when I came   354
H: How firm a foundation   407

Epiphany 2 [2]
G: I sing the praise   50
E: God of change and   177
E: Many are the lightbeams   163
P: Come, O Fount of   459
P: Immortal, invisible, God   1

Epiphany 3 [3]
G: Go tell it on   154
G: "I am the light"   584
G: Praise with joy the   273
E: God of change and   177
E: In Christ there is   394, 395
E: Many are the lightbeams   163
E: O God in whom   401

Epiphany 4 [4]
G: Amen, Amen   161
E: Ekolu mea nui   496
E: Gracious Spirit, Holy   61
E: Let us hope when   461
E: Praise the Source of   411
E: We plant a grain   540

Epiphany 5 [5]
G: Jesus calls us, o'er   171, 172
G: Tú has venido a   173
E: There is a name   52
H: Let all mortal flesh   345
H: Take my life, God   448
H: Send me, Lord   360

Epiphany 6 [6]
G: Blessed are the poor   180
G: We yearn, O Christ   179
E: There is a name   52
H: Like a tree beside   313

(*Year C continued*)

Epiphany 7 [7]
G: Spirit of Jesus, if 590
G: They asked, "Who's 541
G: Your ways are not 170
E: Giver of life, where'er 603

Epiphany 8 [8]
G: My hope is built 403
G: We would be building 607
E: Each winter as the 435
E: Steal away 599
E: What wondrous love is 223
H: Isaiah the prophet has 108
H: Mikotoba o kudasai 317

Epiphany 9 [9]
G: O Christ, the healer 175
G: We yearn, O Christ 179
P: Alabanza 34
H: For the healing of 576

Epiphany Last/Transfiguration
G: Jesus, take us to 183
G: O Christ, the healer 175
G: O wondrous sight, O 184
G: We have come at 182
E: Love divine, all loves 43
E: There's a sweet, sweet 293

Ash Wednesday
(*See* Year A)

Lent 1
G: Forty days and forty 205
G: Lord Jesus, who through 211
G: O love, how vast 209
E: Sekai no tomo 72
P: Be not dismayed 460

Lent 2
G: Jesus, take us to 183
G: O Jesus Christ, may 212
G: O wondrous sight, O 184
G: We have come at 182

Lent 3
G: Come to tend God's 586
G: Cristo es la peña 45
G: There's a wideness in 23
P: Salup na ang adlaw 97

Lent 4
G: Ah, what shame I 203
G: O God, how we 202
E: Camina, pueblo de Dios 614
E: Love divine, all loves 43
E: My life flows on 476

Lent 5
G: A woman came who 206
G: Said Judas to Mary 210
G: Savior, an offering 536
E: Awake, my soul, stretch 491
E: Before your cross, O 191
E: When I survey the 224
P: Let us hope when 461

Palm Sunday
G: All glory, laud, and 216, 217
G: Mantos y ramos 214

Passion Sunday (*See also*
HOLY WEEK, 218–229)
G: Jesus took the bread 343
G: Let us break bread 330
G: Una espiga 338
E: Alas! and did my 199, 200
E: All hail the power 304
E: In a lowly manger 162
E: O love, how vast 209
E: O loving founder of 111

Monday in Holy Week
(*See* Year A)

Tuesday in Holy Week
(*See* Year A)

Wednesday in Holy Week
(*See* Year A)

Holy Thursday (*See* Year A)

Good Friday (*See* Year A)

Holy Saturday
(*See* Good Friday, Year A)

Easter Vigil (*See* Year A)

Easter (*See* Year A)

Easter Evening (*See* Year A)

Easter 2 (*For additional Easter
Season hymns, see 246–256*)
G: Yours be the glory 253
G: Jesus, Sovereign Savior 255
G: Not with naked eye 406
G: O sons and daughters 244
G: These things did Thomas
254
G: We live by faith 256

Easter 3
G: Jesus calls us, o'er 171, 172
G: Listen to your savior 250
E: Canticle to the Lamb p. 735
E: Unite and join your 617
E: What wondrous love is 223
P: Wake, my soul 91

Easter 4
E: Behold the host all 296
E: Blessed assurance 473
E: Crown with your richest 301
E: Lift high the cross 198
E: O saints in splendor 380
P: God is my shepherd 479
P: My shepherd is the 247
P: Such perfect love my 248

Easter 5
G: Un mandamiento nuevo 389
E: Camina, pueblo de Dios 614
E: I want to be 616

E: O holy city, seen 613
P: Creating God, your 462
P: To you, O God 17

Easter 6
G: Peace I leave with 249
G: Womb of life, and 274
E: Christ will come again 608
E: For the healing of 576
E: Shall we gather at 597
P: God of Abraham and 20

Ascension (*See* Year A)

Easter 7
(*See also* ASCENSION, 257–260)
G: Eternal Christ, 390
G: Help us accept each 388
G: O Christ Jesus, sent 47
G: O love, how vast 209
G: You walk along our 504
E: Where cross the 543

Pentecost
(*See* PENTECOST, 261–272)
G: Christ Jesus, please be 375
E: Baptized into your name 324
E: Come forth, O Love 289
E: Fire of God, undying 64
E: Holy Spirit, ever dwelling 59
E: Joys are flowing like 284
E: O Christ, the great 387
E: O holy Dove of 285
E: O Spirit of God 60
E: Soplo de Dios viviente 56
E: They did not build 373
E: This is the day 84
P: Spirit, spirit 286

Trinity Sunday (*See* TRINITY
SUNDAY, 273–280)
G: Come now, Almighty 275
G: Holy Spirit, come, 264
G: O Trinity, your face 280
E: Amazing grace, 547, 548
E: Creator God, creating 278
P: God reigns o'er all 21
H: O Holy Spirit, Root 57
H: O Wisdom breathed 740

Proper 4 [9]
(*See* Epiphany 9, Year C)

Proper 5 [10]
G: Love divine, all loves 43
G: O for a thousand 42
E: Jesu, Jesu, fill us 498
P: Wake, my soul 91
H: Though falsely some 477

Proper 6 [11]
G: An outcast among 201
E: Alas! and did my 199, 200
E: I heard the voice 489

Proper 7 [12]
G: I'm so glad, Jesus 474
E: In Christ there is 394, 395
E: Many are the lightbeams 163
E: The church of Christ 306

E: When minds and bodies 399
P: As pants the hart 481

Proper 8 [13]
G: Come to tend God's 586
G: O Jesus, I have 493
E: Savior, who dying gave 452
E: Spirit of God, descend 290
E: Spirit of the living 283
H: God of the prophets 358

Proper 9 [14]
G: Come, labor on 532
G: Let us talents and 347
E: Beneath the cross of 190
H: Bring many names 11
H: I've got peace like 478
H: Mothering God, 467

Proper 10 [15]
G: Born of God, Eternal 542
G: From the crush of 552
G: Jesu, Jesu, fill us 498
G: They asked, "Who's 541
G: Through all the world 587
E: For all the saints 299
H: Let justice flow like 588

Proper 11 [16]
G: Jesus, I live to 457
G: We love your realm 312
E: Canticle to Christ p. 736
E: O Christ, the great 387
E: Of the Parent's heart 118
E: When peace, like a 438
E: Won't you let me 539
H: We are dancing Sarah's 501

Proper 12 [17]
G: Eternal Spirit of the 520
G: I look to you 463
G: Prayer is the soul's 508
G: Renew your church 311
E: What ruler wades 169
P: Lead us from death 581

Proper 13 [18]
G: We cannot own the 563
E: At the font we 308
P: We sing to you 9
H: Like a mother who 583

Proper 14 [19]
G: Keep awake, be always 112
G: Keep your lamps 369
E: Faith of the martyrs 381
E: For the faithful who 384
E: Forward through the 377
E: I sing a song 295

Proper 15 [20]
G: O Day of God 611
E: Faith of the martyrs 381
E: For all the saints 299
E: For the faithful who 384
E: My faith, it is 418
E: Standing at the future's 538

Proper 16 [21]
G: How can I say 14

(Year C continued)

E: Come, we who love   379, 382
E: Standing at the future's   538
E: Strengthen all the weary   612
P: O my soul, bless   13
H: Lead on eternal   573

Proper 17 [22]
G: We are your people   309
G: Won't you let me   539
E: How firm a foundation   407
E: Jesus, the joy of   329
E: We offer Christ   527

Proper 18 [23]
G: "Take up your cross"   204
G: Be now my vision   451
G: Somos pueblo que   340
G: When I survey the   224
P: O God of strength   534
H: Now in the days   350

Proper 19 [24]
G: "I am the light"   584
G: Come, O Fount of   459
G: Savior, like a shepherd   252
E: Amazing grace,   547, 548
E: Immortal, invisible,   1
E: There's a wideness in   23

Proper 20 [25]
G: Born of God, Eternal   542
G: More love to you   456
G: O Love that will   485
G: You servants of God   305
E: Father almighty, bless us   518
E: We offer Christ   527
H: There is a balm   553

Proper 21 [26]
G: Through all the world   587
E: All my hope on   408
E: Canticle of the Mystery   p. 737

E: Let all mortal flesh   345
E: We shall not give   437
P: Be not dismayed   460

Proper 22 [27]
G: Savior, an offering   536
G: We plant a grain   540
E: Like a mother who   583
P: I will trust in   416

Proper 23 [28]
G: Amazing grace,   547, 548
G: An outcast among   201
G: How can I say   14
G: O for a world   575
E: Jesus, I live to   457
E: Jesus, still lead on   446

Proper 24 [29]
G: O God, my God   515
G: O Source of all   513
G: There is a balm   553
G: What a friend we   506
E: Christian, rise and act   537
P: Unto the hills we   466

Proper 25 [30]
G: Give me a clean   188
G: Not my brother, nor   519
G: If I have been   544
E: Awake, my soul, stretch   491
P: How lovely is your   600, 601
H: Profetiza, Pueblo mío   578

Proper 26 [31]
G: Come, O Fount of   459
G: Pass me not, O   551
E: Thank our God for   397
H: O God, my God   515

All Saints (*See also* ALL
SAINTS DAY, 295–299)
G: Blessed are the poor   180

E: A hymn of glory   259
E: Alleluia!   257
E: Give thanks for life   297

Proper 27 [32]
G: Camina, pueblo de Dios   614
G: Giver of life, where'er   603
G: I'm pressing on the   442
E: I want Jesus to   490
P: To God compose a   36

Proper 28 [33]
G: Be not dismayed   460
G: By gracious powers   413
G: Incarnate God,   414
G: Profetiza, Pueblo mío   578
E: O Source of all   513
P: To God compose a   36
H: We shall overcome   570

Reign of Christ (*See also*
REIGN OF CHRIST, 300–305)
G: An outcast among   201
G: Canticle of Zechariah   p. 733
G: Eternal Christ, you rule   302
G: Now bless the God   110
G: The royal banners   221
E: Adoro te devote   339
E: Canticle to Christ   p. 736
E: ¡Cristo vive!   235
E: En santa hermandad   392
E: Glorious is your name   53
E: When morning gilds the   86
P: A mighty fortress is   439, 440

Thanksgiving (*See also*
THANKSGIVING, 419–425)
G: Somos pueblo que   340
G: There's a spirit in   294
E: Por la mañana   88
E: Take my life, God   448
P: All people that on   7

Years A,B,C

Annunciation
G: Beautiful Jesus   44
G: Jesus, Jesus, oh, what   136
G: Mary, woman of the   123
G: O God, whose steadfast   426
G: O Wisdom breathed   740
G: Once in royal David's   145

Visitation
G: Canticle of Mary   p. 732
G: Mary, woman of the   123
G: My heart sings out   106
G: My soul gives glory   119
G: O God, whose steadfast   426
E: God, whose giving   565
E: Shadow and substance   398
E: We are your people   309
E: Your ways are not   170
H: My heart is overflowing   15

Presentation
G: Canticle of Simeon   p. 734
G: O sing a song   51
G: Song of Simeon   805, 806,
    807, 808
E: O God, we bear   585
P: How lovely is your   600, 601
P: Lift up your heads   117

Holy Cross
G: As Moses raised the   605
G: God loved the world   208
G: God our Author and   530
G: In the cross of   193, 194
G: Lift high the cross   198
G: Sing, my tongue   220
G: When I survey the   224
P: To God compose a   36

TOPICAL INDEX

ADORATION AND PRAISE
God (1–39)
By whatever name we call you 560
Lord, make me more holy 75
Come, O thankful people, come 422
Come, we who love God's name 379, 382
De colores 402
En santa hermandad 392
For the faithful who have answered 384
For the fruit of all creation 425
God of the ages, who with sure command 592
Great is your faithfulness 423
Heaven and earth, and sea and air 566
Holy God, we praise your name 276
Holy, holy, holy 277
Let us break bread together 330

Now thank we all our God 419
O how glorious, full of wonder 558
O saints in splendor sing 380
Praise our God above 424
Praise the Source of faith and learning 411
Praise to God, your praises bring 430
Rising in darkness 90
Someone asked the question 523
Stars and planets flung in orbit 567
Thank our God for sisters, brothers 397
We praise you, O God 420

Jesus Christ (40–55)
All hail the power of Jesus' name! 304
Alleluia! Gracious Jesus! 257
Blessed assurance 473
Crown with your richest crowns 301

I'll shout the name of Christ who lives 234
Jesus, the joy of loving hearts 329
Lift high the cross 198
O holy radiance, joyous light 739
Of the Parent's heart begotten 118
Rejoice, give thanks and sing 303
Take me to the water 322
We have gathered, Jesus dear 74
When morning gilds the skies 86
You servants of God, your Sovereign proclaim 305

Holy Spirit (56–64)
O holy Dove of God descending 285
There's a sweet, sweet Spirit 293

ADVENT (101–123)
(*See also* JESUS CHRIST: Advent)

AFFIRMATION OF FAITH
(See FAITH AND ASPIRATION)

ALL SAINTS DAY (295–299)
(See also CHURCH: Communion of Saints)
God of change and glory 177
Lift your head, O martyrs, weeping 445

ANNIVERSARIES
(See CHURCH: Anniversaries and
Dedications)

ANNUNCIATION, THE
Beautiful Jesus 44
Jesus, Jesus, oh 136
Mary, woman of the 123
O God, whose steadfast love 426
O Wisdom breathed from God 740
Once in royal David's city 145

ANXIETY (See PEACE: Inner; STRUGGLE
AND CONFLICT)

ARTS AND MUSIC
Colorful Creator 30
Now let us all, in hymns of praise 529
O grant us, God, a little space 516
Praise the Source of faith and learning 411
Sing praise to God, who has shaped 22
Spirit of love 58
When in our music God is glorified 561
When the morning stars together 453

ASCENSION (257–260)
(See also JESUS CHRIST: Ascension)

ASH WEDNESDAY (185–188)
(See also CONFESSION OF SIN;
FORGIVENESS OF SIN)
O God, how we have wandered 202

ASPIRATION
(See FAITH AND ASPIRATION)

ASSURANCE
(See COMFORT AND ASSURANCE)

ATONEMENT
(See JESUS CHRIST: Savior)

AUTUMN
(See SEASONS: Changing)

BAPTISM, HOLY (322–328)
God, when I came into this life 354
Great work has God begun in you 353
My God, accept my heart this day 352

BAPTISM OF JESUS (167–169)

BEATITUDES, THE
Blessed are the poor in spirit 180

BEGINNING OF WORSHIP
(See OPENING OF WORSHIP)

BENEDICTIONS
(See CLOSE OF WORSHIP)

BIBLE, HYMNS ABOUT THE (315–321)
I love to tell the story 522
Jesus loves me! 327

BIBLICAL NAMES
As Moses raised the serpent up 605
Come, you faithful, raise the strain 230
Deep in the shadows of the past 320
"Gentle Joseph, Joseph dear" 105
God of Abraham and Sarah 20
"I come to the garden alone" 237
I want to be ready 616
Jerusalem, my happy home 378
Jesus calls us, o'er the tumult 171
Jesus, take us to the mountain 183
Lo, how a Rose e'er blooming 127
Nearer, my God, to you 606
Not with naked eye, 406
O God, whose steadfast love 426
O holy city, seen of John 613
O sons and daughters, let us sing 244
O wondrous sight, O vision fair 184
Ruler of life, we crown you now 228
Said Judas to Mary 210
Savior, an offering costly and sweet 536
The God of Abraham praise 24
There is a balm in Gilead 553
These things did Thomas count 254
They asked, "Who's my neighbor?" 541
We have come at Christ's own bidding 182
When Israel was in Egypt's land 572

BURIAL AND MEMORIAL (365–368)
Abide with me 99
Blessed be the tie that binds 393
For all the saints 299
Give thanks for life 297
God is my shepherd 479
Immortal Love, forever full 166
In the bulb there is a flower 433
Jesus, keep me near the cross 197
My life flows on in endless song 476
My shepherd is the living God 247
O what their joy 385
Precious Lord, take my hand 472
Pues si vivimos 499
Shall we gather at the river 597
What wondrous love is this 223

CALL OF CHRIST (See DISCIPLESHIP;
ORDINATION; VOCATION)

CANTICLES (See also CANTICLES AND
ANCIENT SONGS, 732–740)

Benedictus (Song of Zechariah) 733
Now bless the God of Israel 110

Magnificat (Song of Mary) 732
My heart sings out with joyful praise 106
My soul gives glory to my God 119

Nunc Dimittis (Song of Simeon) (805–808)

Song of Hannah
My heart is overflowing 15

CHANGING SEASONS
(See under SEASONS)

CHILDREN
All glory, laud, and honor 216, 217
Child of blessing, child of promise 325
Deep in the shadows of the past 320
Great God of earth and heaven 579
"Hosanna, loud hosanna" 213
Jesus loves me! 327

Little children, welcome! 323
Now the day is over 98
O God, who teaches us to live 359
O God, whose steadfast love 426
Once in royal David's city 145
Pray for the wilderness 557
Touch the earth lightly 569
Wonder of wonders, here revealed 328

CHRIST (See JESUS CHRIST)

CHRISTIAN UNITY (386–402)
(See also CHURCH: Nature and Unity)
Called as partners in Christ's service 495
Come, let us join with faithful souls 383
Community of Christ 314
From the crush of wealth and power 552
God, bless our homes 429
God made from one blood 427
How beautiful, our spacious skies 594
I come with joy 349
Now is the time approaching 609
O for a world 575
O God of strength 534
O God, the Creator 291
O God, we bear the imprint 585
O praise the gracious power 54
Praise with joy the world's Creator 273
Una espiga 338
Unite and join your cheerful songs 617
We are your people 309
We plant a grain of mustard seed 540
We shall not give up the fight 437
Won't you let me be your servant? 539

CHRISTMAS (124–153)
(See also JESUS CHRIST: Birth and Infancy)
Amen, Amen 161
Go tell it on the mountain 154
In a lowly manger born 162
Jesus the Light of the World 160
Love came down at Christmas 165

CHURCH (306–314)
Anniversaries and Dedications (369–373)
Christ is made the sure foundation 400
God is here! As we your people meet 70
Like a tree beside the waters 313
Now let us all, in hymns of praise 529
O day of radiant gladness 66
O God of all your people past 374
Renew your church 311
The church's one foundation 386

Communion of Saints (374–385)
(See also ALL SAINTS DAY)
All hail the power of Jesus' name! 304
Behold the host all robed in light 296
Christ the Victorious 367
Lift your head, O martyrs, weeping 445
Now let us all, in hymns of praise 529
Rising in darkness 90
Unite and join your cheerful songs 617
We are not our own 564
We are your people 309

Mission in the World
(See also SERVICE; WITNESS)
Called as partners in Christ's service 495
Come, God, Creator, be our shield 69
Come, O Spirit, dwell among us 267
Come, O Spirit, with your sound 265

Come to tend God's garden 586
Community of Christ 314
For the fruit of all creation 425
Forward through the ages 377
God of grace and God of glory 436
In the midst of new dimensions 391
Jesu, Jesu, fill us with your love 498
Let every Christian pray 261
Let us talents and tongues employ 347
O Christ, the great foundation 387
O God in whom all life begins 401
O Spirit of the living God 263
O Word of God incarnate 315
Peace I leave with you, my friends 249
Profetiza, Pueblo mío 578
Renew your church 311
Said Judas to Mary 210
Sent forth by God's blessing 76
The church of Christ, in every age 306
You walk along our shoreline 504

Nature and Unity
At the font we start our journey 308
Children of God 533
Christ is made the sure foundation 400
Draw us in the Spirit's tether 337
Filled with the Spirit's power 266
God is here! As we your people meet 70
God, we thank you for our people 376
In Christ there is no East or West 394, 395
Like the murmur of the dove's song 270
Little children, welcome! 323
O Christ Jesus, sent from heaven 47
O God of all your people past 374
O Spirit of the living God 263
Sekai no tomo 72
Somos pueblo que camina 340
Spirit of love 58
Thank our God for sisters, brothers 397
The church of Christ, in every age 306
The church's one foundation 386
They did not build in vain 373
We love your realm, O God 312
Womb of life, and source of being 274

Worship and Prayer
All people that on earth do dwell 7
Christ, mighty Savior 93
Enter, rejoice, and come in 73
God is here! As we your people meet 70
God is truly with us 68
Holy Spirit, ever dwelling 59
Hoy celebramos con gozo al Dios 246
I come with joy 349
I woke up this morning 85
Let me enter God's own dwelling 67
O day of radiant gladness 66
O God in heaven 279
O Jesus Christ, may grateful hymns 212
O Spirit of God 60
The day you gave us, God, is ended 95
We gather together 421
We have come at Christ's own bidding 182
We have gathered, Jesus dear 74
When in our music God is glorified 561
When the morning stars together 453

CITIZENSHIP (591–594)

CITY
O Jesus Christ, may grateful hymns 212

CITY OF GOD
Come, we who love God's name 379, 382
Glorious things of you are spoken 307
Jerusalem, my happy home 378
O holy city, seen of John 613
O what their joy 385
You are salt for the earth, O people 181

CLOSE OF WORSHIP (75–82)
At the font we start our journey 308
Blessed be the tie that binds 393
Father almighty, bless us 518
Great work has God begun in you 353
Guide me, O my great Redeemer 18, 19
In Christ there is no East or West 394, 395
Jesus shall reign 300

CLOUD OF WITNESSES (See ALL SAINTS
DAY; CHURCH: Communion of Saints)

COMFORT AND ASSURANCE (472–490)
Abide with me 99
Amazing grace, 547, 548
Be not dismayed 460
Blessed are the poor in spirit 180
Break now the bread of life 321
"Comfort, comfort O my people" 101
Hush, Hush, Somebody's calling my name
604
I heard my mother say 409
I look to you in every need 463
Jesus, lover of my soul 546
My hope is built on nothing less 403
Now the day is over 98
O for a thousand tongues to sing 42
O what their joy 385
On River Jordan's banks I stand 598
Our God, to whom we turn 37
Pass me not, O gentle Savior 551
Pues si vivimos 499
Softly and tenderly 449
Sun of my soul, O Savior dear 96
Sweet hour of prayer! 505
The weaver's shuttle swiftly flies 464
There is a balm in Gilead 553
'Tis winter now; the fallen snow 432
Wake, my soul 91
We sing to you, O God 9
What a friend we have in Jesus 506
When peace, like a river 438

COMMANDMENTS (See GOD: Law of)

**COMMISSIONING; ORDINATION;
INSTALLATION (355–360)**
Called as partners in Christ's service 495
Tú has venido a la orilla 173

COMMITMENT
(See CONSECRATION; DISCIPLESHIP)

COMMUNION, HOLY (329–349)
Alleluia! Gracious Jesus! 257
At the font we start our journey 308
Christ at table there with friends 227
Christ, enthroned in heavenly splendor 258
Great work has God begun in you 353
Hoy celebramos con gozo al Dios 246
It was a sad and solemn night 225
Mothering God, you gave me birth 467

Such perfect love my Shepherd shows 248
This is a day of new beginnings 417
Un mandamiento nuevo 389
We are not our own 564
When minds and bodies meet as one 399

COMMUNION OF SAINTS
(See under CHURCH)

COMMUNITY IN CHRIST
(See CHRISTIAN UNITY)

CONFESSION OF SIN
(See also FORGIVENESS OF SIN)
Ah, holy Jesus 218
Ah, what shame I have to bear 203
Alas! and did my Savior bleed 200
Come, Holy Spirit, heavenly Dove 281
Eternal Christ, who, kneeling 390
From the crush of wealth and power 552
Give me a clean heart 188
God, we thank you for our people 376
I must tell Jesus 486
O for a closer bond with God 450
O God, as with a potter's hand 550
O God, we bear the imprint of your face 585
O sacred Head, now wounded 226
Rock of ages, cleft for me 596
If I have been the source of pain, O God 544
Spirit of Jesus, if I love my neighbor 590

CONFIDENCE (See COMFORT AND
ASSURANCE; FAITH AND
ASPIRATION; TRUST)

CONFIRMATION (350–354)
(See also CONSECRATION)
O Jesus, I have promised 493
Rejoice, you pure in heart 55
Tú has venido a la orilla 173

CONFLICT
(See STRUGGLE AND CONFLICT)

CONSECRATION (448–457)
(See also STEWARDSHIP AND CREATION)
As with gladness those of old 159
Baptized into your name most holy 324
Born of God, Eternal Savior 542
Breathe on me, Breath of God 292
Children of God 533
Christian, rise and act your creed 537
Dear God, embracing humankind 502
Ekolu mea nui 496
God, speak to me, that I may speak 531
God, when I came into this life 354
I sing the praise of Love almighty 50
I was there to hear your borning cry 351
I would be true 492
Jesus, the joy of loving hearts 329
Just as I am 207
Let me enter God's own dwelling 67
Let there be light, O God of hosts! 589
Lift up your heads, O mighty gates 117
My God, accept my heart this day 352
O God, as with a potter's hand 550
O kou aloha no 580
O Love that will not let me go 485
O Morning Star, how clear and bright 158
O Source of all that is 513

Savior, an offering costly and sweet 536
Sois la semilla 528
Sovereign and transforming Grace 512
Spirit of God, descend upon my heart 290
Spirit of the living God 283
They did not build in vain 373
We are not our own 564
What ruler wades through murky 169
When I survey the wondrous cross 224

CONSOLATION
(*See* BURIAL AND MEMORIAL;
    COMFORT AND ASSURANCE)

CONSTANCY
Great is your faithfulness 423
I've got peace like a river 478
Jesus, still lead on 446
Keep your lamps trimmed and burning 369
Over my head 514
Surely no one can be safer 487
We who would valiant be 494
We would be building 607
Why should I feel discouraged 475

COSMOS
(*See* GOD: Works in Creation;
    STEWARDSHIP AND CREATION)

COURAGE
(*See also* STRUGGLE AND CONFLICT)
Jesus, priceless treasure 480
My life flows on in endless song 476
O Jesus Christ, may grateful hymns 212
Strengthen all the weary hands 612
We shall overcome 570
We who would valiant be 494

COVENANT
(*See* GOD: Covenant and Promises of)

CREATION
(*See* GOD: Works in Creation;
    STEWARDSHIP AND CREATION)

CROSS
(*See* JESUS CHRIST: Passion and Cross)

CROSS OF BELIEVERS
Beneath the cross of Jesus 190
Nearer, my God, to you 606
Ruler of life, we crown you now 228
"Take up your cross," the Savior said 204
We are climbing Jacob's ladder 500
Your ways are not our own 170

DEATH
(*See* BURIAL AND MEMORIAL;
    COMFORT AND ASSURANCE;
    ETERNAL LIFE)

DEDICATIONS (*See* CHURCH:
    Anniversaries and Dedications)

DELIVERANCE (*See also* JESUS CHRIST:
    Savior)
By gracious powers 413
Guide me, O my great Redeemer 18, 19
In Egypt under Pharaoh 574
O God of earth and altar 582

Rock of ages, let our song 10
There's a voice in the wilderness 120
When Israel was in Egypt's land 572

DEVOTION (*See* CONSECRATION;
    DISCIPLESHIP)

DISCIPLESHIP (491–504)
Baptized into your name most holy 324
Before your cross, O Jesus 191
Children of God 533
Christian, rise and act your creed 537
Come, labor on 532
Filled with the Spirit's power 266
God our Author and Creator 530
God, whose giving knows no ending 565
Help us accept each other 388
"I am the light of the world!" 584
I am yours, O Lord 455
Jesus calls us, o'er the tumult 171, 172
Mark how the Lamb of God's 167
Mary, woman of the promise 123
O God of strength 534
Send me, Lord 360
Sent forth by God's blessing 76
Sois la semilla 528
"Take up your cross," the Savior said 204
Teach me, O Lord, your holy way 465
Tú has venido a la orilla 173

DISCOURAGEMENT
(*See* COMFORT AND ASSURANCE)

DIVERSITY (*See* PLURALISM)

DOMINION OF GOD
(*See* REALM OF GOD)

DOUBT
O God, my God 515
These things did Thomas count 254
Yours is the glory, Resurrected One! 253

DUTY (*See* SERVICE)

EASTER (230–245)
(*See also* JESUS CHRIST: Resurrection)

EASTER SEASON (246–256)

ECOLOGY
Pray for the wilderness 557
Touch the earth lightly 569
We are not our own 564

ECUMENISM (*See* CHRISTIAN UNITY;
    CHURCH: Nature and Unity)

EDUCATION
(*See also* TRUTH; YOUTH)
Come, teach us, Spirit of our God 287
O God, who teaches us to live 359
Praise the Source of faith and learning 411
Teach me, O Lord, your holy way 465

EPIPHANY (154–181)
(*See also* JESUS CHRIST: Life and Ministry)

ETERNAL LIFE (595–606)
(*See also* BURIAL AND MEMORIAL;

CHURCH: Communion of Saints;
    JESUS CHRIST: Resurrection)
Be still, my soul 488
Beams of heaven, as I go 447
Behold the host all robed in light 296
Give thanks for life 297
God loved the world 208
Graced with garments 334
Hail the day that sees Christ rise 260
I want to be ready 616
I'm pressing on the upward way 442
Jerusalem, my happy home 378
Jesus, I live to you 457
Let us hope when hope seems 461
O God, our help in ages past 25
O mighty God, when I survey 35
On a hill far away 195
Pass me not, O gentle Savior 551
Softly and tenderly 449
The church's one foundation 386
The strife is o'er 242
Wakantanka taku nitawa 3
Wake, my soul 91
We are often tossed and driven 444
What wondrous love is this 223

EUCHARIST
(*See* COMMUNION, HOLY)

EVANGELISM
(*See* CHURCH: Mission in the World)

EVENING (92–100)
God be with you 81
I heard my mother say 409
May the Sending One defend you 79
Savior, again to your dear name 80

FAITH AND ASPIRATION (403–418)
(*See also* CONSECRATION; PRAYER;
    TRUST)
Alas! and did my Savior bleed 199
An outcast among outcasts 201
As pants the hart for cooling streams 481
Ask me what great thing I know 49
At the font we start our journey 308
Breathe on me, Breath of God 292
Come, O Fount of every blessing 459
Each winter as the year grows older 435
Faith of the martyrs 381
Great Spirit God 341
Here, Savior, in this quiet place 555
How can I say thanks 14
I want to be ready 616
I'm pressing on the upward way 442
In the bulb there is a flower 433
Jesus, keep me near the cross 197
Let me enter God's own dwelling 67
Let us hope when hope seems hopeless 461
Lift every voice and sing 593
Lord, I want to be a Christian 454
More love to you, O Christ 456
Nearer, my God, to you 606
O for a closer bond with God 450
O Savior, for the saints 298
O Savior, let me walk with you 503
Renew your church 311
Savior, an offering costly and sweet 536
Shall we gather at the river 597
Some glad morning 595

This little light of mine 524 525
We have the strength to lift and bear 178
We limit not the truth of God 316
We live by faith and not by sight 256
We shall overcome 570

FAITHFULNESS (*See* CONSTANCY)

FAMILY (*See* SEASONS: Festival of the
   Christian Home)

FEARS
Jesus, Savior, pilot me 441
What a covenant 471
Yours is the glory, Resurrected One! 253

FELLOWSHP (*See* CHRISTIAN UNITY)

FESTIVAL OF THE CHRISTIAN HOME
(*See* under SEASONS)

FOREBEARS (*See* CHURCH: Communion
   of Saints; CITIZENSHIP; HERITAGE)

FORGIVENESS OF SIN
All praise be yours, my God, 100
Down at the cross 189
Give me a clean heart 188
God loved the world 208
Great God of earth and heaven 579
Here, O my Lord, I see you 336
Mikotoba o kudasai 317
O God, as with a potter's hand 550
O kou aloha no 580
O my soul, bless your Creator 13
Salup na ang adlaw 97
Touch the earth lightly 569

FREEDOM AND LIBERATION

Spiritual
Beams of heaven, as I go 447
¡Cristo vive! 235
Glory, glory hallelujah 2
God marked a line and told the sea 568
God of grace and God of glory 436
I'm so glad, Jesus lifted me 474
It's the old ship of Zion 310
Listen to your savior call 250
If I have been the source of pain, 544
Some glad morning 595
Someone asked the question 523
Spirit of Jesus, if I love my neighbor 590
We shall overcome 570

National
God marked a line and told the sea 568
God the Omnipotent! 577
How beautiful, our spacious skies 594
In Egypt under Pharaoh 574
We shall not give up the fight 437
We shall overcome 570
When Israel was in Egypt's land 572

FUNERALS
(*See* BURIAL AND MEMORIAL)

GOD

Covenant and Promises of
Amazing grace, how sweet 547, 548
De colores 402

God of Abraham and Sarah 20
My heart sings out with joyful praise 106
My soul gives glory to my God 119
Now bless the God of Israel 110
Profetiza, Pueblo mío 578
Wonder of wonders, here revealed 328

Creator
(*See* GOD: Works in Creation)

Dominion of
(*See* GOD: Realm of)

Fatherhood, Motherhood of
Be now my vision 451
Bring many names 11
Child of blessing, child of promise 325
Father almighty, bless us 518
Go, my children, with my blessing 82
How like a gentle spirit 443
Like a mother who has borne us 583
Mothering God, you gave me birth 467
O God, whose steadfast love 426
O Wisdom breathed from God 740
Surely no one can be safer 487
The care the eagle gives her young 468
Womb of life, and source of being 274

Goodness of
(*See* GOD: Providence and Goodness of)

Grace of
Amazing grace, how sweet 547, 548
Bless God, O my soul! 549
Christ rose up from the dead 239
Come, O Fount of every blessing 459
Creating God, your fingers trace 462
God created heaven and earth 33
How deep the silence of the soul 509
I need you every hour 517
O for a thousand tongues to sing 42
On Pentecost they gathered 272
There's a wideness in God's mercy 23
When, like the woman at the well 196

Guidance of
Be now my vision 451
God of our life 366
God of the ages, who with sure 592
God, who stretched the spangled 556
God's actions, always good and just 415
Guide me, O my great Redeemer 18 19
How lovely is your dwelling 600
I sing as I arise today! 83
I will lift the cloud of night 482
If you but trust in God to guide you 410
O grant us light 469
O splendor of God's glory bright 87
Savior God above 602
Shadow and substance 398

Judgment of
My eyes have seen the glory 610
O Day of God, draw near 611

Justice of
My heart is overflowing 15
To God compose a song of joy 36

Law of
God marked a line and told the sea 568
The God of Abraham praise 24

Love of
A woman came who did not 206

As Moses raised the serpent up 605
En santa hermandad 392
Father almighty, bless us 518
God our Author and Creator 530
Gracious Spirit, Holy Ghost 61
Hear the voice of God, so tender 174
How like a gentle spirit 443
Immortal Love, forever full 166
Let us hope when hope seems 461
Like a tree beside the waters 313
Mikotoba o kudasai 317
O how shall I receive you 102
O Love that will not let me go 485
O Trinity, your face we see 280
Out of the depths, O God, we call 554
There are some things I may not know 405
There's a wideness in God's mercy 23

Mercy of
Bless God, O my soul! 549
Grant us wisdom to perceive you 510
I love my God, who heard my cry 511
Lead us from death to life 581
Salup na ang adlaw 97
Surely no one can be safer 487
There's a wideness in God's mercy 23

Power and Majesty of
All people that on earth do dwell 7
Come now, Almighty God 275
God the Omnipotent! 577
Holy, holy, holy 277
Immortal, invisible, God only wise 1
Let heaven your wonders proclaim 29
The care the eagle gives her young 468
We worship you, God 26

Presence of
Bring many names 11
By gracious powers 413
Come, God, Creator, be our shield 69
Day is done 92
Fire of God, undying Flame 64
God is truly with us 68
God reigns o'er all the earth! 21
How deep the silence of the soul 509
I need you every hour 517
I sing the mighty power of God 12
In solitude, in solitude 521
Let it breathe on me 288
Not with naked eye, 406
O grant us, God, a little space 516
There are some things 405
Though falsely some revile or hate me 477
Where charity and love prevail 396

Providence and Goodness of
All my hope on God is founded 408
Be not dismayed 460
Be still, my soul 488
Give up your anxious pains 404
God is my shepherd 479
God moves in a mysterious way 412
God of Abraham and Sarah 20
God of our life 366
God, whose giving knows no ending 565
Golden breaks the dawn 470
Great is your faithfulness 423
Heaven and earth, and sea and air 566
I look to you in every need 463
I will lift the cloud of night 482
If you but trust in God to guide you 410

Immortal, invisible, God only wise 1
My heart is overflowing 15
Now thank we all our God 419
O God, how we have wandered 202
O God of all your people past 374
O my soul, bless your Creator 13
Por la mañana 88
Praise to God, your praises bring 430
Praise to the living God 8
Shadow and substance 398
'Tis winter now; the fallen snow 432
Unto the hills we lift our longing eyes 466
When minds and bodies meet as one 399
Why should I feel discouraged 475

Realm of
Come now, Almighty God 275
"Comfort, comfort O my people" 101
God reigns o'er all the earth! 21
Holy God, we praise your name 276
Isaiah the prophet has written of old 108
Keep awake, be always ready 112
Lead on eternal Sovereign 573
On River Jordan's banks I stand 598
We love your realm, O God 312
You are salt for the earth, O people 181

Righteousness of
God the Omnipotent! 577
In Egypt under Pharaoh 574
Let justice flow like streams 588
O God of earth and altar 582

Shepherd, The
God is my shepherd 479
My shepherd is the living God 247
Though falsely some revile or hate me 477

Strength and Refuge of
A mighty fortress is our God 439, 440
As pants the hart for cooling streams 481
Giver of life, where'er they be 603
How firm a foundation 407
How lovely is your dwelling 600
I look to you in every need 463
I will lift the cloud of night 482
Lift your head, O martyrs, weeping 445
O God, our help in ages past 25
Rock of ages, let our song 10
Unto the hills we lift our longing eyes 466
We sing to you, O God 9

Works in Creation
All beautiful the march of days 434
All things bright and beautiful 31
Cantemos al Creador 39
Colorful Creator 30
Creating God, your fingers trace 462
De colores 402
God created heaven and earth 33
God of the sparrow God of the whale 32
God, who stretched the spangled 556
Golden breaks the dawn 470
Great Spirit God 341
How can I say thanks 14
I sing the mighty power of God 12
Let us with a joyful mind 16
"Lift up your hearts!" 38
O God, the Creator 291
O God, we bear the imprint of your face 585
O how glorious, full of wonder 558
Our God, to whom we turn 37
Praise to God 5

Praise to the living God 8
Sing praise to God, our highest good 6
Stars and planets flung in orbit 567
The weaver's shuttle swiftly flies 464
Wakantanka taku nitawa 3
When the morning stars together 453

GOOD FRIDAY
(See also JESUS CHRIST: Passion and Cross)
Ah, holy Jesus 218
Alas! and did my Savior bleed 200
Journey to Gethsemane 219
My song is love unknown 222
O sacred Head, now wounded 226
Sing, my tongue 220
Were you there 229
When I survey the wondrous cross 224

GOSPEL CALL AND RESPONSE
All my hope on God is founded 408
Before your cross, O Jesus 191
Christian, rise and act your creed 537
Come, labor on 532
Dear God, embracing humankind 502
God, who summons through all ages 356
"I am the light of the world!" 584
Jesus calls us, o'er the tumult 171, 172
Let us talents and tongues employ 347
Like a mother who has borne us 583
Mantos y ramos 214
Mary, woman of the promise 123
My eyes have seen the glory 610
"O come to me, you weary" 484
O Jesus, I have promised 493
Tú has venido a la orilla 173
We cannot own the sunlit sky 563
We gather together 421
You walk along our shoreline 504
Your ways are not our own 170

GRACE (See under GOD)

GRATITUDE (See THANKSGIVING)

GRIEF
(See COMFORT AND ASSURANCE; see
    also BURIAL AND MEMORIAL)

GUIDANCE (See under GOD; JESUS
    CHRIST: Guide and Leader; Presence)

HARVEST
(See SEASONS: Thanksgiving Day)

HEALING (544–555)
Ask me what great thing I know 49
Cristo es la peña de Horeb 45
For the healing of the nations 576
God, bless our homes 429
Immortal Love, forever full 166
Joys are flowing like a river 284
Lead us from death to life 581
Listen to your savior call 250
Now the green blade rises 238
O God of love, O God of peace 571
O Jesus Christ, may grateful hymns 212
O radiant Christ, incarnate Word 168
"Silence! Frenzied, unclean spirit" 176
We have the strength to lift and bear 178
We yearn, O Christ, for wholeness 179

HEALTH AND WHOLENESS
Christ will come again 608
O Christ, the healer, we have come 175
This is a day of new beginnings 417
We yearn, O Christ, for wholeness 179

HEAVEN (See ETERNAL LIFE)

HERITAGE (See also CHURCH: Anniver-
    saries and Dedications, Communion of
    Saints; CITIZENSHIP)
God, creation's great designer 371
My eyes have seen the glory 610
This is my song 591
What gift can we bring 370

HOLY NAME DAY
O for a thousand tongues to sing 42

HOLY SPIRIT
(See also ADORATION AND PRAISE: Holy
    Spirit; PENTECOST)

Baptism
Soplo de Dios viviente 56
There's a sweet, sweet Spirit 293

Comforter
Come forth, O Love divine 289
Holy Spirit, come, confirm us 264
In solitude, in solitude 521
Joys are flowing like a river 284
Like the murmur of the dove's song 270
O holy Dove of God descending 285
O Holy Spirit, Root of life 57
O Spirit of God 60
Soplo de Dios viviente 56

Fruits of
God of change and glory 177
Gracious Spirit, Holy Ghost 61
O God in whom all life begins 401

Illuminator
Come forth, O Love divine 289
Come, O Spirit, with your sound 265
Come, teach us, Spirit of our God 287
Eternal Spirit of the living Christ 520
Holy Spirit, truth divine 63
O for a closer bond with God 450
O Spirit of God 60
O splendor of God's glory bright 87
Spirit of Jesus, if I love my neighbor 590

Power of
Come, O Spirit, dwell among us 267
Come, O Spirit, with your sound 265
Come, share the Spirit 62
Filled with the Spirit's power 266
Fire of God, undying Flame 64
God the Spirit, guide and guardian 355
Holy Spirit, ever dwelling 59
Holy Spirit, truth divine 63
Let every Christian pray 261
Like the murmur of the dove's song 270
Spirit, spirit of gentleness 286
There's a spirit in the air 294
Wind who makes all winds that blow 271

Renewal of
Come, Holy Spirit, heavenly Dove 281
Dust and ashes touch our face 186
Fire of God, undying Flame 64

Hear the voice of God, so tender 174
Holy Spirit, come, confirm us 264
Let every Christian pray 261
Let it breathe on me 288
O Spirit of the living God 263
On Pentecost they gathered 272
Soplo de Dios viviente 56
This is a day of new beginnings 417
Wind who makes all winds that blow 271

Sanctifier
Breathe on me, Breath of God 292
Creator Spirit, come, we pray 268
Holy Spirit, come, confirm us 264
Spirit of the living God 283
Sweet delight, most lovely 269
There's a sweet, sweet Spirit 293

HOLY WEEK (218–229)

HOME AND FAMILY (See MARRIAGE;
SEASONS: Festival of the Christian
Home)

HOPE
All my hope on God is founded 408
Blessed assurance 473
Day is done 92
Ekolu mea nui 496
Give thanks for life 297
Hope of the world 46
Jesus shall reign 300
Let us hope when hope seems hopeless 461
Lift every voice and sing 593
Lift your head, O martyrs, weeping 445
My hope is built on nothing less 403
O for a world 575
Sovereign and transforming Grace 512
The weaver's shuttle swiftly flies 464
We have the strength to lift and bear 178
We shall overcome 570
We would be building 607
We yearn, O Christ, for wholeness 179

HUNGER AND POVERTY
Through all the world, a hungry Christ 587

ILLNESS (See HEALING; HEALTH AND
WHOLENESS)

IMMORTALITY (See BURIAL AND
MEMORIAL; CHURCH: Communion
of Saints; ETERNAL LIFE)

INCARNATION (See JESUS CHRIST:
Birth and Infancy; Divinity; Epiphany)

INSTALLATIONS (355–360)
Called as partners in Christ's service 495

INTERCESSIONS (See PRAYER)

JESUS CHRIST
(See also ADORATION AND PRAISE)

Advent (101–123)
Let all mortal flesh keep silence 345

Ascension (257–260)
Hail O festal day! 262

Baptism of (167–169)

Birth and Infancy (124–153)
Awake! awake, and greet 107
Watcher, tell us of the night 103
With joy draw water 109

Crucifixion
(See JESUS CHRIST: Passion and Cross)

Divinity
Beautiful Jesus 44
In a lowly manger born 162
Incarnate God, immortal Love 414
Jesus, take us to the mountain 183
O Christ Jesus, sent from heaven 47
O come, all you faithful 135
O Trinity, your face we see 280
Of the Parent's heart begotten 118

Epiphany and Youth (154–166)

Friend
I must tell Jesus 486
Jesus, priceless treasure 480
My song is love unknown 222
O Jesus, I have promised 493
What a friend we have in Jesus 506

Guide and Leader
Eternal Christ, who, kneeling 390
I thank you, Jesus 41
Jesus, Savior, pilot me 441
Jesus, still lead on 446
Jesus the Christ says 48
My faith, it is an oaken staff 418
Sekai no tomo 72
Teach me, O Lord, your holy way 465
You are the way 40

Lamb of God
Christ, enthroned in heavenly 258
Hail the day that sees Christ rise 260
Jesus, priceless treasure 480
Just as I am 207
Lift high the cross 198
O saints in splendor sing 380
Sing, my tongue 220
Unite and join your cheerful songs 617
You servants of God, 305

Life and Ministry
Amen, Amen 161
O love, how vast, how flowing free 209
O sing a song of Bethlehem 51
There was Jesus by the water 545
They asked, "Who's my neighbor?" 541
When, like the woman at the well 196

Light
A hymn of glory let us sing 259
Arise, your light is come! 164
Christ, mighty Savior 93
"I am the light of the world!" 584
I heard the voice of Jesus say 489
Jesus, the joy of loving hearts 329
Jesus the Light of the World 160
Now all the woods are sleeping 94
O Morning Star, how clear and bright 158
O radiant Christ, incarnate Word 168
O splendor of God's glory bright 87
We have gathered, Jesus dear 74

Love of
Eternal Christ, you rule 302
Eternal Spirit of the living Christ 520
I love to tell the story 522

I sing the praise of Love almighty 50
I thank you, Jesus 41
Incarnate God, immortal Love 414
Jesu, Jesu, fill us with your love 498
Jesus loves me! 327
Jesusthe very thought to me 507
Listen to your savior call 250
O Christ, the healer, we have come 175
O how shall I receive you 102
O love, how vast, how flowing free 209
There is a name I love to hear 52
You are called to tell the story 357

Passion and Cross
(See also LENT; GOOD FRIDAY)
Christ at table there with friends 227
Journey to Gethsemane 219
My song is love unknown 222
O Bread of life 333
O praise the gracious power 54
What wondrous love is this 223

Presence of
(See also COMMUNION, HOLY)
Abide with me 99
Alleluia! Gracious Jesus! 257
Break now the bread of life 321
Christ Jesus, please be by our side 375
Glorious is your name, O Jesus 53
"I come to the garden alone" 237
I heard the voice of Jesus say 489
I want Jesus to go with me 490
Jesus loves me! 327
Jesus, Sovereign, Savior 255
Jesusthe very thought to me 507
Joys are flowing like a river 284
O Christ Jesus, sent from heaven 47
O Jesus, I have promised 493
Precious Lord, take my hand 472
Sun of my soul, O Savior dear 96
There's a spirit in the air 294
Though falsely some revile or hate me 477
We yearn, O Christ, for wholeness 179
What ruler wades through murky 169
Where cross the crowded ways of life 543

Presentation of
O sing a song 51
Song of Simeon 805–808

Resurrection
(See also EASTER)
Amen, Amen 161
Camina, pueblo de Dios 614
Come, you faithful, raise the strain 230
Hail O festal day! 262
Sing, my tongue 220
Yours is the glory, Resurrected One! 253

Return of
Born in the night, Mary's Child 152
Born of God, Eternal Savior 542
Christ will come again 608
Come, O long–expected Jesus 122
Let all mortal flesh keep silence 345
O Christ, the great foundation 387
O how shall I receive you 102
Peace I leave with you, my friends 249
Toda la tierra 121
We hail you God's anointed 104

Savior (See also ADORATION AND
PRAISE: Jesus Christ)
Alleluia! Alleluia! Hearts to heaven 243

An outcast among outcasts 201
As Moses raised the serpent up 605
Beneath the cross of Jesus 190
Blessed assurance 473
Come, O Fount of every blessing 459
De colores 402
Down at the cross 189
God loved the world 208
Great Spirit God 341
I greet you, sure Redeemer 251
Lift high the cross 198
My heart sings out with joyful praise 106
My life flows on in endless song 476
O loving founder of the stars 111
On a hill far away 195
Pass me not, O gentle Savior 551
Rejoice, give thanks and sing 303
Rock of ages, cleft for me 596
Savior, like a shepherd lead us 252
Savior, when in tears and dust 185
Savior, who dying gave 452
Sing, my tongue 220
We offer Christ 527
What wondrous love is this 223
When peace, like a river 438

Shepherd
Savior, like a shepherd lead us 252
Such perfect love my Shepherd shows 248

Sovereignty and Reign (300–305)
A hymn of glory let us sing 259
Beautiful Jesus 44
Christ is made the sure foundation 400
Each winter as the year grows older 435
Hail the day that sees Christ rise 260
Hope of the world 46
I greet you, sure Redeemer 251
Jesus, Sovereign, Savior 255
Lift up your heads, O mighty gates 117
O loving founder of the stars 111
Once in royal David's city 145
The royal banners forward fly 221
We hail you God's anointed 104

Strength and Refuge
Jesus, lover of my soul 546
My hope is built on nothing less 403
Rock of ages, cleft for me 596
What a friend we have in Jesus 506

Teacher
O Savior, let me walk with you 503
Sekai no tomo 72

Temptation of
Forty days and forty nights 205
Lord Jesus, who through forty days 211
Mark how the Lamb of God's 167

Transfiguration of (182–184)

Triumphal Entry
All glory, laud, and honor 216, 217
"Hosanna, loud hosanna" 213
Mantos y ramos 214
Ride on! Ride on in majesty! 215

JOY
Cantemos al Creador 39
Hoy celebramos con gozo al Dios 246
Jesus the very thought to me 507
Someone asked the question 523
Strengthen all the weary hands 612
This little light of mine 524 525

JUSTICE AND PEACE (570–590)
(See also GOD: Justice of; Righteousness of)
Christ will come again 608
Community of Christ 314
God made from one blood 427
I will trust in the Lord 416
O Day of God, draw near 611
O holy city, seen of John 613
Pray for the wilderness 557
Somos pueblo que camina 340
Standing at the future's threshold 538
We cannot own the sunlit sky 563
You are salt for the earth, O people 181

LABOR (See WORK AND VOCATION)

LAST SUPPER
(See MAUNDY THURSDAY)

LAW (See under GOD)

LENT (189–212) (See also ASH WEDNES-
DAY; MAUNDY THURSDAY; GOOD
FRIDAY; JESUS CHRIST: Passion and
Cross; Temptation of)

LIBERATION
(See FREEDOM AND LIBERATION)

LOVE (See CHRISTIAN UNITY; GOD:
Love of; JESUS CHRIST: Love of)

MARRIAGE (361–364)
Go, my children, with my blessing 82
I was there to hear your borning cry 351
We plant a grain of mustard seed 540

MAUNDY THURSDAY
(See also COMMUNION, HOLY)
Christ at table there with friends 227
It was a sad and solemn night 225
Jesu, Jesu, fill us with your love 498
Un mandamiento nuevo 389
Where charity and love prevail 396

MEMORIAL DAY
(See CITIZENSHIP; HERITAGE)

MERCY (See under GOD)

MINISTRY
(See also ORDINATION)
Called as partners in Christ's service 495
God, speak to me, that I may speak 531
God the Spirit, guide and guardian 355
God, who summons through all ages 356
O God in whom all life begins 401
O God, who teaches us to live 359
O Savior, let me walk with you 503
Send me, Lord 360
You are called to tell the story 357
You walk along our shoreline 504

MISSION
(See CHURCH: Mission in the World)

MORNING (83–91)
Cantemos al Creador 39
Este es el día 65
Holy, holy, holy 277

MOTHER'S DAY (See SEASONS: Festival
of the Christian Home)

MUSIC (See ARTS AND MUSIC)

NATION, THE (See CITIZENSHIP)

NATIVITY, THE
(See JESUS CHRIST: Birth and Infancy)

NATURE
(See GOD: Works in Creation)

NEIGHBOR
(See DISCIPLESHIP; SERVICE)

NEW CREATION
Alabanza 34
Camina, pueblo de Dios 614
Creator God, creating still 278
Isaiah the prophet has written of old 108
Love divine, all loves excelling 43
Now is the time approaching 609
O Day of God, draw near 611
O Holy Spirit, Root of life 57
Pray for the wilderness 557
Stars and planets flung in orbit 567
Womb of life, and source of being 274

NEW YEAR, THE
(See under SEASONS)

NURTURE
Come, teach us, Spirit of our God 287
Creator God, creating still 278
Creator Spirit, come, we pray 268
Grant us wisdom to perceive you 510
Guide my feet 497
Incarnate God, immortal Love 414
Like a tree beside the waters 313
O Wisdom breathed from God 740
Sweet delight, most lovely 269

OBEDIENCE
God marked a line and told the sea 568
Once in royal David's city 145
Teach me, O Lord, your holy way 465

OFFERTORIES (783–785)
(See also SERVICE MUSIC)
God, whose giving knows no ending 565
"Lift up your hearts!" 38
Savior, who dying gave 452
Stars and planets flung in orbit 567
Take my gifts 562
The weaver's shuttle swiftly flies 464
We praise you, O God 420
What gift can we bring 370

OPENING OF WORSHIP (65–74)
(See also ADORATION AND PRAISE;
MORNING; PROCESSIONAL HYMNS)
Come, share the Spirit 62
God reigns o'er all the earth! 21
Sing praise to God, who has shaped 22
We gather together 421
When in our music God is glorified 561

ORDINATION (355–360)
(See also DISCIPLESHIP; MINISTRY)

Called as partners in Christ's service 495
Spirit of the living God 283
Tú has venido a la orilla 173

PAIN AND SUFFERING
Be still, my soul 488
Here, Savior, in this quiet place 555
I love my God, who heard my cry 511
In Egypt under Pharaoh 574
Lead us from death to life 581
Mikotoba o kudasai 317
O Bread of life 333
O Christ, the healer, we have come 175
"O come to me, you weary" 484
O God in heaven 279
O God, my God 515
O Love that will not let me go 485
"Silence! Frenzied, unclean spirit" 176
Sweet hour of prayer! 505
Through all the world, a hungry 587
Where cross the crowded ways of life 543

PALM SUNDAY
(See JESUS CHRIST: Triumphal Entry)

PARDON (See FORGIVENESS OF SIN)

PASSION SUNDAY (See JESUS CHRIST:
    Passion and Cross; GOOD FRIDAY)

PATRIOTISM (See CITIZENSHIP)

PEACE (See also JUSTICE AND PEACE)

Inner
Beams of heaven, as I go 447
Dear God, embracing humankind 502
Glorious is your name, O Jesus 53
Here, O my Lord, I see you face to face 336
How deep the silence of the soul 509
How like a gentle spirit 443
In the cross of Christ I glory 193 194
Jesus, priceless treasure 480
Let there be light, O God of hosts! 589
"O come to me, you weary" 484
Out of the depths, O God, we call 554
Peace I leave with you, my friends 249
Pues si vivimos 499
Savior, again to your dear name 80
What a covenant 471
When peace, like a river 438

World
God of the ages, who with sure 592
Great God of earth and heaven 579
How beautiful, our spacious skies 594
It came upon the midnight clear 131
Let there be light, O God of hosts! 589
Now is the time approaching 609
O God of love, O God of peace 571
This is my song 591

PENITENCE (See CONFESSION OF SIN;
    FORGIVENESS OF SIN)

PENTECOST (See also ADORATION AND
    PRAISE: Holy Spirit; CHURCH:
    Nature and Unity)

Day of (261–272)
Come forth, O Love divine 289
Come, Holy Spirit, heavenly Dove 281

Come, share the Spirit 62
O holy Dove of God descending 285
Spirit, spirit of gentleness 286

Hymns of the Spirit (281–294)
Creator Spirit, come, we pray 268
Hear the voice of God, so tender 174
Sweet delight, most lovely 269
Wind who makes all winds that blow 271

Trinity Sunday (273–280)
(See also TRINITY, THE HOLY)

PILGRIMAGE
At the font we start our journey 308
Awake, my soul, stretch every nerve 491
Behold the host all robed in light 296
For the faithful who have answered 384
Forward through the ages 377
Guide my feet 497
How firm a foundation 407
I sing as I arise today! 83
In the midst of new dimensions 391
It's the old ship of Zion 310
Jesus, Savior, pilot me 441
Jesus, still lead on 446
Lead on eternal Sovereign 573
Lift every voice and sing 593
My faith, it is an oaken staff 418
O Jesus, I have promised 493
Savior God above 602
Shall we gather at the river 597
Siyahamb' ekukhanyen' kwenkhos' 526
Somos pueblo que camina 340
We shall overcome 570
We who would valiant be 494
Won't you let me be your servant? 539

PLURALISM (See also CHRISTIAN
    UNITY; CHURCH: Nature and Unity;
    JUSTICE AND PEACE)
Come, let us join with faithful souls 383
God of change and glory 177
O for a world 575
Praise with joy the world's Creator 273
We are your people 309

PRAISE
(See ADORATION AND PRAISE)

PRAYER (505–521)
(See also CHURCH: Worship and Prayer)
Every time I feel the Spirit 282
Give up your anxious pains 404
I am yours, O Lord 455
I must tell Jesus 486
Let there be light, O God of hosts! 589
More love to you, O Christ 456
Nearer, my God, to you 606
O kou aloha no 580
Out of the depths I call 483
Out of the depths, O God, we call 554
Por la mañana 88
Precious Lord, take my hand 472
Rising in darkness 90
Spirit of God, descend upon my heart 290
Wake, my soul 91

PRESENTATION OF JESUS
(See JESUS CHRIST: Presentation of)

PROCESSIONAL HYMNS
(See also OPENING OF WORSHIP)
All glory, laud, and honor 216, 217
All hail the power of Jesus' name! 304
Angels, from the realms of glory 126
As with gladness those of old 159
Crown with your richest crowns 301
For the beauty of the earth 28
From all that dwell below the skies 27
Glorious things of you are spoken 307
Hail O festal day! 262
Holy, holy, holy 277
Immortal, invisible, God only wise 1
Joyful, joyful, we adore you 4
Lift high the cross 198
"Lift up your hearts!" 38
Love divine, all loves excelling 43
Praise with joy the world's Creator 273
Rejoice, give thanks and sing 303
Rejoice, you pure in heart 55
The church's one foundation 386
The God of Abraham praise 24
The royal banners forward fly 221
To you, O God, all creatures sing 17
We worship you, God 26
When morning gilds the skies 86
You are salt for the earth, O people 181

PROCLAMATION (See WITNESS)

PROPHETS
"Comfort, comfort O my people" 101
God of the prophets 358
Little Bethlehem of Judah 113
Profetiza, Pueblo mío 578
Spirit, spirit of gentleness 286
The Baptist shouts on Jordan's shore 115
There's a voice in the wilderness 120

PROVIDENCE (See under GOD)

PSALM PARAPHRASES
(See also Psalter section (621–731))
A mighty fortress is our God 439 440
All people that on earth do dwell 7
As pants the hart for cooling streams 481
Creating God, your fingers trace 462
Enter, rejoice, and come in 73
Este es el día 65
From all that dwell below the skies 27
God is my shepherd 479
Let heaven your wonders proclaim 29
Let us with a joyful mind 16
My shepherd is the living God 247
O God, our help in ages past 25
O how glorious, full of wonder 558
O my soul, bless your Creator 13
Out of the depths I call 483
This is the day 84
To God compose a song of joy 36
To you, O God, all creatures sing 17
Unto the hills we lift our longing eyes 466
We worship you, God 26

REALM OF GOD (607–617)
(See also GOD: Realm of)

RECONCILIATION (See CHRISTIAN
    UNITY; FORGIVENESS OF SIN)

REDEMPTION
(*See* JESUS CHRIST: Savior)

REFORMATION DAY
A mighty fortress is our God 439 440
I greet you, sure Redeemer 251
Lift your head, O martyrs, weeping 445
Now thank we all our God 419

REIGN OF CHRIST (300–305)
(*See also* JESUS CHRIST: Ascension;
    Sovereignty and Reign)

REPENTANCE
(*See also* FORGIVENESS OF SIN)
Dear God, embracing humankind 502
Dust and ashes touch our face 186
Eternal Spirit of the living Christ 520
Help us accept each other 388
How beautiful, our spacious skies 594
O God, how we have wandered 202
Savior, when in tears and dust 185
Through all the world, a hungry Christ 587

REST
All praise be yours, my God, this night 100
Christ, mighty Savior 93
Giver of life, where'er they be 603
I heard the voice of Jesus say 489
It came upon the midnight clear 131
On River Jordan's banks I stand 598
The day you gave us, God, is ended 95

RESURRECTION
(*See under* JESUS CHRIST)

RURAL LIFE
Awake, awake to love and work! 89
Come, O thankful people, come 422
Praise our God above 424

SACRAMENTS (*See* BAPTISM, HOLY;
    COMMUNION, HOLY)

SAINTS (*See* ALL SAINTS DAY;
    CHURCH: Communion of Saints)

SALVATION
Amazing grace, how sweet 547, 548
Camina, pueblo de Dios 614
I love to tell the story 522
In a lowly manger born 162
Love divine, all loves excelling 43
O mighty God, when I survey in wonder 35
Strengthen all the weary hands 612
There are some things I may not know 405

SANCTIFICATION
(*See* HOLY SPIRIT: Sanctifier)

SCHOOLS
(*See* EDUCATION; YOUTH)

SCIENCE AND TECHNOLOGY
God, who stretched the spangled heavens
    556
O grant us, God, a little space 516
Praise the Source of faith and learning 411

SCRIPTURES
(*See* BIBLE, HYMNS ABOUT THE)

SEASONS

Changing (430–435)
All things bright and beautiful 31

Festival of the Christian Home (426–429)
Come, let us join with faithful souls 383
When love is found 362
Your love, O God, has called us here 361

New Year, The
All beautiful the march of days 434
By gracious powers 413
Now greet the swiftly changing year 431
This is a day of new beginnings 417

Thanksgiving Day (419–425)
I sing the mighty power of God 12
We sing to you, O God 9

SECURITY
(*See* GOD: Strength and Refuge; JESUS
    CHRIST: Strength and Refuge)

SERENITY (*See* PEACE: Inner)

SERVICE (532–543) (*See also* CHURCH:
    Mission in the World; DISCIPLESHIP)
Awake, awake to love and work! 89
Come to tend God's garden 586
For the healing of the nations 576
God, speak to me, that I may speak 531
God, whose giving knows no ending 565
Like a mother who has borne us 583
O Christ Jesus, sent from heaven 47
O holy city, seen of John 613
O Source of all that is 513
There's a spirit in the air 294
We cannot own the sunlit sky 563
We would be building 607

SERVICE MUSIC (741–815)
(*See Contents*)

SIN
(*See* CONFESSION OF SIN;
    FORGIVENESS OF SIN)

SOCIAL JUSTICE
(*See* JUSTICE AND PEACE; SERVICE)

SORROW (*See* COMFORT AND
    ASSURANCE; PEACE: Inner)

SPRING (*See* SEASONS: Changing)

**STEWARDSHIP AND CREATION
(556–569)** (*See also* ECOLOGY; GOD:
    Works in Creation)
A woman came who did not 206
Awake, awake to love and work! 89
Born of God, Eternal Savior 542
Take my life, God, let it be 448
When the morning stars together 453

STRUGGLE AND CONFLICT (436–447)
By gracious powers 413
Each winter as the year grows older 435
Forty days and forty nights 205
God made from one blood 427
How firm a foundation 407
I want Jesus to go with me 490
In solitude, in solitude 521

Lead on eternal Sovereign 573
Lord Jesus, who through forty days 211
O God, my God 515
Rock of ages, let our song 10
When love is found 362

SUFFERING (*See* PAIN AND SUFFERING)

SUMMER (*See* SEASONS: Changing)

TEACHERS (*See* COMMISSIONING;
    CONFIRMATION; EDUCATION;
    YOUTH)

TEMPTATION (*See* CONFESSION OF
    SIN; JESUS CHRIST: Temptation of;
    STRUGGLE AND CONFLICT)

TESTIMONY (*See* WITNESS)

THANKSGIVING
For the beauty of the earth 28
Give thanks for life 297
God of the sparrow God of the whale 32
God, we thank you for our people 376
How can I say thanks 14
Hoy celebramos con gozo al Dios 246
"Lift up your hearts!" 38
O Word of God incarnate 315
Praise to God 5
Take my gifts 562
Thank our God for sisters, brothers 397
To you, O God, all creatures sing 17
What gift can we bring 370

THANKSGIVING DAY
(*See under* SEASONS)

TRANSFIGURATION (182–184)

TRAVELERS
Lord, make me more holy 75
God be with you 81
My faith, it is an oaken staff 418
Now the day is over 98
Savior, again to your dear name 80

TRIALS
(*See* STRUGGLE AND CONFLICT)

TRINITY, THE HOLY
(*See also* PENTECOST: Trinity Sunday)
Baptized into your name most holy 324
Christ Jesus, please be by our side 375
Come, God, Creator, be our shield 69
Come, O Spirit, dwell among us 267
En santa hermandad 392
God the Spirit, guide and guardian 355
Lord, dismiss us with your blessing 77
Mothering God, you gave me birth 467
O day of radiant gladness 66
O holy radiance, joyous light 739
O Wisdom breathed from God 740
Un mandamiento nuevo 389
When minds and bodies meet as one 399

TRUST
(*See also* COMFORT AND ASSURANCE;
    FAITH AND ASPIRATION)
Give up your anxious pains 404
Giver of life, where'er they be 603

God moves in a mysterious way 412
God of our life 366
God's actions, always good and just 415
I love my God, who heard my cry 511
I will trust in the Lord 416
If you but trust in God to guide you 410
I've got a feeling 458
Lead on eternal Sovereign 573
O God of love, O God of peace 571
Out of the depths I call 483
Por la mañana 88
Savior, like a shepherd lead us 252
Softly and tenderly 449
Such perfect love my Shepherd shows 248
Sweet hour of prayer! 505
We are often tossed and driven 444
We have the strength to lift and bear 178
Why should I feel discouraged 475

TRUTH
My eyes have seen the glory 610
O grant us light 469
We limit not the truth of God 316

UNITY (See CHRISTIAN UNITY;
   CHURCH: Nature and Unity)

VISITATION OF MARY TO ELIZABETH
Mary, woman of the promise 123
My heart sings out 106
My soul give glory 119

VOCATION (See WORK AND VOCA-
   TION; See also CONFIRMATION;
   STEWARDSHIP AND CREATION)

WINTER (See SEASONS: Changing)

WITNESS (522–531)
(See also CHURCH: Mission in the World)
Ask me what great thing I know 49
Faith of the martyrs 381
For all the saints 299
For the faithful who have answered 384
I sing a song of the saints of God 295
Lift your head, O martyrs, weeping 445
Standing at the future's threshold 538
You are called to tell the story 357

WORD OF GOD
(See BIBLE, HYMNS ABOUT THE)

WORK AND VOCATION
O grant us, God, a little space 516
Take my gifts 562

WORSHIP
(See CHURCH: Worship and Prayer)

WORSHIP RESOURCES (816–887)
(See Contents)

YOUTH (See also CHILDREN; CONFIR-
   MATION; EDUCATION)
Come, teach us, Spirit of our God 287
Great work has God begun in you 353
I was there to hear your borning cry 351
I would be true 492
Now in the days of youth 350
Rejoice, you pure in heart 55
Take my life, God, let it be 448
We shall overcome 570
We would be building 607

ZEAL
Awake, awake to love and work! 89
Awake, my soul, stretch every nerve 491
Christian, rise and act your creed 537
Come, labor on 532
Come, we who love God's name 379, 382
Faith of the martyrs 381
Lead on eternal Sovereign 573
We who would valiant be 494

ZION
(See also CHURCH; CITY OF GOD)
Come, we who love God's name 379, 382
Glorious things of you are spoken 307

First Line Index

Indentation and italics are used to indicate a first line or name by which a hymn is also known, or a translation.

A hymn of glory let us sing 259
A mighty fortress is our God..............439, 440
A toi la gloire, ô Ressuscité! 253
A woman came who did not count the cost 206
Abide with me 99
Adeste, fideles 135
Adoro te devote 339
Again we keep this solemn fast 187
Ah, holy Jesus 218
Ah, what shame I have to bear...............203
Alabanza 34
Alas! and did my Savior bleed 199, 200
All beautiful the march of days 434
   All creatures of our God and King 17
   All earth is waiting 121
All glory, laud, and honor 216, 217
All hail the power of Jesus' name!...............304
All my hope on God is founded 408
All people that on earth do dwell 7
All praise be yours, my God, this night 100
All things bright and beautiful 31
Alleluia! Alleluia! Hearts to heaven 243
Alleluia! Gracious Jesus! 257
   Alleluia! Sing to Jesus! 257
Almighty God, your Word is cast 318
Amazing grace, how sweet the sound 547, 548
Amen, Amen 161
An outcast among outcasts 201
Angels, from the realms of glory 126
Angels we have heard on high 125

Arise, your light is come! 164
As Moses raised the serpent up 605
As pants the hart for cooling streams 481
   As shepherds filled with joy 149
   As the rain is falling 34
As we gather at your table 332
As with gladness those of old 159
Ask me what great thing I know 49
   At early dawn 88
   At the Cross 199
At the font we start our journey...............308
Awake! awake, and greet the new morn 107
Awake, awake to love and work! 89
Awake, my soul, stretch every nerve 491
Away in a manger 124

Baptized into your name most holy 324
Be known to us in breaking bread 342
Be not dismayed 460
Be now my vision...............451
Be still, my soul 488
   Be thou my vision 451
Beams of heaven, as I go 447
Beautiful Jesus 44
   Beautiful Savior 44
Because you live, O Christ 231
   Before the cross of Jesus 191
Before your cross, O Jesus 191
   Behold a host all robed in white 296
Behold the host all robed in light 296

Behold us, Lord, a little space 516
Beneath the cross of Jesus 190
Bless God, O my soul! 549
Blessed are the poor in spirit 180
Blessed assurance 473
Blessed be the tie that binds 393
Blessed Jesus, at thy word 74
Blessed Quietness 284
Born in the night, Mary's Child 152
Born of God, Eternal Savior 542
Bread of the world, in mercy broken 346
Break forth, O beauteous heavenly light 140
Break now the bread of life 321
Break thou the bread of life 321
Breath of the living God 56
Breathe on me, Breath of God 292
Brightest and best 156, 157
Bring many names 11
By gracious powers 413
By whatever name we call you 560

Called as partners in Christ's service 495
Camina, pueblo de Dios 614
Cantemos al Creador 39
Carol our Christmas 141
Child of blessing, child of promise 325
Children of God 533
Children of the heavenly Father 487
Christ at table, there with friends 227
Christ, enthroned in heavenly splendor 258
Christ is living 235
Christ is made the sure foundation 400
Christ is the Mountain of Horeb 45
Christ Jesus, please be by our side 375
Christ, mighty Savior 93
Christ rose up from the dead 239
Christ the Lord is risen today 233
Christ the Victorious 367
Christ will come again 608
Christian, rise and act your creed 537
Colorful Creator 30
Come, celebrate with thanksgiving 246
Come down, O Love divine 289
Come forth, O Love divine 289
Come, gather in this special place 335
Come, God, Creator, be our shield 69
Come, Holy Ghost, our souls inspire 268
Come, Holy Spirit, heavenly Dove 281
Come, labor on 532
Come, let us join with faithful souls 383
Come, my soul 91
Come, my Way, my Truth, my Life 331
Come now, Almighty God 275
Come, O Creator Spirit 268
Come, O Fount of every blessing 459
Come, O long-expected Jesus 122
Come, O Spirit, dwell among us 267
Come, O Spirit, with your sound 265
Come, O thankful people, come 422
Come, share the Spirit 62
Come, teach us, Spirit of our God 287
Come, thou almighty King 275
Come, thou fount of every blessing 459
Come, thou long-expected Jesus 122
Come to tend God's garden 586
Come unto me, ye weary 484
Come, we who love God's name 379, 382
Come, we who love the Lord 379, 382
Come ye thankful people, come 422
Come, you faithful, raise the strain 230

"Comfort, comfort O my people" 101
Community of Christ 314
Crashing waters at creation 326
Creating God, your fingers trace 462
Creator God, creating still 278
Creator God we sing 39
Creator of the stars of night 111
Creator Spirit, come, we pray 268
Cristo es la peña de Horeb 45
¡Cristo vive! 235
Crown him with many crowns 301
Crown with your richest crowns 301

Day is done 92
De colores 402
De tierra lejana venimos 155
Dear God, embracing humankind 502
Dear Lord and Father of mankind 502
Deck thyself, my soul, with gladness 334
Deep in the shadows of the past 320
Down at the cross 189
Draw us in the Spirit's tether 337
Dust and ashes touch our face 186

Each winter as the year grows older 435
Ekolu mea nui 496
En santa hermandad 392
Enter in the realm of God 615
Enter, rejoice, and come in 73
Es ist ein' Ros entsprungen 127
Este es el día 65
Eternal Christ, who, kneeling 390
Eternal Christ, you rule 302
Eternal Spirit of the living Christ 520
Every time I feel the Spirit 282

Fairest Lord Jesus 44
Faith of our fathers 381
Faith of the martyrs 381
Father almighty, bless us 518
Father, we praise thee 90
Filled with excitement 214
Filled with the Spirit's power 266
Fire of God, undying Flame 64
For all the saints 299
For the beauty of the earth 28
For the faithful who have answered 384
For the fruit of all creation 425
For the healing of the nations 576
Forty days and forty nights 205
Forward through the ages 377
From all that dwell below the skies 27
"From heaven above to earth I come" 130
"From heaven unto earth I come" 130
From the crush of wealth and power 552

"Gentle Joseph, Joseph dear" 105
Give me a clean heart 188
Give thanks for life 297
Give to the winds thy fears 404
Give up your anxious pains 404
Giver of life, where'er they be 603
Glad tidings 146
Glorious is your name, O Jesus 53
Glorious things of you are spoken 307
Glory, glory hallelujah 2
Go forth, O people of God 614
Go, my children, with my blessing 82
Go tell it on the mountain 154
Go to dark Gethsemane 219

God be with you...81
God, bless our homes.................................429
God created heaven and earth 33
God, creation's great designer 371
   God himself is with us.............................68
God is here! As we your people meet..........70
God is my shepherd....................................479
God is truly with us.......................................68
God loved the world....................................208
God made from one blood.........................427
God marked a line and told the sea..........568
God moves in a mysterious way 412
God of Abraham and Sarah..........................20
God of change and glory............................177
God of grace and God of glory 436
   God of our fathers, whose almighty hand 592
God of our life...366
God of the ages, who with sure command 592
God of the prophets...................................358
God of the sparrow God of the whale.........32
God our Author and Creator......................530
God reigns o'er all the earth!.......................21
God, speak to me, that I may speak 531
God the Omnipotent!..................................577
God the Spirit, guide and guardian 355
God, today bless this new marriage 364
God, we thank you for our people.............376
God, when I came into this life...................354
God, who stretched the spangled heavens.........556
God, who summons through all ages.........356
God, whose giving knows no ending.........565
   God Will Take Care of You 460
God, you have set us 372
God's actions, always good and just 415
   God's Eye Is on the Sparrow......................475
Golden breaks the dawn.............................470
Good Christian friends, rejoice 129
Graced with garments of great gladness..........334
Gracious Spirit, Holy Ghost..........................61
Grant us wisdom to perceive you.............510
Great God of earth and heaven 579
Great is your faithfulness 423
Great Spirit God...341
Great work has God begun in you 353
Guide me, O my great Redeemer...........18, 19
   Guide me, O thou great Jehovah 18, 19
Guide my feet..497

Hail, O festal day!..262
Hail the day that sees Christ rise 260
   Hail thee festal day 262
   Hail to the Lord's anointed 104
Halleluja...236
Hark! the herald angels sing......................144
Hark! the herald angels sing (Jesus, the Light)..........160
   He arose 239
   He who would valiant be 494
Hear the voice of God, so tender...............174
Heaven and earth, and sea and air...........566
Help us accept each other 388
   Here, O God, Your Servants Gather 72
Here, O my Lord, I see you face to face..........336
Here, Savior, in this quiet place 555
   Higher Ground 442
   His Eye Is on the Sparrow 475
Hitsuji wa nemurere....................................137
   Holy Ghost, dispel our sadness 269
Holy God, we praise your name.................276
Holy, holy, holy 277
Holy Spirit, come, confirm us 264

Holy Spirit, ever dwelling 59
Holy Spirit, truth divine 63
Hope of the world...46
"Hosanna, loud hosanna" 213
How beautiful, our spacious skies.............594
How blessed are they who trust in Christ..........365
   How brightly beams the Morning Star 158
   How Can I Keep from Singing 476
How can I say thanks....................................14
How deep the silence of the soul..............509
How firm a foundation.................................407
How like a gentle spirit 443
How lovely is your dwelling 600, 601
Hoy celebramos con gozo al Dios..............246
   Humbly I adore thee 339
Hush, Hush, Somebody's calling my name..........604

"I am the light of the world!" 584
I am yours, O Lord 455
I come to the garden alone.........................237
I come with joy 349
   I greet thee, who my sure Redeemer 251
I greet you, sure Redeemer 251
I heard my mother say................................409
I heard the voice of Jesus say.....................489
I look to you in every need 463
I love my God, who heard my cry 511
   I love the Lord, who heard my cry 511
   I love thy Kingdom, Lord 312
I love to tell the story 522
I must tell Jesus...486
I need you every hour.................................517
I sing a song of the saints of God 295
I sing as I arise today!...................................83
I sing the mighty power of God 12
I sing the praise of Love almighty 50
   I sing the praise of love unbounded 50
I thank you, Jesus 41
I want Jesus to go with me..........................490
   I want Jesus to walk with me 490
I want to be ready 616
I was there to hear your borning cry..........351
I will lift the cloud of night.........................482
   I will make the darkness light 482
I will trust in the Lord.................................416
I woke up this morning.................................85
I would be true..492
If I have been the source of pain, O God..........544
   If thou but suffer God to guide thee 410
If you but trust in God to guide you 410
   I'll Fly Away 595
I'll shout the name of Christ who lives......234
I'm pressing on the upward way 442
I'm so glad, Jesus lifted me 474
Immortal, invisible, God only wise 1
Immortal Love, forever full 166
In a lowly manger born 162
   In all our living 499
In Christ there is no East or West 394, 395
In Egypt under Pharaoh 574
In solitude, in solitude................................521
In the bleak midwinter 128
In the bulb there is a flower 433
In the cross of Christ I glory 193, 194
   In the Garden 237
In the midst of new dimensions 391
Incarnate God, immortal Love 414
Isaiah the prophet has written of old 108
It came upon the midnight clear 131
   It Is Well with My Soul 438

It was a sad and solemn night 225
It's the old ship of Zion 310
I've got a feeling 458
I've got peace like a river 478

Jerusalem, my happy home 378
Jesu, Jesu, fill us with your love 498
    Jesus a new commandment has given us 389
Jesus calls us, o'er the tumult 171, 172
Jesus Christ is risen today..240
    Jesus, I live to thee 457
Jesus, I live to you 457
Jesus is here right now 348
Jesus, Jesus, oh, what a wonderful child 136
Jesus, keep me near the cross 197
    Jesus, lead thou on 446
Jesus, lover of my soul 546
Jesus loves me! 327
Jesus, our brother, strong and good 138
Jesus, priceless treasure 480
Jesus, Savior, pilot me 441
Jesus shall reign..300
Jesus, Sovereign, Savior...255
Jesus, still lead on 446
Jesus, take us to the mountain 183
Jesus the Christ says..48
Jesus, the joy of loving hearts 329
    Jesus, the Light of the World 160
    Jesus, the very thought of thee 507
Jesus—the very thought to me................................507
    Jesus, thou joy of loving hearts 329
Jesus took the bread 343
Journey to Gethsemane 219
Joy dawned again on Easter Day 241
Joy to the world! 132
Joyful, joyful, we adore you 4
Joys are flowing like a river 284
Just as I am 207

Keep awake, be always ready 112
Keep your lamps trimmed and burning 369

Lead on eternal Sovereign 573
    Lead on, O King eternal 573
Lead us from death to life 581
    Leaning on the Everlasting Arms 471
Let all mortal flesh keep silence 345
Let every Christian pray 261
Let heaven your wonders proclaim 29
Let it breathe on me 288
Let justice flow like streams 588
Let me enter God's own dwelling 67
Let there be light, O God of hosts! 589
Let us break bread together 330
    Let us even now go to Bethlehem 142
Let us hope when hope seems hopeless 461
Let us talents and tongues employ 347
    Let us with a gladsome mind 16
Let us with a joyful mind 16
Lift every voice and sing 593
Lift high the cross 198
    Lift thy head, O Zion, weeping 445
Lift up your heads, O mighty gates 117
"Lift up your hearts!" 38
Lift your head, O martyrs, weeping 445
Like a mother who has borne us 583
Like a tree beside the waters 313
Like the murmur of the dove's song 270
Listen to your Savior call 250
Little Bethlehem of Judah 113

Little children, welcome! 323
Lo, how a Rose e'er blooming 127
    Lord, bless our homes 429
    Lord, dear Lord above 602
Lord, dismiss us with your blessing 77
    Lord, enthroned in heavenly splendor 258
    Lord God of hosts 534
Lord, I want to be a Christian 454
    Lord Jesus Christ, be present now 375
Lord Jesus, who through forty days........................211
Lord, make me more holy 75
    Lord, speak to me, that I may speak 531
    Lord, we thank thee for our brothers 397
    Lord, when I came into this life 354
    Lord, who throughout these forty days 211
Los magos que llegaron a Belén 155
Love came down at Christmas 165
Love divine, all loves excelling 43

    Make a gift of your holy Word 317
Malipayong adlaw'ng natawhan 428
Manglakat na kita sa Belen 142
Mantos y Ramos 214
    Many and great, O God, are your works 3
Many are the lightbeams 163
    Many Gifts, One Spirit 177
Maoz tsur y'shuati 10
Mark how the Lamb of God's selfoffering 167
Mary, woman of the promise 123
    Master, no offering costly and sweet 536
May the Sending One defend you 79
Mikotoba o kudasai 317
    Mine eyes have seen the glory..............................610
More love to you, O Christ 456
Mothering God, you gave me birth 467
My eyes have seen the glory 610
My faith, it is an oaken staff 418
My God, accept my heart this day 352
My heart is overflowing 15
My heart sings out with joyful praise 106
My hope is built on nothing less 403
My life flows in endless song 476
My shepherd is the living God 247
    My shepherd will supply my need 247
My song is love unknown 222
My soul gives glory to my God 119
    My Soul Overflows with Praise 88

Nearer, my God, to you 606
Not my brother, nor my sister 519
Not with naked eye, not with human sense 406
Now all the woods are sleeping 94
Now bless the God of Israel....................................110
Now greet the swiftly changing year 431
Now in the days of youth 350
Now is the time approaching 609
Now let us all, in hymns of praise 529
Now thank we all our God 419
Now the day is over 98
Now the green blade rises 238
    Now the sun is setting 97
Nu oli! 146
Nun danket alle Gott 419

    O beautiful for spacious skies 594
O Bread of life 333
    O brother man, fold to thy heart 533
O Christ Jesus, sent from heaven 47
O Christ, the great foundation 387
O Christ, the healer, we have come 175

O come, all you faithful 135
O come, O come, Emmanuel 116
"O come to me, you weary" 484
O Day of God, draw near 611
   O day of God, draw nigh 611
O day of radiant gladness 66
   O day of rest and gladness 66
O for a closer bond with God 450
   O for a closer walk with God 450
O for a thousand tongues to sing 42
O for a world 575
O God, as with a potter's hand 550
O God, how we have wandered 202
O God in heaven 279
O God in whom all life begins 401
O God, my God 515
O God of all your people past 374
O God of earth and altar 582
O God of love 363
O God of love, O God of peace 571
O God of strength 534
O God, our help in ages past 25
O God, the Creator 291
O God, we bear the imprint of your face 585
O God, who teaches us to live 359
O God, whose steadfast love 426
O grant us, God, a little space 516
O grant us light 469
O holy city, seen of John 613
O holy Dove of God descending 285
O holy God, whose gracious power 535
O holy radiance, joyous light 739
O Holy Spirit, Root of life 57
O how glorious, full of wonder 558
   O How I Love Jesus 52
O how shall I receive you 102
O Jesus Christ, may grateful hymns 212
O Jesus, I have promised 493
O kou aloha no 580
O little town of Bethlehem 133
   O Lord of life, where'er they be 603
   O Love, how deep, how broad, how high 209
O love, how vast, how flowing free 209
O Love that will not let me go 485
O loving founder of the stars 111
   O Master, let me walk with thee 503
O mighty God, when I survey in wonder 35
O Morning Star, how clear and bright 158
   O my soul, bless God, the Father 13
O my soul, bless your Creator 13
O praise the gracious power 54
O radiant Christ, incarnate Word 168
O sacred Head, now wounded 226
O saints in splendor sing 380
   O Sapientia 740
O Savior, for the saints 298
O Savior, let me walk with you 503
O sing a song of Bethlehem 51
O sons and daughters, let us sing 244
O Source of all that is 513
O Spirit of God 60
   O spirit of life 60
O spirit of the living God 263
O splendor of God's glory bright 87
O Trinity, your face we see 280
O what their joy and their glory must be 385
O Wisdom breathed from God 740
O wondrous sight, O vision fair 184
O Word of God incarnate 315
   O worship the King 26
   Of the Father's love begotten 118

Of the Parent's heart begotten 118
On a hill far away 195
On Christmas night all Christians sing 143
   On Jordan's stormy banks I stand 598
On Pentecost they gathered 272
On River Jordan's banks I stand 598
Once in royal David's city 145
Onuniyan tehanl waun 548
   Open now thy gates of beauty 67
Our God, to whom we turn 37
Out of the depths I call 483
Out of the depths, O God, we call 554
Over my head 514

Part in peace! 78
Pass me not, O gentle Savior 551
Pastores a Belén 149
Peace I leave with you, my friends 249
   Pero Queda Cristo 88
Por la mañana 88
Praise our God above 424
Praise the Source of faith and learning 411
Praise to God 5
Praise to God, your praises bring 430
Praise to the living God 8
Praise with joy the world's Creator 273
   Praise ye the Lord, the Almighty 22
Pray for the wilderness 557
Prayer is the soul's sincere desire 508
Precious Lord, take my hand 472
Profetiza, Pueblo mío 578
Pues si vivimos 499

Rejoice, give thanks and sing 303
   Rejoice, the Lord is King! 303
Rejoice, you pure in heart 55, 71
Renew your church 311
Return, my people 114
Ride on! Ride on in majesty! 215
Rising in darkness 90
Rock of ages, cleft for me 596
Rock of ages, let our song 10
Ruler of life, we crown you now 228

Said Judas to Mary 210
Salup na ang adlaw 97
Savior, again to your dear name 80
Savior, an offering costly and sweet 536
Savior God above 602
Savior, like a shepherd lead us 252
   Savior, thy dying love 452
Savior, when in tears and dust 185
Savior, who dying gave 452
See the little baby 147
Sekai no tomo 72
   Send Me, Lord 360
Sent forth by God's blessing 76
Shadow and substance 398
Shall we gather at the river 597
   Sheaves of summer 338
   Sheep fast asleep 137
Sheltered by God's loving Spirit 368
Si fui motivo de dolor, oh Dios 544
"Silence! Frenzied, unclean spirit" 176
Silent night, holy night 134
Sing a different song 150
Sing, my tongue 220
   Sing of colors 402
Sing praise to God, our highest good 6
Sing praise to God, who has shaped 22
   Sing praise to God who reigns above 6

Sing them over again to me 319
Siyahamb' ekukhanyen' kwenkhos' 526
Softly and tenderly 449
Sois la semilla 528
Some Day 447
Some glad morning 595
Someone asked the question 523
Somos pueblo que camina 340
Son of God, eternal Savior 542
Soplo de Dios viviente 56
Sovereign and transforming Grace 512
Spirit of God, descend upon my heart 290
Spirit of Jesus, if I love my neighbor 590
Spirit of love 58
Spirit of the living God 283
Spirit, spirit of gentleness 286
Standing at the future's threshold 538
Standing in the Need of Prayer 519
Stars and planets flung in orbit 567
Steal away 599
Strengthen all the weary hands 612
Strong Son of God, immortal Love 414
Such perfect love my shepherd shows 248
Sun of my soul, O Savior dear 96
Surely no one can be safer 487
Sweet delight, most lovely 269
Sweet hour of prayer! 505
Sweet, Sweet Spirit 293

Take me to the water 322
Take my gifts 562
Take my life and let it be 448
Take my life, God, let it be 448
"Take up your cross," the Savior said 204
Teach me, O Lord, your holy way 465
Thank our God for sisters, brothers 397
Thank you, God 559
The Baptist shouts on Jordan's shore 115
The care the eagle gives her young 468
The church of Christ, in every age 306
The church's one foundation 386
The day of resurrection! 245
The day thou gavest, Lord, is ended 95
The day you gave us, God, is ended 95
The duteous day now closeth 94
The first Nowell 139
The God of Abraham praise 24
The King of love my shepherd is 248
The magi who to Bethlehem did go 155
The Old Rugged Cross 195
The Queen's Prayer 580
The royal banners forward fly 221
The Song of Hannah 15
The strife is o'er 242
The time was early evening 344
The weaver's shuttle swiftly flies 464
There are some things I may not know 405
There is a balm in Gilead 553
There is a name I love to hear 52
There was Jesus by the water 545
There's a spirit in the air 294
There's a sweet, sweet Spirit 293
There's a voice in the wilderness 120
There's a wideness in God's mercy 23
These things did Thomas count 254
They asked, "Who's my neighbor?" 541
They did not build in vain 373
Thine is the glory 253
This is a day of new beginnings 417
This is my song 591
This is the day 84

This is the day 65
This joy I have 524
This joyful Eastertide 232
This little light of mine 524, 525
Thou art the way 40
Though falsely some revile or hate me 477
Three Greatest Things 496
Through all the world, a hungry Christ 587
Thuma mina 360
'Tis the old ship of Zion 310
'Tis winter now; the fallen snow 432
To God compose a song of joy 36
To you, O God, all creatures sing 17
Toda la tierra 121
Touch the earth lightly 569
Truth whom we adore 339
Tú has venido a la orilla 173
'Twas in the moon of wintertime 151
'Twas on that dark and doleful night 225

Un mandamiento nuevo 389
Una espiga 338
Unite and join your cheerful songs 617
United by God's love 392
Unto the hills we lift our longing eyes 466

Wakantanka taku nitawa 3
Wake, my soul 91
Watcher, tell us of the night 103
We are climbing Jacob's ladder 500
We are dancing Sarah's circle 501
We are marching in the light of God 526
We are not our own 564
We are often tossed and driven 444
We are people on a journey 340
We are your people 309
We cannot own the sunlit sky 563
We come unto our fathers' God 374
We gather together 421
We hail you God's anointed 104
We have come at Christ's own bidding 182
We have gathered, Jesus dear 74
We have the strength to lift and bear 178
We limit not the truth of God 316
We live by faith and not by sight 256
We love your realm, O God 312
We offer Christ 527
We plant a grain of mustard seed 540
We praise you, O God 420
We shall not give up the fight 437
We shall overcome 570
We sing to you, O God 9
We who would valiant be 494
We worship you, God 26
We would be building 607
We yearn, O Christ, for wholeness 179
We'll Understand It Better By and By 444
Were you there 229
What a covenant 471
What a fellowship 471
What a friend we have in Jesus 506
What a glad day 428
What child is this 148
What gift can we bring 370
What ruler wades through murky streams 169
What wondrous love is this 223
Whate'er my God ordains is right 415
When I, O Lord, behold thy vast creation 35
When I survey the wondrous cross 224
When in our music God is glorified 561
When Israel was in Egypt's land 572

When Jesus wept 192
When, like the woman at the well 196
When love is found 362
When minds and bodies meet as one 399
When morning gilds the skies 86
When peace, like a river 438
When the morning stars together 453
Where charity and love prevail 396
Where cross the crowded ways of life 543
Who would think that what was needed 153
Why should I feel discouraged 475
  Why We Sing 523
Wind who makes all winds that blow 271
With joy draw water 109
Womb of life, and source of being 274
Wonder of wonders, here revealed 328
  Wonderful Words of Life 319

Won't you let me be your servant? 539

  Ye servants of God, your Master proclaim 305
  Yes, God Is Real 405
Yigdal elohim chai 24
You are called to tell the story 357
You are salt for the earth, O people 181
  You are the seed 528
You are the way 40
  You have come down to the lakeshore 173
You servants of God, your Sovereign proclaim 305
  You shall prophesy, all my people 578
You walk along our shoreline 504
Your love, O God, has called us here 361
Your ways are not our own 170
  Yours is the glory, Resurrected One! 253

DESCANT INDEX

Come, O thankful people, come 422
Good Christian friends, rejoice 129
Holy, holy, holy 277
I sing the mighty power of God 12
Lead us from death to life 581

Sent forth by God's blessing 76
The first Nowell 139
To you, O God, all creatures sing 17
'Twas in the moon of wintertime 151
We shall not give up the fight 437